Why Do You Need this New Edition?

If you are wondering why you should buy this new edition of Social Problems in a Diverse Society, here are 10 good reasons:

Statistics are thoroughly updated throughout the text, and include important findings from the 2010 Census.

New research is incorporated in every chapter.

Chapter 3, "Video Games, Racial Stereotypes of Native Americans, and Glamorized Violence" takes a look at the seldom-discussed issue of prejudice against Native Americans and how it is glamorized in video games.

Chapter 5, "Where Have All the Older Women Gone? Fashion Magazines for the Young Only!" examines how many of the most popular fashion magazines, even though supposedly for older women, almost exclusively have young celebrities or models on their front covers and in much of the magazine content.

Chapter 6, "A Mixed Bag: Praise and Criticism for Young Lesbian and Gay Characters in *Glee*" discusses the popular hit TV series about high school life for members of a glee club and delves into how the media have become more positive in representations of gay and lesbian characters in recent years.

Chapter 8, "Framing of Alcohol Use in Reality TV Series," describes how many reality shows, including *The Real World, Bachelor and Bachelorette, and the Real Housewives* … franchise, rely on excessive alcohol consumption to help carry along the "story" of high-stakes romance and social life supposedly among a chosen few.

Chapter 9, "Murder in the Social Media: Stories That Get Attention," takes a close look at how the social media have become so prominent in providing a platform for everyday people to express their opinion and render legal advice even if they do not really know what is going on in a criminal trial or courtroom. The 2011 Casey Anthony case is used as an example of "stories that get attention."

Chapter 11, "Social Media in the 21st Century: Posting One's Fertility (or Infertility) on Facebook" is a cutting-edge analysis of the anxiety and stress that women who are unable to bear children feel when they learn by way of Facebook or Twitter that one of their friends is pregnant.

Chapter 13, "The Media and the Underground Economy" discusses how designer handbags are so widely advertised in the media that they become highly valued in the underground economy as well. The box also looks at the issue of "fake" Apple stores that sprung up in China in 2011.

Chapter 18, "Covering Hurricane Katrina and the BP Oil Spill: Similar Location but Different Issues" describes how media coverage of these two disasters in the same region was similar in some ways but also highly different in others because one was a natural disaster and the other was a technological, man-made disaster.

PEARSON

Social Problems

IN A DIVERSE SOCIETY

SIXTH EDITION

Diana Kendall

Baylor University

PEARSON

Boston   Columbus   Indianapolis   New York   San Francisco   Upper Saddle River
Amsterdam   Cape Town   Dubai   London   Madrid   Milan   Munich   Paris   Montréal   Toronto
Delhi   Mexico City   São Paulo   Sydney   Hong Kong   Seoul   Singapore   Taipei   Tokyo

Editorial Director: Craig Campanella
Editor in Chief: Dickson Musslewhite
Publisher: Karen Hanson
Editorial Assistant: Joseph Jantas
Director of Marketing: Brandy Dawson
Executive Marketing Manager: Kelly May
Marketing Assistant: Diane Griffin
Managing Editor: Denise Forlow
Digital Media Editor: Tom Scalzo
Digital Media Project Manager: Nikhil Bramhavar
Senior Manufacturing and Operations Manager
    for Arts & Sciences: Mary Fischer

Operations Specialist: Alan Fischer
Design Manager: John Christiana
Art Director: Anne Bonanno Nieglos
Interior and Cover Designer: Irene Ehrmann
Cover Photo: Jen Grantham/iStockphoto
Lead Media Project Manager: Thomas Scalzo
Associate Editor: Mayda Bosco
Full-Service Project Management: Element LLC
Composition: Element LLC
Printer/Binder: R.R. Donnelley/Willard
Cover Printer: Lehigh/Phoenix Color
Text Font: 10/12 Minion Pro

Credits and acknowledgments borrowed from other sources and reproduced, with permission, in this textbook appear on appropriate page within text (or on pages 470–474).

Many of the designations by manufacturers and seller to distinguish their products are claimed as trademarks. Where those designations appear in this book, and the publisher was aware of a trademark claim, the designations have been printed in initial caps or all caps.

Library of Congress Cataloging-in-Publication Data
Kendall, Diana Elizabeth.
    Social problems in a diverse society / Diana Kendall. — 6th ed.
        p. cm.
    Includes bibliographical references and index.
    ISBN-13: 978-0-205-15290-2
    ISBN-10: 0-205-15290-2
    1. Social problems.   I. Title.
    HN17.5.K457 2012b
    361.1—dc23
                                                2012001617

10 9 8 7 6 5 4 3 2 1

Student Edition:
ISBN 10: 0-205-15290-2
ISBN 13: 978-0-205-15290-2

Instructor's Review Copy:
ISBN 10: 0-205-86518-6
ISBN 13: 978-0-205-86518-5

Books a la carte:
ISBN 10: 0-205-86732-4
ISBN 13: 978-0-205-86732-5

Preface

In the preface to the previous edition of *Social Problems in a Diverse Society* I wrote, "A glimpse at the headline of any daily newspaper or at the TV screen shows us that we are living in difficult times: Our social problems are many in number, diverse in their causes and consequences, and often global in their reach." As I now write the Sixth Edition preface, this statement remains highly relevant. In the intervening three years, numerous social problems have emerged, and many national and global problems have intensified or become more complex. National and international economic structures continue in a state of upheaval, and political leaders frequently appear unable, or unwilling, to create social policies or laws that will benefit larger segments of the population. The richest individuals have accumulated even greater wealth while a significant portion of middle- and lower-income families have seen employment opportunities dry up, household incomes diminish, and, in some cases, their homes be taken away through foreclosures by mortgage-lending institutions. Although some social problems are constantly discussed in the media, others are barely mentioned. Some media sources frame their presentations of the news based on their own political and ideological slants. This kind of slanted media representation, coupled with the unprecedented use of text messaging and social networks such as Facebook and Twitter, produces a sense of "media overload" in many people. Sometimes it is easy to become discouraged, thinking that social problems can't be reduced or solved.

However, studying social problems helps us think about ways in which social change might occur because this course provides us with new insights on problems in our nation and world. Although we live in challenging times, the social problems course provides us with an excellent way in which to develop our critical thinking skills and to learn how to use sociological perspectives to analyze concerns ranging from terrorism and war to inequalities rooted in factors such as race, ethnicity, nationality, class, gender, age, and sexual orientation.

My first and foremost goal in writing this book is to make the study of social problems *interesting* and *relevant* to you, the student. To stimulate your interest in reading the chapters and participating in class discussions, I have used lived experiences (personal narratives of *real* people) and statements from a wide variety of analysts to show how social problems affect people at the individual, group, and societal levels. Moreover, I have applied the sociological imagination and relevant sociological perspectives to all the topics in a systematic manner. I think that one of the most important contributions of this new edition is that I have thoroughly revised and updated information throughout the book. In this age of instant communications, it is very important to have the latest data available at the time the text is being written, and I have worked toward this goal throughout all eighteen chapters.

Like previous editions of *Social Problems in a Diverse Society,* the sixth edition focuses on the significance of social inequality and race, class, and gender as key factors in our understanding of problems in the United States and worldwide. Throughout this text, all people—but particularly people of color and white women—are shown not merely as "victims" of social problems but as individuals who resist discrimination and inequality and seek to bring about change in families, schools, workplaces, and the larger society. To place specific social problems within a larger social inequality framework, Chapters 2 through 6 conduct a systematic evaluation of wealth and poverty, racial and ethnic inequality, gender inequality, and inequalities based on age and sexual orientation. Thereafter, concepts and perspectives related to race, class, and gender are intertwined in the discussion of specific social problems in institutions such as education and health care.

Social Problems in a Diverse Society is balanced in its approach to examining social problems. It includes a comprehensive view of current feminist and other contemporary perspectives on a vast array of subjects—such as the effect of new technologies on social life and how the media depict social issues. As a sociologist who specializes in social theory, I was disheartened by the minimal use of sociological theory to analyze social problems in many texts. Similarly, some texts give the impression that social problems can be solved if people reach a consensus on what should be done, but *Social Problems in a Diverse Society*, Sixth Edition, emphasizes that the way people view a social problem is related to how they believe the problem should be reduced or solved. Consider poverty, for example: People who focus on individual causes of poverty typically believe that individual solutions (such as teaching people the work ethic and reforming welfare) are necessary to reduce the problem, whereas those who focus on structural causes of poverty (such as chronic unemployment and inadequate educational opportunities) typically believe that solutions must come from the larger society. Moreover, what some people perceive as a *problem* is viewed by others as a *solution* for a problem (e.g., the sex industry as a source of income, or abortion to terminate a problematic pregnancy). In the final chapter (Chapter 18), I ask students to more fully explore the question, "Can Social Problems Be Solved?"

Finally, I wrote *Social Problems in a Diverse Society*, Sixth Edition, to provide students and instructors with a text that covers all the major social concerns of our day but does not leave them believing that the text—and perhaps the course—was a "depressing litany of social problems that nobody can do anything about anyway," as one of my students stated about a different text. I believe the sociological perspective has much to add to our national and global dialogues on a host of issues such as environmental degradation; terrorism and war; discrimination based on race, class, gender, age, sexual orientation, or other attributes; and problems in education. Welcome to an innovative examination of social problems—one of the most stimulating and engrossing fields of study in sociology!

NEW TO THIS EDITION
SOCIAL PROBLEMS IN THE MEDIA

Social Problems in the Media   Box 8.1

Framing of Alcohol Use in Reality TV Series

- "Mommy needs a drink"—Alex McCord, *Real Housewives of New York City*, asking for one of many drinks consumed by the women who star in the "housewives" franchise on BRAVO TV network (author's files, 2011).
- "In the meantime, enjoy your cocktail party, and remember that only one of you will receive the first impression rose tonight." Chris Harrison, host of *The Bachelor* and *The Bachelorette*, introduces the first of many cocktail parties where eligible marriage partners are plied with alcohol and left to impress that season's bachelor or bachelorette (author's files, 2011).

Many reality shows on television feature alcohol consumption with mixed results. If we think about how social drinking is framed on these programs, it is easy to identify at least three frames. One is the "social drinking is fun" framework, which carries the message that participants

contrite for their overconsumption; in other cases, they are simply shown as being hung over or in need of "the hair of the dog," another drink that allegedly will take the edge off their previous overindulgence.

The third framing method used to show excessive alcohol consumption on some television entertainment news shows is the "rehab as a revolving door" approach that has been popularized in coverage of hard-partying celebrities such as Lindsay Lohan. Celebrity "news" programs, such as *E News* and ABC TV's *Entertainment Tonight*, carry "glamour" stories about heavy consumption of alcohol by high-profile individuals and then follow up with stories about their "stints" in rehab. Some shows report on celebrities who briefly enter rehab and come out miraculously cured; others show the revolving door effect as the same individuals are readmitted on numerous occasions to gain sobriety. Celebrities entering

Because one of my areas of specialization is the media, I have chosen to do an extensive update of the "Social Problems in the Media" boxes throughout the book.

Here are a few examples of new or revised topics:

Chapter 3: "Video Games, Racial Stereotypes of Native Americans, and Glamorized Violence" takes a look at the seldom-discussed issue of prejudice against Native Americans and how it is glamorized in video games.

Chapter 5: "Where Have All the Older Women Gone? Fashion Magazines for the Young Only!" examines how many of the most popular fashion magazines, even though supposedly for older women, almost exclusively have young celebrities or models on their front covers and in much of the magazine content.

Chapter 6: "A Mixed Bag: Praise and Criticism for Young Lesbian and Gay Characters on *Glee*" discusses the popular hit TV series about high school life for members of a glee club and delves into how the media have become more positive in representations of gay and lesbian characters in recent years.

Chapter 8: "Framing of Alcohol Use in Reality TV Series" describes how many reality shows, including *The Real World, Bachelor* and *Bachelorette*, and the *Real Housewives* rely on excessive alcohol consumption to help carry along the "story" of high-stakes romance and social life supposedly among a chosen few.

Chapter 9: "Murder in the Social Media: Stories That Get Attention" takes a close look at how the social media have become prominent in providing a platform for everyday people to express their opinions and render legal advice even if they do not really know what is going on in a criminal trial or courtroom. The 2011 Casey Anthony case is used as an example of "stories that get attention."

Chapter 11: "Social Media in the Twenty-First Century: Posting One's Fertility (or Infertility) on Facebook" is a cutting-edge analysis of the anxiety and stress that women who are unable to bear children feel when they learn by way of Facebook or Twitter that one of their friends is pregnant.

Chapter 13: "The Media and the Underground Economy" discusses how designer handbags are so widely advertised in the media that they become highly valued in the underground economy as well. The box also looks at the issue of "fake" Apple stores that sprang up in China in 2011.

Chapter 18: "Covering Hurricane Katrina and the BP Oil Spill: Similar Location but Different Issues" describes how media coverage of these two disasters in the same region was similar in some ways but also highly different in others because one was a natural disaster and the other was a technological, human-made disaster.

CRITICAL THINKING AND YOU

Critical Thinking and You   Box 8.3

Calling on a Higher Power or Using Self-Reliance? Alcohol and Drug Abuse Programs

Dr. Mary F. Holley, an obstetrician, founded Mothers against Methamphetamine (MAMa) because her brother Jim became hooked on meth at age 22 and committed suicide at 24 years of age. By starting this organization, Dr. Holley hoped to catch the attention of people who are addicted to crystal meth. Mothers against Methamphetamine (MAMa). MAMa is based on two key principles: (1) that addicts need help from other people to overcome their addiction and, perhaps even more important, and (2) that addicts need help from God or a power greater than themselves to overcome their addiction.

not required to acknowledge God or to confess their problems to other members. The ideas of individual willpower and group support, for example, are expressed in the motto of Women for Sobriety (2011): "We are capable and competent, caring and compassionate, always willing to help another; bonded together in overcoming addictions." MAMa, AA, and NA represent one approach to dealing with a social problem at the individual level; RR, SOS, and WFS represent another. Consider the following questions in thinking about these divergent approaches to dealing with alcohol and drug abuse.

The boxed feature "Critical Thinking and You" encourages students to use the sociological imagination in thinking and answering questions about issues such as:

- "Determining What Constitutes a Social Problem" (Chapter 1, "Studying Social Problems in the Twenty-First Century")

- "Is Reality TV Important to You?" (Chapter 14, "Problems in the Media")

- "Do We Have a Problem or Not? Learning from Environmental Sociology" (Chapter 15, "Population, Global Inequality, and the Environmental Crisis")

- "The 'Cosmopolitan Canopy': Civility for Persons of Color in the City?" (Chapter 16, "Urban Problems")

- "Applying Sociology to the Ordinary and the Extraordinary in Everyday Life" (Chapter 18, "Can Social Problems Be Solved?")

EXCITING FEATURES

A number of special features have been designed to incorporate race, class, and gender into our analysis of social problems and to provide new insights on the social problems that we hear about in the news.

Lived Experiences Throughout Each Chapter

These authentic, first-person accounts are used as vignettes—"real words from real people"—to create interest and show how the problems being discussed affect people as they go about their daily lives. Lived experiences provide opportunities for instructors to systematically incorporate into lectures and class discussions examples of relevant, contemporary issues that have recently been on the evening news and in newspaper headlines, and for you to examine social life beyond your own experiences ("to live vicariously," as one student noted). Some examples of NEW lived experiences in the Sixth Edition include:

- Hailey, a college student, describes how she felt when her college was on "lockdown" because there was

allegedly a person carrying a gun on campus. This example shows how gun violence on college campuses and elsewhere continues to be a pressing social problem (Chapter 1, "Studying Social Problems in the Twenty-First Century").

- Danielle describes how a social food bank has helped reduce her problems with lack of food and hunger (Chapter 2, "Wealth and Poverty: U.S. and Global Economic Inequalities").

- The opening lived experience in Chapter 3, "Racial and Ethnic Inequality," looks at a Super Bowl commercial that may perpetuate racist and sexist stereotypes of men and women of color.

- The U.S. Supreme Court decision in the Walmart discrimination lawsuit is the topic of the lived experience in Chapter 4, "Gender Inequality."

- Being "too young" or "too old" to find employment is the topic of the lived experience in Chapter 5, "Inequality Based on Age."

- Chapter 7, "Prostitution, Pornography, and the Sex Industry" contains a lived experience by a porn film star who works in the sex industry so that she can support herself and her three children.

- Elite criminals, such as Raj Rajaratnam, provide the lived experience for Chapter 9, "Crime and Criminal Justice."

- The lived experience in Chapter 10, "Health Care: Problems of Physical and Mental Illness," is provided by a patient with multiple chronic illnesses who is able to find a social network of individuals with similar problems.

- A Latino single father provides the opening lived experience for Chapter 11, "The Changing Family."

- Chapter 13, "Problems in Politics and the Global Economy," offers lived experiences of how a collapse in the mining industry in Europe and of factories in the United States harms the communities in which they are located and the people who live therein.

- Zainub Razvi in Pakistan and Amanda Hirsch in the United States describe their similar problems with Internet addiction because they spend large amounts on time online to the exclusion of people and other activities (Chapter 14, "Problems in the Media").

- The 2011 Oslo terrorist attack is the subject of the lived experience in Chapter 17, "Global Social Problems: War and Terrorism."

- The BP Gulf oil spill and the Hurricane Katrina disaster are the foundation for the lived experiences in Chapter 18, "Can Social Problems Be Solved?"

Interesting and Highly Relevant Boxed Features

In addition to the "Critical Thinking and You" boxes, four other types of boxes—"Social Problems in the Media," "Social Problems and Social Policy," "Social Problems in Global Perspective," and "Social Problems and Statistics"—highlight important current topics regarding pressing social problems:

- *Social Problems and Social Policy:* Boxes include "'Packing Heat': Should College Students Be Allowed to Carry Guns on Campus?" (Chapter 1, "Studying Social Problems in the Twenty-First Century"); "Paying for Health Care: Can We Learn from Canada, the United Kingdom, and Sweden?" (Chapter 10, "Health Care: Problems of Physical and Mental Illness"); and "Journalism Ethics 101: The Media and People They Cover" (Chapter 14, "Problems in the Media").

Social Problems and Social Policy · Box 8.2

Legalizing Marijuana: An Issue That Never Goes Away

The controversy over marijuana has been going on for a long time and is still far from being resolved. Advocates of legalization suggest that marijuana use should no longer be subject to legal control. Some states have adopted some form of decriminalization for the possession of small amounts—usually less than one ounce or so—of marijuana. Other states have passed medical marijuana laws that permit use of the drug under specific medical circumstances. Advocates of these laws believe that doctors should be allowed to prescribe marijuana or that the federal government should lift the ban on the medical use of this drug altogether. Advocates of medical legalization believe that marijuana's benefits in treating certain medical conditions far outweigh its possible adverse consequences. For example, marijuana can help control glaucoma, an eye disease that eventually produces blindness. It also can forestall AIDS-related complications, ease the nausea

Michigan, Montana, Nevada, New Jersey, New Mexico, Oregon, Rhode Island, Vermont, and Washington) and the District of Columbia currently allow the use of marijuana for medical purposes, and several state have decriminalized its recreational use so that the fine for possession of marijuana in limited amounts is about the equivalent of a traffic ticket. However, that does not mean that a person cannot be prosecuted for marijuana use. The U.S. Supreme Court ruled in 2005 that medical marijuana users could be federally prosecuted because federal drug laws take precedence over state drug laws—and under federal law, marijuana is a *controlled substance*, which makes distribution of the drug a crime, even if it is being used for medicinal purposes. Marijuana is defined as a controlled substance because it is listed as a Schedule I drug under the 1970 Controlled Substances Act. Schedule I substances have a high potential for abuse, no cur-

---

- *Social Problems in Global Perspective:* Boxes include "What Do France and the United States Have in Common? Complex Racial and Immigration Issues, for One Thing" (Chapter 3, "Racial and Ethnic Inequality"); "An International Message for Gay Teens: Problems Remain Worldwide but 'It Gets Better'" (Chapter 6, "Inequality Based on Sexual Orientation"); "Motherhood from Afar: Parenting Other People's Children to Give One's Own Children a Better Future" (Chapter 11 "The Changing Family"); "The Malling of Dubai: Transnational Corporations in the Midst of Affluence

---

Social Problems in Global Perspective · Box 2.1

World Hunger, Food Losses, and Food Waste?

The most heartbreaking thing about starving children is their equanimity. They don't cry. They don't smile. They don't move. They don't show a flicker of fear, pain or interest. Tiny, wizened zombies, they shut down all nonessential operations to employ every last calorie to stay alive.

—New York Times columnist Nicholas D. Kristof (2009) laments the overwhelming sight of malnourished children in West Africa

Roughly one-third of the edible parts of food produced for human consumption gets lost or wasted

Food Program's senior food security analyst, explains the cause of food riots: "The human instinct is to survive, and people are going to do no matter what to survive. And if you're hungry you get angry quicker" (Lacey, 2008:A11). However, some of the world's poorest people do not riot at all and merely suffer in silence because they are physically too weak to engage in activism or they must channel what little energy they have into survival for themselves and their children, as journalist Nicholas Kristof described earlier.

Why does so much hunger exist worldwide? The most popular answer to this question typically relates to the issue of *scarcity*, and the solution is seen as more effectively producing and distributing food so that fewer people

---

and Poverty" (Chapter 13, "Problems in Politics and the Global Economy"); and "Anti-Muslim Blogs That Travel around the World" (Chapter 17, "Global Social Problems: War and Terrorism").

- *Social Problems and Statistics:* Boxes include "Poverty in the United States" (Chapter 2, "Wealth and Poverty"); and "Accurate and Inaccurate Comparisons" (Chapter 3, "Racial and Ethnic Inequality").

Social Problems and Statistics · Box 2.2

Poverty in the United States

Is the problem of poverty in the United States a larger or smaller problem today than it was in the past? The good news is that during the past four decades, the *poverty rate*—the percentage of the U.S. population that the government defines as being "poor"—declined from 21 percent early in the 1960s to 14.3 percent in 2009 (DeNavas-Walt et al., 2010). The bad news is that the *total number of people living in poverty* is still 43.6 million people

notes that statistics play an important role in campaigns to create or to refute claims about social problems. If statistics indicate that a social condition adversely affects large numbers of people, that condition may be defined as a social problem that requires that a society do something about it. However, if the statistics indicate that fewer people are adversely affected or that the number of people so affected is going down, that condition may be downgraded as a con-

the expansion of some public policies and to demand the end of others (such as "welfare as we know it"). Instead of using statistics to reaffirm our political perspective, we may gain more by looking at these figures from a sociological perspective. An increase in the total number of people living below the poverty line, as also reported by the U.S. Census Bureau, is a statistic that can be used to validly argue that poverty remains as serious a social problem today, and

---

BUILT-IN STUDY FEATURES

These pedagogical aids promote students' mastery of sociological concepts and perspectives.

- *New to This Edition:* "Did You Know?" is a three-bullet response to the question at the beginning of each chapter that provides students with several concise points to think about as they read the chapter. Each chapter also contains a new "Independent Research" suggestion in one of the boxed features to encourage students to engage in personal observation and note-taking or to conduct Internet research on specific topics so that they can expand their sociological insights on pressing issues.

DID YOU KNOW

- Jobs traditionally associated with men tend to pay better than jobs associated with women, even for the same level of education and skill.

- About 40 percent of working women are employed in "female" occupations such as nursing and teaching.

- Women employed in "male" occupations still earn less, on average, than their male counterparts in similar jobs.

- *Thinking Sociologically.* A bulleted list of critical thinking questions at the beginning of each chapter gives students an overview of major topics.

- *Summary in Question-and-Answer Format.* Each chapter concludes with a concise summary in a convenient question-and-answer format to help students master the key concepts and main ideas in each chapter.

- *Key Terms.* Major concepts and key terms are defined and highlighted in bold print within the text. Definitions are provided the first time a concept is introduced; they are also available in the Glossary at the back of the text.

Gender Inequality

CHAPTER
4

THINKING SOCIOLOGICALLY

- Why should we be concerned about sexual harassment? How is sexual harassment related to gender inequality?
- What types of gender socialization influence our ideas about what it means to be a woman or a man?
- How does gender-segregated work contribute to the larger picture of gender inequality in a society?

Marginal annotations link to relevant content to review and explore in MySocLab.

ORGANIZATION OF THIS TEXT

Social Problems in a Diverse Society, Sixth Edition, has been organized with the specific plan of introducing disparities in wealth and poverty, race and ethnicity, gender, age, and sexual orientation early on, so that the concepts and perspectives developed in these chapters may be applied throughout the text. Chapter 1 explains the *sociological perspective* and highlights the issue of violence to draw students into an examination of such debates as whether "guns kill people" or "people kill people."

Chapter 2 looks at *wealth and poverty* in the United States and around the world. The chapter provides new insights on wealth compared with income inequality and on problems such as homelessness, low-income and poverty-level neighborhoods, and the relationship between "cheap labor" and the global economy. Chapter 3

integrates the previous discussion of class-based inequalities with an examination of *racial and ethnic inequality.* Chapter 4 discusses *gender inequality* and highlights factors such as mainstream gender socialization and social barriers that contribute to the unequal treatment of women in the workplace and family and at school and other social institutions. Ageism and *inequality based on age* are discussed in Chapter 5. *Inequality based on sexual orientation* is examined in Chapter 6, where concerns such as how gay men and lesbians are portrayed on television shows are discussed and problems regarding an accurate count of the number of gays and lesbians are described.

Chapter 7 links previous discussions of race, class, and gender to an analysis of *prostitution, pornography, and the sex industry.* In Chapter 8, *alcohol and other drugs* are discussed in depth, and students are provided with information about the so-called date rape drug and the abuse of prescription drugs, over-the-counter drugs, and caffeine. Chapter 9 discusses *crime and criminal justice* and takes an incisive look at sociological explanations of crime.

Beginning with Chapter 10, a look at *health care and its problems,* we examine some of the major social institutions in our society and note aspects of each that constitute a social problem for large numbers of people. Chapter 10 discusses the Affordable Care Act, its possible effects on health care in the United States, and the legal challenges associated with this attempt to bring about more universal health coverage in this country. The chapter also explores global enemies of health in low-income nations. Chapter 11 analyzes *the changing family,* emphasizing diversity in intimate relationships and families, and child-related family issues such as problems with day care. Chapter 12 presents contemporary *problems in education,* tracing the problems to such issues as what schools are supposed to accomplish, how they are financed, and why higher education is not widely accessible. Chapter 13 focuses on *problems in politics and the global economy* and provides a variety of perspectives on political power and the role of the military-industrial complex in U.S. politics and the economy. Chapter 14, a discussion of *problems in the media,* looks at how newer social media and concentration in existing mainstream media affects the news and entertainment that people receive. Chapter 15 provides a survey of problems associated with *population and the environmental crisis,* particularly focusing on the causes and consequences of overpopulation and high rates of global migration. Chapter 16, a look at *urban problems,* details the powerful impact of urbanization on both high-income and low-income nations of the world. Chapter 17 discusses *global social problems related to war and terrorism*. After discussing such topics as militarism, military technology, and war in historical context, the text examines current issues of war and terrorism. Chapter 18 asks, "*Can social problems be solved?*" and includes a review of the sociological theories used to explain social problems, plus an analysis of attempts at problem solving at the microlevel, midrange, and macrolevel of society.

SUPPLEMENTS

Instructor's Manual and Test Bank <**ISBN** 0205249752> Each chapter in the Instructor's Manual offers a variety of the following types of resources: Chapter Summary, New to This Chapter (for revisions), Chapter Outline, Learning Objectives, Critical Thinking Questions, Activities for Classroom Participation, Key Terms, Weblinks, Suggested Readings, and Suggested Films. Designed to make your lectures more effective and to save preparation time, this extensive resource gathers useful activities and strategies for teaching your course.

Also included in this manual is a test bank offering multiple-choice, true/false, fill-in-the-blank, and/or essay questions for each chapter. The Instructor's Manual with test bank is available to adopters at www .pearsonhighered.com.

MyTest <**ISBN** 0205249787> This computerized software allows instructors to create their own personalized exams, to edit any or all of the existing test questions, and to add new questions. Other special features of this program include random generation of test questions, creation of alternate versions of the same test, scrambling question sequence, and test preview before printing. For easy access, this software is available within the instructor section of the **MySocLab**, or at www .pearsonhighered.com.

PowerPoint Presentations <**ISBN** 0205249779> The PowerPoint presentations for *Social Problems in a Diverse Society, Sixth Edition,* are informed by instructional and design theory. You have the option in every chapter of choosing from any of the following types of slides: Lecture & Line Art, Clicker Response System, and/or Special Topics PowerPoints. The Lecture PowerPoint slides follow the chapter outline and feature images from the textbook integrated with the text. The Clicker Response System allows you to get immediate feedback from your students regardless of class size. The Special Topics PowerPoint slides allow you to integrate rich supplementary material into your course with minimal preparation time. Additionally, all of the PowerPoints are uniquely designed to present concepts in a clear and succinct manner. They are available to adopters at www .pearsonhighered.com.

MYSOCLAB

MySocLab <**ISBN** 0205877893> is an engaging student and faculty learning system for sociology courses. It allows students to test their mastery of the concepts in the book by providing chapter-by-chapter diagnostic pretests, post-tests, and exams, all of which have been revised for the Census Update edition of the text. Results from the diagnostic tests build a customized study plan, and students are provided rich supplementary content, including flashcards and recommendations for further reading, to help them learn any concepts they have not yet mastered.

MySocLab allows instructors to track the progress of both individual students and the class as a whole. Based on the diagnostic results of the class, instructors receive a suggested customized lesson plan. The customized lesson plan enables the instructor to modify classroom activities to reflect student performance.

MySocLab also features chapter-specific Media Assignments, including Social Explorer®, which provides easy access to demographic information about the United States using interactive data maps, and Associated Press videos and interactive activities addressing current news events.

Students can use MySocLab to access the Pearson eText, making it easy to search the text and take notes electronically. Updated chapter-by-chapter audio files accompany the Pearson eText. MySocLibrary, another feature of MySocLab, offers electronic versions of over 100 classic and contemporary readings in sociology that include introductions, multiple choice questions, and essay/discussion questions for each reading.

MySocLab is available as a premium Web site with no course management features or requirements, or it can be accessed through either BlackBoard or WebCT course management platforms.

Succeed with **MySocLab**   www.mysoclab.com

The new MySocLab delivers proven results in helping students succeed, provides engaging experiences that personalize learning, and comes from a trusted partner with educational expertise and a deep commitment to helping students and instructors achieve their goals.

Here are a few activities you will find for this chapter:

Watch on mysoclab.com   **Core Concepts** video clips feature sociologists in action, exploring important concepts in the study of Social Problems. Watch:
• Women in the Workplace

Explore on mysoclab.com   **Social Explorer** is an interactive application that allows you to explore Census data through interactive maps. Explore:
• Social Explorer Activity: Changing Household Size Between 1970 and 2000

Read on mysoclab.com   **MySocLibrary** includes primary source readings from classic and contemporary sociologists. Read:
• The Way We Weren't: The Myth and Reality of the "Traditional" Family

ACKNOWLEDGMENTS

I wish to thank personally the many people who have made this Sixth Edition a reality. First, I offer my profound thanks to the following reviewers who provided valuable comments and suggestions on how to make this text outstanding. Whenever possible, I have incorporated their suggestions into the text. The reviewers are:

Sixth Edition
Stephen Morewitz, San Jose State University
Christabel Rogalin, Purdue University, North Central
Gerald Titchener, Des Moines Area Community College
Suzanne Weber, Broward College

Fifth Edition
Michele Bogue, Texas Christian University
Leslie Cintron, Washington & Lee University
Brian Hawkins, University of Colorado–Boulder
Jason Mazaik, Massbay Community College

Fourth Edition
Todd F. Bernhardt, Broward Community College
Ann Marie Hickey, University of Kansas
Amy Holzgang, Cerritos College
Dr. Fred Jones, Simpson College
Dr. Gordon W. Knight, Green Mountain College

Third Edition
Joanne Ardovini-Brooker, Sam Houston State University
Bernadette Barton, Morehead State University
Tody Buchanan, Dallas Baptist University
Janice DeWitt-Heffner, Marymount University
Marcie Goodman, University of Utah
Judith Greenberg, Georgia State University
Patricia A. Joffer, Mesa State College
Thomas G. Sparhawk, Central Virginia Community College

Second Edition
Susan Cody, Brookdale Community College
William A. Cross, Illinois College
Jennifer A. John, Germanna Community College
James J. Norris, Indiana University, South Bend
Anne R. Peterson, Columbus State Community College

First Edition
Allan Bramson, Wayne County Community College
Scott Burcham, University of Memphis
Keith Crew, University of Northern Iowa
Mike Hoover, Western Missouri State College
Mary Riege Laner, Arizona State University
Patricia Larson, Cleveland State University
Kathleen Lowney, Valdosta State College
Edward Morse, Tulane University
Charles Norman, Indiana State University
James Payne, St. Edward's University
Anne R. Peterson, Columbus State Community College
Margaret Preble, Thomas Nelson Community College
Dale Spady, Northern Michigan University
John Stratton, University of Iowa

This Sixth Edition of *Social Problems in a Diverse Society* has involved the cooperative efforts of many people who have gone above and beyond the call of duty to make the book possible. I wish to thank Karen Hanson, publisher, for her efforts throughout the publishing process. Likewise, I wish to thank Heidi Allgair of Element LLC, who made everything run smoothly. I am extremely grateful to Denise Forlow at Pearson. I wish to especially thank Elsa Peterson, an excellent researcher and publications specialist, for her guidance and assistance on the Sixth Edition.

To each of you reading this preface, I wish you the best in teaching or studying social problems and hope that you will share with me any comments or suggestions you have about *Social Problems in a Diverse Society,* Sixth Edition. The text was written with you in mind. Let's hope that our enthusiasm for "taking a new look at social problems" will spread to others so that together we may seek to reduce or solve some of the pressing social problems we encounter during our lifetime.

DIANA KENDALL

Studying Social Problems in the Twenty-First Century

THINKING SOCIOLOGICALLY

- Why are social problems everybody's problem?

- How does sociology differ from "common sense" in explaining social problems?

- Do you agree with this statement: "Guns don't kill people; people kill people"? Is this sound sociological thinking?

So we were all freaking out, and it was . . . I don't know . . . it was scary. . . . Oh my gosh. There could be someone else out there. But there was literally cops everywhere you turned. There were a couple of policemen standing right there and blocking off certain areas where they didn't know if it was safe to walk yet.

—*"Hailey," a University of Texas sophomore, explains how she felt as she watched from her classroom during a university-wide lockdown when SWAT teams swarmed her campus university after another student opened fire with an assault rifle, shooting randomly into both the air and the ground, before killed himself (Klaus, 2010; Fleming, 2010).*

None of us thought it was gunshots. [The shooter] didn't say a single word the whole time. He didn't say get down. He didn't say anything. He just came in and started shooting. . . . I'm not sure how long it lasted. It felt like a really long time but was probably only a minute or so. He looked like, I guess you could say, serious. He didn't look frightened at all. He didn't look angry. Just a straight face.

—*Trey Perkins, a Virginia Tech University student, describes a scene of violence in the lecture hall where his German class met. Before the lone gunman ended his shooting spree, thirty-three people were dead and more than two dozen others were wounded (msnbc.com, 2007).*

For those of us who spend our days in a college setting, few things scare us more than the thought that violence might shatter our "protected" social environment in a lecture hall or other campus facility. Sadly, however, such shootings are becoming an all-too-common occurrence in educational settings, from elementary and secondary schools to colleges and universities across the United States. And schools are only one of the many settings in which seemingly random acts of violence, typically involving guns and multiple injuries or deaths, take place. Violence has also become all too common in locations such as shopping malls, workplaces, hospitals, and other public spaces. Regardless of where the violence occurs, it leaves behind shock and anguish. **Violence is the use of physical force to cause pain, injury, or death to another or damage to property**. On an almost daily basis, the Internet and global television news channels quickly spread word of the latest bombing, the latest massacre, or the latest murder. In the United States today, gunfire is one of the leading causes of death—only vehicular accidents take a higher toll on the lives of young people in this country. Indeed, the United States has the highest homicide rate of any high-income nation. In this chapter, we explore what we can learn from sociology about social problems such as this.

USING SOCIOLOGICAL INSIGHTS TO STUDY SOCIAL PROBLEMS

Sociologists who specialize in the study of social problems often focus on violence as a pressing social issue because it inflicts harm not only on victims and their families but also on entire communities and the nation. The study of social problems is one area of inquiry within *sociology*—the **academic discipline that engages in the systematic study of human society and social interactions**. A sociological examination of social problems focuses primarily on issues that affect an entire *society* —**a large number of individuals who share the same geographic territory and are subject to the same political authority and dominant cultural expectations**—and the groups and organizations that make up that society. *Culture* **refers to the knowledge, language, values, customs, and material objects that are passed from person to person and from one generation to the next in a human group or society**. Culture helps us define what we think is right or wrong and identify the kinds of behavior we believe should be identified as a social problem.

What Is a Social Problem?

A *social problem* is a social condition (such as poverty) or a pattern of behavior (such as substance abuse) that harms some individuals or all people in a society and that a sufficient number of people believe warrants public concern and collective action to bring about change. Social conditions or certain patterns of behavior are defined as social problems when they systematically disadvantage or harm a significant number of people or when they are seen as harmful by many of the people who wield power, wealth, and influence in a group or society. Problems that disadvantage or harm a significant number of people include violence, fear of crime, environmental pollution, and inadequate access to health care.

Problems that may be viewed as harmful to people who have power, wealth, and influence are conditions that adversely affect their economic livelihood and social well-being, such as a weakening economy, inadequate schools that do not produce the quality of workers that employers need, and high rates of crime that threaten their safety and security. To put it another way, social problems are social in their causes, consequences, and sources of possible resolution. Because social problems are social in their causes, public perceptions of what constitutes a social problem change over time (see Table 1.1). It is no surprise, for

example, that concerns about economy, unemployment, and the federal budget deficit are important to people in the United States today given the difficult times that many people have experienced in recent years as well as extensive media coverage of economic concerns as dominant national issues.

Sociologists apply theoretical perspectives and use a variety of research methods to examine social problems. Some social problems—such as violence and crime—are commonly viewed as conditions that affect all members of a population. Other social problems—such as racial discrimination—may be viewed (correctly or incorrectly) as a condition that affects some members of a population more than others. However, all social problems may be harmful to all members in a society whether they realize it or not. As an example, sociological research has documented the extent to which racial discrimination by whites against African Americans and other people of color wastes the energies and resources of those individuals who engage in such racist actions as well as harming the targets of their actions (see Feagin and Vera, 1995).

TABLE 1.1 Changing Perceptions of What Constitutes a Social Problem, 1950–2011

Nationwide polls taken over the last half century reflect dramatic changes in how people view social problems. Notice how responses to the question "What do you think is the most important problem facing the country today?" have changed over the years.

1950		1965		1975	
War	40%	Civil rights	52%	High cost of living	60%
The economy	15%	Vietnam War	22%	Unemployment	20%
Unemployment	10%	Other international problems	14%	Dissatisfaction with government	7%
Communism	8%	Racial strife	13%	Energy crisis	7%
1990		**2005**		**2011**	
Budget deficit	21%	War in Iraq	19%	Economy in general	26%
Drug abuse	18%	The economy/jobs	18%	Unemployment	19%
Poverty, homelessness	7%	Terrorism (general)	6%	Federal budget deficit	17%
The economy	7%	Health care	5%	Dissatisfaction with government	13%
		Social Security	4%	Health care	9%
		Moral/family values	4%	Education	6%

Sources: *The New York Times*, 1996b; The Polling Report, 2005; J. Jones, 2011.

Social problems often involve significant discrepancies between the ideals of a society and their actual achievement. For example, the United States was founded on basic democratic principles that include the right to "Life, Liberty, and the pursuit of Happiness," as set forth in the Declaration of Independence. The rights of individuals are guaranteed by the U.S. Constitution, which also provides the legal basis for remedying injustices. Significant discrepancies exist, however, between the democratic ideal and its achievement. One such discrepancy is *discrimination*—**actions or practices of dominant group members (or their representatives) that have a harmful impact on members of subordinate groups**. Discrimination may be directed along class, racial, gender, and age lines. It also may be directed against subordinate group members whose sexual orientation, religion, nationality, or other attributes are devalued by those who discriminate against them. Sometimes, discrimination is acted out in the form of violence. This type of violent act is referred to as a *hate crime*—**a physical attack against a person because of assumptions regarding his or her racial group, ethnicity, religion, disability, sexual orientation, national origin, or ancestry**. Hate crime laws have been adopted on the federal and state level that increase the penalties for crimes committed when the perpetrator is motivated by the race, color, national origin, religion, sexual orientation, gender, or disability of the victim. For example, some states have laws criminalizing interference with religious worship. However, hate crime laws vary widely, and five states have no hate crime laws and any complaints would have to be dealt with as a civil action. Among those states that have passed hate crime laws, some of the laws do not protect sexual orientation, which remains a heavily debated issue regarding hate crime legislation. For many people, hate crimes are a personal problem because they believe that they have been the victim of violent attacks based on their race, ethnicity, religion, sexual orientation, or other devalued attributes.

When hate crimes have been reported prominently by the news media, some political leaders have taken a stronger stand against such violence, thus moving the problem from the personal to the social level. For example, when an African American man in New York City was attacked with a baseball bat, leaving him with a fractured skull, the city's mayor made public appearances around the city to show that the city would actively confront racial violence and would not tolerate it. As Mayor Michael R. Bloomberg stated, "I cannot stress it enough: We are going to live together, and nobody, nobody, should ever feel that they will be attacked because of their ethnicity, their orientation, their religion, where they live, their documented status, or anything else. Period. End of story" (quoted in Rutenberg and Kilgannon, 2005:A15). Public statements such as this and corresponding changes in social policy and law are the point at which personal problems and social issues begin to connect. Sociologists use a perspective known as the sociological imagination to explain this phenomenon.

The Sociological Imagination: Bringing Together the Personal and the Social

How do our personal problems relate to the larger social problems in our society and around the world? Although each of us has numerous personal problems, ranging from how to pay our college tuition and where to find a job to more general concerns about safety, health, and war, we are not alone in these problems, and there are larger societal and global patterns that we can identify that are related to these issues. In one of the most popular phrases in the social sciences, sociologist C. Wright Mills uniquely captured the essence of how our personal troubles are related to the larger social issues in society. According to Mills, the *sociological imagination* **is the ability to see the relationship between individual experiences and the larger society**. The sociological imagination enables us to connect the private problems of individuals to public issues. Public issues (or social problems) are matters beyond a person's control that originate at the regional or national level and can be resolved only by collective action. Mills (1959b) used unemployment as an example of how people may erroneously separate personal troubles from public issues in their thinking. The unemployed individual may view his or her unemployment as a personal trouble concerning only the individual, other family members, and friends. However, widespread unemployment resulting from economic changes, corporate decisions (downsizing or relocating a plant abroad), or technological innovations (computers and advanced telecommunications systems displacing workers) is a public issue. As another example, it is easy for the victims of violent crimes and their families to see themselves as individual victims rather than placing such attacks within the larger, collective context of a society that often tolerates violence. The sociological imagination helps us shift our focus to the larger social context and see how personal troubles may be related to public issues.

Enron employees leave the company's headquarters after being laid off December 3, 2001, in Houston, Texas. Business scandals such as the one involving Enron Corporation show the wide gap between those corporate executives who made millions of dollars from questionable business practices that eventually brought down their companies and the employees who lost their jobs and benefits when those companies folded.

Sociologists make connections between personal and public issues in society through microlevel and macrolevel analysis. ***Microlevel analysis* focuses on small-group relations and social interaction among individuals**. Using microlevel analysis, a sociologist might investigate how fear of unemployment affects workers and their immediate families. In contrast, ***macrolevel analysis* focuses on social processes occurring at the societal level, especially in large-scale organizations and major social institutions such as politics, government, and the economy**. Using macrolevel analysis, a sociologist might examine how the loss of about 7.9 millions jobs in Great Recession of 2007–2009 affected the U.S. economy. As Mills suggested, a systematic study of a social problem such as unemployment gives us a clearer picture of the relationship between macrolevel structures such as the U.S. economy and microlevel social interactions among people in their homes, workplaces, and communities.

What can we gain by using a sociological perspective to study social problems? A sociological examination of social problems enables us to move beyond myths and common-sense notions, to gain new insights into ourselves, and to develop an awareness of the connection between our own world and the worlds of other people. According to sociologist Peter Berger (1963:23), a sociological examination allows us to realize that "things are not what they seem." Indeed, most social problems are multifaceted. When we recognize this, we can approach pressing national and global concerns in new ways and make better decisions about those concerns. By taking a global perspective on social problems, we soon realize that the lives of all people are closely intertwined and that any one nation's problems are part of a larger global problem. Examining violence as a social problem, for example, makes it possible for us to look at the causes and consequences of this type of behavior on a global basis. It also makes it possible for us to look more closely at our own society to see how we respond to such problems through social policy. An example is the renewed call by many members of society for gun control in the aftermath of each new episode of gun-related violence and the contradictory assertion from organizations such as the National Rifle Association that gun-control laws are neither needed nor effective (see Box 1.1). As this example shows, what constitutes a social problem and what should be done about that problem is often a controversial topic.

DO WE HAVE A PROBLEM? SUBJECTIVE AWARENESS AND OBJECTIVE REALITY

A subjective awareness that a social problem exists usually emerges before the objective reality of the problem is acknowledged. Subjective awareness tends to be expressed as a feeling of uneasiness or skepticism about something, but the feeling is not founded on any concrete evidence that a problem actually exists. A subjective awareness that there is potential for violent acts in public settings such as schools, day-care centers, businesses, and churches exists even when there has been no recent violence in one of these settings. However, when new killings take place, our subjective awareness shifts to being an objective reality.

Consider, for example, the differences in subjective awareness and objective reality when it comes to violence in the media. Many people feel uncomfortable with the increasingly graphic nature of portrayals of violence on television and in films and video games.

Social Problems and Social Policy

Box 1.1

"Packing Heat": Should College Students Be Allowed to Carry Guns on Campus?

It's strictly a matter of self-defense. I don't ever want to see repeated on a Texas college campus what happened at Virginia Tech, where some deranged, suicidal madman goes into a building and is able to pick off totally defenseless kids like sitting ducks.

—Texas State Senator Jeff Wentworth comments on why he supported legislation in Texas to give college students and professors the right to carry guns on campus (Vertuno, 2011)

There is no scenario where allowing concealed weapons on college campuses will do anything other than create a more dangerous environment for students, faculty, staff and visitors.

—Glen Johnson, Oklahoma Chancellor of Higher Education, explains why he is opposed to concealed handguns on campus (Vertuno, 2011).

Although few states have actually enacted a law expressly allowing individuals to carry concealed weapons on public college campuses, the issue of whether students, faculty, and staff (in addition to public safety personnel) should be allowed to possess guns or other concealed weapons on campuses comes up quite often. Social policy questions regarding this issue typically are framed in terms of "concealed weapons," but the focus of these discussions is primarily on guns. As Katherine S. Newman and her associates found in a study of public school violence, gun availability is a key reason why many school shootings are so deadly: "Mass murders tend not to happen—in school or anywhere else—when knives are the only weapon available" (Newman, Fox, Harding, Mehta, and Roth, 2004:69). To curb the high number of deaths related to firearms in this nation, pro-gun-control advocates believe that we need social policies that regulate the gun industry and gun ownership. However, opponents of gun-control measures argue that regulation will not curb random violence perpetrated by a few disturbed or frustrated individuals.

What is social policy and how is it supposed to alleviate such problems as violence in society? Social scientists use the term *social policy* to refer to a written set of ideas and goals that are formally adopted by a relevant decision-making body, for example, a government bureaucracy, a state legislature, or the U.S. Congress. According to sociologist Joel Best (1999:143), we often think of social policy as a means of "declaring war" on a social problem. Social policy discussions on gun-related violence at the state and federal levels have focused on how to win the "war" on guns. However, as Best (1999:147) notes, "Warfare presumes that fighting

the enemy is a common cause for the entire society; individuals should set aside their doubts and reservations and join in the larger struggle. . . . Declaring war, then, is a call for a united, committed campaign against a social problem."

In the case of gun-related violence, however, there is a profound lack of societal consensus on the causes of the problem and what should be done about it. Some favor regulation of the gun industry and gun ownership; others believe that regulation will not curb random violence perpetrated by frustrated individuals. Underlying the arguments for and against gun control are these words from the Second Amendment to the U.S. Constitution: "A well regulated Militia, being necessary to the security of a free State, the right of the people to keep and bear Arms, shall not be infringed." Those in favor of legislation to regulate the gun industry and gun ownership argue that the Second Amendment does not guarantee an individual's right to own guns: The right to keep and bear Arms applies only to those citizens who do so as part of an official state militia. However, the U.S. Supreme Court ruled in 2008 that the Second Amendment protects an individual's right to own a gun for personal use. In other words, people have a constitutionally protected right to keep a loaded handgun at home for self-defense. This is in keeping with an argument long made by spokespersons for the National Rifle Association (NRA), a powerful group with about 4.3 million members nationwide, which has stated that gun control regulations

To curb the high number of deaths related to firearms in this nation, pro-gun-control advocates believe that we need social policies that regulate the gun industry and gun ownership. However, opponents of gun-control measures argue that regulation will not curb random violence perpetrated by a few disturbed or frustrated individuals.

Social Problems and Social Policy

Box 1.1 continued

violate the individual's constitutional right to own a gun and would not be an effective means of curbing random acts of violence on school campuses and elsewhere.

What solutions exist for the quandary over gun regulations? Declaring war on a social problem such as gun-related violence is difficult for several reasons. First, social problems are not simple issues: Most problems have multiple causes and a variety of possible solutions. Second, it is difficult to determine what constitutes victory in such a war. Third, it takes a long time to see the outcome of changes in social policies, and efforts to produce change may receive reduced funding or be eliminated before significant changes actually occur. Finally, it is impossible to rally everyone behind a single policy, and much time is therefore spent arguing over how to proceed, how much money to spend, and who or what is the real enemy. In the final analysis, the problem of gun violence is a chronic problem in the United States that has yet to be successfully addressed by social policy and its implementation.

In the meantime, we return to the question we initially raised about students possessing guns at college. Those persons who believe that students should be allowed to carry guns on campus for self-defense assert that no acts of violence have occurred at universities where students are legally allowed to carry concealed handguns. They also note that many states set the legal age limit at twenty-one for obtaining a concealed handgun license, which means that the students who obtain such a license typically are juniors or seniors, not beginning college students. By contrast, those individuals and organizations that strongly object to non–law enforcement personnel "packing heat" on college campuses argue that when guns are readily available, there is a greater likelihood of lethal outcomes because people have violent force right at their fingertips when they fear for their safety or become involved in an emotionally volatile situation.

What will be the future of guns on college campuses? If gun rights lobbyists have their way, more states will allow concealed guns on college campuses; if most people in the academic community and other concerned citizens are listened to when they declare their opposition to laws granting students the right to carry firearms at their college or university, we hopefully will not have the deadly mix of students, guns, and campus life in the name of "self-defense." How do you feel about this very polarizing social policy issue? Would you feel more—or less—safe if you knew that many people were carrying concealed weapons on your campus?

Initially, parents have a subjective awareness that these depictions might be harmful for their children and perhaps for the larger society. However, it is only when we have facts to support our beliefs that there is a link between media violence and actual behavior that we move beyond a subjective awareness of the issue. Indeed, numerous studies show that media violence, including excessive use of violent video games, influences how young people think and act. For example, children who frequently watch violence on television may become less sensitive to pain and suffering of others. They may become more fearful of the world around them, and ultimately, they may be more likely to behave in aggressive or harmful ways toward other people. As researchers gather additional data to support their arguments, the link between extensive media watching and the potential for violence grows stronger, moving into the realm of objective reality rather than being merely a subjective awareness of isolated individuals. Of course, most studies are not without their critics, and this is the case for studies on media and violence. Debates flourish in scholarly journals between some researchers who believe that the risks of media violence have been exaggerated (such as Ferguson and Kilbrun, 2010) and other scholars (such as Bushman, Rothstein, and Anderson, 2010) whose findings support the belief that violent media, including video games, increase aggressive thoughts, angry feelings, and aggressive behaviors and decrease empathic feelings and prosocial behaviors.

However, even the gathering of objective facts does not always result in consensus on social issues. Individuals and groups may question the validity of the facts, or they may dispute the facts by using other data that they hope demonstrate a different perspective. Examples of objective conditions that may or may not be considered by everyone to be social problems include environmental pollution and resource depletion, war, health care, and changes in moral values. Religious and political views influence how people define social problems and what they think the possible solutions might be. Often, one person's solution to a problem is viewed as a problem by another person. For example, some people see abortion as a solution to an unwanted pregnancy, whereas others believe that abortion is a serious social problem. Abortion and end-of-life decisions (such as assisted suicide and "right to die" cases) are only two of the many issues that are strongly influenced by religion and politics in the United States. To analyze the conditions that must be met before an objective reality becomes identified as a social problem, see Box 1.2.

Just like other people, sociologists usually have strong opinions about what is "good" and "bad" in society and what might be done to improve conditions. However, sociologists know their opinions are often subjective. Thus, they use theory and systematic research techniques and report their findings to other social scientists for consideration. In other words, sociologists strive to view social problems *objectively*. Of course, complete objectivity may not be an attainable—or desirable—goal in studying human behavior. Max Weber, an early German sociologist, acknowledged that complete objectivity might be impossible but pointed out that *verstehen* ("understanding" or "insight") was critical to any analysis of social problems. According to Weber, *verstehen* enables individuals to see the world as others see it and to empathize with them. *Verstehen*, in turn, enables us to use the sociological imagination and employ social theory rather than our own opinions to analyze social problems.

USING SOCIAL THEORY TO ANALYZE SOCIAL PROBLEMS

To determine how social life is organized, sociologists develop theories and conduct research. A *theory* is a **set of logically related statements that attempt to describe, explain, or predict social events**. Theories are useful for explaining relationships between social concepts or phenomena, such as age and unemployment. They also help us interpret social reality in a distinct way by giving us a framework for organizing our observations. Sociologists refer to this theoretical framework as a *perspective*—**an overall approach or viewpoint toward some subject**. Three major theoretical perspectives have emerged in sociology: the functionalist perspective, which views society as a basically stable and orderly entity; the conflict perspective, which views society as an arena of competition and conflict; and the interactionist perspective, which focuses on the everyday, routine interactions among individuals. The functionalist and conflict perspectives are based on macrolevel analysis because they focus on social processes occurring at the societal level. The interactionist

---

Critical Thinking and You
Box 1.2

Determining What Constitutes a Social Problem

Which of the following is defined as a major social problem in the United States?

- Driving a motor vehicle, which results in approximately 32,708 U.S. deaths each year
- Playing contact sports in school, which results in many injuries and deaths among young people
- Hunting for wild game, which results in numerous injuries and deaths among hunters and bystanders

If you answered "None of the above," you are correct. Although driving a motor vehicle, playing contact sports, and hunting may have hazardous potential consequences, few people view these actions in and of themselves as being a social problem. In other words, not all behavior that may result in violence or even death is classified as a social problem.

What questions should we ask to determine if something is a social problem? Here are a few suggestions:

1. Is there a public outcry about this conduct or this condition? Are people actively discussing the issue and demanding that a resolution be found?

2. Does the conduct or condition reflect a gap between social ideals and social reality? What social ideals are involved? What is the social reality about the situation?

3. Are a large number of people involved in defining the problem and demanding that a solution be found? Does the matter have national attention? If not, is a special-interest group the primary source of demands that something be done about the condition?

4. Can a solution be found for the problem? If not, can we reduce the problem or alleviate the suffering of some victims of the problem?

Based on these questions, what pressing social issues are we overlooking in our nation or on a global basis that should be considered as social problems requiring immediate action? What issues receive too much attention from the media and the public? How do culture, religion, and politics influence our definition of what constitutes a social problem?

perspective is based on microlevel analysis because it focuses on small-group relations and social interaction.

The Functionalist Perspective

The functionalist perspective grew out of the works of early social thinkers such as Auguste Comte (1798–1857), the founder of sociology. Comte compared society to a living organism. Just as muscles, tissues, and organs of the human body perform specific functions that maintain the body as a whole, the various parts of society contribute to its maintenance and preservation. According to the *functionalist perspective*, **society is a stable, orderly system composed of a number of inter-related parts, each of which performs a function that contributes to the overall stability of society** (Parsons, 1951). These interrelated parts are social institutions (such as families, the economy, education, and the government) that a society develops to organize its main concerns and activities so that social needs are met. Each institution performs a unique function, contributing to the overall stability of society and the well-being of individuals (Merton, 1968). For example, the functions of the economy are producing and distributing goods (such as food, clothing, and shelter) and services (such as health care and dry cleaning), whereas the government is responsible for coordinating activities of other institutions, maintaining law and order, dealing with unmet social needs, and handling international relations and warfare.

Manifest and Latent Functions

Though the functions of the economy and the government seem fairly clear-cut, functionalists suggest that not all the functions of social institutions are intended and overtly recognized. In fact, according to the functionalist perspective, social institutions perform two different types of societal functions: manifest and latent. *Manifest functions* are intended and recognized consequences of an activity or social process. A manifest function of education, for example, is to provide students with knowledge, skills, and cultural values. In contrast, *latent functions* are the unintended consequences of an activity or social process that are hidden and remain unacknowledged by participants (Merton, 1968). The latent functions of education include the babysitter function of keeping young people off the street and out of the full-time job market and the matchmaking function whereby schools provide opportunities for students to meet and socialize with potential marriage partners. These functions are latent because schools were not created for babysitting or matchmaking, and most organizational participants do not acknowledge that these activities take place.

Dysfunctions and Social Disorganization

From the functionalist perspective, social problems arise when social institutions do not fulfill their functions or when dysfunctions occur. *Dysfunctions* are the undesirable consequences of an activity or social process that inhibit a society's ability to adapt or adjust (Merton, 1968). For example, a function of education is to prepare students for jobs, but if schools fail to do so, then students have problems finding jobs, employers have to spend millions of dollars on employee training programs, and consumers have to pay higher prices for goods and services to offset worker training costs. In other words, dysfunctions in education threaten other social institutions, especially families and the economy.

Dysfunctions can occur in society as a whole or in a part of society (a social institution). According to functionalists, dysfunctions in social institutions create social disorganization in the entire society. **Social disorganization refers to the conditions in society that undermine the ability of traditional social institutions to govern human behavior.** Early in the twentieth century, sociologists Robert E. Park (1864–1944) and Ernest W. Burgess (1886–1966) developed a social disorganization theory to explain why some areas of Chicago had higher rates of *social deviance*, which they defined as a pattern of rule violation, than other areas had. Social disorganization causes a breakdown in the traditional values and norms that serve as social control mechanisms, which, under normal circumstances, keep people from engaging in nonconforming behavior. **Values are collective ideas about what is right or wrong, good or bad, and desirable or undesirable in a specific society** (R. M. Williams, 1970). Although values provide ideas about behavior, they do not state explicitly how we should behave. Norms, on the other hand, have specific behavioral expectations. **Norms are established rules of behavior or standards of conduct.** French sociologist Emile Durkheim (1858–1917) suggested that social problems arise when people no longer agree on societal values and norms. According to Durkheim, periods of rapid social change produce *anomie*—a loss of shared values and sense of purpose in society. During these periods, social bonds grow weaker, social control is diminished, and people are more likely to engage in nonconforming patterns of behavior such as crime.

Explore the Concept

Social Explorer Activity: The Dissipation of the Agricultural Industry on mysoclab.com

Early sociologists, examining the relationship between social problems and rapid industrialization and urbanization in Britain, western Europe, and the United States in the late nineteenth and early twentieth centuries, noted that rapid social change intensifies social disorganization. *Industrialization* **is the process by which societies are transformed from a dependence on agriculture and handmade products to an emphasis on manufacturing and related industries**. At the beginning of the Industrial Revolution, thousands of people migrated from rural communities to large urban centers to find employment in factories and offices. New social problems emerged as a result of industrialization and *urbanization,* **the process by which an increasing proportion of a population lives in cities rather than in rural areas**. During this period of rapid technological and social change, a sharp increase occurred in urban social problems such as poverty, crime, child labor, inadequate housing, unsanitary conditions, overcrowding, and environmental pollution.

Applying the Functionalist Perspective to Problems of Violence

Some functionalists believe that violence arises from a condition of anomie, in which many individuals have a feeling of helplessness, normlessness, or alienation. Others believe that violence increases when social institutions such as the family, schools, and religious organizations weaken and the main mechanisms of social control in people's everyday lives are external (i.e., law enforcement agencies and the criminal justice system).

One functionalist explanation of violence, known as the *subculture of violence hypothesis*, **states that violence is part of the normative expectations governing everyday behavior among young males in the lower classes**. Violence is considered a by-product of their culture, which idealizes toughness and even brutality in the name of masculinity. According to criminologists Marvin E. Wolfgang and Franco Ferracuti (1967), who originated this theory, violent subcultures (for example, violent juvenile gangs and organized crime groups) are most likely to develop when young people, particularly males, have few legitimate opportunities available in their segment of society and when subcultural values accept and encourage violent behavior. In this context, young people come to consider aggression or violence a natural response to certain situations. More recent studies have linked the subculture of violence hypothesis to neighborhood codes of violence that are disproportionately found in violent inner-city neighborhoods

with large minority populations (Matsueda, Drakulich, and Kubrin, 2006). For many years, however, this perspective has been criticized for exclusively focusing on violence among young males, often persons of color, in the lower classes because it does not provide any explanation regarding violence perpetrated by people in the middle or upper classes.

Still other functionalist explanations of violence focus on how changes in social institutions put some people at greater risk of being victims of violent crime than others. According to the *lifestyle-routine activity approach*, **the patterns and timing of people's daily movements and activities as they go about obtaining the necessities of life—such as food, shelter, companionship, and entertainment—are the keys to understanding violent personal crimes and other types of crime in our society**. Looking at violence crime, for example, social institutions and people's lifestyle may contribute to the rate of certain types of offenses. Even when rates of violent crime in the United States dropped to the lowest level in nearly 40 years in 2011, cities such as Flint, Michigan, and New York City saw the number of violent crimes increase for all four types of violent crime—murder, rape, robbery, and aggravated assault (Oppel, 2011). What factors might contribute to these increases? We can only speculate because many variables are involved. However, a few structural factors we might consider in Flint, Michigan, are the closing of automobile and parts manufacturing plants, creating high rates of structural unemployment, and the prevalence of drugs and gangs. By contrast, structural factors contributing to high rates of violent crime in New York City might include the following:

- Many people reside in close proximity to each other but remain virtual strangers who are less likely to notice if something unusual happens.
- Many people live alone (because of being single, widowed, or divorced) and do not have others who look out for them.
- Many people walk or take public transportation and thus have greater vulnerability to unscrupulous individuals.
- Many people have variable work and leisure schedules that place them on the streets at all hours of the day and night and make them more vulnerable to violent attack.

These are just a few of the many factors related to the social structure and fabric of urban life that may increase the odds of being murdered, raped, robbed, or assaulted in some cities. The lifestyle-routine activity approach suggests that people who willingly put themselves in situations that expose them to the potential for violent crime should modify their behavior or that society should provide greater protection for people whose lifestyle routine leaves them vulnerable to attackers. The lifestyle-routine activity approach is good as far as it goes, but it does not address other issues such the causes of violence in the home and other supposedly safe havens in society.

How would a functionalist approach the problem of violence? Most functionalists emphasize shared moral values and social bonds. They believe that when rapid social change or other disruptions occur, moral values may erode and problems such as school violence or hate crimes are likely to occur. Functionalists believe that to reduce violence, families, schools, religious organizations, and other social institutions should be strengthened so that they can regenerate shared values and morality. Most functionalists also believe that those who engage in violent criminal behavior should be prosecuted to the full extent of the law.

The functional approach to social problems has been criticized for its acceptance of the status quo and for its lack of appreciation of how problems in society are associated with vast economic and social inequality, racism, sexism, ageism, and other forms of discrimination that keep our society from being an equal playing field for everyone.

The Conflict Perspective

The *conflict perspective* **is based on the assumption that groups in society are engaged in a continuous power struggle for control of scarce resources.** Unlike functionalist theorists, who emphasize the degree to which society is held together by a consensus on values, conflict theorists emphasize the degree to which society is characterized by conflict and discrimination. According to some conflict theorists, certain groups of people are privileged while others are disadvantaged through the unjust use of political, economic, or social power. Not all conflict theorists hold the same views about what constitutes the most important form of conflict. We will examine two principal perspectives: the value conflict perspective and the critical-conflict perspective.

The Value Conflict Perspective

According to value conflict theorists, social problems are conditions that are incompatible with group values. From this perspective, value clashes are ordinary occurrences in families, communities, and the larger society, in which individuals commonly hold many divergent values. Although individuals may share certain core values, they do not share all values or a common culture. As previously stated, culture refers to the knowledge, language, values, customs, and material objects that are passed from person to person and from one generation to the next in a human group or society.

Discrepancies between ideal and real culture are a source of social problems in all societies. *Ideal culture* refers to the values and beliefs that people claim they hold; *real culture* refers to the values and beliefs that they actually follow. In the United States, for example, members of the National Association for the Advancement of Colored People (NAACP), La Raza, the Ku Klux Klan, and the White Aryan Resistance all claim to adhere to ideal cultural values of equality, freedom, and liberty; however, these ideal cultural values come into direct conflict with real cultural values when issues of racial-ethnic relations arise. Peaceful celebrations held by members of the NAACP to celebrate the birthday of slain African American civil rights leader Martin Luther King, Jr., and KKK rallies in states such as Kentucky and Virginia to reclaim "White Power" are concrete examples of the clash between ideal and real cultural values. Groups may claim that they advocate for peace, justice, and fairness but their real culture, the values and beliefs they actually follow, are quite different (for an example, visit this website: http://kkkknights.com).

Critical-Conflict Perspective

Unlike the value conflict approach, critical-conflict theorists suggest that social problems arise out of the major contradictions inherent in the way societies are organized. Some critical-conflict perspectives focus on class inequalities in the capitalist economic system; others focus on inequalities based on race, ethnicity, or gender.

Most class perspectives on inequality have been strongly influenced by Karl Marx (1818–1883), a German economist and activist, who recognized that the emergence of capitalism had produced dramatic and irreversible changes in social life. *Capitalism* **is an economic system characterized by private ownership of the means of production, from which personal profits can be derived through market competition and without government intervention.** In contemporary capitalist economies, businesses are privately owned and operated for the profit of owners and corporate shareholders. According to Marx, members of the *capitalist class* (*the bourgeoisie*), who own and control the means of production (e.g., the land, tools, factories, and money for investment), are at the top of a system of social stratification that affords them different lifestyles and life chances from those of the members of the *working class* (the *proletariat*), who must sell their labor power (their potential ability to work) to capitalists. In selling their labor power, members of the working class forfeit control over their work, and the capitalists derive excessive profit from the workers' labor.

Marx believed that capitalism led workers to experience increased levels of impoverishment and alienation—a feeling of powerlessness and estrangement from other people and from oneself (Marx and Engels, 1847/1971:96). He predicted that the working class would eventually overthrow the capitalist economic system. Although Marx's prediction has not come about, Erik Olin Wright (1997) and other social scientists have modified and adapted his perspective to apply to contemporary capitalist nations. In today's capitalist nations, according to Wright, ownership of the means of production is only one way in which people gain the ability to exploit others. Two other ways in which individuals gain control are through control of property and control over other people's labor. In this view, upper-level managers and others in positions of authority gain control over societal resources and other individuals' time, knowledge, and skills in such a manner that members of the upper classes are able to maintain their dominance (Wright, 1997; Wright and Rogers, 2010).

Some critical-conflict perspectives focus on racial and gender subordination instead of class-based inequalities. Critical-conflict theorists who emphasize discrimination and inequality based on race or ethnicity note that many social problems are rooted in the continuing exploitation and subordination of people of color by white people. For example, Native Americans have the highest rates of poverty in the United States because of extended periods of racial subordination and exploitation throughout this country's history.

Critical-conflict theorists who use a feminist approach focus on *patriarchy*, a system of male dominance in which males are privileged and women are oppressed. According to a feminist approach, male domination in

Unions and other workers' organizations empower workers to voice their concerns in the capitalist system. Since the economic downturn that began in 2008, members of unions such as the United Auto Workers have joined in protests against what they see as destructive banking practices, excessive profits, and corporate tax breaks that destroy communities and hurt working families.

society contributes not only to domestic violence, child abuse, and rape but also to poverty and crimes such as prostitution. Feminist scholars state that gender inequality will not be eliminated in the home, school, and workplace until patriarchy is abolished and women and men are treated equally.

Finally, some critical-conflict theorists note that race, class, and gender are interlocking systems of privilege and oppression that result in social problems. For

Critical-conflict theorists observe that African American women are disproportionately affected by flooding, property damage, and housing displacement from hurricanes and other natural disasters.

example, black feminist scholar Patricia Hill Collins (1991, 2005) has pointed out that race, class, and gender are simultaneous forces of oppression for women of color, especially African American women. Critical-conflict analysts focusing on these intersections believe that equality can come about only when women across lines of race and class receive equal treatment (Andersen and Collins, 2009; Collins, 2005). Throughout this text, we will use critical-conflict theory (rather than the value conflict approach) to highlight the power relations that result in social problems.

Applying the Conflict Perspective to Problems of Violence

Conflict theorists who focus on class-based inequalities believe that the potential for violence is inherent in capitalist societies. In fact, say these theorists, the wealthy engage in one form of violence, and the poor engage in another. They note that the wealthy often use third parties to protect themselves and their families from bodily harm as well as to secure their property and investments in this country and elsewhere in the world. For example, the wealthy who live in the United States or other high-income nations and own factories (or own stock in factories) in middle- and low-income nations use the governments and police of those nations—third parties—to control workers who threaten to strike. The wealthy also influence U.S. government policy. For instance, they are likely to support U.S. military intervention—and thus violence—in nations where they have large investments at stake. However, sometimes the wealthy want the U.S. government to look the other way and not intervene in these nations in order to protect investments in countries in which dictators have made their investments profitable.

In contrast, these theorists say, when the poor engage in violence, the violence is typically committed by the individual and is a reaction to the unjust social and economic conditions he or she experiences daily on the bottom rung of a capitalist society. The economic exploitation of the poor, these theorists note, dramatically affects all aspects of the individual's life, including how the person reacts to daily injustices, stress, and other threatening situations. In violent street crimes, the vast majority of offenders—as well as victims—are poor, unemployed, or working in low-level, low-paying jobs. In fact, most violent street crime is an intraclass phenomenon: Poor and working-class people typically victimize others who are like themselves.

The conflict perspective argues that the criminal justice system is biased in favor of the middle and upper classes. Because it is, its definition of violence depends on where a person's race, class, and gender locate him or her in the system of stratification. In this way, violent crimes are but one part of a larger system of inequality and oppression. Sexism and racism are reinforced by the overarching class structure that benefits the powerful at the expense of the powerless. Exploitation of people of color and the poor creates a sense of hopelessness, frustration, and hostility in them that may boil over into violent acts such as rape or murder. At the same time, it is important to note that violent acts, including murder, occur across all class and racial-ethnic categories in the United States.

The conflict perspective that focuses on feminist issues specifically examines violence against women, for example, rape and most spousal abuse. One feminist perspective suggests that violence against women is a means of reinforcing patriarchy. According to the feminist perspective, in a patriarchal system, the sexual marketplace is characterized by unequal bargaining power, making transactions between men and women potentially coercive in nature. Gender stratification is reinforced by powerful physical, psychological, and social mechanisms of control, including force or the threat of force. Fear of violence forces women to change their ways of living, acting, and dressing and thus deprives them of many basic freedoms (Hunnicutt, 2009). The conflict perspective that focuses on racial-ethnic inequalities points out that racism is an important factor in explaining such violent acts as hate crimes. For example, contemporary brutality against African Americans, particularly men, may be traced to earlier periods when hanging or dragging was used to punish slave insurrections and to keep African Americans subservient during the Reconstruction and the subsequent years of legal racial segregation in the South.

No matter what approach conflict theorists take, they all agree on one thing: Violence is unlikely to diminish significantly unless inequalities based on class, gender, and race are reduced at the macrolevel in society. However, social problems must also be examined at the microlevel, where individuals actually live their daily lives.

The Symbolic Interactionist Perspective

Unlike the conflict perspective, which focuses on macrolevel inequalities in society, the symbolic interactionist perspective focuses on a microlevel analysis of how people act toward one another and how they make sense of their daily lives. The *symbolic interactionist perspective* views society as the sum of the interactions of individuals and groups. Most symbolic interactionists study social problems by analyzing how certain behavior comes to be defined as a social problem and how individuals and groups come to engage in activities that a significant number of people and/or a number of significant people view as a major social concern.

What is the relationship between individuals and the society in which they live? One early sociologist attempted to answer this question. German sociologist Georg Simmel (1858–1918), a founder of the interactionist approach, investigated the impact of industrialization and urbanization on people's values and behavior within small social units. Simmel (1902/1950) noted that rapid changes in technology and dramatic urban growth produced new social problems by breaking up the "geometry of social life," which he described as the web of patterned social interactions among the people who constitute a society. According to Simmel, alienation is brought about by a decline in personal and emotional contacts. How people interpret the subjective messages that they receive from others and the situations that they encounter in their daily life greatly influences their behavior and their perceptions of what constitutes a social problem.

Labeling Theory and the Social Construction of Reality

While Simmel focused on how people interpret their own situations, other symbolic interactionists have examined how people impose their shared meanings on others. According to sociologist Howard Becker (1963), *moral entrepreneurs* are people who use their own views of right and wrong to establish rules and label others as deviant (nonconforming). Labeling theory, as this perspective is called, suggests that behavior that deviates from established norms is deviant because it has been labeled as such by others. According to this theory, deviants (nonconformists) are people who have been successfully labeled as such by others. Labeling theory raises questions about why certain individuals and certain types of behavior are labeled as deviant but others are not.

According to some symbolic interaction theorists, many social problems can be linked to the *social construction of reality*—the process by which people's perception of reality is shaped largely by the subjective meaning that they give to an experience (Berger and Luckmann, 1967). From this perspective, little shared reality exists beyond that which people socially create. It is, however, this social construction of reality that influences people's beliefs and actions.

Other symbolic interactionists suggest that how we initially define a situation affects our future actions. According to sociologist W. I. Thomas (1863–1947), when people define situations as real, the situations become real in their consequences. Elaborating on Thomas's idea, sociologist Robert Merton (1968) has suggested that when people perceive a situation in a certain way and act according to their perceptions, the end result may be a *self-fulfilling prophecy*—the process by which an unsubstantiated belief or prediction results in behavior that makes the original false conception come true. For example, a teenager who is labeled a "juvenile delinquent" may accept the label and adopt the full-blown image of a juvenile delinquent as portrayed in television programs and films: wearing gang colors, dropping out of school, and participating in gang violence or other behavior that is labeled as deviant. If the teenager subsequently is arrested, the initial label becomes a self-fulfilling prophecy.

Applying Symbolic Interactionist Perspectives to Problems of Violence

Symbolic interactionist explanations of violence begin by noting that human behavior is learned through social interaction. Violence, they state, is a learned response, not an inherent characteristic, in the individual. Some of the most interesting support for this point of view comes from studies done by social psychologist Albert Bandura, who studied aggression in children (1973). Showing children a film of a person beating, kicking, and hacking an inflatable doll produced a violent response in the children, who, when they were placed in a room with a similar doll, duplicated the person's behavior and engaged

> **Read the Document**
> *Is Violence Against Women About Women or About Violence?* on mysoclab.com

in additional aggressive behavior. Others have noted that people tend to repeat their behavior if they feel rewarded for it. Thus, when people learn that they can get their way by inflicting violence or the threat of violence on others, their aggressive behavior is reinforced.

Symbolic interactionists also look at the types of social interactions that commonly lead to violence. According to the *situational approach,* violence results from a specific interaction process, termed a "situational transaction." Criminologist David Luckenbill (1977) identified six stages in the situational transaction between victim and offender. In the first stage, the future victim does something behavioral or verbal that is considered an affront by the other (e.g., a glare or an insult).

"If It Bleeds, It Leads"? News Reporting on Violence

At least 125 people killed and over 1,000 injured in deadly tornado in Joplin, Missouri.

Local man shoots his wife and two children, and then turns the gun on himself.

Animal control officers confiscate 23 neglected dogs and cats at a local residence.

Will it rain anytime soon? Stay tuned and we'll tell you all about it.

Anyone who has watched the evening news on local television has heard "teasers" such as these. On both local and national news, the lead story is often about war- or terror-related violence, followed by violence in the United States or the local community. Then a human interest story follows to grab viewers' attention and give them a feeling of revulsion about the brutal mistreatment of children or animals. Frequent viewers are aware that stations use routine formulas for putting together the nightly news;

however, many are less aware of how stories are written and presented. For this reason, sociologists with an interest in the media study how journalists, producers, and others frame news stories about events and social problems. Members of the media have the power to determine what makes the news, including which stories get covered, what news items get the most attention, how journalists organize and present their stories, and what effects a particular story might have on viewers. To study social problems effectively we must be aware of how both politics and media processes shape popular understanding and policy responses to pressing social issues such as violence.

In an analysis of media processes, we use the term *media framing* to describe the process by which information and entertainment is packaged by the media (newspapers, magazines, radio and television networks and stations, and the Internet) before being presented to an audience. How

In the second, the offended individual verifies that the action was directed at him or her personally. In the third, the offended individual decides how to respond to the affront and might issue a verbal or behavioral challenge (e.g., a threat or a raised fist). If the problem escalates at this point, injury or death might occur in this stage; if not, the participants enter into the fourth stage. In this stage, the future victim further escalates the transaction, often prodded on by onlookers siding with one party or the other. In the fifth stage, actual violence occurs when neither party is able to back down without losing face. At this point, one or both parties produce weapons, which may range from guns and knives to bottles, pool cues, or other bludgeoning devices, if they have not already appeared, and the offender kills the victim. The sixth and final stage involves the offender's actions after the crime; some flee the scene, others are detained by onlookers, and still others call the police themselves.

The situational approach is based, first, on the assumption that many victims are active participants in the violence perpetrated against them and, second, on the idea that confrontation does not inevitably lead to violence or death. In the first four stages of the transaction, either the victim or the offender can decide to pursue another course of action.

According to symbolic interactionists, reducing violence requires changing those societal values that encourage excessive competition and violence. At the

macrolevel, how the media report on violence may influence our thinking about the appropriateness of certain kinds of aggressive behavior (see Box 1.3). However, change must occur at the microlevel, which means that agents of socialization must transmit different attitudes and values toward violence. The next generation must learn that it is an individual's right—regardless of gender, race, class, religion, or other attributes or characteristics—to live free from violence and the devastating impact it has on individuals, groups, and the social fabric of society.

DID YOU KNOW

Statistics show that the following crimes are committed with a firearm:

- 68 percent of all murders
- 42 percent of all robberies
- 22 percent of all aggravated assaults

USING SOCIAL RESEARCH METHODS TO STUDY SOCIAL PROBLEMS

Sociologists use a variety of research methods to study social problems such as violence. Research methods are strategies or techniques for systematically collecting

Social Problems in the Media

Box 1.3 continued

the media frame stories about social problems influences how we ourselves view the causes, effects, and possible solutions to the problem (Kendall 2011).

In the process of framing a news story, journalists engage in frame amplification, meaning that they highlight some issues, events, or beliefs while downplaying or neglecting other seemingly less important concerns. When news frames highlight some key details or privilege certain stories over others, we say that the highlighted factors are elevated in salience—they are made more noticeable, meaningful, or memorable to audiences. One way in which the reporting of violence is given salience, for example, is the extent to which a few stories garner most of the media coverage, and, in the most widely publicized cases, gain twenty-four-hour coverage of the "latest breaking news." Sensational murder trials are covered around the clock, even when journalists have nothing new to report.

Another way in which the reporting of violence is given salience is through episodic news framing, which focuses on the role of the individual while discounting societal factors. Episodic framing tells a news story in terms of personal experience, focusing on the part that individuals play in a situation. As one report concluded, "Generally speaking, newspaper and television journalists report a small percentage of individual violent incidents at great length and with great precision" (J. E. Stevens, 2001:7); however, this approach typically neglects the bigger picture of factors that may increase the risk of violence. These factors include "the ready availability of firearms and alcohol, racial discrimination, unemployment, violence in the media, lack of education, abuse as a child, witnessing violence in the home or neighborhood, isolation of the nuclear family, and belief in male dominance over females" (J. E. Stevens, 2001:8). Episodic framing highlights the importance of individual responsibility for acts of violence and reinforces the dominant ideology that individuals must be held accountable for their actions. This type of framing suggests to media audiences that public officials, business leaders, and other influential people are not accountable for any part that they may have played in creating a situation that produced the violence. For example, lobbyists who pressure legislators to pass lenient gun-control legislation (or none at all) are seldom held accountable for gun-related deaths, nor are the legislators and politicians who control the political process.

Standing in sharp contrast to episodic framing is thematic framing, which provides a more impersonal view of what the nature of the social problem is. Journalists using thematic framing often tell the story through the use of statistics and discussions of trends ("Is the problem growing worse?" "Should we fear for our safety?"). Thematic framing emphasizes "facts" based on statistical data, such as the number of people killed in drive-by shootings or school violence in recent years. Thematic framing does not focus on the human tragedy of social problems such as violence or poverty, and when bombarded by continuous coverage of this sort, television viewers may conclude that little can be done about the problem. Rather than hearing from the victims of gun violence or poverty, for example, media reports typically emphasize "expert opinion" from "talking heads" who provide information that often supports the reporter's own point of view.

Questions for Consideration

1. Do you think guns should be allowed on college campuses? Why or why not?
2. Would you feel more or less safe if you knew that students and professors might be carrying a weapon?

Independent Research

What effect do blogs and comments on social networking sites such as Facebook and Twitter have on how we think about social problems? Visit your favorite sites to compare how people frame issues on social media as opposed to mainstream media outlets such as television, radio, the Internet, and newspapers.

---

data. Some methods produce *quantitative data* that can be measured numerically and lend themselves to statistical analysis. For example, the Uniform Crime Reports (UCRs), published annually by the Federal Bureau of Investigation (FBI), provide crime statistics that sociologists and others can use to learn more about the nature and extent of violent crime in the United States. Other research methods

Watch on **mysoclab.com**
Qualitative vs. Quantitative Research on **mysoclab.com**

produce *qualitative data* that are reported in the form of interpretive descriptions (words) rather than numbers. For example, *qualitative data* on violence in the United States might provide new insights on how the victims or their families and friends cope in the aftermath of a violent attack such as school shootings or terrorist bombings.

Sociologists use three major types of research methods: field research, survey research, and secondary analysis of existing data. Although our discussion focuses on each separately, many researchers use a combination of methods to enhance their understanding of social issues.

Field Research

Field research **is the study of social life in its natural setting: observing and interviewing people where they live, work, and play.** When sociologists want firsthand information about a social problem, they often use participant observation—field research in which researchers collect systematic observations while participating in the activities of the group they are studying. Field research on social problems can take place in many settings, ranging from schools and neighborhoods to universities, prisons, and large corporations.

Using field research, sociologists have studied gang violence and found that gang members are not all alike. Some do not approve of violence; others engage in violence only to assert authority; still others may engage in violence only when they feel threatened or want to maintain their territory.

Field research is valuable because some kinds of behavior and social problems can be studied best by being there; a more complete understanding can be developed through observations, face-to-face discussions, and participation in events than through other research methods. For example, field research over the past 40 years on the effects of violence in the media on children have indicated that some children behave more aggressively after viewing violence. Children were shown episodes of either *Batman* and *Spiderman* or *Mister Rogers' Neighborhood* (a children's show featuring "Mr. Rogers" who encouraged children to be kind and share with others) for several weeks, after which they were observed for an additional two weeks to see how they behaved. Children who saw the violent cartoons were more likely to interact aggressively with other children than those who watched *Mr. Rogers' Neighborhood* and became more willing to share their toys and cooperate with others. Other studies exposed children to shows such as *Mighty Morphin Power Rangers* and the results were similar: Children who saw episodes containing violence were more prone to aggressive behavior, such as hitting, kicking, shoving, and insulting others, than were children who did not see the episode (Kaiser Family Foundation, 2003).

Sociologists who use field research must have good interpersonal skills. They must be able to gain and keep the trust of the people they want to observe or interview. They also must be skilled interviewers who can keep systematic notes on their observations and conversations. Above all, they must treat research subjects fairly and ethically. The Code of Ethics of the American Sociological Association provides professional standards for sociologists to follow when conducting social science research.

Survey Research

Survey research is probably the research method that is most frequently used by social scientists. **Survey research is a poll in which researchers ask respondents a series of questions about a specific topic and record their responses.** Survey research is based on the use of a sample of people who are thought to represent the attributes of the larger population from which they are selected. Survey data are collected by using self-administered questionnaires or by interviewers who ask questions of people in person or by mail, telephone, or the Internet.

The U.S. Bureau of Justice Statistics, for example, conducts survey research every year with its national crime victimization survey (NCVS), which fills in some of the gaps in the UCR data. The NCVS interview 100,000 randomly selected households to iden not. victims, whether the crime has been re com- These surveys indicate that the num reported mitted is substantially higher th to study a in the UCR.

Survey research 's and over periods of large population 's and over periods of in that popul search does have certain may be co time. How limitations. The use of standardized questions limits the types of information researchers can obtain from respondents. Also, because data can be reported numerically, survey research may be misused to overestimate or underestimate the extent of a specific problem such as violence.

Secondary Analysis of Existing Data

Whereas the NCVS is primary data—data that researchers collected specifically for that study—sociologists often rely on *secondary analysis of existing data*—a **research method in which investigators analyze data that originally were collected by others for some other purpose**. This method is also known as *unobtrusive research* because data can be gathered without the researcher's having to interview or observe research subjects. Data used for secondary analysis include public records such as birth and death records, official reports of organizations or governmental agencies such as the U.S. Census Bureau, and information from large databases such as the general social surveys, which are administered by the National Opinion Research Center.

Secondary analysis often involves *content analysis*, a systematic examination of cultural artifacts or written documents to extract thematic data and draw conclusions about some aspect of social life. Although it is a number of years old, the National Television Violence Study is the most definitive study of violence on television. During a nine-month period each year from October 1994 to June 1997, researchers at several universities selected a variety of programs, including drama, comedy, movies, music videos, reality programs, and children's shows on twenty-three television channels, thus creating a composite of the content in a week of television viewing. The viewing hours were from 6:00 A.M. until 11:00 P.M., for a total of seventeen hours a day across the seven days of the week (National Television Violence Study, 1998). Although the study's findings are too numerous to list all of them, here are a few (TVS, 1998:26–31):

- a. [...] the [...] television violence is glamorized, sanitized, [...]ized. Characters seldom show remorse for [...] and there is no criticism or penalty for [...] Across [...] in 60 per[...] time that it occurs.
- a few of w[...] of the study, violence was found networks a[...] [...] of provision programs taped—only portion of pr[...] [...]vision programs taped—only [...] violence themes—and the [...]ions increased the pro-[...] [...]lence during prime

time (the three-hour period each night that draws the most viewers).
- "High-risk" depictions (those that may encourage aggressive attitudes and behaviors) often involve (1) "a perpetrator who is an attractive role model," (2) "violence that seems justified," (3) "violence that goes unpunished," (4) "minimal consequences to the victim," and (5) "violence that seems realistic to the viewer."
- The typical preschool child who watches cartoons regularly will come into contact with more than 500 high-risk portrayals of violence each year. For preschoolers who watch television for two to three hours a day, there will be, on average, about one high-risk portrayal of violence per hour in cartoons.

Clearly, researchers can learn much from content analysis that they could not learn through other research methods because it allows them to look in more depth at a specific topic of concern and to systematically analyze what they find.

A strength of secondary analysis is its unobtrusive nature and the fact that it can be used when subjects refuse to be interviewed or the researcher does not have the opportunity to observe research subjects firsthand. However, secondary analysis also has inherent problems. Because the data originally were gathered for some other purpose, they might not fit the exact needs of the researcher, and they might be incomplete or inaccurate.

IS THERE A SOLUTION TO A PROBLEM SUCH AS GUN VIOLENCE?

Sociologists view social problems from a variety of perspectives. As shown in Table 1.2, each sociological perspective is rooted in different assumptions, identifies differing causes of a problem, and suggests a variety of possible solutions for reducing or eliminating a social problem such as gun violence.

Functionalists, who emphasize social cohesion and order in society, commonly view social problems as the result of institutional and societal dysfunctions, social disorganization, or cultural lag, among other things. Conflict theorists, who focus on value conflict or on structural inequalities based on class, race, gender, or other socially constructed attributes, suggest that social problems arise either from disputes over divergent values or from exploitative relations in society, such as those between capitalists and workers or between women and men. In contrast, symbolic interactionists focus on

TABLE 1.2 Sociological Perspectives on Social Problems

Perspective	Analysis Level	Nature of Society and Origins of Social Problems	Causes and Solutions to Violence
Functionalism	Macrolevel	Society is composed of interrelated parts that work together to maintain stability within society. Social problems result from dysfunctional acts and institutions.	The weakening of social institutions such as schools, families, and religion has produced an increase in violent behavior. Social institutions must be strengthened, and individuals should be taught to conform to society's rules, which must be reinforced by the criminal justice system.
Conflict theory	Macrolevel	Society is characterized by conflict and inequality. Value conflict theory attributes social problems to lack of agreement on values. Critical-conflict theory focuses on oppression due to class, race, gender, and other social divisions.	Factors such as sharp divisions on values, increasing social inequality, and unresolved discrimination contribute to violence in capitalist societies. To significantly reduce violence, fundamental changes are needed in political and economic institutions to bring about greater equality.
Symbolic interactionism	Microlevel	Society is the sum of the interactions of people and groups. Social problems are based on the behavior people learn from others; how people define a social problem is based on subjective factors.	Violence is learned behavior, and children must be taught attitudes and values that discourage such behavior. At the societal level, we must change those societal values that encourage excessive competition and violence.

individuals' interactions and on the social construction of reality. For symbolic interactionists, social problems occur when social interaction is disrupted and people are dehumanized, when people are labeled deviant, or when the individual's definition of a situation causes him or her to act in a way that produces a detrimental outcome.

No matter what perspectives sociologists employ, they use research to support their ideas. All research methods have certain strengths and weaknesses, but taken together, they provide us with valuable insights that go beyond commonsense knowledge about social problems and stereotypes of people. Using multiple methods and approaches, sociologists can broaden their knowledge of social problems such as violence in the United States and other nations.

In this chapter, we have looked at violence from these sociological perspectives. Like many other social problems, people do not always agree on the extent to which gun violence really is a major social problem in the United States or if the media tend to overblow each isolated incident because it can easily be sensationalized by tying it to other, previous occurrences. For example,

how was the shooting at Virginia Tech similar to, or different from, the one that occurred at Northern Illinois University? Just as people do not share a consensus on what constitutes a social problem, they often do not agree on how to reduce or solve problems such as gun violence.

Functionalist/Conservative Solutions

Those who adhere to a functionalist approach argue that violence can be reduced by strengthening major social institutions (such as the family, education, and religion) so that agents (such as parents, teachers, and spiritual leaders) can be effective in instructing children and young adults and thereby repressing negative attitudes and antisocial behaviors that might otherwise result in violent behavior, such as school and mall shootings.

Some people who embrace a functionalist theoretical perspective on violence also view themselves as being aligned with conservative political sectors that are comprised of individuals who believe that people should be free of government intervention and control when it comes to their "fundamental" rights, including the right to bear arms. From this side of the political arena, social policy solutions to reducing violence, such as passing and enforcing more stringent gun-control measures, are unacceptable means of trying to reduce the number of acts of violence that take place each year. Some political conservatives argue that gun control constitutes an aggressive disarmament strategy that violates the individual's constitutional rights while undermining the nation's overall well-being as a democratic and "free" society.

To reduce violence in the United States, the functionalist approach would suggest that it is important to maintain and preserve traditional moral and social values. Functionalists and political conservatives also believe that we should reinforce the importance of conformity to society's rules and laws through effective use of the criminal justice system, including the passage of tougher laws, more aggressive policing, and the imposition of more severe penalties in the courtroom. Conservative political viewpoints tend to reaffirm this approach by suggesting that positive social behavior, as well as violent behavior, is passed down from generation to generation through families. As a result, positive behavior must be reinforced through positive family life. Child abuse, domestic violence, and other antisocial behavioral problems within the family must not be tolerated because these contribute to larger societal problems of violence and crime.

Conflict/Liberal Solutions

Unlike functionalist sociological perspectives and conservative political approaches to solving the problem of violence, conflict theorists and liberal political analysts generally view increasing social inequality and unresolved discrimination as major factors that contribute to violence in societies. Some conflict theorists highlight the ways in which social problems are linked to the lack of agreement on values in our society. Critical-conflict theorists emphasize that oppression—based on class, race, gender, and other social divisions—is a major factor that contributes to social problems such as gun violence. In the political arena, liberal analysts similarly emphasize how a lack of economic opportunities encourages violence in a society. Based on these viewpoints, if we are to significantly reduce violence in our society, we must push for major changes in our nation's political and economic institutions.

From this approach, one factor contributing to gun violence is poverty and growing inequality. Research has shown, for example, that the risk of sustaining a firearm injury is greatest for young males who have already been involved in the criminal justice system and who have few opportunities for legitimate jobs. Although functionalist theorists might view this situation as being one in which behavioral interventions should occur that target these high-risk people and those individuals who supply them with guns and other contraband items, conflict analysts argue that the problem can be solved only if underlying problems such as poverty, racism, and chronic unemployment are systematically addressed rather than focusing on the people who commit gun-related violence or on suppressing the availability of firearms throughout the nation. From this approach, ways to eventually reduce gun-related violence might include passing legislation that requires that workers be paid a wage high enough that they can adequately support their families; improving public schools so that young people will receive a better education and be able to find decent jobs; and having community, state, and national economic development programs that create good jobs and benefit all people, not just a small percentage of the world's wealthiest people. This approach is most useful in explaining violence in low-income urban areas and other communities where few legitimate opportunities exist for individuals and most economic opportunities are of an illegal nature. It does not explain, however, why recent gun violence has been perpetrated by middle- and upper-middle-class high school students living in the suburbs and by college students with good academic records who appear to have a bright future in front of them.

Symbolic Interactionist Solutions

Finally, symbolic interactionist perspectives focus on how violence is learned behavior that comes from people's interactions in their daily lives. As a result, if we are to prevent violence, we must teach children the attitudes and values that discourage such behavior. If children are exposed to aggressive behavior or violence in their own homes, they may come to view such behavior as the norm rather than the exception to the norm. Some analysts believe that those children who spend large amounts of unsupervised time watching violence in films and on television or playing violent video games will demonstrate more violent behavior themselves. However, other analysts disagree with this assessment, claiming that violence in the media and gaming worlds provides people with an opportunity to vicariously vent their frustrations and feelings without ever actually engaging in violence themselves. Since peer groups are an important source of social learning for children and young people, some symbolic interactionists might suggest that parents, teachers, and other adult caregivers must become aware of the friends and acquaintances of the children for whom they are responsible.

Based on symbolic interactionist perspectives, one way to reduce violence is to teach people of all ages to engage in nonviolent conflict resolution where they learn how to deal with frustrating situations, such as when tensions are running high among individuals or social relationships are breaking down. The focus on competition in nations such as ours encourages people to think of everyone else as their competitors and that, in all situations, what one individual gains is another person's loss. Beliefs such as this tend to foster conflict rather than cooperation, and individuals who think that they have been marginalized (and thus taken out of the competition for friends, material possessions, or other valued goods, services, or relationships) may act out toward their perceived enemies in an aggressive or violent manner. If people learn socially acceptable ways of responding to conflict and intense competition, they may be less likely to engage in violent behavior. However, according to symbolic interactionists and other theorists who use a microlevel approach, we must first recognize as a community or nation that violence is a problem that must be solved, and then we must work collectively to reduce the problem. Although the symbolic interactionist approach is a microlevel perspective, some advocates suggest that changes must also be made at the societal level if we hope to change those societal values that encourage excessive competition and may contribute to negative behavior including gun violence.

Critique of Our Efforts to Find Solutions

How successful are our attempts to solve the problem of gun violence? The answer to this question is mixed. The United States has been somewhat successful in reducing certain types of violence, at least for several years running; however, most of our efforts have focused on particular types of violence or particular populations or categories of people, rather than on bringing about systemic change throughout the nation. Unless our nation and its political leaders face up to the fact that violence in this country is a major social problem that may lie dormant for a period of time but then rise up to leave us frightened and astonished, we are unlikely as a nation to seriously deal with the underlying causes and consequences of such violent actions, which is a necessary prerequisite for reaching the point where we might successfully reduce the problem.

When we think about the problem of gun violence or other pressing social issues that we will examine in this book, we must acknowledge that these problems have existed for many years. We have a long way to go in identifying real solutions to many of these problems, and that is why it is important that you are enrolled in this course and pursuing new ideas for the future. Please join me now as we explore a number of crucial problems we face in the second decade of the twenty-first century.

SUMMARY

✓•—⌐Study and Review on mysoclab.com

■ **How do sociologists define a social problem?**
According to sociologists, a social problem is a social condition (such as poverty) or a pattern of behavior (such as substance abuse) that people believe warrants public concern and collective action to bring about change.

■ **How do sociologists view violence?**
Sociologists view violence as a social problem that involves both a subjective awareness and objective reality. We have a subjective awareness that violence can occur in such public settings as schools, day-care centers, businesses, and churches. Our subjective awareness becomes an objective reality when we can measure and experience the effects of violent criminal behavior.

■ **How do sociologists examine social life?**
Sociologists use both microlevel and macrolevel analyses to examine social life. Microlevel analysis focuses on small-group relations and social interaction among individuals; macrolevel analysis focuses on social processes occurring at the societal level, especially in large-scale organizations and major social institutions.

■ **How does the functionalist perspective view society and social problems?**
In the functionalist perspective, society is a stable, orderly system composed of interrelated parts, each of which performs a function that contributes to the overall stability of society. According to functionalists, social problems such

as violence arise when social institutions do not fulfill the functions that they are supposed to perform or when dysfunctions occur.

■ **How does the conflict perspective view society and social problems?**

The conflict perspective asserts that groups in society are engaged in a continuous power struggle for control of scarce resources. This perspective views violence as a response to inequalities based on race, class, gender, and other power differentials in society.

■ **How does the value conflict perspective differ from the critical-conflict perspective?**

According to value conflict theorists, social problems are conditions that are incompatible with group values. From this perspective, value clashes are ordinary occurrences in families, communities, and the larger society, in which people commonly hold many divergent values. In contrast, critical-conflict theorists suggest that social problems arise out of major contradictions inherent in the way societies are organized.

■ **Why are there so many different approaches in the conflict perspective?**

Different conflict theorists focus on different aspects of power relations and inequality in society. Perspectives based on the works of Karl Marx emphasize class-based inequalities arising from the capitalist system. Feminist perspectives focus on patriarchy—a system of male dominance in which males are privileged and women are oppressed. Other perspectives emphasize that race, class, and gender are interlocking systems of privilege and oppression that result in social problems. However, all of these perspectives are based on the assumption that inequality and exploitation, rather than social harmony and stability, characterize contemporary societies.

■ **How does the symbolic interactionist perspective view society and social problems?**

Unlike the functionalist and conflict perspectives, which focus on society at the macrolevel, the symbolic interactionist perspective views society as the sum of the interactions of individuals and groups. For symbolic interactionists, social problems occur when social interaction is disrupted and people are dehumanized, when people are labeled deviant, or when the individual's definition of a situation causes him or her to act in a way that produces a detrimental outcome.

■ **How do sociological research methods differ?**

In field research, sociologists observe and interview people where they live, work, and play. In survey research, sociologists use written questionnaires or structured interviews to ask respondents a series of questions about a specific topic. In secondary analysis of existing data, sociologists analyze data that originally were collected for some other purpose.

KEY TERMS

capitalism, p. 11
conflict perspective, p. 11
culture, p. 2
discrimination, p. 4
field research, p. 17
functionalist perspective, p. 9
hate crime, p. 4
industrialization, p. 10
lifestyle-routine activity approach, p. 10
macrolevel analysis, p. 5

microlevel analysis, p. 5
norms, p. 9
perspective, p. 8
secondary analysis of existing data, p. 18
self-fulfilling prophecy, p. 14
situational approach, p. 14
social disorganization, p. 9
social problem, p. 2
society, p. 2

sociological imagination, p. 4
sociology, p. 2
subculture of violence hypothesis, p. 10
survey research, p. 17
symbolic interactionist perspective, p. 13
theory, p. 8
urbanization, p. 10
values, p. 9
violence, p. 2

QUESTIONS FOR CRITICAL THINKING

1. The functionalist perspective focuses on the stability of society. How do acts of violence undermine stability? Can a society survive when high levels of violence exist within its borders? Do you believe that violence can be controlled in the United States?

2. Value conflict theorists suggest that social problems are conditions that are incompatible with group values. How would value conflict theorists view debates over gun-control laws?

3. Some critical-conflict theorists believe that social problems arise from the major contradictions inherent in capitalist economies. What part do guns play in a capitalist economy?

4. Using feminist and symbolic interactionist perspectives, what kind of argument can you make to explain why males are more frequently involved in acts of physical violence than females? What do your own observations tell you about the relationship between social norms and aggressive or violent behavior?

Succeed with MySocLab®   www.mysoclab.com

The new MySocLab delivers proven results in helping students succeed, provides engaging experiences that personalize learning, and comes from a trusted partner with educational expertise and a deep commitment to helping students and instructors achieve their goals.

Here are a few activities you will find for this chapter:

Watch on **mysoclab.com**

Core Concepts video clips feature sociologists in action, exploring important concepts in the study of Social Problems. Watch:
- Qualitative vs. Quantitative Research

Explore on **mysoclab.com**

Social Explorer is an interactive application that allows you to explore Census data through interactive maps. Explore:
- Social Explorer Activity: The Dissipation of the Agricultural Industry

Read on **mysoclab.com**

MySocLibrary includes primary source readings from classic and contemporary sociologists. Read:
- Is Violence Against Women About Women or About Violence?

Wealth and Poverty: U.S. and Global Economic Inequities

THINKING SOCIOLOGICALLY

- How important is a person's social class in getting ahead in the United States?

- Why do great disparities exist between the rich and the poor in the United States and around the world?

- How do sociologists explain poverty?

- *Each year the children and staff members of Orca K-8 School in Southeast Seattle, Washington, march through the streets to celebrate the birthday of fallen civil rights leader Dr. Martin Luther King, Jr. and to contribute food and money to the Rainier Valley Food Bank. (rainiervalleypost.com, 2011).*

- *In Oklahoma, a teenager sold a steer and donated the money to a program that provides Food for Kids (News9.com, 2011).*

- *Difficult economic times have affected many families, and some have had nothing left over to share with others. However, some families have encouraged their children to share what they have with those who are less fortunate they they are. Food pantries and home-less shelters throughout the nation attempt to help individuals and families put food on their tables and sometimes a roof over their head.*

When many of us think about people who rely on food pantries to meet some of their nutritional needs, we may picture these individuals as home-less persons who live on the streets or in shelters. Sometimes we may see them as single men who suffer from substance abuse and other problems. However, these perceptions about what the face of hunger looks like do not accurately reflect who the hungry really are in contemporary America. Today, approximately 50 million Americans (1 in 6 people) struggle with hunger, and many of the hungry are children. They are individuals like you and me; they are young mothers with children. They are families where adults hold down several jobs trying to make ends meet, but they cannot afford to purchase adequate food to meet their basic needs. Difficult economic times that were inten-sified by the collapse of the housing market and the Great Recession of 2007–2009 and its lingering aftermath have left many people with tremendous economic hardships related to unemployment, high debt, foreclosure on their home, and other financial and personal problems. Limited hope and opportunity to get ahead stands in stark contrast to what this nation has stood for in the eyes of people throughout the world.

For centuries, the United States has been described as the "land of opportunity"—home of the American Dream. Simply stated, the American Dream is the belief that each generation can have a higher standard of living than that of its parents. Implicit in the American Dream is the belief that all people—regardless of race, creed, color, national origin, sex, sexual orientation, or religion—should have an equal opportunity for success. But do all the people in this nation have an equal opportunity for success?

In this chapter, we look at inequality and poverty in the U.S. class system and worldwide. A ***class system*** **is a system of social inequality based on the ownership and control of resources and on the type of work people do**. A primary characteristic of any class system is social mobility. *Social mobility* refers to the upward or downward movement in the class structure that occurs during a person's lifetime and from one generation to another. The research of many social analysts and journalists suggests that upward social mobility is an elusive goal for many people.

WEALTH AND POVERTY IN GLOBAL PERSPECTIVE

Although disparity exists in the distribution of economic resources in the United States, disparities are even wider across nations. Looking first at the United States, we see that there are both very wealthy and very poor individuals and families.

DID YOU KNOW

Wealth and Poverty in Global Perspective

- The top 20 percent of U.S. households own 85 percent of all privately held wealth.

- One out of seven people in the United States poverty.

- 925 mill

25

Consider, for example, that the top 1 percent of households (the upper class) owned 34.6 percent of all privately held wealth in 2007, and the next 19 percent (the managerial, professional, and small-business stratum) had 50.5 percent, which means that just 20 percent of the people owned a remarkable 85 percent. Surprisingly, what this means is that only 15 percent of the wealth is left for the entire bottom 80 percent of all wage and salary workers (Domhoff, 2011). To learn more about differences in wealth and income inequality in the United States, visit the website of sociologist G. William Domhoff (http://sociology.ucsc.edu/whorulesamerica/power/wealth.html), who has studied this issue extensively for more than four decades.

When sociologists conduct research on wealth and poverty around the world, they frequently analyze secondary data that were originally collected by organizations such as the World Bank and the United Nations. These data focus on quality-of-life indicators such as wealth; income; life expectancy; health; sanitation; the treatment of women; and education for high-income, middle-income, and low-income nations. *High-income nations* **are countries with highly industrialized economies; technologically advanced industrial, administrative, and service occupations; and relatively high levels of national and per capita (per person) income**. Examples of high-income economies ($12,196 or more per year) are Australia and New Zealand, Japan, Republic of Korea, the European nations, the Persian Gulf states, several Caribbean nations, and the United States and Canada. *Middle-income nations* **are countries undergoing transformation from agrarian to industrial economies**. Recently, the World Bank subdivided middle-income nations into two categories: upper-middle-income economies ($3,946 to $12,195 per year) and lower-middle-income economies ($996 to $3,945 per year). Examples of countries in the upper-middle-income category are Mexico, some Central American countries such as Costa Rica and Panama, and some South American countries such as Brazil, Columbia, Peru, and Venezuela. Albania, Bosnia and Herzegovina, Bulgaria, and the Russian Federation are ʌ among the eastern European nations included in ʌegory. In the lower-middle-income category are ʌ nations such as China, India, and Pakistan; ʌ nations such as the Arab Republic of ʌ, and Syrian Arab Republic; and ʌ ntries such as Guatemala and

ʌ **primarily agrarian** ʌ**ialization and low**

levels of national and personal income. Examples of low-income economies ($995 or less per year) are many countries in sub-Saharan Africa, which have experienced little or no benefit from changes in global economic markets and have also suffered from political upheavals, corruption, and high rates of HIV/AIDS. Today, low-income nations include countries such as Afghanistan, Bangladesh, Cambodia, Ethiopia, Haiti, Nepal, Rwanda, and Tajikistan (World Bank, 2011).

Comparisons of high-income and low-income nations reveal a growing gap between the rich and the poor, both within and among nations. Income disparities are not the only factor that defines poverty and its effect on people. Although the average income per person in lower-income countries has doubled in the past thirty years and for many years economic growth has been seen as the primary way to achieve development in low-income economies, the United Nations since the 1970s has more actively focused on human development as a crucial factor in fighting poverty. In 1990 the United Nations Development Programme (UNDP) introduced the Human Development Index (HDI), establishing three new criteria for measuring the level of development in a country: life expectancy, education, and living standards. Beginning in 2010 the *Human Development Report* included a new top category of nations, "Very High Human Development." People who live in countries in the highest human development categories can expect to be better educated, to live longer, and to earn more. For all categories of development, three dimensions are included in the HDI: (1) life expectancy at birth, (2) mean years of schooling and expected years of schooling, and (3) gross national income (GNI) per capita. The top four countries identified as having "Very High Human Development" are Norway, Australia, New Zealand, and the United States. By contrast, the bottom three countries in the "Low Human Development" (bottom) category are Niger, Democratic Republic of the Congo, and Zimbabwe (United Nations Development Programme, 2010). To show how these categories translate into real life, consider the fact that a child born in Norway in 2010 has a life expectancy of 81 years, as contrasted with a life expectancy of 47 for a child born in the same year in Zimbabwe. Or compare the GNI per capita of $176 (U.S. currency) in Zimbabwe to GNI of $58,810 in Norway. How does the United States compare with these? The 2010 life expectancy rate for the United States was 79.6 years and the GNI was $47,094.

Vast differences in income and development are reflected in disparity in people's life chances in each nation. *Life chances* **are the extent to which individuals have access to important societal resources such as food, clothing, shelter, education, and health care.** Poverty, food shortages, hunger, and rapidly growing populations are pressing problems in many middle- and low-income nations (see Box 2.1). It is important to note that poverty goes far beyond inadequate income: It includes poor health and nutrition, low education and skills, inadequate livelihoods, bad housing conditions, social exclusion, lack of participation, and many other detrimental conditions that negatively affect human beings (United Nations Development Programme, 2010). Consequently, the United Nations introduced the Multidimensional Poverty Index (MPI) to help identify overlapping deprivations that are suffered by households in health, education, and living standards. About 1.75 billion people in the 104 countries covered by the MPI experience multi-dimensional poverty. By contrast, approximately 1.44 billion people are defined as poor when income alone (living on $1.25 a day or less) is used as the key poverty indicator.

Social Problems in Global Perspective | Box 2.1

World Hunger, Food Losses, and Food Waste?

The most heartbreaking thing about starving children is their equanimity. They don't cry. They don't smile. They don't move. They don't show a flicker of fear, pain or interest. Tiny, wizened zombies, they shut down all nonessential operations to employ every last calorie to stay alive.

—New York Times *columnist Nicholas D. Kristof (2009) laments the overwhelming sight of malnourished children in West Africa*

Roughly one-third of the edible parts of food produced for human consumption gets lost or wasted globally, which is about 1.3 billion tons per year. Food waste is more of a problem in rich countries and food loss during production is a bigger issue in poor countries because of poor infrastructure and technology.

—*Findings from a Food and Agriculture Organization of the United Nations (2011) report titled "Global Food Losses and Food Waste: Extent, Causes and Prevention"*

Hunger and other problems associated with poverty can be found around the globe as grain prices soar and the cost of food continue to rise. Estimates suggest that of the world's population of 7 billion, nearly 1 billion people are chronically hungry, or the equivalent of one in seven people worldwide (worldhunger.org, 2011). Some analysts believe that social unrest, including food riots, will continue as millions of people find themselves deeper in poverty and without adequate food to survive. Food riots across North Africa in 2011 are thought to have helped set off revolutions responsible for overthrowing governments in Tunisia and Egypt (Rudolf, 2011). Arif Husain, the World

Food Program's senior food security analyst, explains the cause of food riots: "The human instinct is to survive, and people are going to do no matter what to survive. And if you're hungry you get angry quicker" (Lacey, 2008:A11). However, some of the world's poorest people do not riot at all and merely suffer in silence because they are physically too weak to engage in activism or they must channel what little energy they have into survival for themselves and their children, as journalist Nicholas Kristof described earlier.

Why does so much hunger exist worldwide? The most popular answer to this question typically relates to the issue of *scarcity*, and the solution is seen as more effectively producing and distributing food so that fewer people will be hungry (Lappé, 2008). However, many analysts believe that this explanation is seriously flawed. According to social scientist Frances Moore Lappé (2008), hunger is not *caused* by scarcity: Hunger is a *symptom* of deeper causes, including widely held beliefs that create *artificial* scarcity. In other words, wealthy and powerful individuals and corporations make decisions that serve their best interests while casting aside millions of the world's people who are deprived of life's most basic and important necessities, such as food, as a result of those decisions. For example, India and Africa have millions of hungry people even though these areas export millions of tons of food to higher-income nations around the globe (Lappé, 20?e Consider that domestic animals (not humans) ?ore about one-third of all grain that is produced ?one-half than one-sixth of all grain goes into the ?d humans fuels, starch, and other uses. In ?World hunger (or less) of all grain production?n the Food and (Kristof, 2011). ?e United Nations

Another important ? was highlighted in ? Agricultural Or?

Social Problems in Global Perspective

Box 2.1 continued

High food prices and food shortages contributed to the 2011 bloody riots in Tunisia and Algeria when people were confronted with the realities of poverty in daily life.

(2011): A tremendous amount of food—at least one-third of all food produced globally—is either lost or wasted each year. Food loss in industrialized nations typically is caused by retailers and consumers who throw "perfectly edible foodstuffs" into the trash. According to the FAO (2011):

> Food can be wasted due to quality standards, which reject food items not perfect in shape or appearance. At the consumer level, insufficient purchase planning and expiring "best-before-dates" also cause large amounts of waste, in combination with the careless attitude of those consumers who can afford to waste food.

The average consumer in North America and Europe wastes between 209.4 and 253.5 pounds of food per year, as sharply contrasted with only 13.2 to 24.3 pounds of food wasted in sub-Saharan Africa, south Asia, and Southeast Asia. Food waste in medium- and high-income countries can be reduced by making consumers, retailers, and others in the food industry more aware of good and beneficial ways to use safe food that is presently being thrown away.

Unlike food waste in rich countries that occurs at the consumption stage, poorer nations experience food loss early during the production phase, which occurs in the middle stages of the food supply chain. What this means is that many problems occur because of limited harvesting techniques, in storage and cooling facilities in difficult climates, and in packaging and marketing. To reduce food loss in developing nations will have to organize, diversify, and upscale marketing. However, this will

be a difficult task because many small farmers live on the margins of food insecurity themselves. On the other hand, reducing food losses would have an immediate and significant effect not only on their livelihood but also on their access to food for their own families.

Faced with the problems of food loss and food waste, is there anything that can be done about hunger around the world? If we are to curb world hunger, we must focus on human needs and values, not on profits that are enjoyed by only a tiny percentage of the world's population. According to Lappé, the real roots of world hunger lie in the answers to questions such as these: (1) Who owns and controls the land where food can be grown? (2) Why do small farmers and producers continue to see their share of profits shrink while global transnational corporations have extremely high profit margins? (3) Why do trade rules favor those who are already wealthy? and (4) Why does the debt burden—the debt repayments that poor nations make to wealthy nations each year—fall disproportionately on poor people? Although these questions may cause us to think that we cannot do much to alleviate world hunger, we must have hope that the situation can change (Lappé, 2008). For example, we may encourage people to view hunger as more than a lack of basic resources and instead to see how the problem is rooted in large-scale economic inequalities and social injustices in the twenty-first century. The first step in applying our sociological imagination to the problem is to view hunger as everyone's problem, not as something that affects only people living in the poorest, most distressed nations of the world and on the margins of life in the United States. Consider these challenging words of Lappé (2008):

> It is tempting to view hunger as a moral crisis, when it is more usefully understood as a crisis of imagination. . . . Humanity is trapped in a failed frame, a way of seeing that underestimates both nature's potential and the potential of human nature. . . . Mounting sociological evidence reveals that most humans have, inherently, what it takes to end hunger: deep needs for fairness, efficacy and meaning. The challenge is therefore to reframe hunger as a crisis of human relationships that is within our proven power to address, to search out and broadcast lessons of success, and most importantly, to fearlessly engage oneself.

Questions for Consideration

1. What steps might you take in your own community to reduce the problem of hunger?
2. What social policies do you think the United States might implement to help alleviate world hunger?

The three dimensions of the MPI, health, education, and living standards, are subdivided into ten indicators:

- Health—nutrition and child mortality
- Education—years of schooling and school attendance
- Living standards—cooking fuel, toilet, water, electricity, flooring in residence, and assets (such as a radio, TV, telephone, bike, or motorbike)

Using the MPI, sub-Saharan Africa has the highest incident of multidimensional poverty (for example, 93 percent in Niger); however, more than half (844 million) of the world's multidimensionally poor live in south Asia. Overall, the less-developed countries of south Asia and sub-Saharan Africa and the poorest countries of Latin America have more multidimensional inequality and poverty.

At a poverty line of $1.25 per day, more than 1.4 billion people live in *absolute poverty*, **a condition that exists when people do not have the means to secure the most basic necessities of life.** Absolute poverty is often life threatening. People living in absolute poverty may suffer from chronic malnutrition or die from hunger-related diseases. Current estimates suggest that more than 600 million people suffer from chronic malnutrition and more than 40 million people die each year from hunger-related diseases. To put this figure in perspective, the number of people worldwide dying from hunger-related diseases each year is the equivalent of more than 300 jumbo jet crashes a day with no survivors and half the passengers being children. Even those who do not live in absolute poverty often experience hardships based on *relative poverty,* **a condition that exists when people can afford basic necessities such as food, clothing, and shelter but cannot maintain an average standard of living in comparison to that of other members of their society or group.** An example is individuals who live in an extremely hot or cold region but cannot afford adequate protection from environmental conditions while others in their community enjoy heated or air-conditioned residences and wear clothing appropriate to current weather conditions.

Despite the disparity in life chances and the prevalence of poverty, experts project that the populations of middle- and low-income nations will increase by almost 60 percent by the year 2025 while the populations of high-income nations will increase by about 11 percent. Because half of the world's population of more than 6 billion people already lives in low-income nations (see Map 2.1 on page 30), this rapid increase in population can only compound existing problems and increase inequality on a global basis.

How do social scientists explain the disparity between wealth and poverty in high-income and low-income nations? According to the "new international division of labor" perspective, the answer lies in the global organization of manufacturing production. Today, workers in a number of low-income nations primarily produce goods such as clothing, electrical machinery, and consumer electronics for export to the United States and other high-income nations. Using this global assembly line, transnational corporations find that they have an abundant supply of low-cost (primarily female) labor, no corporate taxes, and no labor unions or strikes to interfere with their profits. Owners and shareholders of transnational corporations, along with subcontractors and managers in middle- and low-income nations, thus benefit while workers remain in poverty despite long hours in sweatshop conditions.

ANALYZING U.S. CLASS INEQUALITY

Despite the American Dream, one of this country's most persistent social problems is that the United States is a highly stratified society. *Social stratification* **is the hierarchical arrangement of large social groups on the basis of their control over basic resources.** Today, the gap between the rich and the poor in the United States has a dramatic effect on everyone's life chances and opportunities. Affluent people typically have better life chances than the less affluent because the affluent have greater access to quality education, safe neighborhoods, high-quality nutrition and health care, police and private security protection, and an extensive array of other goods and services. In contrast, people who have low and poverty-level incomes tend to have limited access to these resources.

How are social classes determined in the United States? Most contemporary research on class has been influenced by either Karl Marx's means of production model or Max Weber's multidimensional model. In Marx's model, class position is determined by people's relationship to the means of production. Chapter 1 described Marx's division of capitalist societies into two classes: the bourgeoisie, or capitalist class, which owns the means of production, and the proletariat, or working class, which sells its labor power to the capitalists to survive. According to Marx, inequality and poverty are inevitable by-products of the exploitation of workers by capitalists.

Like Karl Marx, early German sociologist Max Weber (1864–1920) believed that economic factors were important in determining class location and studying social inequality. Consequently, Weber developed also believed that other factors were relevant.

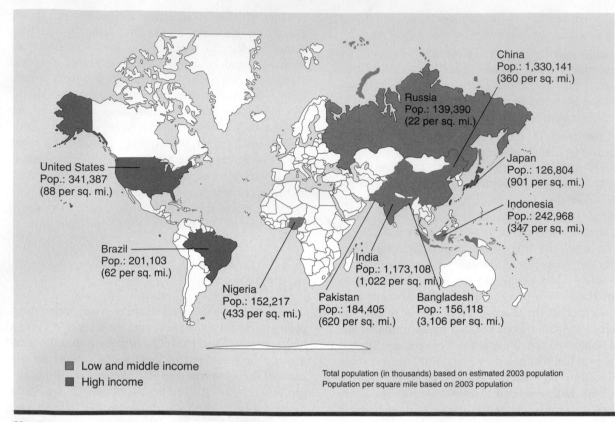

China
Pop.: 1,330,141
(360 per sq. mi.)

Russia
Pop.: 139,390
(22 per sq. mi.)

Japan
Pop.: 126,804
(901 per sq. mi.)

Indonesia
Pop.: 242,968
(347 per sq. mi.)

United States
Pop.: 341,387
(88 per sq. mi.)

Brazil
Pop.: 201,103
(62 per sq. mi.)

India
Pop.: 1,173,108
(1,022 per sq. mi.)

Nigeria
Pop.: 152,217
(433 per sq. mi.)

Pakistan
Pop.: 184,405
(620 per sq. mi.)

Bangladesh
Pop.: 156,118
(3,106 per sq. mi.)

■ Low and middle income
■ High income

Total population (in thousands) based on estimated 2003 population
Population per square mile based on 2003 population

Map 2.1   The most rapid population growth is occurring primarily in low- and middle-income nations that can least afford to take care of greater numbers of people.
Source: U.S. Census Bureau, 2011b

a multidimensional class model that focused on the interplay of wealth, power, and prestige as determinants of people's class position. **Wealth is the value of all economic assets, including income, personal property, and income-producing property**. While some people have great wealth and are able to live off their investments, others must work for wages. **Power is the ability of people to achieve their goals despite opposition from others**. People who hold positions of power can achieve their goals because they can control other people; on the other hand, people who hold positions that lack power must carry out the wishes of others. **Prestige is the respect, esteem, or regard accorded an individual or group by others**. Individuals who have high levels of prestige tend to receive deferential treatment from those with lower levels of prestige.

Contemporary theorists have modified Marx's and Weber's theories to the sociologist economic inequality. According to Weber's multidimensional. Wright (1997), neither model of wealth, power,

and prestige nor Marx's two-class system fully defines classes in modern capitalist societies or explains economic inequality. Wright sets forth four criteria for placement in the class structure: (1) ownership of the means of production, (2) purchase of the labor of others (employing others), (3) control of the labor of others (supervising others on the job), and (4) sale of one's own labor (being employed by someone else). On the basis of these criteria, Wright (1979, 1985) has identified four classes in the U.S. economy: the capitalist class, the managerial class, the small-business class, and the working class. Based on this approach, issues pertaining to contemporary inequality are directly linked to how the U.S. class structure works (Wright and Rogers, 2010).

Wealth versus Income Inequality

For the first time in a number of years, Microsoft's Bill Gates does not lead the list of the world's richest billionaires. That distinction goes to Carlos Slim Helu, telecom entrepreneur of Mexico (*Forbes*, 2010). However, Gates's wealth remains at approximately $52 billion (down from a 1999 high of $85 billion) despite the fact that he has made donations exceeding $28 billion to the Bill & Melinda Gates Foundation and other organizations that work to reduce deaths from AIDS, malaria, tuberculosis, and polio, and to those that fight hunger. For some of the wealthiest people in the world, extreme riches means a life of ease and luxury; for others, it means helping with philanthropic causes. Overall, how much wealth a person has is an important indicator of access to positive life chances such as high-quality education, business and entrepreneurial opportunities, legal and medical services, and comfort and safety in housing.

Accumulation of wealth provides opportunities for people in ways that earned income alone does not, and disparities in wealth across lines of race and ethnicity are evident in the United States. For example, the average white household had fifteen times as much wealth as the average African American or Latino/a household in 2007. Research conducted over more than a decade by social scientists Melvin Oliver and Thomas Shapiro (2006) shows that African Americans continue to have fewer chances to accumulate wealth than white Americans because whites, especially well-off whites, have had many years to amass assets and pass them on from generation to generation, whereas African Americans have not. According to Oliver and Shapiro, African Americans have experienced the cumulative effects of racial discrimination as evidenced in inadequate schooling, high unemployment rates, low wages, and higher rates of certain types of crime. As a result, it is difficult for younger generations of African Americans to amass more wealth, which keeps many people cemented to the bottom of the U.S. economic hierarchy. Of course, a growing number of African Americans, particularly sports figures and music stars like Tiger Woods, Michael Jordan, "Magic" Johnson, Kobe Bryant, Bill Cosby, and "Jay Z," have achieved great wealth as measured in the hundreds of millions of dollars, but not in billions, which remains the exclusive domain of media magnet, Oprah Winfrey (*Forbes*, 2010).

Like wealth, income is extremely unevenly divided in the United States. ***Income* is the economic gain derived from wages, salaries, income transfers (governmental aid such as Temporary Assistance for Needy Families, known as TANF), or ownership of property.** The income gap between the richest and poorest U.S. households has been wide for many years. The top 20 percent of households earned about half of the nation's aggregate income in 2005 and the top 5 percent alone

earned more than 20 percent of aggregate income (see Figure 2.1). As shown in Figure 2.2, median income for households across racial and ethnic lines has remained relatively constant over the last decade. Although African Americans and Latinas/os have made some

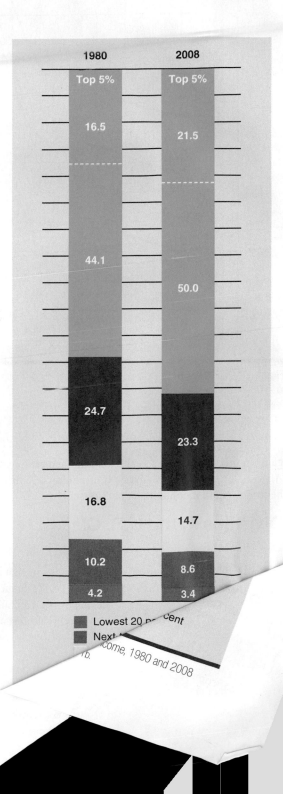

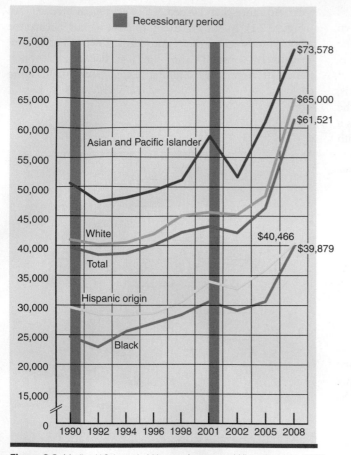

Figure 2.2 Median U.S. household income by race and Hispanic origin, 1990 to 2008 (median income in 2008 dollars)

Note: People of Hispanic origin may be of any race. Data points represent the midpoints of the respective years.

Source: U.S. Census Bureau, 2011b

gains in income in recent years, median income for both African American and Latina/o households remains far behind median income for white households.

Divisions in the U.S. Class Structure

The United States has a number of class divisions that are ~~characterized~~ by widely diverse lifestyles and life chances. The *upper*, or capitalist, *class*—the wealthiest and most powerful class—is made up of investors, heirs, and executives. Some members of the [upper class derive their income] from investments in [media] conglomerates,

high-rise hotels, apartment buildings, and office parks; others earn their wealth as entrepreneurs, presidents of major corporations, sports or entertainment celebrities, or top-level professionals. For example, the *Wall Street Journal's* 2010 list of the top ten corporate executives showed that these top earners had salaries, bonuses, and stock options ranging from about $24.5 million to more than $87 million. The *upper-middle class* is composed of professionals (for example, physicians and attorneys), business analysts, owners of small businesses, stockbrokers, and corporate managers. These individuals generally do not own the means of production but have substantial control over production and other workers (Wright, 1979, 1985).

The *middle class* includes white-collar office workers, middle-management personnel, teachers, and people in support positions (for example, medical technologists, nurses, and legal and medical secretaries), semiprofessionals, and nonretail sales workers, such as insurance salespeople and real estate agents. Over time, with increased professionalization of civil employees such as police officers and firefighters, more of whom now hold college degrees, some definitions of the middle class have expanded to include a wider diversity of occupations. In recent years, middle-class families have been having a more difficult time because the cost of essentials, such as housing, health care, transportation, and college, have increased faster than income. The middle class has also been hard hit by the Great Recession of 2007–2009, when higher rates of unemployment and diminished job security made it more difficult for people in this category to stay even, much less get ahead.

Unlike the middle class, which has traditionally been defined by education and occupational achievements, and aspirations for upward mobility, the *working class* is composed of people who work as semiskilled machine operators in industrial settings and unionized workers in goods-producing industries. Others in the working class include people employed in routine, semiskilled positions such as day-care workers, checkout clerks, cashiers, and counter help in fast-food restaurants. Although jobs in industrial settings and unionized jobs have decreased dramatically over the past three decades, working-class jobs in routine, semiskilled positions have seen rapid growth as big-box stores such as Walmart and Home Depot, and national, franchised fast-food restaurants such as Subway, McDonald's, and KFC have made substantial inroads throughout the nation.

The *working poor class* includes most service workers and the lowest-paid operatives and sales and clerical workers. Examples include hotel cleaning staff, lawn maintenance workers, and other low-wage jobs that often were filled in the 2010s by immigrant workers, some of whom would be classified by government officials as undocumented workers. Many of the working poor hold down more than one job in an effort to make ends meet, but they still remain at the edge of poverty. In addition to earning less than a living wage, many workers in this class must contend with jobs that have unpleasant or dangerous working conditions and offer no benefits, such as health insurance, holidays, or vacations, and provide no job security.

The *chronically poor* category is composed working-age people are unemployed or outside the labor force and children who live in poor families caught in long-term deprivation. Individuals who are unable to work because of age or disability and single mothers who are heads of households are overrepresented among the chronically poor. At best, a few of the chronically poor hold part-time or seasonal employment that pays very low wages and has no job security. The term *underclass* is sometimes used to refer to the chronically poor, but

some social scientists argue that this derogatory label puts poor people outside the mainstream of society and suggests that all of them are responsible for their own problematic situation.

Although these classes shift slightly over time in regard to factors such as the amount of money that people earn and the specific kinds of work that are included in each category, the U.S. class structure has largely remained unchanged since the post–World War II era of the 1950s. What has changed is the nature of work, such as the introduction of information age, high-tech employment, and the decline of occupations in factory and industrial settings. What has not changed is the persistence of poverty and the difficulty that people in poverty have when they attempt to move up the class ladder and improve their family's life chances and overall quality of life.

POVERTY IN THE UNITED STATES

In any given year, between 13 and 17 percent of all Americans fall below the official poverty line, and some analysts estimate that about 40 percent of the U.S. population may have fallen below the poverty line at some point in time within a ten-year span. Approximately 43.6 million people (14.3 percent of the

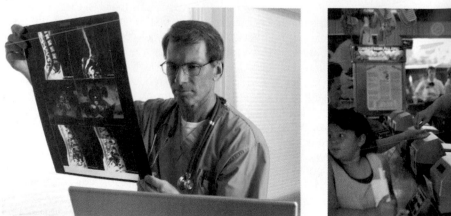

Upper-middle-class professionals, such as the doctor shown on the left, are one segment of the U.S. class structure, wher... working class, including these fast-food workers on the right, constitute another segment. How do functionalist and conflict views di... ...tions of the U.S. class structure?

U.S. population) fell below the poverty threshold in 2009, which ranged from $10,830 for a single-person household to $22,050 for a family of four. The percentage of people living in poverty in 2009 was the highest since 1984 (see Figure 2.3).

The United States has the highest poverty rate of any advanced industrial nation. The **poverty rate is the proportion of the population whose income falls below the government's official poverty line—the level of income below which a family of a given size is considered to be poor**. As is discussed in Box 2.2, the U.S. poverty rate declined over the four decades from the mid-1960s to the mid-2000s, but both the rate and the number of people living in poverty rose between 2006 and 2010. The official poverty line is based on money income and cash government assistance

programs such as Social Security payments; however, it does not reflect the value of in-kind benefits such as public housing subsidies, Medicare, or Medicaid.

The Poverty Line

How is the U.S. poverty line determined? When first established in 1965 by the Social Security Administration, the poverty line was based on an assumption that the average family must spend about one-third of its total income on food. Thus, the official poverty line was determined by a minimum family *market basket*—a low-cost food budget that contains a minimum level of nutrition for a family—multiplied by three to allow for nonfood costs such as rent and utilities. The federal Office of Management and Budget (OMB) updates the

---

Social Problems and Statistics

Box 2.2

Poverty in the United States

Is the problem of poverty in the United States a larger or smaller problem today than it was in the past? The good news is that during the past four decades, the *poverty rate*—the percentage of the U.S. population that the government defines as being "poor"—declined from 21 percent early in the 1960s to 14.3 percent in 2009 (DeNavas-Walt et al., 2010). The bad news is that the *total number of people living in poverty* is still 43.6 million people (see Figure 2.3).

How statistics are created and how they are used are important factors in assessing the nature and extent of a social problem. Statistics can be stated as numbers that can be compared with other numbers or as numbers that can be compared. *Lies and percentages. In Damned Lies and Statistics: Untangling Numbers from the Media, Politicians, and Activists,* Joel Best (2001)

notes that statistics play an important role in campaigns to create or to refute claims about social problems. If statistics indicate that a social condition adversely affects large numbers of people, that condition may be defined as a social problem that requires that a society do something about it. However, if the statistics indicate that fewer people are adversely affected or that the number of people so affected is going down, that condition may be downgraded as a concern or even cease to be defined as a social problem.

Statistics regarding poverty in the United States are an example. Consider, for example, increases and declines in the poverty rate, as reported by the U.S. Census Bureau. When the poverty rate goes down, this statistic can be used to argue that poverty is less of a social problem today. When the poverty rate goes up, this statistic can be used to advocate for

the expansion of some public policies and to demand the end of others (such as "welfare as we know it").

Instead of using statistics to reaffirm our political perspective, we may gain more by looking at these figures from a sociological perspective. An increase in the total number of people living below the poverty line, as also reported by the U.S. Census Bureau, is a statistic that can be used to validly argue that poverty remains as serious a social problem today, and that proactive measures must be taken to reduce or alleviate this problem. In fact, the *actual number* of people who are poor today is greater than the number of individuals who were poor about fifty years ago because more people are living in the United States today, and the same percentage of a larger population obviously results in a larger total number.

Regardless of which statistics are used or how they are interpreted,

Social Problems and Statistics

Box 2.2 continued

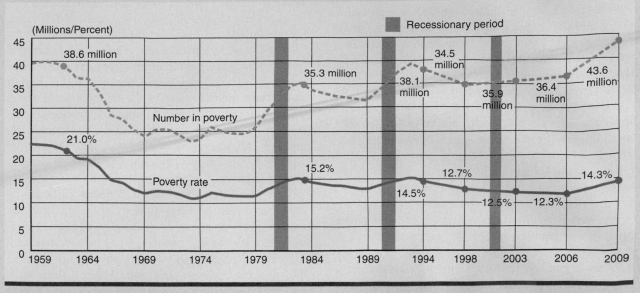

Figure 2.3 Poverty in the United States, 1959 to 2009
Source: DeNavas-Walt et al., 2010.

poverty is a social problem in the United States. Is the problem increasing or is it decreasing? At least until the Great Recession of 2007–2009, the answer was mixed: The rate of poverty was down, but the total number of people living in poverty was up. Likewise, the gap between the rich and the poor in this country continued to increase throughout this time period.

As we see data regarding poverty in the United States, and statistics about other social problems, it is important for us to read between the lines, to seek to understand what the statistics really mean. By knowing and understanding those statistics (and the source of those statistics—are they real or, in Best's terminology, "mangled"?), we can come closer to understanding the implications of poverty and of other social problems that are discussed throughout this book.

poverty line annually; it is also adjusted for the number of people in the household.

Today, many social analysts argue that the official poverty line is too low. According to economist Patricia Ruggles (1990, 1992), the poverty line is based on outdated (pre-1960) standards that were established at a time when fewer households were composed of two working parents or of single parents who faced employment-related expenses such as work clothes, transportation, child care, and quick and convenient foods. More than twenty years ago, Ruggles argued that poverty thresholds should be increased by at least 50 percent.

Who Are the Poor?

If poverty were equally distributed among all social groups in the United States, all people regardless of their age, race, or ethnicity, sex, household composition, or other attributes would have an equal statistical chance of being among the poor in any given year. However, poverty is not distributed equally: People poverty th

Age, Gender, Household Composition, and Poverty

The vast majority of poor people in the United States are women and children. Children under age eighteen—24.3 percent of the U.S. population—account for more than 35 percent of the poor. About one in five children age eighteen and under lives in poverty (see Table 2.1). The percentage of children under six years of age who live in poverty-level households is even higher: In 2009 about one in four was considered poor. When children under age six live in households headed by women with no adult male present, more than 54 percent are poor (DeNavas-Walt, Proctor, and Smith, 2010).

About two-thirds of all adults living in poverty are women; households headed by women are the fastest-growing segment of the overall poverty population. Researchers have discovered a number of reasons why single-parent families headed by women are at such a great risk of poverty. Single-parent families typically have fewer employed adults in them and therefore a lower annual income than most two-parent households in the first place, and women generally earn less money than men, even for comparable work. Thus, a single-parent family headed by a woman usually faces a greater risk of poverty than a single-parent family headed by a man. In 2009, about one-third of all families headed by women (with no husband present) were poor and nearly 15 percent lived in deep poverty. Women bear the major economic burden for their children. Contributions from absent fathers in the form of child support and alimony payments accounted for a very small percentage, if any, of family income. By contrast, only 18 percent of single-parent families headed by men were poor, and 8 percent lived in deep poverty. For children living in a married-couple family, the economic outlook is much better than for children who live in single female-headed families and are more than four times as likely to be living in poverty, and six times as likely to be living in deep poverty (National Center for Legal and Economic Justice, 2010).

The association between gender and poverty is referred to as the *feminization of poverty*—**the trend whereby women experience poverty at far higher rates than men** (Pearce, 1978). In the United States and throughout the world, women experience poverty at higher rates than men. However, women are not the only ones who are disadvantaged by poverty: The high rate of poverty among children is directly linked to poverty among women. High rates of female poverty are related to women's unique vulnerability to event-driven poverty—poverty resulting from the loss of a job, disability, desertion by a spouse, separation, divorce, or widowhood. Other social structural factors contributing to women's poverty are shifts in the nation's economy and demographic shifts such as childbearing outside marriage and higher divorce rates. Women's poverty rates have decreased slightly in recent decades, partly due to an increase in the proportion of women in the paid labor force and some improvement in the gender wage gap (whereby men earn more money than women even when they are performing similar kinds of work). Ironically, however, the gender gap may not have narrowed because women are making *more* money but because men are making *less* money as jobs in manufacturing and other well-paid employment sectors have grown fewer in number or disappeared altogether. In the next section we examine race, ethnicity, and poverty, so it is important to note that women of color, particularly African American

TABLE 2.1 Children (Under 18 Years Old) Below the U.S. Poverty Level, 1990 and 2009					
Year	**Percentage below Poverty Level**				
	All Races	Non-Hispanic White	Asian or Pacific Islander	African American	Hispanic Origin
1990	20.6	12.3	17.6	44.8	38.4
2009	...7	11.9	14.0	35.7	33.1

Source: Da...vas-Walt et al., 2010.

women and Latinas, are especially disadvantaged by both the feminization of poverty and issues of racial inequality. For this reason, the term *racial feminization of poverty* has been introduced to describe the intersectionality of gender and racial inequalities in problems associated with poverty.

Race, Ethnicity, and Poverty

Despite fluctuations in poverty rates over time, African Americans, Latinos/as (Hispanics), and Native Americans consistently remain overrepresented among people living in poverty (see Figure 2.4). In the United States, approximately 38.1 million people list their race as African American or black, a figure that amounts to 12.4 percent of the U.S. population. As compared to 12.4 percent of the overall population, about 25.8 percent of African Americans were among the officially poor in 2009. This figure was similar to 25.3 percent of Hispanics (Latinas/os), and sharply higher than 9.4 percent for non-Latino/a whites and 12.5 percent for Asian Americans (DeNavas-Walt et al., 2010). Poverty rates for Native Americans and Alaska Natives are not provided by the U.S. Census Bureau, and current estimates place poverty rates for this category in a range from 24 and 33 percent; however, this is guesswork because of the lack of official data.

Those who experience poverty are also likely to experience unemployment, hunger, and income and educational disparities. These conditions are particularly harmful for children, and more than a third (35.7 percent) of all African American and Hispanic children live in poverty, as 11.9 percent of white (non-Hispanic) Americans. Although any number of children living in poverty is harmful, the persistent disparity across racial and ethnic lines creates a situation where people of color are living in economic hardship and experiencing "recession-like" conditions even when the U.S. economy was strong. Sociological research examining the relationship between race, ethnicity, and poverty has consistently shown that past discrimination has a long-term, detrimental effect on the life chances and opportunities of persons of color in the United States. In Chapter 3, we look more closely at racial and ethnic

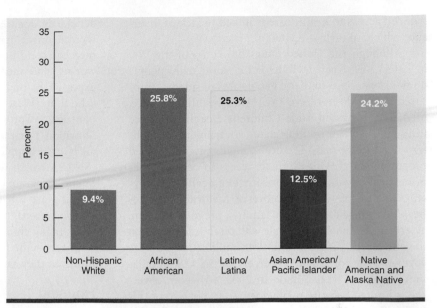

Figure 2.4 People below the U.S. poverty level, 2009, by race
Source: DeNavas-Walt et al., 2010.

inequalities and explore various explanations for the persistence of this problem in our nation.

Consequences of Poverty

Poverty statistics are more than just a snapshot of who is poor and how the poor live: These statistics are predictors. As such, they tend to predict a grim future for individuals who live below the poverty line and for the entire nation. Individuals and families in poverty do not have the chance to contribute to society, and in turn, they do not have access to the same privileges and opportunities as those who are more affluent. Of special concern are issues of health and nutrition, housing, and education.

Health and Nutrition

Poverty is related to health disparities. Lower-income individuals average fewer healthy days per year and have higher rates of infant mortality; greater prevalence and hypertension, diabetes, and other chronic, particu- shorter life expectancy rates. The prole. hyper- larly great as individuals grow. Statistics tension ("high blood press well as other show that persons li, e prescription drugs, uninsured person ly with insurance (CDC tension und ly Report, 2011). In sum, proper Morbi reduced access to health care is linked to lack of insurance which, in turn, is related to poverty.

Although the United States has some of the best high-tech health care facilities in the world, many people do not have access to them. People are considered uninsured if they do not have any private health insurance, Medicare, Medicaid, state Children's Health Insurance Program coverage, or other state-, government-, or military health care plan. Medicaid, a government-funded program that provides limited access to certain types of medical care, is the major source of health care coverage for people living in poverty. Medicaid provides health coverage for children, families, pregnant women, elderly individuals, and people with disabilities based on income levels. In 2009, almost 48 million people were covered by Medicaid (15.7 percent of the U.S. population), up from 42.6 million in 2008. However, coverage is limited because many doctors do not accept this form of payment, and some patients cannot afford to pay the initial deductible or copayment. For the working poor and unemployed, lack of health insurance is a major problem: More than 26 percent of all people earning below $25,000 a year are uninsured. In 2009, 32 percent of Latinos/as, 21 percent of African Americans, and 10 percent of all persons below the age of eighteen (regardless of race and ethnicity) were uninsured (DeNavas-Walt et al., 2010). Many states have established the Children's Health Insurance Program (CHIP) for families earning less than about $45,000 per year for a family of four, but premiums and cost-sharing are required of some families.

Like health care, good nutrition is essential to an individual's well-being. Good nutrition depends on the food purchased, and when people are poor, they are more likely to go without food or to purchase cheap but filling foods such as beans, rice, and potatoes that typically do not meet all daily nutritional requirements. Poor children particularly are at risk for inadequate nutrition, food insecurity, and sometimes hunger. *Food insecurity* refers to the lack of consistent access to adequate food for active, healthy living. One in seven U.S. households ¥ million) are considered to be food insecure at some ho⋯ring the year, and for African American house‐ curil⋯tio is one in four, or 3.6 million. Food inse‐ in po⋯pro⋯sed in recent years because of increases and well-b⋯ployment rates. nutrition are⋯ecurity is detrimental to health of illness and⋯are hungry or lack adequate developmental o⋯ and are at greater risk ⋯rity affects children's ⋯lems such as iron

deficiency anemia and poor socioemotional development. Hunger may also contribute to or result in other medical conditions such as rickets, scurvy, parasitic worms, and mental retardation. More people would experience food insecurity were it not for national school breakfast and lunch programs, community food pantries, and programs such as the Special Supplemental Nutrition Program for Women, Infants, and Children (WIC), the Supplemental Nutrition Assistance Program (SNAP), which was formerly referred to as the Food Stamp Program. Problems associated with food and housing are intricately linked. When parents have to decide between paying the rent and putting food on the table, many choose to pay the rent in hopes of keeping a roof over the heads of family members. Sometimes, however, they cannot afford to do either.

Housing

Many regions of the United States lack affordable housing for low-income families. Across the nation, housing costs have risen dramatically even for marginal places of residence. The problem has been heightened by the loss of many lower-cost housing units. In cities with rapid urban and suburban growth patterns, low-cost housing units have been replaced by expensive condominiums or single-family residences for affluent residents. This shift to condominiums and single-family residences has made finding housing even more difficult for people living in poverty. When low-income housing is available, it may be located in areas that are plagued by high crime rates and overcrowded conditions. The housing often has inadequate heating and plumbing facilities, cockroach and rodent infestation, and dangerous structural problems due to faulty construction or lack of adequate maintenance.

Over the last several years, many more low-income families have had to rely on shared housing and frequent moves to keep a roof of their heads. Today, it is not uncommon to find multiple generations of family members, such as a mother raising her children in her parents' home, living together in crowded conditions. Shared housing situations are referred to as being "doubled-up," and economic hardship means that some people are staying with relatives for extended periods of time because they do not have the financial resources to go elsewhere. Some people lack housing stability regardless of the nation's economic conditions; however, many of those who are doubling up or moving from place to place trying to have somewhere to stay are people who have lost their job or been removed from their homes due to foreclosure. Shared housing produces many problems for poorer individuals, including overcrowding, the necessity of moving from place to play when they "wear out their welcome," and safety concerns because of feeling compromised by having to live with others who may intimidate or threaten them with bodily harm if their rules and demands are not met. For some individuals and families it is just one step from shared housing to homelessness.

In recent years, the nation's homeless population has continued to increase, and more people are experiencing homelessness for the first time. The number of homeless at any given time in the United States varies widely based on which agency is collecting data. However, standard estimates place the homeless population at between 1 and 1.3 million, with about 23 percent of those individuals being "permanent homeless" persons who have been on the streets for one year or more. The number of chronically homeless people has remained about the same over the past five years. Most people go into and out of homelessness, often using shelters if they are not able to double up, as discussed previously. But, some data indicate that nearly four in ten homeless persons live on the street, in a car, or in another place not intended for human habitation. Although the homeless population includes both single individuals and families, the number of homeless families increased by about 30 percent between 2007 and 2010, while the number of homeless individuals remained about the same

or dropped slightly in various regions of the country. The main causes of homelessness among families with children are unemployment, lack of affordable housing, poverty, domestic violence, and low-paying jobs. Like homeless families, single homeless individuals also list lack of affordable housing and poverty as major contributing factors in their homelessness; however, they also indicate other factors, such as mental illness and substance abuse, combined with a lack of needed services that worsened the problem (National Alliance to End Homelessness, 2011). Despite other factors that may come into play, most researchers argue that homelessness is most often caused by poverty and job loss, and these concerns intensify as economic conditions worsen across all states and the nation as a whole.

Education

Poverty and education are deeply intertwined. Children who do not have adequate housing and food are at a disadvantage from the first day they enter a classroom. Some schools offer low-income children additional services, such as free meal programs and tutors, to help them gain a more equal footing in their studies, but some problems are difficult to overcome. One is the extent to which the parents of children living in poverty are able to become involved in their children's education and the amount of cultural capital they are able to

Housing is one reflection of larger economic inequalities that exist in the United States. What economic realities are shown by this multistory house in a wealthy suburban neighborhood (left) as compared with these apartment units in a low-income urban area (right)?

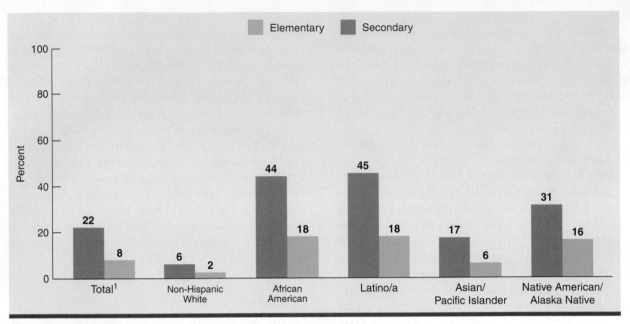

Figure 2.5 Percentage of public school students in high-poverty schools, 2008 to 2009

Note: Total includes students whose racial-ethnic group was not reported.

Source: National Center for Education Statistics, 2011.

pass on to them. We will look at these issues in greater detail in later chapters. For now, it is important to note that a crucial relationship exists between educational opportunities and life chances. Children from low-income families tend to have inadequate educational opportunities, which keep them at the bottom of the class system. They get fewer years of schooling and are less likely to graduate from high school or college than are children from more affluent families.

A recent U.S. Department of Education study shows that the number of so-called high-poverty schools—identified as schools where more than 75 percent of students come from low-income and poverty-level families and thus are eligible for a subsidized lunch program—has increased in the United States. As shown in Figure 2.5, the highest percentages of students in high-poverty schools are African Americans and Latinos/as in the elementary grades. In high-poverty schools, only 68 percent of twelfth graders graduated in 2008, compared to 91 percent in low-poverty schools, and graduates from high-poverty schools are far less likely to enroll in college. The schools that poor children of all ages attend are more likely to be in areas with lower property values and more limited funding bases for education than are the schools attended by more affluent students, who often live in property-rich suburbs. Schools located in high-poverty rural areas or central

cities often are in need of repairs and improvements, have underpaid and overworked teachers, and must rely on outdated equipment and teaching materials. Lack of educational opportunity results in lower levels of educational attainment among people from lower-income and poverty-level families and tends to perpetuate poverty by making it significantly more difficult for these individuals to acquire well-paying jobs or a more secure economic future.

SOCIAL WELFARE IN THE UNITED STATES

The initial wave of social welfare in the United States was enacted under President Franklin D. Roosevelt's New Deal during the Great Depression of the 1930s. Including farm subsidies, fair housing standards, a minimum wage and maximum workweek, protections for organized labor, jobs programs such as the Works Progress Administration (WPA), and the Social Security system, the New Deal marked the beginning of the *welfare state*—a system in which the government takes the chief responsibility for providing for the social and economic security of residents by providing them with certain services and benefits, such as education, health care, insurance against disability, sickness, and

Sympathetic versus Negative Framing of Stories about the Poor

She trudged languorously along the thrumming streets of Elmhurst, Queens, lost in her early evening thoughts. . . . Walking consumes time, and in the awkward caution of her life it drains her of troubled memories. . . . This is a doleful life that Anna Berroa never anticipated. It seems to catch her unawares. One moment she was middle class, envisioning a placid old age, and then a series of untoward events ambushed her. . . . Poverty is particularly frightening from the lens of old age, when there are few, if any, opportunities to enhance one's prospects and the only escape hatch seems to be death.

—Journalist N. R. Kleinfeld (2003) paints a sympathetic picture of the life of Anna Berroa, who is portrayed as representative of other older individuals who are forced from a relatively comfortable economic status to poverty

Sharon Jasper has been victimized. Sharon Jasper has been rapidly wronged. She has become a Section 8 carcass, the victim of ever changing public housing policies. Sharon Jasper has spent 57 of her 58 years dedicated to one cause and one cause only, and has nothing to show for her dedicated servitude. She has lived in Section 8 housing all but one of her 58 years. This legacy was passed down from her parents, who moved into Section 8 housing in 1949 when Sharon was six months old. She has passed the legacy down to her own children, but fears they may have to get jobs to pay for the utilities and deposits that Section 8 is now requiring. She laments about her one year hiatus from the comfort of her Section 8 nirvana, "I tried it for a year . . . you know. . . working and all. It's not anything I would want to go though again, or wish on anyone in my family, but I am damn proud of that year."

—"Jim Byrd," author of "A Skewed View" Internet blog (www.jimbyrd.com), attempts to satirize Sharon Jasper's efforts on behalf of the tenants' association of the St. Bernard Housing Development in New Orleans to keep their homes in the aftermath of Hurricane Katrina. At that time the city council was considered a redevelopment plan to replace St. Bernard with more expensive housing and a PGA golf course.

The first media narrative (about Anna Berroa) uses sympathetic framing to show empathy for an older woman who has worked hard all of her life but is reduced to poverty. In the second narrative (about Sharon Jasper), an

Internet blogger uses negative-image framing to influence public opinion about welfare and public housing. In the blog, the woman's life is satirized and negative stereotypes attributed to individuals who live in public housing are exaggerated. Let's look more closely at these two media framing approaches to see how they might affect the thinking of some nonpoor people regarding poverty and dependency.

In Chapter 1, we discussed the difference between thematic and episodic framing in the media. As you will recall, thematic framing provides a more impersonal view of the nature of a social problem (such as the primary use of statistical data in an article about homelessness or poverty). By contrast, episodic framing tells a story in terms of

Star Parker, a syndicated columnist and political commentator who often appears on major television networks, is a former welfare receipient and founder of a conservative think tank advocating market-based public policy to transition America's poor from what she sees as government dependency.

Social Problems in the Media

Box 2.3 continued

personal experience, focusing on the part that individuals play in the situation. Both of the previous stories are examples of episodic framing: They highlight the personal experiences of individuals living in poverty to represent a larger category of people who are undergoing extreme economic hardship. In the process, this kind of media framing gives poverty a human face (Kendall, 2011). However, the "faces" are extremely divergent in the two examples. The journalist writing about Anna Berroa's situation frames her story sympathetically and seeks to show that Anna's situation is not unique among older people living in large cities like New York. Sympathetic framing is most likely to be used when the individuals in the story are children, elderly individuals, or persons with an illness or disability.

Unlike sympathetic framing that shows the societal and individual problems associated with poverty, negative-image framing focuses on the dependency and/or deviance of persons in the media report. Welfare in its many forms is one issue that often receives negative-image media framing. A keyword search for "welfare dependency" by this author yielded more than 3,500 newspaper articles, TV news reports, and Internet blogs on welfare between the early 1990 and 2010 (see Kendall, 2011). Negative-image framing of poor women of color often employs controlling images of the women as "welfare mothers" who are chronically on public assistance, live in housing projects with multiple generations present, lack ambition, have a poor work ethic, and are unwilling to get

off the "public dole." Many of these frames are evident in the blog about Sharon Jasper.

What effect does media framing of poverty stories have on audiences? Sympathetic framing may produce some degree of empathy on the part of viewers and readers for the plight of people who are living in conditions that are assumed to be beyond their control. By contrast, negative-image framing emphasizes the shortcomings of individuals, in this case the poor and those living in public housing, and suggests to those who are better off that these less-fortunate individuals created their own problems.

Question for Consideration

1. Have U.S. audiences seen too much, or too little, of the true nature of poverty as a result of the kinds of frames that media "voices" use when they cover stories about the poor?

Independent Research

Search the Internet for websites and blogs (such as www. jimbyrd.com) that discuss issues pertaining to poverty, gender, race, and social inequality. Make a list of the ones you consider to be fair and balanced in their discussions and a second list of ones that you believe are distorted and perpetuate classism, racism, sexism, ageism, or other forms of biased thinking about persons living in poverty in the United States or other nations.

unemployment, and retirement pensions. From their inception, government assistance programs have been viewed as "good" if recipients are thought to be deserving of assistance and "bad" if recipients are considered undeserving. This issue has become more polarized as many traditional media sources, bloggers, and social media users have emphatically expressed their views on this topic (see Box 2.3).

The second wave of welfare programs began with the passage of the Economic Opportunity Act of 1964 and the implementation of President Lyndon Johnson's War on Poverty programs, which focused on education and vocational training for low-income children and adults to help them escape poverty. These programs included preschool education (Head Start), compensatory education, and vocational training programs such as Job Corps, Neighborhood Youth Corps, and Manpower Development. With these programs in place, the percentage of people living in poverty dropped from

22 percent in 1960 to 12 percent in 1976 (Kelso, 1994). However, in the 1980s and early 1990s, funding for many of these programs was greatly reduced or eliminated, and in 1996, President Clinton signed into law the Personal Responsibility and Work Opportunity Reconciliation Act, a welfare reform plan that dramatically changed the U.S. welfare system by requiring recipients to work in exchange for time-limited assistance (see Box 2.3).

The third wave of welfare programs is somewhat different from the earlier ones in that it involves tweaking and attempting to fund existing welfare legislation. For example, the Work Opportunity Tax Credit (WOTC), authorized by the Small Business Job Protection Act of 1996, provided federal tax credits for employers who hire certain categories of job seekers, including welfare recipients who have received Temporary Assistance for Needy Families for at least a nine-month period. In 2010, President Obama signed the Tax Relief Unemployment Insurance Reauthorization and Job Creation Act, which further extended the WOTC so that employers would receive tax credits (of about $9,000 each) for each new long-term (at least eighteen consecutive months) TANF recipient hired over a two-year period. SNAP (food stamps) recipients, some veterans, individuals receiving Supplemental Security Income benefits, and ex-felons are also included in the tax credit. Along with unemployment insurance, Medicaid, and funding for education for the disadvantaged, tax benefits and funding of this type has been the primary way in which social welfare in the United States has been dealt with in the twenty-first century.

What have been the results so far? According to some policy analysts, without initiatives such as these the poverty level would have risen even more than it did, particularly in view of the economic crises in the first decade of this century and the aftermath that will linger well into the second decade. In the words of President Barack Obama, "the most important anti-poverty effort is growing the economy and making sure there are enough jobs out there" (quoted in Bernstein, 2010). SNAP (food stamps), unemployment insurance benefits, and Social Security are the three major programs that were expanded by the American Recovery and Reinvestment Act of 2009 and they proved to be particularly useful in keeping families above the poverty line or helping them not sink deeper into poverty if they were already there (Bernstein, 2010).

Are welfare programs a problem or a solution for poverty? The answer to this question depends on how poverty itself is explained.

Explanations for Poverty

Poverty can be explained in individualistic, cultural, or structural terms. The framework that is applied influences people's beliefs about how poverty might be reduced. Individual explanations for poverty view poverty as the result of either attitudinal and motivational problems that cause individuals to be poor or the amount of human capital that a person possesses. Attitudinal and motivational explanations focus on the United States as the "land of opportunity" and suggest that people who do not succeed have no one to blame but themselves for their lack of motivation, laziness, or other flaws. In contrast, human capital explanations of poverty highlight the individual's lack of human capital—the assets that

Read the Document
Racial Stratification and Education in the United States: Why Inequality Persists on **mysoclab.com**

a person brings to the labor market such as education, job training, experience, and specialized knowledge or skills. Those favoring human capital explanations of poverty have noted, for example, that the introduction of new workplace technologies has resulted in many people having limited human capital to bring to the job market. To some sociologists, individual explanations of poverty amount to **blaming the victim—a practice used by people who view a social problem as emanating from within the individual who exhibits the problem** (Ryan, 1976). Proposed laws that require drug testing of welfare and/or unemployment applicants and beneficiaries are contemporary examples of this concept and support its usefulness more than 30 years after psychologist William Ryan originally coined the term in the 1970s. Victim blaming often has a racist and/or sexist component, as is evidenced in old stereotypes of the "black welfare mother" when, in actuality, many individuals who benefit from public assistance programs are neither persons of color nor women. For six decades, media representations have contributed to myths and negative stereotypes about the poor and how they live (see Box 2.3).

Cultural explanations of poverty focus on how cultural background affects people's values and behavior. Among the earliest of these explanations is the culture of poverty thesis by anthropologist Oscar Lewis (1966). According to Lewis, some—but not all—poor people develop a separate and self-perpetuating system of attitudes and behaviors that keeps them trapped in poverty. Among these attitudes and behaviors are an inability to defer gratification or plan for the future; feelings of apathy, hostility, and suspicion toward others; and deficient speech and communication patterns. The culture of poverty thesis has provided political leaders and social analysts with a rationale for labeling the poor as lazy and perpetually dependent on "government handouts."

More recent cultural explanations of poverty have focused on the lack of **cultural capital—social assets such as the values, beliefs, attitudes, and competencies in language and culture that are learned at home and required for success and social advance** (Bourdieu and Passeron, 1990). From this perspective, low-income people do not have cultural capital to function in a competitive economy. According to some sociologists, cultural explanations of poverty and deflect attention from structural explanations of shift blame from the economy to the poor and powerless.

Unlike individualistic and cultural explanations of poverty, wh

explanations of poverty focus on the macrolevel, the level of social organization that is beyond an individual's ability to change. One structural explanation of poverty points to changes in the economy that dramatically alter employment opportunities for people, particularly those who have the least wealth, power, and prestige. We have seen much evidence supporting this structural explanation during the Great Recession in the first two decades of the twenty-first century. Millions of jobs have been lost in the U.S. economy, causing more workers to experience long-term unemployment. Even in periods of greater economic growth and prosperity in the United States, little of the growth has found its way into workers' paychecks in more than four decades.

Another structural explanation for poverty suggests that poverty is a side effect of the capitalist system: The rich get richer, and the poor either get poorer or remain about the same. Using this explanation, analysts note that workers are increasingly impoverished by the stagnation of real earnings, which have not increased in constant dollars for a number of years. *Constant dollars* is the term used to indicate that dollars have been adjusted for the effects of inflation, as opposed to *current dollars*, which are actual dollars paid or received at a specific point in time. Using constant dollars to measure earnings makes it possible for researchers to make meaningful comparisons about wages and how much products cost over an extended period of time. For example, a business executive who earned $50,000 annually in the 1930s in current dollars would actually have been earning more than $500,000 in constant dollars.

According to the U.S. Bureau of Labor Statistics (2011b), real average hourly earnings for all employees declined in 2001, further contributing to the *wage squeeze*, which is the steady downward pressure on the real take-home pay of workers that has occurred over the past three decades. During these same decades, shareholders in major corporations have had substantial increases in dividends and chief executive officers have received extremely lucrative salaries and compensation packages. Corporate downsizing, off-shoring of poorly paid workers in other nations, and use of immigrant labor enhanced capitalists' profits and contributed to the impoverishment of workers wages of a more permanent poverty class. In affluent intense quest for profit results in low and impo ide disparity in the life chances of eople, and the unemployment people.

IS THERE A SOLUTION TO POVERTY?

As we saw in Chapter 1, how people view a social problem has a direct effect on how they believe the problem should be reduced or solved. Poverty, hunger, and social inequality are no exception. Functionalist analysts and those who follow a conservative political outlook typically view these issues quite differently—and offer different solutions—from conflict or symbolic interactionist theorists and liberal political analysts, who possess divergent assumptions about the causes for, effects of, and possible solutions to these pressing social problems.

Functionalist/Conservative Solutions to the Problem of Poverty

How big a problem is poverty in the United States? Some functionalist theorists and conservative political analysts begin any discussion of poverty by noting that, although poverty *is* a problem, it is not *as big a problem* as some people might believe. To some of these analysts, for example, "official" poverty statistics issued by agencies of the federal government and some other organizations exaggerate the nature and extent of poverty in this country. Some functionalists and conservatives believe that, if we take into account all of the available antipoverty benefits (including Medicaid, Social Security, subsidized housing, and SNAP [food stamps]), the number of people living in poverty is much lower than many estimates suggest. In other words, if we include all of the benefits available to so-called poor people when we calculate rates of poverty, we will find that the real poverty rate is much lower official statistics might indicate.

From a functionalist viewpoint, there will always be poverty in any society: Some people will earn more than other people, there will always be people on the "bottom rungs" of society, and those on the bottom rungs will live in poverty when contrasted with those who earn more. The issue, from this point of view, is not whether society can eliminate poverty but rather what can be done to strengthen those social institutions that help individuals lift themselves out of poverty. Based on functionalist and conservative perspectives, putting more resources into welfare benefits for the poor is the equivalent of simply throwing away money in an effort to solve the problem. According to one political leader who advocated this philosophy, "What poor Americans, like all other Americans, need are jobs, not more government benefits" (Committee on Ways and Means, 2011). From this approach, you do not eliminate poverty by paying people to stay poor and/or unemployed. Throwing money at the problem of poverty therefore neither reduces the nation's poverty rate nor helps poor individuals become self-sufficient. Instead, it increases public spending and adds billions of dollars to the national debt.

Based on this functionalist/conservative assessment of the causes of poverty, what are the possible ways to reduce or eliminate poverty? Those who adhere to a functionalist approach often argue that poverty-related problems can be reduced by strengthening our major social institutions. We must promote private-sector job creation, improve our schools, and strengthen our families, churches, and communities so that these groups can more effectively meet the needs of people. By motivating low-income and poverty-level people to change their attitudes, beliefs, and work habits, they will have a better chance of escaping poverty. According to some analysts, we must educate children and young people in low-income or poverty-level families to stay out of poverty by completing their education, not get pregnant outside marriage, and get a job.

Conflict/Liberal Solutions to the Problem of Poverty

Some of the strongest critiques of functionalist/conservative perspectives on poverty come from conflict theorists and liberal political analysts who argue that this approach amounts to "blaming the victim." When we blame people living in poverty for their own plight, we place the focus on their "faulty" beliefs, values, or actions; we do not give proper attention to larger societal issues such as the role that out-of-control capitalists or greedy and corrupt political elites play in maintaining and perpetuating vast inequalities and social injustices in society. This perspective is in keeping with the ideas of Karl Marx, who believed that poverty was a side effect of capitalism, an economic system that made a few people very wealthy but pushed the vast majority further and further into poverty.

Different schools of thought within the larger umbrella of conflict theory offer different views of poverty and what its solutions might be. According to feminist conflict theorists, for example, poverty is partly based on gender. Patriarchy in society and discrimination against women in the home and workplace produce a harmful effect on women and children. The feminization of poverty makes women particularly vulnerable to event-driven poverty such as the loss of a job

or a downturn in the economy that makes it more difficult for those on the lower rungs of the economic ladder to find a job at all, much less to find decent-paying work. From this perspective, solving the problem of poverty requires solving problems within the labor market itself, especially the problems that women face within that market.

Conflict theorists who focus on the issue of racial and ethnic inequality believe that poverty is rooted in past and present prejudice and discrimination that keeps people of color out of the economic mainstream. The high poverty rate among African Americans, Latinos/as, and other people of color is caused by structural factors such as substandard schools, inadequate housing, and crime-ridden neighborhoods. The lack of social policies that address ongoing problems of economic inequality, such as the large number of subordinate-group members who do not have health insurance or access to legal counsel, also contributes to the continued subordination of these populations. Based on this perspective, the problem of poverty can be solved only if we are able to reduce racial and ethnic inequality, as well as economic inequality, in our nation.

Overall, conflict theorists and liberal political analysts view increased social inequality and unresolved race, class, and gender discrimination as major factors that contribute to the problem of poverty: These structural problems are beyond the control of individuals who live in poverty. Liberal political analysts argue that, to reduce the problem of poverty, federal and state governments must play a larger role by enacting and implementing social policies that stimulate the economy, create new jobs, and provide workers with a living wage: People must be better rewarded for working by creating a living wage that makes it possible for people to have adequate food, clothing, shelter, and other necessities of life. We must also overhaul housing policies and strengthen job-training programs. In other words, to significantly reduce poverty, we must not blame people for being poor. Our nation's political and business leaders must devise new ways to fund needed social service programs and must cut excessive "corporate welfare" programs that primarily benefit the wealthiest

Symbolic Interactioni... ...ons to the Problem of P...

...ing a symbolic ...us on how human ...interaction and how ...anings on others. One

As discussed in Cha... interactionist per... behavior is le... people i...

of the ways in which meanings—both positive and negative—are shared is through the labeling of other individuals and groups. *Labeling theory* is based on the assumption that how people are viewed by others has a strong influence on how they perceive themselves, particularly if they accept the label placed on them as being valid. When people are labeled as "deviant," for example, they have fewer resources and opportunities than those who are not so labeled. Persons labeled as "deviant" are more likely to engage in nonstandard patterns of behavior, and they have a much greater chance of being stigmatized by others. *Stigma* is a negative social label that singles out people as "deviants" because of some characteristic they possess that is devalued by other individuals.

In the United States, being financially self-sufficient is the minimum norm for social acceptance by many people. Individuals who are poor are considered to be a burden on society and may be labeled as "lazy," "ignorant," or "useless" in a society that values high achievement and self-sufficiency. In sociologist Erving Goffman's (1963) discussion of social stigma, he stated that individuals are stigmatized when their appearance, behavior, or assumed beliefs and attitudes go against cultural norms. Those who are stigmatized experience social disapproval from others and are blamed for being the cause of their own problems. Although some of the poor, homeless, and hungry individuals in our nation may escape stigmatization because they are largely invisible to middle- and upper-class people, poverty-level individuals who are visible on the streets and busy corners in major cities are often the object of labeling ("Bum!") and derision ("Get a job!"). They also experience informal and official stigmatization (such as city ordinances that prohibit homeless people from being on the streets if they have no visible means of support). Based on Goffman's assessment of stigma, we may assume that labeling and stigmatization strongly affect people and have a profound effect on human interactions across class lines.

Symbolic interactionists suggest that, to reduce or eliminate poverty we should find more constructive ways think about poor people individually and better ways ... on what might reduce poverty at a societal level. poor ... proving how affluent people perceive of the issue ... immediately resolve the larger structural process ... duce vast economic inequalities, the ... ople's perceptions about the poor

might result in significant social policy changes. When poor people are viewed as *being the problem*, our political, business, and social leaders see little reason to take action to reduce poverty. By contrast, if the poor are viewed as *needing assistance to overcome poverty* because of factors largely beyond their control, political leaders may be more likely to seek ways to provide that assistance.

People who are poor are hurt psychologically and socially by being stigmatized and have little chance of escaping poverty. According to Goffman, going through the process of stigmatization spoils a person's identity and makes the individual feel inadequate and even inferior. If poor individuals who are labeled as having some sort of personal flaw that keeps them in poverty come to accept this label, they may lose any motivation to try to rise out of poverty: Why try to escape poverty when it is an inevitable consequence of their own personal flaws?

Although the symbolic interactionist perspective does not provide a list of ways to deal with social problems such as poverty, it does provide us with insights on the sociopsychological issues that are associated with being poor, such as how labeling and stigmatization may affect individuals living in poverty. This approach makes us aware that social change must occur at both the microlevel and macrolevel to reduce poverty. Many individuals living in poverty are not passive victims of their situation: They want to bring about positive changes in their own lives and that of their families if they are only given the opportunity to do so. Amazingly, many people living in poverty have not given up on the American Dream of upward mobility for themselves and their children. About two decades ago, a woman named Sara described the common struggles of people across time and place to find opportunities to get out of poverty and improve their quality of life:

> I got my vision, I got my dreams. . . . I have goals—I want to be something different from what I have right now. . . . I guess to be somebody in poverty, to see that generation that's coming behind us—it's sad, it's real sad, what do they have to strive for? . . . I just got to believe I only can make the difference . . . even though obviously the system doesn't really want you to succeed. . . . I can become what statistics has designed me to be, a nothing, or I can make statistics a lie. . . . Today, I am making statistics a lie. (Polakow, 1993:73)

SUMMARY

✔● Study and Review on mysoclab.com

Why is social stratification a social problem?

Social stratification refers to the hierarchical arrangement of large social groups based on their control over basic resources. In highly stratified societies, low-income and poor people have limited access to food, clothing, shelter, education, health care, and other necessities of life.

What are the major problems of the low-income nations?

Studies of global inequality distinguish between high-income nations (countries with highly industrialized economies and relatively high levels of national and per capita [per person] income), middle-income nations (countries that are undergoing transformation from agrarian to industrial economies), and low-income nations (countries that are primarily agrarian with little industrialization and low levels of national and personal income). Poverty, food shortages, hunger, and rapidly growing populations are pressing problems in many low-income nations.

How does the "new international division of labor" perspective explain global inequality?

According to this perspective, transnational corporations have established global assembly lines of production in which workers in middle- and low-income nations, earning extremely low wages, produce goods for export to high-income nations such as the United States and Japan.

How is the U.S. class structure divided?

The U.S. population is divided into a number of classes. The upper, or capitalist, class is the wealthiest and most powerful class and is made up of investors, heirs, and executives. The upper-middle class is composed of professionals, business analysts, owners of small businesses, stockbrokers, and corporate managers. The middle class includes white-collar office workers, middle-management personnel, people in technical-support positions, semiprofessionals, and nonretail sales workers. Members of the working class hold occupations such as semiskilled machine operators and counter help in fast-food restaurants. The chronically poor include individuals of working age who are outside the labor force and children who live in poor families.

Who are the poor in the United States?

The major categories of poor people in the United States are women, children under age eighteen, and people of color, especially African Americans, Latinas/os, and Native Americans.

What are individual and cultural explanations of poverty?

Individual explanations of poverty focus on the attitudinal and motivational problems of individuals or the amount of human capital a person possesses. Cultural explanations of poverty focus on how cultural background affects people's values and behavior. These explanations focus on the microlevel, and many sociologists view them as attempts to blame the victim for the problem.

What are structural explanations of poverty?

Structural explanations of poverty focus on the macrolevel, the level of social organization that is beyond an individual's ability to change. These explanations consider how changes in the economy have altered employment opportunities or how inequality and exploitation are inherent in the structure of class relations in a capitalist economy.

What solutions have been suggested for poverty?

Most individual and cultural solutions focus on the importance of work. Individual perspectives suggest that people should work harder. Cultural perspectives suggest enhancing people's cultural capital to make them better prepared for employment. Structural perspectives are based on the assumption that society can reduce poverty by creating job and training programs and investing in people through provision of child care, health care, and affordable housing.

KEY TERMS

absolute poverty, p. 29
blaming the victim, p. 43
class system, p. 25
cultural capital, p. 43
feminization of poverty, p. 36
high-income nations, p. 26

income, p. 31
life chances, p. 27
low-income nations, p. 26
middle-income nations, p. 26
poverty rate, p. **34**
power, p. 30

prestige, p. 30
relative poverty, p. 29
social stratification, p. 29
wealth, p. 30
welfare state, p. 40

QUESTIONS FOR CRITICAL THINKING

1. You have decided to study wealth and poverty in your community. Which of the research methods described in Chapter 1 would provide the best data for analysis? What secondary sources might provide useful data? What kinds of information would be easiest to acquire? What kinds of information would be most difficult to acquire?

2. What would happen if all the wealth in the United States were redistributed so that all adults had the same amount? Some analysts suggest that within five years, most of the wealth would be back in the possession of the people who hold it today. What arguments can you give to support this idea? What arguments can you give to disprove this idea?

3. How do the lives of assembly-line workers in middle- and low-income nations compare with the lives of people who live in poverty in central cities and rural areas of the United States? Should U.S. foreign policy include provisions for reducing the problems of people in middle- and low-income nations? Should it be U.S. government policy to help disadvantaged people in our own country? Why or why not?

4. Pretend that cost is no object and develop a plan for solving the problem of poverty in the United States. What are your priorities and goals? How long will your plan take to implement? Who will be the primary beneficiaries of your plan? Will the plan have any effect on you?

Succeed with MySocLab®   www.mysoclab.com

The new MySocLab delivers proven results in helping students succeed, provides engaging experiences that personalize learning, and comes from a trusted partner with educational expertise and a deep commitment to helping students and instructors achieve their goals.

Here are a few activities you will find for this chapter:

Watch on **mysoclab.com**   **Core Concepts** video clips feature sociologists in action, exploring important concepts in the study of Social Problems. Watch:
- Social Class in the United States: Fact or Fiction?

Explore on **mysoclab.com**   **Social Explorer** is an interactive application that allows you to explore Census data through interactive maps. Explore:
- Social Explorer Activity: Children Living in Poverty & Single Parent Households

Read on **mysoclab.com**   **MySocLibrary** includes primary source readings from classic and contemporary sociologists. Read:
- Racial Stratification and Education in the United States: Why Inequality Persists

Racial and Ethnic Inequality

THINKING SOCIOLOGICALLY

- How does a sociological definition of race differ from a biological one?

- Why are some forms of discrimination more difficult to identify and remedy than others?

- What similarities can we identify in the experiences of various subordinate racial and ethnic groups in the United States? What are some of the differences?

Super Bowl Commercial for Pepsi Max: "Love Hurts"

The commercial shows an African American couple, interacting—the guy eats too much fast food and the wife takes it away. At the end of the commercial, the woman is about to take away a Pepsi from him but stops when she sees that the soda has no calories. They both begin to enjoy cans of Pepsi Max on a park bench just as a blond jogger catches the husband's eye. The wife throws the Pepsi can at her husband, he ducks, and the blond woman gets knocked out. The couple run away together.

—Lori Kozlowski (2011) describes a Super Bowl commercial of Pepsi Max

Classy black ladies, do you remember when I told you that we must hold the media and commercial companies accountable for the negative stereotypes they put out there about black women? Well the Pepsi commercial that aired during the Super Bowl this evening is a perfect example of what I mean. Have you seen this racist Pepsi commercial that negatively stereotypes black women as angry and violent yet? In it a black woman bullies her black husband for eating bad things and at the end throws a can of Pepsi at a white woman he smiles at. . . . This video was part of a Pepsi contest and guess what? It won and was displayed for millions to view.

—This blog by "Classy Black Lady" (2011) reveals the frustration that a number of viewers felt when they watched a popular Super Bowl commercial that portrayed an "angry black woman" supposedly physically abusing her husband for eating junk food and then throwing a Pepsi Max can that accidentally hits an attractive white woman dressed in shorts and a tank top.

What does a commercial selling soft drinks have to do with a discussion about racial and ethnic inequality? Portrayals found in ads may trivialize our nation's larger problems regarding racial and ethnic discrimination. When the media attempt to satirize racial differences and poke fun at people based on their appearance or perceived attributes they actually open wider the doors of prejudice and discrimination with these "humorous" spots. In this chapter, we examine both overt and covert forms of discrimination, ranging from "joking" media portrayals to larger-scale discrimination in education, employment, law enforcement, and other areas of social life. As was described in Chapter 1, *discrimination* is the actions or practices of dominant-group members that have a harmful impact on members of subordinate groups (Feagin and Feagin, 2011). Like many other social problems, racial and ethnic discrimination signals a discrepancy between the ideals and realities of U.S. society today. Although equality and freedom for all—regardless of race, color, creed, or national origin—are stated ideals of this country, many subordinate-group members experience oppression regardless of their class, gender, or age.

RACIAL AND ETHNIC INEQUALITY AS A SOCIAL PROBLEM

Race is among the most divisive social problems facing the United States today. However, regardless of our racial or ethnic background, we all share certain interests and concerns that cross racial and class boundaries. Some of the problems are unemployment and job insecurity, declining real wages, escalating medical and housing costs, a scarcity of good-quality child-care programs, inadequate public education, and the toll of crime and drug trafficking in all neighborhoods. From this perspective, racial and ethnic inequality is a problem for everyone, not just for people of color.

✳── Explore the Concept
Social Explorer Activity: Patterns of Unemployment and Race on mysoclab.com

What Are Race and Ethnicity?

Many sociologists view race as a social construct—a classification of people based on social and political values—rather than a biological given. How does a sociological definition of race differ from a biological one? A biological definition of a race is a population that differs from other populations in the incidence of some genes. In the past, some anthropologists classified diverse categories of peoples into races on the basis of skin color (pigmentation) and features and build (morphology). However, contemporary anthropologists classify races in terms of genetically determined immunological and biochemical differences. In the process, they have concluded that no "pure" races exist because of multiple generations of interbreeding.

In contrast with the biological definition of race, sociologists define a *racial group* **as a category of people who have been singled out, by others or themselves, as inferior or superior, on the basis of subjectively selected physical characteristics such as skin color, hair texture, and eye shape**. African American, Native American, and Asian American are examples of categories of people that have been designated racial groups.

Sociologists note that racial groups usually are defined on the basis of real or alleged physical characteristics; ethnic groups are defined on the basis of cultural or nationality characteristics. An *ethnic group* **is a category of people who are distinguished, by others or by themselves, as inferior or superior primarily on the basis of cultural or nationality characteristics** (Feagin and Feagin, 2011). Briefly stated, members of an ethnic group share five main characteristics: (1) unique cultural traits, (2) a sense of community, (3) a feeling that one's own group is the best, (4) membership from birth, and (5) a tendency, at least initially, to occupy a distinct geographic area (such as Chinatown and Little Saigon). "White ethnics," such as Irish Americans, Italian Americans, and Jewish Americans, are also examples of ethnic groups.

"Official" Racial and Ethnic Classifications

Racial and ethnic classifications have been used for political, economic, and social purposes for many years. During the sixteenth century, northern Europeans used the concept of race to rationalize the enslavement of Africans, who were deemed an "inferior race" (Feagin and Feagin, 2011).

Before the Civil War, race was used to justify the subordination of African Americans—whether they were classified as "slaves" in the South or "freemen" in the North. In some southern states, people were classified on the basis of the "one-drop rule"—a person with any trace of African blood was considered "black" and treated as inferior. For example, in 1911 an Arkansas law created the one-drop rule in that state thereby making interracial cohabitation a felony and defining as "Negro" any person who had "any negro blood whatsoever" (Sweet,

2005). Other states traced "black blood" by fractions, such as one-sixteenth African ancestry, or used an "eyeball test" based on physical features such as hair texture, eye color, and shape of nose, ears, lips, and skull (Sweet, 2005). Being classified as "Negro," "black," or "colored" had a profound effect on people's life chances and opportunities during slavery and the subsequent era of legally sanctioned segregation of the races. Gregory Howard Williams describes how he felt when he learned from his father in the 1950s that he was "colored" rather than white, as he previously had been led to believe:

> [My father said,] "Life is going to be different from now on. In Virginia you were white boys. In Indiana, you're going to be colored boys. I want you to remember that you're the same today that you were yesterday. But people in Indiana will treat you differently. . . ."
>
> No, I answered, still refusing to believe. I'm not colored, I'm white! I look white! I've always been white! I go to "whites only" schools, "whites only" movie theaters, and "whites only" swimming pools! I never had heard anything crazier in my life! How could Dad tell us such a mean lie? I glanced across the aisle [of the bus] to where he sat grim-faced and erect, staring straight ahead. I saw my father as I never had seen him before. . . . My father was a Negro! We were colored! After ten years in Virginia on the white side of the color line, I knew what that meant. (G. H. Williams, 1996:33–34)

When Williams and his younger brother went to live with their African American grandmother in Muncie, Indiana, they quickly saw the sharp contrast between the "white" and "black" worlds: The first was one of privilege, opportunity, and comfort, and the second was one of deprivation, repression, and struggle. Since that time, Williams has become a lawyer and a law school dean; however, his memories of the prejudice and discrimination he experienced in Muncie because of the change in his racial classification remain with him (G. H. Williams, 1996).

In the past, government racial classifications were based primarily on skin color. One category existed for "White" (persons who may vary considerably in actual skin color and physical appearance); all the remaining categories are considered "nonwhite." In 2000, the U.S. Census Bureau required respondents to choose from the categories of White, Black, Asian and Pacific American, American Indian, Eskimo or Aleut, or "Other" in designating their racial classification. The 2000 census also allowed people to place themselves in more than one racial category.

For the 2010 Census, two questions were asked about Hispanic origin and race (see Figure 3.1). In regard to the first question, the Census Bureau defines Hispanic origin as "the heritage, nationality group, lineage, or country of birth of the person or the person's parents or ancestors before their arrival in the United States" (Humes, Jones, and Ramirez, 2011). "Hispanic or Latino" refers to a person of Cuban, Mexican, Puerto Rican, South or Central American, or other Spanish culture or origin regardless of race. In other words, people who identify their origin as Hispanic, Latino, or Spanish may be of any race, and it should be noted that these terms are often used interchangeably. In regard to the second question about race, 15 response categories were provided, and people could select more than one choice, plus having the option to write in more detailed information about their race.

Census data regarding Hispanic origin and race and ethnicity are important for a number of reasons. One factor is that these data are often considered when policy decisions are being made at all levels of the government. These classifications affect people's access to federal aid, education, employment, housing, health care, social services, and many other valued goods and services in our nation. A second factor is that the data are also used in the redistricting process carried out by the states and may have an effect on how congressional districts are drawn. Finally, data about race and Hispanic origin are used in monitoring how well local areas comply with the federal Voting Rights Act. In the past, subordinate-group members often were deprived of the right to vote or intimidated if they attempted to exercise their right to select the local, state, and national political leadership.

DID YOU KNOW

- *Minority group* is a figure of speech that refers to power rather than number of people.
- California had the largest minority population in 2010.
- Census data on population affect enforcement of laws such as civil rights, voting, fair housing, equal opportunity, and legislative redistricting.

Dominant and Subordinate Groups

The terms *majority group* and *minority group* are widely used, but their meanings are less clear as the composition of the U.S. population continues to change. Accordingly, many sociologists prefer the terms *dominant* and *subordinate* to identify power relationships that are based on perceived racial, ethnic, or other attributes and identities. A **dominant (majority) group is one that is advantaged and has superior resources and rights in a society** (Feagin and Feagin, 2011). Dominant groups (sometimes referred to as majority groups regardless of their proportion in the overall U.S. population) often are determined on the basis of race or ethnicity, but they can also be determined on the basis of gender, sexual orientation (homosexuality, heterosexuality, or bisexuality), or physical ability. A **subordinate (minority) group is one whose members, because of physical or cultural characteristics, are disadvantaged and subjected to unequal treatment by the majority group and regard themselves as objects of collective discrimination** (Wirth, 1945). In the United States, people of color, all women, people with disabilities, and gay men and lesbians tend to be considered subordinate-group members.

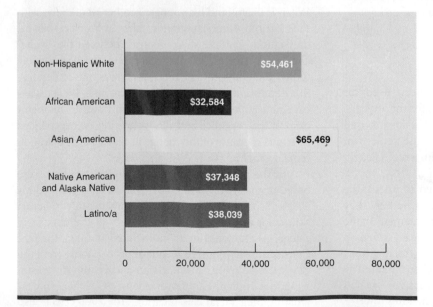

Figure 3.1   Median U.S. family income by race and Hispanic origin of householder, 2009.
Source: DeNavas-Walt et al., 2010.

In the United State   hnic dominant group typically is asso   hite-skin privi-lege, which is afforded   trace their an-cestry to northern Eu   themselves as European Americans   Anglo-Saxon Protestants). Women's   eggy McIntosh has described white p   ntless, invisible knapsack that makes it   nt-group mem-bers to go about their e   without having to explain themselves t   fy their actions based on race. Accord   skin color has given white people an u   e because they live in a society that val   onstructed ra-cial category over others and confers dominance to their group while identifying other categories as being subor-dinate (see Kimmel and Ferber, 2009).

·Most white Americans are unaware of the benefits that they derive from white-skin privilege. Nevertheless, the advantage–disadvantage and power–exploitation re-lationships of dominant and subordinate groups in this country are deeply rooted in patterns of racial prejudice and discrimination.

RACISM, PREJUDICE, AND DISCRIMINATION

Racism **is a set of attitudes, beliefs, and practices used to justify the superior treatment of one racial or eth-nic group and the inferior treatment of another racial or ethnic group**. In the United States, racism is some-times referred to as white racism. *White racism* refers to socially organized attitudes, ideas, and practices that deny people of color the dignity, opportunities, free-doms, and rewards that are typically available to white Americans (Feagin, 2010). From this per-spective, people of color pay a *direct, heavy, and immedi-ately painful price* for

◉—Watch on mysoclab.com

Racial Stereotypes and Discrimination on **mysoclab.com**

racism, while white discriminators pay an *indirect and seldom-recognized price*. For example, white Americans must deal with inherent contradictions between the ide-als of the United States and the realities of injustice and inequality that often are related to differential treatment of individuals and groups based on their perceived ra-cial, ethnic, or national origins.

Prejudice **is a negative attitude based on faulty generalizations about members of selected racial and ethnic groups**. These generalizations may involve such characteristics as race, age, religion, or sexual orienta-tion. If we think of prejudice as a set of negative attitudes toward members of another group simply because they belong to that group, we quickly realize that all people have prejudices, whether or not they acknowledge them. Prejudice is rooted in *ethnocentrism*—**the assumption that one's own group and way of life are superior to all others**. For example, most school children are taught that their own school and country are the best. The school song, the pledge to the flag, and the national anthem are forms of *positive ethnocentrism*. However, *negative ethnocentrism* can result if individuals come to believe, because of constant emphasis on the superiority of one's own group or nation, that other groups or nations are inferior and should be treated accordingly (Feagin and Feagin, 2011). Negative ethnocentrism is manifested in stereotypes that adversely affect many people.

Although the United States has come a long way in race relations, we are reminded that unresolved issues remain when debates about affirmative action emerge once again.

Stereotypes **are overgeneralizations about the appearance, behavior, or other characteristics of all members of a group.** For example, second-generation Filipino American Steven De Castro and his friends were the objects of stereotyping throughout their school years:

"What's up, monkey?" "Hey Ching Chong! Hey eggroll!" "Here comes the gook!" If you are Filipino in America, that is what you grow up hearing in the schoolyard. All you want to do is belong, but white and black classmates never let you forget that you will never belong in their America. (De Castro, 1994:303–304)

Box 3.1 discusses stereotyping and discrimination in nations with diverse populations. Discrimination may be carried out by individuals acting on their own or by individuals operating within the context of large-scale organizations or institutions such as schools, corporations, and government agencies.

Individual discrimination **consists of one-on-one acts by members of the dominant group that harm members of the subordinate group or their property** (Carmichael and Hamilton, 1967). Individual discrimination results from the prejudices and discriminatory actions of bigoted people who target one or more subordinate-group members. An example of individual discrimination is a college athlete who refers to another player by a derogatory name because he or she does not like something the other player said or did.

In contrast, *institutional discrimination* **consists of the day-to-day practices of organizations and institutions that have a harmful impact on members of subordinate groups.** Institutional discrimination is carried out by the individuals who implement policies and procedures that result in negative and differential treatment of subordinate-group members. An example is the practice of *reverse redlining*. In the past, *redlining* referred to banks or other lending agencies that refused loans to people of color in "white" neighborhoods. Recently, reverse redlining lawsuits have been filed against some financial institutions on the basis that these banks had steered African Americans toward predatory loans as opposed to more conventional ones. Predatory loans are those with high interest rates and ballooning payments that increase over the term of the mortgage, making it difficult for borrowers to keep up with their payments. As a result, many African American families in cities such as Memphis and Baltimore lost their homes to foreclosure. Although numerous banks have steered borrowers of all racial and ethnic categories toward the more expensive subprime loans (which led to the near-collapse of the U.S. housing market in 2008), if African Americans borrowers were specifically targeted for these high-risk loans because of race, this practice clearly fits the definition of institutional discrimination.

The United States has a long history of institutional discrimination. Jewish immigrants in the late 1800s experienced discrimination in accommodations and employment. Signs in hotel windows often read "No Jews Allowed," and many "help wanted" advertisements stated "Christians Only" (Levine, 1992:55). Such practices are referred to as *anti-Semitism*—**prejudice and discriminatory behavior directed at Jews.** In 2011, worldwide news media and social networking sites were filled with stories about alleged anti-Semitic remarks made by John Galliano, a high-fashion clothing designer, who was subsequently fired by the French fashion house Christian Dior. Because it is against the law in France to incite racial hatred, the designer could be fined or imprisoned for up to six months if anti-Semitism is proven (Saltmarch, 2011). Although few situations draw this much media attention, race and ethnic researchers still find patterns of discrimination that exist against Jewish persons today.

PERSPECTIVES ON RACIAL AND ETHNIC INEQUALITY

Over the course of the past 100 years, sociologists have developed different perspectives to explain why racial and ethnic inequality occurs and why it persists. Some perspectives are social-psychological; others focus on sociological factors such as migration, assimilation, conflict, and exploitation.

Social-Psychological Perspectives

Are some people more prejudiced than others? Social-psychological perspectives on prejudice emphasize psychological characteristics or personality traits. We will look at the frustration-aggression hypothesis and the authoritarian personality.

Aggression is behavior intended to hurt someone, either physically or verbally (Weiten and Lloyd, 1994). According to the *frustration-aggression hypothesis*, individuals who are frustrated in their efforts to achieve a highly desired goal tend to develop a pattern of aggression toward others (Dollard et al., 1939). If they have a very high level of frustration and are unable to strike out at the source of their frustration, they may

What Do France and the United States Have in Common? Complex Racial and Immigration Issues, for One Thing

Paris, France
February 12, 2011

> In a televised debate last March [Éric Zemmour, a French radio, newspaper, and television commentator] argued that blacks and Arabs were the targets of illegal racial profiling by the French police because the majority of traffickers are black and Arab; "that's how it is, it's a fact." The same day, on another channel, he suggested that French employers "have the right" to deny employment to blacks or Arabs.
>
> *—Scott Sayare (2011), a journalist for the New York Times, explains why one of France's best-known media commentators was charged with defamation and "provocation to racial discrimination."*

The use of stereotypes that are derogatory regarding a person's race, ethnicity, nationality, or religion is not new in global politics. Over the centuries, immigrants to countries such as England, France, Sweden, and the United States have often been stereotyped as "criminals," "cheap labor," or "the Other," who threaten the quality of life for longer-term residents. Whether the stereotypes are of Muslims in France, low-wage Latvian construction workers in Sweden, or Latinos/as in the United States, these negative images fuel a fear of outsiders and heighten citizens' anxieties about jobs and economic security. Stereotypes of "cheap labor" typically are contradictory: Immigrant workers are portrayed as wanting jobs so badly that they will work for less money and take more hazardous jobs than longer-term residents, but they are also depicted as being ignorant, lazy, and deviant individuals who will place an unnecessary burden on the nation's schools, hospitals, and welfare system.

In France, race and immigration are intertwined with religion to the extent that media commentators express strong opinions about France's immigrant population and single out Muslims who remain "unassimilated," such as Islamic women who wear the burka that covers them in black from head to toe, and/or the hijab (full facial veil). In 2010, the French government fueled public debate by deciding to impose a $185 (U.S. dollars) fine and possibly "citizenship classes" on women who wear the veil in public (Cody, 2010).

Like France, the United States has had extensive debates about immigration reform, particularly in regard to amenity paths (for illegal immigrants) to citizenship and special workers' visa programs. Hostility toward Latinos/as (Hispanics) and other immigrant groups has largely focused on jobs, education, health care, and other concerns that some U.S. citizens believe they are losing to immigrant workers. In France, a similar story exists: Animosity toward Muslims has grown in France as citizens have become more aware of an increasingly visible Muslim population of more than 5 million in their midst, the largest number in western Europe. Derogatory remarks and stereotypes increase the distance between diverse populations, and in both the United States and France, many are quick to stereotype, name-call, and play on the suspicions and fears of people about special "Hispanic" or "Muslim" immigration problems.

What will be the future of immigration and integration in France and the United States? Some social analysts believe that in times of national economic downturns and global recessions, there will always be animosity and discrimination against recent immigrants and racial and ethnic minorities who are primarily on the lower-rungs of the social stratification system. Other analysts argue that, without greater inclusion of immigrants and persons with diverse backgrounds, entire nations are weaker not only in dealing with their own problems at home but in finding a niche in the global economy and the wider world.

Questions for Consideration

1. Do media commentators influence how people think about individuals of other racial and ethnic groups and nationalities by the manner in which they frame social issues and public policy?

2. Can you think of any media personalities in the United States who make similar comments to the ones discussed in this box? What is your reaction to those comments?

3. Is it possible to create communities and nations in which people from diverse backgrounds can come together and live in peace and harmony? Why or why not?

take out their hostility and aggression on a *scapegoat*—**a person or group that is blamed for some problem causing frustration and is therefore subjected to hostility or aggression by others**. For example, undocumented workers in the United States, sometimes referred to as "illegal immigrants" or "illegal aliens," are blamed for a wide variety of societal woes, including running up education and health care costs by having multiple children after they enter this country. However, the United States is not alone in treating migrant workers as scapegoats and taking out feelings of frustration and sometimes aggression on them (see Box 3.1).

Another major social-psychological perspective suggests that people who have an authoritarian personality are most likely to be highly prejudiced. According to psychologist Theodor W. Adorno and his colleagues (1950), the *authoritarian personality* is characterized by excessive conformity, submissiveness to authority, intolerance, insecurity, a high level of superstition, and rigid, stereotypic thinking. Individuals with this type of personality typically view the world as a threatening place and are highly intolerant of members of subordinate racial, ethnic, or religious groups.

Symbolic Interactionist Perspectives

Somewhat related to social-psychological explanations of prejudice and discrimination are theories based on the symbolic interactionist perspective. One symbolic interactionist approach emphasizes how racial socialization contributes to feelings of solidarity with one's own racial-ethnic group and hostility toward all others. *Racial or ethnic socialization* is a process of social interaction that contains specific messages and practices concerning the nature of one's racial-ethnic status as it relates to (1) personal and group identity, (2) intergroup and interindividual relationships, and (3) one's position in the social stratification system. Although racial and ethnic socialization may occur through direct statements about race made by parents, peers, teachers, and others, it may also include indirect modeling behaviors, which occur when children imitate the words and actions of parents and other caregivers (Hughes et al., 2011). Racial and ethnic socialization also occurs indirectly through media representations of people in various racial and ethnic categories. As we saw at the beginning of the chapter, advertising is a form of persuasion and social learning that may influence how people think about race and ethnicity. Video games are another example: Some video games use racial stereotyping to create a digital cast of characters that players encounter as they play the game (see Box 3.2).

Racial and ethnic socialization affects how people view themselves, other people, and the world. Racial socialization helps make race a prism through which African Americans and other people of color view their daily lives (Marable, 1995). During the process of socialization in families, schools, and churches, some minority group members learn to understand and interpret the effects of prejudice and racial discrimination in their daily life.

> Though all groups practice racial and ethnic socialization, white racial socialization emphasizes white racial bonding. According to Christine E. Sleeter (1996), white racial bonding occurs when white people act in ways that reaffirm the common stance on race-related issues and draw we–they boundaries, thus perpetuating racism and discrimination. Such people choose to live near other whites, to socialize with other whites, and to vote for other whites, thus maintaining racial solidarity. Although many whites do not support racist beliefs, actions, or policies, they fear breaking bonds with other whites and may simply remain silent in the face of prejudice and discrimination (Sleeter, 1996).

Functionalist Perspectives

To functionalists, social order and stability are extremely important for the smooth functioning of society. Consequently, racial and ethnic discord, urban unrest, and riots are dysfunctional and must be eliminated or contained. One functionalist perspective focuses on *assimilation*—**the process by which members of subordinate racial and ethnic groups become absorbed into the dominant culture**. Functionalists view assimilation as a stabilizing force that minimizes differences that otherwise might result in hostility and violence (Gordon, 1964). In its most complete form, assimilation becomes *amalgamation,* **also referred to as the *melting-pot model,* a process in which the cultural attributes of diverse racial-ethnic groups are blended together to form a new society incorporating the unique contributions of each group**. Amalgamation occurs when members of dominant and subordinate racial-ethnic groups intermarry and procreate "mixed-race" children.

Early assimilation in the United States focused primarily on the Anglo-conformity model, rather than the melting-pot model. The *Anglo-conformity model* **refers to a pattern of assimilation whereby members of**

Video Games, Racial Stereotypes of Native Americans, and Glamorized Violence

Tomahawks, bows and arrows, feathered headdresses, a connection to the spiritual world—these are just a few of the stereotypical elements associated with the "Indians" of popular culture. . . . A few notable Native American characters that have appeared in video games include Mortal Kombat's Nightwolf, a tribal warrior donning feathers and face paint, who wields a bow and arrows, a tomahawk, and can also transform into a wolf to defeat his adversaries, Street Fighter's equally stereotypical Thunder Hawk, and Banjo Tooie's magical shaman Humba Wumba, who lives in a "wigwam". . . . We tend to glance over these highly stereotypical portrayals as fun and harmless, but can these simplified, misleading images of Native Americans have a negative impact on consumers? Many of these stereotypes, whether they have some sort of basis in history or not, are certainly not relevant to the contemporary Native American.

—*Video game reviewer Charles Sharam (2011) discusses the portrayal of Native Americans in video games and decries what he refers to as "The Digitized Indian."*

Since the introduction of video games, media analysts have argued about what effect these games have on players. Central concerns focus on the use of excessive violence and sexualized representations to make the games more exciting and "fun" for players. However, another issue is also important: How are characters portrayed in regard to race and ethnicity?

Consider Native Americans, for example. Few Native American characters have been portrayed in video games; however, many of those who have been portrayed in a negative manner, framing the "storyline" through old stereotypes (such as "Indian scalping" of white men when the reverse was sometimes true) that have been used to justify violence against Native Americans. The Association for American Indian Development took a stand against games such as GUN, which contains racist and genocidal images of Native Americans. However, violence against Native Americans has not drawn much attention from mainstream media sources or the general public. Perhaps,

this is because many people, including the most frequent users of video games, have come to view racial stereotypes and violence against subordinate-group members are nothing more than a part of contemporary social life.

Many violent video games are primarily played by suburban white males; however, many of the characters in these games are based on racial or ethnic stereotyping that shows men of color and recent immigrants as comprising the vast majority of the criminal population in the United States. In earlier games, such as the *Grand Theft Auto* series, and its Xbox 360 successor, the *Saint's Row* series, racism is primarily evident in stereotypical street gangs and the dialog they used. The only white person in *Saint's Row,* for example, is Troy, the gang leader's right-hand man who is actually a police officer working undercover. Games such as these portray few, if any, positive images of subordinate-group members. Some reviewers argue that this portrayal is not a problem because the games are an "equal opportunity" situation in which African Americans, Mexican Americans, Cuban Americans, Haitians, Italian Americans, Russian Americans, and members of all other ethnic groups are shown in the same (negative) light.

What effect does racial stereotyping in video games have on young people? Manufacturers of video games emphasize that their games are geared for an audience over the age of seventeen and that younger people should not be playing them at all. However, many younger individuals play the games for hours at a time. Video-game makers say that the games are just a way for people to relax and have fun; however, critics warn that some games may have harmful consequences as they reinforce negative images of subordinate-group members and perpetuate violence.

Questions for Consideration

1. In violent video games, does the overrepresentation of characters patterned on subordinate racial or ethnic groups influence our thinking regarding race in this country? Why or why not?
2. Should any controls be placed on the content of video games and other forms of entertainment? If so, should the government, parents, or the purchasers of video games be the primary agents of social control?

subordinate racial-ethnic groups are expected to conform to the culture of the dominant (white) Anglo-Saxon population. Assimilation does not always lead to full social acceptance. For example, for many years, successful African Americans and Jewish Americans were

excluded from membership in elite private clubs and parties in the homes of coworkers. This practice has not entirely ended even with greater diversity in the nation and more social awareness of the problems inherent in discrimination in the twenty-first century.

Political conservatives focus on assimilation and, particularly, adopting English as the country's official language. In her now-classic book *Out of the Barrio* (1991), social analyst Linda Chavez states that Latinas/os in the United States must learn English and adopt the dominant culture if they want economic success and social acceptance. According to Chavez, Latinos/as should forget about entitlement programs such as affirmative action and focus on assimilating into the U.S. economic mainstream. Although Chavez's work is now more than twenty years old, it continues to be an inspiration for advocates who press for full assimilation of Hispanics or Latinos/as. And it appears that this issue is far from over. In 2011, for example, Republicans in both the U.S. House and U.S. Senate introduced legislation that would declare English the official language of the United States and require that all individuals who apply for U.S. citizenship must pass an English language test. Although this legislation had not passed in 2011, it no doubt will be introduced again in future congressional sessions (Kasperowicz, 2011).

Another functionalist perspective emphasizes *ethnic pluralism*—**the coexistence of diverse racial-ethnic groups with separate identities and cultures within a society**. In a pluralistic society, political and economic systems link diverse groups, but members of some racial-ethnic groups maintain enough separation from the dominant group to guarantee that their group and ethnic cultural traditions continue (Gordon, 1964). Ethnic pluralism in the United States typically has been based on *segregation* because subordinate racial-ethnic groups have less power and privilege than do members of the dominant group. *Segregation* **is the spatial and social separation of people by race/ethnicity, class, gender, religion, or other social characteristics**. Sociological studies have found that when high levels of racial segregation are followed by interracial contact, racial competition often ensues, bringing with it an increase in tension and sometimes violence (Olzak, Shanahan, and McEneaney, 1996). An example of ethnic pluralism linked to tension is politics in Bronx, New York. In the past Jewish Americans and Puerto Ricans formed coalitions that constituted a voting block to help specific candidates get elected to office. However, as large waves of immigrants moved into the area, greater interracial competition has ensued among people who trace their origins to the Dominican Republic, Ecuador, Mexico, the Republic of Korea, and other nations of the world. So, the question remains when diverse racial and ethnic groups come into close proximity to each other is the pattern that emerges one of ethnic pluralism or conflict?

This brings us to the conflict perspective which argues that conflict between groups is inevitable in racial and ethnic relations.

Conflict Perspectives

Conflict theorists explain racial and ethnic inequality in terms of economic stratification and access to power. As was discussed in Chapter 1, there are a number of conflict perspectives. However, in this chapter, we focus on the critical-conflict approach, which explains racial and ethnic inequality in terms of economic stratification and unequal access to power. We will briefly examine class perspectives, split-labor market theory, gendered racism, internal colonialism, and the theory of racial formation.

Class perspectives on racial and ethnic inequality highlight the role of the capitalist class in racial exploitation. For example, according to sociologist Oliver C. Cox (1948), the primary cause of slavery was the capitalist desire for profit, not racial prejudice. African Americans were enslaved because they were the cheapest and best workers that owners of plantations and mines could find to do the heavy labor. One contemporary class perspective suggests that members of the capitalist class benefit from a split-labor market that fosters racial divisions among workers and suppresses wages. According to the *split-labor market theory*, the U.S. economy is divided into two employment sectors: a primary sector composed of higher-paid workers in more secure jobs ("good jobs") and a secondary sector composed of lower-paid workers in jobs that often involve hazardous working conditions and little job security ("bad jobs") (Bonacich, 1972, 1976). Dominant-group members are usually employed in primary-sector positions; subordinate-group members usually are employed in the secondary sector. Bonacich (1972, 1976) found that workers in the two job sectors tend to have divergent interests and goals; therefore worker solidarity was unlikely. Members of the capitalist class benefit from these divisions because workers are less likely to bind together and demand pay increases or other changes in the workplace. In the twenty-first century, more than four decades after Bonacich's research, studies of the split-labor market, and similar research based on dual-labor-market theory, show that the United States today is even more polarized into good and bad job segments. Similarly, income inequality has increased drastically over the past four decades. Some analysts believe that the racial-ethnic inequality still exists in a split- or dual-labor market, but other researchers argue that factors other than race are equally or more important (see Hudson, 2008).

A second critical-conflict perspective links racial inequality and gender oppression. *Gendered racism* **may be defined as the interactive effect of racism and sexism in exploiting women of color.** According to social psychologist Philomena Essed (1991), not all workers are exploited equally by capitalists. For many years, the majority of jobs in the primary sector of the labor market were held by white men, while most people of color and many white women were employed in secondary-sector jobs. Below the secondary sector, in the underground sector of the economy, many women of color and undocumented immigrants from African and the Caribbean nations work in marginal jobs, sweatshops, and the sex trade to survive. Work in the underground sector is unregulated, and people who earn their income in it are vulnerable to exploitation by many people, including unscrupulous employers. For example, recent studies have found that employers increasingly are breaking or evading worker-protection laws and standards to the detriment of workers and often consumers. Referred to as the "gloves-off economy," more employers are now violating workers' rights not only in marginal sector employment, such as sweatshops, but also in other low-wage sectors of the labor market. Although all workers are harmed by these practices, people of color are often more disadvantaged and powerless in the face of blatant violations of their rights by owners and managers (see Bernhardt et al., 2008).

A third critical-conflict perspective examines *internal colonialism*—**a process that occurs when members of a racial-ethnic group are conquered or colonized and forcibly placed under the economic and political control of the dominant group.** According to sociologist Robert Blauner (1972), people in groups that have been subjected to internal colonialism remain in subordinate positions in society much longer than do people in groups that voluntarily migrated to this country. For example, Native Americans and Mexican Americans were forced into subordination when they were colonized by European Americans. These indigenous groups lost property, political rights, components of their culture, and often their lives. Meanwhile, the capitalist class acquired cheap labor and land, frequently through government-sanctioned racial exploitation (Blauner, 1972). Vestiges of internal colonialism remain visible today in the number of Native Americans who live in poverty on government reservations, as well as Mexican Americans in *colonias*—poor subdivisions that usually lack essential services such as water, electricity, and sewage disposal—located along the U.S.–Mexico border.

The last critical-conflict perspective we will look at is the *theory of racial formation*, **which states that the government substantially defines racial and ethnic relations.** From this perspective, racial bias and discrimination tend to be rooted in government actions ranging from passage of race-related legislation to imprisonment of members of groups that are believed to be a threat to society. According to sociologists Michael Omi and Howard Winant (1994), the U.S. government has shaped the politics of racial inequality in this country through actions and policies that have resulted in the unequal treatment of people of color. Immigration legislation, for example, reveals specific racial biases. The Naturalization Law of 1790 permitted only white immigrants to qualify for naturalization, and the Immigration Act of 1924 favored northern Europeans and excluded Asians and southern and eastern Europeans. In the twenty-first century, new and highly contested immigration laws in states such as Arizona specifically targeted Hispanics and posed a potential threat to the civil rights of Latinos/as who are American citizens (Pew Hispanic Center, 2010).

INEQUALITIES AMONG RACIAL AND ETHNIC GROUPS

Although all subordinate racial and ethnic groups have been the objects of prejudice and discrimination and share many problems, each has its own unique identity and concerns. In our examination of Native Americans and Alaska Natives, African Americans, Latinos/as (Hispanics), and Asian and Pacific Americans, we will note commonalities and differences in the discriminatory practices each group has experienced when in contact with members of the dominant group.

Native Americans (American Indians) and Alaska Natives

Although Native Americans have received more attention than Alaska Natives in popular and scholarly writing, both groups have experienced discrimination throughout history. Alaska Natives are the indigenous peoples of Alaska, and include groups such as the Inupait and Yupik, who primarily live along the northern and western coasts; Aleuts who reside on the Aleutian Islands; coastal Indians, primarily Tlingits and Haidas; and the Athapascan Indians in the central regions of the state. Native Americans (American Indians) reside in the forty-eight contiguous states; however, both Native

Americans and Alaska Natives are believed to have originally migrated from Asia to North America thousands of years ago, moving across Beringia, a natural bridge of land, into what is now Alaska. Further migration brought some of them to Canada, the United States, and South America.

Colonized Migration and Genocide

When Christopher Columbus arrived in 1492, approximately 15 million indigenous people lived on this continent. They had many distinct cultures, languages, social organizations, technologies, and economies (R. Thornton, 1987; Sale, 1990; Mohawk, 1992). The arrival of the white Europeans changed the native inhabitants' ways of life forever as *colonization migration*—a process whereby a new immigrant group conquers and dominates an existing group in a given geographic area— occurred (Lauber, 1913; Feagin and Feagin, 2011). *Colonization* is the term used to describe how a nation exerts its powers of governance over lands, cultures, and peoples outside its own national borders. Alaska's indigenous peoples experienced colonization under Spain, Britain, and Russia from 1741 until the 1800s, and then, from the 1800s forward, under the U.S. government. As the process of colonization moves forward, indigenous people are frequently displaced, or dominated by their oppressors, or killed. During these periods of conquest, white European immigrants engaged in **genocide, the deliberate, systematic killing of an entire people or nation**. Hundreds of thousands of Native Americans died during this period. This widespread murder was rationalized by stereotypes depicting Native Americans as subhuman "savages" and "heathens" (Takaki, 1993).

Forced Migration and "Americanization"

After the Revolutionary War in the United States, the newly founded federal government negotiated treaties with various Native American nations to acquire additional land for the rapidly growing white population. Even with these treaties in place, federal officials ignored boundary rights and gradually displaced Native Americans from their lands. When the demand for land escalated, Congress passed the Indian Removal Act of 1830, forcing entire nations to move to accommodate white settlers. During the "Trail of Tears," perhaps the most disastrous of the forced migrations, over half of the Cherokee nation died while being relocated from the southeastern United States to what was called the Indian Territory in Oklahoma during the bitter cold winter of 1832 (R. Thornton, 1984). After the forced

relocation, Native Americans were made wards of the government—a legal status akin to that of a minor or a mental incompetent—and by 1920, about 98 percent of all native lands were controlled by the U.S. government (McDonnell, 1991).

Because Native Americans were regarded as less "civilized" than whites, Native American children were subjected to an extensive Americanization process. Boarding schools and mission schools, cosponsored by the government and churches, were located some distance from the reservations to facilitate assimilation. In these schools, white teachers cut Native American boys' braids, eliminated the children's traditional clothing, handed out new names, and substituted new religious customs for old ones (Oxendine, 1995). Thousands of Alaska Native young people also were removed from their villages and sent to boarding schools far from home where teachers attempted to purge them of their languages and cultural traditions.

Contemporary Native Americans and Alaska Natives

In popular culture, Native Americans and Alaska Natives have been represented as artifacts of "Indian culture" rather than as real people. As such, they are associated with turquoise jewelry and deerskin clothing, "Indian" Barbie dolls, vehicles such as the Jeep "Cherokee," and the stereotypical images utilized by sports teams with names like "Braves," "Redskins," "Chiefs," and "Seminoles." Tens of thousands of tourists travel to Alaska to admire the totem poles of the Alaska Natives and to purchase replicas of native artifacts without learning the authentic history of the groups that have been oppressed for centuries.

Today, Native Americans and Alaska Natives number about 5.2 million, including those who reported more than one race in the 2010 Census. They make up about 1.7 percent of the total U.S. population. States where American Indians and Alaska Natives are the largest racial or ethnic group are Alaska, Montana, North Dakota, Oklahoma, and South Dakota. However, many Native Americans also live in California, Arizona, Texas, New Mexico, and New York. The median family income of Native Americans and Alaska Natives is $37,348, as compared with a national median of $49,777 for all races. Almost a quarter (23.5 percent) of all Native Americans and Alaska Natives fell below the official poverty line in 2009 (factfinder.census.gov, 2010).

Native Americans and Alaska Natives have experienced many forms of discrimination. They lost extensive amounts of land to the federal government and to business interests that have not compensated them adequately for their losses. As a result, they have actively opposed mining, logging, hunting, and real estate development on native lands without permission or compensation. But the losses have gone even deeper for those who believe their culture and way of life have been stripped away from them. Consequently, rates of alcoholism, drug abuse, diabetes, cardiovascular disease and suicide are high, particularly for people living on government-run reservations. About 12 percent of deaths among Native Americans and Alaska Natives are alcohol related. This figure is more than three times as high as for the United States as a whole. The largest percentage of alcohol-related deaths occurs on remote reservations in the Northern Plains.

Historically, Native Americans have had very limited educational and employment opportunities. In the 2010s, efforts were made to establish a network of tribal colleges that would provide more Native Americans with the education they need to move into better jobs. More Native American and Alaska Native youth have also attended four-year colleges in recent years. Today, more Native Americans own and operate small businesses than in the past. However, some of the more problematic forms of new revenue for Native American and Alaska Native groups are casino gambling and cigarette shops that are operated on Native American lands. Although businesses such as these have increased revenues and produced more income for tribal nations, many social analysts believe that these businesses have also contributed to social problems for Native Americans, including alcoholism, gambling addiction, and smoking-related health problems.

Some Native American groups on government-controlled reservations have found a new source of revenue through ownership and operation of casinos. However, these casinos have not been without controversy.

African Americans

The term *African American* does not reflect the diversity of the more than 42 million African Americans, including those who identify themselves as being of more than one race. African Americans currently make up 13.6 percent of the U.S. population. There is a lack of consensus about whether *African American* or *black* is the most appropriate term to refer to black residents of the United States (including those who reported more than one race). Those who prefer the term *black* point out that it incorporates many African-descent groups living in this country that do not use *African American* as a racial or ethnic self-description. For example, people who trace their origins to Haiti, Puerto Rico, or Jamaica typically identify themselves as "black" but not as "African American." Although some are descendants of families that have been in this country for many generations, others are recent immigrants from the West Indies, South America, Africa, and the Caribbean. Many also have Native American, white, or Latino/a (Hispanic) ancestors (Feagin and Feagin, 2011). African Americans reside throughout the United States; however, eighteen states have an estimated black population of at least 1 million. About 3.5 million African Americans lived in New York State in 2009, but Mississippi had the largest share of blacks (38 percent) in its total population.

Slavery and the Racial Division of Labor

It is believed that the earliest African Americans arrived in North America with the Spanish conquerors in the fifteenth century. Most historians trace their arrival to about 1619, when the first groups of indentured servants were brought to the colony of Virginia. Between 1619 and the 1860s, about 500,000 Africans were forcibly brought to North America, primarily to work on southern plantations, and these actions were justified by the devaluation and stereotyping of African Americans. Some analysts believe that the central factor associated with the development of slavery in this country was the plantation system, which was heavily dependent on cheap and dependable manual labor. Slavery was primarily beneficial to the wealthy southern plantation owners, but many of the rationalizations used to justify slavery were eventually institutionalized in southern custom and practice, such as the sharecropper system and later in legalized racial segregation. Slavery became illegal in the northern states by the late 1700s, but it continued in the South until 1863, when it was abolished by the Emancipation Proclamation.

Who benefited most from slavery? From its beginnings in 1619, when the first Africans were brought to North America for forced labor, slavery created a rigid, caste like division of labor between white slave owners and overseers and African slave labor. Southern plantation owners derived large profits from selling raw materials harvested by the slaves. Northern capitalists became rich by converting those raw materials into finished products that could be sold at market (e.g., the cotton fiber used in textile manufacturing). Even white immigrants benefited from slavery because it provided the abundant raw materials necessary to keep factories running so that they would have jobs.

Segregation and Lynching

After slavery was abolished in 1863, this division of labor was maintained through *de jure segregation*, the passage of laws that systematically enforced the physical and social separation of African Americans from whites in all areas of public life, including schools, churches, hospitals, cemeteries, buses, restaurants, water fountains, and restrooms. (These laws were referred to as *Jim Crow laws* after a derogatory song about a black man.) African Americans who did not stay "in their place" were subjected to violence by secret organizations such as the Ku Klux Klan and by lynch mobs (Franklin, 1980).

While African Americans in the South experienced de jure segregation, those who migrated to the North experienced *de facto segregation*—racial separation and inequality enforced by custom. African Americans seeking northern factory jobs encountered *job ceilings*—specific limits on the upward job mobility of targeted groups—set up by white workers and their unions (see Baron, 1969; Allen, 1974). Because African American men were barred from many industrial jobs, African American women frequently became their families' primary breadwinners. Most African American women were employed as domestic workers in private households or as personal service workers such as hotel chambermaids (Higginbotham, 1994).

Protests and Civil Disobedience

During World War II, new job opportunities opened up for African Americans in northern defense plants, especially after the issuance of a presidential order prohibiting racial discrimination in federal jobs. After the war, increasing numbers of African Americans demanded an end to racial segregation. Between the mid-1950s and 1964, boycotts, nonviolent protests, and *civil disobedience*—nonviolent action seeking to change a policy or

law by refusing to comply with it—called attention to racial inequality in the United States. The civil rights movement culminated in passage of the Civil Rights Acts of 1964 and 1965, which signified the end of *de jure* segregation; however, *de facto* segregation was far from over.

Contemporary African Americans

Since the 1960s, African Americans have made substantial gains in politics, education, and median income, but inequality remains persistent. The most visible political gain was the election of the nation's first African American president, Barack Obama, in 2008. However, large gains have not been made at the national level in the number of congressional seats occupied by African Americans. Since 1995, the number of African Americans serving in Congress has remained in a constant range between thirty-nine and forty-two. However, all of these elected officials are in the U.S. House of Representatives; no African American is serving in the U.S. Senate (as of 2011). Even more telling is the fact that twenty-five states have never elected an African American to Congress. More African Americans have won state and city elections, including mayoral races in some of the nation's major cities that have large African American populations, such as Houston, Philadelphia, New Orleans, Atlanta, and Washington, DC. Overall, however, black Americans remain significantly underrepresented in the political arena.

The proportion of African Americans in professional and managerial occupations grew steadily for several decades but slowed during two recessions in the 2000s. About 29 percent of employed black Americans held managerial, professional, and related occupations in 2009, while another 25 percent held service occupations in health care, protective services, food preparation, building and grounds cleaning and maintenance, and personal care and service occupations. As these percentages show, for employed African Americans, a distinct divide exists between middle- and upper-middle-class professional positions and those in the working-class service sector. The continuation of a racial division of labor is still evident across all occupational sectors, including the top positions in major corporations. Consider *Fortune* 500 companies (the 500 highest revenue-producing companies), for example; only five had African American chief executive officers (CEOs) in 2011. One of the five, Ursula Burns, chair and CEO of Xerox, was the first African American woman in history to head a *Fortune* 500 company. In the final analysis, African Americans are still underrepresented in board-level corporate leadership: Blacks comprise 13.6 percent of the U.S. population but hold only 7 percent of *Fortune* 500 board seats (Morial, 2011).

Unemployment rates and median household income also reveal inequalities in education and employment opportunities for African Americans. The unemployment rate for African Americans (16 percent in May 2011) has remained twice as high as that for white Americans (7.7 percent in May 2011) for more than three decades (U.S. Bureau of Labor Statistics, 2011a). As is shown in Figure 3.1, a wide disparity exists between the median income of white Americans and that of African Americans. Whereas African American households had median earnings of $32,587 in 2009, the median earnings of white non-Latino families ($54,461) were about 67 percent higher (DeNavas-Walt et al., 2010).

Contemporary scholars have suggested that past discriminatory practices by banks, real estate agencies, mortgage lenders, and other businesses have resulted in the high percentage of racially segregated neighborhoods, schools, workplaces and churches that exist in the present (Feagin and Feagin, 2011). Since 2000, residential segregation by race decreased to the lowest level in the past 100 years; however, it persists in many areas, and even increased in 25 of the 100 largest metropolitan areas in the United States. In 2010, a typical African American lived in a neighborhood that was 46 percent black, whereas the typical white person lived in a neighborhood that was 79 percent white (Ellinwood, 2010). Residential segregation produces a ripple effect on all other areas of social life, including the schools that children attend, the quality of education they receive, the types of jobs people have access to, and the availability and quality of public facilities such as hospitals and transportation systems. Residential segregation is also intertwined with the problem of resegregation of schools in the post–civil rights era: The U.S. Supreme Court has ruled that most of the voluntary means used by school districts to increase integration in classrooms are unconstitutional (Orfield and Lee, 2007). And, in segregated neighborhoods it is impossible to integrate schools without a variety of selection processes that do not adhere to the "neighborhood school concept," which means that younger students attend classes in a school that is in their neighborhood or close by.

Latinos/as (Hispanic Americans)

Between 2000 and 2010, the Latino/a (Hispanic American) population in the United States grew by 43 percent, increasing by 15.2 million people to a high of 50.5 million. In 2010, Latinos/as made up 16 percent of the total U.S. population, and two-thirds are of Mexican origin. After Mexican Americans, who make up 66 percent of the Hispanic-origin people in the United States, the next largest groups of Latinos/as are Puerto Ricans (9 percent), Cuban Americans (4 percent), Salvadoran Americans (3 percent), and Dominican Americans (3 percent) (Ennis, Rios-Vargas, and Albert, 2011). Other Latinos/as trace their ancestry to elsewhere in Central and South America. Over half of the Hispanic population in the United States lives in just three states: California, Texas, and Florida. Other states with relatively large Hispanic populations include New York, Illinois, Arizona, New Jersey, and Colorado (Ennis et al., 2011). How these states became home to most Hispanic Americans (Latinos/as) was largely based on geographic proximity from their country of origin and treatment by the U.S. government.

Internal Colonialism and Loss of Land

Beginning in the late 1400s and continuing into the early 1500s, Spanish soldiers took over the island of Puerto Rico, Central America, and that area of the United States now known as the Southwest. Although Mexico gained its independence from Spain in 1810, it lost Texas and most of the Southwest to the United States in 1848. Under the treaty ending the Mexican-American War, Texans of Mexican descent (Tejanos/as) were granted U.S. citizenship; however, their rights as citizens were violated when Anglo-Americans took possession of their lands, transforming them into a landless and economically dependent laboring class.

When Spain lost the Spanish-American War, it gave Puerto Rico and the Philippine Islands to the United States. Gradually, U.S.-owned corporations took over existing Puerto Rican sugarcane plantations, leaving peasant farmers and their families with no means of earning a living other than as seasonal sugarcane laborers. In time, nearly one-third of the Puerto Rican population migrated to the U.S. mainland. The majority of this population settled in the Northeast and found work in garment factories or other light manufacturing.

Migration

In the late 1950s and early 1960s, waves of Latinos/as escaping from Fidel Castro's Communist takeover of Cuba were admitted to the United States. Unlike Puerto Ricans, who have been allowed unrestricted migration between the mainland and the island since Puerto Rico became a U.S. possession in 1917 (Melendez,

1993), these immigrants were admitted as political refugees (Rogg, 1974). Mexicans have been allowed to migrate to the United States whenever there has been a need here for agricultural workers. However, during times of economic depression or recession in this country, Mexican workers have been excluded, detained, or deported.

Many Latinos/as have experienced discrimination as a result of the Immigration Reform and Control Act (IRCA) of 1986. Although IRCA was passed to restrict illegal immigration into the United States, it has adversely affected many Latinos/as. To avoid being penalized for hiring undocumented workers, some employers discriminate against Latinas/os who "look foreign" on the basis of facial features, skin color, or clothing. In 2010, the state of Arizona enacted a controversial law that authorized local police to check the immigration status of anyone they reasonably suspect of being in the United States illegally. Before the law was enforced, a federal judge imposed an injunction preventing major sections of the law from going into effect due to questions about its constitutionality (enforcing immigration law is a federal issue). This controversy has reached a federal appeals court, and many legal analysts believe this case will ultimately be heard by the U.S. Supreme Court. In the meantime, Arizona's law has polarized many individuals and advocacy groups who have strong opinions on immigration reform. Not to be confused with the 2010 law, another Arizona law passed in 2007 that allows the state to shut down businesses that hire illegal immigrants was upheld by the Supreme Court in 2011. This is one of many contentious debates that will continue in the future as the United States grows even more diverse as a nation.

Contemporary Latinos/as

Today, Latinos/as comprise a rapidly growing percentage of the U.S. population (see Box 3.3). Although the full effect of this young and growing populace has not yet been fully evidenced in U.S. politics and business, many analysts predict that Latinos/as will be increasingly visible in all areas of public life by 2020. The 2010 U.S. Census estimates that by 2050, one out of every four Americans will be of Hispanic decent. However, progress has been slow: Hispanic Americans, who represent 16 percent of the U.S. population, occupy only 4 percent of the total corporate board of director seats on *Fortune* 1000 companies (Hispanic Association on Corporate Responsibility, 2004). In secondary-sector employment, the other end of the employment spectrum, low wages, hazardous workplaces, and unemployment are pressing

problems for Latinos/as. The unemployment rate for Latinos/as was 11 percent in May 2011 as compared with 7.7 percent for white (non-Hispanic) Americans. In 2009, more than one-fourth (25.3 percent) of Latinas/os lived below the official U.S. poverty line (DeNavas-Walt et al., 2010).

Problems in employment are intensified by problems in schooling and levels of educational attainment among Hispanics in the United States, particularly those who are foreign born. For example, about one-third (34.6 percent) of all foreign-born Latinos/as ages twenty-five and older have less than a ninth-grade education, and only 9.7 percent are college graduates. Among native-born Latinos/as, the percentages are somewhat better in that 29.2 percent are high school graduates, 22.2 percent have some college, and 16.6 percent are college graduates. For comparison, slightly less than one-third (31.3 percent) of non-Hispanic white Americans and almost half (49.9 percent) of all Asian Americans are college graduates (Pew Hispanic Center, 2010). Like African Americans, many Hispanic students attend low-performing, segregated schools in states such as California. According to recent reports, Hispanic students are segregated in Southern California schools because of ethnic origin, poverty, and language. As compared to 1970 when the average Latina/o student in Los Angeles attended a school that was 45 percent white, Hispanic students in 2008 attended schools where the student population with only 6 percent white (non-Hispanic). Latinos/as make up more than 80 percent of public school students in some school districts in California, New Mexico, and Texas. Education scholars believe that lack of diversity and racial-ethnic segregation in schools diminishes all students' learning opportunities, but Hispanic students are among the most adversely affected.

Housing is another problem for Latinas/os. Studies have found that more Hispanic adults believe that discrimination in housing is a growing problem in the 2010s. Factors contributing to housing discrimination are immigration status (particularly regarding illegal or undocumented immigrants) and lack of English language skills. In the past, landlords, realtors, and bankers in many communities colluded to keep Mexican Americans segregated in barrios and away from predominantly Anglo neighborhoods (Menchaca, 1995); however, this practice appears to be less of a problem today if prospective residents are financially qualified to rent or purchase a resident. The foreclosure crises harmed Latino/a families that lost their homes because of an inability to pay high mortgages in the recession, but it also

Social Problems and Statistics   Box 3.3

Accurate and Inaccurate Comparisons

According to data from the U.S. Census Bureau for 2010, 16.3 percent of the U.S. population is of Hispanic (or Latino/a) origin, representing a significant increase from previous years. Looking at the number of people who chose one race only on Census 2010, approximately 72.4 percent of the population is white, 12.6 percent is black or African American, 4.8 percent is Asian American, 0.9 percent is Native American or Alaska Native, 0.2 percent is Native Hawaiian or other Pacific Islanders, and 2.9 percent is of two or more races (see Figure 3.2). These are valid statistics, and they come from a very good source of data: the U.S. Census Bureau.

On the basis of these statistics, we can conclude that Latinos/as comprise the largest subordinate racial-ethnic group in the United States and that African Americans (who previously were the largest such group) comprise the second-largest subordinate racial-ethnic group. However, it would be incorrect to conclude that Latinos/as (16.3 percent) and African Americans (12.6 percent) represent 28.9 percent of the U.S. population. Why is this true?

Whereas African Americans are considered to be members of a racial group, Latinos/as are considered to be members of an ethnic group. A Latino/a may be of any one or more racial categories: Some Latinos/as are also whites; other Latinos/as are also African American, Asian American, and/or Native American. Therefore, the Census Bureau asks separate questions regarding a person's race and regarding whether or not he or she is of Hispanic origin, and each person answers both questions.

The thing to be noted here is that in using statistics, it is important that we not make inaccurate comparisons of statistics. As sociologist Joel Best (2001:97–98) states,

Good comparisons involve comparable items: they pair apples with

apples, and oranges with oranges. Comparable statistics count things in the same ways. Comparisons among statistics that are not comparable confuse and distort. Before accepting any statistical comparison, it is important to ask whether the numbers are comparable.

As was noted, it would be inappropriate to add the percentage of the U.S. population that is African American to the percentage that is Latino/a and conclude that these two categories represent 28.9 percent of the overall U.S. population: Because one is based on race and the other on ethnicity, there is some overlap between the two. For the same reason, combining the percentage of the U.S. population that is white with the percentage that is Latino/a would not produce a useful statistic: Most Latinos/as self-identify as white.

However, the census data in Figure 3.2 do provide valid bases for other comparisons. For example, the proportion of the U.S. population that is Latino/a (about 16.3 percent) can be compared with the proportion that is non-Hispanic (about 83.7 percent) to validly conclude that the vast majority of the population

is non-Latino/a, although Latinos/as are a significant and growing minority of the U.S. population. Likewise, the proportion that is Latino/a (16.3 percent) can be compared with the proportion that is African American (12.6 percent) to validly conclude that these two categories are of somewhat similar size although there are slightly more persons who self-identify as Latino/a as compared to African American. Similarly, the proportion that is African American can be compared with the proportion that is Asian American, and so on. In each instance, these are good comparisons involving comparable items.

In each instance in this text where comparisons are made, every effort is made to ensure that they involve comparable statistics. Even so, that can be a difficult task: As Figure 3.2 reflects, 2.9 percent of the U.S. population self-identifies as being of two or more races, meaning that we must keep in mind that the statistics shown represent only those people who self-identify as being of only one race and that such statistics therefore ignore the growing number of people in this country who see themselves as being of mixed racial backgrounds.

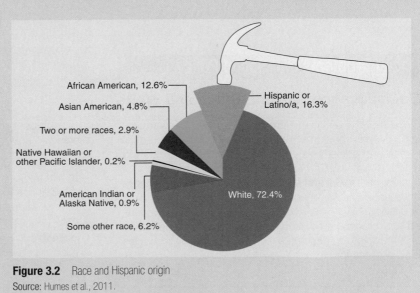

Figure 3.2 Race and Hispanic origin
Source: Humes et al., 2011.

benefited those who were able to purchase residences in neighborhoods that previously were less welcoming.

Asian and Pacific Americans

Asian and Pacific Americans are one of the fastest-growing racial-ethnic groups in the United States; their numbers have risen from 1 million in 1960 to more than 17 million in 2010, including those who identify themselves as being of more than one race. Constituting about 5.6 percent of the U.S. population, most Asian and Pacific Americans reside in California, New York, Hawaii (U.S. Census Bureau, 2011b); however, cities such as Seattle, Washington, and Washington, DC, have high-percentage Asian American populations as well.

Immigration and Oppression

Among the first Asian and Pacific people to arrive in this country were Chinese immigrants, who came between 1850 and 1880. Some were fleeing political oppression and harsh economic conditions in China; others were recruited to build the transcontinental railroad. Almost immediately, these immigrants were labeled "the yellow peril," a reflection of nineteenth-century prejudice that Asians constituted a threat to Western civilization. In response to demands from white workers who were concerned about cheap labor (employers paid Chinese laborers far less than white workers [Takaki, 1993]), Congress passed the Chinese Exclusion Act of 1882, bringing all Chinese immigration to an abrupt halt. This law wasn't repealed until World War II, when Chinese American workers contributed to the U.S. war effort by working in defense plants (see Chan, 1991).

Facing high levels of overt discrimination, many Chinese Americans opened laundries, stores, and restaurants, doing business primarily with each other (Takaki, 1993). More recently, however, young second- and third-generation Chinese Americans have left these ethnic niches to live and interact with people from diverse racial-ethnic groups.

Internment

Although Japanese Americans experienced high levels of prejudice and discrimination almost as soon as they arrived in this country, their internment in U.S. concentration camps during World War II remains the central event of the Japanese American experience (Kitano and Daniels, 1995). After Japan bombed Pearl Harbor in 1941, anti-Japanese sentiment soared in the United States. Japanese Americans were forcibly removed to concentration camps on remote military bases surrounded by barbed wire fences and guard towers. During their internment, which lasted for more than two years, most Japanese Americans lost their residences, businesses, and anything else they had owned. Four decades later, the U.S. government issued an apology for its actions and agreed to pay $20,000 to each Japanese American who had been detained in a camp (Kitano and Daniels, 1995). For Japanese Americans and other Asian and Pacific Americans, the struggle for rights has often been played out in the U.S. Supreme Court and other judicial bodies (see Box 3.4).

Social Problems and Social Policy

Box 3.4

Social Justice: Beyond Black and White

Since the civil rights movement of the 1960s, many social analysts have defined issues pertaining to social justice and social policy primarily in terms of "black and white" (Chin, 1999). However, throughout the history of this country, racial and ethnic groups, ranging from Native Americans and Mexican Americans to Jewish Americans and Asian Americans and Pacific Islanders, have protested against what they perceive to be racist social policies, and many groups have played key roles in the struggles for civil rights for all.

Think about these laws and social policies that have affected Asian Americans and Pacific Islanders:

- In the 1880s, Chinese Americans pooled their resources to hire lawyers to fight such unfair immigration laws as the Chinese Exclusion Act of 1882 and other laws that prohibited them from owning land, attending "white-only" public schools, or gaining citizenship (Chin, 1999).
- In *People v. Hall* (1854), the California Supreme Court ruled that a white man had been wrongfully convicted

Social Problems and Social Policy

Box 3.4 continued

of murder because Chinese witnesses had testified against him. The court ruled that the testimony was inadmissible because, according to the justices, the Chinese could be considered "constructive blacks" and thus were covered under a statement in the California state constitution that prohibited "blacks and Indians" from testifying against white Americans (see Foner and Rosenberg, 1993).

- Because of fears that Japanese Americans would undermine U.S. efforts against Japan during World War II, Executive Order 9066, issued in 1942, called for the internment of all people of Japanese descent living on the West Coast. More than 120,000 Japanese Americans were sent to "relocation camps" (concentration camps) as a result of this order. Fred Korematsu, a Japanese American living in San Francisco, and several others sought to avoid internment. Korematsu was arrested, convicted, and sent to an internment camp in Utah. In *Korematsu v. United States* (1944), the U.S. Supreme Court upheld his conviction, but the Court never examined the constitutionality of the government policy on internment. In 1983, Korematsu (then in his eighties) was finally exonerated, and his case encouraged other Japanese Americans to seek reparations for their internment (Chin, 1999).

- U.S. medical schools and a number of state university systems, including the University of California, changed their admissions eligibility rules so that more students from underrepresented racial-ethnic groups will be eligible for admission. Although this produced a favorable outcome for more minority applicants, Asian Americans were not included in the "underrepresented" category: Only African Americans, Latinos/as, and American Indians (Native Americans) are *underrepresented* in higher education today, whereas the percentage of Asian American students in undergraduate and medical school populations has been consistently higher than any other minority group.

As these examples show, the issue of social justice is wide-ranging and encompasses the concerns of people of all racial and ethnic groups. In eras of overt discrimination, laws and social policies have directly targeted persons of color who were deemed unworthy or ineligible for admission to this country or to the institutions of this nation, such as colleges and professional schools. In the 2010s, the questions become even more complex: When

does a law or social policy benefit some racial or ethnic category at the expense of individuals in other racial or ethnic categories?

Clearly, some past laws were directly discriminatory toward Asian Americans. Today, the controversy in higher education is about how to bring about greater inclusion of students from all racial and ethnic categories, as well as more diversity in college populations, and in an effort to reach these goals may indirectly and unintentionally harm some Asian Americans and non-Hispanic white Americans. Many social analysts believe that social policies must be designed to improve racial and ethnic relations in this country. For such a change to occur, people must become more aware of the vital role that individuals from diverse racial and ethnic groups play in the daily life of this nation. Affirmative action was never intended to be a cure-all solution to inequality. Rather, it was intended only to redress discrimination in workplace hiring and academic admissions. In assessing the value of affirmative action, the central question is this: In the absence of sweeping societal reforms—unlikely to take place anytime soon—does affirmative action or other proactive eligibility rules help counteract the continuing injustice caused by discrimination? According to some social scientists, the answer to this question is yes. To those who believe that opportunities are a zero-sum game ("if you win, I lose"), then the answer is probably an unequivocal no!

Question for Consideration

1. This box specifically addresses social justice issues for Asian Americans. What other groups can you think of that have been systematically discriminated against by laws and social policies that excluded them from the United States or social institutions—such as schools, courts, businesses, and medical facilities—in this country?

Independent Research

How is diversity encouraged in higher education? What statements do colleges and universities make about diversity today? Find out how your college or university advocates diversity by visiting your school's website. See also the "Diversity" section at the University of California website (www.universityofcalifornia.edu/diversity/) or the University of Texas at Austin (www.utexas.edu/diversity/index.php).

Colonization

A bloody guerrilla war between Filipino Islanders and U.S. soldiers followed Spain's surrender of the Philippine Islands, as well as Puerto Rico, to the United States in the aftermath of the Spanish-American War. When the battle ended in 1902, the United States established colonial rule over the islands, and Filipinos were "Americanized" by schools that the U.S. government established (Espiritu, 1995).

Most early Filipino migrants were recruited as cheap labor for sugar plantations in Hawaii, agriculture in California, and fish canneries in Seattle and Alaska. Like members of other racial-ethnic groups, Filipino Americans were accused of stealing jobs and suppressing wages during the Great Depression, and Congress restricted Filipino immigration to fifty people per year until after World War II.

Newer Waves of Asian Immigration

Since the 1970s, many Indochinese American refugees have arrived in the United States from Vietnam, Cambodia, Thailand, and Laos. About half of these immigrants live in western states, especially California, but their numbers continue to grow in Texas and the Gulf Coast region, Chicago and the Midwest, and other regions of the nation. Although many early Vietnamese refugees were physicians, pharmacists, and engineers who were able to reenter their professions in the United States, more recent immigrants have had less formal education, fewer job skills, and therefore much higher rates of unemployment. For this reason, many Vietnamese Americans have become small-business owners and ethnic entrepreneurs of establishments such as nail parlors and restaurants. Many of the children and grandchildren of these immigrant entrepreneurs have worked toward college degrees and are entering well-paid jobs in managerial and professional occupations, high-tech firms, and medicine.

Today, many of the Asian and Pacific immigrants arriving from India and Pakistan also are highly educated professionals. About 1.6 million Asian Indian immigrants reside in the United States, which makes them the third largest immigrant group after Mexican and Filipino immigrants. Nearly half of all Asian Indian immigrants reside in one of our states: California, New Jersey, New York, and Texas. About 25 percent of employed Indian-born men work in information technology, and about 33 percent work in management, business, finance, and in information technology. Overall, Asian Indians are less likely to live in poverty than U.S.-born natives. Although Asian Indians have education and income levels about the national average, this did not keep them from becoming objects of discrimination after the September 11, 2001 (9/11), attacks on the United States. Similarly, Pakistani Americans have been subject to discrimination because of fears about connections between their Muslim religion and terrorist activity. Many Pakistani Americans today are well educated and are employed in professions such as law, medicine, and higher education. Others own their own businesses and hire other family members to work with them. While it might appear that full assimilation has occurred for Pakistanis and other Asian Indians, they still experience discrimination based on their religious beliefs, if nothing else.

Although some immigrants from Korea are also professionals, many have few years of formal schooling. In the past, initial contact between Korean Americans and African Americans produced conflict because they had no mutual understanding and other racial tensions were running strong in cities such as Los Angeles and New York. Over time, these tensions appear to have dissipated and some Korean Americans have developed ethnic niches in "Koreatowns," which are actually multicultural neighborhoods where various racial and ethnic groups interact relatively successfully. In Los Angeles, for example, many Korean Americans learn Spanish so that they can communicate with customers and employees in their shops (DeWolf, 2007).

Native Hawaiians and Pacific Islanders

More than 1.2 million people are Native Hawaiians or other Pacific Islanders, including those who identify themselves as being of more than one race. People in this category make up 0.4 percent of the total U.S. population. Native or part-native Hawaiians can trace their ancestry to the original Polynesian inhabitants of the islands. Originally governed as a monarchy and then as a republic, the Hawaiian Islands were annexed by the United States in 1898. In 1959, Congress passed legislation that made Hawaii the fiftieth state. Because of widespread immigration and high rates of intermarriage, contemporary Hawaiians include people of virtually every ancestry on earth, including significant numbers of people with Chinese, Japanese, Filipino, Korean, and Puerto Rican ancestry.

Contemporary Asian and Pacific Americans

Asian and Pacific Americans have high educational levels compared to the overall U.S. population. Nearly nine out of ten Asian and Pacific Americans age twenty-five and over are high school graduates. Asian and Pacific Americans are almost twice as likely to have a bachelor's degree than are non-Latina/o whites: Almost 50 percent of Asian and Pacific Americans age twenty-five and over hold at least a bachelor's degree, and 19 percent hold an advanced degree (master's or doctor's degree, for example).

The median income of households in this population category exceeded that of non-Latino/a whites: $65,469 in 2009 (DeNavas-Walt et al., 2010). In fact, the median family income of Japanese Americans is more

Many Asian Americans have created economic niches such as ownership of nail salons, restaurants, or other small businesses to provide them with a livelihood. Creation of economic niches has contributed to the financial survival of many immigrant groups throughout U.S. history.

than 30 percent above the national average. Today, about 12.5 percent of all Asian and Pacific American families live below the official poverty line.

IS THERE A SOLUTION TO RACIAL AND ETHNIC INEQUALITY?

Although most sociologists acknowledge that there will always be some inequality in the distribution of wealth, power, and prestige in the United States, some analysts are concerned about the vast social inequalities that exist along racial and ethnic lines. These inequalities affect people's opportunities, quality of life, and access to important goods and services such as education, housing, and health care. Discrimination based on race and ethnicity is a significant factor in determining people's life chances and their opportunities. Racial and ethnic inequality is intertwined with class-based inequality to produce strong distinctions in the life chances and opportunities for people who are in dominant, privileged groups and those who are in subordinate, oppressed groups where they may be subjected to unequal treatment and collective discrimination. Sociologists who apply functionalist, conflict, and symbolic interactionist perspectives to the study of racial and ethnic inequalities typically offer different analyses of the problem and suggest different ways to reduce or eliminate race- or ethnicity-based injustice and inequality. Similarly, social analysts applying various political approaches to the problem provide divergent outlooks on what causes racial inequality and what the possible solutions might be to this problem.

Functionalist/Conservative Solutions to the Problem of Racial and Ethnic Inequality

How do functionalists suggest reducing racial-ethnic inequality? High rates of immigration in the United States have raised new questions in recent decades about how to maintain social order and stability when people from throughout the world are arriving in this country, bringing with them a wide variety of languages, cultures, and traditions that are different from those of established residents. Older functionalist models of assimilation—based on the belief that members of subordinate racial and ethnic groups should absorb the dominant culture as soon as possible and become somewhat indistinguishable from it—are no longer effective in producing a homogeneous population where everyone speaks the same language, shares the same holidays, and participates in the same cultural traditions. Instead, these racial and ethnic differences have become a source of identity and pride for many people. But these differences are often used to "explain" why inequalities exist in educational attainment, job opportunities, income, health, and other valued goods and services along lines of race, ethnicity, and national origin. Based on this approach, individuals and groups are at least partly responsible for their own subordination because of decisions they make along the way.

For some functionalist analysts and political conservatives, lack of assimilation by recent immigrant groups is a major problem that can be reduced only by heightening legal requirements for entry into the country as well as for employment and housing, controlling the borders more effectively, and demanding that people become part of the mainstream culture by making English the "official language." Functionalists and political conservatives often view families, schools, and churches as being key institutions that should foster achievement in minority youths by helping them to accept dominant U.S. cultural patterns. As previously discussed, some political analysts strongly advocate that people living in the United States should learn English and speak this language in public places. They also believe that individuals should adopt the dominant culture if they want to achieve academic and economic success, as well as social acceptance in the larger society. According to some conservative analysts, if subordinate-group members continue to be the objects of prejudice and discrimination in the United States, they have no one to blame but themselves because they have been unwilling to embrace the dominant culture. Conservatives typically view programs such as affirmative action or others that are designed to specifically benefit minority-group members as being divisive and harmful. By contrast, functionalist analysts and conservative political observers believe that individual achievement should be encouraged and highly rewarded because individuals such as Oprah Winfrey can serve as role models for other minority youths on how to get ahead in the United States and other nations.

Conflict/Liberal Solutions to the Problem of Racial and Ethnic Inequality

From a conflict perspective, racial and ethnic inequality can be reduced only through struggle and political action. Conflict theorists believe that if inequality is based on the exploitation of subordinate groups by the dominant group, political intervention is necessary to bring about economic and social change. They agree that people should mobilize to put pressure on public officials. Many people believe that racial inequality will not be reduced until there is significant national support and leadership for addressing social problems directly and forcefully.

Among the problems that conflict theorists and liberal political analysts believe need to be systematically addressed in the United States are persistent patterns of prejudice and discrimination, both at the individual and institutional levels. Conflict theorists who use a class perspectives approach often point out that discrimination in the workplace must be reduced before racial and ethnic inequality can be eliminated. Discrimination based on race and class play a key part in determining the amount of education people have, the kinds of jobs that they hold, how much they earn, what kind of benefits (if any) they have, and what opportunities they may have for future advancement. If the deck is stacked against people of color and recent immigrants in the labor market, these individuals will have few opportunities to get ahead in American society.

Conflict theorists and liberal political analysts who believe that the government substantially defines racial and ethnic relations emphasize that solutions to the problem of inequality will be found only through government programs that specifically attack racial inequality and actively reduce patterns of discrimination. For this reason, many conflict/liberal solutions to the problem are based on the assumption that we have reduced or eliminated affirmative action programs before they have been fully effective in bringing about social change. Clearly, affirmative action programs in the past opened up opportunities for many college students, workers, and minority businesses that otherwise would have remained out of the economic and social mainstream. Now, if conflict/liberal theorists' assertions are correct, programs such as this are still needed if all people are to have equal opportunities in this nation. For this to occur, political activism will be required because such changes typically occur only because of organized political pressure. Ironically, when the U.S. economy is in a recession and people are concerned about having a job and earning a living wage, it sometimes becomes more difficult to mobilize them to demand economic justice, even when they are low-income individuals and/or subordinate-group members who are the most likely to be harmed by the vast divide between the rich and the poor.

Symbolic Interactionist Solutions to the Problem of Racial and Ethnic Inequality

According to symbolic interactionists, prejudice and discrimination are learned, and what is learned can be unlearned. As sociologist Gale E. Thomas (1995:339) notes, "In the areas of race, ethnic, and human relations, we must learn compassion and also to accept and truly embrace, rather than merely tolerate, differences . . . through honest and open dialogue and through the formation of genuine

The Jack and Jill of America Foundation, which focuses on the African American community, is a membership organization of mothers with children ages 2 to 19. It is dedicated to nurturing future leaders by supporting children through leadership development, volunteer service, philanthropic giving and civic duty.

friendships and personal experiential . . . exchanges and interactions with different individuals and groups across cultures." In other words, only individuals and groups at the grass-roots level, not government and political leaders or academic elites, can bring about greater racial equality.

Racial socialization and personal identity are central to symbolic interactionist perspectives on inequality because how people are socialized has a profound effect on how people view themselves and other people. For this reason, children and young adults should be taught about cultural diversity and American history, including how members of some subordinate groups were treated by some members of dominant groups. They should also be encouraged to think of positive ways in which individuals of all races can acquire a positive self-concept and interact positively with each other. By developing a better understanding of the past, it is reasoned, children and young adults of all races will be able to understand how race is a prism through which African Americans and other people of color view their lives. To reduce racial and ethnic inequality will require a better understanding of people across racial and ethnic categories. This must begin with a new social construction of reality that requires that people abandon those traditional prejudices that make it impossible for them to view others as people who are deserving of social justice and equality.

Whether or not the people of the United States work for greater equality for all racial-ethnic groups, one thing is certain: The U.S. population is becoming increasingly diverse at a rapid rate. Although an examination of the racial and ethnic composition of the U.S. population in Census 2010 shows that the non-Hispanic white alone population is still the largest in number and proportion in the nation, the Hispanic population accounts for more than half of the growth of the total U.S. population (see Figure 3.3 on page 72). The Asian population alone increased by 43 percent, and was the fastest-growing major racial group. (Recall that the Hispanic/Latino/a classification is an ethnic category.) By the year 2050, a number of U.S. residents will trace their roots to Africa, Asia, the Hispanic countries, the Pacific Islands, and the Middle East, not white Europe. We must recognize the challenges posed by increasing racial-ethnic and cultural diversity and develop a visionary and inclusive perspective so that our nation can meet the challenges of a rapidly changing world in which conflict, terrorism, natural disasters, and geopolitical turmoil are constant sources of news.

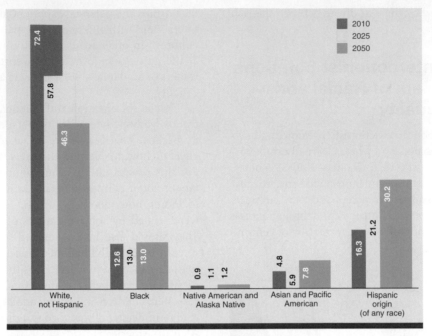

Figure 3.3   Percentage of U.S. population by race and Hispanic origin (for those indicating one race only): 2010, 2025, and 2050 (middle-series projections)
Source: Humes et al., 2011.

SUMMARY

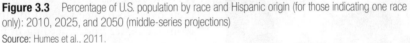

((•─ **Listen** to the **Chapter Audio** on **mysoclab.com**

■ **How do racial and ethnic groups differ?**
According to sociologists, racial groups are defined on the basis of real or alleged physical characteristics, and ethnic groups are defined on the basis of cultural or nationality characteristics.

■ **What are dominant and subordinate groups?**
Although the terms *majority group* and *minority group* are widely used, many sociologists prefer the terms *dominant* and *subordinate* to identify power relationships that are based on perceived racial, ethnic, or other attributes and identities. A dominant (majority) group is one that is advantaged and has superior resources and rights in a society. A subordinate (minority) group is one whose members, because of physical or cultural characteristics, are disadvantaged and subjected to unequal treatment by the dominant group, and regard themselves as objects of collective discrimination.

■ **How are prejudice and discrimination related?**
Prejudice is a negative attitude that might or might not lead to discrimination, which is an action or practice of dominant-group members that has a harmful impact on subordinate-group members.

■ **How do individual discrimination and institutional discrimination differ?**
Although individual discrimination and institutional discrimination are carried out by individuals, individual discrimination consists of one-on-one acts by members of the dominant group; institutional discrimination refers to actions and practices that are built into the day-to-day operations of large-scale organizations and social institutions.

■ **How do the interactionist and functionalist perspectives view racial and ethnic relations?**
Interactionists focus on microlevel issues such as how people develop a racial-ethnic identity and how individuals from diverse racial-ethnic groups interact with each other. Functionalists focus on macrolevel issues such as how entire groups of people assimilate into the mainstream of the society.

■ **What are the major conflict explanations for racial-ethnic inequality?**
Conflict perspectives include class perspectives, split-labor market theory, gendered racism, internal colonialism, and racial formation theory.

■ **What types of discrimination have been experienced by Native Americans, African Americans, Latinos/as, and Asian and Pacific Americans in the United States?**

Native Americans have experienced internal colonization, genocide, forced migration, and Americanization. African Americans have experienced slavery, *de jure* segregation (Jim Crow laws), and *de facto* segregation—racial separation and inequality enforced by custom. Latinos/as have experienced internal colonialism, exclusionary immigration policies, and segregation in housing and education. Asian and Pacific Americans also have experienced exclusionary immigration policies; Japanese Americans uniquely experienced internment during World War II.

■ **What commonalities can be seen in the experiences of all subordinate racial-ethnic groups?**

Members of most subordinate racial-ethnic groups have these commonalities in their experiences in the United States: (1) Each has been the object of negative stereotypes and discrimination, (2) each has resisted oppression and continued to strive for a better life for its members and their children, and (3) each has been the object of some government policy that has shaped its place (or lack thereof) in U.S. race and ethnic relations over the past two centuries.

KEY TERMS

amalgamation, p. 56
Anglo-conformity model, p. 56
anti-Semitism, p. 54
assimilation, p. 56
dominant (majority) group, p. 52
ethnic group, p. 51
ethnic pluralism, p. 58
ethnocentrism, p. 53

gendered racism, p. 59
genocide, p. 60
individual discrimination, p. 54
institutional discrimination, p. 54
internal colonialism, p. 59
melting-pot model, p. 56
prejudice, p. 53
racial group, p. 51

racism, p. 53
scapegoat, p. 56
segregation, p. 58
stereotypes, p. 54
subordinate (minority) group, p. 52
theory of racial formation, p. 59

QUESTIONS FOR CRITICAL THINKING

1. Given the U.S. Census Bureau choices, what racial or ethnic classification (or classifications) do you believe most closely applies to you? In what specific ways might your life be different if you were in one or more of the other classifications?

2. Sociologists suggest that we acquire beliefs about ourselves and others through socialization. What specific messages have you received about your racial-ethnic identity? What specific messages have you received about dealing with people from other racial-ethnic groups?

3. Have all white Americans, regardless of class, gender, or other characteristics, benefited from racial prejudice and discrimination in the United States? Why or why not?

4. Compare recent depictions of Native Americans, African Americans, Latinos/as, and Asian and Pacific Americans in films, television shows, and advertisements. To what extent have we moved beyond the traditional stereotypes discussed in this chapter? To what extent have the stereotypes remained strong?

Succeed with MySocLab®   www.mysoclab.com

The new MySocLab delivers proven results in helping students succeed, provides engaging experiences that personalize learning, and comes from a trusted partner with educational expertise and a deep commitment to helping students and instructors achieve their goals.

Here are a few activities you will find for this chapter:

Watch on **mysoclab.com**

Core Concepts video clips feature sociologists in action, exploring important concepts in the study of Social Problems. Watch:
- Racial Stereotypes and Discrimination

Explore on **mysoclab.com**

Social Explorer is an interactive application that allows you to explore Census data through interactive maps. Explore:
- Social Explorer Activity: Patterns of Unemployment and Race

Read on **mysoclab.com**

MySocLibrary includes primary source readings from classic and contemporary sociologists. Read:
- Race Matters

Gender Inequality

THINKING SOCIOLOGICALLY

- Why should we be concerned about sexual harassment? How is sexual harassment related to gender inequality?

- What types of gender socialization influence our ideas about what it means to be a woman or a man?

- How does gender-segregated work contribute to the larger picture of gender inequality in a society?

New York Times, **June 20, 2011:**

"Justices Rule for Wal-Mart in Bias Case"

WASHINGTON—*The Supreme Court on Monday threw out the largest employment discrimination case in the nation's history. The suit, against Wal-Mart Stores, had sought to consolidate the claims of as many as 1.5 million women on the theory that the company had discriminated against them in pay and promotion decisions. . . . The court did not decide whether Wal-Mart had in fact discriminated against the women, only that they could not proceed as a class.*

—Journalist Adam Liptak (2011) describes the Supreme Court's decision in a massive Walmart lawsuit that claimed that the corporation discriminated against female employees who were paid less than men in similar positions and given fewer promotions. The Court ruled that the case could not move forward as a class-action suit against the giant corporation, leaving the women plaintiffs to move forward individually with a claim if they so chose. Four Supreme Court justices, including Justice Ruth Bader Ginsburg, dissented in part on the Court's decision. The follow is an excerpt from Justice Ginsburg's opinion:

Supreme Court of the United States, June 20, 2011:

The named plaintiffs, led by Betty Dukes, propose to litigate, on behalf of the class, allegations that Wal-Mart discriminates on the basis of gender in pay and promotions. They allege that the company "relies on gender stereotypes in making employment decisions such as . . . promotion[s] and pay." Wal-Mart permits those prejudices to infect personnel decisions, the plaintiffs contend, by leaving pay and promotions in the hands of "a nearly all male management workforce" using "arbitrary and subjective criteria." . . . Women fill 70 percent of the hourly jobs in the retailer's stores but make up only "33 percent of management employees" [in 2001]. "The higher one looks in the organization the lower the percentage of women.". . . Wal-Mart's supervisors do not make their discretionary decisions in a vacuum. The District [lower] Court reviewed means Wal-Mart used to maintain a "carefully constructed . . . corporate culture," such as frequent meetings to reinforce the common way of thinking, regular transfers of managers between stores to ensure conformity throughout the company, monitoring of stores "on a close and constant basis," and "Wal-Mart TV broadcast into all stores." The plaintiff's evidence, including class members' tales of their own experiences, suggests that gender bias suffused Wal-Mart's company culture.

—Justice Ruth Bader Ginsburg (2011) explains in her dissenting opinion on the Supreme Court's decision in Wal-Mart Stores Inc., Petitioner v. Betty Dukes et al. why she believes there is more than enough uniting the claims of the women plaintiffs to show that Walmart's delegation of discretion over pay and promotions is a policy that is uniform throughout all the corporation's stores.

In what may have been the largest employment discrimination cases in U.S. history, a number of current and former female employees claimed that Walmart discriminated against women in recruitment, promotion, and pay. One issue in the case was the extent to which Walmart as a corporation is responsible for the decisions of individual male employees in various stores throughout the country. The business community has sided with Walmart as this case has moved up through the court system and finally reached the U.S. Supreme Court. Other corporations feared that if the women won this lawsuit, a flood of class-action lawsuits pertaining to sexual discrimination would follow, some of which might affect their own organizations. By contrast, groups that promote women's rights, civil rights, and consumer groups have been advocates for the women plaintiffs, believing that they have uncovered longstanding problems of women in the workplace. As a sociological issue, the Walmart case calls out to the problem of discrimination and gender inequality in the workplace while, at the same time, raising interesting questions about what constitutes sexism and gender-based discrimination in specific "corporate cultures" and other settings in the twenty-first century.

What is sexism? **Sexism is the subordination of one sex, usually female, based on the assumed superiority of the other sex**. Lewd comments, derogatory jokes, indecent gestures, and other conduct that makes women feel uncomfortable constitutes sexist behavior. In the Walmart lawsuit, for example, Justice Ginsburg comments on sexist practices of male supervisors, such as "Senior management often refer to female associates as 'little Janie Qs'" and "[M]en are here to make a career and women's aren't." Sexist behavior may create in-group solidarity among men, particularly in male-dominated groups and occupations, but it marginalizes women and makes them "sex objects," thus perpetuating gender inequality. From this perspective, pervasive sexism (along with racism and class-based inequalities) is deeply rooted in society, where it has a negative effect on women and men alike.

GENDER INEQUALITY AS A SOCIAL PROBLEM

Just as subordinate racial-ethnic group members experience discrimination based on innate characteristics, women experience discrimination based on their sex. Because 51 percent of the people in the United States are female, women constitute the numerical majority. However, they sometimes are referred to as the country's largest minority group because, typically, they do not possess as much wealth, power, or prestige as men.

Defining Sex and Gender

What is the difference between sex and gender? Although many people use these terms interchangeably, sociologists believe that there are significant differences in their meanings. **Sex is the biological differences between females and males**. A person's sex is the first label he or she receives in life. Before birth or at the time of birth, we are identified as male or female on the basis of our sex organs and genes. In comparison, **gender is the culturally and socially constructed differences between females and males that are based on meanings, beliefs, and practices that a group or society associates with "femininity" or "masculinity."** For many people, being masculine means being aggressive, independent, and not showing emotions; being feminine means the opposite—being unaggressive, dependent, and very emotional. Understanding the difference between sex and gender is important, according to sociologists, because what many people think of as sex differences—for example, being aggressive or independent—are actually socially constructed gender differences based on widely held assumptions about men's and women's attributes. In other words, males are supposed to be aggressive and independent not because they have male sex organs but because that's how people in this society believe males should act.

Biological and Social Bases for Gender Roles

To study gender inequality, sociologists begin with an examination of the biological and social bases for gender roles, which are the rights, responsibilities, expectations, and relationships of women and men in a society. Gender roles have both a biological and a social basis. The biological basis for gender roles is rooted in the chromosomal and hormonal differences between men and women. When a child is conceived, the mother contributes an X chromosome, and the father contributes either an X chromosome (which produces a female embryo) or a Y chromosome (which produces a male embryo). As the embryo's male or female sex glands develop, they secrete the appropriate hormones (androgens for males, estrogens for females) that circulate through the bloodstream, producing sexual differentiation in the external genitalia, the internal reproductive tract, and possibly some areas of the brain. At birth, medical personnel and family members distinguish male from female infants by their *primary sex characteristics:* the genitalia that are used in the reproductive process. At puberty, hormonal differences in females and males produce *secondary sex characteristics*, the physical traits that, along with the reproductive organs, identify a person's sex. Females develop secondary sex characteristics such as menstruation, more prominent breasts, wider hips and narrower shoulders, and a layer of fatty tissue throughout the body. Male secondary sex characteristics include the development of larger genitals, a more muscular build, a deeper voice, more body and facial hair, and greater height. Although both males and females have androgens and estrogens, it is the relative proportion of each hormone that triggers masculine or feminine physical traits.

Is there something in the biological and genetic makeup of boys or girls that makes them physically aggressive or unaggressive? As sociologist Judith Lorber (1994:39) notes, "When little boys run around noisily, we say 'Boys will be boys,' meaning that physical assertiveness has to be in the Y chromosome because it is manifest so early and so commonly in boys." Similarly, when we say, "She throws like a girl" we mean, according to Lorber, that "she throws like a female child, a carrier of XX chromosomes." However, Lorber (1994:39) questions these widely held assumptions: "But are boys universally, the world over, in every social group, a vociferous, active presence? Or just where they are encouraged to use their bodies freely, to cover space, take risks, and play outdoors at all kinds of games and sports?"

According to Lorber, boys and girls who are given tennis rackets at the age of three and encouraged to become champions tend to use their bodies similarly. Even though boys gradually gain more shoulder and arm strength and are able to sustain more concentrated bursts of energy, after puberty girls acquire more stamina, flexibility, and lower-body strength. Coupled with training and physical exercise, these traits enhance, compensate for, or override different physical capabilities (Lorber, 1994). Thus, the girl who throws like a girl is probably a product of her culture and time: She has had more limited experience than many boys at throwing the ball and engaging in competitive games at an early age.

The social basis for gender roles is known as the *gender belief system*—the ideas of masculinity and femininity that are held to be valid in a society (Lorber, 1994). The gender belief system is reflected in what sociologists refer to as the *gendered division of labor*—**the process whereby productive tasks are separated on the basis of gender**. How do people determine what constitutes "women's work" or "men's work"? Evidence from cross-cultural studies shows that social factors, more than biological factors, influence the gendered division of labor in societies. In poor agricultural societies, for example, women work in the fields and tend to their families' daily needs; men typically produce and market cash crops but spend no time in household work. In high-income nations, an increasing proportion of women are in paid employment but still have heavy household and family responsibilities. Across cultures, women's domain is the private and domestic, and men's domain is the public, economic, and political. This difference in how labor is divided and how workers are rewarded affects access to scarce resources such as wealth, power, and prestige. Given their domain, men have greater access to wealth, power, and prestige, a situation that leads to gender inequality in other areas.

To explain gender inequality, some sociologists use a *gender-role approach*, focusing on how the socialization process contributes to male domination and female subordination. Other sociologists use a structural approach, focusing on how large-scale, interacting, and enduring social structures determine the boundaries of individual behavior. Let's look first at how socialization can perpetuate gender stereotyping and inequality.

GENDER INEQUALITY AND SOCIALIZATION

Numerous sociological studies have found that gender-role stereotyping is one of the enduring consequences of childhood gender socialization. Socialization into appropriate "feminine" behavior makes women less likely than men to pursue male-dominated activities, and socialization into appropriate "masculine" behavior makes men more likely than women to pursue leadership roles in education, religion, business, politics, and other spheres of

◉ **Watch** on **mysoclab.com**

Gender Socialization on **mysoclab.com**

public life. We learn our earliest and often most lasting beliefs about gender roles from a variety of socializing agents—people, groups, or institutions that teach us what we need to know to participate in society. Among the most significant socializing agents are parents, peers, teachers and schools, sports, and the media.

Gender Socialization by Parents

From birth, parents create and maintain gender distinctions between girls and boys through differential treatment. Because boys are thought to be less fragile than girls, parents are more likely to bounce an infant son, to hold him up in the air, and to play with him more vigorously than they are an infant daughter. Parents tend to cuddle infant girls, treat them gently, and provide them with verbal stimulation through cooing, talking, and singing to them.

Parents reinforce gender distinctions through their selection of infants' and children's clothing. Most parents dress boys in boldly colored "rough and tough" clothing and girls in softly colored "feminine" clothing. They purchase sweatshirts that are decorated with hearts and flowers or female characters such as Cinderella, Ariel (the Little Mermaid), or Rapunzel for girls and sweatshirts that feature male superheroes, athletic motifs, or characters such as Mickey Mouse, Spider-Man, or Superman for boys.

Parents further reinforce gender stereotyping and gender distinctions through the toys they buy. For example, parents buy blocks and building sets, vehicles, sporting equipment, and action toys such as guns, tanks, and soldiers for boys and dolls, doll clothing, dollhouses, play cosmetics, and homemaking items such as dishes and miniature ovens for girls. However, toys and games do more than provide fun and entertainment; they develop different types of skills and can encourage children to participate in gender-typed activities.

DID YOU KNOW

- Jobs traditionally associated with men tend to pay better than jobs associated with women, even for the same level of education and skill.

- About 40 percent of working women are employed in "female" occupations such as nursing and teaching.

- Women employed in "male" occupations still earn less, on average, than their male counterparts in similar jobs.

Chores also reinforce gender distinctions. Most research confirms that parents use toys and chores to encourage their sons more than their daughters toward greater independence. Thus, boys frequently are assigned such maintenance chores as carrying out the garbage, cleaning up the yard, or helping dad or an older brother. Girls, on the other hand, are given domestic chores such as shopping, cooking, clearing the table, and doing laundry. When parents purchase gender-specific toys and give children gender-specific household assignments, they send a powerful message about the gendered division of labor. However, gender socialization by parents does not stop at the end of childhood. Parents play a pivotal role in what many children do—and how they perceive of themselves in regard to gender, as well as class—well into adolescence and adulthood (see Box 4.1).

Critical Thinking and You   Box 4.1

Does Class Position Influence How We Think about Gender?

My mother is of a culture that believes girls aren't worth educating. . . . [My father thought] why reach for the sky when you can be happy on earth. My dad was trying to save me from disappointment. The daughter of peasant stock shouldn't strive to be in the ruling class, he thought. . . . If I had had parents who backed me, I could've owned my own company by now. I was always struggling against my parents.

— *"Donna" (not her real name), a journalist for a national magazine, describes how her working-class parents thought that if the "working-class life was good enough for us, it's good enough for you, too" (quoted in Lubrano, 2004:33–34).*

Being a debutante helped to define who I am as a woman and where I belong. I'm glad my mother insisted that I "come out" even though, at the time, I didn't want to because I thought it was "old fashioned" and "elitist." I think being a deb showed me I can be a woman with good manners and represent my family's position well.

— *"Mary" (not her real name), a twenty-five-year-old white upper-class woman, explains how she felt about being presented as a society debutante at the encouragement of her mother (author's files, 2002).*

Although Donna and Mary are both women living in America, they have had different experiences as women based on their class location and what their families thought their "place" was in the social order. Donna represents those individuals who are raised in a blue-collar family but now live a white-collar, middle-class lifestyle. By contrast, Mary represents individuals who are raised in an upper-class family and continue to live a privileged lifestyle. Both women's stories reflect an interesting intersection of gender and class. To participate in the debutante ritual, Mary had to come from the "right families" with the proper social credentials and sufficient resources to pay for the many expenses associated with this ritual, while Donna's early life was a struggle, not only in regard to getting an education but also in facing parents who believed that she should not aspire to be upwardly mobile.

The lived experiences of these two women, as described by a sociologist (Kendall, 2002) and by a reporter for the *Philadelphia Inquirer* (Lubrano, 2004), are typical of thousands of women and men living in the United States where to be "male" or "female" does not fully explain a person's life chances and opportunities: Class is also a critical factor in understanding each individual's life. Consider, for example, how the intersections of gender and class have influenced the lives of people you know.

Questions for Consideration

1. Think of a community you know well (perhaps your hometown or a city in which you lived for a lengthy period of time) and identify several families you consider to be in each of these categories: upper class, middle class, and working class. What are the key work and leisure activities of the men in each class? What are the key work and leisure activities of the women in each class?

2. Do these activities reflect the socialization of women and men based on their gender? Based on their class location?

3. What commonalities exist among women across class lines in the activities they typically perform? What activities are specific to women in the upper class? The middle class? The working class?

4. When is gender more important than class in helping us understand human behavior? When is class more important?

5. What type of sociological research might help you further explore the intersections of gender and class in your community?

Peers and Gender Socialization

Peer groups are powerful socializing agents that can reinforce existing gender stereotypes and pressure individuals to engage in gender-appropriate behavior. Peer groups are social groups whose members are linked by common interests and, usually, by similar age. Children are more widely accepted by their peer group when they conform to the group's notion of gender-appropriate behavior. Male peer groups place more pressure on boys to do "masculine" things than female peer groups place on girls to do "feminine" things. For example, most girls today wear jeans, and many play soccer and softball, but boys who wear dresses or play hopscotch with girls are banished from most male peer groups.

During preadolescence, male peer groups also reinforce gender-appropriate emotions in boys. In a study of a Little League baseball team, for example, sociologist Gary Fine (1987) found that the boys were encouraged by their peers to engage in proper "masculine" behavior—acting tough even when they were hurt or intimidated, controlling their emotions, being competitive and wanting to win, and showing group unity and loyalty. Boys who failed to display these characteristics received instantaneous feedback from their teammates.

Peers are important in both women's and men's development of gender identity and their aspirations for the future. Among college students, for example, peers play an important part in career choices and the establishment of long-term, intimate relationships. Even in kindergarten and the early grades, peers influence how we do in school and our perceptions of ourselves and others.

Education and Gender Socialization

Like parents and peers, teachers may reinforce gender distinctions by communicating to students that males and male-dominated activities are more important than females and female-dominated activities. Research on education continues to show the existence in schools of *gender bias*—**a situation in which favoritism is shown toward one gender**. For example, education scholars Myra Sadker and David Sadker (1994) found that teachers subtly convey the message to their students that boys are more important than girls by devoting more time, effort, and attention to boys than to girls. In day-to-day interactions, teachers are more likely to allow boys to interrupt them and give boys more praise, criticism, and suggestions for remediation than girls. Boys are more likely to be called on in class, whether they volunteer or

not. When boys make comments, teachers often follow up with additional questions or suggestions; but when girls make comments, teachers often respond with a superficial "OK" and move on to the next student. Teachers praise girls for their appearance or for having a neat paper, but boys are praised for their accomplishments.

Some educational analysts have suggested that, contrary to the assumption that gender bias in schools harms only girls and young women, what actually occurs in the classroom is that male students are now at a disadvantage because classrooms and teachers' attitudes have been remodeled to serve the needs of girls. Journalist Peg Tyre (2008) argues that educational emphasis in the 1990s that focused on helping girls succeed has put boys at a disadvantage because, by nature, boys are more active and noisy, and teachers in the early years of schooling are usually young and female and have little tolerance for the way boys behave and express themselves. According to this perspective, a form of reverse sexism has developed in recent decades that places boys at a disadvantage in learning environments that are less structured and focus less on grades and competition (Sommers, 2001). Other analysts have suggested that an emphasis on reading and language arts skills puts boys at a disadvantage because girls typically pick up reading earlier than boys (Whitmire, 2010). As this debate continues regarding the relative advantages or disadvantages of female and male students, we can still conclude that gender does matter in the classroom, and what takes place there has a lasting effect on gender socialization. Moreover, the American Association of University Women (AAUW, 2008) has found in recent research that girls' successes in education do not come at the expense of boys, an issue that we will examine in greater detail in Chapter 12.

Despite this ongoing controversy, research continues to show that teachers use gender-segregated activities to organize classroom and playground activities ("Boys line up on the left; girls on the right"). Teachers may do this out of convenience or for disciplinary purposes, not because they have any intent to engage in gender bias. For example, they may want to eliminate the amount of class time that is lost dealing with students' complaints, such as "Jose pulled my hair" or "She hit me," by keeping girls and boys separated.

However, there are times when gender bias clearly is visible, as in the case of sexual harassment. When teachers take a "boys will be boys" attitude about derogatory remarks and aggressive behavior against girls, a hostile learning environment is created not only for girls but also for all students. *Sexual harassment*—**unwanted sexual**

Take a close look at this picture. What do you notice about the two lines? Social scientists have pointed out that gender socialization occurs in many ways, including how teachers organize school activities by sex.

advances, requests for sexual favors, or other verbal or physical conduct of a sexual nature—is frequently overlooked by teachers and school administrators. Unfortunately, media stories like the one about the first-grade boy who was suspended from school for kissing a female classmate on the cheek trivialize gender bias and sexual harassment, both of which create a hostile environment that makes it more difficult for many girls and young women to learn and accomplish as much as their male counterparts (see Orenstein, 1996; Sadker and Sadker, 1994). Researchers have found that in some schools, male students regularly refer to girls as "sluts," "bitches," and "hos" without fear of reprimand from teachers, and the girls' fear of reprisal keeps them from speaking out against their harassers (Orenstein, 1996). One high school student described her experience in a shop class in this way:

> The boys literally pushed me around, right into tables and chairs. They pulled my hair, made sexual comments, touched me, told sexist jokes. And the thing was that I was better in the shop class than almost any guy. This only caused the boys to get more aggressive and troublesome. (Sadker and Sadker, 1994:127)

However, girls are not the only ones to experience sexual harassment at school. A now-classic report by the AAUW and based on a national survey of more than 2,000 public school children in the eighth through eleventh grades states that 83 percent of girls and 79 percent of boys reported having experienced harassment at least once and that one in four of the students had experienced sexual harassment often (AAUW Educational Foundation, 2001). Nonphysical harassment (such as other students making comments or spreading rumors about them) and physical harassment (such as someone pulling off or down their clothing in a sexual way or forcing them to do something sexual other than kissing) were concerns of many of the students in the study. However, girls were more likely than boys to report negative consequences of these actions: Many stated that such harassment made them feel "self conscious," "embarrassed," or "less confident" (AAUW Educational Foundation, 2001). Other studies have also found that girls and women are vulnerable to sexual harassment on their way to and from school. Little notice is given to the number of girls and young women who are followed, verbally harassed, and touched by boys and men as they walk to school or ride a school bus or the subway, particularly once the female student reaches puberty (AAUW Dialogue, 2009).

Boys often are limited by stereotypical notions of masculinity and gender-appropriate behavior. According to Sadker and Sadker (1994:220), boys confront "frozen boundaries" of the male role at every turn in their school life. They are taught to "Be cool, don't show emotion, repress feelings, be aggressive, compete, and win"—the same messages that sociologist Gary Fine (1987) found Little Leaguers using to reinforce each other. Such teachings not only limit the range of emotions boys are allowed to feel but also encourage boys to see themselves—and other males—as better than girls and to distance themselves from any activity that is considered "feminine," even if it is an activity they enjoy. Male gender norms, which require boys to be active, aggressive, and independent, often conflict with school norms, which require students to be quiet, passive, and conforming. Many boys walk a tightrope between compliance and rebellion. They tend to receive lower grades than girls do and are more likely to drop out of school (Sadker and Sadker, 1994).

Studies in the twenty-first century have confirmed the findings of various researchers who conducted their studies in the 1980s and 1990s. In a study by the AAUW, researchers found that sexual harassment is common on college campuses, but it is most common at large universities, four-year institutions, and private colleges (Hill and Silva, 2005). Both men and women are likely to be harassed, but the form that the harassment takes is different, and females and males often respond in different ways. According to the AAUW report, female students are more likely to be the object of sexual jokes, comments, gestures, and looks. By contrast, male students are more likely to be teased about being gay or referred to by a homophobic name. Overall, men are more likely than women to be the ones who harass men or women (Hill and Silva, 2005) At the bottom line, victims typically do not report that they have been the victims of sexual harassment, and those who do the harassing think that their actions are "funny." For this reason, sexual harassment is difficult to identify and eradicate on college campuses and other public settings.

In sum, although the media and popular culture have spotlighted "mean girls" and portrayed girls and young women as constant rivals with each other, studies from the 1990s and after remain valid as they describe how gender socialization in schools seeks to turn "boys into men" and "girls into women" may work to the detriment of both genders, but women, having been the subordinate sex for centuries, are often the biggest losers when it comes to issues of self-confidence, self-esteem, and earning ability in previously male-dominated schooling and employment.

Sports and Gender Socialization

Although girls' participation in athletics has increased dramatically since the 1972 passage of Title IX, which mandates equal opportunities in academic and athletic programs, boys' participation is about one and one-half times that of girls. Emphasis on greater gender equity in sports has contributed to a more positive outlook for girls and women with regard to participation in a wider variety of athletic endeavors. For example, when students in a 1990 study were asked about sports participation, most students listed all sports as male domains with the exception of figure skating, gymnastics, and jumping rope, which were identified as female activities (Michigan Department of Education, 1990). Although this perception has changed in recent years as a much wider range of opportunities in sports has become available to women, some critics argue that women's gains have been at the expense of men in college sports and others have suggested that colleges and universities have been less than forthcoming in meeting the requirements of this law (see Box 4.2).

Social Problems and Social Policy   Box 4.2

Title IX and Gender Quotas in College Sports

I'm not opposed to women getting an opportunity to do anything they want, but when you start eliminating men's sports to pay for it, there is some inequity. When Title IX was initiated, the wrestling program in my college, William & Mary, was wiped out.

—*Ben Smith, a former member of his high school and college wrestling teams, explains why he has mixed feelings about Title IX (quoted in Connelly, 2011).*

If we are forced to have gender quotas in college sports, men's programs will lose out to women's programs.

—*An often-repeated statement made by critics of Title IX of the Education Amendments of 1972*

Have these statements proved to be true over the past forty years since Title IX was enacted? Have men's teams felt great pain while women's teams obtained an advantage in college athletics? To gain insights on this controversial social policy, let's first look at what Title IX is all about.

Title IX prohibits discrimination on the basis of sex in any educational program or activity receiving financial assistance from the U.S. government and has been applied to athletic programs as well as to other academic endeavors. A three-part test was established to help colleges determine if they provide sufficient opportunities for female athletes to participate in athletic programs:

- Does the college have the same proportion of students and athletes who are female?

- Does the college have a "history and continuing practice" of expanding opportunities for women?

- Can the college show that it is fully and effectively accommodating the interests and abilities of women on campus?

Overall, statistics show that Title IX has had a very favorable effect on women's participation in college athletic programs. Consider, for example, the more than 500 percent increase in the number of women competing in college sports between 1972 and 2011. Fewer than 30,000 female athletes competed in 1972, as compared to 186,000 a year in the 2010s. Statistics—in this instance, data about athletic participation—show that

Social Problems and Social Policy

Box 4.2

some women's teams have made progress in regard to equity, but that this typically has not been at the expense of men's athletic programs. As a result of Title IX, many more women are playing collegiate sports today than before this law was enacted, but the percentage *increase* in athletic participation during that period of time has not been as high for females as it has been for males: More men are playing varsity sports today than in the past, even as their numbers on college campuses have become a smaller percentage of the undergraduate student population. Although there has been a significant increase in the number of female athletes competing in college sports, the representation of female athletes remains far from proportional to the number of female students at most colleges. Consider, for example, that in 2004–2005, 41 percent of athletic participants in college sports were women, but during that same period of time, women made up about 55 percent of all full-time undergraduate students at U.S. colleges (Cheslock, 2007). At the same time that more women have become involved in college athletic programs, women have come to dominate undergraduate enrollments, making it more difficult to demonstrate the effect of Title IX in regard to athletic participation.

At the bottom line—the dollar figures—we can particularly see that men's athletic programs have not been losing out to women's programs. Men's collegiate sports still receive the lion's share of the money when it comes to budgets, coaches' salaries, facilities, and other resources. Some of the complaints of coaches and male athletes—particularly in programs such as swimming, wrestling, and other less visible sports—that they are losing out to women's programs might better be directed toward other men's programs, specifically football and basketball, that remain the powerhouses for both bringing in the money and spending it (Cheslock, 2007).

Each year, colleges and universities are required to report their female and male participation numbers to the Department of Education. Unfortunately, recent reports have found that a number of institutions attempt to comply by using unique, and perhaps unorthodox methods, for counting male and female athletes and programs. For example, some Division I sports programs, such as women's basketball, count male players who practice with women's teams as female participants. Other schools double or triple count women in sports such as track because athletes frequently participate in more than one kind of competition (Thomas, 2011a). Rather than adding more female athletes or teams, other institutions have eliminated some lower-profile, less-profitable men's sports, such as wrestling and swimming, so that they will be in compliance with the proportionality necessary between men's and women's sports (Thomas, 2011b).

Title IX has created new opportunities for women in sports, and hopefully, these advances will not be undermined during difficult economic times by budget cuts or lack of good will in fulfilling the letter and spirit of the law.

Questions for Consideration

1. Why is it important for women to have equal opportunities to participate in competitive sporting events in college?

2. How does this box relate to discussions about the socialization process in this chapter?

Independent Research

What policy does your college or university use to bring about greater gender equity in sports? To do more research on college sports, or find information about National Collegiate Athletic Association (NCAA) sports, go to the NCAA website at www.ncaa.org. Click on "Research" to learn more about topics such as recent legislation pertaining to college sports, academic progress of student-athletes, and the probability of high school athletes going pro.

Overall, for both women and men, sports participation is an important part of gender socialization. Across lines of race, ethnicity, and gender, sports and other extracurricular activities provide students with important opportunities for leadership and teamwork and for personal contact with adult role models. Consequently, athletic participation must be viewed as more than just "play"; it constitutes an important part of the learning experience and can promote greater equality in society or leave some people behind.

The Media and Gender Socialization

The media—including newspapers, magazines, television, movies, and the Internet—are powerful sources of gender stereotyping. Although some critics argue that the media simply reflect existing gender roles in society, others point out that the media have a unique ability to shape ideas. From children's cartoons to adult shows, television programs offer more male than female characters. Furthermore, the male characters act in a strikingly different manner from female ones. Male characters in both children's programs and adult programs are typically aggressive, constructive, and direct, while some female characters use their feminine wiles to get what they want by acting helpless, seductive, or deceitful.

Reality TV shows are an example of gender socialization that may perpetuate negative stereotypes. As television scheduling in prime-time has increasingly moved away from entertainment shows, such as scripted sitcoms, competitive- and relationship-oriented reality shows (that are modeled on the structure of fictionalized episodic television programming) have increasingly taken their place. The ultimate prize on many reality shows is either winning money or "winning" a person who is increasingly dehumanized and sexualized as the series progresses. Consider *The Bachelor* and *The Bachelorette*, for example. Twenty-five or more contestants complete for the "prize"—a human being who is supposed to be the person of the winner's dreams. In the process of playing the game, contestants put their dignity on the line and engage in highly sexualized activities that result in some being labeled with terms such as "Bitch," "Bimbo," "Gold-digger," "Tramp," "Nerd," "Loser," or similar slurs.

What effect do reality TV shows and similar forms of entertainment have on gender socialization? Like many other forms of media framing, the portrayal of "real" men and women as one-dimensional characters who should be judged on the basis of their attractiveness and their

Television reality shows such as *The Bachelor* often rely on stereotypical portrayals of women's behavior, such as these young women who are supposedly "out to get" a man at virtually any cost. How might such representations of women and men affect viewers' perceptions on what constitutes gender-appropriate behavior?

cunning ways has a negative effect on how individuals view each other and reinforces a pattern of gender stereotyping that promotes the idea that human beings are nothing more than commodities that can be bought and sold. Often those who show that they lack loyalty and cannot be trusted (as in Donald Trump's *The Apprentice* franchise) reap the rewards at the end, after lengthy discussions about gender-based characteristics that are valued or devalued by the other players. Often the devalued characteristics and attributes (such as being a Madonna, whore, crybaby, or bitch) are those most frequently associated with women.

Television and films influence our thinking about the appropriate behavior of women and men in the roles they play in everyday life. Because it is often necessary for an actor to overplay a comic role to gain laughs from the viewing audience or to exaggerate a dramatic role to make a quick impression on the audience, the portrayal of girls and women may (either intentionally or inadvertently) reinforce old stereotypes or create new ones. Consider, for example, the growing number of women who are depicted as having careers or professions (such as law or medicine) in which they may earn more income and have more power than female characters had in the past. Some of these women may be portrayed as well-adjusted individuals; however, many female characters are still shown as being too emotional and unable to resolve their personal problems or as sexual objects. An example is ABC TV's *Grey's Anatomy* where a number of the male and female characters have had sexual encounters or longer-term intimate relationships with each other. Some of these encounters occur while they are at work and supposedly busy saving patients' lives. Female characters who are supervisors or bosses are often portrayed as loud, bossy, and domineering individuals. Mothers in situation comedies frequently boss their children around and may have a Homer Simpson–type husband who is lazy and incompetent or who engages in aggressive verbal combat or crafty maneuvers to get around having to do something the woman has suggested.

Advertising further reinforces ideas about women and physical attractiveness. Women are bombarded with media images of ideal beauty and physical appearance, and eating problems such as anorexia and bulimia are a major concern associated with many media depictions of the ideal body image for women. With anorexia, a person has lost at least 25 percent of body weight owing to a compulsive fear of becoming fat. With bulimia, a person consumes large quantities of food and then purges the food by induced vomiting, excessive exercise, laxatives, or fasting. In both forms of eating disorders, distorted body image plays an important part, and this distorted image may be perpetuated by media depictions and advertisements. According to a now-classic study by media scholar Jean Kilbourne (1994:395):

> The current emphasis on excessive thinness for women is one of the clearest examples of advertising's power to influence cultural standards and consequent individual behavior. Body types, like clothing styles, go in and out of fashion, and are promoted by advertising. . . . The images in the mass media constantly reinforce the latest ideal—what is acceptable and what is out of date. . . . Advertising and the media indoctrinate us in these ideals, to the detriment of most women.

Clearly, Kilbourne's research remains relevant nearly two decades later. Although eating disorders cannot be attributed solely to advertising and the mass media, images of ultra-thin women constantly paraded before girls and women of all shapes and sizes do create an unrealistic expectation among all females that they should be extremely thin.

Why is awareness of gender socialization important for understanding sex discrimination and gender inequality? Social analysts who use a gender-role approach say that because parents, peers, teachers, and the media influence our perceptions of who we are and what our occupational preferences should be, gender-role socialization contributes to a gendered division of labor, creates a wage gap between women and men workers, and limits the occupational choices of women and men. However, some social analysts say that no direct evidence links gender role socialization to social inequality and that it is therefore important to use social structural analysis to examine gender inequality (see Reskin and Hartmann, 1986). In other words, these analysts believe that the decisions that people make (such as the schools they choose to attend and the occupations they choose to pursue) are linked not only to how they were socialized, but also to how society is structured. We now examine structural features that contribute to gender inequality.

CONTEMPORARY GENDER INEQUALITY

How do tasks in a society come to be defined as "men's work" or "women's work" and to be differentially rewarded? Many sociologists believe that social institutions and structures assign different roles and responsibilities to women and men and, in the process, restrict women's opportunities. According to feminist scholars, gender inequality is maintained and reinforced through individual and institutionalized sexism. The term *individual sexism* refers to individuals' beliefs and actions that are rooted in antifemale prejudice and stereotypic beliefs. The term *institutionalized sexism* refers to the power that men have to engage in sex discrimination at the organizational and institutional levels of society. This pattern of male domination and female subordination is known as *patriarchy*—**a hierarchical system of social organization in which cultural, political, and economic structures are controlled by men**. According to some analysts, the location of women in the workplace and on the economic pyramid is evidence of patriarchy in the United States (Epstein, 1988). In this section, we focus on five structural forms that contribute to contemporary gender inequality: the gendered division of labor, the wage gap, sexual harassment, the glass ceiling and the glass escalator, and the double shift.

The Gendered Division of Paid Work

Whether by choice or economic necessity, women have entered the paid labor force in unprecedented numbers in recent years. Women's employment participation is significantly higher today than it was in 1970 when 43 percent of U.S. women were in the labor force. In 2009, 59.2 percent of women were in the labor force, and this share has remained relatively stable (in the 59 percent range) throughout the first decade of this century. Among white women ages twenty-five to fifty-four, the increase is even more dramatic: nearly 76 percent of U.S. women currently are either employed or looking for a job. In fact, a higher proportion of women of all races, ages, and marital status groups are employed or seeking work than ever before (see Figure 4.1). At the same time, the proportion of male employees in the United States has declined from almost 80 percent in 1970 to 72 percent in 2009. Numerous events have contributed to this decline, but top factors include the closing of many factories and other industrial sites, decline of labor unions, and globalization of the workforce (where jobs go abroad and do not come back) are considered to be top factors. The Great Recession and the slow recovery in the 2000s had a negative effect on the job market. Between January 2007 and December 2009, 6.9 million workers were displaced from jobs they had held for at least three years, and men accounted for about 60 percent of those displaced (U.S. Bureau of Labor Statistics, 2010). Many men have been hard hit by lengthy periods

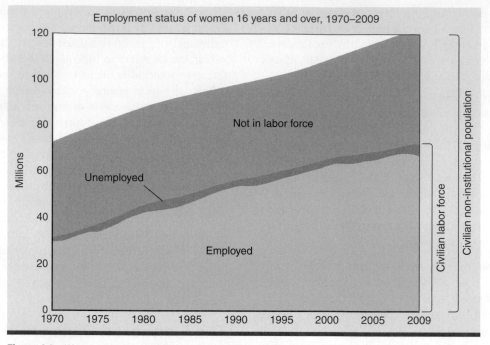

Figure 4.1   Women in the U.S. labor force, 1970 to 2009
Source: U.S. Bureau of Labor Statistics, 2010.

of unemployment or underemployment where job seekers take positions that pay less and have few benefits than their previous employment in hopes that something better will come along soon.

Although many people who know these statistics are optimistic about the gains women in the United States have made in employment, it should be noted that women's position as a social category in the labor force is lower than men's in terms of status, opportunities, and salaries. Today, most women and men are employed in occupations that are segregated by gender (see Table 4.1). The term *gender-segregated work* refers to the extent to which men and women are concentrated in different occupations and places of work (Reskin and Padavic, 1994). For example, women are predominant in word-processing pools and child-care centers, while men are predominant in the construction trades. Other individuals are employed in settings where both men and women are present. In these settings, however, women are employed predominantly in clerical or other support positions, while men hold supervisory, managerial, or other professional positions. Even in professions such as law, a gap remains. Despite an increase in the number of women entering the legal profession, about 84 percent of all law firm partners (owners) are men (U.S. Bureau of Labor Statistics, 2010). Gender-segregated work is most visible in occupations that remain more than 90 percent

female (for example, preschool and kindergarten teachers, registered and vocational nurses, receptionists, and word processors) or more than 90 percent male (for example, various kinds of construction workers, firefighters, truck drivers, and engineers) (U.S. Bureau of Labor Statistics, 2010).

Observers who are optimistic about women's gains point out that government statistics show women employed in a wide variety of organizations and holding nearly every kind of job. It is important to note, however, that the types of work women and men do still vary significantly and many employed women in the United States today are concentrated in **pink-collar occupations—relatively low-paying, nonmanual, semiskilled positions that are held primarily by women**—such as clerical workers; hosts and hostesses at restaurants, lounges, and coffee shops; medical assistants, and child-care workers. In twenty-first-century recession, women fared better than men in regard to employment largely became many females remain concentrated in so-called pink-collar jobs with lower pay levels.

Historically, women have also been overrepresented in the contingent workforce. **Contingent work is part-time work, temporary work, or subcontracted work that offers advantages to employers but can be detrimental to workers' welfare**. Many employers stress that having more contingent workers and fewer

TABLE 4.1 Employment Percentages by Occupation and Sex, 2009

Occupation	Men	Women
Total percentage[1]	100	100
Managerial and professional specialty	34.5	40.5
Management, business, and financial operations	16.7	13.9
Professional and related occupations	17.2	26.6
Sales and office occupations	17.0	32.2
Sales and related occupations	10.7	11.7
Office and administrative support	6.3	20.4
Service occupations	14.3	21.3
Production, transportation, and material moving occupations	17.0	5.2
Production occupations	7.5	3.3
Transportation and material moving	9.5	1.9
Natural resources, construction, and maintenance occupations	17.3	.9

[1] Percentages might not add to 100 because of rounding.

Source: U.S. Bureau of Labor Statistics, 2010.

permanent, full-time employees helps the company's bottom line and keeps corporations competitive in the global marketplace. Several employer benefits are associated with high rates of contingent work—cost containment, the ability to meet variations in product demand or labor supply, the desire to protect the employment of permanent staff, and the degree of complexity of laws associated with laying off permanent staff. However, this type of employment typically is not as beneficial for the worker as holding a full-time position that provides health insurance coverage, paid vacations and holidays, and employer-sponsored contributions to a pension plan. Some contingent workers, particularly parents of younger children, take contingent jobs because they need to take care of family responsibilities. Some women are drawn to contingent work for this reason; others find that they have few, if any, other options for employment.

Although the degree of gender segregation in the workplace and in professions, such as accounting, law, and medicine, has declined in the last three decades, occupational segregation by race and ethnicity persists. Today, a larger percentage of Asian American women (47 percent) and white women (41 percent) hold management, professional, and related occupations than black

or African American women (34 percent) or Latinas (25 percent). By contrast, in service occupations such as private household workers and cleaning crews in office buildings and hotels, we find a higher percentage of Latinas (32 percent) and African American women (29 percent) than white women (20 percent). Across racial and ethnic lines, women continue to be concentrated in jobs in which they receive lower wages and fewer benefits on average than men (U.S. Bureau of Labor Statistics, 2010).

The Wage Gap

The *wage (pay) gap*—**the disparity between women's and men's earnings**—is the best-documented consequence of gender-segregated work (Reskin and Padavic, 1994). Despite changing times and women's increased labor force participation, in 2009, women working full time in the United States still earned just 77 percent, on average, of what men earned. This 23 percent pay gap makes a significant difference in median annual earnings for women and for men in many occupations. Since families have increasingly

Explore the Concept
Social Explorer Activity: Income Inequality by Gender on mysoclab.com

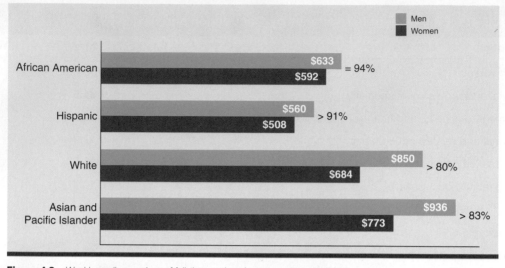

Figure 4.2 Weekly median earnings of full-time workers by race and gender, 2010
Source: U.S. Bureau of Labor Statistics, 2011.

relied on women's income to make ends meet, how much women earn is of concern to everyone, not just women. In some families women are the only wage earners. For example, about one-third of employed mothers are the sole breadwinners for their families because they are single parents or their spouses are unemployed or otherwise not in the paid labor force (AAUW, 2011).

No matter what their race or ethnic group, men earn more than women of the same racial or ethnic group (see Figure 4.2). The weekly median earnings for women who worked full time in 2010 were $669 per week compared to $824 for men. This means that a woman who works full time makes about 81 cents for every dollar that a man makes. The pay gap varies by race-ethnicity as well as gender. Hispanic (Latino/a) women earn 91 cents for every dollar that a Hispanic (Latino) man makes, based on $560 in weekly wages for men and $508 for women. A similar pattern exists in the weekly median earnings of African American men ($633) and women ($592); in this case, women earn 94 percent of what males earn. In sharp contrast, Asian American men earn $936 in weekly median earnings, as compared to $773 for Asian American women (or 83 cents for every dollar earned). For white Americans, women earn 80 percent of what men earn, based on men's weekly earnings of $850 as compared to women's earnings of $684. Because white American men constitute the largest demographic group in the labor force, they are often used for comparison purposes: Hispanic women (Latinas) earn 60 cents for every dollar that white men earn; African American women earn 70 cents; white American women earn 80

cents; and Asian American women earn 91 cents for every dollar that white men earn (AAUW, 2011).

The wage gap varies by age: The older the worker, the larger the gap. This may be true in part because younger workers tend to have about the same amount of work experience and to be concentrated in entry-level jobs. Thus, between the ages of twenty and twenty-four, women earn an average of 93 cents for every dollar that men earn. However, women between the ages of twenty-five and thirty-four earn only 89 cents for every dollar that men earn. Women between the ages of thirty-five and forty-four earn only 77 cents per dollar; and by ages fifty-five to sixty-four, the amount has dropped to 75 cents for each dollar men earn (AAUW, 2011).

Social analysts suggest that the higher wage gap for older workers probably reflects a number of factors, including the fact that women in those age groups tend to have, on average, less overall work experience and less time with their present employer than have men of the same age (Herz and Wootton, 1996). As Figure 4.3 shows, the wage gap has narrowed somewhat between women and men over the last few years, but much of the decrease in wage disparity can be attributed to a decline in men's average earnings (adjusted for inflation) rather than to a significant increase in women's earnings.

For pay equity to occur between men and women, there has to be a broad-based commitment to **compa-rable worth—the belief that wages ought to reflect the worth of a job, not the gender or race of the worker**. To determine the comparable worth of different kinds of jobs, researchers break a specific job into components

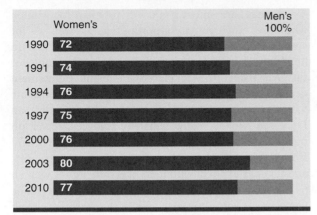

Figure 4.3   The U.S. wage gap: Women's earnings as a percentage of men's earnings, selected years 1990 to 2010
Source: U.S. Bureau of Labor Statistics, 2010.

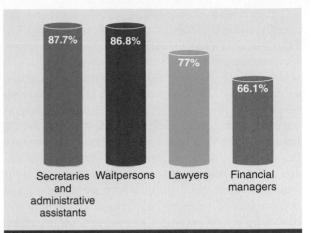

Figure 4.4   U.S. wage gap in selected occupations

- *Across cultures, parents tend to socialize daughters and sons differently, including the clothes that the children are encouraged to wear. What gender-related messages do clothes convey? What messages about gender did you receive from your parents? Do you wish to convey the same messages to your children?*

- *Take a close look at this picture. What do you notice about the two lines? Social scientists have pointed out that gender socialization occurs in many ways, including how teachers organize school activities by sex.*

- *As more women have entered the paid workforce, they have encountered a double shift at home. According to researchers, employed women still do most of the daily household chores such as taking care of the children. Is this photo a hopeful sign for the future?*

- *According to conflict and feminist perspectives, many women continue to face sexism even after they attain top positions in the workplace. Zoe Cruz, shown here, was fired from Morgan Stanley, a Wall Street financial services firm, where she had risen to upper management because her boss "lost confidence" in her ability. www.CartoonStock.com*

Source: U.S. Bureau of Labor Statistics, 2010.

to determine (1) how much education, training, and skills are required; (2) how much responsibility a person in that position has for others' work; and (3) what the working conditions are. Researchers then allocate points for each component to determine whether or not men and women are being paid equitably for their work (Lorber, 1994). For pay equity to exist, men and women in occupations that receive the same number of points must be paid the same. However, pay equity exists for very few jobs. (See Figure 4.4 for a comparison of men's and women's earnings in selected occupations.)

Comparable worth is an important issue for men as well as women. Male workers in female-dominated jobs such as nursing, secretarial work, and elementary teaching pay an economic penalty for their choice of work. If women were compensated fairly, an employer could not undercut men's wages by hiring women at a cheaper rate (Kessler-Harris, 1990).

Sexual Harassment

Sexual harassment is a form of intentional gender discrimination that includes all unwelcome sexual attention that affects an employee's job conditions or creates a hostile work environment such as the one alleged in the Walmart lawsuit discussed at the beginning of this chapter. According to the U.S. Equal Employment Opportunity Commission (EEOC), sexual harassment in the workplace is a form of sex discrimination that violates Title VII of the Civil Rights Act of 1964:

> Unwelcome sexual advances, requests for sexual favors, and other verbal or physical conduct of a sexual nature constitutes sexual harassment when

submission to or rejection of this conduct explicitly or implicitly affects an individual's employment, unreasonably interferes with an individual's work performance or creates an intimidating, hostile or offensive work environment. (U.S. Equal Employment Opportunity Commission [EEOC], 2002)

As this definition suggests, sexual harassment can occur in various forms, including supervisor–subordinate harassment, subordinate–supervisor harassment, and peer–peer harassment. It also occurs in other types of institutions. Although most reported cases of sexual harassment involve the harassment of women by men, the victim as well as the harasser may be a woman or a man (U.S. EEOC, 2002).

People who are accused of sexual harassment frequently claim that their actions were merely harmless expressions of (supposedly) mutual sexual attraction. However, sexual harassment is not about attraction; it is about abuse of power. Sexual harassment constitutes a form of intimidation and aggression: The recipient has no choice in the encounter or has reason to fear repercussions if she or he declines. Some men are able to harass because they hold economic power over women (e.g., bosses and supervisors who control promotions and raises; college professors who give grades and write letters of recommendation); others are able to harass because they hold gender-based power (e.g., boyfriends, husbands, and others who have power rooted in cultural patterns of male dominance and backed up by the threat of violence and the ability to rape).

Sexual harassment occurs in a wide variety of settings and across lines of race, ethnicity and class. However, some of the individuals must vulnerable to harassment are low-income women, particularly recent immigrants who may be in the country illegally and fear deportation. Alleged sexual assaults of hotel housekeepers and nannies in private households are examples of situations in which powerless women come into contact with powerful males who use their prominent positions and their physical strength as men to assault women who they think will not come forward to complain and who, if they do report the attack, will not be believed by others because of their subordinate position in the workplace and the world. In reporting these alleged crimes, the media keep readers informed, but they may also sensationalize the stories to sell papers, improve TV ratings, or increase the number of website hits.

The media often sensationalize cases of sexual assault. In August of 2011, hotel workers provided a media opportunity outside a New York City court building where French politician Dominique Strauss-Kahn had been ordered to appear on charges of sexually assaulting a hotel housekeeper. The so-called "DSK" case made headlines for weeks.

Sexual harassment is a costly problem for women who lose employment opportunities, as well as for employers who may lose millions of dollars a year in litigation, low productivity, absenteeism, and employee turnover related to workplace harassment. Harassment occurs not only at work but often during the commute to work in cities such as New York, Chicago, and San Francisco where many female employees travel on public sidewalks or public transportation to get to and from work. After being the object of catcalls, groping, and sexually explicit comments, it is difficult for women to perform their jobs. Frequent harassment in public places on the way to work and in the workplace itself contributes to lack of job satisfaction, and high rates of absenteeism and turnovers (Kearl, 2010). Sexual harassment and other forms of blatant and subtle discrimination in the workplace also contribute to the institutional barriers that limit women's opportunities to rise to the top positions in corporations and other occupational settings.

The Glass Ceiling and the Glass Escalator/Elevator

Feminist researchers have used the advancement (or lack of advancement) of women into top-tier management jobs as a litmus test for how well women are faring in the labor force as a whole. Studies continue to confirm that women hold a small percentage of the top positions. Although more women have moved up the corporate ladder, many of them have encountered a variety of barriers as they tried to enter the lucrative and prestigious top positions of their occupations. This effect is known as the *glass ceiling*—**the invisible institutional barrier, based on attitudinal or organization bias, that prevents qualified and deserving people from advancing upward to top management-level positions in their organization**. Such barriers exist because of prejudice on the basis of sex, age, political or religious affiliation, weight-based appearance norms, or potentially devalued attributes or characteristics. Discrimination against individuals on the basis of these characteristics is illegal; however, this does not keep such practices from being prevalent in most countries. Research has highlighted the glass ceiling in businesses and organizations ranging from college sports administration and higher education to investment banking, surgery, and other medical specialties.

The glass ceiling is particularly evident in the nation's *Fortune* 500 companies (the 500 largest companies based in the United States). In 2010, men held close to 85 percent of all board seats. White men accounted for most of this percentage at 77.6 percent, as compared to minority men who held 6.8 percent. White women held 12.7 percent of board seats, and only fifteen of those companies had a woman as chief executive officer of the corporation (see Table 4.2). Collectively, minority women held less than 3 percent of *Fortune* 500 board seats, with African American women holding 1.9 percent, Hispanic women 0.7 percent, and Asian Pacific Islander women 0.3 percent. Overall, women of all racial and ethnic categories and people of color lost ground on *Fortune* 500 boards between 2004 and 2010. Even though more qualified women and minorities were available for board service than in the past, few were chosen for these positions. This suggests a persistent glass ceiling that contributes to a significant underrepresentation of women (and minorities) in board leadership positions. These figures also suggest that corporations are not gaining valuable input from women and minority men who make up 66 percent of the U.S. population because of the lack of inclusion

of individuals from diverse populations in the corporate powerhouses (UnityFirst.com, 2011).

As previously mentioned, the glass ceiling exists in many occupations and professions. In investment banking where macho risk-taking has been the norm in recent years, only 17 women are among the 220 most senior bankers on executive committees at 20 of the biggest investment banks, and 8 of those are heads of human resources or communications. These positions are considered to be more women oriented and they are not high-profile positions that participate in deal making (*Wall Street Journal*, 2011). Shifting to higher education, many women have experience the glass ceiling in terms of tenure, promotion, access to grants, and the ability to move to top administrative positions, if they so desire (Gardiner, Tiggermann, Kearns, and Marshall, 2007). In college sports administration, a similar picture emerges: underrepresentation of women in athletic administration positions may be partly attributed to the perceived view among those doing the hiring that masculinity—as evidenced by attributes such as aggressiveness and competitiveness—is necessary to successful perform these management roles (Henderson, Grappendorf, and Burton, 2011).

Now to shift to a profession where popular perception holds that women are getting ahead quickly—becoming a physician or surgeon. Although the number of women graduating from medical schools has nearly doubled over the past thirty years, and three times as many women have become surgical residents and surgeons since 1970, researchers believe that they have found a persistent glass ceiling that prevents female surgeons from attaining full professorships at medical schools throughout the United States. The pipeline grows even narrower at the top: Women account for less than one-third of all surgeons who move into senior ranks at medical institutions (Eckhard, 2011). Consider, for example, the disproportionate rate of female full professors in surgery, as compared to the rate for men: About 35 percent of male surgeons become full professors, as sharply contrasted to slightly more than 10 percent of women seeking similar positions (Eckhard, 2011).

Overall, women are most likely to reach top positions in the service sector (for example, banking and diversified finance, publishing, retailing, food services, and entertainment), a sector in which they have traditionally been employed in great numbers. Women fare worse in male-dominated businesses such as mining, crude oil, brokerages, and manufacturing.

Unlike women who enter male-dominated occupations, men who enter female-dominated occupations

TABLE 4.2 *Fortune* 500 Companies with a Woman as CEO

Company	Rank
Sara Lee	180
Yahoo	343
WellPoint	31
Sunoco	78
Western Union	413
Xerox	152
Avon Products	228
Reynolds American	272
DuPont	86
TJX	119
PepsiCo	50
Kraft Foods	53
Rite Aid	89
BJ's Wholesale Club	232
Archer Daniels Midland	27

Source: theathleticmindset.com, 2011.

are apt to find little difficulty in rising to the top of their occupation. In research on men working as registered nurses, elementary teachers, librarians, and social workers, sociologist Christine L. Williams (1995) found that men tended to rise in disproportionate numbers to administrative positions at the top of these occupations. Williams (1995:12) calls the upward movement of men in "women's professions" the glass escalator effect because, as she notes, "like being on an invisible 'up' escalator, men must struggle to remain in the lower (i.e., 'feminine') levels of their professions." Other researchers have used the term *glass elevator* to convey a similar meaning: On an elevator, a person has to do even less physically to "move up." According to Williams (1995), when men move up in traditionally female-dominated occupations, they tend to move into more "masculine" specialties. Male librarians, for example, often move into high-technology computer information specialties and administration. In contrast, women in male-dominated occupations typically find they are bumping their heads on the glass ceiling.

Other research using data from a national sample of registered nurses found that, contrary to the *vertical* pattern of occupational stratification represented by the glass escalator/elevator metaphor, sex segregation is often *horizontal* because men and women are disproportionately clustered in specific gendered specialties. Male nurses often gravitate toward areas of nursing that are more "masculine," such working in the emergency room as opposed to labor and delivery (K. A. Snyder and Green, 2008).

The Double Shift

Although there have been dramatic changes in the participation of women in the labor force, the division of labor by sex has remained essentially unchanged in many families. Although more married women now share responsibility for earning part—or all—of the family income, many married men do not participate in routine domestic chores (Reskin and Padavic, 1994). Consequently, many employed women must deal with a double work load. In the words of sociologist Arlie Hochschild (1989), women with dual responsibilities as wage earners and unpaid household workers work "the second shift." In countries such as India, the problem is great enough that some analysts use the term *double-shift stress syndrome*,

> **▶ Read the Document**
> *Thinking About the Baby: Gender and Divisions of Infant Care* on **mysoclab.com**

which they attribute to symptoms of stress combined with psychosocial factors of constantly trying to get a variety of tasks done and maintain personal and family time as well (*Times of India*, 2011).

Not only does the relative number of hours spent on housework differ widely between women and men, but the kinds of chores men and women do also vary significantly. Women do many of the daily chores such as taking care of children, making beds, and cooking and cleaning up after meals. Men are more likely to do chores that do not have to be done every day. For example, men typically mow the lawn, repair cars or other equipment, and do home improvements (Shelton, 1992). Although some kinds of housework can be put off, young children's needs cannot be ignored or delayed, so daily domestic duties in families with young children consume a great deal of time and energy. A sick child or a school event that cannot be scheduled around work causes additional

As more women have entered the paid workforce, many man are more actively involved in childcare. How might this change influence gender roles in the future?

stress for parents, especially mothers. Furthermore, more and more women are becoming members of "the sandwich generation." In other words, they are caught, sandwiched, between the needs of their young children and those of older relatives for whom they are often the primary caregivers. In an effort to keep up with family obligations while working full time or part time, many women spend a large portion of their earnings on day-care and elder-care centers, prepared foods and meals from fast-food restaurants, and laundry and dry cleaning (Bergmann, 1986).

When sociologists conduct research on participation in household work, both men and women state that working couples should share household responsibilities. However, when it gets down to who actually does what, most studies find that women, even those who hold full-time jobs, do most of the work. According to Arlie Hochschild (1989), many women try to solve their time crunch by forgoing leisure activities and sleep.

PERSPECTIVES ON GENDER INEQUALITY

Unlike functionalist and conflict perspectives, which focus on macrolevel sources of gender inequality, interactionist perspectives typically focus on social constructs such as language. It is language, interactionists say, that structures our thinking and discourse about domination and subordination.

The Symbolic Interactionist Perspective

For symbolic interactionists, who view society as the sum of all people's interactions, language is extremely significant in defining social realities because it provides people with shared meanings and social realities. Historically, what men have thought, written, and concluded have been the givens of our discourse (Peterson and Runyan, 1993). Today, however, English and other languages are being criticized for *linguistic sexism*—that is, for words and patterns of communication that ignore, devalue, or make sex objects of one sex or the other, most often women.

Linguistic sexism, some analysts believe, perpetuates traditional gender role stereotypes and reinforces male dominance. These analysts note that the idea that women are secondary to men in importance is embedded in the English language: The masculine form (*he*) is used to refer to human beings generally, and words such as *chairman* and *mankind* are considered to include both men and

women (C. Miller and Swift, 1991). When a woman enters a profession such as medicine or law, she is frequently referred to as a "female doctor" or "woman lawyer"; such terms linguistically protect these male-dominated professions from invasion by females (Lindsey, 1994).

Language can also be used to devalue women by referring to them in terms that reinforce the notion that they are sex objects. Terms such as *fox*, *bitch*, *babe*, or *doll* further devalue women by ascribing petlike, child-like, or toylike attributes to them (K. L. Adams and Ware, 1995). According to one analyst, at least 220 terms exist for sexually promiscuous women, but only 22 terms exist for promiscuous men (Stanley, 1972).

Research by scholars in a variety of disciplines has demonstrated not only the importance of language in patterning our thoughts, but also how gender—and the hierarchy it constructs—is built into the English language (Peterson and Runyan, 1993). According to sociologists Claire M. Renzetti and Daniel J. Curran (1995:151), "Given that women are denigrated, unequally defined, and often ignored by the English language, it serves not only to reflect their secondary status relative to men in our society, but also to reinforce it."

According to symbolic interactionists, male dominance is also perpetuated through nonverbal communication such as bodily movement, posture, eye contact, use of personal space, and touching. Men typically control more space than women do, whether they are sitting or standing. Men tend to invade women's personal space by standing close to them, touching them, or staring at them. Such actions are not necessarily sexual in connotation, but to symbolic interactionists, they reinforce male dominance. However, when a man nudges and fondles a flight attendant or a coworker in the office, these actions do have sexual overtones that cannot be dismissed. Sexual harassment cases show that women do not appreciate such acts and feel threatened by them, especially if the toucher is the employer (Lindsey, 1994:79).

Although the symbolic interactionist perspective has been criticized for ignoring the larger, structural factors that perpetuate gender inequality, it is important to note that language and communication patterns are embedded in the structure of society and pass from generation to generation through the socialization process.

The Functionalist Perspective

In focusing on macrolevel issues affecting gender inequality, functionalists frequently examine employment opportunities and the wage gap between men and women.

According to such early functionalists as Talcott Parsons (1955), gender inequality is inevitable because of the biological division of labor: Men generally are physically stronger than women and have certain abilities and interests, whereas women, as the only sex able to bear and nurse children, have their own abilities and interests. Given the biological attributes, Parsons said, men find themselves more suited to *instrumental* (goal-oriented) *tasks* and women to *expressive* (emotionally oriented) *tasks*. In the home, therefore, men perform such instrumental tasks as providing economic support and making the most important decisions for the family, while women perform such expressive tasks as nurturing children and providing emotional support for all family members. The division of labor by gender ensures that important societal tasks—such as procreation and the socialization of children—are fulfilled and that the family is socially and economically stable.

According to Parsons, this division of labor continues in the workplace, where women again do expressive work and men again do instrumental work. Thus, women cluster in occupations that require expressive work, such as elementary school teaching, nursing, and secretarial work, because of their interests and abilities. Women also are concentrated in specific specialties within professions such as law and medicine because of their aptitude for expressive work and their desire to spend more time with their families than men, who are in more lucrative specialties, are able to spend. For example, many women in law specialize in family law, and many women in medicine specialize in pediatrics (infants and children), obstetrics and gynecology (women), or family practice. In corporations, women are thought to be more adept at public relations and human resources, positions in which many women are clustered; men are viewed as more adept at financial management. In recent years, however, critics have rejected the dichotomy between men's instrumental work and women's expressive work set forth by functionalists. These critics have noted that the functionalist explanation of gender inequality does not take into account sex discrimination and other structural barriers that make some educational and occupational opportunities more available to men than to women. It also fails to examine the underlying power relations between women and men and does not consider the fact that society places unequal value on tasks assigned to men and women.

Other functionalist explanations of gender inequality focus on the human capital that men and women bring to the workplace. According to human capital explanations, what individuals earn is based on choices

Many women in law specialize in family law, and many women in medicine specialize in pediatrics (infants and children), obstetrics and gynecology (women), or family practice. In corporations, women are thought to be more adept at public relations and human resources, positions in which many women are clustered; men are viewed as more adept at financial management.

they have made, including choices about the kinds of training and experience they accumulate. For example, human capital analysts argue that women diminish their human capital when they leave the labor force to engage in childbearing and child-care activities. While women are out of the labor force, their human capital deteriorates from nonuse. When they return to work, they earn lower wages than men do because the women have fewer years of work experience and their human capital in the form of education and training may have become obsolete.

Critics of the human capital model note that it is based on the false assumption that all people, regardless of gender, race, or other attributes, are evaluated and paid fairly on the basis of their education, training, and other job-enhancing characteristics. It fails to acknowledge that white women and people of color tend to be paid less even when they are employed in male-dominated occupations and take no time off for family duties.

Conflict and Feminist Perspectives

Conflict perspectives on gender inequality are based on the assumption that social life is a continuous struggle in which members of powerful groups (males, in this case) seek to maintain control of scarce resources such as social, economic, and political superiority. By dominating individual women and commanding social institutions, men maintain positions of privilege and power. However, conflict theorists note, not all men

are equally privileged: Men in the upper classes have greater economic power because they control elite positions in corporations, universities, the mass media, and government.

Conflict theorists using a Marxist approach believe that gender inequality results primarily from capitalism and private ownership of the means of production. Basing their work on this Marxist approach, socialist feminists state that under capitalism, men gain control over property and over women. Thus, capitalism exploits women in the workplace, and patriarchy exploits women at home. According to this perspective, capitalists benefit from the gendered division of labor in the workplace because they can pay women lower wages and derive higher profits. At the same time, individual men benefit from the unpaid work women do at home. The capitalist economic system is maintained because women reproduce the next generation of workers while providing current employees (often including themselves) with food, clean clothes, and other goods and services that are necessary for those who must show up at the workplace each day (Hartmann, 1976).

Unlike socialist feminists, *radical feminists* focus exclusively on patriarchy as the primary source of gender inequality. From this perspective, men's oppression of women is deliberate, with ideological justification provided by other institutions such as the media and religion. *Liberal feminists* believe that gender inequality is rooted in gender-role socialization, which perpetuates women's lack of equal civil rights and educational opportunities. *Black feminists* believe that women of color face inequalities based on the multiplicative effect of race, class, and gender as simultaneous forces of oppression (Andersen and Collins, 2009).

Conflict and feminist perspectives have been criticized for their emphasis on male dominance without a corresponding analysis of how men might be oppressed by capitalism and/or patriarchy.

GLOBAL GENDER INEQUALITY

Many social analysts argue that patriarchy and capitalism have maintained and perpetuated gender inequality worldwide. Today, millions of girls and women are the victims of physical and sexual abuse, and authorities believe that the number of cases is so seriously underreported that we do not know the full nature and extent of this problem. According to the United Nations, approximately one out of every three women in the world has been beaten, coerced into sex, or otherwise abused in her lifetime, usually by someone she knows (Yost and

Rodriguez, 2010). Similarly, a World Bank study found that gender-based violence (such as rape and domestic violence) is a greater cause of ill health and death among women between the ages of fifteen and forty-four than cancer, motor vehicle accidents, war, or malaria (Yost and Rodriguez, 2010). Likewise, social policies such as China's one-child rule have reduced the number of girls born in that nation (see Box 4.3 on page 96), and patterns of female genital mutilation and violence against girls and women perpetuate women's powerless condition. Although infant mortality rates typically are higher for boys than for girls, there are regions of the world where gender-based discrimination has served to outweigh any biological advantage that girls otherwise might have. In regard to female genital mutilation, UN studies estimate that in some African countries, more than half of all girls and women have been subjected to female genital mutilation (referred to by some as "female circumcision").

Systematic patterns of gender discrimination are the result of centuries of maltreatment of girls and women, and these patterns are maintained and perpetuated based on tradition, customs, religious beliefs, family socialization, and prevalent economic and political conditions. Breaking the virtual chains that currently bind many women is extremely difficult. Despite calls from some international organizations for greater gender equality, women remain significantly underrepresented worldwide in governments, political parties, and at the United Nations.

Is paid employment the solution for producing greater gender equality? This is a difficult question to answer. It appears that employment alone does not greatly reduce the problem: Worldwide, more women are employed outside the household today than in previous decades. In all regions except northern Africa and western Asia, women constitute at least one-third of the workforce. In middle- and low-income nations, self-employment, part-time work, and home-based jobs have offered some opportunities for women, but these forms of employment typically provide little security, few benefits, and low income and sometime bring hazardous materials into the women's homes. Outside employment frequently is not much better: These jobs are often concentrated in a few occupations within employment sectors that are characterized by low wages, little or no authority and benefits for employees, and virtually no job security. From high-income nations (such as the United States and Japan) to low-income nations, women typically earn less than men in the paid workforce, and women's opportunities to attain the better-paid positions are restricted.

Revisiting the One-Child Policy in China

When a son is born, Let him sleep on the bed,

Clothe him with fine clothes, And give him jade to play . . .

When a daughter is born, Let her sleep on the ground,

Wrap her in common wrappings, And give broken tiles to play . . .

—*Traditional Chinese thinking on the divergent value of male and female babies as recorded in the 1000–700 BC "Book of Songs"(quoted in Baculinao, 2004)*

This age-old bias against girls, combined with a one-child-only policy implemented in China in the late 1970s and early 1980s, has produced international interest and concern about baby girls in China because of parents' distinct preference for male children. Recently, government officials announced that they were intensifying efforts to protect girls and to address the gender imbalance of newborn babies (BBC News, 2010). What is the gender imbalance? In 2010, the ratio of births in China was close to 120 boys for every 100 girls, as contrasted with the international average of about 106 boys to every 100 girls (BBC News, 2010). How did this imbalance occur? In the past, with China's strict family planning policies, some parents wanted to prevent female births so that they can count on their sons to help them out with the work and to take care of them when they are older. Over the decades, some reports showed an increase in sex-selective abortions; however, Chinese officials and social analysts around the world have debated the extent to which these abortions actually occurred (Denoble, 2010). Sex-selective abortion refers to a situation in which an individual or couple decides to terminate a pregnancy solely on the basis of the sex of the fetus. This type of abortion does not include situations where an abortion is chosen for health-related concerns or any reason other

than that the fetus is a member of the unwanted sex. In some cases, the parents kill their infant daughters (infanticide). Other parents sell their infant girls to families who want a daughter or put them up for international adoption. Some reports indicate that as many as three million babies in China are hidden by their parents every year to sidestep the one-child policy (M. Moore, 2010).

In 2011, sex ratios at birth and in the first years of life show that millions of female fetuses and infant girls are "missing" in China. Practices such as sex-selective abortion, infanticide, and the selling of baby girls constitute a global social problem that is harmful not only to girls and women in China but that also produces adverse effects on these nations—and their citizens—for decades to come. One effort to reduce the imbalance between male and female infants encourages the birth of girls and suggests that people should show more respect for females. The program speaks out against female infanticide, pre-birth sex selection, and other types of behavior that are detrimental to baby girls. Other analysts believe that the one-child policy will die off on its own accord given the rapidly aging population of China where the first children born under the one-child policy now face a future that includes taking care of elderly parents alone and paying into massive pension plans for the care of ever-increasing numbers of elderly persons.

Questions for Consideration

1. Do people in the United States equally value male children and female children? What examples can you give to support your answer?

2. How do social policy and law influence what we think of as the "ideal family"?

3. Should the government of any nation play a central role in determining how many children a couple should have? In determining the gender of the children?

Problems of economic opportunity for women are further complicated by high rates of global illiteracy and low levels of educational attainment. It is estimated that women account for 64 percent of the nearly 800 million illiterate people worldwide, and there is little hope that these numbers will be reduced in the early decades of the twenty-first century (United Nations Educational, Scientific and Cultural Organization [UNESCO], 2011). The levels of educational attainment in some countries among those women who are literate is also problematic.

In most nations girls and women actively seek educational opportunities when they are able to do so; however, oppressive political regimes and local customs have conspired to keep women undereducated. This is a problem not only for the women but also for their children and other family members. It means that the women will be less equipped to educate their children for changing times in their nation and that the women will not have the necessary skills for becoming economically self-sufficient. Although the gender gap is closing somewhat in the United States, women worldwide still lag far behind men in educational attainment. This disparity is particularly pronounced in some countries in Africa and southern Asia.

Around the globe, women's problems—including violence, illiteracy, and lack of educational and employment opportunity—are further exacerbated by poor medical facilities and health crises such as HIV/AIDS. Although life expectancy has generally been increasing worldwide, AIDS has taken a devastating toll on the population in regions such as southern Africa, particularly among girls and women. Women now account for almost half of all HIV/AIDS cases worldwide, and in regions with high HIV prevalence such as southern Africa, young women are at greater risk than young men. Another major problem is the high rate of maternal mortality (dying from pregnancy-related causes). Inadequate health care facilities and lack of access to the medical care that does exist contribute to high rates of maternal mortality and shorter life expectancies for many women. The disparities in maternal mortality vary widely across regions. According to one report, a Nigerian woman's lifetime risk of dying from pregnancy-related complications is 1 in 7 as opposed to 1 in 48,000 in Ireland. As people in the United States and other high-income nations continue to be concerned about economic instability, political and economic leaders often turn their attention to issues other than the rights of women, but as some women's advocacy groups have pointed out, the problems of girls and women worldwide are the problems of all people.

IS THERE A SOLUTION TO GENDER-RELATED INEQUALITY?

Although the rights and working conditions of women in the United States have improved during the past forty years, much remains to be done before gender equality truly can exist. In many families and in many workplaces, women's roles have changed significantly, and men's roles have undergone important changes as well. Men have greater opportunities to express their emotions, be active fathers in the lives of their children, and sometimes feel less pressure to be the sole or primary financial provider in the family. However, changes for both men and women have extracted their price as changing roles, responsibilities, and social norms have brought about new stresses and conflict within families, occupations, and the larger society.

With regard to how we might specifically go about reducing or solving gender inequality, a point that was made in previous chapters bears repeating: How we view social problems affects how we think the problem should be solved.

Functionalist/Conservative Solutions to the Problem of Gender Inequality

Some functionalist analysts believe that although women and men have different gender roles, this does not necessarily mean that gender inequality exists. From this approach, the division of labor by gender ensures that important societal tasks, such as childbearing and the socialization of children, are fulfilled and that families remain stable, dependable social institutions. If we accept the assumption that *gender differences* do not necessarily equal *gender inequality*, then a social problem does not truly exist.

Most functionalists and conservative analysts acknowledge that, in day-to-day life, gender differences can *contribute* to the problems that at least some women face. By way of example, sexual harassment is more likely to be encountered by women than by men; some women may find job and pay opportunities limited by their lack of human capital in the workplace; and child-care responsibilities in some families are unequally and unfairly divided between the father and the mother. However, these are issues relating to specific aspects of social life, rather than a "catchall" category of sexism and gender inequality. In other words, there is not an all encompassing gender "problem," and there is no overall solution that would eliminate or reduce gender-related problems.

From this perspective, the primary "solution" to problems arising from gender differences is to be found in better education and in the strengthening of existing social institutions. Education contributes to women's human capital and thus to their ability to earn wages and hold positions that are comparable to those of men. Strengthening other social institutions such as the family promotes having a two-parent household in which both parents share household responsibilities and are active participants in rearing their children.

Conflict/Liberal Solutions to the Problem of Gender Inequality

Some conflict theorists view elimination of all gender-based discrimination as the primary solution for gender inequality, and they strongly disagree with functionalist/conservative ideas that efforts to promote gender equality are a threat to family life and family values. Instead, theorists using a Marxist approach state that gender equality will come about only when capitalism and patriarchy are abolished: Capitalism exploits women in the workplace, and patriarchy exploits women in the home. However, it would be extremely difficult, if not impossible, to end capitalism as we know it and to abolish all forms of male domination over women, so many theorists and political analysts look for less sweeping solutions to this problem. For example, some social activists and women's organizations establish funds to help women file lawsuits when they believe they have been the objects of sexual harassment or discrimination in the workplace. Although such activities do not solve the problem of gender inequality at the societal level, they call attention to the fact that such problems still exist, and they may help individuals and small groups of workers gain opportunities and social justice.

Liberal feminists and liberal political analysts typically believe that gender inequality can be reduced through legislation that seeks to reduce discrimination and by programs that provide more opportunities for women. These analysts emphasize the importance of equality in all areas of social life, including families, education, politics, and work. From this perspective, the best way to produce change is through government policies that are designed to bring about greater gender equality in activities ranging from college sports teams and politics to hiring and promotion in the workplace. Similarly, sexual harassment and violence against women must be actively discouraged, and perpetrators of such offenses must be vigorously prosecuted. Some liberal analysts also highlight the ways in which race, class, gender, and age intersect to produce multiple dimensions of inequality that are particularly harmful for women of color: Social change to reduce gender inequality must simultaneously deal with issues of race, class, and age if equality for all women is the goal.

Symbolic Interactionist Solutions to the Problem of Gender Inequality

Symbolic interactionists think that gender inequality can be reduced only when people redefine social realities and eliminate problems such as linguistic sexism. In their view, language is one way in which male superiority over women is expressed and reinforced in the culture. As a result, language should be modified so that it no longer conveys notions of male superiority and female inferiority, which are then transmitted intergenerationally through the socialization process.

Since symbolic interactionists focus on microlevel processes, one way to reduce or eliminate gender inequality is to change the process of socialization. Emphasis in popular culture on sexualized images of women contributes to the devaluation of all women, particularly those who are not young, thin, and comparable to media portrayals of what women should be like and how they should act. Similarly, the representation of men as either strong, wealthy, and powerful, or as "dudes," slackers, and evil men in media portrayals creates distorted images of men that others may seek to imitate. According to some symbolic interactionists, media representations such as these must be modified before people will truly accept the wider range of roles and responsibilities that should be available to women as well as men.

Finally, to some symbolic interactionists, gender and issues of gender inequality are—like beauty—"in the eye of the beholder," and individuals typically have their own perceptions about the social interactions that occur in their own life. Although symbolic interactionist views on the solution to gender inequality focus primarily on microlevel issues, these observations highlight the ways in which social interaction and popular culture influence not only our individual thinking but also beliefs and values that are embedded in the larger structure of society.

What do you think might reduce gender inequality in the United States? Could your solutions be applied to similar problems in other nations? Why or why not?

SUMMARY

✓ Study and Review on mysoclab.com

■ **How does sex differ from gender?**
Sex is the biological aspects of being male or female; gender is the socially constructed differences between females and males. In short, sex is what we (generally) are born with; gender is what we acquire through socialization.

■ **What are the primary socializing agents?**
The key socializing agents are parents, peers, teachers and schools, sports, and the media, all of which may reinforce gender stereotypes and gender-based inequalities as they attempt to teach gender-appropriate behavior.

■ **How are sexism and patriarchy related?**
Individual and institutional sexism are maintained and reinforced by patriarchy, a hierarchical system in which cultural, political, and economic structures are dominated by males.

■ **What are some of the primary causes of gender inequality?**
Gender inequality results from economic, political, and educational discrimination against women as evidenced in gender-segregated work, which in turn results in a disparity—or wage gap—between women's and men's earnings. Even when women are employed in the same job as men, on average they do not receive the same (or comparable) pay.

■ **What is the second shift, and why is it a problem for women?**
The second shift is the unpaid household work performed by employed women. Many women have a second shift because of their dual responsibilities in the workplace and at home. The typical woman in the United States who combines paid work in the labor force and family work as a homemaker does not have enough hours in the average day to fulfill all her responsibilities, and many men have

been unwilling or unable to pick up some of the slack at home.

■ **How do functionalist and conflict analysts explain the gendered division of labor?**
According to functionalist analysts, women's caregiver roles in contemporary industrialized societies are crucial in ensuring that key societal tasks are fulfilled. While the husband performs the instrumental tasks of economic support and decision making, the wife assumes the expressive tasks of providing affection and emotional support for the family. According to conflict analysts, the gendered division of labor within families and the workplace results from male control and dominance over women and resources.

■ **What are the major feminist perspectives and how do they explain gender inequality?**
In liberal feminism, gender equality is connected to equality of opportunity. In radical feminism, male dominance is seen as the cause of oppression. According to socialist feminists, women's oppression results from capitalism and patriarchy and women's dual roles as paid and unpaid workers. Black feminism focuses on race and class in analyzing gender inequality.

KEY TERMS

comparable worth, p. 88
contingent work, p. 86
gender, p. 77
gender bias, p. 80

gendered division of labor, p. 78
glass ceiling, p. 90
patriarchy, p. 85
pink-collar occupations, p. 86

sex, p. 77
sexism, p. 76
sexual harassment, p. 80
wage (pay) gap, p. 87

QUESTIONS FOR CRITICAL THINKING

1. Examine the various administrative and academic departments at your college. What is the gender breakdown of administrators and faculty in selected departments? Can you identify a gender-related pattern associated with women's and men's majors at your school? What conclusions can you draw about the relationship between gender and education on the basis of your observations?

2. Will the increasing numbers of women in higher education, the workplace, and the military tip the balance of power between men and women and result in greater gender equality in the future? Explain your answer.

3. What kind of study might you develop to examine the effects of children's clothing and toys on the socialization of children? How could you isolate the clothing or toy variable from other variables that influence children's socialization?

4. What steps do you think should be taken to reduce sexism and bring about greater gender equality in the United States? What resources would you need to implement your plan?

Succeed with MySocLab®   www.mysoclab.com

The new MySocLab delivers proven results in helping students succeed, provides engaging experiences that personalize learning, and comes from a trusted partner with educational expertise and a deep commitment to helping students and instructors achieve their goals.

Here are a few activities you will find for this chapter:

Watch on **mysoclab.com**

Core Concepts video clips feature sociologists in action, exploring important concepts in the study of Social Problems. Watch:
- Gender Socialization

Explore on **mysoclab.com**

Social Explorer is an interactive application that allows you to explore Census data through interactive maps. Explore:
- Social Explorer Activity: Income Inequality by Gender

Read on **mysoclab.com**

MySocLibrary includes primary source readings from classic and contemporary sociologists. Read:
- Thinking About the Baby: Gender and Divisions of Infant Care

Inequality Based on Age

THINKING SOCIOLOGICALLY

- How is our age related to what people expect of us? Is age always a good indicator of our abilities?

- What are some of the major problems experienced by older people?

- How do key sociological perspectives explain the aging process and how ageism contributes to social inequality?

I'm worried all the time. I'm worried because I have bills to pay.

—Ana Galindo, a nineteen-year-old looking for work, is very concerned about her chances of finding a job with a teen unemployment rate of 24 percent in the United States (quoted in Whitaker, 2011).

People with Masters [degrees are] trying to work at McDonald's. They're going to get hired before I do.

—John Reed-Torres, another job-hunting teen, who worries that overqualified applicants will be hired for almost any job before he will (quoted in Whitaker, 2011).

I think it's my age. I think it's working against me. I have friends my age that are struggling. And we're all near that 50 bracket, over-50 bracket. And there's so many young people coming out today that will do the job for a lot less.

—Sam Wade, a former office manager who has been looking for work for more than a year, believes that her age is a major factor holding her back from finding employment: She knows the statistic that, for people over fifty, the chance of finding a job within a year is only 24 percent (quoted in Smith, 2011).

These comments from teens and over-fifty job seekers sound like a zero-sum game ("If I win, you lose") because the younger applicants believe that the older ones will get the jobs because of their age and experience; the older applicants believe that the younger ones will get the jobs because of their youth and willingness to work for less. Which is it? The answer to this question is more complex than it initially might appear. Although U.S. unemployment is a problem for at least 13.5 million people who are considered officially unemployed, the situation particularly affects teen workers between the ages of sixteen and nineteen and older workers, who have been referred to as "America's new unemployables" (T. Smith, 2011). To be "officially unemployed" means that a person is actively seeking work and may be drawing unemployment benefits, as compared to "discouraged workers" who have given up searching for a new position. Teen unemployment is further complicated by the fact that many young people in the past found summer jobs at public parks, pools, and other facilities that have been affected by cuts in federal funding. Older workers also face employment barriers, but for a different reason: Many employers do not want to have to pay the higher salaries and provide benefits (such as health insurance and retirement plans) that they believe more experienced workers over age forty are likely to expect. While some analysts see higher rates of unemployment among teens and older workers as a fluke, social scientists who specialize in the study of aging might view this problem as age-based inequality.

In this chapter, we discuss how age-based inequality has a variety of sources, and how these inequalities are exacerbated by stereotypes of young people and older individuals. These stereotypes are harmful to the individual's self image, and—if they are widely believed by the general population—they limit the opportunities of youth and older adults. Age-based inequality is linked to age discrimination, which by definition involves negative and differential treatment of people over forty years of age.

AGEISM AS A SOCIAL PROBLEM

Ageism—prejudice and discrimination against people on the basis of age—is a social problem that particularly stigmatizes and marginalizes older people. Gerontologist Robert Butler (1969) introduced the term *ageism* to describe how myths and misconceptions about older people produce age-based discrimination. According to Butler, just as racism and sexism perpetuate stereotyping and discrimination against people of color and all women, ageism perpetuates stereotyping of older people and age-based discrimination. Most research has therefore focused on the negative impact ageism has on older people.

▷◻⌐ Read the **Document**
Ageism in the American Workplace on
mysoclab.com

Age-Based Stereotypes

There are more stereotypes about the physical and mental abilities of older people than there are about the abilities of people in any other age category. This does not mean that children and adolescents are exempt from age-based stereotypes. Comedians often refer to very young children as "crumb crunchers," "curtain climbers," and "little ankle biters." Animated television characters such as the *Rugrats* and young characters in many situation comedies and movies are simply stereotypic depictions of children and young adolescents.

Older people, however, are stereotyped in numerous ways. Some stereotypes depict them as slow in their thinking and movement; as living in the past and unable to change; and as cranky, sickly, and lacking in social value. Other stereotypes suggest that older people are "greedy geezers," living an affluent lifestyle and ignoring the needs of future generations. When many people accept age-based stereotypes, they can affect how people vote and what types of social policies legislators enact. Negative stereotypes of older people reinforce ageism and influence how younger people interact with older people.

Although most of us do not believe that we engage in stereotypical thinking about older people, researcher William C. Levin (1988) found that college students in his study evaluated people differently on the basis of their assumed age. When Levin showed three photographs of the same man, who had been made up to appear twenty-five in the first photo, fifty-two in the second,

and seventy-three in the third, to the students and asked them to evaluate these (apparently different) men for employment purposes, many students described the "seventy-three-year-old" as less competent, less intelligent, and less reliable than the "twenty-five-year-old" and the "fifty-two-year-old." Clearly, our place in the social structure changes during our life course, and if we live long enough, any of us may become the target of stereotyping and discrimination directed at older people (Hooyman and Kiyak, 2011).

DID YOU KNOW

- The U.S. population is growing at a faster rate in the older age categories than in the younger ages.
- 37.2 years is the median age (half of the population is older and half is younger) in the United States: This is a new high.
- U.S. counties of 100,000 or more where a large university is located typically have the lowest median ages in the nation.

Social Inequality and the Life Course

To study age and social inequality, many sociologists and social gerontologists focus on the life course—the age-based categories through which people pass as they grow older. In the United States, the life course tends to be divided into infancy and childhood, adolescence and young adulthood, middle age, later maturity, and old age. The field of gerontology examines the biological, physical, and social aspects of the aging process. We will focus primarily on *social gerontology*—**the study of the social (nonphysical) aspects of aging**—as we examine age classifications in the United States.

Childhood

Infants (birth to age two) and children (ages three to twelve) are among the most powerless individuals in society. In the past, children were seen as the property of their parents, who could do with their children as they chose. Although we have a more liberal attitude today, children remain vulnerable to problems such as family instability, poverty, maltreatment by relatives and other caregivers, and sexual exploitation.

"My mom and dad are still very sharp."

The Children's Defense Fund (2010) points out some of the perils of childhood in the United States:

- One out of every five children lives in poverty, including more than 40 percent of African American and more than 33 percent of Hispanic children.
- Family stability and financial resources are limited because more than one-third of all children are being born to unmarried mothers, 71 percent of African American children, 50 percent of Hispanic children, and 27 percent of white children.
- States together spend almost three times as much per prisoner as per public school pupil.
- 7.4 million children annually are reported to be victims of child abuse and neglect.
- Nine children and teens a day are killed by guns.

These are only a few of the many problems associated with childhood in the contemporary United States. The deep recession and slow economic recovery this country is experiencing heightens the perils that many children face. As Marian Wright Edelman, the founder and president of the Children's Defense Fund, emphasizes:

> Children have only one childhood and it is right now. Millions of children in our nation require emergency attention in our recession ravaged economy.... If the foundation of your house is crumbling, you don't say you cannot afford to fix it. Children are the foundation of America's future. We need to invest in their health, early childhood development, and education. Today is tomorrow.... [However] children are the poorest age group and the younger the children are, the poorer they are. We rank highest among industrialized nations in relative child poverty and in the gap between rich and poor, and last in protecting children against gun violence. (Children's Defense Fund, 2010:v)

In her call for change, Edelman points out several of national social problems—including health, education, poverty, violence, and gun-related deaths—that not only harm the 74 million children (one-fourth of the U.S. population) in this country but the rest of us as well.

Adolescence and Emerging Adulthood

Before the twentieth century, the concept of adolescence did not exist. When children grew big enough to do adult work, they were expected to fulfill adult responsibilities such as making money to support their families. Today, the line between childhood and adolescence is blurred, as is the line between adolescence and emerging adulthood. Adolescence is defined as the period between puberty and legal adulthood, or the teenage years (ages thirteen to seventeen). Emerging adulthood signifies the phase of the life span between adolescence and full-fledged adulthood, or the years between ages of eighteen and twenty-five (Arnett, 2004).

Adolescence One of the most significant phrases in an individual's life is between childhood and adulthood. Adolescents are not treated as children, but they are not afforded the full status of adulthood. Early teens are considered too young to drive, to drink alcohol, to stay out late, and to do other things that are considered to be adult behavior by the media, particularly television and movies, and by members of some peer groups. Adolescents face an identity crisis in which they must figure out who they are and what they want to become. They also face difficult decisions pertaining to their sexuality and their relationships with people of the same sex and the opposite sex. Teen pregnancy and parenthood are major concerns for many adolescents. Overall, a defining factor in adolescence is puberty, particularly the psychological and social consequences that go along with that period of rapid physical growth and psychological change that culminates in sexual maturity.

Adolescents must deal with conflicting demands from parents, teachers, friends, classmates, and others. At the same time, they are in the process of creating a stable identity and determining what they want to do with the rest of their live. In the past, the five hallmarks of being an "adult" were completing school, leaving home, becoming financially independent, getting married, and having a child. Analysts now believe that preparing to take these major steps constitutes the key developmental tasks of adolescence (based on Perkins, 2011):

- Achieving new and more mature relations with boys and girls in the same age bracket
- Achieving a masculine or feminine social role
- Dealing with changes brought about by puberty and accepting one's own body-build
- Achieving emotional independence from parents and other adults
- Preparing for marriage and family life
- Preparing for an economic career
- Developing an ideology that provides a set of values and an ethical system to guide behavior
- Desiring and achieving socially responsible behavior

These development tasks increase anxiety on the part of adolescents and frequently contribute to conflicts between young people and their parents about issues such as parental control and supervision, household chores, finances, schooling, and privacy rights.

Social problems in the larger society often become the individual problems for adolescents. Drinking, drug abuse, the widespread availability of sexually explicit media ranging from video games to television and film, high dropout rates and violence in schools, and the nearly 25 percent unemployment rate among teens, all have a negative effect on individuals attempting to make the transition from adolescence to emerging adulthood and beyond. For example, unemployment rates for adolescents, particularly African American males, are extremely high. Available jobs are in the service sector, such as fast-food restaurants, which usually pay minimum wage or slightly above. Perceiving a lack of opportunity for themselves in the adult world, some teens, especially males, join gangs and/or engage in criminal activity. Between the ages of ten and seventeen, an African American child is five times as likely as a white youth to be arrested for a violence crime, and African American youths are more than four times as likely as white youths to be detained in a juvenile correctional facility (Children's Defense Fund, 2010). Because of the complexity of modern social life and the number of young people who did not appear ready to move from adolescence to the young adulthood stage of the life course, psychologist Jeffrey Jensen Arnett coined the term "emerging adulthood" to identify the twenties as a distinct life stage.

Emerging adulthood As previously stated, emerging adulthood is the span between adolescence and full-fledged adulthood, usually between the ages of eighteen and twenty-five. The term best applies to young people in high-income, developed nations who are not parents and have not assumed all the responsibilities associated with adulthood. Emerging adulthood is characterized as a period of frequent change, as described by a journalist for the *New York Times*:

> The traditional cycle seems to have gone off course, as young people remain untethered to romantic partners or to permanent homes, going back to school for lack of better options, traveling, avoiding commitments, competing ferociously for unpaid internships or temporary (and often grueling) Teach for America jobs, forestalling the beginning of adult life. (Henig, 2010)

As studies have shown, about one-third of people in their twenties relocate their residence every year, with forty percent moving back home with parents at least once. During their twenties, young people have an average of seven jobs. Marriage occurs later than in the past, and at least two-third of people in this age category live with a romantic partner for a period of time without getting married.

Structural factors in the larger society have contributed to the development of emerging adulthood. Among these are the time necessary to complete sufficient education to survive in an information-based economy, limitations on the number of available entry-level jobs, and less pressure to marry early because of greater acceptance of premarital sex, cohabitation, and birth control. Similarly, women feel less pressure to have children at an early age and are more likely to pursue higher levels of education and more career options before getting married and having children.

Social problems associated with this stage of development include the issue that states and the federal government use a variety of ages to signify when young people are eligible or competent to engage in specific kinds of behavior. Consider, for example, that young people can join the military at age eighteen but not drink until they are twenty-one years of age. They can drive a motor vehicle at age sixteen but not rent a car until age twenty-five unless they pay an extra premium. Young people can vote at eighteen, but some states will not allow them to age out of foster care until they reach their twenty-first birthday. And, finally, this one is well-known to college students: "Parents have no access to their child's college records if the child is over 18, but parents' income is taken into account when the child applies for financial aid up to age 24" (Henig, 2010). These are only a few examples that show the blurred edges of the transitions between adolescence and emerging adulthood, as well as between emerging adulthood and young adulthood in contemporary societies.

In developing the concept of emerging adulthood, Arnett argues that it is period of self-focus that is valuable for individual self-discovery, but other analysts ask this question: Is this a middle- and upper-class phenomenon? Arnett answers that he included working-class young people and persons of color in his study. In the final analysis, emerging adulthood appears to be a period for people who have sufficient financial resources to afford a "time out" before assuming the full responsibilities of adulthood (Henig, 2010).

Young Adulthood

In the past, young adulthood was described as beginning in the early to mid-twenties and lasting to about age thirty-nine. However, if we add emerging adulthood as another stage in the life course, young adulthood now encompasses the years between twenty-six and thirty-nine. In this developmental period, people acquire new roles and experience a sense of new freedom. However, many also experience problems finding their niche, particularly when it appears doubtful that they will have as high a standard of living as their parents had. Some analysts believe that an age thirty transition may occur when people begin to question the original decisions they made about career and home life, and some of them will make changes to try to reestablish their original dream of the twenties. Subsequent chapters examine a variety of issues affecting young adults, including alcohol and drug abuse, divorce, and employment instability. During their thirties, people may become more focused on their careers and on trying to create stability in their friendships and family life before entering a "midlife" transition that brings them into their forties.

Middle Age

Because life expectancy was lower in the past, the concept of middle age (age forty to sixty-five) did not exist until fairly recently. *Life expectancy*—an estimate of the average lifetime of people born in a specific year—increased dramatically during the twentieth century. Today, life expectancy at birth in the United States is approximately 78.4 years, compared to only forty-seven years in 1900.

As people progress through middle age, some compare their accomplishments with their earlier aspirations and decide if they have reached their goals. Individuals who feel positive about their accomplishments are more likely to have good physical and mental health. Those who think that "my life is more than half over, and I haven't done anything" tend to experience higher levels of stress and have more health problems, including hypertension and depression.

During middle age people also experience *senescence (primary aging)*, which results from molecular and cellular changes in the body. Some signs of senescence are visible (e.g., wrinkles and gray hair); others are not (e.g., arthritis or stiffness in connective tissue joints; a gradual dulling of senses such as taste, touch, and vision; and slower reflexes). Vital systems also undergo gradual change; lung capacity diminishes; and the digestive, circulatory, and reproductive systems gradually decline in efficiency (Atchley, 2004). In addition to primary aging, people experience *secondary aging*, which has to do with environmental factors and lifestyle choices. A MacArthur Foundation study on aging identified several factors that contribute to "successful aging," including regular physical activity, continued social connections, resiliency (the ability to bounce back readily after suffering a loss), and

self-efficacy (a feeling of control over one's life). According to one gerontologist, "Only about 30 percent of the characteristics of aging are genetically based; the rest—70 percent—is not" (Brody, 1996:B9).

Some people fight the aging process by spending billions of dollars on cosmetic and beauty products that promise "No Wrinkles" and "Eternal Youth." Others have cosmetic surgery. In 2010, people between the ages of thirty-five and fifty had the most elective procedures. Almost 10 million surgical and nonsurgical cosmetic procedures were performed in 2010 in the United States, marking a 155 percent increase in the total number of procedures since 1997. The top five surgical cosmetic procedures were breast augmentation, liposuction, eyelid surgery, abdominoplasty ("tummy tuck"), and breast reduction. Botox injection was the top nonsurgical cosmetic procedure. In one sociological study, an interviewee explained that she decided to undergo liposuction (a surgical procedure in which fat is removed) because she was getting a lot of "crepeyness" in her neck and her jowls were "coming down" because of aging (Dull and West, 1991:57). As her remarks suggest, the United States is a youth-oriented society that tends to equate beauty, stamina, and good health with youth. Because of this, many of the changes associated with growing older are viewed as something to be avoided at all costs. Popular culture contributes to this perception by suggesting that middle-aged women are invisible or that they become unattractive if they do not endeavor to prevent the aging process and remain sexy (see Box 5.1).

Whereas women in middle age may believe that they have become less sexually attractive than they were, middle-aged men tend to realize that their physical strength and social power over others are limited. As if to reinforce their awareness of the passage of time, many women and men also may have to face the fact that their children have grown and left home. However, for some people, middle age is a time of great contentment; their income and prestige are at their peak, the problems of raising their children are behind them, they are content with their spouse of many years, and they may have grandchildren who give them a tie to the future. Even so, all middle-aged people know that their status will change significantly as they grow older.

Later Maturity and Old Age

Later maturity is usually considered to begin in the sixties. The major changes associated with this stage are social. Although many people in their sixties retain sufficient physical strength to be able to carry on an active

Where Have All the Older Women Gone? Fashion Magazines for the Young Only!

Essence:
>   Proportion of readers over age 50 = 22 percent
>   Proportion of women over 40 portrayed = 9 percent

Harper's Bazaar:
>   Proportion of readers over age 50 = 23 percent
>   Proportion of women over 40 portrayed =
>   8.8 percent

Elle Magazine:
>   Proportion of readers over age 50 = 19 percent
>   Proportion of women over 40 portrayed =
>   2.7 percent

W Magazine:
>   Proportion of readers over age 50 = 14 percent
>   Proportion of women over 40 portrayed = 5 percent

Vogue:
>   Proportion of readers over age 50 = 20 percent
>   Proportion of women over 40 portrayed =
>   7.3 percent

>   *D. C. Lewis, Medvedev, and Seponski, 2011*

If a woman over age 50 picks up a fashion magazine, she should not expect to see someone like her peering back from the cover (Pappas, 2011). Listed above are popular fashion magazines where women over the age of fifty make up 14 to 23 percent of the readership. But, notice the second figure under each magazine: Even when researchers dropped the age category by ten years (to age forty), few older women are portrayed in these magazines, especially on the cover.

If women over fifty are loyal reader of magazines such as *Vogue, W, InStyle, Essence, Elle,* and *Cosmopolitan,* is it possible for a middle-aged woman to find other women in her age category in these publications? According to recent research, the answer is a resounding no! In a systematic study of ageism in fashion magazines, researchers found that these magazines largely exclude women over age forty from magazine covers, editorial pages, and advertising. Although some publications carry items for the baby boomer generation, the women shown are thin, youthful, and wrinkle-free. Analysts fear that the absence of older women in publications that target women will further contribute to the negative body image of women that is associated with eating disorders and extensive cosmetic surgeries in hopes of regaining a youthful appearance. Looking at magazine advertising, companies selling antiwrinkle creams and other treatments for "aging" use young women or, when older women are used, they have an unusually youthful appearance for their age.

Does the absence of older women in publications they read have any effect on them? Researchers believe that

the absence of older women in media portrayals may produce internalized ageism, a condition where women feel negatively about themselves because the natural aging is considered a form of deviance that must be masked from the public eye unless women aggressively work to defeat the process. Showing only those women who are young or who continually work to "improve" their face and body to appear more youthful may have a detrimental effect on all women. Middle-aged women are immediately affected by the lack of representation of women like themselves because they must be hidden from sight because they are growing older. Younger women may fear the natural

Some people fight the aging process by spending billions of dollars on cosmetic and beauty products that promise "No Wrinkles" and "Eternal Youth." Others have cosmetic surgery. The United States is a youth-oriented society that tends to equate beauty, stamina, and good health with youth. Because of this, many of the changes associated with growing older are viewed as something to be avoided at all costs.

Social Problems in the Media

Box 5.1 continued

process of aging because they perceive that growing old devalues women as they become unattractive and irrelevant, or worse yet, they disappear altogether.

At the bottom line, even magazines and ads that claim to celebrate the older woman actually are not *celebrating middle age itself* but rather are encouraging readers to *avoid looking or acting middle-aged* by purchasing products or services that claim to allow a woman to at least temporarily evade the inevitable process of aging. But middle-aged women are not the only ones who are targeted by advertisers for antiaging products. Recently, advertisers have reached out to men and to younger women (in their twenties and thirties), informing them that "Now is the time to fight the aging process, before it's too late!" According to some media analysts, ads such as these reflect our cultural obsession with appearance over substance and with youth over age.

Questions for Consideration

1. What values in our society might contribute to women's fear of looking "old"?
2. Do these same values apply to men? Why or why not?
3. How do television programs promote ideas about what it means to be young, middle-aged, or old in America?

Independent Research

What magazine portrayals or advertisements can you find that reaffirm the worth of women and men across age categories, racial and ethnic groupings, and class locations? Do these publications and ads primarily emphasize the physical appearance of people? What other attributes do the publications and ads highlight?

Explore the **Concept**

Social Explorer Activity: Where are the Elderly? [report] on **mysoclab.com**

social life, their peer groups shrink noticeably as friends and relatives die. Many people in later maturity find themselves caring for people of their own age and older people.

Sociologists use an age pyramid to show the distribution of a given population by age and sex groupings at various points in time. As Figure 5.1 shows, the U.S. population is aging due to an increase in life expectancy combined with a decrease in the birthrate. This is a long-term trend, and as Box 5.2 shows, it is important to differentiate between short-term changes and long-term trends when we are comparing statistics.

When does "old age" begin? A lack of consensus exists about when a person stops getting older and actually reaches old age. Researchers consistently find that the older people get, the older they say a person must be to be thought of as "old." According to a study by the Pew Research Center (2009), people under twenty believe that old age begins at sixty; those between the ages of thirty and forty-nine place old age at sixty-nine; those who are fifty to sixty-two years old place old age at seventy-two; and individuals sixty-five and older believe that old age begins at seventy-four. This tells us a great deal about the social construction of old age, which is primarily based on personal and social perceptions about age and what it means to be "old," more than on any concrete evidence that old age has been reached.

Some people link old age to retirement, but the age of retirement has been shifting upward in recent years. One reason that people are working longer is the persistent recession and the losses older people experienced in pension plans when stocks plummeted in the 2000s. Another reason people are working longer is a change in Social Security benefits: Age sixty-two is the earliest a person can start receiving Social Security retirement benefits of any amount; however, there is about a 30 percent reduction in the amount paid annually over what the person might receive if he or she had waited until the full retirement age which eventually will be sixty-seven years of age. Supposedly, people will receive about the same amount of Social Security benefits over their lifetime whether they retire at an earlier age and take a smaller amount of money paid over a longer period of time, or they retire at a later age and take a larger amount of money for a shorter period of time. Although some people continue to work past age seventy, most have left paid employment by their seventieth birthday. Today, about 16 percent of people sixty-five and older are in the paid labor force.

Some problems of older people are economic or social, whereas others are health related. Although some older individuals live in poverty or have economic distress as they support other family members, the poverty rate for people sixty-five and older (8.9 percent) is relatively lower than it is for other age categories. Medicare, Medicaid, and Social Security benefits have reduced the rate of elder poverty in this country; however, some

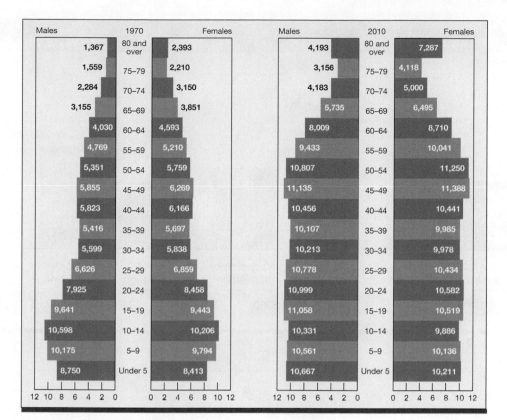

Figure 5.1 U.S. age pyramid by age and sex, 1970 and 2010.
Source: U.S. Census Bureau, 2010.

political leaders and social analysts fear that these entitlement programs will be unsustainable in the future. Psychosocial concerns are another problem: Some older people report that they feel sad or depressed; others state

that they feel like they are not needed or are a burden to other people (Pew Research Center, 2009).

Psychosocial concerns and health problems are closely related. Some people over sixty-five report that

---

Social Problems and Statistics   Box 5.2

Drawing the Wrong Conclusion

In its 2000 survey, the U.S. Census Bureau found that for the first time, the population age sixty-five years and over did not increase at a faster rate than the rate of the total U.S. population (see Figure 5.2 on page 110 for comparison). On the basis of this statistic, it would have been easy to draw the conclusion that the aging of the U.S. population has occurred and would decrease in the future. However, this would have been an

inaccurate assumption because, as Figure 5.2 shows, between 2000 and 2010, the population age sixty-five and over grew at a faster rate (15.1 percent) than the population under age forty-five. The slower growth rate in the number of people age sixty-five and older in 2000 was actually a reflection of low rates of birth in the 1920s and early 1930s, but it was not an accurate reflection of the sixty-five and over population in 2010 or

beyond. The Census Bureau predicts that the number of people sixty-five and over will increase from 39.6 to 88.5 million by 2050, when people in this age category would comprise 20 to 21 percent of the total U.S. population. Whenever we compare statistics at different points in time or over different periods of time, we need to keep in mind what this example shows: that a short-term change is not necessarily proof of a long-term trend.

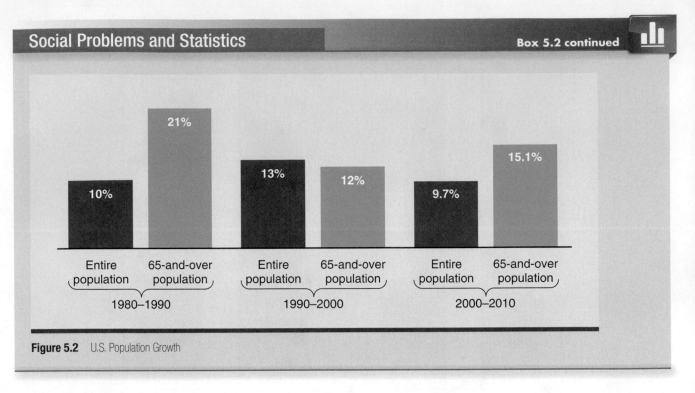

Figure 5.2   U.S. Population Growth

they have some degree of memory loss, serious illness, and/or orthopedic problems. Although everyone has some difficulty recalling names of people and certain facts, about one-in-four persons age sixty-five and older report that they have experienced memory loss to the extent that it concerns them. This fear is intensified by our growing awareness of Alzheimer's disease and its harmful and deadly consequences on the human body, as discussed later in the chapter. In addition to a heightened chance of heart attacks, strokes, and cancer, older people typically have more orthopedic problems, falls, and a decline in the senses. As persons grow older, their bones become more porous and brittle; a simple fall can result in broken bones that take longer to heal than those of a younger person. Strength, mobility, and height may decline; and the abilities to see, hear, taste, touch, and smell may diminish. Because taste and smell work together to allow us to enjoy food, eating may become less pleasurable and so contribute to poor nutrition in some older adults. Although it is not true of all elderly people, older individuals do not always react as rapidly (physically or mentally) as younger persons, particularly when they are engaged in intense activities such as driving a vehicle or running machinery.

As older people have begun to live longer, gerontologists have come to realize that there are significant differences among the "young-old" (ages sixty-five to seventy-four), the "old-old" (ages seventy-five to eighty-four), and the "oldest-old" (ages eighty-five and older). Although more than half of all people age sixty-five and older are in the young-old category, the oldest-old category has grown more rapidly over the past three decades than has any other age group in the United States. In 2010, about 72,000 people were 100 years of age or older in the United States (U.S. Census Bureau, 2011a).

Death and Dying

In previous generations, death was a common occurrence in all stages in the life course, but today most deaths occur among older people. The leading causes of death among people age sixty-five and over are diseases of the heart, malignant neoplasm (cancer), and cerebrovascular diseases (stroke, aneurysm, or other circulatory disorders affecting the brain). Because of medical advances and the increase in life expectancy, death is now viewed as that stage of the life course that usually occurs in old age. According to social gerontologists, the increased association of *death* with the process of *aging* has caused many people to deny the aging process and engage in ageism as a means of denying the reality of death, particularly their own. Researchers have found, however, that many people do not actually fear death itself as much as they fear the possibility of pain and suffering, loss of control, and the consequences of their death for survivors (Marshall and Levy, 1990). Given a chance to choose, most people would choose a painless death over prolonged physical and mental deterioration and the prospect of being a burden on their families. Some researchers have also found that older people have less fear of death than younger people do; others have found that education and religious beliefs are important factors in how people view death and dying (Kalish, 1985).

There are four widely known frameworks for explaining how people cope with the process of dying: the *stage-based approach*, the *trajectories of grief approach*, the *dying trajectory*, and the *task-based approach*. The *stage-based approach* was popularized by Elisabeth Kübler-Ross (1969), who proposed five stages in the dying process: (1) denial ("Not me"), (2) anger ("Why me?"), (3) bargaining and asking for divine intervention to postpone death ("Yes me, but . . ."), (4) depression and sense of loss, and (5) acceptance. According to some social scientists, Kübler-Ross's study is limited because she focused primarily on the attitudes of younger people who had terminal illnesses. These scientists argue that the same stages might not apply to older people who believe that they have already lived a full life (Marshall, 1980; Kalish, 1985). Some have pointed out that these stages have never been conclusively demonstrated or comprehensively explained.

Another framework, the *trajectories of grief approach,* was introduced by the clinical psychologist George Bonanno (2009, 2010), who claims that bereavement studies have disproved the stages of grief approach and helped researchers identify four common trajectories of grief:

- **Resilience**—the ability of people to maintain a relatively stable, healthy level of psychological and physical functioning while they are dealing with a highly disruptive event such as the death of a relative or a life-threatening situation
- **Recovery**—a gradual return to previous levels of normal functioning after experiencing a period of psychological stress such as depression or posttraumatic stress disorder

- **Chronic dysfunction**—lengthy suffering (sometimes several years or more) and the inability to function after experiencing grief
- **Delayed grief or trauma**—experiencing what appears to be a normal adjustment after the loss of a loved one but then having an increase in distress and other symptoms months later (based on Bonanno, 2010)

To explain his views on grief-related behavior, Bonanno coined the term *coping ugly* to describe how some seemingly inappropriate or counterintuitive behavior (such as telling jokes or laughing) may seem odd at the time but help a person move on after a loss. Although Bonanno's ideas about persistent resilience have been embraced by some gerontologists and bereavement specialists, others disagree and see this condition as a form of denial that might necessitate counseling or other treatment.

A third approach, referred to as the *dying trajectory,* focuses on the perceived course of dying and the expected time of death. For example, a dying trajectory may be sudden, as in the case of a heart attack, or it may be slow, as in the case of lung cancer. According to the dying-trajectory approach, the process of dying involves three phases: the acute phase, characterized by the expression of maximum anxiety or fear; the chronic phase, characterized by a decline in anxiety as the person confronts reality; and the terminal phase, characterized by the dying person's withdrawal from others (Glaser and Strauss, 1968).

Finally, the *task-based approach* is based on the assumption that the dying person can and should go about daily activities and fulfill tasks that make the process of dying easier on family members and friends, as well as on the dying person. Physical tasks can be performed to satisfy bodily needs, whereas psychological tasks can be done to maximize psychological security, autonomy, and richness of experience. Social tasks sustain and enhance interpersonal attachments and address the social implications of dying. Spiritual tasks help people identify, develop, or reaffirm sources of spiritual energy and foster hope (Corr, Nabe, and Corr, 2003). In the final analysis, however, how a person dies or experiences the loss of a loved one is shaped by many social and cultural factors. These endeavors are influenced by an individual's personality and philosophy of life, as well as the social context in which these events occur.

Technological advances in medicine have helped focus attention on the physical process of dying and, in recent years, the needs of dying patients and their families. Many people are choosing to sign a *living will*—

a document stating their wishes about the medical circumstances under which their life should be allowed to end. Some people reject the idea of being kept alive by elaborate life-support systems and other forms of high-tech medicine, choosing to die at home rather than in a hospital or nursing home. The hospice movement has provided additional options for caring for the terminally ill. *Hospices* **are organizations that provide a homelike facility or home-based care (or both) for people who are terminally ill.** Some hospices have facilities where care is provided, but hospice is primarily a philosophy that affirms life, not death, and offers holistic and continuing care to the patient and family through a team of visiting nurses, on-call physicians, and counselors. Home care enables many people to remain in familiar surroundings and maintain dignity and control over the dying process.

PROBLEMS ASSOCIATED WITH AGING

Age stratification—the inequalities, differences, segregation, or conflict between age groups—occurs throughout the life course (Atchley, 2004). Stratification based on age is a determinant of how education, jobs, and other scarce resources and opportunities are allocated in society. But this type of stratification also limits roles and opportunities. Many people automatically assume that at age fourteen, a person should be in school; that at age thirty, a person should be married; and that at age sixty-five, a person should retire from full-time employment. Such perceptions about age may create problems for people in all age categories, but the problems typically are most pronounced among older people.

Workplace Discrimination

Despite passage of the Age Discrimination in Employment Act of 1967 to protect workers age forty and above from unfair employment practices based on age, many subtle forms of age discrimination in the workplace remain. In times of deep recession and economic crisis, finding a desirable job is difficult for people of all ages. However, in either good or bad economic conditions, some employers prefer younger workers to older workers, based on widely held assumptions that older workers have more health problems than younger workers, and that older employees may be overqualified and more "bossy" than their younger counterparts.

Employers might also hire younger workers because they believe that they can pay them less than older workers and make more demands on their time and energy. Older employees might find that their employers have downgraded their job descriptions, have failed to promote them or grant them raises, and sometimes are trying to push them out of their jobs so that cheaper workers can be hired. Despite the negative stereotypes, some employers have found it profitable to hire older employees. In the 2010s slightly more than one-fourth of employees at *Fortune* 500 companies are age fifty or older. Among the industries with the highest number of older employees are airlines, utilities, and insurance companies. By contrast, food and beverage companies typically have the largest number of young employees (Brandon, 2011). Of course, it is important to distinguish between companies that are currently employing a large number of older workers and those who are hiring older workers: Frequently, companies with older workers have employees who have remained with the company for many years and have "aged on the job" rather than being recently hired. Organizations with unionized workers often have a larger proportion of older workers because the union system protected those who had been on the job the longest from being laid off when firms downsized their workforce: "Last hired, first fired" was the official motto of some union and labor leaders. However, at some point, retirement becomes an expected part of the life course of individuals.

Older people have been stereotyped as being behind the times and not keeping up with new technology. However, this stereotype is inaccurate for people, like the couple shown here, who use computers regularly for sending e-mail, gathering information, and paying bills.

Retirement and Changing Roles

Retirement is the institutionalized separation of an individual from her or his occupational position, with continuation of income from a retirement pension based on prior years of service. In the past, mandatory retirement allowed employers to force all employees to retire at a certain age, usually sixty-five, regardless of their health or desire to continue working. This practice was widespread in the United States in the 1960s and 1970s, but Congress outlawed mandatory retirement before age seventy by an extension of the Age Discrimination Act. In 1986, Congress abolished mandatory retirement altogether.

Changes in compulsory retirement laws have contributed to a change in how many people view retirement. In the past it was believed that people were unable to adequately perform their jobs after a certain age. Now, retirement was seen less as a sign of decline than as a newfound period of leisure and opportunity for adaptation and reflection. For some, however, adapting to less income, increased dependency, and the loss of roles and activities is very difficult. As a result, many older people continue to work full time or part time or become involved in volunteer activities that fill some of the time they used to spend in the workplace.

Typically, retirement for poor white Americans, African Americans, and Latinos/as is different from retirement for white Americans. Low-wage jobs and racial discrimination in the workplace diminish the earning power of many people, so those who have held

lower-paying positions throughout their lifetime often have no employer-sponsored or self-purchased pension plans, only Social Security. Even if these individuals in the bottom tier of the dual-labor market do have pension plans with defined benefits, their pension checks, which are based on income during the working years, are small, leaving many with no choice but to work into their seventies. However, many currently employed people do not have the traditional, defined benefit pension coverage that many retirees have because most employers no longer offer this benefit. A *defined benefit* retirement plan is one in which the employer guarantees to pay the employee at retirement a fixed monthly income for the rest of his or her life. The plans provided by some states for their employees are an example. "Service credits" are calculated for the number of years the employee worked, and then these are put into a formula that includes the amount of money the employee made while working for the organization to determine how much the retiree's monthly income will be for life. By contrast, a *defined contribution* retirement plan is one in which the employer agrees to contribute a fixed amount to the employee's pension fund each year in which the employee is employed. However, the amount of income the employee receives during retirement depends on investing the retirement money so that more can accumulate to give the employee enough to live on for the rest of his or her life. Private sector 401(k) plans and public and nonprofit sector 403(b) plans are examples of defined contribution plans, but these often have a greater market risk associated with changes in the value of the investments in the plan. To

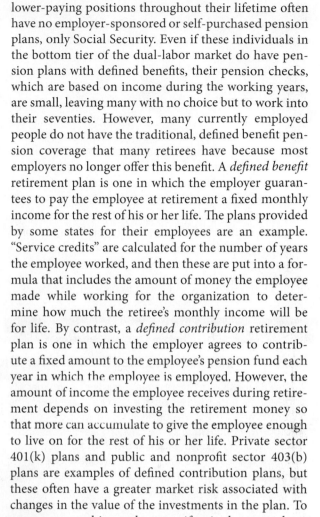

put this another way, if retired persons have most of their investment in the stock market, and the stock market takes a tumble, so does their retirement account—the amount of money they have set aside to live on for the rest of their life.

Health, Illness, and Health Care

At age ninety-three, Malcolm Clarke plays doubles tennis four times a week and sails his boat; he also shops and cooks for himself (Brody, 1996). Although Clarke attributes his longevity and good health to "luck," studies show that many older people are not developing the disabling diseases that were common in the past, and the vast majority functions quite well. Improvement in the health status

Assisted living facilities are a popular housing option for many middle- and higher-income older people because they provide needed services but offer more homelike settings and greater freedom than other long-term care facilities such as nursing homes.

of older people has been attributed, at least in part, to better education (knowing what to do and not do to stay healthy), nutrition, and health insurance through Medicare and sometimes Medicaid (see Box 5.3). Because most people over age sixty-five are covered by Medicare, health care coverage is a greater problem for the young and middle-aged. Lack of health insurance affects substantial portions of all age groups below age sixty-five. In 2009, it was estimated that 50.7 million people were uninsured, and 7.5 million of those were children (DeNavas-Walt et al., 2010).

Watch on **mysoclab.com**

Physical Challenges of Living Longer on **mysoclab.com**

Malnutrition is a life-threatening problem for some older people. Although malnutrition is sometimes related to poverty, nutritionists suggest that the condition is pervasive even among older people, especially over the age of seventy, who are not poor. Some older individuals may eat too little, lack nutritious food, or have digestive problems related to aging. Researchers have become concerned about malnutrition among older individuals because of its link to isolation, loneliness, and mortality among elderly individuals. Older people with strong social networks are more likely to eat sufficient food to sustain them.

Most deaths of older individuals are from chronic illness or disease. About seven out of every ten deaths among older people are due to heart disease, cancer, stroke, pneumonia, Alzheimer's disease, or diabetes. One of the leading killers of persons over age sixty-five is heart disease. Among white women, heart disease is the leading cause of death; breast cancer and lung cancer are responsible for nearly half of all cancer deaths in women. African American women are more likely than white women to die from diabetes. Men are highly

---

Social Problems and Social Policy   Box 5.3

Government-Funded Health Care for Older People: Medicare

Are people entitled to health care regardless of their ability to pay? For years, this has been a disputed question in the United States. The issue of health care for older people was partially addressed in 1965 when Congress enacted the Medicare program, a federal program for people age sixty-five and over who are covered by Social Security or railroad retirement insurance or who have been permanently and totally disabled for two years or more. Funded primarily through Social Security taxes paid by current workers, Medicare is an *entitlement program*. Those who receive benefits must have paid something to be covered. Medicare Part A (hospital insurance) provides coverage for some inpatient hospital expenses, including critical-access hospitals and skilled-nursing facilities. It also helps cover hospice care and limited home health care. Part B (medical insurance) helps cover doctors' services and outpatient care. It covers some of the services of physical and occupational therapists, and some home health care. Most people pay a monthly premium for Part B. Beginning in 2006, Medicare prescription drug coverage became available to everyone covered under Medicare. Private companies provide the coverage, and beneficiaries choose the drug plan and pay a monthly premium.

Clearly, Medicare has created greater access to health care services for many older people, but it has serious limitations. Medicare primarily provides for acute, short-term care and is limited to partial payment for ninety days of hospital care and for a restricted amount of skilled nursing care and home health services. It also has a deductible and copayments (fees paid by people each time they see a health care provider), and it pays only 80 percent of *allowable* charges, not the *actual amount* charged by health care providers. Medicare spending has grown rapidly in the past decade. For example, Medicare spending grew 7.2 percent to $431.2 billion in 2007, which followed a growth of 18.5 percent in 2006, because of the one-time implementation of Medicare Part D (prescription coverage).

Some low-income older people are eligible for Medicaid, a joint federal-state *means-tested welfare program* that provides health care insurance for poor people of any age who meet specific eligibility requirements. However, Medicaid recipients have been stigmatized because Medicaid is a "welfare program." Furthermore, because the administrative paperwork is burdensome and reimbursements are so low, many physicians have refused to take Medicaid patients for a number of years. The number of physicians now refusing Medicaid patients is growing rapidly because of further reductions in Medicaid funding as many states look for ways to make massive budget cuts. Chapter 10 discusses U.S. health care in greater detail.

Questions for Consideration

1. What impact do you think the aging of the U.S. population will have on government-funded programs such as Medicare and Medicaid?
2. What solutions can you suggest for providing more adequate health care for older people at less cost?

vulnerable to prostate, lung, and colorectal cancers. Many people over age eight-five die of heart disease, multiple organ failure, or pneumonia. Recently, the number of AIDS cases has risen among older people, and AIDS educators are seeking to make older people aware of the risk of becoming infected with HIV, the virus that causes AIDS.

Perhaps the most dreaded health concern of older people is Alzheimer's disease, an "irreversible, progressive brain disease that slowly destroys memory and thinking skills and, eventually, the ability to carry out the simplest tasks of daily living" (National Institute on Aging, 2010). Alzheimer's is the most common form of dementia; an estimated 5.4 million Americans had the disease in 2011. Although medical scientists are not completely sure where Alzheimer's originated or what its effects are, they believe it is caused by various diseases and conditions that result in damaged brain cells or connections between brain cells. It is a degenerative disease that gradually brings about a decline in memory and other cognitive skills, including the ability to speak coherently, to recognize or identify objects, to execute motor activities, and to think abstractly. People with dementia may initially seem forgetful and easily confused; in time, they may cease to recognize people they have always known. In advanced stages of the disease, they may lose the ability to speak, get dressed alone, bathe and use the toilet without assistance, and even feed themselves. The likelihood of developing Alzheimer's disease doubles for every five-year interval beyond age sixty-five (National Institute on Aging, 2010). No treatment is available to slow the deterioration of brain cells or cure Alzheimer's, but some drugs are available that appear to slow the early progression of symptoms

People age sixty-five and older account for more than one-third of all dollars spent on health care, and this figure is expected to rise dramatically with the aging of the U.S. population. People spend more money on health care as they grow older because they experience chronic diseases that are resource intensive, requiring regular treatment by health care personnel and expensive medications to control the effects of these problems. Many believe the cost problems associated with health care will be further intensified by the feminization of aging—the increasing proportion of older women in the population—because women, on average, live longer than men born in the same year. Older women typically are living on a fixed income that makes it impossible for them to pay the difference between the amount that Medicare pays on a medical bill and the actual amount owed for services they receive. Chapter 10 discusses health care issues in greater detail.

Victimization

Although older people are in fact less likely than younger people to be victims of violent crime, they fear this type of crime more than people in other age categories do. However, as discussed at the beginning of this chapter, older people are often the target of other types of crime. Con artists frequently contact them by snail mail, e-mail, or telephone to perpetrate scams that often promise prizes or involve a "stockbroker" selling a "hot" stock or other commodity. The Internet has made it easier, rather than more difficult, for scan artists to take advantage of older persons who believe they have received e-mail or other messages from old friends or a financial institution they do business with, leading the older person to divulge personal information that can be used to take money from the individual.

Another form of victimization is elder abuse. According to the U.S. Administration on Aging, the abuse may be physical, emotional, sexual, financial, and/or the result of neglect. According to the best available estimates, between 1 and 2 million people over age sixty-five in the United States have been injured, exploited, or otherwise mistreated by someone on whom they depended for care (see National Center on Elder Abuse, 2005). Many analysts believe that elder abuse is underreported because people who know of the abuse are unwilling to report it and older people who are the victims are either too ashamed or afraid to notify authorities. Although some analysts initially believed that younger people were likely to exploit older people who were psychologically and economically dependent on them, just the opposite has often proven true: Younger people are more likely to exploit elders on whom they themselves are dependent (Atchley, 2004).

Family Problems and Social Isolation

Older people can easily become socially isolated from their families. Younger members who once asked for advice stop asking, perhaps because they think that their older relatives are out of touch or perhaps because of some miscommunication. Sometimes, younger family members feel unduly burdened by the concerns of their elders, which don't seem truly important to them. For one reason or another, older people come to believe (rightly or wrongly) that they are isolated from the rest of the family.

In 2008, 40 percent of women and 20 percent of men age sixty-five and above lived alone (Federal Interagency Forum on Aging-Related Statistics, 2010). Many older people live alone voluntarily, but others live by themselves because they are divorced, widowed, or single. Living alone is not the equivalent of social isolation. Many older people have networks of friends with whom they engage in activities. To a large degree, the extent to which they associate with others has to do with social class: People with more money are able to pursue a wider array of activities and take more trips than are those with more limited resources. Unfortunately, older people who live alone are more likely than other older people who live with their spouses to be in poverty.

Perhaps one of the saddest developments in contemporary society is the growing number of older people who are homeless. Some older homeless people have lived on the streets for many years; others have become homeless because they have been displaced from low-income housing such as single-room occupancy (SRO) hotels. In recent years, many SROs in cities such as New York and San Francisco have been replaced by high-rise office buildings, retail space, and luxury condominiums. Older people who are homeless typically lack nutritious food, appropriate clothing, adequate medical care, and a social support network. They tend to die prematurely of disease, crime victimization, accidents, and weather-related crises such as a winter blizzard, when an individual without shelter can freeze to death on a park bench. Fortunately, the picture is not this bleak for many older people who remain in residences they have occupied for many years.

Housing Patterns and Long-Term Care Facilities

Many people mistakenly assume that a large number of older people live in long-term care facilities such as nursing homes. In fact, however, only 4 percent of people age sixty-five and over live in long-term care facilities. More than people of any other age category, older people are likely to reside in the housing in which they have lived for a number of years and own free and clear of debt. White Americans are significantly more likely than African Americans and Latinas/os to own their homes, and married couples are more likely to own their homes than are single people. Among women over age sixty-five, white women and African American women were more likely than women of other races to live alone as compared to older Asian

American women and Hispanic (Latina) women who were more likely to live with relatives other than a spouse (Federal Interagency Forum on Aging-Related Statistics, 2010).

Some low-income older people live in planned housing projects that are funded by federal and local government agencies or private organizations such as religious groups. Older people with middle and upper incomes are more likely to live in retirement communities (for example, Sun City) or in *congregate housing*, which provides amenities such as housekeeping, dining facilities, and transportation services (Hooyman and Kiyak, 2011). In recent years, religious organizations and for-profit corporations have developed *multilevel* facilities, which provide services ranging from independent living and assisted living to skilled nursing care all at the same site. Such facilities often are quite expensive. Residents may have to purchase their housing units, pay a substantial initial entry fee, and/or sign life care contracts, which provide for nursing home care if it becomes necessary.

Today, only 1.1 percent of people between the ages of sixty-five to seventy-four live in long-term care facilities such as nursing homes; however, the percentage increases to 15 percent among people age eighty-five and over. Because of their greater life expectancy, higher rates of chronic illness, and higher rates of being unmarried, women account for three out of every four residents of nursing homes. According to social gerontologists, the primary factors related to living in a nursing home are age (eighty-five and over), being female, having been in the hospital recently, living in retirement housing, having no spouse at home, and having some cognitive or physical impairment that interferes with the activities of daily living.

Although some nursing home facilities may be excellent, others have undergone extensive media scrutiny and public criticism for violations of regulations and harmful practices such as elder abuse. As a result, many people select home care, adult day care, or assisted living for older relatives rather than institutional settings.

PERSPECTIVES ON AGING AND SOCIAL INEQUALITY

Although each of the major sociological perspectives focuses on different aspects of aging and social inequality, they all provide insights into how people view the aging process and how ageism contributes to social inequality in society.

The Functionalist Perspective

According to functionalists, dramatic changes in such social institutions as the family and religion have influenced how people look at the process of growing old. Given this, both the stability of society and the normal and healthy adjustment of older people require that they detach themselves from their social roles and prepare for their eventual death (Cumming and Henry, 1961). Referred to as *disengagement theory*, this theory suggests that older people want to be released from societal expectations of productivity and competitiveness. At the same time, disengagement facilitates a gradual and orderly transfer of statuses and roles from one generation to the next instead of an abrupt change, which might result in chaos. Retirement policies, then, are a means of ensuring that younger people with more up-to-date training (for example, high-tech programming) move into occupational roles while ensuring that older workers are recognized for years of service (Williamson, Rinehart, and Blank, 1992).

Critics of this perspective object to the assumption that disengagement is functional for society and that all older people want to disengage even though they are still productive and gain satisfaction from their work. In fact, according to some social analysts, disengagement as evidenced by early retirement policies has been dysfunctional for society. Social Security and other pension systems have been strained by the proportionately fewer workers who are paying into the plan to support an increasing number of retired workers. Contrary to disengagement theory, these analysts say, older people may disengage not by choice but because of a lack of opportunity for continued activity.

The Symbolic Interactionist Perspective

Symbolic interactionist perspectives on aging and inequality focus on the relationship between life satisfaction and levels of activity. The interactionist *activity theory* is based on the assumption that older people who are active are happier and better adjusted than are less active older persons. According to this theory, older people shift gears in late middle age and find meaningful substitutes for previous statuses, roles, and activities (Havighurst, Neugarten, and Tobin, 1968). Those who remain active have a higher level of life satisfaction than do those who are inactive or in ill health (Havighurst et al., 1968). In contrast to disengagement theory, activity theory suggests that older people must deny the existence of old age by maintaining middle-aged lifestyles for as long as possible.

Other symbolic interactionist perspectives focus on role and exchange theories. Role theory poses the question "What roles are available for older people?" Some theorists note that industrialized, urbanized societies typically do not have roles for older people (Cowgill, 1986). Other theorists note that many older people find active roles within their own ethnic group. Although their experiences might not be valued in the larger society, they are esteemed within their ethnic subculture because they are a rich source of ethnic lore and history. According to sociologist Donald E. Gelfand (1994), older people can exchange their knowledge for deference and respect from younger people.

In a capitalist economy, older people are viewed as a growing consumer market for services and products that promise to reduce the effects of aging.

Conflict and Feminist Perspectives

Conflict theorists focus on the political economy of aging in analyzing the problems of older people in contemporary capitalistic societies. From this perspective, class constitutes a structural barrier to older people's access to valued resources, and dominant groups attempt to maintain their own interests by perpetuating class inequalities. According to conflict theorists, aging itself is not the social problem. The problem is rooted in societal conditions that older people often face without adequate resources such as income and housing. People who were poor and disadvantaged in their younger years become even more so in old age.

In the capitalist system, middle- and upper-income older people might be viewed as consumers to whom a range of products and services can be sold specifically based on the consumers' age. As the "baby boomers," those born between 1946 and 1964, grow older, advertisers focus on them as a target audience for pharmaceutical products, such as pills to reduce the effects of arthritis, high blood pressure, and sexual impotency, and for foods and automobiles that are thought to be appropriate for older individuals (*The Economist*, 2002). In this way, people over age sixty might be more positively portrayed as having active and healthy lifestyles, but these lifestyles appear to be available only to those people who purchase the particular products or services that are being advertised. According to some conflict analysts, this is yet another way in which people are exploited by capitalist societies, in which the primary emphasis is on profits rather than on the real needs of individuals.

Rooted in the conflict tradition, feminist theorists suggest that aging creates greater problems for some women than for men because of the double standard of aging that is linked to conventional expectations about what the attitudes, roles and appearance for each sex should be. For women, the loss of a youthful appearance is more likely to bring social devaluation; for men, growing older (at least to some point) brings the appearance of power, influence, and experience that many people value, especially in professionals who control large sums of money or provide advice (such as physicians, attorneys, and certified public accountants) about what patients or clients should do. Researchers using a feminist approach point to the popularity of elective cosmetic surgery among women for providing females of all ages with what they consider to be a more pleasing or youthful appearance. However, in the past two decades, more men have availed themselves of surgical procedures to enhance their appearance as well.

IS THERE A SOLUTION TO AGE-BASED INEQUALITY?

As we have seen, technological innovations and advances in medicine have contributed to the steady increase in life expectancy in the United States. Advances in the diagnosis, prevention, and treatment of diseases associated with old age, such as Alzheimer's disease, may revolutionize people's feelings about growing older. Technology may bring about greater equality and freedom for older people. Home-based computer services such as banking and shopping make it possible for older people to conduct their daily lives without having to leave home to obtain services. Computerized controls on appliances, lighting, and air conditioning make it possible for people with limited mobility to control their environment. Technology also brings recreation and education into the home. For example, Senior Net is a nationwide computer network that encourages discussion of diverse topics and provides hands-on classes in computer use. Robotics and computer systems may eventually be used by frail older people who otherwise would have to rely on family or paid caregivers to meet their needs or move to a nursing home. However, class is again a factor: More than 75 percent of home accessibility features currently are paid for by users or their families (Hooyman and Kiyak, 2011).

Economic concerns loom large in the future as baby boomers have begun to retire, bringing about a dramatic shift in the **dependency ratio—the number of workers necessary to support people under age fifteen and over age sixty-three.** Instead of *five* workers supporting one retiree by paying Social Security taxes, *three* workers will be providing support for each retiree. Extensive media discussion about Medicare costs and other benefits for older people have increased the animosity of some younger people toward the older population. Blogs and social networking communications often have screeds against older people who take advantage of the system, keep jobs that younger workers would like to have, and generally use up the resources of society without regard to the needs of younger individuals. Some analysts have suggested that conflict across age categories will grow more intense in future decades of the twenty-first century because of the rapid movement of the large baby boomer population into the older age categories and the increasing demands on health care, Social Security, and other social welfare programs that may go with that booming population. However, advocates of *productive aging* suggest that instead of pitting young and old against each other, we should change our national policies and attitudes. We should encourage older people to continue or create their own roles in society, not to disengage from it. Real value should be placed on unpaid volunteer and care giving activities, and settings should be provided in which older people can use their talents more productively (Hooyman and Kiyak, 2011). To distribute time for family responsibilities and leisure more evenly throughout the life course, changes must occur in the workplace. Today, younger workers struggle to care for their families, without the support of employers in many cases, and leisure is associated with old age and "being put out to pasture." But people who have had no opportunity to engage in leisure activities earlier in their life are unlikely to suddenly become leisure-oriented. Employment, family responsibilities, and leisure must become less compartmentalized, and changes in technology and employment may make this possible. At present, however, it is difficult for most people to have *free time* and *money* at the same time.

Functionalists suggest that changes must occur in families and other social institutions if we are to resolve problems brought about by high rates of divorce, single-parent households, and cohabitation by unmarried couples, which tend to reduce the individual's commitment to meet the needs of other family members. These analysts argue that individuals must be socialized to care for an increasing number of living generations in their family and must be given economic incentives such as tax breaks for fulfilling their responsibility to children and older relatives. Because adult children might have to provide economic and emotional support for aging parents and grandparents at the same time as they are caring for their own children, more community services are needed, particularly for adult children who are "suitcase caregivers" for frail, elderly relatives living many miles away (Foreman, 1996). Communities should create or expand existing facilities such as daycare centers for children and seniors; provide affordable housing; and build low-cost, community-based health facilities.

Other social analysts suggest that people need to rely more on themselves for their retirement and old age. Younger workers should be encouraged to save money for retirement and not to assume that Social Security, Medicare, and other entitlement programs will be available when they reach old age. As conflict theorists have pointed out, however, many young people do not have jobs or adequate income to meet their current economic needs, much less their future needs. Many people with children under age eighteen cannot afford to save for their children's education or pay their college tuition bills during the same years that they should be putting aside money for their own retirement (E. Brandon, 2009). Those who have experienced lengthy periods of unemployment during the Great Recession often cannot afford to save money for either.

From the conflict perspective, age-based inequality is rooted in power differentials, and short of dramatic changes in the structure of political and economic power in society, the only way for older people to hold onto previous gains is through continued activism. However, this approach does not take into account the fact that some older people have benefited more than others from social programs such as Medicare, Social Security, and the Older Americans Act (the federal law that authorizes and funds direct services such as senior centers, nutrition programs, and referral services). Groups such as the Gray Panthers and the American Association of Retired Persons (AARP) work for passage of specific legislation that has benefited many older people. Nevertheless, older people as a category are devalued in a society that prizes youth over old age and in a social structure that defines productivity primarily in terms of paid employment.

According to interactionists, however, individuals who maintain strong relationships with others and remain actively involved throughout their lifetime have reason to be optimistic about life when they reach old age. Indeed, in studies of older adults, Barbara Resnick and her colleagues found positive interpersonal relationships and a sense of purpose to be among the top qualities contributing to resilience (Resnick et al., 2011:200).

SUMMARY

✔•─ **Study** and **Review** on **mysoclab.com**

■ **What is ageism and why is it considered a social problem?**
Ageism is prejudice and discrimination against people on the basis of age. Ageism is a social problem because it perpetuates negative stereotypes and age-based discrimination, particularly against older people.

■ **What is the life course and why are different stages problematic for some people?**
The life course is generally divided into infancy and childhood, adolescence and young adulthood, middle age, later maturity, and old age. During infancy and childhood, we are dependent on other people and so are relatively powerless in society. Adolescence is a stage in which we are not treated as children but also are not afforded the full status of adulthood. In young adulthood, we acquire new roles and have a feeling of new freedom but also may have problems ranging from alcohol and drug abuse to employment instability that may make life complicated. In emerging and young adulthood, we seek a sense of identity and acquire new roles and a new sense of freedom. During middle age, we begin to show such visible signs of aging as wrinkles and gray hair, and roles begin to change in the workplace and family as children leave home. In later maturity, we increasingly find ourselves involved in caring for people of our own age and older people. Problems of older adults vary widely because of the diverse needs of the young-old (ages sixty-five to seventy-four), the old-old (ages seventy-five to eighty-four), and the oldest-old (ages eighty-five and older).

■ **What types of problems do older people face today?**
Despite laws to the contrary, older workers may experience overt or covert discrimination in the workplace. Retirement brings about changing roles and a loss of status for those older people whose identity has been based primarily on their occupation. For some older people, malnutrition, disease, and lack of health care are life-threatening problems. Older people may become the victims of scams by con artists and elder abuse by family members or nursing home personnel.

■ **How do people cope with the process of dying?**
Four explanations have been given for how people cope with dying. Kübler-Ross identified five stages that people go through: (1) denial, (2) anger, (3) bargaining, (4) depression, and (5) acceptance. By contrast, the trajectories of grief approach suggests that people have more than one way of dealing with grief: (1) resilience, (2) recovery, (3) chronic dysfunction, and (4) delayed grief or trauma. The dying trajectory suggests that individuals do not move toward death at the same speed and in the same way. The task-based approach suggests that daily activities can still be enjoyed during the dying process and that fulfilling certain tasks makes the process of death easier on everyone involved (not just the dying person).

■ **How do functionalist and symbolic interactionist explanations of age-based inequality differ?**
According to functionalists, disengagement of older people from their jobs and other social positions may be functional for society because it allows the smooth transfer of roles from one generation to the next. However, symbolic interactionists suggest that activity is important for older people because it provides new sources of identity and satisfaction later in life.

■ **How do conflict theorists explain inequality based on age?**
According to conflict theorists, aging itself is not a social problem. The problem is rooted in societal conditions that older people often face when they have inadequate resources in a capitalist society. In the capitalist system, older people are set apart as a group that depends on special policies and programs. Analysts using a feminist approach focus on how aging uniquely affects women in societies that value youth over age and men more than women.

KEY TERMS

ageism, p. 102
dependency ratio, p. 118
hospices, p. 112
social gerontology, p. 103

QUESTIONS FOR CRITICAL THINKING

1. If you were responsible for reducing ageism, what measures would you suggest to bring about greater equality? What resources would be required to fulfill your plan?

2. Should retirement be compulsory for people in some occupations and professions but not others? Consider, for example, neurosurgeons (brain surgeons), airline pilots, police officers, and firefighters? Explain your answer.

3. Which sociological theory more closely reflects how you plan to spend your later years? What other approaches to aging can you suggest?

4. Will future technological advances change how people view growing old? Explain your answer.

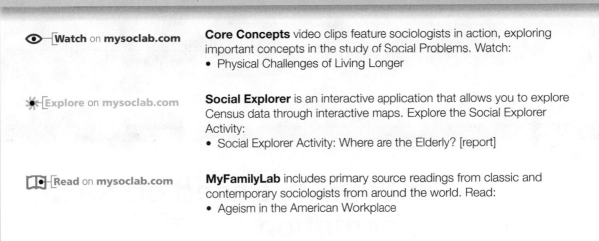

Succeed with MyFamilyLab® www.myfamilylab.com

The new MySocLab delivers proven results in helping students succeed, provides engaging experiences that personalize learning, and comes from a trusted partner with educational expertise and a deep commitment to helping students and instructors achieve their goals.

Here are a few activities you will find for this chapter.

Watch on mysoclab.com

Core Concepts video clips feature sociologists in action, exploring important concepts in the study of Social Problems. Watch:
- Physical Challenges of Living Longer

Explore on mysoclab.com

Social Explorer is an interactive application that allows you to explore Census data through interactive maps. Explore the Social Explorer Activity:
- Social Explorer Activity: Where are the Elderly? [report]

Read on mysoclab.com

MyFamilyLab includes primary source readings from classic and contemporary sociologists from around the world. Read:
- Ageism in the American Workplace

6

Inequality Based on Sexual Orientation

THINKING SOCIOLOGICALLY

○ Why is sexual orientation an emotionally charged legal and social issue in the United States?

○ What types of discrimination are based on sexual orientation?

○ How do biological and psychological explanations differ from sociological perspectives on sexual orientation?

Many times throughout my life people have been shocked when they find out my father is gay. "I had no idea," they say. "You'd never know just by looking at you." They make me feel like a rare species as their eyes scan me for any abnormalities they missed that could have tipped them off. Ladies and Gentlemen, step right up! Look closely at the child of a gay dad. No horns! No tail! In fact, she could pass for anybody's child.

—*Author Abigail Garner (2005:13) explains in her book,* Families Like Mine, *how she and other children*

of gay parents feel when they are treated differently and stigmatized by individuals who are sure they know what the child of a gay parent should look like.

It's hard to grow up under a microscope. As kids, we are expected to talk about very adult issues—sex, civil rights, legal and political issues. What other situations are there where people talk to kids and then legislate from there?

—*Jesse Gilbert, age thirty, describes how the children of gay or lesbian parents feel when they are constantly asked about their parents (Garner, 2005:13).*

The comments by these two individuals show the extent to which the children of lesbian and gay parents may be stereotyped by individuals who identify themselves as heterosexual. When Abigail Garner (in one of the opening vignettes) was five years old, her parents divorced, her father came out as gay, and she found herself in the middle of many discussions regarding the children of people who are lesbian, gay, bisexual, or transgender (LGBT). As a result, she wrote a book describing the unique issues and problems that such children face, including negative stereotyping and homophobia at school. Garner's research shows that LGBT parents and their children experience discrimination based on *sexual orientation*—**a preference for emotional-sexual relationships with individuals of the same sex (homosexuality), the opposite sex (heterosexuality), or both (bisexuality).**

People in LGBT families have been widely criticized because some people believe that gay and lesbian parents are not only different from heterosexual parents but that they are inferior to them because of their sexual orientation, lifestyle, and acceptance of non-traditional family values (O'Briant, 2008). The terms *homosexual* and *gay* are most often used in association with males who prefer same-sex relationships; the term *lesbian* is used in association with females who prefer same-sex relationships. Heterosexual individuals, who prefer opposite-sex relationships, are sometimes referred to as *straight* (e.g., "What's it like to be straight?"). It is important to note, however, that heterosexual people are much less likely to be labeled by their sexual orientation than are people who are gay, lesbian, or bisexual.

◉—⌐ **Watch** on **mysoclab.com**
Alternative Sexual Orientation on **mysoclab.com**

What criteria do social scientists use to classify individuals as gay, lesbian, or bisexual? In a definitive study of sexuality published in the mid-1990s, researchers at the University of Chicago established three criteria for identifying people as homosexual or bisexual: (1) sexual *attraction* to persons of one's own gender, (2) *sexual involvement* with one or more persons of one's own gender, and (3) *self-identification* as a gay man, lesbian, or bisexual (Michael et al., 1994). According to these criteria, then, engaging in a homosexual act does not necessarily classify a person as homosexual. In fact, many respondents in the Chicago study indicated that although they had had at least one homosexual encounter when they were younger, they no longer were involved in homosexual conduct and never identified themselves as lesbian, bisexual, or gay.

NATURE AND EXTENT OF INEQUALITY BASED ON SEXUAL ORIENTATION

How many gays, lesbians, bisexuals, and transgender persons are there in the United States? First, it is important to note that estimates of how many people report any *lifetime* same-sex sexual behavior and any same-sex sexual attraction are much higher than those who actually identify as LGB. Nearly 25.6 million people in the United States (11 percent of the population) have acknowledged in one survey or another that they have experienced as least some same-sex sexual attraction.

As for having engaged in same-sex sexual behavior, about 19 million people (8.2 percent of the population) in the United States have stated that, on at least one occasion, they have had such an encounter.

Why is it difficult to determine the number of people who identify as LGBT if they are willing to self-report their sexual orientation on questionnaires or in other kinds of research? What about the U.S. Census Bureau count, for example? Although the U.S. Census Bureau keeps track of numbers in sex, age, and racial-ethnic categories, it does not ask about sexual orientation or gender identity in its surveys. LGBT persons living with a spouse or partner can identify their relationship by checking either the "husband or wife" or "unmarried partner" box. In 2009, the Census Bureau estimated that 581,000 same-sex couples were living in the United States, but it did not count gay singles. Census 2010 will be the first to officially report on same-sex partners and same-sex spouses; however, this information is not available at the time of this writing. Additional information may also be available on the transgender population: Census 2010 asked a question about each person's sex, and transgender persons were asked to select only one sex—the one with which they most strongly identify.

Read the Document

The Five Sexes: Why Male and Female Are Not Enough on **mysoclab.com**

Because of the lack of official data, determining how many people identify as LGBT involves estimates and guesswork. The Williams Institute at the University of California at Los Angeles School of Law estimates that 9 million people (about 3.8 percent of all Americans) identify as gay, lesbian, bisexual, or transgender. According to this report, bisexuals make up 1.8 percent of the U.S. population, with more women than men typically identifying as bisexual. Only a slightly smaller proportion (1.7 percent) identify as being gay or lesbian. Transgender adults make up 0.3 percent of the population (Gates, 2011). However, as previously noted, the exact percentages are not known (see Box 6.1).

Why is homosexuality a controversial issue? Although homosexuality has existed in most societies throughout human history, for most of the last 2,000 years, there have been groups—sometimes entire societies—that considered homosexuality "a crime against nature," "an abomination," or "a sin" (Doyle, 1995:224). Most societies have norms pertaining to *sexuality*—**attitudes, beliefs, and practices related to sexual attraction and intimate relationships with others**. The norms are based on the assumption that some forms of attraction and sexual relationships are *normal* and appropriate and others are *abnormal* and *inappropriate*. In many societies, homosexual conduct has been classified as a form of *deviance*—**a behavior, belief,**

Social Problems and Statistics

How Many People Are Lesbian, Gay, Bisexual, and Transgender?

According to sociologist Joel Best (2001:87), "bad statistics often take on a life of their own." In other words, when statistics are frequently repeated, they are assumed to be valid and are taken for granted. Best uses the discrepancy between estimates of how many gays and lesbians live in the United States as one example. Today, most research focuses not only on gay and lesbian persons but also bisexual and transgender people, which makes counting even more difficult.

The earliest estimates of the number of gays and lesbians residing in the United States arose from studies by biologist Alfred Kinsey and his colleagues in the 1930s and 1940s. On the basis of interviews with more than 11,000 people, the researchers developed the so-called Kinsey Report (Kinsey et al., 1948), which suggested that about 10 percent of the male population and a slightly lower percentage of the female population in the United

States was more or less exclusively homosexual at some point between the ages of sixteen and fifty-five. Although Kinsey's research has been widely criticized because it included a much higher proportion of prisoners (who did not have options for heterosexual sexual encounters), middle-class whites, and college-educated people than resided in the general population, the 10 percent figure became widely accepted.

Other studies have produced estimates quite different from that of the Kinsey Report. On the basis of a 1992 survey of more than 3,000 noninstitutionalized U.S. residents, for example, Edward O. Laumann and colleagues (1994) concluded that about 2.8 percent of adult males and 1.4 percent of adult females in this country self-identify as gays or lesbians and that about 4.9 percent of males and 2.7 percent of females had engaged in homosexual conduct at some point since age eighteen.

or condition that violates social norms. This classification can make people targets of prejudice, discrimination, and even death. Extreme prejudice toward gay men and lesbians is known as *homophobia—excessive fear or intolerance of homosexuality*. According to sociologists, homophobia is a *socially determined prejudice*, not a medically recognized *phobia*. Homophobia is intensified by the ideology of *compulsory heterosexism*, a belief system that denies, denigrates, and stigmatizes any gay, lesbian, or bisexual behavior, identity, relationship, or community. Somewhat like institutional racism and sexism, compulsory heterosexism is embedded in a society's social structure and maintained by ideologies that are rooted in religion and law.

IDEOLOGICAL BASES OF INEQUALITY BASED ON SEXUAL ORIENTATION

How does inequality based on sexual orientation differ from prejudice and discrimination against racial or ethnic groups, women, older people, and individuals in other devalued categories? Social analyst Bruce Bawer (1994:81) has forcefully argued that homophobia differs from other forms of bigotry in everyday life:

> In a world of prejudice, there is no other prejudice quite like [homophobia]. Mainstream writers, politicians, and cultural leaders who hate Jews or blacks or Asians but who have long since accepted the unwritten rules that forbid public expression of those prejudices still denounce gays with impunity. For such people, gays are the Other in a way that Jews or blacks or Asians are not. After all, they can look at Jewish or black or Asian family life and see something that, in its chief components—husband, wife, children, workplace, school, house of worship—is essentially a variation of their own lives; yet when they look at gays—or, rather, at the image of gays that has been fostered both by the mainstream culture and by the gay subculture—they see creatures whose lives seem to be different from theirs in every possible way.

DID YOU KNOW

- Consensual sexual acts between adults of the same sex are illegal in more than seventy-five countries worldwide.

- An estimated 3.8 percent of the adult population in the United States identify as lesbian, gay, bisexual, or transgender.

- Growing numbers of TV series geared toward teens are showing gay and lesbian characters dealing with issues associated with sexual orientation.

Box 6.1

In the 2000s more surveys have included questions that make it possible for researchers to estimate the size of the LGBT population, but these estimates also vary widely. An an example, scholarly Gary J. Gates (2011) of the Williams Institute at the University of California Los Angeles School of Law points out that the 2008 General Social Survey-found 1.1 percent of respondents in one study identified as bisexual, and 1.7 percent as gay/lesbian, for a total of 2.9 percent. By contrast, two other studies cited by Gates found higher percentages: the 2009 California Health Interview Survey found 1.4 percent bisexual and 1.8 percent gay/lesbian, for a total of 3.2 percent, while the 2009 National Survey of Sexual Health and Behavior found the largest percentages—3.1 percent for bisexual and 2.5 percent for gay/lesbian. These studies all focused on people who identify themselves as lesbian, gay, or bisexual because the transgender category is more difficult to determine other than on the basis of self-identification (Gates, 2011).

Differences in estimates of the LGBT population may be attributed to a number of factors. First, how representative is the population that is being surveyed in comparison with the overall population that the statistics allegedly represent? Second, how accurate are the responses with regard to the conclusions that are drawn from those responses? By way of example, in face-to-face interviews, will people sometimes give inaccurate responses with regard to questions about things such as sexual orientation or conduct? Either of those factors (and many others) can greatly skew the results of the survey. As a result, we should be careful in assuming that statistics about such subjects are accurate.

As gay rights advocates suggest, however, regardless of how many people are LGBT in the United States or elsewhere, the central issue is not about numbers but rather about reducing discrimination. Social policy should seek to do this, regardless of the exact number of people the policy affects.

According to Bawer, heterosexuals cannot identify with the daily lives of lesbians and gay men, who—unlike them—exist as identifiable categories primarily because there is such strong antigay prejudice in the United States. In fact, the stereotypic beliefs that dominant (heterosexual) group members hold about gay men and lesbians are a major impediment to achieving gay rights and reducing inequalities based on sexual orientation. Stereotypic beliefs about lesbians and gay men often equate people's sexual *orientation* with sexual *practice*. For example, all gay men and lesbians, regardless of the nature and extent of their sexual activity, are stereotyped as being sexually compulsive and possibly predatory.

Media depictions often reinforce stereotypes of gay men as being more excitable and emotional than heterosexual men, and lesbians are portrayed as overly muscular and athletic, aggressive, and sometimes strident. Recently, some television shows have sought to bring gay lifestyles into prime-time programming. Although a few of these shows have perpetuated negative stereotypes about lesbians and gay men, others have attempted to change public perceptions about issues related to sexual orientation (see Box 6.2). Religion and law have been two primary social institutions that have strongly influenced how sexual orientation is viewed and how it has been dealt with by societies throughout history.

Social Problems in the Media

Box 6.2

A Mixed Bag: Praise and Criticism for Young Lesbian and Gay Characters on *Glee*

Coming-out stories are standards, almost a cliché on television shows dealing with gay characters and this goes back to the '70s and '80s. What's probably different now is that the age is becoming younger, and I think this reflects the fact that the sort of battleground for gay people in society includes high school and probably even includes middle school. It's moved younger in the past decade or so, I think in part . . . because young people are becoming more aware of their identities.

—*Larry Gross, director of the University of Southern California's Annenberg School for Communication and Journalism, discusses how more gay and lesbian characters are now portrayed on TV shows targeting younger audiences (quoted in Friedlander, 2011).*

In the aftermath of media reports of physical and cyberbullying of gay teens and young adults, some of which resulted in suicide, controversy continues to surround the portrayal of gay and lesbian characters on TV shows appealing to younger audiences. FOX network's *Glee* is an example of a show that has received both acclaim and protest. This comedy-drama series, set at the fictitious William McKinley High School in Lima, Ohio, shows the glee club director's efforts to restore the club to its former glory even as other faculty and students ridicule the club and its members. However, a subplot emerges in *Glee* that involves what it is like to be a gay or lesbian in high school, why students are fearful about what other

people will think if they find out that a person is a lesbian or gay, and how lesbian, gay, and bisexual students determine whether they should come out or remain secretive about their orientation.

In addition to network TV series such as *Glee*, cable shows such as *The L World* (shown here) now feature more gay, lesbian, bisexual and transgendered characters in recent years. Does this mean that problems associated with sexual orientation will soon be eliminated? Why or why not?

Glee involves a number of characters who have emerged as gay or lesbian as the series has progressed. Kurt Hummel (Chris Colfer), one of the most visibly gay characters, is bullied by football player Dave Karofsky (Max Adler) who constantly threatens Kurt, knocks him into school lockers, and throws slushies all over him. In one episode, Karofsky kisses Kurt while they are in the middle of an intense argument. Kurt tells Karofsky that he knows he is gay and that he should be honest with himself and come out. Karofsky's response is to threaten to kill Kurt if he tells anyone. Karofsky eventually acknowledges that he is gay and apologizes to Kurt for how badly he has treated him but he still does not want anyone to find out that he is gay. As the series developed, additional gay, lesbian, and bisexual characters were introduced and more issues confronting LGBT persons in high school were included in the storyline.

LGBT advocates have praised the show for its candor and for raising public awareness about problems of gay and lesbian students. In 2011, *Glee* was named Outstanding Comedy Series by the Gay & Lesbian Alliance Against Defamation (GLAAD). However, the series has also been the target of criticism from so-called conservative and religious media spokespersons. Examples include conservative media critic Dan Gainor's description of *Glee* as a "depraved initiative" of the show's creator Ryan Murphy "to promote his gay agenda" (huffingtonpost.com, 2011). According to Gainor, "This is clearly Ryan Murphy's vision of what growing up should be, not most of America's. It's a high school most parents would not want to send their kids to" (huffingtonpost.com, 2011). Gainor's comments echo the sentiments of numerous other conservative and religious commentators who believe that shows such as *Glee* "shove the gay thing down our throats" and portray a "disgusting gay teen sex romp" (huffingtonpost.com, 2011).

What will the future hold for gay-friendly TV shows? A study conducted by GLADD found that, of the 587 series regular characters shown across 84 programs on five broadcast networks (ABC, CBS, The CW, FOX, and NBC) in the 2010 to 2011 season, 23 characters (3.9 percent) were LGBT while 564 (96.1 percent) were straight (heterosexual). The breakdown of LGBT characters was as follows: 14 characters (2.4 percent) were gay men; 7 characters (1.2 percent) were bisexual females; and 2 characters (0.3 percent) were lesbians (GLADD, 2011). Spokespersons for GLAAD and similar organizations suggest that we have a long way to go in proportionate representation of gays and lesbians in the media and in their treatment in everyday life: These individuals are often viewed as one-dimensional people rather than as whole persons who possess many different—and praiseworthy—attributes and talents.

Question for Consideration

1. How do you think the portrayal of people based on their sexual orientation might be improved on television, in films, and in other forms of popular entertainment?

Independent Research

Conduct your own study to identify positive and negative examples of how various media forms portray people based on their sexual orientation. Compare your findings with reports found on the GLAAD website (www.glaad.org).

Religion and Sexual Orientation

Most of the major religions of the world—Judaism, Christianity, Islam, and Hinduism, as well as Confucianism—historically have regarded homosexuality as a sin. Indeed, the only major world religion that does not condemn homosexuality is Buddhism (Dynes, 1990). Religious fundamentalists in particular denounce homosexual conduct as a sign of great moral decay and societal chaos. In the Judeo-Christian tradition, religious condemnation of homosexuality derives from both the Hebrew Scriptures (e.g., Genesis 19 and Leviticus 18:33) and the New Testament (e.g., Romans 1:26–27 and I Corinthians 6:9) (Kosmin and Lachman, 1993).

Since the early 1990s, same-sex marriages and the ordination of "practicing" lesbians and gay men have been vigorously debated by various religious organizations. For example, the Vatican has directed Roman Catholic bishops in the United States to oppose laws that protect homosexuals, promote public acceptance of homosexual conduct, or give gay relationships

equal footing with traditional, heterosexual marriage. However, many Roman Catholics disagree with the directive, stating that it is based on the faulty assumption that lesbians and gay men seek to influence the sexual orientation of children or youths with whom they live or work, that gay people are erotically attracted to every person of their own gender, and that they cannot control their sexual impulses in same-sex environments (cited in Bawer, 1994). Roman Catholics are not the only religious group debating same-sex marriage and the ordination of lesbians and gay men: The Southern Baptist Convention voted to expel two congregations—one for blessing the union of two gay men and the other for licensing a gay divinity student to preach. Although Baptist congregations usually are allowed to be autonomous, religious leaders determined that this autonomy did not extend to "acts to affirm, approve or endorse homosexual behavior" because these acts are deemed to be "contrary to the Bible on human sexuality and the sanctity of the family" (cited in Kosmin and Lachman, 1993:230). In 2011, the Southern Baptist Convention voted to take corrective measures that would help increase racial and ethnic diversity in congregations and overcome past racism; however, when gay and lesbian advocates asked leaders of the convention to apologize for antihomosexual policies and "destructive efforts to 'cure' people of homosexuality," the convention refused by reaffirming the church's official position that homosexual behavior is a sin as dictated by the Bible (Eckholm, 2011:A20) By contrast, a breakthrough occurred for gay and lesbian persons in the Presbyterian Church (U.S.A.) in 2011 when the 2.1 million member denomination changed its ordination policy so that openly gay and lesbian persons in same-sex relationships could be ordained as ministers, elders, and deacons in the church (Colbert, 2011). Other mainline Protestant churches, including the United Church of Christ and the Episcopal and Evangelical Lutheran churches, have also accepted gay and lesbian clergy. Church leaders in these denominations have been careful to state that changes in policy do not mean that local churches will be required to ordain gay and lesbian clergy; the change means that it is now acceptable under church rules if the congregations wish to do so.

As opposed to looking to traditional denominations for church membership, some lesbians and gays have carved out their own niches by forming religious bodies of their own, such as the Metropolitan Community Church, that focus on the spiritual needs of the gay community. Others have turned to websites such as gay-church.org, which claims to be one of the largest gay and lesbian affirming Christian church directories and bulletin boards in the world.

Law and Sexual Orientation

Throughout U.S. history, moral and religious teachings have been intertwined with laws that criminalize homosexual conduct. In the past, the law looked at homosexual *conduct* differently from the way it deals with *homosexuality*. The thinking was that to be a homosexual was not a crime, but to engage in homosexual conduct was a crime, at least in those states that had passed *sodomy laws* criminalizing oral or anal intercourse between persons of the same sex. Under these state laws, it was possible to imprison persons who engaged in oral or anal intercourse regardless of their sexual orientation. In 1986, in *Bowers v. Hardwick*, the U.S. Supreme Court upheld the constitutionality of a Georgia state law that criminalized oral and anal sex in private between consenting adults whether or not the conduct was between persons of the same sex. For homosexuals, the Court's ruling virtually eliminated protection for sexual activities and created the impression that gay or lesbian

couples had no privacy rights. Seventeen years later, the Supreme Court reversed *Bowers v. Hardwick* in its 2003 decision in *Lawrence v. Texas*, which invalidated sodomy laws in all fourteen states that had such laws on their books.

Gay rights activists and other civil rights advocates who had long advocated for change in state laws pertaining to sodomy expressed their approval of the Supreme Court's decision because they saw it not only as benefiting individuals but also as another step forward in the long battle for gay rights in the United States.

DISCRIMINATION BASED ON SEXUAL ORIENTATION

As campaigns for equal rights and an end to antigay discrimination have progressed, more people have come forward to declare that they are gay, lesbian, or bisexual and to indicate their support for gay organizations. Many lesbian or gay couples have sought the statutory right to marry, to obtain custody of children, to adopt, and to have their property pass to one another at death—in sum, to do all the things that people in heterosexual marriages are permitted to do. However, because ideas about marriage and the family are at the core of many people's moral or religious objections to homosexuality, gay marriage is still among the more controversial social issues today.

The Fight for Marital Rights

In June 2011, New York joined the District of Columbia and Connecticut, Iowa, Massachusetts, New Hampshire, and Vermont to become the sixth (and by far the most populous) U.S. state to allow gay and lesbian couples to enter into legally recognized marital relationships. As of that date, four additional states (Maryland, New Mexico, New York, and Rhode Island) had pledged that they would not discriminate against marriages between same-sex couples from other states, but these states had not officially opened the door to same-sex marriage in their own state. The issue is complicated from a legal standpoint because states have the right to regulate marriage within their own borders, and some states have passed constitutional amendments that limit marriage to a union between a man and a woman while others have enacted statutes that restrict marriage to two persons of the opposite sex.

Adding an additional layer to various decisions made by the states, the federal government, during the administration of President Bill Clinton, passed the 1996

Defense of Marriage Act that bars federal recognition of same-sex marriage. More recently, the Obama administration declared that the Defense of Marriage Act is unconstitutional and that the U.S. Justice Department will no longer defend the law in court. President Obama's decision in this regard created yet another great political and moral divide between gay rights advocates who praised the change and political conservatives who denounced the decision. Recent polls have shown that the U.S. public generally favors equal rights for gay and lesbian people with one exception—the right of same-sex couples to marry. The outcome of the gay marriage issue remains to be seen; however, many social analysts believe that if the "marriage" barrier is removed, it will open the door to many other legal challenges, including state laws about adoption and federal laws pertaining to noncitizen spouses applying for legal residency (Savage and Stolberg, 2011).

Today, as in previous decades, many same-sex partners who have united but are unable to legally marry have chosen to cohabit. *Cohabitation* refers to the practice in which partners live together in a sexual relationship where they assume the same responsibilities as a "married couple" but are not considered by law to have all of the rights and privileges of those who are considered to be legally "married."

Some cities and states have given legal recognition to the concept of a **domestic partnership—a household partnership between two individuals of the same gender who live together in a long-term relationship of indefinite duration and share a common domestic life but are not legally married or joined by a civil union**. Initially, some gay rights advocates saw the recognition of domestic partnerships as a major step forward because it was believed that same-sex partners would derive more of the rights and benefits, such as health insurance coverage through employers, that were provided to heterosexual married couples. However, gay and lesbians quickly found that certain rights came only with a marriage license and that there was strong opposition to efforts by unmarried lesbian or gay couples to attempt to exercise such rights as joint parenting through birth or adoption; the right to file joint income tax returns; legal immigration and residency for partners from other countries; benefits such as annuities, pensions, and Social Security for surviving spouses; wrongful death benefits for surviving partners; and immunity from having to testify in court against a spouse.

Because of the many limitations placed on domestic partnerships and the desire to be legally married, many same-sex couples in the United States have chosen to get married in countries such as Canada, Belgium, Spain, and the Netherlands, which provide legal recognition for same sex unions. Other couples have chosen to marry in states where same-sex marriages are currently recognized.

As battles over same-sex marriage have continued in states such as California, some analysts have compared the discrimination faced by lesbian and gay couples with that of earlier bans on interracial marriage in the United States. In deciding a case regarding same-sex marriage in the California Supreme Court, for example, the Chief Justice quoted from that court's 1948 decision in *Perez v. Sharp* that struck down a state ban on interracial marriage: "The essence of the right to marry is freedom to join in marriage with the person of one's choice" (quoted in Liptak, 2008:A10). However, opponents of same-sex marriage argue that this comparison is not valid because they believe marriage has nothing to do with *race* and everything to do with the union of *a man and a woman* (Liptak, 2008). It remains to be seen what the longer-term implications of the California Supreme Court's decision and similar ones will be for the future of marital rights for gay and lesbian couples. Yet another murky area of rights that contributes to inequality based on sexual orientation is the issue of parental rights in the United States.

Although more states have legalized same-sex marriage, controversy continues over the rights of gay and lesbian couples in the United States.

Parental Rights

Like the fight for marital rights, the LGBT community has struggled for many years to gain the same parental rights as heterosexual couples. What are parental rights? The term *parental rights* refers to all of the legal rights, and corresponding legal obligations, that are attached to being the parent of a child. These rights include, but are not limited to, the following: (1) the right to legal and physical custody of the child, (2) the right to physical access or visitation with the child, (3) the right to inherit property from the child and to have the child inherit property from the parent, (4) the right to consent to medical care and treatment for the child, (5) the right to consent to the marriage of the child or to the child's enlistment in military service, and (6) the ability to contract on behalf of the child. The corresponding legal obligations include the following duties: (1) financial support for the child, (2) legal defense in legal proceedings, (3) care and supervision of the child, (4) legal liability for some damages the child may cause, (5) responsibility for seeing that the child attends school, and (6) the obligation to protect the child and provide a safe environment for the child (Adoption Glossary, 2011). If gay and lesbian couples are denied parental rights by law and in the courts of the land, they have little or no legal recourse and are unable to exert authority over their children's lives, health care, property, or much else about them. For this reason, gay and lesbian advocates have combined their efforts with organizations such as the American Civil Liberties Union to staunchly defend the rights of LGBT parents in regard to the care, custody, and control over their children.

Estimates suggest that between 8 and 10 million children are being raised by gay or lesbian parents in the United States. Data from Census 2010 show that child rearing among same-sex couples is more prevalent in the southern regions of the United States, and many of these couples are either African American or Latino. According to gay rights advocates, the data do not match the stereotypical image of gay parents as being white, affluent, urban, and living in the Northeast or on the West Coast (Tavernise, 2011) .

How do gay and lesbian couples parent children? Many gay and lesbian couples entered into their current relationship after first having children in heterosexual relationships. In this situation, one LGB partner typically is the biological and legal parent of the child. In some court custody cases, the nonbiological parent has been deemed to have no legal standing because he or she has neither biological nor legal ties to the child. To prevent this situation from occurring, some lesbian and gay couples have drafted their own parenting contracts, but for the most part, these agreements are not enforceable in court and can be revoked by the biological parent at any time. Many couples rely on legal documents such as special powers of attorney, wills, and guardianship agreements to protect both partners' rights, but these documents do not have the legal force of formal adoption. As more states allow unmarried partners—whether gay or straight—to adopt children, more same-sex couples are actively seeking joint legal custody of their children.

Other children come into the gay family through adoption, surrogacy through in vitro fertilization (IVF), or foster parenting. According to preliminary Census 2010 data, about 19 percent of same-sex couples *who are raising children* reported that they had an adopted child living in the house. This is more than double the 8 percent who reported in the 2000 Census that they had adopted a child (Tavernise, 2011). This percentage should not be confused with the estimated 1.6 percent of *all* lesbian and gay households (totaling approximately 3.1 million) in the United States that reportedly included an adopted child under the age of eighteen. This would add up to nearly 52,000 children. States with the largest number of adopted children living with lesbian and gay parents include California, New York, Massachusetts, Texas, and Washington. At the time of this writing (June 2011) only two states—Mississippi and Utah—specifically prohibit same-sex couples from adopting a child; however, twenty-five states have barriers to adoption because same-sex couples cannot legally marry in those states.

Recent data from the Census Bureau suggest that increasing numbers of lesbian and gay couples are adopting children in spite of the fact that issues pertaining to children's rights and protection in this situation have not been resolved. Two factors have contributed to this increase: (1) the large number of children currently in need of a home and waiting for adoption, and (2) changes in social attitudes and greater acceptance of gays and lesbians in the United States (Tavernise, 2011). Ironically, in some states, gay singles are permitted to adopt children whereas gay couples face stronger prohibitions. Part of the burden on gay and lesbian parents attempting to adopt a child is the necessity of showing that they will be fit parents and that the child's development will not be affected by the parents' sexual orientation.

In addition to adoption (or prior parenting from an opposite-sex relationship), lesbian couples often choose artificial insemination to produce a child. Insemination is the medical procedure by which sperm is inserted into a woman's uterus in an effort to create a pregnancy. The sperm may be from a donor known to one or both of the partners, or it may come from a sperm bank. As more lesbian couples have chosen IVF to become parents, issues have arisen about the rights of nonbiological gay parents, whose claims often are the least recognized. For this reason, advocacy groups believe that legal standing must be given to both parents of children conceived through artificial insemination or traditional surrogacy.

Among gay men, some couples prefer surrogacy because there is a chance for at least one of the partners to be biologically related to the child and be named on the child's birth certificate. Two main types of surrogacy are used: traditional surrogacy and Gestational surrogacy which is done via IVF. Traditional surrogacy is done by artificial insemination: The surrogate uses her own eggs and may use the sperm of one partner in the gay couple. Gestational surrogacy is done by IVF: The gay partners select an egg donor and these eggs may be fertilized by one of the gay couple or a donor, or they may be divided into two batches for fertilization by each partner. In this case, one embryo created by each partner is implanted in the surrogate mother. If a child is conceived, the partners can, if they so desire, have genetic testing performed at a later date to determine the identity of the biological father. Costs for procedures range from a low of $15,000 or $20,000 upward to $150,000 and above. Only affluent lesbian and gay couples can afford some of the more expensive procedures or the repeated use of such procedures, which may be necessary before conception occurs.

Foster parenting is another key concern for many lesbians and gays. Foster care is a state-run program that provides stand-in parents ("foster parents") for minor children who have been removed from the home of their biological parents. Some children have been removed because of abuse or neglect; others were living in families that suffered from financial hardship or other psychosocial problems that could not be taken care of sufficiently to meet the requirements of child welfare agencies. If these issues are eventually cleared up, the parent might regain custody of the child or children. Many in the LGBT community have experienced discrimination when they sought to become foster parents. Widespread myths about the "homosexual lifestyle" lead to the notion that children living with lesbian or gay parents may witness immoral conduct or be recruited into homosexuality. Most states do not prohibit LGBT persons from becoming foster parents per se, but some states (such as Utah) draw the line at letting unmarried,

"Sometimes I think you only married me for the political statement."

cohabiting couples become fosters. This policy results in discrimination against gay and lesbian couples who seek to become foster parents in states where they are not permitted to legally marry. Recently, efforts to restrict gays and lesbians who want to become foster parents or adopt children have been thwarted by public opinion and successful activism on the part of organized advocacy groups that use compelling arguments such as asking this question: "Is it really true that children are better off with *no* home at all rather than living in a gay home?"

Gay rights advocates are cautiously optimistic that social norms and laws are gradually changing. They hope that, in time, sexual orientation alone will not be grounds for denying gay or lesbian couples the opportunity to adopt children or become foster parents. Similarly, LGBT advocates seek laws that afford more equitable parental custody and visitation rights to lesbian or gay parents. Advocates argue that the courts should rule solely on the basis of whether or not individuals and couples will make good parents or, in the case of relationships and marriages that are being dissolved, which parent can provide a better home for the child.

Housing Discrimination

Housing laws have been passed at the federal, state, and local levels to prohibit housing discrimination in the sale, rental, or financing of homes. The earliest federal housing discrimination law, passed in 1866, prohibited racial discrimination; however,

Explore the Concept
Social Explorer Activity: Cohabitation Among Unmarried Same-Sex Couples on mysoclab.com

this law was not widely enforced until the U.S. Supreme Court interpreted that statute to apply to private real estate transactions. The Federal Fair Housing Act was also passed by Congress in 1968, and amended in 1988, to provide legal remedies when individuals were found to be the victims of housing discrimination. The original act specifically focused on discrimination on the basis of race, color, religion, sex, and national origin. In 1988, the act was amended to include discrimination against families with children and persons with physical and/or mental disabilities. However, the Fair Housing Act does not provide protection against housing discrimination for LGBT people. Gays and lesbians have been discriminated against in a number of ways, including by real estate agents who refuse to show them houses in certain "family oriented" apartment or condo buildings or neighborhoods, as well as by finance or insurance companies that treat same-sex couples differently than other prospective homebuyers or lessees. Transgender people have been particularly harmed by discriminatory practices in housing. Transgender respondents in one study were nearly four times more likely to live in extreme poverty, and one in five respondents stated that they experienced homelessness because of their gender identity (thetaskforce.org, 2011).

Like federal law, most state and local law focused primarily on race, color, and national origin until recent decades when more state laws and city ordinances began to prohibit discrimination on the basis of sexual orientation. Based on regional divisions used by the U.S. Census Bureau, the District of Columbia and the following states have laws prohibiting such discrimination: western regional states—Hawaii, California, Oregon, Washington, Nevada, Colorado, and New Mexico; northeastern regional states—Maine, New Hampshire, Vermont, Massachusetts, Rhode Island, Connecticut, New York, and New Jersey; midwestern regional states—Wisconsin, Illinois, Minnesota, and Iowa; and southern regional states—Delaware and Maryland. Conspicuously missing from this list are a large number of southern states, some of which are colloquially referred to as "The Bible Belt," where religious conservatives have been a strong voice in opposition to equal rights for LGBT people.

However, the turbulent rental and housing market in the 2010s brought about some changes in the attitudes of landlords, apartment managers, realtors, mortgage loan financiers, and others in regard to gay and lesbian tenants and owners. When more affluent gay or lesbian couples sought to purchase houses and condominiums, particularly in so-called gay-friendly cities such as San Francisco or Austin, Texas, they found that they

had few, if any, problems with discrimination. Property managers and owners are far less likely than in the past to refuse to rent or sell property to LGBT persons or to make derogatory comments about the individuals or their lifestyles. However, this does not mean that the problem of housing discrimination is been resolved for gays and lesbians. The U.S. Department of Housing and Urban Development is conducting a nationwide study to determine the extent of housing discrimination based on sexual orientation and gender identity. The department is also proposing regulations to ensure that LGBT persons will not be denied public housing or government housing vouchers because of their sexual orientation. However, the U.S. Conference of Catholic Bishops is urging federal housing officials not to adopt proposed rules that would bar groups that receive federal funds from discriminating against LGBT persons in housing programs. According to the bishops' conference, the new rules would force some religious groups to compromise their beliefs or quit Housing and Urban Development programs because some faith-based organizations make housing placements based on their religious beliefs, particularly those pertaining to cohabitation, whether they are heterosexual or homosexual couples (Burke, 2011).

Discrimination in Medical Care

Like housing, medical care is not exempt from discrimination based on sexual orientation. A recent study by Lambda Legal, an LGBT advocacy group, found that health care discrimination experienced by LGBT people and people living with HIV was pervasive (365gay.com, 2010). The study found that many LGBT people had been turned away or faced discrimination when they were sick or seeing medical care. Like many in the heterosexual population, large numbers of LGBT people have been unable to afford the high cost of health insurance coverage. However, unlike the heterosexual community, many LGBT persons have not been able to acquire employer-provided health insurance, particularly because they often cannot be counted as a dependent under their partner's insurance plan. Still other LGBT individuals were denied insurance on the basis of preexisting conditions such as HIV. The problem was especially pronounced among transgender people, some of whom reported that they had been refused care because of bias. Transgender respondents also had over four times the national average of HIV infection, which contributes to some health care professionals' lack of desire to provide medical treatments. Examples include refusing to touch patients or using excessive precautions, as well as using harsh or abusive language and blaming a patient for his or her health status. According to the Lambda study, almost 56 percent of LGBT respondents experienced some type of discrimination in care, as compared to 70 percent of transgender and gender-nonconforming respondents (www.365gay.com, 2010). Further confounding the problem of discrimination was the race, ethnicity, and/or class of LGBT persons: More persons of color and/or low-income individuals experienced discrimination or substandard care than white Americans with higher incomes.

Currently, doctors in a number of states (see the previous list) that have laws protecting LGBT persons against differential treatment, or refusal to treat, cannot withhold treatment or provide substandard treatment because of a patient's sexual orientation or gender identity. The American Medical Association's ethics rules prohibit discrimination, and the AMA has developed guidelines calling for equal treatment of LGBT patients, doctors, and medical students, which are available at the AMA website (www.ama-assn.org).

Despite laws and ethical guidelines to the contrary, all health care providers do not comply with nondiscrimination requirements. LGBT persons continue to fight for equal rights in the important area of health care, and advocates are focusing on the Affordable Care Act of 2010 as a means by which many LGBT persons may be able to afford health insurance coverage or apply for Medicaid. Advocates are particularly concerned that the new health care law should provide broad inclusion of all people regardless of their real or perceived sexual orientation or gender identity. Four key areas have been identified by LGBT advocates as being of great important to their community (Baker and Krehely, 2011):

- Achieving comprehensive nondiscriminatory protection in health insurance exchanges
- Establishing LGBT-inclusive data collection policies
- Recognizing and including LGBT families in all health reform activities
- Supporting community-based health interventions that are LGBT-inclusive

The Affordable Care Act and other issues pertaining to health care are discussed in Chapter 10.

Workplace Discrimination

Despite laws in many states that prohibit discrimination in employment on the basis of sexual orientation, openly LGBT people continue to face widespread discrimination in hiring, retention, and promotion in private and public sector employment. Estimates suggest that from 15 to 43 percent of gay people have experienced some form of discrimination and harassment at the workplace. Transgender people have a more staggering rate of reported discrimination: 90 percent indicate that they have experienced some form of harassment or mistreatment on the job (Burns and Krehely, 2011).

The Williams Institute of Sexual Orientation Law and Public Policy surveyed numerous studies to assess the extent of workplace discrimination and identified the following major forms of discrimination: being passed over for a job or fired because of sexual orientation or gender identity; receiving a negative performance evaluation or being passed over for promotion because they were gay or transgender; and experiencing verbal or physical abuse or having their workplace vandalized because of their sexual orientation (Burns and Krehely, 2011). Problems of workplace discrimination based on sexual orientation or gender identity were not identified by LGBT persons only: Straight coworkers also reported that they were aware of discrimination and harassment against LGBT employees at their place of employment.

In 2011, a landmark bill was introduced in both houses of Congress to ban workplace discrimination based on sexual orientation and gender identity. The Employment Non-Discrimination Act (ENDA) is designed to fill gaps in existing state civil rights laws that make many LGBT people and their families vulnerable to employment discrimination. At the time of this writing, employers in twenty-nine states could refuse to hire someone, or fire them, because they were gay, lesbian, or bisexual. Transgendered workers could be denied employment or fired in thirty-seven states. The passage of ENDA would provide legal protection for LGBT persons in the workplace (American Civil Liberties Union [ACLU], 2011).

Sexual harassment of LGBT workers has also been an ongoing concern in the workplace. Although the Equal Employment Opportunity Commission, a federal agency, acknowledges that same-sex sexual harassment occurs in the workplace, the problem has not always been taken seriously. To prove sexual harassment, victims must show that the harasser targeted a specific category of people such as gay men; therefore charges of harassment reflect the victim's sexual orientation. Victims of same-sex harassment may be blamed for causing the incident. Many fear that they will lose their job if they file a grievance, even though gay rights advocates believe that sexual orientation should be irrelevant in determining whether harassment has occurred.

Discrimination in the Military

In the past, the U.S. military, the nation's largest employer, held that lesbians and gay men were unfit to serve their country, especially if they made their sexual orientation known to others. Although many closeted gay men and lesbians served in various branches of the military over the years, the official government policy was one of exclusion, based on the myth that homosexuals were a security risk because they might be blackmailed by someone who found out about their sexual orientation. Accordingly, tens of thousands of gay and lesbian military service personnel sought to appear as conventional as possible and to behave like heterosexual people. This course of action often had devastating personal consequences for closeted soldiers and sailors (see Shilts, 1993).

When President Bill Clinton attempted to overturn an existing ban on gay service members, the outcry by many military and religious leaders forced the administration to promulgate a compromise policy known as "Don't Ask, Don't Tell," which was made law in 1993. Under this policy, commanders could no longer ask about a serviceperson's sexual orientation, and gay men and lesbians could serve in the military as long as they did not reveal their sexual orientation and refrained from homosexual acts. President George W. Bush supported the "Don't Ask, Don't Tell" policy throughout his two terms in office. Although some social analysts believed that the policy provided gay men and lesbians with the same opportunity to serve their country as heterosexuals had, others believed that this compromise was a form of institutionalized discrimination and continued their efforts to get the policy overturned.

When Senator Barack Obama was running for president, he stated that he would end "Don't Ask, Don't Tell" if elected. After the election, President Obama knew that his administration would have to defend the constitutionality of the law if it were not repealed, and he began the process of getting the law overturned. In 2010, both houses of Congress voted to repeal the "Don't Ask, Don't Tell" policy and sent the provision to President Obama, who signed it into law. What effect this change will have on the military will not be evident for some period of time: The repeal did not go into effect immediately, and there has been some indication that all vestiges of the policy are far from removed in all branches of the U.S. military.

Victimization and Hate Crimes

Before the early 1990s, few acts of violence against gays and lesbians were ever reported in the media. Indeed, hate crimes against gay men and lesbians were not acknowledged as such, even though civil rights groups had been tracking increasing violence motivated by group prejudice for over a decade.

Hate crimes appear to be most prevalent where homophobic attitudes and behaviors are tolerated or at least overlooked. However, some behaviors are too reprehensible to be overlooked. One of the most brutal hate crimes perpetrated against a gay man occurred when Matthew Shepard, a college student, was brutally murdered because of his sexual orientation. In 1999, Shepard's killer, a twenty-two-year-old man, was given two life sentences for beating the gay University of Wyoming student to death. Shepard had been lured from a bar by two men posing as homosexuals. They drove him to the outskirts of Laramie, Wyoming, tied him to a fence, savagely pistol-whipped him, and left him to die in a snowstorm. Had it not been for an appeal for mercy in remarks to the jury by Matthew's father, Dennis Shepard, the killer might have received the death penalty. But Dennis Shepard ended his remarks with one final comment to the killer: "You robbed me of something very precious, and I will never forgive you for that" (Matthew's Place, 1999). In 2009, Congress passed the Matthew Shepard Act to expand the 1969 U.S. Federal Hate Crime Law to include crimes motivated by a victim's actual or perceived gender, sexual orientation, gender identity, or disability.

The Shepard incident was not an isolated hate crime. In numerous incidents around the country across the years, pipe-wielding youths yelling "Kill the faggot" beat a gay man unconscious in Laguna Beach, California; a gay man

The brutal murder of Matthew Shepard, a gay college student in Wyoming, produced an outcry from many people. Some were concerned that hate crimes against individuals because of race, class, gender, or sexual orientation might go unpunished; others used their own beliefs or moral values to harshly judge categories of people who often are the victims of hate crimes.

was so seriously injured in an act of "gay bashing" in Boston; and another gay man was killed by an antigay cruiser who had "picked up" his victim on the Internet. More recently, the world became aware of the suicide of Tyler Clementi, a gay first-year student at Rutgers University, who jumped to his death after his roommate secretly filmed him during a same-sex encounter in his dorm room and posted it live on the Internet. The issue was viewed by many not only as bullying but also as an example of antigay hatred and homophobia on the part of the male roommate and his female companion.

Harassment and violent incidents against younger LGBT persons contribute to a hostile environment that harms not only the well-being of those individuals who are physically and emotionally harmed by others or who commit suicide because of their harsh treatment but also other persons who are aware that many in the LGBT community are victims of verbal and physical harassment and that they themselves much continue to live and work in unsafe spaces such as schools. This problem is not unique to the United States, as explained in Box 6.3, which looks at homophobia in schools in

---

Social Problems in Global Perspective   Box 6.3

An International Message for Gay Teens: Problems Remain Worldwide but "It Gets Better"

Syndicated columnist and author Dan Savage and his partner, Terry, created a YouTube video so that supporters around the world could tell LGBT youth that life does get better if they are currently living in fear or are the victims of bullying. This site, available at (www.itgetsbetter.org/), helps inform young people that growing up isn't easy, especially for individuals in the LGBT community.

Shortly after the It Gets Better Project was started, it turned into a worldwide movement that includes its own website with submissions from celebrities, politicians, and media personalities around the globe. LGBT young people can visit the site and find hope for the future while straight persons can support friends and relatives who are LGBT.

Some people may wonder why it would be necessary for LGBT young people to receive a message of hope from other individuals around the world. The answer is simple: Even in "gay-friendly" countries such as Canada, studies continue to find that LGBT high school students routinely experience homophobic and transphobic incidents at school. This is a surprise to many people because Canada is typically portrayed as one of the world's most open and accepting nations to LGBT persons. Canada affords LGBT Canadians with most of the same legal rights as non-LGBT citizens, and Canada legalized civil marriage rights to same-sex couples nationwide in 2005.

Although this sounds positive for Canada's LGBT population, recent studies of LGBT youth in Canadian schools have shown otherwise. When Egale, Canada's national LGBT rights organization, undertook national studies of 3,700 high school students between 2007 and 2009, researchers found that more than two-thirds of LGBT students reported that they feel unsafe at school because of physical threats based on their perceived or actual sexual orientation. The two school areas where LGBT youth most

commonly felt unsafe were gender-segregated locations such as the physical education changing rooms and washrooms. Transgender students (49 percent) had the highest rate of sexual harassment in school, followed by 45 percent of students with LGBT parents, 43 percent of female bisexual students, 42 percent of male bisexual students, 40 percent of gay male students, and 33 percent of lesbian students. The most common forms of discrimination were verbal harassment and homophobic and transphobic comments such as "faggot," "lezbo," and "dyke," which were reported by 70 percent of all respondents, including both LGBT and non-LGBT students, who participated in the study (Egale Canada, 2011).

One of the goals of the Egale study was to provide educators and administrators with adequate information so that schools would see the necessity of putting antihomophobic policies into place and enforcing them, thereby letting people know that homophobic and transphobic bullying will not be tolerated. As the case of Canada shows, discrimination against LGBT students is an international problem that occurs even in countries that have explicit policies against such behavior. LGBT students in Canada and elsewhere are exposed on a daily basis to language that insults their dignity. They experience verbal, physical, and sexual abuse, and teachers frequently look the other way and do not become involved when they see these events occurring (Egale Canada, 2011).

Questions for Consideration

1. Is it possible to develop school policies that will reduce or eliminate harassment and discrimination based on sexual orientation?

2. Thinking back to your own high school, can you identify areas you would consider to be "unsafe spaces"? If so, what changes could be made so that all students might feel more safe in the school environment?

Canada, one of the most egalitarian nations when it comes to providing the same legal rights for LGBT residents at for non-LGBT citizens.

The Hate Crimes Statistics Act of 1990 reports hate crimes classified on the basis of race, ethnicity/national origin, religion, sexual orientation, and disability. In 2009, law enforcement agencies reported 1,436 hate crime offenses based on sexual-orientation bias. Of these offenses:

- 55.6 percent were motivated by antimale homosexual bias.
- 26.2 percent resulted from antihomosexual bias.
- 15.0 percent were prompted by antifemale homosexual bias.
- 1.7 percent were classified as antibisexual bias.
- 1.5 percent were the result of antiheterosexual bias. (FBI, 2010b)

It is important to recall that these are *reported* offenses and do not include *all* incidents of such crimes. For example, LGBT advocates emphasize that many people do not report a crime in which they were the victim, particularly when the offense is related to sexual orientation or gender identity. Transgender persons are particularly vulnerable to hate crimes and are less likely to report such offenses because they believe that nothing will be done and that they themselves may become the object of investigation.

PERSPECTIVES ON SEXUAL ORIENTATION AND SOCIAL INEQUALITY

Sexual orientation and social inequality can be understood from various perspectives. Psychological approaches examine mental processes and childhood experiences, among other factors, in explanations and descriptions of people who identify as LGBT. Sociological explanations focus primarily on how sexual orientation and homophobia are associated with social learning and/or social structural factors in society.

Psychological Perspectives

According to some perspectives, homosexuality—like heterosexuality—is an ascribed characteristic, present from birth, that cannot be changed through counseling or therapy. By contrast, some psychological approaches associate homosexuality with mental processes and childhood experiences. Early psychological approaches considered homosexuality a form of maladjustment.

Sigmund Freud, founder of the psychodynamic approach, believed that humans are constitutionally bisexual—meaning that masculine and feminine currents coexist in everyone—but that as children progress toward adulthood, they move toward heterosexuality. According to Freud, not everyone makes it down the difficult path to heterosexuality because it is fraught with dangers and problems. According to Freud, for example, sons whose mothers were domineering and overprotective found it difficult to achieve heterosexuality. Following in Freud's footsteps, psychologists in the mid-twentieth century equated heterosexuality with good mental health and homosexuality with mental illness.

In 1942, the American Psychiatric Association formally classified homosexuality as a form of mental illness and suggested that treatments ranging from castration to electroshock therapy might remedy the problem (Marcus, 1992). However, the association's classification did not go undisputed. By administering standard personality tests to two groups of men—one heterosexual and the other homosexual—and asking a panel of psychiatrists and psychologists to tell her the sexual orientation of each subject on the basis of those tests, psychologist Evelyn Hooker (1957, 1958) showed that not all homosexual individuals are maladjusted or mentally ill. The judges were unable to differentiate between heterosexual and homosexual respondents. In 1973, the American Psychiatric Association removed homosexuality from its list of mental disorders.

Many psychologists believe that biological and psychosocial factors interact in the formation of sexual orientation. Psychologist Daryl J. Bem, for example, thinks that genetic factors and gender roles in childhood interact to produce sexual orientation. According to Bem, children typically are raised to feel more like children of their own sex and different from children of the opposite sex. These feelings of similarity and difference are often formed on the playground, where boys are more aggressive than girls. Over time, children's belief that people of the opposite gender are different—and somewhat mysterious—translates into heterosexual desire. However, some children see themselves as more similar to children of the opposite gender. For example, boys who do not like rough-and-tumble play or sports but like to play with dolls or other "girls' toys" might grow up feeling different from other boys. Similarly, girls who prefer "boys' sports" frequently feel awkward around other girls. According to Bem, the best predictor of sexual orientation is the degree to which children are gender-conforming or nonconforming; children who fit in sometimes but not others are likely to become bisexual.

Advocates of Bem's theory point out that it is supported by earlier studies showing that 66 percent of gay men (compared to 10 percent of heterosexual men) did not enjoy activities typical of their own gender. Critics point out that Bem's theory does not take into account the fact that what is defined as gender-appropriate behavior differs widely across cultures and over time. For example, thirty years ago, girls who wanted to play soccer might have been viewed as tomboys with few female friends, whereas today, many girls—and boys—play soccer, and their sports participation does not single them out as different from others of their gender. Bem's theory also does not explain the stages in the process of taking on a homosexual identity or how labeling by others may influence people's perceptions of themselves as homosexual, heterosexual, or bisexual.

Symbolic Interactionist Perspectives

In contrast to biological and psychological perspectives, symbolic interactionist perspectives view heterosexual and homosexual conduct as learned behavior and focus on the process by which individuals come to identify themselves as gay, lesbian, bisexual, or straight. According to symbolic interactionists, most people acquire the status of *heterosexual* without being consciously aware of it because heterosexuality is the established norm and they do not have to struggle over their identity. But the same is not true of people who identify themselves as *homosexual* or *bisexual*. In fact, some sociologists suggest that sexual orientation is a master status for many gay men, lesbians, and bisexuals (Schur, 1965). **A *master status* is the most significant status a person possesses because it largely determines how individuals view themselves and how they are treated by others.** Master status based on sexual orientation is particularly significant when it is linked to other subordinate racial-ethnic group statuses. For example, working-class gay Latinos are more hesitant than white, middle-class gay men to come out to their families because of cultural norms pertaining to *machismo* (masculinity) and the fear that relatives will withdraw the support that is essential for surviving at the subordinate end of race and class hierarchies (see Almaguer, 1995).

Symbolic interactionists have identified several stages in the process of accepting a lesbian, gay, or bisexual identity (Weinberg, Williams, and Pryor, 1994). First, people experience identity confusion—a situation in which they feel different from other people and struggle with admitting that they are attracted to individuals

of the same sex. For example, someone who identified himself as a fourteen-year-old boy posted the following note on an Internet newsgroup:

> I feel like my life is over. Am I gay? God, I hope not. I walk around going, "God, I hope not." I walk around going, "Do I like him?" "Do I like her?" "How would it feel to do it with him/her?" WHY DOES THIS HAVE TO HAPPEN TO ME!! The funny thing is, I absolutely detest everything about sex with men, and relationships with men. But somehow, I feel attracted to them anyway!! (Gabriel, 1995b:1)

In the past, many gay and lesbian people had nowhere to turn in their quest for answers and support from others; today, many use the Internet and other forms of global communication to connect with others who share their concerns (Gabriel, 1995b).

The second stage in establishing a lesbian or gay identity is seeking out others who are openly lesbian or

Individuals seem to accept their identities as lesbian, gay, or bisexual in stages. Initially there is identity confusion. But seeking out others who are open about their sexual orientation and experimenting sexually can eventually lead to acceptance.

gay and perhaps engaging in sexual experimentation or making other forays into the homosexual subculture. In the third stage, people attempt to integrate their self-concept and acceptance of a label such as "homosexual," "gay," or "lesbian" by pursuing a way of life that conforms to their definition of what those labels mean (Coleman, 1981–1982; Ponse, 1978; Cass, 1984). Like most "stage" theories, however, not all people go through these stages. Even those who do might not go through each stage in the same way, and some move back and forth between stages (Weinberg et al., 1994).

Studies on how people come to accept their sexual identity as gay, bisexual, or lesbian show the significance of labeling and how it can create barriers to full participation in American society. However, these studies typically are based on a relatively narrow selection of people, which makes it difficult to generalize the findings to larger populations. That is, respondents who openly identify themselves as gay or bisexual might not be characteristic of the larger homosexual or bisexual population (Weinberg et al., 1994).

Functionalist and Conflict Perspectives

Unlike the symbolic interactionist approach, which focuses primarily on how individuals come to identify themselves as homosexual, bisexual, or heterosexual, functionalist perspectives focus on the relationship between social structure and sexual orientation. To functionalists, social norms and laws are established to preserve social institutions and maintain stability in society. From this perspective, then, many societies punish homosexual conduct because it violates the social norms established by those societies and thus undermines the stability of the societies. Sociologist David P. Aday, Jr., provides an overview of this perspective:

> Marriage and family are structural arrangements that contribute to the continuity of our contemporary society. . . . [Homosexuality undermines] arrangements that currently operate to replace societal members in an orderly way—that is, the arrangement has survival value. . . . If homosexual conduct were allowed to exist unchallenged and unpunished, then it might in time undermine norms and laws that underpin monogamous marital sex, at least some of which results in the production of offspring to repopulate the society. . . . The punishment of homosexual conduct, from ridicule and discrimination to imprisonment, reinforces expectations about heterosexual and marital sex and defines the boundaries of society. (Aday, 1990:25)

The functionalist perspective explains why some people do not believe that homosexual conduct or marriages between lesbian or gay couples should be protected legally. It also explains why some religious and political leaders call for a renewal of "family values" in this country.

Critics suggest that the functionalist approach supports the status quo and ignores a need for new definitions of marriage and family. If marriage is understood to be the decision of two people to live together in a partnership—to be a family—then the intention or the capacity to have children should not be a condition. These critics say that nothing but custom mandates that marital partners must be of different genders.

Whereas the functionalist approach focuses on how existing social arrangements create a balance in society, the conflict approach focuses on *tensions* in society and *differences* in interests and power among opposing groups. From this perspective, people who hold the greatest power are able to have their own attitudes, beliefs, and values—about sexual orientation, in this case—represented and enforced while others are not (Aday, 1990). Therefore, norms pertaining to *compulsory heterosexuality* reflect the beliefs of dominant group members who hold high-level positions in the federal and state government, the military, and other social institutions. However, critics assert that the conflict approach fails to recognize that some people who have wealth and power are gay or lesbian yet take no action to reduce discrimination based on sexual orientation.

Does this photo tend to support or reject some functionalist analysts' assumption that gay or lesbian families destroy "family values" in this country? Why or why not?

According to Karl Marx, conflicts over values are an essential element of social life, and less-powerful people often challenge the laws imposed on them by those in positions of power. For example, adverse decisions by state courts and the U.S. Supreme Court often result in increased political activism by gay and lesbian rights groups. In recent years, more openly lesbian and gay people can be found in public office as elected or appointed officials, in the medical and legal professions, as educators and business leaders, and in all walks of life. However, regardless of their location in the power structure, most gay men, lesbians, and bisexuals remain acutely aware that many social barriers have not been lifted and there has not been a major shift in people's attitudes toward homosexuality and bisexuality.

With rapid Internet communications, lesbians and gay men around the world keep informed about political decisions that may adversely affect them. Many coalitions have been formed to organize gay pride marches and protests around the world. For example, the International Lesbian, Gay, Bisexual and Trans and Intersex Association brings together more than 600 groups from around the world to actively campaign for LGBT rights in about 110 countries around the world.

IS THERE A SOLUTION TO INEQUALITY BASED ON SEXUAL ORIENTATION?

As we have emphasized in previous chapters, how people view a social problem is related to how they believe the problem should be reduced or solved. Inequality based on sexual orientation is no exception because there are many divergent views and policies related to sexual orientation, and some people have very strong feelings about this issue.

Functionalist/Conservative Solutions to the Problem

According to functionalist and conservative perspectives, social norms and laws exist to protect the family and maintain stability in society. Given this, sexual orientation becomes a social issue: Gay activists' demands for equal rights, such as legal recognition of same-sex marriage, become major threats to the stability of society. Conservative political leaders and media analysts continue to blame same-sex marriages for destabilizing families because they are thought to detach procreation from the institution of marriage in the public's view. As a result of this belief, some functionalist theorists

and conservative politicians argue that members of the LGBT community are not in need of protection by the government in regard to issues of equal rights or anti-gay discrimination laws. Family values and morality are often indicated as key reasons why public policies should not be changed to take into account gay rights issues. However, the tide of public opinion appears to be shifting away from this perspective. In 2010, for the first time, Americans' support for the moral acceptability of gay and lesbian relations reached 52 percent in Gallup's annual Values and Beliefs survey (Saad, 2010). Most of the change in opinion was attributed to men, particularly men younger than fifty. However, a slight majority (53 percent) of all respondents still opposed legalization of gay marriage (Saad, 2010), reaffirming the strength of the conservative viewpoint on issues of concern to LGBT advocates.

In sum, many functionalist and conservative analysts view gays, lesbians, bisexuals, and transgender persons as part of the *problem* rather than as part of the *solution* for bringing about stability to families and society in the twenty-first century. They believe that homosexuality is dysfunctional for society in that it does not contribute to society's need for new members, and it undermines social norms and laws that preserve the family unity and maintain stability in society.

Conflict/Liberal Solutions to the Problem

Conflict theorists believe that prejudice and discrimination based on sexual orientation are embedded in the social structure of society and are reinforced by those who hold the greatest power and thus are able to perpetuate their own attitudes, beliefs and values about what constitutes "normal" sexual conduct. From this perspective, homophobia is similar to racism, sexism, and ageism, and the overt and covert discrimination that gays and lesbians experience is similar to the discrimination experienced by people of color, all women, and older people.

According to the conflict approach, the best way to reduce inequality based on sexual orientation is to repeal laws prohibiting sexual acts between consenting adults and to pass laws that ban all forms of discrimination against people who are lesbian, gay, bisexual, or transgender. However, to gain equality rights, conflict and liberal analysts acknowledge that activism and continued zeal is necessary.

In sum, conflict and liberal political analysts believe that political activism is important because members of the LGBT community need to have a "voice" in political decisions and to be treated in the same manner as any other person in the United States. They should be granted the same rights as heterosexual individuals with regard to all aspects of life.

Symbolic Interactionist Solutions to the Problem

From a symbolic interactionist perspective, homosexual conduct is learned behavior, and people go through stages in establishing a lesbian or gay identity. Society should therefore be more tolerant of people as they come to accept their sexual identity. Legal and social barriers that prevent people who are gay, lesbian, bisexual, or transgender from fully participating in society should be removed, thus making the complex psychological and social process of coming out to friends, family, and coworkers easier for those who choose to do so.

If we apply a symbolic interactionist approach to reducing inequality based on sexual orientation, we might look at ways in which society could make it easier for people to accept an identity as gay, lesbian, bisexual or transgender. It is difficult for individuals to accept a master status based on sexual orientation when that status is stigmatized by others in society. Although many people do not overtly stigmatize other individuals or ridicule them to their face, labeling continues in the United States as long as high-profile comedians and ordinary people tell "jokes" about sexual orientation and freely use slang terms to refer to individuals based on their real or imagined sexual orientation. Young people might be socialized, for example, not to use derogatory terms that are related to sexual orientation when they are "putting down" their friends. If symbolic interactionists are correct in their assessment of the importance of labeling in determining how people perceive of themselves and others,

then the manner in which individuals refer to each other, even when "just joking," should be a topic for sensitivity training and for socialization throughout the life course.

In sum, although there is more acceptance of gays and lesbians today compared to a few years ago, much remains to be done in regard to eliminating prejudice and discrimination, including verbal abuse and sometimes physical violence, based on sexual orientation. Policy issues identified as important by members of the LGBT community are far from being resolved in the United States, and gains typically have been measured one state at a time. What the future holds for social inequality based on sexual orientation is unclear; however, public opinion and many policymakers appear to be focusing more on LGBT rights and greater equality rather than reconstructing barriers to withhold or reduce those rights. In the United States, the Obama administration has been emphasizing the importance of gay rights both domestically and internationally. The United Nations also passed a resolution backing gay rights for the first time in 2011. The declaration expressed grave concern about abuses because of sexual orientation and established the groundwork for an international report on discrimination against gays. Asked what this measure would do for gays and lesbians in countries that opposed the resolution, U.S. Deputy Assistant Secretary Daniel Baer responded:

> It is a signal that there are many people in the international community who stand with them and who support them, and that change will come. It's a historic method of tyranny to make you feel that you are alone. One of the things that this resolution does for people everywhere, particularly LGBT people everywhere, is remind them that they are not alone. (quoted in Jordans, 2011)

SUMMARY

✓—**Study** and **Review** on **mysoclab.com**

■ **What criteria do sociologists use to study sexual orientation?**
Sociologists define sexual orientation as a preference for emotional-sexual relationships with persons of the same sex (homosexuality), the opposite sex (heterosexuality), or both (bisexuality). Recent studies have used three criteria for classifying people as homosexual or bisexual: (1) sexual attraction to persons of one's own gender, (2) sexual involvement with one or more persons of one's own

gender, and (3) self-identification as a gay man, lesbian, or bisexual.

■ **How do religion and law influence people's beliefs about homosexuality?**
Most major religions regard homosexuality as a sin. Contemporary religious fundamentalists denounce homosexual conduct as a sign of great moral decay and societal chaos. Throughout American history, moral and religious

teachings have been intertwined with laws that criminalize homosexual conduct. Some states have sodomy laws or other laws pertaining to "deviant sexual conduct," "crimes against nature," or "unnatural intercourse" whereby people can be imprisoned for oral or anal intercourse.

How does cohabitation differ from domestic partnership?

In cohabitation, same-sex or opposite-sex partners live together without being legally married. Many gay or lesbian couples cohabit in this country because they cannot enter into legally recognized marital relationships. However, some cities and states have given legal recognition to domestic partnerships—household partnerships in which unmarried couples live together in a committed, sexually intimate relationship and are granted the same rights and benefits as those accorded to married couples. Domestic partnership agreements benefit some couples by providing health insurance coverage and other benefits that were not previously afforded them.

What types of discrimination do gay and lesbian people experience?

Although lesbians and gay men experience discrimination in most aspects of daily life, some of the principal areas are (1) child custody and adoption, (2) housing, (3) medical care, and (4) the workplace. In each of these areas, gains have been made over the past four decades. However, discrimination against LGBT persons remains among the most blatant of all forms of prejudice and discrimination experienced by members of subordinate groups.

How have changes in the definition of hate crimes affected gay men and lesbians?

Before the early 1990s, hate crimes against gay men and lesbians were not acknowledged. The enactment of the Hate Crime Statistics Act of 1990 enabled hate crimes to be classified on the basis of sexual orientation, race, ethnicity, religion, or other characteristics that are devalued or "hated." Hate crimes against gays and lesbians appear to be most prevalent where homophobic attitudes are tolerated or overlooked.

How do psychologists explain sexual orientation?

Until fairly recently, some psychologists associated homosexuality with maladjustment or mental illness. Today, however, social psychologists believe that genetic and social factors combine to produce sexual orientation. According to Bem's theory, the best predictor of sexual orientation is the degree to which children are gender-conforming or nonconforming; children who fit in sometimes but not at other times are likely to become bisexual.

How do symbolic interactionists explain problems associated with sexual orientation?

According to symbolic interactionists, most people acquire the status of heterosexual without being consciously aware of it. For LGBT persons, sexual orientation can be a master status because it largely determines how individuals view themselves and how they are treated by others. Symbolic interactionists identify several stages in the process of accepting the identity of lesbian, gay, or bisexual: (1) experiencing identity confusion, (2) seeking out others who are openly lesbian or gay and sometimes engaging in sexual experimentation, and (3) attempting to integrate self-concept and acceptance of a label such as "homosexual," "gay," or "lesbian."

How do functionalists explain problems associated with sexual orientation?

Functionalists focus on how social norms and laws are established to preserve social institutions, such as the family, and to maintain stability in society. They also analyze reasons why societies find it necessary to punish sexual conduct that violates social norms prohibiting nonmarital sex and same-sex sexual relations. According to functionalists, homosexual conduct is punished because it undermines social institutions and jeopardizes the society.

How do conflict theorists explain problems associated with sexual orientation?

Conflict theorists believe that the group in power imposes its own attitudes, beliefs, and values about sexual orientation on everyone else. Thus, norms enforcing compulsory heterosexuality reflect the beliefs of dominant-group members in the government, military, and other social institutions. According to conflict theorists, social change can occur only if people demand that laws be changed to bring about greater equality.

How have gay rights advocates sought to reduce inequality based on sexual orientation?

Advocates have argued that lesbians and gay men are citizens and entitled to the same rights and protections that other citizens enjoy, including the right to equal employment and housing, legally sanctioned marriage, and protection from harassment and hate crimes. Some analysts suggest that future social change depends on the continued vigilance of gay and lesbian advocacy organizations.

KEY TERMS

deviance, p. 124

domestic partnership, p. 129

homophobia, p. 125

master status, p. 137

sexuality, p. 124

sexual orientation, p. 123

QUESTIONS FOR CRITICAL THINKING

1. How is homophobia similar to racism, sexism, and ageism? How is it different?

2. As a sociologist, how would you study the problem of discrimination against LGBT persons? What are the strengths and weaknesses of using survey research, interviews, and observations to study discrimination based on sexual orientation?

3. The laws in more states have been changed to give legal recognition to same-sex marriage. How would you find out what students at your college or university believe about this issue? If LGBT student organizations exist on your campus, how might you find out about members' beliefs on this topic? Do you think their responses would differ from those of a cross section of the student population? Why or why not?

4. In Chapters 2 through 6, we have examined inequality and discrimination as it relates to class, race-ethnicity, gender, age, and sexual orientation. If you could do one thing to reduce these problems, what would it be? What resources would be needed to implement your plan?

Succeed with MyFamilyLab® www.myfamilylab.com

The New MyFamilyLab is designed just for you. Each chapter features a pre-test and post-test to help you learn and review key concepts and terms. Experience Marriages and Families in action with dynamic visual activities, videos, and readings to enhance your learning experience.

Here are a few activities you will find for this chapter.

Watch on mysoclab.com

Core Concepts video clips feature sociologists in action, exploring important concepts in the study of Social Problems. Watch:
• Alternative Sexual Orientation

Explore on mysoclab.com

Social Explorer is an interactive application that allows you to explore Census data through interactive maps. Explore:
• Social Explorer Activity: Cohabitation Among Unmarried Same-Sex Couples

Read on mysoclab.com

MyFamilyLab includes primary source readings from classic and contemporary sociologists. Read:
• The Five Sexes: Why Male and Female Are Not Enough

CHAPTER 7

Prostitution, Pornography, and the Sex Industry

THINKING SOCIOLOGICALLY

- Why are prostitution and pornography referred to as the sex industry? What factors have contributed to the growth of the global sex industry?

- Is prostitution a legitimate career choice or is it a form of social deviance? How do sociological perspectives explain the persistence of prostitution worldwide?

- Does the availability of smart phones and tablet computers raise new questions about the ability of society to control pornography if individuals choose to view it?

143

I was sitting in my office at school when a former Sociology of Law student came in carrying a magazine and said, "Dr. Kendall, you need to read this." The student was shocked about an article she read on sex trafficking of young girls in the United States (see Collins, 2011). In our class we talked about global sex trafficking of young women, and this student was surprised to read in the magazine that many young American girls were entering—or being dragged into—the commercial sex industry. The article suggested that as many as 300,000 girls and young women are in the U.S. sex-for-hire business and many of them are now as young as 13 years of age. The article further suggested that the girls are either manipulated through violence or controlled through violence. "What kind of life is that?" my student asked. "Is there anything we can do about it?

Many people believe that sex work is a way to bring money into a household or it is a career choice—with willing buyers and sellers, a purely economic exchange—that is no more or less degrading than any other profession; however, many women—and some men—find out otherwise. Certainly in this country, it is a thriving multibillion-dollar industry that includes prostitution, the adult film and video trade, printed pornography, escort services, massage parlors, and strip and table dancing clubs. Prostitution and other types of sex work have always been controversial; not all social scientists even agree on whether or not the sex industry is a social problem. Human trafficking is often another matter, however, because it involves the commercial sexual exploitation of another person, especially children, and young women, by use of street prostitution, strip clubs, escort services, and the Internet. To better understand the controversy over prostitution, pornography, and other work in the sex industry, let's look at what constitutes deviant behavior.

DEVIANCE, THE SEX INDUSTRY, AND SOCIAL PROBLEMS

In Chapter 6, *deviance* was defined as a behavior, belief, or condition that violates social norms. To learn about deviance, sociologists ask such questions as, Why are some types of behavior considered deviant while others are not? Who determines what is deviant? Whose interests are served by stigmatizing some people as deviants but not others?

Sociologists generally take one of three approaches in studying deviance. The first approach assumes that deviance is *objectively given*: A deviant is any person who does not conform to established social norms—specifically, folkways, mores, and laws. Folkways are informal norms or everyday customs that may be violated without serious consequences. Contemporary U.S. folkways include eating certain foods with silverware and shaking hands when introduced to someone. In comparison, mores are strongly held norms that have moral and ethical connotations. College football players who scalp (sell at inflated prices) the free game tickets they receive from their school for their family members and friends behave unethically and violate social mores. Laws are formal, standardized norms that are enacted by legislatures and enforced by formal sanctions such as fines and imprisonment. Laws may be either civil or criminal. *Civil law* deals with disputes between people or groups, such as an argument between a landlord and a tenant over the provisions of an apartment lease. *Criminal law* deals with public safety and well-being and defines the behaviors that constitute a **crime—a behavior that violates criminal law and is punishable by a fine, a jail term, or other negative sanctions.** Crimes range from relatively minor offenses, such as traffic violations, to major offenses, such as murder.

If deviance is considered to be objectively given, then prostitution and pornography are viewed as violations of deeply held convictions (folkways or mores) about good taste or morality or as significant departures from existing criminal laws. To limit the amount of deviance and criminal behavior in society, in this view, societies employ social control mechanisms. **Social control refers to the systematic practices developed by social groups to encourage conformity and discourage deviance.** Social control can be either internal or external. Internal social control occurs through socialization:

People learn to adhere to the norms of social groups and the larger society. Internal social control mechanisms are strengthened by external mechanisms such as the criminal justice system, which enforces laws whether or not individuals choose to adhere to them.

The second approach to studying deviance considers it to be *socially constructed:* A behavior, belief, or condition is deviant because it is labeled as such. Sociologist Howard S. Becker (1963:8) summed up this approach when he wrote, "Social groups create deviance by making rules whose infraction constitutes deviance, and by applying those rules to particular people and labeling them as *outsiders.*" According to Becker and other interactionists, deviance is not a quality of any act the person commits; rather, a deviant is one to whom the label of deviant has been successfully applied. Thus, street prostitutes who openly solicit customers ("johns") are more likely to be labeled deviant than are women and men who work for high-priced escort services, even though their actions are essentially the same.

The third approach assumes that deviance is rooted in *the social structure of society,* particularly in power relations. In fact, according to this approach, deviance is defined—initially and disproportionately—by the most powerful members of the dominant class, racial, and gender groups. Rule makers and rule enforcers protect the power and privilege of dominant-group members, often at the expense of subordinate-group members. Thus, prostitutes are more likely than their customers or pimps to be apprehended and punished for their alleged sexual deviance.

What is sexual deviance? Although all societies have social norms regulating sexual conduct, not all societies regulate it in the same way. In the United States alone, definitions of what is sexually deviant have varied from time to time, from place to place, and from group to group. Traditionally, at least four types of sexual conduct between heterosexual partners have been regarded as deviant: (1) premarital sex or fornication—sexual relations between two people who are not married to each other; (2) extramarital sex or adultery—sexual relations between a married person and a partner other than her or his spouse; (3) promiscuous sex—casual sexual relations with many partners; and (4) underage sex or statutory rape—sexual relations with children below the age of consent as defined by state law, usually about age fourteen, fifteen, or sixteen. Prostitution crosses several lines of *proscribed* (prohibited) sexual conduct and is viewed as deviance because it involves promiscuous behavior between two (or more) people, who might be married to other people, and sometimes involves underage sex.

Despite changes in prescribed rules of sexual conduct during the twentieth century, the United States is one of the few highly industrialized nations that still defines prostitution as a crime.

DID YOU KNOW
- Prostitution is legal and regulated in twenty-two countries.
- Sex trafficking is a $58 billion industry.
- Sunday is the most popular day of the week for viewing pornography; Thanksgiving Day is the least popular.

PROSTITUTION IN GLOBAL PERSPECTIVE

Narrowly defined, **prostitution is the sale of sexual services (of oneself or another) for money or goods and without emotional attachment.** More broadly defined, systems of prostitution refer to any industry in which women's and/or children's—and sometimes men's—bodies are bought, sold, or traded for sexual use and abuse. According to this definition, systems of prostitution include pornography, live sex shows, peep shows, international sexual slavery, and prostitution as narrowly defined. The vast majority of prostitutes around the globe are women and children. A certain amount of male prostitution does exist, although most boys and men in the sex industry engage in sexual encounters with other males.

Read the Document Prostitution: Facts and Fictions on mysoclab.com

The World's Oldest Profession?

Prostitution has been referred to as the "world's oldest profession" because references to it can be found throughout recorded history. Still, over the past 4,000 years, prostitution has been neither totally accepted nor completely condemned. For example, although prostitution was widely accepted in ancient Greece, where upper-class prostitutes were admired and frequently became the companions of powerful Greek citizens, the prostitutes themselves were refused the status of wife—the ultimate affirmation of legitimacy for women in Greek society—and were negatively compared with so-called virtuous women in a "bad woman–good woman" dichotomy.

Explore the Concept Social Explorer Activity: Patterns of Inequality Among Women on mysoclab.com

In other eras, attitudes and beliefs about prostitution have ranged from generally tolerant to strongly averse. Such early Christian leaders as St. Augustine and St. Thomas Aquinas argued that prostitution was evil but encouraged tolerance toward it. According to Aquinas, prostitution served a basic need that, if unmet, would result in greater harm than prostitution itself. Later Christian leaders, such as Martin Luther in sixteenth-century Europe, believed that prostitution should be abolished on moral grounds.

In the nineteenth-century feminist movement, women for the first time voiced their opinions about prostitution. Some believed that prostitution led to promiscuity and moral degeneracy in men and should therefore be eradicated. Others believed that prostitution should be legitimized as a valid expression of female sexuality outside of marriage. Recently, some advocates have suggested that prostitution should be viewed as a legitimate career choice for women (prostitute as sex worker), but others have argued that prostitution is rooted in global gender inequality (prostitute as victim of oppression).

The Global Sex Industry

The past four decades have seen the industrialization, normalization, and globalization of prostitution. Although *industrialization* typically refers to the mass production of manufactured goods and services for exchange in the market, sociologist Kathleen Barry (1995:122) suggests that this term should also apply to commercialized sex manufactured within the human self. Prostitution becomes *normalized* when sex work is treated as merely a form of entertainment and there are

Social Problems in Global Perspective

Childhood Sexual Slavery: Buying and Selling Girls

M. is an ebullient girl, age 10, who ranks near the top of her fourth-grade class and dreams of being a doctor. Yet she, like all of India, is at a turning point, and it looks as if her family may instead sell her to a brothel. . . . I'm here in Kolkata [India] with America Ferrera, the actress from "Ugly Betty," to film a television documentary. Ferrera fell in love with M., and M. with Ferrera; they spent much of their time giggling together. "When I look at her, I see all the 10-year-old girls I've ever known." Ferrera said. "She's bubbly, silly, and optimistic. It would be heartbreaking to lose such a beautiful spirit to a life of violence and prostitution."

—*Nicholas D. Kristof (2011), an award-winning journalist for the* New York Times, *describes how young girls in India (among other nations) may be sold into prostitution so that their families can have the money.*

Although it is impossible to know exactly how many child prostitutes there are in the world, recent estimates suggest that as many as 1.8 million children a year enter the commercial sex trade (United Nations Children's Fund [UNICEF], 2009). Initially, social analysts believed that economic development would help end or reduce child trafficking and prostitution in Asian nations such as China, Japan, Thailand, and India. But this has not happened. Instead, sex tourism has grown as families have learned that their children can be a source of income from the sex industry. Estimates suggest that sex trafficking is the fastest growing criminal industry in the world, bringing in more than $58 billion annually. According to studies by the United Nations Children's Fund (2009), women make up the largest proportion of traffickers in one-third of the countries that provide information about the gender of *traffickers*—persons are involved in the recruitment, transportation, transfer, harboring, and receiving of children for the purpose of exploitation. Girls and young women are especially vulnerable as victims to trafficking because fear of contracting HIV/AIDS has dramatically increased the demand for younger prostitutes who have not been exposed to sexually transmitted diseases (STDs). In some countries, brothel owners purchase girls as young as ten or twelve years of age and force them to become house prostitutes. Girls such as M., introduced by Kristof, have little chance of escaping once they are forced into brothels. Those who try to escape are caught, severely beaten, and sometimes starved. While imprisoned in the brothel, they are forced to have sex with many customers each night. Since M.'s mother is a prostitute and her family belongs to a subcaste whose girls are expected to become prostitutes, M.'s chances of avoiding the same plight appear bleak (Kristof, 2011).

Sex tourism helps fuel the child prostitution business in nations such as Thailand where most of the prostitutes are younger than fifteen years old. In impoverished areas, young girls' opportunities in the labor market are

no legal impediments to promoting it as a commodity. The *globalization* of prostitution refers to the process by which the sex industry has become increasingly global in scope (e.g., international conglomerates of hotel chains, airlines, bars, sex clubs, massage parlors, brothels, and credit card companies that have an economic interest in the global sex industry), which has occurred as people's political, economic, and cultural lives have become linked globally. For evidence of this globalization, one has only to look at studies of the use of child prostitutes in the sex tourism industry (see Box 7.1).

The global sex industry thrives because of sex trafficking. The term ***sex trafficking* is applied to situations in which an adult is coerced, forced, or deceived into prostitution, or maintained in prostitution through coercion.** Persons who have participated in recruiting, transporting, harboring, receiving, or obtaining an individual for that purpose have committed a trafficking crime. Sex trafficking is coercive and often involves debt bondage, a situation in which women and girls are forced to continue working as prostitutes because of "debt" that was allegedly incurred when they were being transported, recruited, or sold. It is referred to as debt bondage because the women must pay off their so-called debt before they can be free. Some persons initially consent to participate in prostitution but are later held through psychological manipulation or physical force against their will.

The demand for prostitution is greatest when large numbers of men are congregated for extended periods of time in the military or on business far from home. A connection between wartime rape and increased prostitution was documented for the Vietnam War, the wars in El Salvador in the 1980s and in Bosnia in

Box 7.1

These prostitutes are waiting for potential customers outside a bar in Bangkok, Thailand's, downtown redlight district. What global, social, and economic factors contribute to the growing number of girls and young women working in the sex industry worldwide?

limited because of lack of education and the predominance of extremely low-wage jobs. Sex-based tourism in Thailand is considered to be one of the country's chief attractions by some visitors. Analysts have suggested that the prostitution industry has become more thoroughly capitalistic and globalized than ever before. Although a number of advocacy groups such as UNICEF, Not for Sale (www.notforsalecampaign.org), and other human rights organizations fight against child prostitution and human trafficking, fighting the global slave trade is a daunting task that required constant vigilance and much more international cooperation and law enforcement efforts than currently exist.

Questions for Consideration

1. How is the global sex industry linked to the international division of labor and other forms of globalization?
2. Do human rights and international governmental organizations (such as the United Nations) have a responsibility to intervene in cases of child sexual slavery?
3. What can we learn about the status of females worldwide based on information about the sex industry and sex tourism?

Independent Research

After visiting websites developed by advocates seeking to abolish human trafficking and child sex slavery, such as the Not for Sale Campaign (www.notforsalecampaign.org), identify key social problems worldwide that you believe contribute to international sex trafficking.

the 1990s, and the more recent conflicts in Iraq and Afghanistan in the 2000s. Many men also travel around the world on business and remain for extended periods of time. Some nations are more permissive than others in regard to the legality and availability of prostitutes and other sex industry workers to provide the services demanded by global travelers. In some cases, people travel specifically to have sex. The term *sex tourism* refers to travel by a person specifically to engage in sexual activity with prostitutes. Some of the most popular destinations include Brazil, Costa Rico, the Dominican Republic, Kenya, the Netherlands, Philippines, and Thailand.

The global sex industry reflects the economic disparity between the poorest regions of the world—where women and children may be bought, sold, or traded like any other commodity—and the richest regions, such as Europe and North America, where many of the global sex industry's consumers reside. However, some women in the sex trade hope to attain a better life by maintaining ties with customers from whom they receive money and who might help them qualify for visas that allow them to move to another country where they think they will find a better life. According to sociologists Barbara Ehrenreich and Arlie Russell Hochschild (2002:9–10), although many women in low-income nations hope for a better life through prostitution, the men who seek them out as sexual partners typically are looking for something far different, namely a short-term encounter with a woman who embodies "the traditional feminine qualities of nurturance, docility, and eagerness to please. . . . [Some] men seek in the 'exotic Orient' or 'hot-blooded tropics' a woman from the imagined past."

Although research indicates that the global sex industry, especially prostitution, contributes to the transmission of HIV, the virus that causes AIDS, many agencies and governments are not willing or able to come to grips with the problem. For example, Indonesia faces a looming AIDS crisis, particularly among residents that are isolated geographically and socially, such as sex workers, drug users, and LBGT persons, but few efforts are being made to change the situation. Among transgender sex workers, HIV prevalence rates are even higher, reaching about 34 percent of all sex workers in cities such as Jakarta. Yet, despite these figures little is being done to reduce the size of the sex industry or to provide sex education. In fact, the Indonesian government has chosen focus on installing pornography filters on BlackBerry phones rather than dealing with the HIV/AIDS crisis in the sex industry (Terzis, 2011).

Health and Safety Aspects of Prostitution for Women

Although some people view prostitution as nothing more than a job or as a way to make money when few other economic alternatives exist, prostitution should be classified as a hazardous occupation because of its negative physical and psychological effects. Studies of global sexual exploitation have documented that prostitution gravely impairs women's health and constitutes a form of violence. Frequently, women engaged in prostitution suffer physical injuries—such as bruises, broken bones, black eyes, and concussions—similar to those suffered by women who are victims of domestic violence. Although few studies have examined the physical effects of prostitution on male prostitutes, it is likely that boys and men are also vulnerable to physical abuse by individuals who pay for their sexual services.

Safety is a major concern for women in prostitution. Not only are prostitutes vulnerable when it comes to the conduct of their clients, but they also may be brutalized or killed by individuals who may or may not actually use their services. In the 2010s, for example, a serial killer in New York City killed at least five women, some of whom worked the streets and others who advertised their services online. The distinction between the streetwalker and Internet escort has become increasingly blurred, and some female victims and other prostitutes who were interviewed in the aftermath of these killings apparently used both streetwalking and websites advertising their services to acquire new customers (Goldstein and Baker, 2011).

Along with concerns about safety and the ever-present possibility of physical violence, women employed in the global sex industry are vulnerable to numerous health risks, including sexually transmitted diseases such as HIV/AIDS, gonorrhea, herpes, and syphilis. They also have a high risk of chronic gynecological problems such as pelvic pain and pelvic inflammatory disease. Pregnancy and pregnancy-related complications constitute another significant concern for girls and women in prostitution.

Research shows that emotional health is another serious issue associated with prostitution. Some psychologists have found that many prostitutes suffer from what they refer to as a "combat disorder" that is similar to the posttraumatic stress disorders and combat fatigue that veterans of war may experience. Other emotional consequences of prostitution include depression, anxiety, eating disorders, and alcohol and drug abuse. Although some prostitutes remain vigilant about choosing their clients, others are forced by economic necessity and circumstances to become involved with anyone who is willing to pay for their services. This often leads to emotional stress because, as in the case of the serial killer of New York prostitutes, the women must be on their guard at all times for what law enforcement officials refer to as "Jekyll–Hyde switches" in their clients' emotions: If a customer instantly flips between anger and arousal, the prostitute is in greater danger of attack or even death (Goldstein and Baker, 2011).

In contrast to Hollywood films, TV shows, and popular songs that often romanticize the sex industry and relationships between pimps and prostitutes, many women view themselves as being trapped in the global sex industry, a situation that leaves them deeply concerned about the physical and psychological consequences of their work.

PROSTITUTION IN THE UNITED STATES

Trafficking in women and children is as great a problem in the United States as it is in low-income nations. In recent years, organized prostitution networks have been identified in urban, suburban, and rural areas of the country. Women and children from Asia and Mexico have been among the most frequently exploited by smugglers. Prostitutes working in the United States range from solo prostitutes who work alone on the streets or in bars, restaurants, and hotels to large number of women who advertise on websites or work for Internet escort services. According to research by sociologist Sudhir Venkatesh (2010), a rapid transition has occurred from selling sex on the streets to procuring customers on the Internet. For a period of time, Craigslist, the popular provider of Internet classified advertising, published an "adult services" section; however, this practice was discontinued when high-profile business and political leaders were identified as using this means to acquire the services of prostitutes.

The Nature of Prostitution

Clearly, not all prostitutes are alike: Life experiences, family backgrounds, age, years of formal education, locales of operation, types of customers, and methods of doing business vary widely. Sociologists have identified five levels or tiers of prostitution, ranging from Internet-based escort prostitutes to street prostitutes and women who exchange sex for drugs.

Top-tier prostitutes typically are referred to as *escorts* or *call girls* and *call boys*. They are considered the upper echelon in prostitution because they tend to earn higher fees and have more selectivity in their working conditions and customers than do other prostitutes. Escort prostitutes typically have more years of formal education than other types of prostitutes do. Most of them do not think of themselves as prostitutes. Many dress nicely—and often conservatively—so that they do not call undue attention to themselves at luxury hotels, clubs, and apartment buildings. One of the best known sex industry workers in the twentieth century, Sydney Biddle Barrows (1986:69), former owner of a well-known New York escort service, explained the situation this way:

> While good looks were generally important [for escort prostitutes], I was more concerned with the right look. Men have always responded to the way I dress, and I decided that the elegant, classic look that worked for me would also work for the girls. . . . Quite a few of the new girls had no money and nothing appropriate to wear, so I would either lend them something of mine or take them to Saks and charge whatever they needed on my credit card. They would pay me back from their future earnings.

Escort prostitutes work "on call," going out to see customers who are acquired on websites or those who are referred to them by their escort service, pimp, or other procurers such as hotel concierges and taxi drivers who receive a percentage of the prostitute's fees. Although their work is not as visible as that of other prostitutes, they face some of the same hazards, including abusive customers, sexually transmitted diseases, and sometimes violence or death.

The second tier of prostitutes comprises hustlers, strippers, and table (lap) dancers who engage in prostitution on the side. People in this tier work out of nightclubs, bars, and strip joints primarily. The distinction between lap dancers and prostitutes is vague, and a number of state courts have ruled that lap dancing and touching are a form of prostitution that is illegal. Hustlers who operate out of clubs, bars, and strip joints are sometimes referred to as *bar girls* or *bar boys* because it is their job to pressure (hustle) customers to buy drinks. Most hustlers are not paid by the bar but earn their livelihood by negotiating sexual favors with potential customers.

The third tier is made up of *house girls* who work in brothels (houses of prostitution) run by a madam, pimp, or more recently, corporate businessmen, who collect up to half of the fees earned by the women. Customers choose "dates" after they arrive at the brothel or, prior to that, on Internet websites where they make a selection before coming to the brothel. Nevada has been referred to as the Brothel Capital of the United States because it is one of the few states where some of the businesses are legal. Estimates suggest that about twenty legal brothels operate in Nevada, with the most famous being the Chicken Ranch (named for a previous brothel located in LaGrange, Texas, which was popularized in a Broadway hit show, "The Best Little Whorehouse in Texas," and a movie by the same name). Because prostitution is illegal in most states, some prostitute pickup sites operate as massage parlors, body-painting studios, or other seemingly legitimate businesses. Text messaging on cell phones and Internet websites have drastically reduced the need for brothels and similar physical locations for making initial contact between prostitutes and customers.

Near the bottom tier of prostitution are *streetwalkers,* who publicly solicit customers and charge by the "trick." Most street prostitutes feel safer when they are on their own turf and have a pimp who supposedly looks out for their best interests, as a news report explains about a New York City prostitute interviewed in the aftermath of the Long Island prostitute killings:

> One 23-year-old prostitute recalled how her pimp warned her that the Long Island victims had made the mistake of working independently and "didn't tell their daddy [the pimp] where they were." . . . She said she had different safety protocols for each environment; in Hunts Point she would never allow a client to drive her more than three blocks from their meeting point, to stay in a zone where people knew to look for her. She and another worker would sometimes send their pimp a text message containing the license plate of the vehicle she was entering when accepting a date. . . . During most dates, even those arranged online, she surreptitiously called her pimp on her cellphone and left the speakerphone setting on so he could listen in for the duration of the tryst. (Goldstein and Baker, 2011)

As this example shows, the complex relationship between prostitutes and pimps is most prevalent at the streetwalker level. Some streetwalkers believe that they derive protection and even status from their pimp, particularly if they at the top of the pimp's hierarchy. The prostitute who has been with the pimp for the longest or who consistently makes the most money (for the pimp) is usually the top person in the hierarchy. Referred to the *bottom girl,* this woman becomes the business manager who collects money from other prostitutes and generally overseeing the pimp's business interests. According to the FBI, sex traffickers who have more than one victim also have a "bottom" woman who sits atop the hierarchy of prostitutes, disciplining them, and seducing other young people into prostitution. Researchers have documented the exploitive and sometimes violent nature of relationships between pimps and prostitutes, as well as between sex traffickers and prostitutes (Walker-Rodriguez and Hill, 2011). In the Long Island prostitute killings, for example, a number of pimps exploited the fears of the sex workers to their own advantage by using the prostitute-killing spree as a way to increase control over their own female sex workers (Goldstein and Baker, 2011).

The very bottom tier of prostitution is occupied by women who are addicted to crack cocaine and engage in crack-for-sex exchanges (Sharpe, 2005). Researchers have found that poor women, particularly African Americans and recent immigrants, are introduced to crack cocaine by pimps and others who desire to gain power over the women and keep them working as prostitutes for their own economic gain. This places women at high risk for sexually transmitted diseases, including HIV/AIDS, and unplanned pregnancies. Larger structural issues such as poverty, racism, sexism, and classism all contribute to the sex-for-crack barter system because of patterns of exclusion and exploitation that have destroyed the life chances and opportunities of women of color at the bottom of the U.S. class hierarchy (Sharpe, 2005).

Although fewer studies have examined the hierarchy in male prostitution, four main categories have been identified. The *gigolo* is a heterosexual male prostitute who often works at resorts, spas, or on cruise ships where he can easily meet up with lonely, older women who may pay for companionship more than for sex. *Male escorts* may be either heterosexual or homosexual, and increasing numbers of these escorts advertise their services and find dates through online services. *Hustlers* are homosexual male prostitutes who are hired by other males for sexual favors. These individuals tend to hang out in gay bars, gyms, or other neighborhood hangouts known to be frequented by large numbers of unattached gay males. Many male prostitutes in these categories are between the ages of eighteen and twenty-five. Young boys and teens below age eighteen are referred to as "chickens" or "chickenhawks" in the world of male prostitution. Many of these individuals have similar stories to those of young girls who have come to prostitution by way of abusive or nonexistent families, running away from home, living in poverty, and other characteristics common to the victims of sex trafficking.

The Extent of Prostitution

Many attempts have been made to estimate the number of prostitutes in the United States, but these estimates are not based on strong scientific evidence. Child and adolescent prostitution is particularly difficult to quantify. According to the Crimes against Children Research Center at the University of New Hampshire, "[Estimates] are mostly educated guesses or extrapolations based on questionable assumptions. . . . The reality is that we do not currently know how many juveniles are involved in prostitution. Scientifically credible estimates do not exist" (Stransky and Finkelhor, 2008).

Among adults, the Internet has rapidly changed prostitution from an "alleyway business" to an online service (Venkatesh, 2010). Websites, online chat forums, social networking through Twitter and Facebook, as well as other means of communicating without actually having to make contact prior to a "date" have diminished the role of pimps and brothels in the sex industry and made it easier for prostitutes and their customers to meet up, like any other couple, in a restaurant, bar, hotel, or their own home or place of business. Because of these changes in communications technology, it has become more difficult to determine the nature and extent of prostitution in the United States and other nations.

Some analysts believe that as many as 40 million prostitutes are at work worldwide, and official crime statistics show that each year about 80,000 people are arrested for prostitution-related crimes in the United States. Why are accurate estimates so difficult to make? First, there is the question of how prostitution is defined. Second, because of its illegal nature, much prostitution is not reported. Third, arrest records—which are almost the only source of official information on prostitution—do not reflect the extent of prostitution. Finally, many people drift into and out of prostitution, considering it temporary work between full-time jobs or as part-time work while attending school. Although statistics on prostitution arrests provide limited information about many aspects of prostitution, it is possible to gain some idea about who is most likely to be arrested for prostitution-related offenses. As shown in Box 7.2, women are much more likely to be arrested for prostitution in

Social Problems and Statistics  Box 7.2

What We Know and Don't Know about Prostitution

According to U.S. government statistics, 56,640 people were arrested in the United States in 2009 for prostitution and prostitution-related offenses (FBI, 2010). Of this number, women accounted for 39,437 (almost 70 percent) and men accounted for 17,203 (about 30 percent) of the arrests (see Figure 7.1).

Some of the males who were arrested were prostitutes; others were the pimps who procured customers for prostitutes; and yet others were the customers or "johns." It has been estimated that male customers account for about 10 percent of the annual arrests for prostitution-related offenses. Although these statistics tell us something about who is arrested for prostitution, they tell us little about the actual number of individuals who are currently working, or have ever worked, as prostitutes or in prostitution-related work or about the number of people who have paid for the services of a prostitute.

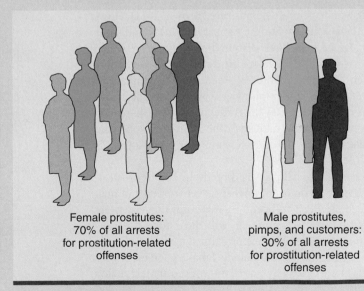

Female prostitutes:
70% of all arrests
for prostitution-related
offenses

Male prostitutes,
pimps, and customers:
30% of all arrests
for prostitution-related
offenses

Figure 7.1 Arrests for prostitution in 2009
Source: FBI, 2010a.

any given year than are men. Only about 10 percent of arrests for prostitution-related crimes are of the sex patrons, who almost exclusively are men.

Prostitution and Age, Class, and Race

Age and prostitution are closely linked. Although some prostitutes are as young as age thirteen or fourteen, the vast majority are between the ages of seventeen and twenty-four. Although prostitutes typically are quite young, with the peak earning age being about twenty-two, the typical male customer is middle-aged, white, and married. Men between the ages of thirty-five and forty-four years of age are the most common customers, according to studies. Some teenage and college-age males also hire prostitutes, particularly for parties or when they are away from home or school on spring break.

Regardless of age, social science research and media accounts suggest that some girls and women enter prostitution by choice while others enter through coercion. According to some reports, many prostitutes were originally runaways who left physically and/or psychologically abusive homes. Other prostitutes were "throwaways"—thrown out of their homes by parents or other family members. Advocates for young sex trade workers have emphasized that sexually exploited youth should primarily be viewed as victims of child abuse, not as criminals who should be sent to juvenile centers or jails where genuine help is rare (Brown, 2011). However, social scientist Sudhir Venkatesh (2011) and some other researchers have disputed the extent to which abuse as a child is a factor in determining why some women become prostitutes. According to Venkatesh's research, many contemporary sex workers made a conscious decision to enter the trade for quick cash—much like a person would take any other part-time job—and because this line of work offers autonomy and a flexible schedule.

Like age, social class is directly linked to prostitution: Lower-income and poverty-level women and men are far more likely to become prostitutes than are more affluent people. Some people with little formal education and few job skills view prostitution as an economic necessity. As one woman stated, "I make good money [as a prostitute]. That's why I do it; if I worked at McDonald's for minimum wage, then I'd feel degraded" (quoted in McWilliams, 1996:340). However, women working for exclusive escort services, and earning as much as $10,000 an hour, are more likely to have attended college and come from the middle or upper-middle class.

Race is also an important factor in prostitution. Sociologist Patricia Hill Collins (2005) suggests that African American women are affected by the widespread image of black women as sexually promiscuous and therefore potential prostitutes. Collins traces the roots of this stereotype to the era of slavery when black women—and black men and children—were at the mercy of white male slave owners and their sexual desires. According to Collins, prostitution exists within an intertwining web of political and economic relationships whereby sexuality is conceptualized along intersecting axes of race and gender. Today, prostitution remains linked to the ongoing economic, political, and social exploitation of people of color, especially women. In 2009, African Americans, who constitute 12.6 percent of the U.S. population accounted for 40.7 percent of all prostitution arrests (see Figure 7.2).

SOCIOLOGICAL PERSPECTIVES ON PROSTITUTION

Sociologists use a variety of perspectives to examine prostitution as a social problem. Functionalists focus on how deviance, including prostitution, serves important functions in society. Interactionists investigate micro-level concerns, such as how and why people become prostitutes and how the stigmatization affects their

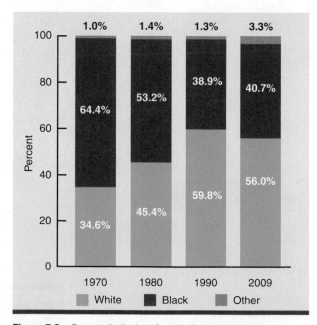

Figure 7.2 Percent distribution of prostitution arrests by race, 1970–2009
Source: FBI, 2010a.

self-esteem. Conflict perspectives seek to explain how the powerful enact their moral beliefs into law and how prostitution is related to capitalism and/or patriarchy.

The Functionalist Perspective

Functionalists believe that the presence of a certain amount of deviance in society contributes to its overall stability. According to early sociologist Emile Durkheim, deviance clarifies social norms and helps societies maintain social control over people's behavior. By punishing those who engage in deviant behavior such as prostitution, the society reaffirms its commitment to its sexual norms and creates loyalty to the society as people bind together to oppose the behavior.

Several generations ago, sociologist Kingsley Davis (1937) predicted that in societies that have restrictive norms governing sexual conduct, prostitution will always exist because it serves important functions. First, it provides quick, impersonal sexual gratification that does not require emotional attachment or a continuing relationship with another person (Freund, Lee, and Leonard, 1991). Second, prostitution provides a sexual outlet for men who do not have ongoing sexual relationships because they are not married or have heavy work schedules. Third, prostitution provides people with the opportunity to engage in sexual practices—such as multiple sex partners, fellatio (oral stimulation of the male genitalia), cunnilingus (oral stimulation of the female genitalia), anal intercourse, or sadomasochism (S&M), including the use of such devices as handcuffs, whips, and chains—that regular sex partners or spouses might view as immoral or distasteful. Fourth, prostitution protects the family as a social institution by making a distinction between "bad girls" or "bad boys"—with whom one engages in promiscuous sexual behavior—and "good girls" and "good boys"—with whom one establishes a family. Finally, prostitution benefits the economy by providing jobs for people who have limited formal education and job skills.

The Symbolic Interactionist Perspective

According to the symbolic interactionist approach, we define any situation according to our own subjective reality and the roles we play in society. In our efforts to communicate with others, we bring to each interaction symbolically charged ideas based on previous experiences. Each of us has a certain amount of emotional energy available for each interaction, and every time we

participate in a new interaction, we have to negotiate the situation all over again. Applying this analysis to the issue of prostitution, we see that, for some prostitutes, impersonal, "for hire" sex is a business deal which can be an efficient, nonemotional way to earn money while satisfying another person's needs. For the interaction to be positive for the prostitute, she must gain control over the situation, as evidenced by this excerpt from an interview with a prostitute named Dolores:

> I set my own schedule. I set my own limits and made my own rules, and I didn't have to answer to anyone. I learned a lot about myself: what I would and would not do for money, and what I was willing to do for the right amount of money. . . . I didn't have to see anyone I didn't want to see. If a man was too boring or too rough or too crude or took too much time, I didn't have to see him again. I loved it. (French, 1988:180)

Although Dolores made these comments more than two decades ago, her remarks capture the still-relevant idea that some people become prostitutes to gain greater freedom and a wider range of career options than they otherwise might have. These reasons fit with sociologist Howard Becker's (1963) suggestion that entering a deviant career is similar in many ways to entering any other occupation. The primary difference is the labeling that goes with a deviant career. Public labeling of people as deviant and their subsequent acceptance or rejection of that label are crucial factors in determining whether or not a person stays in a deviant career such as prostitution.

Unlike Dolores, the subjective reality of many other prostitutes is that they are the objects of exploitation by others, and they have no choice but to remain in the business to survive. Many girls and women see prostitution as a way out of poverty, but they desire to leave the business as soon as possible. From this perspective, the subject reality that drives them is economic necessity and a desire to make the encounter as simple, safe, and emotion-free as possible.

Why do men seek out prostitutes? Numerous researchers have examined the social psychological factors involved in men's decisions to engage the services of prostitutes. Some findings are consistent with symbolic interactionist approaches, particularly the social construction of reality, which suggest that how people *perceive* of a situation is often more important than the *actual* nature of the situation itself. Numerous studies have attempted to answer this question, but it is impossible to come to a consensus about what motivates men to pay for the services of prostitutes because numerous factors, not one single reason, are involved in why men behave as they do (Schwartz, 2008). These are among the reasons given for why men employ prostitutes:

- Misogyny, hatred of women, is a central part of sexist ideology and, as such, is an important basis for the oppression of females in male-dominated societies. Prostitutes are vulnerable to this type of prejudice: Misogyny can be acted out by humiliating women and forcing them to be submissive.
- Some men have a compulsive need for sex and an insatiable desire for sexual pleasure.
- Others believe that real relationships with women are too risky and/or demanding emotionally.
- Still others think they will be unable to have sex without paying for it because of their weight, age, disability, or other characteristics they judge to be unattractive to women.
- Finally, many men work long hours or travel extensively in their work, leaving them with little extra time to meet women or go on dates. (Schwartz, 2008)

The Conflict Perspective

Conflict perspectives emphasize that groups in society are engaged in a continuous struggle involving the allocation of power, wealth, and other scarce resources in a society. Conflict perspectives on prostitution highlight the relationship between power in society and sex work: The laws that make prostitution illegal are created by powerful dominant-group members who seek to maintain cultural dominance by criminalizing sexual conduct that they consider immoral or in bad taste.

Conflict analysts using a liberal feminist framework believe that prostitution should be decriminalized—meaning that laws making prostitution a crime should be repealed. These analysts argue that prostitution a **victimless crime—a crime that many people believe has no real victim because it involves willing participants in an economic exchange.** Therefore, sex workers should not be harassed by police and the courts. From this approach, what is abusive about prostitution is not the profession itself; it is the illegality, humiliation, and degradation that prostitutes experience at the hands of law enforcement officers. Prostitution is often referred to as a victimless crime because there are supposedly consenting adults involved in these activities. From this approach, prostitution involves adults only and is a form of work in the sex industry that should be treated as a labor issue. However, in sharp contrast to this idea that prostitution is a victimless crime, organizers of anti-prostitution campaigns have argued that prostitution

does harm girls and women. Younger sex workers have not always reached the age of adulthood, and some encounters involving prostitutes, pimps, and customers involve exploitation, sexual harassment, rape, and other activities that are far from victimless.

Conflict perspectives using Marxist feminist and radical feminist frameworks suggest that women become prostitutes because of structural factors such as economic inequality and patriarchy. Capitalism and patriarchy foster economic inequality between women and men and force women to view their bodies as simply commodities: "When a man has bought a woman's body for his use as if it were like any other commodity . . . the sex act itself provides acknowledgment of patriarchal right. When women's bodies are on sale as commodities in the capitalist market . . . men gain public acknowledgment as women's sexual masters" (Pateman, 1994:132).

According to Marxist feminists, the only way to eliminate prostitution is to reduce disparities in income levels between women and men and eliminate poverty. However, radical feminists believe that prostitution will not be eliminated until patriarchy is ended.

Conflict theorists who focus on the interrelationship of race, class, and gender in examining social problems suggest that criminalizing prostitution uniquely affects poor women, especially poor women of color, who are overrepresented among street prostitutes. According to these theorists, white male supremacy, which traditionally preserves the best-paying jobs for men, makes women of color particularly vulnerable to recruitment or coercion into prostitution. Analysts using this framework also note that discrimination in law enforcement uniquely affects women of color. For example, law enforcement officials target street prostitutes and other sex workers, particularly when political elites decide to crack down on deviant behavior such as prostitution and pornography.

PORNOGRAPHY

Pornography **is the graphic depiction of sexual behavior through pictures and/or words—including by electronic or other data retrieval systems— in a manner that is intended to be sexually arousing.** Most of these analysts believe that pornography is a pressing social problem. But what kind of social problem is it? Religious groups typically construe pornography as a social

> **Watch** on mysoclab.com
> *Busting Out* on mysoclab.com

problem because they say that it is obscene. On the other hand, social analysts, particularly feminists, usually frame the problem in terms of patriarchy—male oppression of women.

Adding to the confusion over the nature of pornography as a social problem is the difficulty social scientists have in determining what constitutes pornography. Over time, public attitudes change regarding what should be tolerated and what should be banned because of *obscenity*—**the legal term for pornographic materials that are offensive by generally accepted standards of decency.** Who decides what is obscene? According to what criteria? In *Miller v. California* (1973), the U.S. Supreme Court held that material can be considered legally obscene only if it meets three criteria: (1) the material as a whole appeals to prurient interests (lustful ideas or desires); (2) the material depicts sexual conduct in a patently offensive way as defined by state or federal law; and (3) the work as a whole lacks serious literary, artistic, political, or scientific value (Russell, 1993). But according to some analysts, the Court's decision has contributed to the social construction of pornography as a social problem.

Even in the age of high-tech, Internet pornography, many people seek out sexually oriented magazines, videos, and other X-rated merchandise in settings such as the one shown here. Why do many people believe that places of business such as this harm not only individuals and their families but also the larger community?

The Social Construction of Pornography as a Social Problem

The social construction of pornography as a social problem involves both a cognitive framework and a moral framework. The cognitive framework refers to the reality or factualness of the situation that constitutes the "problem." In regard to pornographic materials, one cognitive framework might be based on the assumption that pornography *actually affects* people's actions or attitudes; an opposing cognitive framework might be based on the assumption that pornography is a fantasy mechanism that allows people to express the forbidden without actually engaging in forbidden behavior. The moral framework refers to arguments as to whether something is immoral or unjust. In the case of pornography, moral condemnation arises from the belief that graphic representations of sexuality are degrading, violent, and sinful. From this perspective, pornography is less about sex than about violating taboos in society. The moral framework often distinguishes between pornography and *erotica*—**materials that depict consensual sexual activities that are sought by and pleasurable to all parties involved.** According to sociologist Diana E. H. Russell (1993), materials can be considered erotic—rather than obscene—only if they show respect for all human beings and are free of sexism, racism, and homophobia. Contemporary erotica might include romance novels that describe two consenting adults participating in sexual intercourse. On the other hand, materials depicting violent assault or the sexual exploitation of children would be considered pornographic or obscene. However, the distinction appears to be highly subjective, as feminist scholar Ellen Willis (1981:222) notes: "Attempts to sort out good erotica from bad porn inevitably come down to 'What turns me on is erotic: what turns you on is pornographic.'"

The Nature and Extent of Pornography

As part of the multibillion-dollar sex industry, pornography is profitable to many people, including investors, filmmakers, and owners of stores that distribute such materials. *Hard-core* pornography is material that explicitly depicts sexual acts and/or genitals. In contrast, *soft-core* pornography is suggestive but does not depict actual intercourse or genitals.

Computer telecommunications has become one of the most prevalent ways that pornographic images are made available to people. In the comfort of one's own home or office, an individual can find vast amounts of sexually explicit materials on "X-rated" cable television

One in twelve Internet websites contains pornographic material.

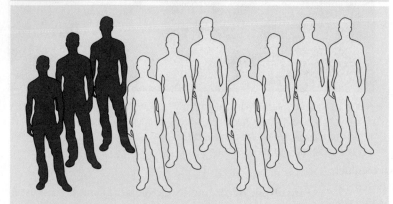

One in three (34%) Internet users report that they have experienced unwanted exposure to pornography through pop-up ads, misdirected links, or e-mails.

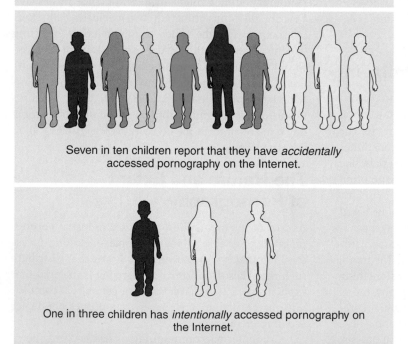

Seven in ten children report that they have *accidentally* accessed pornography on the Internet.

One in three children has *intentionally* accessed pornography on the Internet.

Figure 7.3   Net porns stats, 2010
Source: Duke, 2010; theweek.com, 2010.

channels and sexually oriented websites. Since the Internet is available in so many homes today, children have many more opportunities to view pornographic materials whether or not they choose to do so (see Figure 7.3).

It is estimated that the porn film industry alone is a $10 to $20 billion per year enterprise, a figure that is greater than all of Hollywood's annual box office receipts and does not include revenues from porn magazines, Internet sites, cable adult channels, and the sale of sexual devices. Some individuals in the pornography industry gain wealth from their activities: For top actors at the high end of the pay scale, hourly earnings can be quite high and the work is often glamorously portrayed. Typically, female workers earn about 50 percent more than the men. Although a woman's earnings depend on her looks, a man's career is based more on his ability to perform sexually (Abbott, 2000). Consequently, some men in the porno film industry believe that they are being exploited, as was the case of "Ron," who suggests that profits do not extend to all actors in the films:

You'd have to go a long way to find an industry with worse labor practices. They work people very hard; they pay them very little, really, for what they do. . . . As a porn performer, you're putting up with a couple of days of hard, even abusive, behavior that compromises your ability to do anything else in your life ever again, because the piece of evidence of your past misbehavior continues to exist. . . . But after you've done porn films, you can't do anything else. You can't even do commercials. . . . Another thing. There's an endless appetite for new faces and new bodies, which means they work [actors] to death for about six months or a year, put out twenty to thirty videos with them. And then they can't get work any more. New ones have come along. The audience is sick of looking at the old ones and wants to see new ones. (quoted in Stoller, 1991:209–210)

According to some social analysts, pornography is a prime example of the principle of supply and demand. As long as demand remains high, pornographers will continue to market their goods and services and find new ways to use technology. According to Walter Kendrick, a scholar whose research focuses on pornography:

> Pornographers have been the most inventive and resourceful users of whatever medium comes along because they and their audience have always wanted innovations. Pornographers are excluded from the mainstream channels, so they look around for something new, and the audience has a desire to try any innovation that gives them greater realism or immediacy. (quoted in Tierney, 1994:H18)

Each new development in technology changes the meaning of pornography and brings new demands for regulation or censorship. Today, interactive media presentations and pornography on the Internet are widely believed to be a far more powerful influence on people, especially children, than the printed word is (see Box 7.3).

Social Problems and Social Policy   Box 7.3

Real or Not Real? The Law on Internet Child Pornography

The Internet can bring people a continent away together. It can empower Americans to spread their ideas and innovations across the globe. But the Internet also allows child pornographers to take advantage of speed and anonymity to exploit vulnerable young people and spread horrifying images across the Web. If you don't believe the Internet can cause such harm, all you have to do is listen to Masha's story. When she was just 5, Masha was adopted from a Russian orphanage by a man who began sexually abusing her the night she arrived. Today, after escaping the horrors of this abuse, Masha has come forward to tell her story and raise awareness so others are spared her unspeakable experiences. This courageous 13-year-old has worked tirelessly to close loopholes in child pornography laws that allow predators to download pornographic images of children without significant penalties. . . . Not only was Masha physically abused, but her adoptive father preserved that abuse to revisit himself and to share with the world. This despicable man is in jail but pedophiles spread his revolting photographs across the Web.

—Senator John F. Kerry (2006) explains why he drafted Masha's Law to combat the growing child pornography industry on the Internet and elsewhere.

Masha is a real person who was sexually abused as a child and had pornographic images of her abuse placed on the Internet. This behavior is repugnant to most people; however, some pro-pornography advocates argue that Masha's case, which involves a living person, is different from *virtual child pornography*—which relies on "virtual" actors that are computer-generated images—and that these two types of pornography should be treated differently in social policy. Unlike pro-porn spokespersons, antiporn advocates argue that virtual child pornography is no different from pornography that involves actual children. These arguments moved from theoretical discussions to real cases when law enforcement officials apprehended child pornographers who claimed they used only virtual actors and thus their products were exempt from regulations governing child pornography on the Internet because they did not show real children.

How has social policy shaped the manner in which we look at the issue of real versus virtual child pornography? Initially, the U.S. Congress shaped social policy when it passed the Child Pornography Prevention Act (CPPA) in 1996. According to this act, it was illegal to send or receive depictions of what *appear* to be minors (persons below age eighteen) engaging in sexually explicit conduct. Thus, possession of any type of child pornography would be a criminal offense if the material has been transported in interstate commerce, which includes being sent over the Internet. When this law was challenged and the U.S. Supreme Court heard *Ashcroft v. Free Speech Coalition* in 2002, the Court struck down the CPPA, noting that *virtual* child pornography must be distinguished from child pornography that involves *actual* actors. According to the Court, virtual pornography neither shows a *real* crime being committed nor involves a *real* victim.

However, this is not the end of the story: In 2003, President George W. Bush signed into law the Protect Act—which includes prohibitions against Internet illustrations depicting child pornography, including *computer-generated illustrations* of children—to correct faults the Supreme Court had previously identified in the 1996 Child Pornography Prevention Act. Unlike the CPPA, the Protect Act required that *obscenity* must be proven in regard to the illustrations. Next, the Protect Act was challenged in *United States v. Williams* (2006). In this case, Michael Williams was found guilty of pandering child pornography. Pandering involves advertising, promoting, distributing, or soliciting by any means, including computer, material that causes a person to *believe* that such material is an obscene visual depiction of a minor engaging in sexually explicit conduct, or is a visual depiction of an actual minor engaging in sexually explicit conduct. The Eleventh Circuit Court of Appeals ruled in the *Williams* case that the Protect Act's "pandering provision" violated the First Amendment right of free speech. However, when the Eleventh Circuit's ruling was appealed to the U.S. Supreme Court by the Justice Department in 2008, the Court reversed the Eleventh Circuit's ruling and upheld the 2003 Protect Act. In other words, the Supreme Court upheld the congressional effort to curb the spread of child pornography on the Internet (Greenhouse, 2008). As things stand in 2011,

child pornography on the Internet is illegal, regardless of whether the images shown are real people, computer-generated images, or digitally altered photographs. What effect, if any, future laws, litigation, and court decisions will have on social policy pertaining to pornography remains to be seen. Social policy and law are part of an ever-changing societal landscape that is influenced by various factors, including the political climate at any given time and the actors (such as Supreme Court justices) who play a role in determining what constitutes a crime and how we as a society will deal with those accused of committing these crimes.

Question for Consideration

1. Have we reached the point with recent communications technologies where it is difficult, if not impossible, to distinguish between the real and the virtual or simulated in our society? What do you think?

Research on Pornography

During the past four decades, two presidential commissions have examined pornography and reached contradictory conclusions. The 1970 U.S. Commission on Pornography and Obscenity found no conclusive links between pornography and sex crimes or antisocial behavior. However, the 1986 Attorney General's Commission on Pornography (known as the Meese Commission) concluded that pornography is dangerous, causes sex crimes, increases aggression in males, inspires sexism against women, and encourages *pedophilia* (adults engaging in sexual intercourse with children). Although some members strongly disagreed, the Meese Commission concluded that sexually explicit materials should be further restricted and obscenity laws should be more stringently enforced.

Sociologists do not agree on the extent to which pornography that depicts excessive sex, violence, and the domination of one person by another affects behavior. More than 80 percent of X-rated films in one study included scenes showing women dominated and exploited by men. The vast majority of these films portrayed physical aggression against women, and about half explicitly depicted rape. Explicit violence is also part of many videos in the adult section of video stores. The Internet has made various types of pornography more readily available to people, even in the work-

place. The Internet has also contributed to a massive increase in the availability, accessibility, and volume of child pornography.

Pornography and Age, Gender, Class, and Race

Because viewing pornography is a secretive activity, data on the consumers of various forms are limited. Some studies have found that the typical customer of an adult bookstore is a white, relatively well-educated, married, middle-class man between the ages of twenty-five and sixty-six. Other studies have found that younger and more educated adults express more accepting attitudes toward pornography than do older, less educated adults.

Overall, men watch more sexually explicit material and hold more favorable attitudes toward it than women do. Some analysts attribute this difference to gender role socialization. In a society in which men are socialized to be sexual initiators and often fear rejection, pornography is satisfying because it typically shows a willing female partner. In contrast, women have been socialized to respond negatively to material showing nude bodies and male pleasure that may occur at the expense of a woman's sense of safety and dignity. However, in recent years, more women have become consumers of soft-core pornography and popular materials, such as some women's magazines, that in the past might have been viewed as pornographic in nature but now are thought of as fashionable or trendy. In general, women are more vocal than men in opposing pornography. According to sociologist Michael Kimmel (1990), men are relatively silent for several reasons: embarrassment or guilt for having enjoyed pornography, anger at women's interference in male privilege, lack of interest in what they perceive to be a nonissue, fear that speaking out will lead to questions about their masculinity, and reluctance to talk openly about their sexual feelings.

According to film scholar Laura Kipnis (1996), much of the sentiment against pornography is rooted in class-based elitism: Opposition to pornography is a form of snobbery related to maintaining class distinctions in society. From this perspective, rejecting pornography amounts to rejecting all that is vulgar, trashy, and lower class. Although Kipnis does not suggest that all consumers of pornography are lower class, she believes that members of the upper classes typically view pornography consumers as lower-class people who might imitate the images they see. Similarly, women who appear in pornography or consume it are seen as brainwashed or unenlightened people who lack "class."

In another class analysis of pornography, philosopher Alan Soble (1986) linked men's use of pornography with their feelings of boredom and powerlessness, which are the result of capitalist work relations, the nature of labor, and the centralization of economics and politics. For these men, pornography becomes a diversion—a means of escaping from the dull, predictable world of work. Soble suggests that consumers of pornography use the material to construct fantasies and gain a sense of control; it gives men the opportunity—otherwise rarely available—to organize the world and conduct its events according to their own wishes and tastes. In Soble's eyes, pornography consumption is not an expression of men's power as much as it is an expression of their lack of power (Soble, 1986).

In other research, sociologists Alice Mayall and Diana E. H. Russell (1993) have detailed how different racial-ethnic groups are portrayed in pornography. Examining materials in a heterosexual pornography store, the researchers found that skin color is a highly salient issue: White women were featured in 92 percent of the pornography, perhaps because they fulfill traditional stereotypes equating female beauty with white skin and Caucasian features (Mayall and Russell, 1993).

People of color were more likely to be found in materials featuring rape, bondage and sadomasochism, anal sex, sex with children, and sex between women. Among women of color, African American women were most frequently featured, followed by Asian or Asian American women, and Latinas. African American men who consume pornography have a choice of buying magazines portraying only whites, white men with African American women, or African American men with white women. The researchers were unable to determine whether these options were based on the preferences of consumers or those of the makers of pornography (Mayall and Russell, 1993). Sociologist Patricia Hill Collins (2005) suggests that racism in pornography can be traced to the oppression of black women in slavery: African American women were depicted as animals and used as sex objects for the pleasure of white men. Others have noted that at the same time that the white man was exploiting the black woman, he was obsessive about protecting the white woman from the black man (Gardner, 1994).

IS THERE A SOLUTION TO PROBLEMS ASSOCIATED WITH PROSTITUTION, PORNOGRAPHY, AND THE SEX INDUSTRY?

Despite some efforts to reduce or eliminate prostitution, pornography, and other components of the sex industry, this type of behavior has received little attention in recent years because of a national focus on problems in the economy, the war in Iraq, and other social issues that are considered by many to be more pressing concerns. At the local level, law enforcement officials in areas where prostitution is illegal tend to deal with individual occurrences on a case-by-case basis of whether the behavior is viewed as a public nuisance and how many complaints are received about the people involved. Similarly, pornography seldom raises a stir until the subjects involved are children or the person disseminating pornographic images is in a position of authority, such as a minister, teacher, or college professor, who is held to standards of high moral conduct. Overall, however, enough people tend to view prostitution, pornography, and other services provided by the sex industry as detrimental to society and as a threat to young people that these types of activities remain subject to prosecution when charges are brought against the individuals involved. How might the various theoretical and political perspectives that we have examined offer solutions to these problems?

Sexually explicit sites on the Internet are available to many students through their university Internet accounts. Should colleges and universities be able to restrict students' access to computer pornography? Why or why not?

Functionalist/Conservative Solutions

As you will recall, some functionalist theorists have suggested that some segments of the sex industry, such as prostitution, serve an important function in society because they offer sexual gratification and sexual outlets to people who otherwise have none and might engage in more harmful or illegal activities if these seemingly legitimate avenues of relief were not available to them. However, while some functionalist and conservative analysts acknowledge that the sex industry may produce goods and services that serve as a "safety valve" for some, many believe that these goods and services can be a "trigger" for others. For this reason, a solution to the problems produced by the sex industry is regulation and control. Prostitution and pornography must be carefully controlled, particularly so that children are shielded from these activities and materials. Cities and states where prostitution is legal and pornography is tolerated, for example, often pass ordinances regarding where brothels, X-rated video stores, and similar establishments can be located. Areas typically banned include sites that are near schools, churches, and some residential neighborhoods. To reduce or solve problems associated with such businesses, local law enforcement officials may more closely monitor the area and regulate workers in the industry, including frequent inspections of businesses or requirements that health permits be on display. For workers in the sex industry, practices such as these are often described as "harassment"; however, law enforcement officials, "legitimate" business owners, local residents, and others often see these activities as keeping matters under control and protecting the community's children.

From a *religious conservative* point of view, however, prostitution and pornography are threats to the moral values of society, particularly family values. The presence of prostitution and pornography in a society encourages people to have sexual intercourse outside marriage and to engage in deviant sexual behavior. Both visible prostitutes, in the form of streetwalkers and brothel workers, and invisible prostitutes, such as those who advertise their services on the Internet, are a threat to the moral well-being of society and must be dealt with as such. In regard to pornographic materials, sexually explicit and violent materials should be censored or eliminated outright to protect families and societal values. However, as some critics have pointed out, the controversy over censorship may be rapidly becoming obsolete in a world linked by the Internet and other rapid sources of communication. In such a world, whose community standards should be applied in determining whether materials are obscene? Censorship is a very complicated proposition in the global marketplace.

Conflict/Liberal Solutions

People who advocate a conflict or liberal point of view regarding prostitution and/or pornography emphasize the relationship between power in society and sex work. Laws controlling prostitution and pornography are created by powerful dominant-group members who seek to maintain cultural dominance by criminalizing conduct that they believe to be immoral or in bad taste. For some of these individuals, many aspects of the sex industry are nothing more than victimless crime, and the way to solve the "problem" of prostitution and pornography is to decriminalize these activities and let consenting adults do what they want to as long as it does not harm other people. From this perspective, until other social problems, such as poverty, racism, and sexism, are reduced or solved, there will always be prostitution because it serves as a way to earn money. Similarly, as long as there is a high demand for pornographic materials and people are willing to pay for them, other individuals will be willing to provide them. Critics argue, however, that there is no such thing as a victimless crime. In regard to prostitution, for example, they point out that most women in prostitution, including many who work for "high end" escort services, were sexually abused as children or that they went into the escort business because of economic hardship and the prevalence of racism in the United States (Farley and Malarek, 2008:A27).

Among the conflict/liberal approaches to dealing with prostitution, pornography, and other aspects of the sex industry are those feminist analysts who believe these activities demean and exploit women. According to this approach, pornography is sexist in its portrayal of women, emphasizes male dominance and female submission, and encourages the valuing of women according to their ability to please men, and, therefore, should be done away with. However, not all feminists agree that this is how to solve the problem. Some believe that pornography and prostitution should both be abolished while others believe that we should focus instead on eliminating structural factors that contribute to women's economic inequality and their oppression under patriarchy rather than initially trying to eliminate the sex industry. Other feminists primarily focus on pornography as a form of sexual discrimination and see this problem as a civil rights issue. From this perspective, communities should pass antipornography ordinances so that individuals who are victimized by pornography would be able to sue the pornographers who produced the goods for damages (see Russell, 1993). In sharp contrast, anticensorship feminists do not believe that any single factor such as pornography causes women's subordination. Focusing on pornography as the primary source of sexual oppression, they say, "downplays the sexism and misogyny at work

within all of our most respectable social institutions and practices, whether judicial, legal, familial, occupational, religious, scientific, or cultural" (Segal, 1990:32). Therefore, pornography should not be censored because open discussions about sexuality and sexual practices promote women's sexual freedom and their right to express themselves.

Symbolic Interactionist Solutions

Since symbolic interactionists focus on the process of interaction, this perspective primarily might offer solutions to issues relating to prostitution and the sex industry based on people who are engaged in sex work or those who create, produce, and distribute pornography. What kinds of perceptions do individuals in the sex industry have regarding themselves? What kinds of perceptions do the consumers of goods and services provided by the sex industry have of themselves? The answers to these kinds of questions might help us gain a better understanding of why demands for these types of services may remain strong over time as well as why the supply of prostitutes, pornographic materials, and other sex industry products may also remain constant or increase during specific eras.

According to most symbolic interactionists, people view sex work—including prostitution and pornography—through the lens of their own mores and philosophical beliefs. Prostitution and pornography have gone through a process whereby they have been *socially constructed* as social problems by individuals in some sectors of American society, but not necessarily others, based on individual and collective cognitive and moral frameworks that are used to evaluate these goods and services (as discussed previously in this chapter). From this approach, what might have been identified in the past as "deviant" sexual behavior may now be thought of as relatively normative as it has become more widely accepted in popular culture and everyday life. Similarly, the line between "adult entertainment" and "hard-core pornography" may become blurred as people become more tolerant of certain kinds of language or behavior than in the past.

As some analysts have pointed out, however, the symbolic interactionist perspective is most useful when it is intertwined with what we know about inequalities based on race, class, gender, age, and other social attributes. To gain a better understanding of why people participate in certain kinds of behavior or hold specific beliefs, we must understand where they are located within global hierarchies based on class, gender, or race-ethnicity. For example, in a forum on the topic "Should Prostitution Be Legalized?" University of Chicago Professor of Law and Ethics Martha Nussbaum made this surprising comparison:

> The difference between the sex worker and the professor, who takes money for the use of a particular intimate part of her body, namely her mind, is not the difference between a "good woman" and a "bad woman." It is, usually, the difference between a prosperous well-educated woman and a poor woman with few employment options. (quoted in *The Chronicle of Higher Education*, 2008:B4)

This statement captures both the symbolic interactionists' emphasis on how issues are socially constructed and the larger picture of how inequality and discrimination are an integral component of why people engage in certain kinds of activities.

To reduce problems associated with the sex industry by applying a symbolic interactionist approach, we need to find out more about how people perceive of their actions and what social meanings they attach to their experiences in the sex industry. Do individuals involved in the sex industry have different perspectives on the *self* than those who are not? How does their *self-esteem* compare with individuals who are not involved in, or consumers of, the services offered by prostitutes, pornographers, or other sex workers? According to some symbolic interactionist analysts, for example, the widely used explanation that states that many sex workers suffer from poor self-esteem has major limitations in helping us gain a better understanding of this issue or to identify ways in which prostitution and pornography might be dealt with as social problems in society. As opposed to the notion that "sex workers suffer from low self-esteem," some researchers have concluded that high self-esteem is closely linked to deviant or antisocial behavior such as may be found in some components of the sex industry. If this assumption is correct, it will be impossible to reduce or eliminate the problems associated with prostitution or pornography by merely viewing people who are engaged in this kind of work as being individuals who suffer from "low self-esteem."

By focusing on the micro relations of social life, symbolic interactionist approaches identify social issues and suggest possible resolutions to those issues that are labeled as being *a problem in need of a solution*; this perspective thus helps us look more closely at how the people's interactions add up to larger social concerns. This approach also keeps us from overlooking certain important issues that "big picture" approaches, such as functionalist and conflict theories or conservative and liberal political perspectives, tend to ignore or miss altogether.

SUMMARY

✓•—[Study and Review on **mysoclab.com**

How do sociologists view deviance?
Some sociologists view deviance as objectively given: Social problems such as prostitution and pornography are violations of folkways, mores, or laws. Others view deviance as socially constructed: A behavior, belief, or condition is deviant because it is labeled as such. Still others believe that deviance is rooted in the social structure of society: People who are in positions of power maintain their cultural dominance by defining as deviant the behaviors that they consider immoral, distasteful, or threatening to them.

What kinds of behavior have traditionally been defined as sexual deviance in the United States?
Four types of sexual conduct among heterosexual partners have traditionally been regarded as deviant: premarital sex (fornication), extramarital sex (adultery), promiscuous sex (casual sexual relations with many partners), and underage sex (statutory rape).

What is prostitution and how has it changed in recent years?
Prostitution is the sale of sexual services (one's own or another's) for money or goods and without emotional attachment. According to some social analysts, prostitution has recently become industrialized, normalized, and globalized. The industrialization of prostitution refers to commercialized sex as a product that is manufactured within the human self. Normalization is the process whereby sex work comes to be treated as a form of entertainment with no legal impediments to promoting it as a commodity. The globalization of prostitution refers to the process by which the sex industry has increasingly become global in scope.

What levels, or tiers, of prostitution have sociologists identified?
Sociologists have identified several categories: Escort prostitutes (call girls or call boys) earn higher fees and can be more

selective in their working conditions and customers than other prostitutes. Hustlers (bar girls or bar boys) work out of nightclubs, bars, and strip joints, where they solicit their customers. House prostitutes (house girls) work in brothels, and a substantial portion of their earnings goes to the house madam or pimp. Street prostitutes (streetwalkers) publicly solicit customers and charge by the "trick." At the very bottom of the tiers are those who exchange sex for crack cocaine.

■ **How do functionalists view prostitution?**
Functionalists point out that prostitution, like other forms of deviance, is functional for society. Prostitution continues because it provides people with (1) quick, impersonal sexual gratification without emotional attachment; (2) a sexual outlet for those who have no ongoing sexual relationships; (3) the opportunity to engage in nontraditional sexual practices; (4) protection for the family as a social institution; and (5) jobs for low-skilled people.

■ **How do symbolic interactionists view prostitution?**
Symbolic interactionists believe that prostitution, like other forms of deviance, is socially constructed. Entering a deviant career such as prostitution is like entering any other occupation, but public labeling—and the individual's acceptance or rejection of that label—determines whether a person stays in a deviant career.

■ **How do conflict theorists view prostitution?**
There are several conflict perspectives on prostitution. Liberal feminists consider prostitution a victimless crime, involving a willing buyer and a willing seller, that should be decriminalized. Marxist feminists see prostitution as being linked to the capitalist economy. Radical feminists trace the roots of prostitution to patriarchy in society. Conflict theorists who focus on the intersection of race, class, and gender believe that the criminalization of prostitution is a form of discrimination against poor women, particularly poor women of color.

■ **Does pornography differ from obscenity and erotica?**
Sometimes it is difficult to distinguish among these categories, but *pornography* usually refers to the graphic depiction of sexual behavior through pictures and/or words, including delivery by electronic or other data retrieval systems, in a manner that is intended to be sexually arousing. *Obscenity* is the legal term for pornographic materials that are offensive by generally accepted standards of decency. *Erotica* refers to material depicting consensual sexual activities that are sought by and pleasurable to all parties involved.

■ **Has pornography changed in recent years?**
Yes, technological innovations have greatly increased the variety of pornographic materials available as well as their methods of distribution. According to some analysts, as long as the desire for such materials is high, the multibillion-dollar pornography industry will continue to produce and market goods and services, adapting to new technologies as they become available.

■ **Does research indicate that pornography contributes to sexual violence?**
No conclusive answer has been found to this question. Some studies have found that hard-core pornography is associated with aggression in males and sexual violence in society, but other studies have found no conclusive evidence that pornography contributes to sexual violence. However, most feminist scholars suggest that pornography exploits all women and sometimes men and children.

■ **How do people react to the censorship of pornography?**
Reactions to the censorship of pornography are varied. People with a liberal view of pornography believe that it is a safety valve for society and that censorship, not pornography, is the social problem. Religious conservatives consider pornography a threat to moral values and encourage censorship of some materials. Antipornography feminists view pornography as a primary source of male oppression and violence against women and argue for its restriction or elimination. Anticensorship feminists believe that some pornography is bad but that censorship is worse because it suppresses free speech.

KEY TERMS

crime, p. 144
erotica, p. 155
obscenity, p. 155

pornography, p. 154
prostitution, p. 145
sex trafficking, p. 147

social control, p. 144
victimless crime, p. 154

QUESTIONS FOR CRITICAL THINKING

1. Suppose you are going to participate in a class debate on decriminalizing prostitution. What arguments would you present in favor of decriminalization? What arguments would you present against decriminalization?

2. Are prostitution and pornography the result of sexism, racism, homophobia, and class-based inequality? Why or why not?

3. On the basis of the text discussion of pornography, obscenity, and erotica, find examples from the mainstream media (including films, music videos, talk shows, and fashion ads in magazines) that might fit each category.

4. Peter McWilliams suggests that the problem with censorship can be summed up in two words: Who decides? Who do you think should decide what materials, if any, should be censored as pornographic or obscene? Besides deciding what's acceptable and what isn't, who should decide on the punishment for violating these standards?

Succeed with MySocLab® www.mysoclab.com

The new MySocLab delivers proven results in helping students succeed, provides engaging experiences that personalize learning, and comes from a trusted partner with educational expertise and a deep commitment to helping students and instructors achieve their goals.

Here are a few activities you will find for this chapter:

Watch on **mysoclab.com**

Core Concepts video clips feature sociologists in action, exploring important concepts in the study of Social Problems. Watch:
- Busting Out

Explore on **mysoclab.com**

Social Explorer is an interactive application that allows you to explore Census data through interactive maps. Explore:
- Social Explorer Activity: Patterns of Inequality Among Women

Read on **mysoclab.com**

MySocLibrary includes primary source readings from classic and contemporary sociologists. Read:
- Prostitution: Facts and Fictions

Alcohol and Other Drugs

THINKING SOCIOLOGICALLY

- Is there a relationship between alcohol and drug use and class, gender, age, and race?

- What major health and legal problems are associated with abuse of alcohol and other drugs?

- What drug and alcohol prevention strategies and treatment programs are most widely used to help reduce this social problem?

It's days like today when I just have to stop and be thankful I didn't get myself killed in college. This is a tragic story [of a student's alcohol-related death] and one that happens far too often and comes close to happening enough to make any parent shudder.

I'm 23 now, and I've learned to have a glass of wine with dinner and be content. Two short years ago, I tried to do 21-on-21 with the full support of all my friends. I still have the picture of my arm signed 21 times by all the people who bought me drinks. Lucky for me, the bar we chose was stingy with alcohol and most of my drinks contained less than a half a shot. Still I managed to throw up halfway through the night and "rally" by going right back out to keep drinking.

This night was not an anomaly in my college drinking experience. I made some bad choices, but I think it's

important for parents to be aware that many colleges today have a culture of binge drinking that goes beyond being young and stupid.

I was a serious student—graduating with a 3.9 GPA from a prestigious liberal arts college before going on to medical school. But looking back on how I spent those four years and how many times I encouraged a friend to have "just one more drink" I can't help but feel like I was part of all that is wrong with college culture these days.

—"Liz" responds with her own experiences (in a blog) to a New York Times *article describing the death of Jesse Drews, a college student who attempted to quickly consume twenty-one alcoholic drinks in celebration of his twenty-first birthday (see Parker-Pope, 2008:A1).*

When many people think about death from an alcohol overdose, they typically believe that such events primarily involve routine alcohol abusers or hardcore alcoholics. This is not always the case, however: One-time or occasional drinkers, such as Jesse Drews who went out for one night of "fun," may be seriously harmed or killed by a single alcohol-related incident. In the case of Drews, one night of drinking to celebrate his twenty-first birthday with two college friends resulted in his death. In a popular ritual known as "21-on-21," some young people attempt to drink at least twenty-one shots of liquor as part of their twenty-first birthday coming-of-age ritual. After Drews allegedly consumed between ten and twelve shots of alcohol, his friends took him home because of his inebriated condition. His parents found him unresponsive in the early morning hours, and Drews was later pronounced dead, a result of an alcohol overdose (Parker-Pope, 2008). Tragedies such as this have led a number of parents and advocates for "responsible drinking" to create organizations that will inform people about the dangers associated with excessive alcohol consumption and to encourage them to become responsible drinkers if they are going to drink at all. In this chapter, we examine some of the problems associated with alcohol abuse and with the consumption of other kinds of drugs.

Did You Know
- Approximately 172 to 250 million people worldwide use illicit drugs.
- 21.8 million Americans age twelve or older are current (past month) illicit drug users.
- More than half of all Americans age twelve or older (130.6 million) report that they are current alcohol drinkers; 17.1 million report that they are heavy drinkers.

DRUG USE AND ABUSE

What is a drug? There are many answers to this question, so the definition is not always consistent or clear. For our purposes, a ***drug* is any substance—other than food or water—that when taken into the body alters its functioning in some way.** Drugs are used for either therapeutic or recreational purposes. Therapeutic use occurs when a person takes a drug for a specific purpose such as reducing a fever or controlling pain after surgery. Patients who take prescription drugs for therapeutic purposes may cross the line to drug abuse; for example, a person might exceed the prescribed amount of a drug and try to get extra prescriptions to buy more of it. Recreational drug use occurs when a person takes a drug for no other purpose than achieving some pleasurable feeling or psychological state. Alcohol and tobacco (nicotine) are licit (legal) drugs that are used for recreational purposes; heroin and cocaine are illicit (illegal) recreational drugs (Levinthal, 2011). Licit drugs—which include substances such as vitamins, aspirin, alcohol, tobacco, and prescription drugs—are legal to manufacture, sell, possess, and use. Illicit drugs such as marijuana, cocaine, heroin, and lysergic acid diethylamide (LSD) are socially defined as deviant, and using them is criminal behavior and hence a social problem. We live in a society that is saturated with both licit and illicit drugs, some that are difficult to obtain and others that are as available as drugs at the local convenience store.

Defining Drug Abuse

What is drug abuse? *Drug abuse* is the excessive or inappropriate use of a drug that results in some form of physical, mental, or social impairment. A more difficult question to answer is "What constitutes drug abuse?" When looked at from this perspective, drug abuse has both objective and subjective components. The *objective component* is physical, psychological, or social evidence that harm has been done to individuals, families, communities, or the entire society by the use of a drug. The *subjective component* refers to people's perceptions about the consequences of using a drug and the social action they believe should be taken to remedy the problem.

Sometimes when people talk about drug abuse, the subjective component—the perception of consequences—overrides the objective component. Consider, for example, the subjective and objective components underlying our society's view of the use of marijuana. The subjective component of marijuana use is the general belief that marijuana is harmful and therefore should not be legal, even though there is little evidence that marijuana use is detrimental to health. The subjective component of alcohol use is the general belief that it is harmless and acceptable, even though there is considerable evidence that it impairs more people and produces greater costs to individuals and society than does marijuana use. Therefore, the use of alcohol is legal.

Drug Addiction

The term *drug addiction (or drug dependency)* **refers to a psychological and/or physiological need for a drug to maintain a sense of well-being and avoid withdrawal symptoms.** Drug dependency has two essential characteristics: tolerance and withdrawal. *Tolerance* **occurs when larger doses of a drug are required over time to produce the same physical or psychological effect that was originally achieved by a smaller dose.** Tolerance is a matter of degree: Some drugs produce immediate and profound levels of tolerance, whereas others produce only mild tolerance. For example, when a person first drinks a five-ounce cup of coffee, containing about 100 milligrams of caffeine, the stimulant effect is usually quite pronounced. After that person drinks the

SIGNE
PHILADELPHIA DAILY NEWS
Philadelphia
USA

DRUG-FREE AMERICA

CARTOONISTS & WRITERS SYNDICATE

| AGE 0-4 | 4-12 | 12-18 | 18-24 | 24-38 | 38-65 | 65 — |
| AMOXICILLIN | RITALIN | APPETITE SUPPRESSANTS | NO-DOZ | PROZAC | ZANTAC | EVERYTHING ELSE |

Signe Wilkinson, Cartoonists & Writers Syndicate/cartoonweb.com same amount of coffee over a period of several days or weeks, the effect is greatly diminished, and a second or third cup of coffee (for a total of 200 to 300 milligrams of caffeine) becomes necessary to duplicate the earlier feeling (Levinthal, 2011). **Withdrawal refers to a variety of physical and/or psychological symptoms that habitual drug users experience when they discontinue drug use.** For example, people who suddenly terminate their alcohol intake after long-term, heavy drinking experience various physical symptoms ranging from insomnia to DTs (*delirium tremens,* or mental confusion often accompanied by sweating and tremor) and psychological symptoms such as a reduced sense of self-worth.

ALCOHOL USE AND ABUSE

The use of alcohol—ranging from communion wine in religious ceremonies to beer, wine, and liquor at business and social gatherings—is considered an accepted part of the dominant culture in the United States. *Alcohol* and *alcoholic beverages* are terms that refer to the three major forms in which ethyl alcohol (ethanol) is consumed: *wine,* which is made from fermentation of fruits and contains between 12 and 14 percent ethyl alcohol; *beer,* which is brewed from grains and hops and usually contains 3 to 6 percent alcohol; and *liquor,* which includes whiskey, gin, vodka, and other distilled spirits and usually contains 40 percent (80 proof) to 50 percent (100 proof) alcohol. In the United States, adults consume an average of 2.5 gallons of wine, 21.7 gallons of beer, and 1.4 gallons of liquor a year. In fact, adults consume more alcoholic beverages (25.7 gallons) on average than milk (20.8 gallons) (U.S. Census Bureau, 2011b). But statistics on average alcohol consumption do not indicate how much *each* person drinks during a given year. Some people do not drink at all, and others drink heavily. Among those who drink, 10 percent account for roughly half the total alcohol consumption in this country (Levinthal, 2011).

Many people do not think of alcohol as a drug because it can be purchased legally—and without a prescription—by adults. It is, however, a psychoactive drug that is classified as a *depressant* because it lowers the activity level of the central nervous system. The impairment of judgment and thinking that is associated with being drunk is the result of alcohol depressing the brain's functions. Alcohol also affects mood and behavior. One to two drinks often bring a release from tensions and inhibitions. Three to four drinks affect self-control—including reaction time and coordination of hands, arms, and legs—and judgment, muddling the

person's reasoning ability. Five to six drinks affect sensory perception, and the person might show signs of intoxication such as staggering, belligerence, or depression. At seven to eight drinks, the drinker is obviously intoxicated and may go into a stupor. Nine or more drinks affect vital centers, and the drinker can become comatose or even die. Of course, factors such as body weight, physical build, and recent food and fluid consumption must be taken into account in estimating the rate of alcohol absorption in the body.

Although negative short-term effects of drinking are usually overcome, chronic heavy drinking or alcoholism can cause permanent damage to the brain or other parts of the body. Social scientists divide long-term drinking patterns into four general categories. *Social drinkers* consume alcoholic beverages primarily on social occasions; they drink occasionally or even relatively frequently. *Heavy drinkers* are more frequent drinkers who typically consume greater quantities of alcohol when they drink and are more likely to become intoxicated. *Acute alcoholics* are dependent on alcohol to the point where they plan their schedule around drinking, and crave alcohol when they try to "cut down." *Chronic alcoholics* tend to engage in compulsive behavior such as hiding liquor bottles and sneaking drinks when they are not being observed; they have lost control over their drinking to the point where it impairs their ability to work or to maintain social relationships. Film and television portrayals of alcohol use and abuse sometimes are framed to glamorize this behavior, but other times the stories are framed in such a manner that reveals the problems that chronic alcohol abuse creates for individuals and their families.

Alcohol Consumption and Class, Gender, Age, and Race

Although people in all social classes consume alcohol, income and class differences are associated with alcohol use. For example, studies show that people who earn more than $50,000 a year tend to drink expensive special or imported beers and more wine than liquor, whereas those who earn less than $20,000 tend to consume less expensive domestic beers and drink more beer than wine or liquor (Levinthal, 2011). The relationship between social class and rates of alcohol abuse is not as clear. Some studies show that people in the middle and upper classes are *less* likely to be heavy drinkers or have high rates of alcoholism; however, other studies show that alcohol consumption and abuse tend to be *higher* in the middle and upper classes than in the lower class.

In any case, more affluent people typically have greater resources and more privacy than lower-income individuals have and can often protect themselves from the label "drunk" or "alcoholic." A member of the upper-middle or upper class who drinks to excess at the country club is less visible to the public and less likely to be negatively sanctioned by law enforcement officials—unless the person drives while under the influence—than is a lower-income or poverty-level person who sits on a public sidewalk drinking beer or wine.

Gender, age, and race are also associated with drinking behavior. More men than women drink, and men are more likely than women to be labeled as problem drinkers or alcoholics. In 2009, almost 60 percent of males age twelve or older were current drinkers, as compared with 47 percent of females in the same age category. Women who drink alcoholic beverages tend to be lighter drinkers than men, who are more likely to consume alcohol daily and experience negative personal and social consequences from drinking. However, drinking patterns in the teen years are similar for males and females. Among youths ages twelve to seventeen, the percentage of males who were current drinkers (15 percent) was only slightly higher than the 14 percent rate for females (Substance Abuse and Mental Health Services Administration [SAMHSA], 2010).

Age is also a factor in drinking behavior. Alcoholic beverages are among the most widely used psychoactive substances by young people in the United States. In one study, 14 percent of eighth graders, 29 percent of tenth graders, and 41 percent of twelfth graders admitted that they had consumed an alcoholic beverage in the thirty-day period prior to the survey (Johnston, O'Malley, Bachman, and Schulenberg, 2011). Some researchers have found adolescent drinking is associated with declining academic achievement and increasing emotional distress, although this varies with the extent to which young people drink within the peer context (Balsa, Guiliano, and French, 2011). In a government survey on drug use and health, slightly more than half (52 percent) of people age twelve and older reported that they were current drinkers of alcohol, and 6 percent of respondents reported they were heavy drinkers—those who have engaged in binge drinking on at least five days out of the past thirty days (SAMHSA, 2010). Among young adults between the ages of eighteen and twenty-five, the rate of binge drinking in 2009 was 42 percent, and the rate of heavy drinking was 14 percent (SAMHSA, 2010). Alcohol consumption, including excessive drinking, is often an ingredient of television reality shows, giving the appearance that people who are "cool" and affluent enjoy life more because they drink (see Box 8.1, on p. 170).

Reported alcohol consumption varies across racial and ethnic categories. Among persons age twelve and older, white Americans were more likely than other racial/ethnic groups to report current use of alcohol (57 percent) as compared to persons reporting two or more races (48 percent), Hispanics/Latinos/as (42 percent), American Indians/Alaska Natives and Asian Americans (37 percent) (SAMHSA, 2010). However, these statistics alone do not tell the entire story. Other research has found that higher rates of high-risk drinking are reported among Native Americans and Hispanics. Although white Americans and Native Americans have a greater risk for alcohol use disorders, once alcohol dependence occurs, African Americans and Hispanics (Latinos/as) have higher rates than whites of recurrent or persistent dependence. Moreover, the negative consequences of drinking typically are greater for Native Americans, Hispanics, and African Americans than for white Americans. Researchers attribute these differential effects to a variety of factors, including risky drinking behavior, immigration experiences, racial-ethnic discrimination, economic and neighborhood disadvantage, and variations in alcohol-metabolizing genes (Chartier and Caetano, 2010).

Alcohol-Related Social Problems

Alcohol consumption in the United States has been declining across lines of class, gender, race, and age over the past two decades. Nevertheless, chronic alcohol abuse and alcoholism are linked to many social problems. Here we will examine health problems, workplace and driving accidents, and family problems.

Health Problems

Although not all heavy drinkers and chronic alcohol abusers exhibit the major health problems that are typically associated with alcoholism, their risk of them is greatly increased. For alcoholics, the long-term health effects include *nutritional deficiencies* as a result of poor eating habits. Chronic heavy drinking contributes to high caloric consumption but low nutritional intake. Alcoholism is also associated with fluctuations in blood sugar levels that can cause adult-onset diabetes. Structural loss of brain tissue may produce *alcoholic dementia,* which is characterized by difficulties in problem solving, remembering information, and organizing facts about one's identity and surroundings (Levinthal, 2011).

Framing of Alcohol Use in Reality TV Series

- "Mommy needs a drink"—Alex McCord, *Real House-wives of New York City,* asking for one of many drinks consumed by the women who star in the "housewives" franchise on BRAVO TV network (author's files, 2011).

- "In the meantime, enjoy your cocktail party, and remember that only one of you will receive the first impression rose tonight." Chris Harrison, host of *The Bachelor* and *The Bachelorette*, introduces the first of many cocktail parties where eligible marriage partners are plied with alcohol and left to impress that season's bachelor or bachelorette (author's files, 2011).

Many reality shows on television feature alcohol consumption with mixed results. If we think about how social drinking is framed on these programs, it is easy to identify at least three frames. One is the "social drinking is fun" framework, which carries the message that participants who regularly—and sometimes excessively—consume alcoholic beverages know how to enjoy life, fit in with a group, and maybe even be selected as the "best" marriage partner on series such as ABC's *The Bachelor* and *The Bachelorette*. When the "social drinking is fun" framework is used, drinking is represented as a glamorous and pleasurable activity: Champagne sparkles in fine, crystal glasses, and vibrant toasts are made by expensively dressed participants who engage in animated conversation, thereby sending the message to viewers that it would be fun to be part of the good life, and having a drink might be the place to start.

The second framework used on some reality TV series that show extensive alcohol consumption is the "Excessive drinking makes me talk silly and act stupid, but I really know better." Reality series routinely have participants who consume large amounts of alcohol, become embroiled in heated arguments, and sometime participate in fights or small-scale vandalism. Even when participants go to excess, the cameras continue to roll, giving audiences a voyeuristic view of people acting poorly. In some cases, alcohol abusers are shown as being repentant and

contrite for their overconsumption; in other cases, they are simply shown as being hung over or in need of "the hair of the dog," another drink that allegedly will take the edge off their previous overindulgence.

The third framing method used to show excessive alcohol consumption on some television entertainment news shows is the "rehab as a revolving door" approach that has been popularized in coverage of hard-partying celebrities such as Lindsay Lohan. Celebrity "news" programs, such as *E News* and ABC TV's *Entertainment Tonight,* carry "glamour" stories about heavy consumption of alcohol by high-profile individuals and then follow up with stories about their "stints" in rehab. Some shows report on celebrities who briefly enter rehab and come out miraculously cured; others show the revolving door effect as the same individuals are readmitted on numerous occasions to gain sobriety. Celebrities entering rehab are shown arriving in expensive vehicles, wearing designer clothing and sunglasses, and being whisked into the facility. Meanwhile, photographers are yelling their names and shooting the least flattering photos they can get to sell to celebrity TV news shows and magazines. At the bottom line, it becomes difficult to find reality shows or celebrity news programs that do not feature alcohol consumption.

Questions for Consideration

1. Does it matter how alcohol consumption and abuse are shown on television?

2. What media frames do you think are most often used on other television series and in films to show the problems associated with excessive alcohol consumption and other forms of drug abuse?

3. Are portrayals of alcohol consumption and illegal drug use different when done by male and female participants? What about by people from different racial, ethnic, or national groups? How about individuals from the upper, middle, or lower classes?

Chronic alcohol abuse is also linked to *cardiovascular problems* such as inflammation and enlargement of the heart muscle, poor blood circulation, reduced heart contractions, fatty accumulations in the heart and arteries, high blood pressure, and cerebrovascular disorders such as stroke (Levinthal, 2011). However, studies show that moderate alcohol consumption—such as a glass of wine a day—might improve body circulation, lower

cholesterol levels, and reduce the risk of certain forms of heart disease.

Over time, chronic alcohol abuse also contributes to irreversible changes in the liver that are associated with *alcoholic cirrhosis,* a progressive development of scar tissue in the liver that chokes off blood vessels and destroys liver cells by interfering with their use of oxygen. Chronic liver disease and cirrhosis is the twelfth most frequent cause of death in the United States, and most deaths from it occur between ages forty and sixty-five (Centers for Disease Control and Prevention [CDC], 2010). Given all the possible health problems, perhaps it is not surprising that alcoholics typically have a shorter life expectancy—often by as much as ten to twelve years—than that of nondrinkers or occasional drinkers who consume moderate amounts of alcohol.

Abuse of alcohol and other drugs by a pregnant woman can damage the fetus. The greatest risk of *fetal alcohol syndrome (FAS)*—**a condition characterized by mental retardation and craniofacial malformations that may affect the child of an alcoholic mother**—occurs during the first three months of pregnancy. Binge drinking during the third week of gestation has been linked particularly with this syndrome because that is when crucial craniofacial formation and brain growth take place in the fetus. Using or abusing alcohol at any time during a pregnancy poses extra risks to the fetus. When a pregnant woman drinks alcohol, it easily passes across the placenta to the fetus and can harm the baby's development. Infants born with fetal alcohol syndrome often have poor growth while in the womb and after birth, decreased muscle tone and poor coordination, heart defects, delayed development and functional problems in thinking, speech, movement, or social skills, and facial irregularities such as a small head and narrow, small eyes (National Center for Biotechnology Information, 2009).

Alcohol in the Workplace

Alcohol abuse and alcoholism have a negative impact on safety and productivity in the workplace. According to the U.S. Office of Personnel Management, the cost of alcoholism in the workplace ranges from $33 to $68 billion a year with absenteeism estimated to be four to eight times greater among alcoholics and alcohol abusers (learn-about-alcoholism.com, 2011). Job-related problems associated with drinking include absenteeism, tardiness, poor quality work, strained relationships with coworkers, and accidents on the job site. Excessive alcohol consumption impairs the sensorimotor skills necessary to operate machinery, heavy equipment, and motor vehicles. Numerous studies have shown a relationship between alcohol—and other drugs—and many workplace injuries or fatalities.

Driving and Drinking

Drivers who have been drinking often do not realize how much alcohol they have consumed or what effects it has on their driving ability. As a result, many people drive dangerously even when they are not legally drunk, which in

most states requires a minimum blood alcohol concentration (BAC) of 0.08 or higher and is referred to as driving while intoxicated (DWI) or driving under the influence (DUI). Alcohol-related driving accidents occur, for example, when drivers lose control of their vehicles or fail to see a red traffic light, or a car or pedestrian in the street, or a sharp curve in the road; they also occur when a pedestrian who has had too much to drink is struck by a motor vehicle. In 2009, 33,808 people died in vehicle crashes, and 10,839 of those individuals were killed in alcohol-impaired-driving crashes. Alcohol-impaired-driving fatalities accounted for 32 percent of all fatal crashes in 2009. An average of one alcohol-impaired-driving fatality occurred every forty-eight minutes in 2009 (National Center for Statistics and Analysis [NCSA], 2010). It will come as no surprise that the rate of alcohol impairment among drivers involved in fatal crashes was four times higher at night than during the day in that same year.

Age is once again an important factor: In 2009 fatal vehicle crashes, the highest percentage of drivers with a BAC level of .08 or higher was between the ages of twenty-one and twenty-four (35 percent), followed by ages twenty-five to thirty-four (32 percent), and thirty-five to forty-four (26 percent). Figure 8.1 shows the percentage of drivers involved in fatal crashes with a BAC of 0.08 or higher (NCSA, 2010).

Although traffic fatalities in alcohol-impaired-driving crashes have decreased slightly in recent years, the negative effect of hard-core drunk drivers in fatal

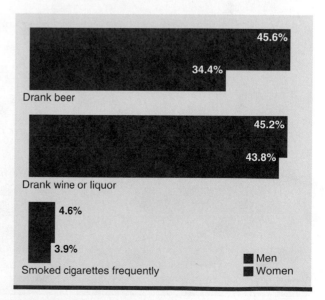

Figure 8.1   Percentage of drivers involved in fatal crashes with blood alcohol levels of 0.08 or higher, 2009, by gender
Source: NCSA, 2010.

crashes has not changed. According to recent reports, the hard-core drunk driver continues to account for an unequal share of alcohol-impaired driving fatalities each year. In 2009, 70 percent of drivers involved in a fatal drunk-driving crash had a BAC of 0.15 or higher. It is also important to note that 44 percent of drivers involved in a fatal motor vehicle crash had a prior DWI conviction and a BAC level of 0.15 or higher (Century Council, 2010). What this means is that drivers with a BAC level of 0.08 or higher in fatal crashes were eight times more likely to have a prior conviction for driving while impaired than were drivers with no alcohol (NCSA, 2010).

Family Problems

Chronic alcohol abuse or alcoholism makes it difficult for a person to maintain social relationships and have a stable family life. For every person who has a problem with alcohol, at least four other people, on average, are directly affected by that individual's drinking on a daily basis (Levinthal, 2011). Domestic abuse and violence in families are frequently associated with heavy drinking and alcohol abuse by one or more family members. Growing up in a family that is affected by alcohol can have a profound impact on children. The extent to which alcohol abuse affects other family

▶ Read the Document
Association is Not Causation: Alcohol and Other Drugs Do Not Cause Violence on **mysoclab.com**

members depends on the degree of alcoholism and the type of alcoholic. Some alcoholic parents are violent and abusive; others are quiet and sullen or withdrawn. To outsiders, the family of an alcoholic might appear to be normal, but family members might feel as though they have an "elephant in the living room," as journalist Joyce Maynard (1994:80–81) explains:

> I grew up in an alcoholic household. But as difficult as it was dealing with my father's drinking, the greater pain for me was the secret keeping. Adult children of alcoholics refer to the phenomenon as "the elephant in the living room": You have a huge, inescapable fact about your life that affects everything in your home, but nobody mentions it, although everybody's behavior is altered to accommodate or deal with it. . . . Our family squeezed past the elephant in the living room, felt his breath on our faces, and rearranged furniture to make room for him. I hid liquor bottles if a friend was coming over. To prevent my father from driving, I even stashed away the keys to his car. But I never uttered a word, and neither did the rest of my family, about what was behind those actions. . . . It wasn't until I became an adult myself that I recognized the unhealthiness of our family's conspiracy of silence.

As Maynard suggests, family members of alcoholics frequently become enablers—people who adjust their behavior to accommodate an alcoholic. Enabling often takes the form of lying to cover up the alcoholic's drinking, absenteeism from work, and/or discourteous treatment of others. Enabling leads many families to develop a pattern of **codependency—a reciprocal relationship between the alcoholic and one or more nonalcoholics who unwittingly aid and abet the alcoholic's excessive drinking and resulting behavior** (Jung, 1994). When codependency occurs, the spouse or another family member takes on many of the alcoholic's responsibilities and keeps the alcoholic person from experiencing the full impact of his or her actions. Children who grow up in alcoholic families tend to have higher than normal rates of hyperactivity, antisocial behavior, low academic achievement, and cognitive impairment (Levinthal, 2011). Unfortunately, children raised

Alcohol abuse and domestic violence are major problems in many families. In a society that glamorizes alcohol consumption, it is difficult for some people to understand the physical and mental harm that excessive drinking may cause.

in alcoholic families may also carry the problematic effects of their childhood experiences and early family environment into their own adult romantic relationships and families (Kearns-Bodkin and Leonard, 2008).

TOBACCO (NICOTINE) USE AS A SOCIAL PROBLEM

The nicotine in tobacco is a toxic, dependency-producing psychoactive drug that is more addictive than heroin. It is categorized as a *stimulant* because it stimulates central nervous system receptors, activating the release of adrenaline, which raises blood pressure, speeds up the heartbeat, and gives the user a sense of alertness. Some people claim that nicotine reduces their appetite, helps them lose weight, and produces a sense of calmness and relaxation. Perhaps these physical and psychological effects of nicotine dependency help to explain why about 21 percent of adults age eighteen and over (46.6 million people) were current smokers in 2009.

When we examine smoking by race-ethnicity, age, gender, and education, we see some striking differences. The breakdown by race and ethnicity for people over age eighteen indicates that the highest rate of smoking (23 percent) is by American Indians/Alaska Natives, followed by white Americans (22 percent), African Americans (21 percent), Hispanic/Latinos/as (15 percent), and Asian Americans (12 percent). The percentage for Asian Americans does not include Native Hawaiians and other Pacific Islanders. The breakdown by age shows that thousands of young people begin smoking every day. Estimates suggest that about 3,450 young people between twelve and seventeen years of age smoke their first cigarette each day, and about 850 persons younger than eighteen years of age begin smoking on a daily basis (cdc.gov/tobacco, 2011). The highest rates of smoking for both men and women are in the eighteen- to forty-four-years category (23 percent) and forty-five to sixty-four years category (22 percent). However, for both age groups, men are more likely than women to be current smokers. The lowest rate of smoking is among adults age sixty-five years and over (10 percent) (CDC, 2010).

Looking at smoking by gender, the percentage of current smokers is higher for men (23 percent) than for women (18 percent) among adults age eighteen years. Similarly, the percentage of females who have never smoked was higher for women (64 percent) than for men (51 percent), while men (26 percent) make up a higher percentage of former smokers than women (18 percent). These estimates are for 2009 but remain relatively consistent across a number of years.

Smoking is hazardous for both men and women, but it is especially problematic for pregnant women. In the United States, it is estimated that about 16 percent of pregnant women smoke during their pregnancies. Not surprisingly, cigarette smoking adversely affects infants and children. Infants who are born to women who smoke typically have lower than average birth weights and sometimes slower rates of physical and mental growth. When a pregnant woman smokes, blood vessels constrict, which reduces the amount of oxygen reaching the fetus. Carbon monoxide transmitted from the mother's blood to the fetus interferes with the distribution of oxygen that does reach the fetus. Nicotine also readily crosses the placenta, and concentrations in the fetus can be as much as 15 percent higher than maternal levels. Nicotine concentrates in fetal blood, amniotic fluid, and breast milk. Combined, these factors can have severe consequences for the fetuses and infants of smoking mothers. These newborns also display signs of stress and drug withdrawal consistent with what has been reported in infants exposed to other drugs. In some cases, smoking during pregnancy may be associated with spontaneous abortions and sudden infant death syndrome (SIDS), as well as learning and behavioral problems and an increased risk of obesity in children. In addition, smoking more than one pack a day during pregnancy nearly doubles the risk that the affected child will become addicted to tobacco if that child starts smoking. Estimates suggest that smoking during pregnancy causes more than 1,000 infant deaths annually, and neonatal care costs related to smoking are estimated to be more than $500 million per year (National Institute on Drug Abuse [NIDA], 2010). Children who grow up in households in which one or both parents smoke are more apt to suffer from frequent ear infections, upper respiratory infections such as bronchitis and sinusitis, allergies, asthma, and other health problems than are children whose parents do not smoke.

Education is another important variable when looking at current smokers: Cigarette smoking is less prevalent among adults who are college graduates compared with those with fewer years of former education. In 2009, about 35 percent of those who had not complete high school were cigarette smokers, as compared to 30 percent of high school graduates who did not attend college, 25 percent for persons with some college, and 13 percent of college graduates (SAMHSA, 2010). Among students currently enrolled in college, full-time students are less likely to be current cigarette smokers than their peers who are not enrolled full time in college. Among young adults between the ages of eighteen and twenty-two years, 27 percent of full-time college students reported that they had used cigarettes in the past month in 2009, as compared to 41 percent of young people in the same age category who were not enrolled full time. The use of smokeless tobacco use by full-time male college students increased sharply from 2008 (9 percent) to 2009 (13 percent). This increase may be partly attributed to the fact that boys and young men have been targeted in advertising by manufacturers of smokeless tobacco products, such as chewing tobacco and moist snuff, which is placed between the cheek and the gum. White teenage boys and young adult males of all racial-ethnic categories, particularly in the South and West, are among the most frequent consumers of these products. However, oral smokeless tobacco is no less harmful to the health of users than cigarette smoking because smokeless tobacco is absorbed through the membranes of the mouth into the bloodstream, increasing the risk of cancer of the tongue, cheeks, gums, and esophagus. Most habitual snuff users have leukoplakia (a white, thick precancerous patch that is visible on tissues in the mouth) and erythroplakia (a red precancerous spot inside the mouth and nasal cavity).

Although the overall proportion of smokers in the general population has declined somewhat since the 1964 surgeon general's warning that smoking is linked to cancer and other serious diseases, tobacco is still responsible for about one in every five deaths annually in the United States. Smoking causes cancer, heart disease, stroke, and lung diseases (including emphysema, bronchitis, and chronic airway obstruction). People who smoke cigarettes, cigars, or pipes have a greater likelihood of developing lung cancer and cancer of the larynx, mouth, and esophagus than nonsmokers do because nicotine is ingested into the bloodstream through the lungs and soft tissues of the mouth (NIDA, 2010). When tobacco burns, it forms carbon monoxide, which disrupts the transport of oxygen from the lungs to the rest of the body and hence contributes to cardiovascular disease and other serious illnesses (Levinthal, 2011).

Smoking typically shortens life expectancy. On average, smokers die thirteen to fourteen years earlier than nonsmokers. Even people who never light up a cigarette are harmed by **environmental tobacco smoke —the smoke in the air as a result of other people's tobacco smoking** (Levinthal, 2011). When someone smokes a cigarette, about 75 percent of the nicotine ends up in the air. Researchers have found that nonsmokers who carpool or work with heavy smokers are more affected by environmental smoke than are nonsmokers who are only occasionally exposed to it. Therefore, smoking has been banned in many public and private facilities throughout the country.

Why do so many people use nicotine if it is so dangerous? Several reasons have been suggested. Nicotine creates a high level of dependency, so once a person has begun to use tobacco regularly, the withdrawal symptoms may be strong enough to make the person light up another cigarette. Some researchers have found that the majority of people who smoke recognize that smoking is bad for them and would like to quit but cannot. In the past, sophisticated marketing campaigns associated smoking with desirable cultural attributes such as achieving maturity, gaining wealth and happiness, or being thin and sexy. Although smokeless tobacco and cigarette manufacturers are no longer allowed to advertise their products in many media venues, other avenues, such as cigarette packaging and NASCAR racing sponsorships, have been found. The U.S. Food and Drug Administration (FDA) continues to try to block these loopholes by first banning NASCAR advertising and then putting requirements in place that by 2012 each cigarette pack required a graphic warning label to cover the top half of the package. Images on the new labels include rotting teeth, lungs that have been darkened by cancer, a man in an oxygen mask, and a corpse. Along with the pictures are blunt warnings such as "Cigarettes cause fatal lung disease," "Smoking can kill you," and "Cigarettes cause strokes and heart disease." Will these graphic images and warnings reduce cigarette smoking, particularly by first-time smokers? Only time will tell; however, if the past is any indications, smokers previously have learned to ignore warning labels on cigarette packages. The best hope may be that younger, potential smokers will heed these warnings and not become smokers in the first place—not only for their own health and well-being but also for their friends, associates, and pets, all of whom may be harmed by secondhand smoke, allergies, and other environmentally related conditions.

PRESCRIPTION DRUGS, OVER-THE-COUNTER DRUGS, AND CAFFEINE

When most people think of drug abuse, they picture unscrupulous drug dealers in dark alleys selling illegal drugs. But legal drugs also can be abused. Legal drugs fall into two categories: *prescription drugs,* which are dispensed only by a registered pharmacist on the authority of a licensed physician or dentist, and *over-the-counter (OTC) drugs,* which are available off the shelf and are restricted only by the customer's ability to pay.

Prescription Drugs

In the last decade, percentage of people in the United States who have taken at least one prescription drug in the past month increased from 44 to 48 percent. Increasing numbers of people also reported that they used two or more drugs, and the use of five or more drugs increased from 6 to 11 percent. Prescription drug use increased with advancing age: Most persons using five or more drugs are age sixty or over. White Americans had the highest percentage of drug use, and Mexican Americans (Hispanics/Latinos/as) had the lowest. Increased usage of prescription drugs came with a stiff price tag as spending more than doubled from 1999 to 2008, when $234.1 billion was spent (Qiuping, Dillon, and Burt, 2010).

The most commonly used types of prescription drugs by age category are bronchodilators for children between the ages of zero and eleven; central nervous system stimulants (attention deficit disorder) for adolescents ages twelve to nineteen; antidepressants for adults ages twenty to fifty-nine; and cholesterol-lowering drugs for adults age sixty and over (Qiuping et al., 2010).

The National Institute on Drug Abuse (NIDA) identifies three classes of prescription drugs that are most often abused—opiates, depressants, and stimulants. Pain medication is probably the prescription drug that is most frequently abused. Millions of people benefit from *narcotics*—natural or synthetic opiates such as OxyContin, Darvon, Vicodin, Dilaudid, Demerol, and Lomotil—that are often prescribed for postoperative pain, or to relieve other forms of pain such as in late-stage cancer, or to suppress coughing, control chronic diarrhea, and reduce heroin withdrawal symptoms. However, there are risks of short-term abuse and long-term psychological and physical dependence. Over time, users develop tolerance for the drug they are taking and must continue to increase dosages to obtain the same effect that was derived from the lower dose. Drug dependency that results from physician-supervised treatment for a recognized medical disorder is called *iatrogenic addiction*. Iatrogenic addiction is most likely to occur with long-term use and/or high dosages of a prescription drug; it most often affects people from the middle or upper class who have no previous history of drug abuse or addiction (Levinthal, 2011).

Other widely used, and sometimes abused, drugs are central nervous system depressants such as Nembutal, Valium, and Xanax, which are used to treat anxiety, panic, and sleep disorders. Drugs such as these are highly addictive and, when taken for long periods of time, become

difficult, if not impossible, to stop without supervision of medical professionals because these drugs have serious physical withdrawal symptoms. The third category of highly abused drugs is stimulants and amphetamines like Dexedrine, Ritalin, and Adderall, which are used for weight loss, to treat sleeping disorders, and to help children with attention deficit hyperactivity disorder (ADHD). According to the American Psychiatric Association, these disorders are characterized by emotionality, behavioral hyperactivity, short attention span, distractibility, impulsiveness, and perceptual and learning disabilities. Although some children are probably correctly diagnosed with this disorder, other analysts believe that stimulants and amphetamines are overprescribed.

Another controversial prescription drug is Prozac, an antidepressant. Introduced in 1987 as a breakthrough medication for clinical depression, Prozac has become a "cure-all for the blues," a far milder form of depression. Advocates believe that the more than 4.5 million prescriptions for Prozac that are filled annually enhance the quality of life for many people, freeing them from depression and suicidal thoughts. But the long-term side effects of the drug are unknown, and there is some evidence that Prozac is associated with intense, violent suicidal thoughts in some patients. Both Prozac and Ritalin are approved by the U.S. Food and Drug Administration (FDA) and are considered safe and effective if taken as directed (Kramer, 1993). Fluoxetine (Prozac) is the only antidepressant approved by the FDA for use in treating depression in children age eight and older. However, the FDA ordered that prominent warnings be placed on all antidepressants indicating that they carry an increased risk of suicidal thinking and behavior in children (Helms, 2005). Some doctors prescribe other drugs on an "off-label" basis to treat depression in children and adolescents. *Off-label use* refers to the practice of prescribing drugs for an unapproved condition or for an unapproved age group, unapproved dose or unapproved form of administration. It is estimated that off-label use of medications is especially common for psychiatric drugs, where the rate may be as high at 31 percent (Radley, Finkelstein, and Stafford, 2006). According to one study, a "hemorrhage of off-label use" in medicine has occurred in recent years (Avorn and Kesselheim, 2011).

Abuse of prescription drugs among teenagers has become an increasing problem in another way as well: Some young people use *legal* medicines *illegally*, even having "pharming parties" where they trade drugs from their families' medicine cabinets with each other. As many as one in five teenagers (20 percent) report that they have taken a prescription drug without a doctor's prescription one or more times during their life. White American youths had a higher rate (23 percent) than Hispanics (17 percent) or African Americans (12 percent) of illegally taking prescription drugs (Eaton et al., 2010).

Compounding the problem of taking painkillers, antianxiety medicines, and ADHD and ADD drugs without proper medical supervision is the fact that many young people combine the drugs with alcohol. Ironically, the problem of taking legal drugs illegally is exacerbated by the fact that it is easier for young people to acquire prescription drugs in their own homes than it is to get illegal ones (C. Banta, 2005).

Over-the-Counter Drugs

A fine line exists between prescription and over-the-counter (OTC) drugs. Today, both types of drugs are advertised directly to the consumer in the electronic and print media with suggestions to "ask your doctor or pharmacist about [our product]." Some drugs are available both by prescription and over the counter, depending on their strength and dosage. For example, allergy medications such as Claritin-D and drugs for acid reflux and stomach ulcers (e.g., Zantac and Tagamet) that are now sold over the counter were previously available only by prescription.

Widely used OTC drugs include analgesics, sleep aids, and remedies for allergies, coughs, and colds. Abuse of aspirin and other analgesics can cause gastric bleeding, problems with blood clotting, complications in surgery patients and pregnant women in labor and delivery, and Reye's syndrome (a potentially life-threatening condition that can arise when children with flu, chicken pox, or other viral infections are given aspirin). Abuse of OTC drugs is perhaps most common among young teens ranging from ages thirteen to sixteen. It is estimated that one out of every eleven teens has abused some sort of OTC medicine.

Cough or cold medicines containing dextromethorphan are the most popular type of OTC drugs to abuse because they are inexpensive and easily accessible in the family medicine cabinet. Overdoses of analgesics such as acetaminophen (e.g., Tylenol and Anacin-3), aspirin, and ibuprofen (e.g., Motrin and Advil) have been linked to cases of attempted suicide, especially by white females between the ages of six and seventeen years. Few of these suicide attempts have resulted in death except when the analgesics were combined with alcohol or other drugs (Levinthal, 2011). Like analgesics, sleep aids are dangerous when combined with alcohol or some cough and cold remedies because they are depressants that slow down the central nervous system. Even cough and cold medications alone have side effects, such as drowsiness,

that can be hazardous if users attempt to drive a car or operate heavy machinery. To counteract drowsiness, some drug companies add caffeine to their product.

Caffeine

Although it is a relatively safe drug, caffeine is a dependency-producing psychoactive stimulant. Caffeine is an ingredient in coffee, tea, chocolate, soft drinks, and stimulants such as NoDoz and Vivarin. Most people ingest caffeine because they like the feeling of mental alertness and reduced fatigue that it produces. Because caffeine blocks the brain's production of adenosine, a brain chemical that calms the brain's arousal centers, it has a "wake-up" effect on people (Medpagetoday.com, 2005).

The extent to which caffeine actually improves human performance is widely debated. Caffeine may increase alertness and reduce fatigue particularly when a person is performing boring or repetitive tasks, and it also improves performance on tasks that require sustained response (A. Smith, 2002). Less is known about the effect of caffeine on complex tasks because this typically involves interactions between the caffeine and other variables (such as amount of sleep and time of day) that increase or decrease alertness (A. Smith, 2002). The short-term physiological effects of caffeine include dilated peripheral blood vessels, constricted blood vessels in the head, and a slightly elevated heart rate (Levinthal, 2011). Long-term effects of heavy caffeine use (more than three cups of coffee or five cups of tea per day) include increased risk of heart attack and osteoporosis—the loss of bone density and increased brittleness associated with fractures and broken bones. In large amounts and over-extended periods of time, excessive use of caffeine can lead to a condition known as *caffeinism*—a combination of caffeine dependency and a variety of unpleasant side effects such as nervousness, irritability, anxiety, insomnia, headaches, and heart palpitations.

Along with physiological disorders, excessive caffeine usage has also been linked to caffeine-induced psychiatric disorders such as caffeine intoxication (overstimulation of the central nervous system through a caffeine overdose), caffeine-induced anxiety disorders (generalized anxiety, panic attacks, and obsessive-compulsive symptoms), and caffeine-induced sleep disorders (inability to sleep or significant disruption in sleep patterns) resulting from long-term, excessive caffeine intake. Overall, some individuals believe that the social problems associated with the abuse of caffeine and prescription and OTC drugs are relatively minor when compared with the social problems associated with illegal drugs, but more similarities exist than many people would like to admit.

ILLEGAL DRUG USE AND ABUSE

Are some drugs inherently bad and hence classified as illegal? What constitutes an illegal drug is a matter of social and legal definitions and therefore is subject to change over time. During the 1800s and early 1900s, people in the United States had fairly easy access to drugs that are currently illegal for general use. In the early 1800s, neither doctors nor pharmacists had to be state licensed. Patent medicines, which sometimes contained such ingredients as opium, morphine, heroin, cocaine, and alcohol, could be purchased in stores, through mail-order advertisements, and from medicine wagons run by people who called themselves doctors and provided free entertainment to attract crowds. Over time, because of the rapidly growing number of narcotics addicts, prescriptions became required for some drugs. Some forms of drug use were criminalized because of their association with specific minority groups. For example, opium could legally be consumed in cough syrup, but smoking the same amount of opium was declared illegal in 1908 because opium smoking was a favorite pastime of the Chinese workers who were building railroads in the western United States. Other forms of opium use were regulated when Congress passed the Harrison Narcotics Act in 1914.

The Harrison Act required anyone who produced or distributed drugs to register with the federal government, keep a record of all transactions, and pay a tax on habit-forming drugs such as heroin, opium, and morphine; it also required that certain drugs be purchased only from physicians. However, the Harrison Act and drug-related legislation that has followed it have not been able to eliminate illegal drug use in this country. Today, the most widely used illegal drugs are marijuana, stimulants such as cocaine and amphetamines, depressants such as barbiturates, narcotics such as heroin, and hallucinogens such as LSD.

Marijuana

Marijuana is the most extensively used drug in the United States. It can be taken orally, mixed with food, and smoked in a concentrated form as hashish. Most people in the United States smoke marijuana in a hand-rolled cigarette known as a *reefer* or a *joint*, in pipes or water pipes, or in other smoking implements such as a hollowed-out cigar (*blunt*). Marijuana is both a central nervous system depressant and a stimulant. In low to moderate doses, the drug produces mild sedation; in high doses, it produces a sense of well-being, euphoria, and sometimes hallucinations. Marijuana slightly increases blood pressure and heart rate and greatly lowers blood glucose levels, causing extreme hunger.

The human body manufactures a chemical that closely resembles tetrahydrocannabinol (THC) and specific receptors in the brain are designed to receive it. Marijuana use disrupts these receptors, impairing motor activity, concentration, and short-term memory. As a result, complex motor tasks such as driving a car or operating heavy machinery are dangerous for a person who is under the influence of marijuana. Some studies show that heavy marijuana use can impair concentration and recall in high school and college students. Users become apathetic and lose their motivation to perform competently or achieve long-range goals such as completing their education. Overall, the short-term effects of marijuana are typically milder than the short-term effects of drugs such as cocaine.

In regard to the long-term effects of marijuana, some studies have found an increased risk of cancer and other lung problems associated with inhaling because marijuana smokers are believed to inhale more deeply than tobacco users. Like other kinds of drugs, use of marijuana during pregnancy is especially problematic. High doses of marijuana smoked during pregnancy can disrupt the development of a fetus and result in lower than average birth weight, congenital abnormalities, premature delivery, and neurological disturbances (Levinthal, 2011).

How strong is marijuana? Controversy exists about whether the average potency of marijuana has risen over the past three decades (erowid.org, 2009). According to spokespersons on one side of the debate, potent marijuana—marijuana with high levels of the plant's primary psychoactive chemical, THC—has existed for many years, but marijuana's potency surpassed 10 percent for the first time in 2009 (Meserve and Ahlers, 2009). The stronger marijuana is of concern because high concentrations of THC have the opposite effect of lower-potency varieties and may bring about paranoia, irritability, and other negative effects (Meserve and Ahlers, 2009). Based on government-funded research analyzing thousands of samples of seized marijuana that are tested at the Potency Monitoring Project at the University of Mississippi each year, findings show that marijuana's concentration of the psychoactive ingredient THC has increased dramatically. By contrast, advocates for the legalization of marijuana argue that studies such as this are government-funded hype designed to convince users and potential users that marijuana is stronger and thus more dangerous for users than it was in the past (erowid.org, 2009). According to marijuana advocates, the average potency of this drug has remained about the same since the early 1980s, meaning that the drug is no more harmful today than it was in the past.

From this perspective, the average potency of marijuana remains at about 8.52 percent, and given that the primary health risk of marijuana comes from the process of smoking itself, then higher potency products actually might be less dangerous because the user can achieve the desired effect by inhaling less (erowid.org, 2009).

Obviously, this debate will continue as long as the battle over legalization of marijuana continues (see Box 8.2).

Is marijuana illegal in all states? No, at least sixteen states and the District of Columbia have legalized marijuana for medical usage, often with specific stipulations regarding residency requirements, limits to the

---

Social Problems and Social Policy   Box 8.2

Legalizing Marijuana: An Issue That Never Goes Away

The controversy over marijuana has been going on for a long time and is still far from being resolved. Advocates of legalization suggest that marijuana use should no longer be subject to legal control. Some states have adopted some form of decriminalization for the possession of small amounts—usually less than one ounce or so—of marijuana. Other states have passed medical marijuana laws that permit use of the drug under specific medical circumstances. Advocates of these laws believe that doctors should be allowed to prescribe marijuana or that the federal government should lift the ban on the medical use of this drug altogether. Advocates of medical legalization believe that marijuana's benefits in treating certain medical conditions far outweigh its possible adverse consequences. For example, marijuana can help control glaucoma, an eye disease that eventually produces blindness. It also can forestall AIDS-related complications, ease the nausea brought on by cancer chemotherapy, and counter some of the symptoms of epilepsy and multiple sclerosis. Advocates envision a physician-controlled, prescription-based system or a legalized regulatory system something like the one that is in place now for alcohol and tobacco. If marijuana were treated as a legal substance, it could be subject to restrictions on advertising, content, purchase age, and other regulations for production, distribution, and sale.

In sharp contrast, opponents of medical marijuana laws or legalization argue that the medical benefits of marijuana are modest at best and the drug is useless or dangerous at worst. Negative effects of marijuana identified in various studies include changes in brain chemistry that can affect memory and attention spans and that can lead to difficulty in concentration and in learning new, complex information. Marijuana also increases heart rate and blood pressure, irritates lungs, and decreases blood flow to the arms and legs, and can reduce sexual performance. Opponents believe that medical marijuana laws or legalization would increase the general level of use and open the door for legalization of drugs such as cocaine, heroin, amphetamines, and hallucinogens.

The debate over legalization of marijuana is far from over. At the time of this writing, sixteen states (Alaska, Arizona, California, Colorado, Hawaii, Maine, Maryland,

Michigan, Montana, Nevada, New Jersey, New Mexico, Oregon, Rhode Island, Vermont, and Washington) and the District of Columbia currently allow the use of marijuana for medical purposes, and several state have decriminalized its recreational use so that the fine for possession of marijuana in limited amounts is about the equivalent of a traffic ticket. However, that does not mean that a person cannot be prosecuted for marijuana use. The U.S. Supreme Court ruled in 2005 that medical marijuana users could be federally prosecuted because federal drug laws take precedence over state drug laws—and under federal law, marijuana is a *controlled substance,* which makes distribution of the drug a crime, even if it is being used for medicinal purposes. Marijuana is defined as a controlled substance because it is listed as a Schedule I drug under the 1970 Controlled Substances Act. Schedule I substances have a high potential for abuse, no currently accepted medical use in treatment, and a lack of accepted safety.

In a more recent turn of events, the U.S. Department of Justice announced in 2009 that it would no longer prioritize the prosecution of individuals who distribute or use marijuana if they comply with state medical marijuana laws. At that time, some political leaders decided to take a more active role in regulating their state's medical marijuana industry. The State of Colorado, among others, established stricter medical pot rules in an effort to curb the dramatic growth of medical marijuana centers that had popped up in that state. Rules established by states typically codify issues such as how much sales volume each medical marijuana center can have and how much of the drug each patient can purchase. In states such as Michigan, a voter referendum to legalize medical marijuana made the issue of enforcement even more complex because law enforcement officials must verify if a person is legally using or selling the drug (as a registered patient or care provider) or if the drug is being used for recreational (nonmedicinal) purposes (Conan, 2011).

What will happen in the future? Will marijuana use for medical purposes be legalized at the federal level? Should states set their own policies regarding the legalization of marijuana and for what purposes? What do you think?

amount of possession, payment of fees, and other conditions as set forth by the states. The Drug Enforcement Administration has identified Marinol, a prescription drug that is a synthetic version of THC in pill form and perhaps an inhaler or patch, as the "legal" medical marijuana. Marinol is used to relieve side effects of chemotherapy, such as nausea and vomiting, for cancer patients, and to help AIDS patients regain their appetite. Currently, there are no FDA-approved medications containing marijuana that are smoked.

How widespread is marijuana use among teens and young people? Nationwide, almost 21 percent of students in one major survey had used marijuana one or more times *during the thirty days prior to the survey* (SAMHSA, 2010). Nearly 37 percent of all students surveyed had used marijuana at one or more times *during their life*, with the rate being higher for males (39 percent) than females (34 percent). More African American and Hispanic males (44 percent) indicated that they had tried marijuana at least once when compared with white American males (39 percent). By contrast, about one-third of females across racial and ethnic categories indicated at they had used this drug at least one time: African American females (38 percent), Hispanic females (36 percent), and white American females (34 percent). Overall, the amount of perceived risk that young people in research studies associate with marijuana use has dropped as the rise in its use has occurred over the past two decades. Perceived risk has declined as availability and use have risen. In 2010, 41 percent of eighth graders, 69 percent of tenth graders, and 82 percent of twelfth graders reported that it is fairly or very easy to get marijuana (Johnston et al., 2011). Marijuana will continue to raise concern, particularly among younger users, because it has been considered a "gateway drug" that may lead to other illicit drug use (see Figure 8.2).

Stimulants

Cocaine and amphetamines are among the major stimulants that are abused in the United States. Both are popular because they increase alertness and give people a temporary sense of well-being. It is quite another matter

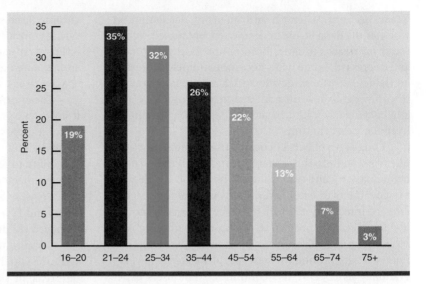

Figure 8.2   Marijuana as first specific drug associated with initiation of illicit drug use among past year illicit drug initiates age twelve or older: 2009

Note: The percentages do not add to 100 percent due to rounding or because a small number of respondents initiated multiple drugs on the same day. The first specfic drug refers to the one that was used on the occasion of first-time use of any illicit drug.

Source: SAMHSA, 2010.

when a user becomes dependent on one of them and experiences withdrawal symptoms. The number and percentage of stimulant users increased in 2009 to 1.3 million from 904,000 people in 2008, partly because of an increase in methamphetamine users.

Cocaine and Crack

Cocaine is an extremely potent and dependency-producing drug derived from the small leaves of the coca plant, which grows in several Latin American countries. In the nineteenth century, cocaine was introduced in the United States as a local anesthetic in medical practice and a mood-enhancer in patent medicines. It was an ingredient in Coca-Cola from the 1880s to the early 1900s. Today, cocaine is the third most widely used psychoactive drug after alcohol and marijuana. Cocaine typically comes in two forms: powder and crack. In its powdered form, users typically sniff, or "snort," the drug into their nostrils or inject it intravenously. Crack is a hardened, potent form of cocaine that is smoked by users.

The effects of cocaine on the human body depend on how pure the dose is and what result the user expects. Because of the effects that cocaine has on the brain, most cocaine users experience an increase in energy, or a powerful high or "rush," in which heart rate, blood pressure, and respiration increase dramatically.

Reactions vary in length and intensity, depending on whether the drug is injected, smoked, or snorted. When the drug wears off, users become increasingly agitated and depressed. Some users become extremely depressed and suicidal; others develop such a powerful craving that they easily become addicted to the drug. Occasionally, cocaine use results in sudden death by triggering an irregular heart rhythm.

Long-term effects of cocaine use include addiction, disturbed moods and irritability, paranoia, restlessness, hallucinations, and serious health problems. People who use cocaine over extended periods of time have higher rates of infection, heart disturbance, internal bleeding, hypertension, cardiac arrest, stroke, hemorrhaging, and other neurological and cardiovascular disorders than nonusers do. Although these problems often develop gradually as cocaine use continues, some users experience the problems after a single dose. Intravenous

Today, cocaine use—in powder and crack form—constitutes the third most widely used psychoactive drug

cocaine users who share contaminated needles and syringes are also at risk for AIDS. The risk of contracting AIDS is especially high in crack houses, where women addicts often engage in prostitution (see Chapter 7) to acquire drugs.

Cocaine use is hazardous during pregnancy because it slows fetal growth and infants tend to be born smaller. Cocaine-exposed children have also been found to have more difficulty with tasks requiring visual attention and the ability to focus on a task at hand, but the problems have not been as great as some experts theorized when analysts were concerned that "crack babies" born in the 1980s and 1990s would become a generation of severely damaged children (Okie, 2009).

Cocaine use has many side effects and hazards, some of which are not readily apparent. In 2011, an outbreak of skin reactions in Los Angeles and New York was blamed on an influx of adulterated cocaine that was being cut with a veterinary medication known as levamisole, which is used for deworming livestock. Some users suffered permanent scarring after smoking or snorting the tainted drug; others developed purple-colored patches of dead skin on their ears, nose, cheeks, and other parts of the body (CBS LosAngeles, 2011).

In 2009, about 1.6 million persons over the age of twelve in the United States reported that they have used cocaine at least once in the past month. According to some studies, more males than females use cocaine, and the majority of users are in their twenties. Initial cocaine usage among young people under age eighteen has declined over the past decade, and most (72 percent) the 0.6 million people who recently used cocaine for the first time were eighteen years of age or older when the first used the drug (SAMHSA, 2010).

Crack cocaine usage has been widely discussed in the media, particularly because of its association with higher rates of use by racial and ethnic minorities and because of disparity in sentencing in drug crimes. President Barack Obama signed the Fair Sentencing Act into effect in 2010 to reduce the disparity in sentencing between those convicted of crimes involving crack cocaine and powder cocaine. Under sentencing guidelines in the Controlled Substances Act, set up during the co-called crack epidemic of the late 1980s, possession of crack could carry the same sentence as the possession of a quantity of cocaine that was 100 times larger. According to the U.S. Sentencing Commission, no other drug is as racially skewed as crack in terms of the number of offenders: 79 percent of crack offenders in 2009 were African American, as compared to 10 percent who were white American and 10 percent who were Hispanic/Latino/a. Consequently, more African Americans were spending more time in prison (with a 115-month average sentence for crack offenses) as contrasted with white Americans (with an 87-month average for crack offenses). The distinction between powder cocaine and crack cocaine has been one of the most divisive issues in drug enforcement and the U.S. court system for several decades (Kurtzleben, 2010).

Amphetamines and Methamphetamines

Like cocaine, amphetamines ("uppers") are a highly potent and highly addictive psychostimulant drugs that increase energy and decrease appetite. Amphetamines in the form of diet pills and pep formulas are legal substances when they are prescribed by a physician, but many people, believing that they cannot lose weight or have enough energy without the pills, become physically and/or psychologically dependent on them.

Some of the most widely used medications containing amphetamine are Adderall, Dexedrine, Benzedrine, and ProCentra. Physical effects of these drugs can include hyperactivity, dry mouth, hypertension, dizziness, insomnia, and numerous other medical conditions, some of which may become life threatening. Psychological effects include euphoria, anxiety, agitation, paranoia, and excessive feelings of many kinds, including power and superiority. Withdrawal effects are often pronounced because the user feels mental fatigue, depression, and increased appetite. Users quickly develop tolerance for amphetamines, and must increase the amounts used so that they can achieve the same effect. Recent trends suggest that younger people, particularly those in grades eight, ten, and twelve, are less likely to be using or experimenting with amphetamines than in the 1980s, when use reached a peak (SAMHSA, 2010).

One subclass of amphetamines is referred to as methamphetamine, which goes by a variety of street names, including speed, chalk, ice, glass, crystal, and meth. Unlike amphetamines, there are no legal uses of methamphetamine and physicians cannot prescribe this drug as a medication. In 2009, the number of methamphetamine users increased to an estimated 502,000 from 314,000 in 2008. In the past these users were referred to as speed freaks: heavy users who injected massive doses of amphetamines several times a day; often did "runs," staying awake for extended periods of time; ate very little; and engaged in bizarre behavior such as counting cornflakes in a cereal box or pasting postage stamps on the wall before "crashing" and sleeping for several days. In the 1960s, a popular phrase was "speed kills." By the 1980s, the most popular form was crystal methamphetamine or "ice," which comes in crystallized, white powdery form that looks like small pieces of rock or glass. These chunks can be heated and the fumes inhaled, much like crack. Crystal meth is often manufactured in illegal labs by amateur chemists. When students in grades eight, ten, and twelve were asked about use of meth in 2010, researchers found rates of use at 1.2 percent, 1.6 percent, and 1.0 percent for each grade, respectively. These rates are lower than measurements from 1999, which found 3.2 percent of eighth graders, 4.6 percent of tenth graders, and 4.7 percent of twelfth graders indicating that they had used any type of methamphetamine in the prior twelve months (Johnston et al., 2011). It is important to note that, although amphetamine and methamphetamine are similar in many ways and have similar effects, methamphetamine breaks down into amphetamine when it is metabolized. What it means is methamphetamine has a stronger effect on the body, acts quickly, and is considered too dangerous to have any therapeutic usage as a prescription drug, unlike amphetamine. Chronic meth use also changes how the brain functions, which may lead to reduced motor skills, impaired verbal learning, and changes in brain areas associated with memory and emotion.

Depressants

Many people who abuse stimulants also abuse depressants—drugs, including alcohol, that depress the central nervous system and may have some pain-killing properties. The most commonly used depressants are barbiturates (e.g., Nembutal and Seconal) and antianxiety drugs or tranquilizers (e.g., Librium, Valium, and Miltown). It is estimated that the number and percentage of nonmedical users of these psychotherapeutic drugs in 2009 was about 7 million persons or 2.8 percent (SAMHSA, 2010). Use of tranquilizers is also at a peak level among students in grades eight (2.8 percent), ten (5.1 percent), and twelve (5.6 percent), even though respondents in this study were asked to exclude any medically prescribed use from their answers (Johnston et al., 2011).

Relatively low oral doses of depressants produce a relaxing and mildly disinhibiting effect; higher doses result in sedation. Users can develop both physical addiction to and psychological dependence on these depressants. Users sometimes use depressants for *potentiation*—the interaction that takes place when two drugs are mixed together to produce a far greater effect than the effect of either drug administered separately.

Heroin users, for example, will sometimes combine heroin and barbiturates in hopes of prolonging their high and extending their heroin supply (Levinthal, 2011).

Rohypnol and GHB (gamma hydroxybutyrate), also known as "Grievous Bodily Harm" or "Liquid X," have been drugs of concern on some college campuses. Rohypnol, also known as "roofies," is used as an anesthetic and sleep aid in other countries, but it is not approved for use in the United States. Before it was banned by the FDA in 1990, GHB was sold in health food stores and used by body builders to increase muscle growth. Currently, GHB is manufactured illegally, and some people acquire the recipe on the Internet. Rohypnol and GHB are popular among young people because they are inexpensive ("lunch money") drugs and produce a "floaty" state, a mild euphoria, increased sociability, and lowered inhibitions. For some people, Rohypnol works like a powerful sleeping pill. For other users, however, the consequences are more dire. Rohypnol is known as the "date rape drug" because a number of women have reported that they were raped after an acquaintance secretly slipped the drug into their drink. The combination of alcohol and Rohypnol or GHB has also been linked to automobile accidents and deaths from overdoses, which occur because it is difficult to judge how much intoxication will result when depressants are mixed with alcohol.

Narcotics

Narcotics or opiates are available in several forms: natural substances (e.g., opium, morphine, and codeine); opiate derivatives, which are created by making slight changes in the chemical composition of morphine (e.g., heroin and Percodan); and synthetic drugs, which produce opiatelike effects but are not chemically related to morphine (e.g., Darvon and Demerol). Because heroin is the most widely abused narcotic, we will focus primarily on its effects.

Who uses heroin? In 2009, as many as 180,000 persons used heroin for the first time within the past year, significantly more than the average annual number from 2002 to 2008 when numbers ranged from 91,000 to 118,000 (SAMHSA, 2010). Young people are among the heaviest heroin users; however, only about 1 percent of people between eighteen and twenty-nine years of age have ever used the drug. Some people who try the drug experience adverse side effects such as nausea and vomiting and never use it again; others become addicted. Current estimates of the number of U.S. heroin abusers range from 300,000 to 700,000. Most studies conclude that the typical heroin abuser is a young male, often a subordinate-group member, under age thirty, who lives in a low-income area of a large urban center such as New York City (Levinthal, 2011).

What effect does heroin have on the body? Most heroin users inject the drug intravenously—a practice known as *mainlining* or *shooting*—which produces a tingling sensation and feeling of euphoria that is typically followed by a state of drowsiness or lethargy. Heroin users quickly develop a tolerance for the drug and must increase the dosage continually to achieve the same effect. Heroin and other opiates are highly addictive; users experience intense cravings for the drug and have physical symptoms such as diarrhea and dehydration if the drug is withdrawn.

What are the long-term effects of heroin? Although some users experience no long-term physical problems, there are serious risks involved in heroin use. In high doses, heroin produces extreme respiratory depression, coma, and even death. Because the potency of street heroin is unknown, overdosing is always a possibility. Street heroin also tends to be diluted with other ingredients that produce adverse reactions in some users. Shooting up with contaminated needles can lead to hepatitis or AIDS. Heroin use also has been linked more directly to crime than have some other types of drug use. Because hard-core users have difficulty holding a job yet need a continual supply of the drug, they often turn to robbery, burglary, shoplifting, pimping, prostitution, or working for the underground drug industry (B. Johnson et al., 1985).

Hallucinogens

Hallucinogens or psychedelics are drugs that produce illusions and hallucinations. In 2009, these drugs were used by 1.3 million persons age twelve or older in the prior month (SAMHSA, 2010). Mescaline (peyote), lysergic acid diethylamide (LSD), phencyclidine (PCP), and methylenedioxy methamphetamine (MDMA) produce mild to profound psychological effects, depending on the dosage. Mescaline or peyote—the earliest hallucinogen used in North America—was consumed during ancient Native American religious celebrations.

LSD was the most widely used hallucinogen for a number of years; however, this is no longer true. In the 1960s, LSD became a well-known hallucinogen because of Dr. Timothy Leary's widely publicized advice, "Turn on, tune in, drop out." LSD is one of the most powerful of the psychoactive drugs; a tiny dose (10 micrograms) of the odorless, tasteless, and colorless drug can produce dramatic, highly unpredictable psychological effects for up to twelve hours. These effects are often referred to as a *psychedelic trip,* and users report experiences ranging from the beautiful (a good trip) to the frightening and extremely depressing (a bad trip). Some studies found that a possibility of *flashbacks* in which the user reexperienced the effects of the drug as much as a year after it was taken. Most long-term psychiatric problems associated with the drug involve people who are unaware that they have been given LSD, who show unstable personality characteristics before taking the drug, or who experience it under hostile or threatening circumstances (Levinthal, 2011).

Among the more recent hallucinogens are PCP ("angel dust") and MDMA ("Ecstasy"), sometimes referred to as "club drugs" because they are popular at night clubs and raves. PCP can be taken orally, intravenously, or by inhalation, but it is most often smoked. Initially, PCP was used as an anesthetic in surgical procedures, but it was removed from production when patients who received it showed signs of agitation, intense anxiety, hallucinations, and disorientation. Production then went underground, and PCP became a relatively inexpensive street drug that some dealers pass off as a more expensive drug to unknowing customers. In the mid-1980s, Ecstasy hit the street market. Manufactured in clandestine labs by inexperienced chemists, Ecstasy, or "E," is a "designer drug" that is derived from amphetamines and has hallucinogenic effects. Users claim that it produces a state of relaxation, insight, euphoria, and heightened awareness. Ecstasy has a high abuse potential and no recognized medical use; however, 760,000 persons indicated that they had used Ecstasy in the past month when surveyed in 2009 (SAMHSA, 2010). It is far easier to explain *what* some of the major drugs taken in contemporary societies are than it is to explain *why* many people abuse drugs.

EXPLANATIONS OF DRUG ABUSE

Why do people abuse drugs? Various explanations have been given. Some focus on biological factors; others emphasize environmental influences. Social scientists believe that drug abuse is associated with continuous and cumulative influences from the time of conception throughout the life course. Thus to answer the question

▸ Watch on **mysoclab.com**
Hidden Addictions?
on **mysoclab.com**

of why people abuse drugs, we must examine the intertwining biological, psychological, and sociological factors that affect people's behavior.

Biological Explanations

Some biological explanations of alcohol and other drug addiction focus on genetic factors. Some studies of alcoholism have found that children who have an alcoholic birth parent have a higher than normal risk of becoming alcoholics themselves, even if they are adopted at birth and reared by nonalcoholic parents. These studies suggest that the child of an alcoholic parent inherits a biological predisposition (or vulnerability) to problem drinking or alcoholism. For example, the child might inherit increased sensitivity to alcohol as indicated by impaired enzyme production, brain function, and physiological responsivity during alcohol intake. The child also might inherit cognitive or learning impairments (e.g., hyperactivity, attention deficit disorder, or language delay) or psychological features (e.g., impulsivity, sensation seeking, anxiety, or aggressiveness) that increase the risk of alcohol abuse by exaggerating the rewarding biological and psychological properties of alcohol (Levinthal, 2011).

Other biological studies focus on the relationship between the brain and drug addiction. These studies have found convincing evidence that drugs such as alcohol, heroin, and cocaine act directly on the brain mechanisms that are responsible for reward and punishment. As the drugs stimulate the areas of the brain that create the sensation of pleasure and suppress the perception of pain, the user receives reinforcement to engage in further drug-taking behavior. According to these findings, then, drugs that provide an immediate rush or intense euphoria (e.g., cocaine and heroin) are more likely to be abused than are drugs that do not. Similarly, drugs that produce pleasant but rapidly dissipating effects (e.g., alcohol) tend to encourage users to take additional doses to maintain the pleasurable effects. Biological explanations provide some insights into drug abuse, but biological factors alone do not fully explain alcoholism and other drug dependency.

Currently, researchers are studying the genetics of alcoholism and drug dependency to assess the extent to which drug abuse is related to biological factors as opposed to the social environment in which a person lives. Does our genetic makeup play a role in alcoholism and dependency on other drugs? Some scientists have found that genetic markers such as the dopamine

D2 receptor are present more often in alcoholics than in nonalcoholics. In animal studies that do not include human beings, this receptor has been associated with brain functions that are related to reward, reinforcement, and motivation to act in a specific manner. Although human genome research might hold promise for identifying genes related to drug dependency, researchers currently have not identified one specific gene that is linked to alcohol-related behavior. It is believed that more than one gene is responsible for vulnerability to drug abuse and that other factors, including psychological influences and the social setting in which a person lives, may play a more significant role in determining an individual's vulnerability to drug addiction.

Psychological Explanations

Psychological explanations of drug abuse focus on either personality disorders or the effects of social learning and reinforcement on drug-taking behavior. Some studies have found that personality disorders—antisocial personality, psychopathy, impulsivity, affective disorder, and anxiety, among others—are more common among drug abusers than among nonabusers (Shedler and Block, 1990). Hyperactivity, learning disabilities, and behavioral disorders in childhood are also associated with a greater risk of substance abuse in adolescence or young adulthood. When people have low self-esteem or lack motivation, their desire to get away from problems is intensified, and drugs often provide the most available option for escape.

Social psychologists explain drug behavior in terms of social learning. According to *social learning theory,* drug and alcohol use and abuse are behaviors that are acquired and sustained through a learning process. Learning takes place through instrumental conditioning (positive reinforcement or punishment) and modeling (imitation) of other people's behavior. Every person learns attitudes, orientations, and general information about drug use from family members, friends, and significant others, so he or she comes to associate positive consequences (positive reinforcement) and negative consequences (punishment) with drug use. Therefore, whether the person abstains from, takes, or abuses drugs depends on the past, present, and anticipated rewards and punishments he or she associates with abstinence, use, or abuse. In a nutshell, the more an individual defines drug behavior as good, or at least excusable, the more that person is likely to use drugs.

Sociological Explanations

The social psychological perspective on drug abuse and the symbolic interactionist perspective overlap. In contrast, functionalists focus on how drug use and abuse fulfills a function in society, and conflict theorists emphasize the role of powerful elites in determining what constitutes legal or illegal drug use.

The Symbolic Interactionist Perspective

Like social psychologists, sociologists who use a symbolic interactionist framework believe that drug behavior is learned behavior that is strongly influenced by families, peers, and other people. In other words, individuals are more likely to use or abuse drugs if they have frequent, intense, and long-lasting interactions with people who use or abuse drugs. For example, some children learn to abuse alcohol or other drugs by watching their parents drink excessively or use illegal drugs. Other young people learn about drug use from their peer group. In his classic study of marijuana users, sociologist Howard S. Becker (1963) concluded that drug users learn not only how to "do" drugs from other users but also what pleasurable reactions they should expect to have from drug use.

People also are more prone to accept attitudes and behaviors that are favorable to drug use if they spend time with members of a *drug subculture*—a group of people whose attitudes, beliefs, and behaviors pertaining to drug use differ significantly from those of most people in the larger society. Over time, people in heavy drinking or drug subcultures tend to become closer to others within their subculture and more distant from people outside the subculture. Given this, participants in hard-core drug subcultures quit taking drugs or drinking excessively only when something brings about a dramatic change in their attitudes, beliefs, and values regarding drugs. Although it is widely believed that most addicts could change their behavior if they chose to do so, according to labeling theory, it is particularly difficult for individuals to discontinue alcohol and other drug abuse once they have been labeled "alcoholics" or "drug addicts." Because of the prevailing ideology that alcoholism and drug addiction are personal problems rather than social problems, individuals tend to be held solely responsible for their behavior.

The Functionalist Perspective

Why does the level of drug abuse remain high in the United States? Functionalists point out that social institutions such as the family, education, and religion, which previously kept deviant behavior in check, have become fragmented and somewhat disorganized. Because they have, it is now necessary to use formal mechanisms of social control to prohibit people from taking illegal drugs or driving under the influence of alcohol or other drugs. External controls in the form of law enforcement are also required to discourage people from growing, manufacturing, or importing illegal substances. Functionalists believe that activities in society continue because they serve important societal functions. Prescription and over-the-counter drugs, for example, are functional for patients because they ease pain, cure illness, and sometimes enhance or extend life. They are functional for doctors because they provide a means for treating illness and help justify the doctor's fee. They are functional for pharmacists because they provide a source of employment; without pills to dispense, there would be no need for pharmacists. But dysfunctions also occur with prescription drugs: Patients can experience adverse side effects or develop a psychological dependence on the drug; doctors, pharmacists, and drug companies might be sued because they manufactured, prescribed, or sold a drug that is alleged to cause bodily harm to users.

Illicit drugs also have functions and dysfunctions. On the one hand, illicit drug use creates and perpetuates jobs at all levels of the criminal justice system, the federal government, and social service agencies that deal with problems of alcoholism and drug addiction. What, for example, would employees at the Drug Enforcement Administration (DEA), the principal federal narcotics control agency, do if the United States did not have an array of illicit drugs that are defined as the "drug problem"? On the other hand, the dysfunctions of illicit drug use extend throughout society. At the individual level, addictive drugs such as heroin, cocaine, and barbiturates create severe physical and mental health problems as well as economic crises for addicts, their families, and acquaintances. At the societal level, drug abuse contributes to lost productivity, human potential and life, and money. Billions of dollars in taxpayers' money that might be used for education or preventive health care are spent making and enforcing drug laws and dealing with drug-related crime and the spread of AIDS by addicts who shoot up with contaminated needles. Addiction to illegal drugs, the abuse of legal drugs, and the abuse of alcohol and tobacco exacerbate the loss of human potential and undermine the stability of society.

The Conflict Perspective

According to conflict theorists, people in positions of economic and political power make the sale, use, and possession of drugs abused by the poor and the powerless illegal. We mentioned earlier that opium smoking was outlawed because it was associated with the Chinese. Similarly, marijuana smoking, which was associated primarily with Mexican workers who were brought to the United States during the 1920s to work in some fields and factories, was restricted by the Marijuana Tax Act of 1937. Although the name of this legislation suggests that its purpose was to raise tax revenues, the intent was to criminalize marijuana and provide a mechanism for driving Mexican workers back across the border so that they would not be a threat to U.S.-born workers who couldn't find jobs during the Great Depression. As middle- and upper-middle-class, college-educated people took up marijuana smoking in the 1950s and 1960s, many states reduced the penalties for its use. In sum, restricting the drugs that members of a subordinate racial-ethnic group use is one method of suppressing the group and limiting its ability to threaten dominant-group members or gain upward mobility in society. Whether a drug is legal or illegal is determined by those who control the nation's political and legal apparatus.

Conflict theorists also point out that powerful corporate interests perpetuate the use and abuse of legal drugs. Corporations that manufacture, market, and sell alcohol, tobacco, and pharmaceuticals reap huge profits from products that exact a heavy toll on the personal health and well-being of abusers, their families and communities, and the larger society. Recent congressional hearings on the tobacco industry's alleged manipulation of nicotine levels to make cigarette smoking more addictive have helped highlight this point. However, by contributing millions of dollars each year to election campaigns, these corporations position themselves to manipulate political decisions that could affect them. Members of Congress who control most tobacco-related regulations typically receive large campaign contributions from political action committees funded by the tobacco industry and often represent districts where tobacco companies are among the largest employers. Using their wealth and political clout, elites in tobacco companies have spent years vigorously fighting measures, including those that would classify and regulate tobacco as a drug; however, they appear to be at least temporarily losing the battle when it comes to advertising and control of the information on their own packaging. The FDA now requires cigarette advertising and labeling on packages to visually show persons suffering from the diseases most frequently associated with cigarette smoking.

IS THERE A SOLUTION TO PROBLEMS ASSOCIATED WITH ALCOHOL AND DRUG ABUSE?

How to prevent abuse of alcohol and other drugs and how to treat drug-related problems after they arise are controversial issues in contemporary society. What kinds of drug abuse prevention programs are available? Will future treatment programs for alcoholics and drug addicts differ from the ones that are available today?

Prevention Programs

Drug and alcohol prevention programs can be divided into three major categories: primary, secondary, and tertiary prevention. *Primary prevention* refers to programs that seek to prevent drug problems before they begin. Most primary prevention programs focus on people who have had little or no previous experience with drugs. In contrast, *secondary prevention* programs seek to limit the extent of drug abuse, prevent the spread of drug abuse to substances beyond those already experienced, and teach strategies for the responsible use of licit drugs such as alcohol (Levinthal, 2011). For example, a program directed at college students who already consume alcohol might focus on how to drink responsibly by emphasizing the dangers of drinking and driving. Finally, *tertiary prevention* programs seek to limit relapses by individuals recovering from alcoholism or drug addiction. The purpose of tertiary prevention is to ensure that people who have entered treatment for some form of drug abuse become free of drugs and remain that way.

In the United States, a variety of primary and secondary prevention strategies have been employed, including (1) reduction in the availability of drugs, (2) punishment of drug addicts, (3) scare tactics and negative education, (4) objective information approaches, (5) promotional campaigns, and (6) self-esteem enhancement and affective education (Levinthal, 2011). We'll look at each in more detail.

> **Explore the Concept**
>
> *Social Explorer Activity: The Rise in Homelessness in the 1970s* on mysoclab.com

In an attempt to reduce the supply and availability of drugs, U.S. law enforcement agencies have expended vast resources to control the domestic production, sale, and consumption of illicit drugs, but their efforts have removed only a small fraction of drugs. The U.S. government has also tried to reduce the influx of drugs from other countries. Despite drug laws and an array of sanctions against drug trafficking, drug use and abuse have not been significantly deterred in the United States or elsewhere.

Map 8.1 shows the volume of drugs that continue to arrive in the United States from other nations. Efforts to punish offenders of U.S. drug laws have clogged the criminal justice system and overcrowded prisons without noticeably reducing the sale and consumption of illegal drugs in this country. In fact, scare tactics and negative education programs have not fared much better; they turn off students and do not achieve their desired goal. In fact, scare tactics appear to pique some students' curiosity about drugs rather than deter their use. Objective information programs often begin in kindergarten and progress through grade twelve. Using texts, curriculum guides, videos, and other materials, teachers impart factual information about drugs to students, but as with scare tactics, students sometimes become more—instead of less—interested in drug experimentation. By contrast, self-esteem enhancement and affective education programs focus on the underlying emotional and attitudinal factors that are involved in drug abuse while building character

The U.S. "war on drugs" has not resulted in significantly reduced rates of drug abuse.

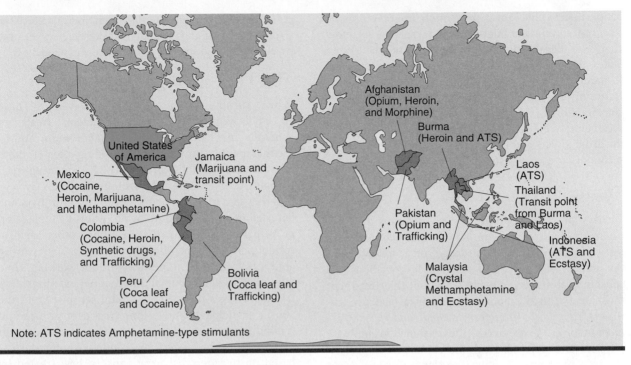

Map 8.1   Main sources of illegal drugs imported into the United States.
Source: U.S. Department of State, 2011.

through teaching positive social values and attitudes. These programs are most effective when they are incorporated into more comprehensive prevention programs.

If the purpose of prevention programs is to reduce actual drug-taking behavior, what types of programs have the greatest likelihood of success? Many social analysts suggest that family- and school-based primary and secondary prevention programs are the most effective. Previously, some prevention programs focused on high school students, but today elementary schools are among the first lines of attack because drug-taking behavior now starts at younger ages. Nearly 75 percent of U.S. public schools have a program known as DARE (Drug Abuse Resistance Education), which is taught by specially trained police officers who teach children how to resist drugs. Critics suggest that police officers, whom many young people view as authority figures, are not the best people to teach adolescents that drug use is not cool. Critics also note that one-shot programs that are forced on students might not prevent drug abuse. Children who have been through the DARE program are no less likely to smoke, drink, or use other drugs than are children who have not been through the program.

Prevention programs for the future that look hopeful emphasize *life skills training*. The Life Skills Training Program developed by Gilbert Botvin (2011) at Cornell Medical School consists of a fifteen-session curriculum directed toward seventh-grade students. Booster sessions are offered in the eighth and ninth grades. The program provides information on the short-term consequences of alcohol or other drug use and teaches participants critical thinking skills, independent decision making, ways to reduce anxiety and resist peer pressure to take drugs, and ways of gaining a sense of personal control and self-esteem. Unlike programs that primarily tell students to stay off drugs, life skills training attempts to give students the tools they need to stay drug free. Examples of activities include teaching students the necessary skills to resist social (peer) pressure, to develop greater self-esteem and self-confidence, and to enable students to cope with anxiety in an effective manner (Botvin, 2011).

Future prevention programs will be family, school, and community based. They will offer alternative activities and outlets to drug use. These programs, like other drug abuse prevention efforts, will take into account issues that affect people differently depending on their race-ethnicity, religion, or other factors. Reaching across lines of race, class, and gender, the next generation of drug abuse prevention programs will use cable television channels to make people aware of the effects of drugs on the human body and how to get help in dealing with alcoholism and drug addiction. The Internet has become a vital source of information, and one that many people turn to first. Future prevention programs provide a source of optimism but only if social structural factors change. If illegal drugs continue to flow into the United States, and television and other media sources continue to glamorize smoking, drinking, and other drug use, the future of preventive programs is bleak. Without social change, efforts will be directed toward apprehension and incarceration of drug offenders and treatment programs for drug addicts and alcoholics, not toward primary or secondary prevention strategies.

Treatment Programs

Tertiary prevention programs are programs that aim to ensure that people who have sought help for some form of drug abuse remain drug free. It follows from the biological and social learning explanations for substance abuse and alcohol addiction that treatment must deal with the body's physiological and psychological responses. Therefore, *alcohol and drug treatment* involves the use of activities designed to eliminate physical and psychological addiction and to prevent relapse—returning to abuse and/or addiction. Most treatment programs are based on a medical model or therapeutic community.

The Medical Treatment Model

The *medical treatment model* considers drug abuse and alcoholism to be medical problems that must be resolved by medical treatment by medical officials. Treatment might take the form of *aversion therapy* or *behavioral conditioning*. For example, drugs such as Cyclazocine and Naloxone are given to heroin and opiate addicts to prevent the euphoric feeling that they associate with taking the drugs. Supposedly, when the pleasure is gone, the person will no longer abuse the drug. Some heroin addicts also receive methadone detoxification to alleviate withdrawal symptoms associated with stopping heroin use. Over a one- to three-week period, the patient receives decreasing doses of methadone, a synthetic opium derivative that blocks the desire for heroin but does not have its negative side effects.

Antabuse is used in the treatment of alcoholism. After the person has been detoxified and no alcohol remains in the bloodstream, Antabuse is administered along with small quantities of alcohol for several consecutive days. Because this combination produces negative effects such as nausea and vomiting, the individual eventually develops an aversion to drinking, which becomes associated with uncomfortable physical symptoms. Although the medical treatment model works for some people, it is criticized for focusing on the physiological effects of alcohol and drug dependency and not dealing with the psychological and sociological aspects of dependency.

The Therapeutic Community

When substance abusers are perceived to have an underlying psychological problem, treatment generally involves counseling, rehabilitation, and/or the therapeutic community. Counseling often employs rehabilitated alcoholics or addicts who encourage participants to take more responsibility for their lives so that they can function better in the community. Some counseling and rehabilitation programs take place on an outpatient basis or as day treatment; others involve residential treatment. *Outpatient programs* allow drug abusers to remain at home and continue working while attending regular group and individual meetings. *Day treatment* takes place in a hospital setting where the abuser participates in day-long treatment groups and individual counseling sessions and returns home in the evening. The *therapeutic community approach* is based on the idea that drug abuse is best treated by intensive individual and group counseling in either a residential or a nonresidential setting. Residential treatment takes place in a special house or dormitory where alcoholics or drug addicts remain for periods of time ranging from several months to several years. One of the most widely known residential treatment centers is the Betty Ford Clinic in California; many others exist throughout the country. Residents in these programs receive therapy and try to establish new behavior patterns outside of their drinking or drug abuse environments.

Perhaps the best-known nonresidential therapeutic community is Alcoholics Anonymous (AA), founded in 1935, and its offshoot, Narcotics Anonymous (NA). Both AA and NA provide members with support in their efforts to overcome drug dependence and addiction. AA was established in 1935 by two alcoholics who were seeking a way of returning to sober life. In 2010, the organization has almost 116,000 groups and more than 2.1 million members. Members use only their first names to ensure anonymity, and recovering alcoholics serve as sponsors and counselors for others. AA and NA are based on a twelve-step program that requires members to acknowledge that they are alcoholics or drug addicts who must have the help of a higher power (usually identified as God) and other people to remain sober or drug free. Other programs continue to be developed to aid alcohol- and drug-addicted individuals. Some are organized around religious principles, such as Mothers

Against Methamphetamine, while others focus on individual willpower (see Box 8.3).

All the approaches for reducing alcohol and drug abuse that we have discussed can help certain individuals, but none address what to do about social structural factors that contribute to the drug problem. Because drug- and alcohol-related problems and their solutions are part of deeper social issues and struggles, they cannot be dealt with in isolation. If the United States sets out to reduce inequalities in all areas of social life, perhaps the drug problem will be alleviated as well. What do you think it would take to make this happen?

Critical Thinking and You   Box 8.3

Calling on a Higher Power or Using Self-Reliance? Alcohol and Drug Abuse Programs

Dr. Mary F. Holley, an obstetrician, founded Mothers against Methamphetamine (MAMa) because her brother Jim became hooked on meth at age 22 and committed suicide at 24 years of age. By starting this organization, Dr. Holley hoped to catch the attention of people who are addicted to crystal meth. Mothers against Methamphetamine (MAMa). MAMa is based on two key principles: (1) that addicts need help from other people to overcome their addiction and, perhaps even more important, and (2) that addicts need help from God or a power greater than themselves to overcome their addiction.

MAMa's approach is similar to Alcoholics Anonymous (AA) and Narcotics Anonymous (NA) in that the founders of these programs emphasized that addicts need the help of a higher power and of other people, especially in a one-on-one, individualized approach where one recovering alcoholic or drug addict helps other recovering drinkers or drug addicts. Over the years, controversies have existed regarding the extent to which religion should play a part in AA and NA meetings—where direct references are made to reliance on God in the Twelve Step recovery program. Part of the debate has focused on people who were ordered to attend AA meetings after being convicted of drunk driving and who believed that they should not be required to do something that involves religion. However, AA leaders state that the belief in God or a power greater than themselves is a fundamental principle of their organization and that this is a necessary belief if addicts are to be successful in their recovery.

Secular alcohol and drug recovery groups (those that use no religious references) have been organized by addicted individuals who found that existing programs did not meet their needs. Among these secular programs are Rational Recovery (RR), Secular Organization for Sobriety (SOS), and Women for Sobriety (WFS), all of which focus on individual willpower and the importance of taking responsibility for one's own actions to overcome addiction. Group support is also important, but members are not required to acknowledge God or to confess their problems to other members. The ideas of individual willpower and group support, for example, are expressed in the motto of Women for Sobriety (2011): "We are capable and competent, caring and compassionate, always willing to help another; bonded together in overcoming addictions." MAMa, AA, and NA represent one approach to dealing with a social problem at the individual level; RR, SOS, and WFS represent another. Consider the following questions in thinking about these divergent approaches to dealing with alcohol and drug abuse.

Questions for Consideration

1. What are the advantages of bringing religion into recovery programs? What problems might be associated with this approach?

2. Is there a difference in a person voluntarily attending meetings of an organization such as AA as compared to being ordered to attend by a judge? If so, what are the key distinctions?

3. If you were asked to design a recovery program, would you more closely follow the approach of AA or of the secular organizations? Why?

Independent Research

Locate organizations in your community or on the Internet that claim to help people recover from illnesses and addictions such as alcohol abuse or drug dependency. Distinguish between nonprofit organizations, such as AA and NA, and for-profit rehabilitation services or facilities that charge a fee for their services and may include residential treatment. What differences can you identify among the various kinds of services and treatments that are being offered? Using your sociological imagination, what types of counseling and treatment do you believe would be most effective in helping a person overcome an addiction to alcohol or drugs such as methamphetamine?

SUMMARY

✔•⌐Study and **Review** on **mysoclab.com**

■ **What are the major patterns of drinking?**

Social scientists divide long-term drinking patterns into four categories: (1) Social drinkers consume alcoholic beverages primarily on social occasions and drink either occasionally or relatively frequently; (2) heavy drinkers are more frequent drinkers who typically consume greater quantities of alcohol when they drink and are more likely to become intoxicated; (3) acute alcoholics have trouble controlling their use of alcohol and plan their schedule around drinking; and (4) chronic alcoholics have lost control over their drinking and tend to engage in compulsive behavior such as hiding liquor bottles.

■ **What are the major hazards associated with tobacco use?**

Nicotine is a toxic, dependency-producing drug that is responsible for about one in every five deaths in the United States. People who smoke have a greater likelihood of developing cardiovascular disease, lung cancer, and/or cancer of the larynx, mouth, and esophagus. Even those who do not smoke may be subjected to the hazard of environmental tobacco smoke—the smoke in the air as a result of other people's tobacco smoking. Infants born to women who smoke typically have lower than average birth weights and sometimes have slower rates of physical and mental growth.

■ **What problems are associated with use of prescription and over-the-counter drugs?**

Some prescription drugs have the potential for short-term abuse and long-term psychological and physical dependence. This form of dependency is known as iatrogenic addiction—drug dependency that results from physician-supervised treatment for a recognized medical disorder. Over-the-counter drugs, which are widely advertised and readily available, may be dangerous when combined with alcohol or other drugs.

■ **Is marijuana illegal in all states?**

No, at least sixteen states and the District of Columbia have legalized marijuana for medical usage, often with specific stipulations regarding residency requirements, limits to the amount of possession, payment of fees, and other conditions as set forth by the states.

■ **In the United States, what are the major stimulant drugs?**

Cocaine and amphetamines are the major stimulant drugs that are abused in the United States. Cocaine is an extremely potent and dependency-producing stimulant drug. Amphetamines can be obtained legally in the form of diet pills and pep formulas when they are prescribed by a physician. One subclass of amphetamines is referred to as methamphetamine, which goes by a variety of street names, including speed, chalk, ice, glass, crystal, and meth.

Unlike amphetamines, there are no legal uses of methamphetamine, and physicians cannot legally prescribe this drug.

■ **What are depressants and what health-related risk do they pose?**

As the name indicates, depressants depress the central nervous system; they also may have some pain-killing properties. The most common depressants are barbiturates and antianxiety drugs or tranquilizers. Users may develop both physical addiction and psychological dependency on these drugs. There is also the risk of potentiation—the drug interaction that takes place when two drugs are mixed together and the combination produces a far greater effect than that of either drug administered separately.

■ **What other drugs are widely abused in the United States?**

Narcotics or opiates, including natural substances (e.g., opium, morphine, and codeine), opiate derivatives (e.g., heroin and Percodan), and synthetic drugs with opiatelike effects (e.g., Darvon and Demerol) are frequently abused. Hallucinogens or psychedelics such as mescaline (peyote), lysergic acid diethylamide (LSD), phencyclidine (PCP), and MDMA (Ecstasy) are also widely abused.

■ **How do biological and psychological perspectives view alcohol and drug addiction?**

Biological explanations of alcohol and drug addiction focus on inherited biological factors and on the effects of drugs on the human brain. Psychological explanations of drug abuse focus on personality disorders and the effects of social learning and reinforcement on people's drug-taking behavior.

■ **How do sociological perspectives view alcohol and drug addiction?**

Symbolic interactionists believe that drug use and abuse are learned behaviors that are strongly influenced by families, peers, and others who serve as role models. People are more prone to accept attitudes and behaviors that are favorable to drug use if they spend time with members of a drug subculture. Functionalists believe that drug-related problems have increased as social institutions such as the family, education, and religion have become fragmented and somewhat disorganized. However, use of alcohol and other drugs serves important functions even though some aspects of their use are dysfunctional for society. According to conflict theorists, people in positions of economic and political power are responsible for making the sale, use, and possession of some drugs illegal. Conflict theorists also point out that powerful corporate interests perpetuate the use and abuse of alcohol, tobacco, and other legal drugs.

■ **What is the purpose of prevention and treatment programs?**

Primary prevention programs seek to prevent drug problems before they begin. Secondary prevention programs seek to limit the extent of drug abuse, prevent the spread of drug abuse to other substances beyond the drugs already experienced, and teach strategies for the responsible use of licit drugs such as alcohol. Tertiary prevention programs seek to limit relapses by individuals recovering from alcoholism or drug addiction. They may be based on either a medical model or the therapeutic community. The best-known therapeutic community is Alcoholics Anonymous (AA).

■ **What other factors must be taken into account in efforts to reduce the drug problem?**

Alcoholism and drug abuse are intertwined with other social problems such as dramatic changes in the economic and technological bases of the society, the growing gap between the rich and poor, and inequalities based on race-ethnicity and gender.

KEY TERMS

codependency, p. 172

drug, p. 166

drug addiction (or drug dependency), p. 167

drug subculture, p. 184

environmental tobacco smoke, p. 174

fetal alcohol syndrome (FAS), p. 171

tolerance, p. 167

withdrawal, p. 168

QUESTIONS FOR CRITICAL THINKING

1. Does public tolerance of alcohol and tobacco lead to increased use of these drugs? Why do many people view the use of alcohol and tobacco differently from the use of illicit drugs?

2. If stimulants, depressants, and hallucinogens have such potentially hazardous side effects, why do so many people use these drugs? If drug enforcement policies were more stringently enforced, would there be less drug abuse in this country?

3. As a sociologist, how would you propose to deal with the drug problem in the United States? If you were called on to revamp existing drug laws and policies, what, if any, changes would you make in them?

4. How have changes in technology and social networking affected the problem of alcohol and drug abuse over the past century? How have changes in the global economy affected drug-related problems in this country and others?

Succeed with MySocLab®   www.mysoclab.com

The new MySocLab delivers proven results in helping students succeed, provides engaging experiences that personalize learning, and comes from a trusted partner with educational expertise and a deep commitment to helping students and instructors achieve their goals.

Here are a few activities you will find for this chapter:

Watch on **mysoclab.com**

Core Concepts video clips feature sociologists in action, exploring important concepts in the study of Social Problems. Watch:
• Hidden Addictions?

Explore on **mysoclab.com**

Social Explorer is an interactive application that allows you to explore Census data through interactive maps. Explore:
• Social Explorer Activity: The Rise in Homelessness in the 1970s

Read on **mysoclab.com**

MySocLibrary includes primary source readings from classic and contemporary sociologists. Read:
• Association is Not Causation: Alcohol and Other Drugs Do Not Cause Violence

9

Crime and Criminal Justice

THINKING SOCIOLOGICALLY

⦿ What do you think of when you hear the word *crime*? Do the media influence how we think about crime?

⦿ Is there a relationship between class and violent crime? Property crime? Corporate crime?

⦿ How do structural explanations of crime differ from those based on a biological or psychological approach?

As the verdicts were read aloud in court, one "guilty" following another, Mr. Blagojevich, who had always proclaimed his innocence, turned, his jaw clenched grimly, to look at his wife, Patti, in the front row. By then, she was already slumped back in the arms of a relative, eyes closed, wiping away tears.

—Journalists Monica Davey and Emma G. Fitzsimmons (2011) describe the scene in court as a jury convicted former Illinois Governor Rod R. Blagojevich of most of the twenty federal counts of corruption against him.

Raj Rajaratnam, the billionaire investor who once ran one of the world's largest hedge funds, was found guilty on Wednesday of fraud and conspiracy by a federal jury in Manhattan. He is the most prominent figure convicted in the government's crackdown on insider trading on Wall Street. Mr. Rajaratnam was convicted on all 14 counts. Mr. Rajaratnam, dressed in a black suit, had no expression as the verdict was read in the overflowing courtroom….

"Raj hated to lose and loved a good fight," one former colleague said. "He's a big sports fan, and I think in some ways he viewed this trial as a contest."

—Journalists Peter Lattman and Azam Ahmed (2011) discuss the appearance and demeanor of Raj Rajaratnam, a self-made billionaire formerly on the Forbes 400 Richest Americans list, after his conviction in an insider trading case involving his Galleon Group, one of the world's largest hedge funds.

When many people think about crime and criminal justice, they primarily focus on violent crimes, police chases, and interrogations that are so popular on TV crime series and in movies. However, recent news headlines have called our attention to the extent to which nonviolent crime has contributed to massive economic losses in the United States and worldwide, and this kind of crime has come about through the dishonest and corruption of political leaders, corporate leaders, top hedge fund managers, and others in high-reward, high-profile positions. As discussed in this chapter, the term "white-collar crime" may be more than seventy years old, but the image it conveys is still relevant today. Originally defined by sociologist Edwin H. Sutherland as "crime committed by a person of respectability and high social status in the course of his occupation," these kinds of offenses are becoming increasingly common in an era when the wealthy, the powerful, and the privileged appear to view themselves as being above the law, not like other ordinary criminals who engage in garden-variety street crimes such as robbery, burglary, assault, and murder.

From one sociological perspective, crime is rooted in *the social structure of society*, particularly in power relations. A *structural approach* to understanding deviance and crime makes us aware that the most powerful members of the dominant racial, class, and gender groups have economic, political, and social power that often protects them from being apprehended and punished. There are exceptions, of course, such as in cases listed previously and others involving high-ranking corporate officials. In this chapter, we examine crimes that are committed by people at all levels of society, ranging from perpetrators of street crimes to CEOs who improperly use millions of dollars in corporate money.

DID YOU KNOW

- Crimes rates have been falling in the United States
- More than 2 million persons under age eighteen are arrested in the United States each year.
- Identity theft is the number one consumer complaint in the United States.
- More than 3,000 inmates are on death row and 42 percent are African American.

CRIME AS A SOCIAL PROBLEM

Many people in the United States fear crime and are somewhat obsessed with it even though they have no direct daily exposure to criminal behavior. Their information about crime comes from the news media and sometimes from watching real-crime television shows such as *America's Most Wanted* or fictionalized crime stories such as *CSI, Criminal Minds, NCIS*, or *Law and Order* on television (Kort-Butler and Hartshorn, 2011). Media coverage of crime is extensive and might in fact contribute to our widespread perception that crime has increased dramatically in this country. The truth, however, is rather different: The rate of serious and violent crime has fallen significantly during the last ten years (FBI, 2010a). That is not to say that crime isn't a problem. Crime statistics tell only part of the story. Crime is a significant social problem because it endangers people's lives, property, and sense of well-being.

Problems with Official Statistics

Over the past three decades, sophisticated computer-based information systems have not only improved rates of detection, apprehension, and conviction of offenders but also have provided immediate access to millions of bits of information about crime, suspects, and offenders. The leading source of information on crimes reported in the United States is the Uniform Crime Report (UCR). It is published annually by the Federal Bureau of Investigation (FBI) and is based on data provided by federal, state, and local law enforcement agencies. The UCR tracks

violent crimes and property crimes. Violent crimes include murder, rape, robbery, and aggravated assault. Examples of property crimes are burglary (breaking into private property to commit a serious crime), motor vehicle theft, arson, and larceny-theft. The UCR also includes a "Crime Clock" (see Figure 9.1), showing how often (on average) certain crimes are committed in this country. In 2009, for example, a murder occurred in the United States on an average of once every thirty-five minutes, a robbery every minute, and a forcible rape every six minutes (FBI, 2010a). During the same year, about 13.7 million arrests were made in the United States for all criminal infractions (excluding traffic violations).

How accurate are these crime statistics? Any answer to this question must take into account the fact that legal definitions of some offenses vary from jurisdiction to jurisdiction and that the statistics reflect only crimes that are reported to law enforcement agencies or that

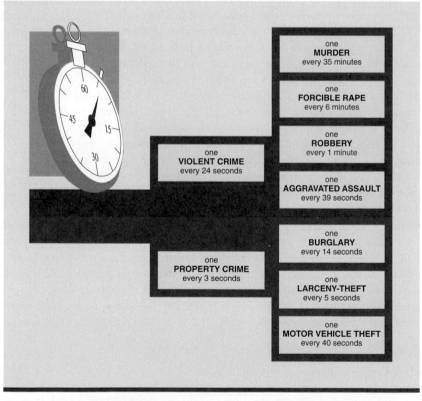

Figure 9.1 Crime clock, 2009: The crime clock should be viewed with care. Being the most aggregate representation of UCR data, it is designed to convey the annual reported crime experience by showing the relative frequency of occurrence of certain offenses. This mode of display should not be taken to imply a regularity in the commission of the offense; rather, it represents the annual ratio of crime to fixed time intervals.
Source: FBI, 2010a.

police officers see occur. According to the UCR, overall rates of crime (number of crimes per 100,000 people), which increased sharply between 1987 and 1991, have (except during 2001) decreased annually since then. Preliminary UCR statistics for 2010, for example, show that violent crime was down 5.5 percent in 2009–2010 from 2008–2009, which the rate of violent crime was also down 5.3 percent from the previous year of 2007–2008. In all major crime categories this pattern holds true: Reported crimes have fallen in all categories each year since 2006–2007 (FBI, 2011b). Because the number of crimes that are reported is not necessarily the number of crimes that are *committed*, the Bureau of Justice Statistics conducts an annual National Crime Victimization Survey (NCVS) of 100,000 randomly selected households to identify crime victims, whether the crime was reported or not. These surveys indicate that the number of crimes that are committed is substantially higher than the number that is reported. However, the NCVS has limitations too: (1) Responses are based on recall, and some people don't remember specifically when a crime occurred; (2) for various reasons, respondents might not be truthful; and (3) the surveys focus on personal crimes and property crimes and do not measure workplace crimes such as embezzlement or bribery.

Defining Crime and Delinquency

Crime is behavior that violates the criminal law and is punishable by fine, jail term, or other negative sanctions. In the United States, criminal laws can be enacted at the local, state, and federal levels. As a result, some laws apply uniformly throughout the states while others vary from state to state or apply only in the local jurisdiction where they were passed. Whether the law that is broken is federal, state, or local, there are two components to every crime: the act itself and *criminal intent*, expressed in the concept of *mens rea*, meaning "guilty mind." An individual's intent in committing a crime can range from willful conduct (hiring someone to kill one's spouse) to an unintentional act of negligence that is defined as a crime (leaving a small child unattended in a locked automobile in extremely hot weather, resulting in the child's death). Criminal law is divided into two major categories: misdemeanors and felonies. **Misdemeanors are relatively minor crimes that are punishable by a fine or less than a year in jail.** Examples include public drunkenness, shoplifting, and traffic violations. **Felonies are more serious crimes, such as murder,** **rape, or aggravated assault, that are punishable by more than a year's imprisonment or even death.** Children and adolescents below a certain age (usually eighteen) who commit illegal or antisocial acts usually are not charged with criminal conduct but are adjudicated as *delinquent* by a juvenile court judge. However, when older juveniles are charged with violent crimes, it is becoming increasingly common to *certify* or *waive* them to adult court.

TYPES OF CRIMES

To make the study of crime—a large and complex subject—manageable, sociologists and criminologists categorize types of crime. In this section, we will look at six categories of crime: violent crime, property crime, occupational crime, corporate crime, organized crime, and juvenile delinquency.

Violent Crime

In the United States, a violent crime occurs on an average of once every twenty-four seconds (FBI, 2010a). **Violent crime consists of actions involving force or the threat of force against others and includes murder, rape, gang violence, and aggravated assault and robbery.** Violent crimes are committed against people; nonviolent crimes are usually committed against property. People tend to fear violent crime more than other kinds of crime because victims are often physically injured or even killed and because violent crime receives the most sustained attention from law enforcement officials and the media.

Murder

The UCR defines **murder as the unlawful, intentional killing of one person by another.** (Killing in self-defense or during wartime is not murder.) By this definition, murder involves not only an unlawful act but also *malice aforethought*—the *intention* of doing a wrongful act. A person who buys a gun, makes a plan to kill someone, and carries out the plan has probably committed murder. In contrast, *manslaughter* is the unlawful, *unintentional* killing of one person by another. An intoxicated person who shoots a gun into the air probably holds no malice toward the bystander who is killed by a stray bullet. Sometimes a person's intentions are clear, but many times they are not, and the lines between intentional, unintentional, and accidental homicides are often blurred.

Mass murder **is the killing of four or more people at one time and in one place by the same person.** Based on this definition, there is no shortage of examples of mass murder in the United States. Among the recent mass murders that have received the most media coverage are the 2011 Arizona shooting of Congresswoman Gabrielle Giffords and the 2010 shooting on the military base at Fort Hood, Texas, where a U.S. Army psychiatrist was accused of shooting and killing a number of military personnel and civilians. According to criminologists, mass murderers tend to kill in the areas where they live, to be males, and to have psychological disorders or serious mental illness.

Serial murder **is the killing of three or more people over more than a month by the same person.** Serial murders account for relatively few victims annually but receive extensive media coverage. Among the best-known serial killers in previous decades were Ted Bundy, John Wayne Gacy, and Jeffrey Dahmer. In the 1990s and early 2000s, the most widely known serial killers included Angel Resendiz ("The Railway Killer"), who wandered the country on trains, allegedly killing at many as twenty-four people nationwide, and Robert L. Yates, Jr. ("The Prostitute Killer"), who murdered at least twelve prostitutes in the Spokane, Washington, area. More recent cases of assumed serial murder have also involved prostitute killings, but no one has been apprehended in some of these violent crimes. Once a serial murderer is apprehended, it is often difficult for law enforcement officials to determine the actual number of victims that individual murdered, and perpetrators sometimes admit to additional killings that cannot be conclusively attributed to the individual.

What are the characteristics of a serial killer? It is difficult to characterize serial killers, outside of the fact that the best-known ones have been white males. Some travel extensively to locate their victims; others kill near where they live. One study identified four basic types of serial killers: (1) *visionaries*, who kill because they hear a voice or have a vision that commands them to commit the murderous acts; (2) *missionaries*, who take it on themselves to rid the community or the world of what they believe is an undesirable type of person; (3) *hedonists*, who obtain personal or sexual gratification from violence; and (4) *power/control seekers*, who achieve gratification from the complete possession of the victim (Robert Holmes, 1988).

Nature and extent of the problem Statistics on murder are among the more accurate official crime statistics available. Murders rarely go unreported, and suspects are usually apprehended and charged. It is estimated that 15,241 persons were murdered in 2009, which is a 7.3 percent decrease from 2008. There were 5.0 murders per 100,000 population in 2009. More than 44 percent of murders were reported in the South, followed by 21 percent in the West, 20 percent in the Midwest and 14 percent reported in the Northeast. Of those 15,241 estimated murders, the FBI (2010a) found more detailed informed on 13,636 of the murders. Referred to as "expanded homicide data" by the FBI, this report provides us with information regarding the age, sex, and race of the murder victim and offender, as well as the type of weapon used, the relationship of the victim to the offender, and the circumstances surrounding the incident. For this reason, the following information is based on the "expanded data," not on the entire estimated 15,241 persons who were believed to have been murdered in 2009.

Of the 13,636 total murder *victims* for which supplemental data were reported in 2009, about 77 percent of the victims (10,496) were male, as compared to 23 percent of female victims. Among both male and female victims, 48.7 percent were white American, 48.6 percent were African American, and 2.7 percent were of other races (FBI, 2010a). Almost half (48.6 percent) of all these murders involved one victim and one offender, and 84 percent of white victims were killed by white offenders, as compared to 91 percent of African American victims who were killed by other African Americans (see Table 9.1). Most murder victims and offenders were age eighteen and over. For murders where the circumstances were known, 41 percent of victims were murdered during an argument, such as a romantic triangle, or in situations where felonies (such as rape, robbery, or burglary) were being committed

TABLE 9.1 Percentage of Single Victim–Single Offender Homicides by Race of Offenders and Victims, 2009

	Offenders		
	White	**Black**	**Other/ Unknown**
White	84%	13%	3%
Black	7%	91%	3%

Note: May add up to more than 100% because of rounding.

Source: FBI, 2010a.

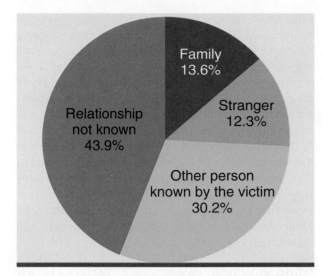

Figure 9.2 Murder by relationship of victim and offender, 2009
Source: FBI, 2010.

(23 percent). The statistics for female murder victims (for whom their relationships to the offenders were known) are particularly striking: Slightly more than one-third (34.6 percent) were murdered by their husbands or boyfriends. In cases where information was available, slightly more than half of all murder victims knew their assailants: About 14 percent were related to their assailant, and 30.2 percent were acquainted with them well enough to at least engage in an argument. Of the remaining victims, 12.3 percent were murdered by strangers, and in about 43.9 percent of cases, the relationship between victim and offender was unknown (see Figure 9.2).

Shifting our focus to homicide *offenders*, 15,760 people were arrested for murder in 2009. However, it is important to recall that alleged offenders who are arrested in a specific year may not have committed the crime during that same year, so information about murder offenders who have been arrested does not necessarily correspond to the estimated number of murders that occur or the number of victims who are identified in a given year such as 2009. Among those arrested for murder and nonnegligent manslaughter in 2009, males accounted for almost 90 percent of all offenders for whom gender was known. Of all offenders for whom race was known, almost 52 percent were African American, 46 percent were white American, and 2.1 percent were of other races. Race was unknown for 4,339 offenders. Of the homicide for which the FBI received weapons data, firearms were used in almost 72 percent of all homicides, and handguns comprised almost 71 percent

of all firearms used in 2009. Although there has been a downward trend in murder rates in the 2010s, murder still has a special newsworthiness in all forms of media.

Rape

Many people think of rape as a sexually motivated crime, but it is actually an act of violence in which sex is used as a weapon against a powerless victim. As defined by the FBI, forcible rape is the carnal knowledge of a female forcibly and against her will. Although both men and women are victimized by rape, the legal definition of *forcible rape* **is the act of forcing sexual intercourse on an adult of legal age against her will.** Sexual assaults or attempts to commit rape by force or threat of force are included in FBI statistics on this crime. Unlike murder or other violent crimes, the age of the victim is a central issue in charging a person with rape. *Statutory rape* **refers to sexual intercourse with a person who is under the legal age of consent as established by state law** (some states now use the term *illegal intercourse* instead of *statutory rape*). In most states, the legal age of consent is between ages sixteen and eighteen. A few states have attempted to include male victims of sexual assault in definitions of rape.

Acquaintance rape **is forcible sexual activity that meets the legal definition of rape and involves people who first meet in a social setting.** Acquaintance rape is sometimes referred to as "date rape," but acquaintance rape is a more accurate term because crime may occur anywhere: It does not have to be on a "date." Acquaintance or date rape excludes spousal (marital) rape and rape by a relative (incest). Acquaintance rape is often associated with alcohol or other drug consumption, especially among college students. Ironically, we probably know much less about the actual number of acquaintance rapes than we do about the number of stranger rapes because victims are more likely to report sexual attacks by strangers and less likely to report attacks perpetrated by individuals they know.

On college campuses, acquaintance rape sometimes takes the form of gang or party rape. Unlike individual acquaintance rape, party or gang rape is used as a reinforcing mechanism for membership in the group of men (Sanday, 2007). In fact, men who rape in groups might never commit individual rape. As they participate in party or gang rape, they experience a special bonding with each other and use rape to prove their sexual ability to other group members and thereby enhance their status among members.

Nature and extent of the problem Although reporting of rape has increased by about one-third over the past two decades, statistics on rape tend to be much lower than the actual rate of occurrence because about 60 percent of rapes and other sexual assaults are not reported to the police. Males account for about 10 percent of all rape and sexual assault victims, but they are the least likely to report such an assault (Rape, Abuse, and Incest National Network [RAINN], 2011). According to the U.S. Department of Justice, if a rape is reported, there is a 51 percent change of an arrest; if the arrest is made, there is an 80 percent change of prosecution; if there is a prosecution, there is a 58 percent change of conviction; and if there is a felony conviction, there is a 69 percent change the offender will spend time in jail. However, the reality is that most rapes are not reported, and fifteen of sixteen rapists will remain free (RAINN, 2011).

In 2009, the number of forcible rapes was estimated at 88,097. The rate of forcible rapes was estimated at 56.6 per 100,000 female inhabitants. Rapes by force made up 93 percent of all reported rape offenses in 2009, and attempts or assaults to commit rape accounted for 7 percent of reported rapes (FBI, 2010a). Like murder, rape follows certain patterns in terms of gender, age, race, and region of the country. Although there is no single profile of a rapist, most rapists tend to be under age twenty-five; their typical victims are also under twenty-five. Although females of all ages are raped, the rate of victimization drops off sharply after age thirty-four.

Offenders and victims are usually of the same race and class. Although numerically more white women are raped than African American women and more white men commit rape than African American men, the probabilities of being a rape victim or an offender are significantly higher for African Americans than for whites (FBI, 2010a). The rate of reported rape varies geographically; the states in the South accounted for 38.4 percent of the total in 2009, followed by states in the Midwest, the West, and the Northeast.

Read the Document

Fraternities and Collegiate Rape Culture: Why Are Some Fraternities More Dangerous Places for Women? on **mysoclab.com**

Social responses to rape As the discrepancies between official statistics and victimization studies indicate, societal attitudes toward rape primarily affect the victims of rape. Many rapes are never reported. The extremely traumatic nature of the crime prevents some victims from coming forward. They might believe that if they don't think about it or talk about it, the experience will "go away." Often, the fear generated by the attack is carried over into a fear that the attacker might try to get even or attack again if the crime is reported. This is a particularly significant issue for women who are still in proximity to their attacker. Suppose the attacker is in the same college class or works at the same place as the victim. How can the woman file a report without disrupting her whole life? Many women also fear how they will be treated by the police and, in the event of a criminal trial, by prosecutors and defense attorneys. Many victims also fear publicity for themselves and their families.

Gang Violence

One particular form of violence has been receiving renewed attention in the 2010s: Gang-related violence has federal authorities and law enforcement officials in some states worried about the 20,000 violent street gangs, motorcycle gangs, and prison gangs with nearly one million members who are criminally active in the United States today. Many gangs are sophisticated and well organized; all use violence to control neighborhoods and boost their illegal money-making activities, which include alien smuggling, armed robbery, assault, auto theft, drug and gun trafficking, extortion, fraud, identity theft, home invasions, and murder. Typically, gangs are composed primarily of young males of the same race or ethnicity. Some gangs are basically peer groups that hang out together, but others are well organized and violent. In recent years, gang activity and gang-related violence have increased significantly not only in large metropolitan areas but also in smaller cities and suburbs. U.S.-based gang members illegally cross the U.S.–Mexico border to smuggle illicit drugs and illegal aliens from Mexico to the United States, a situation that frequently results in violence (National Gang Intelligence Center, 2009). An example was the "Red Zone" investigation that focused on Nuestra Familia, a Mexican American prison-based gang that operates in detention facilities across the state of California, and Nortenos, another gang that acts as the Familia's street-level arm (McKinley, 2011). In operation Red Zone, large quantities of narcotics, firearms, and cash were seized in raids, and some gang members were charged with assault, mayhem, gun possession

Watch on **mysoclab.com**

Crips and Bloods: Clip 1 on **mysoclab.com**

and attempted murder (McKinley, 2011). This is only one of many examples of where law enforcement officials are finding that gangs, drugs, and violent crime all go hand-in-hand and that a holistic approach is necessary to reduce these kinds of crimes. Authorities believe that gangs are responsible for a significant portion of the violent crime committed in many urban communities, and that much of this crime is associated with drug trafficking activities. Violence often erupts in disputes over control of drug territory and enforcement of drug debts in urban areas and over expansion of drug distribution operations in suburban communities. The primary drugs distributed by gangs are marijuana, powder cocaine, crack cocaine, Ecstasy, methamphetamine, and heroin (National Gang Intelligence Center, 2009).

Intervention by law enforcement officials and the criminal justice system has had only limited success in dealing with the structural problems—lack of educational opportunities and jobs, inadequate housing, and racial and ethnic discrimination—that accompany much gang behavior. The monetary rewards for gang involvement often far outweigh what gang members could make in legitimate occupations and enterprises. If there is a solution at all, it appears that the most productive answer comes from former gang members and

This group portrait of the 18th Street gang in California shows members standing in front of a mural and flashing their gang's signs. What factors do you think are most important in determining whether or not a person will join a gang?

former felons who band together to help break the cycle of crime and hopelessness that they believe produces gang violence. For example, the Alliance of Concerned Men of Washington, DC, a collection of middle-aged former felons, substance abusers, and inmates, mediated a truce between two factions of a gang that had been terrorizing a southeast Washington neighborhood. Members of the alliance not only reduced gang violence in the city but also helped gang members find jobs, giving them hope that they would be able to reach their eighteenth birthdays.

Aggravated Assault and Robbery

Two other kinds of violent crime, aggravated assault and robbery are included in the FBI's Uniform Crime Reporting. *Aggravated assault* is the unlawful attack by one person upon another for the purpose of inflicting severe or aggravated bodily harm. Typically, this type of assault involves the display of—or the threat to use—a weapon or other means likely to produce death or great bodily harm. Of the approximately 807,000 aggravated assaults that occurred in 2009, offenders used hands, fists, and/or feet in 27 percent of the attacks; 21 percent used firearms; 19 percent used knives or cutting instruments; and the remaining 34 percent were committed with other weapons (*Note:* Percentages have been rounded and do not add up to 100 percent). Like other kinds of crime, the highest rate of aggravated assault (45 percent) was in the South, followed by the West (23 percent), the Midwest (19 percent), and the Northeast (14 percent). As shown on Map 9.1, the risk of being a crime victim varies by region of the country for both violent crime and property crime.

Arrests for aggravated assault in 2009 included 330,368 individuals, with 78 percent of the arrests being for male offenders (258,467) and 22 percent of the arrests being for female offenders (72,905). In regard to race-ethnicity, white Americans accounted for 64 percent of all arrests for aggravated assault as compared to 34 percent for African Americans, and others making up the remaining 2 percent (FBI, 2010a).

When aggravated assault and larceny-theft occur together, the offense is identified under the category of robbery (FBI, 2010a). *Robbery* is the taking or attempting to take anything of value from the care, custody, or control of a person or persons by force or threat of violence and/or by putting the victim in fear. In 2009, an estimated 408,217 robberies were committed, with an estimated $508 million in losses. The average dollar value of property stolen per reported robbery was

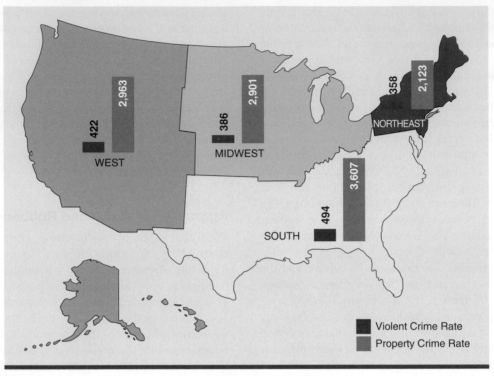

Map 9.1 Violent and property crime by region, 2009 (per 100,000 inhabitants).
Source: FBI, 2010.

$1,244, and the highest average dollar loss was for banks, which lost $4,029 per offense (FBI, 2010a). Arrests for robbery are higher for men than for women: In 2009, males accounted for 88 percent of all robbery arrest, as compared to 12 percent for females. Unlike some other statistics on race-ethnicity and crime we have examined, African Americans had a higher rate (56 percent) of all arrests for robbery, as compared with 43 percent of white Americans. As you will recall, African Americans make up about 12.6 percent of the U.S. population, so this arrest statistic is greatly out of proportion to the total number of black Americans residing in the United States in 2009.

Property Crime

Property crime **is the taking of money or property from another without force, the threat of force, or the destruction of property.** Larceny-theft, burglary, motor vehicle theft, and arson are examples of property crimes. The FBI defines *larceny-theft* as the unlawfully taking or attempting to take property (with the exception of motor vehicles) from another person. About 6.3 million larceny-thefts occurred nationwide in 2009, making up almost 68 percent of all property crimes committed in that year. Larceny-theft includes thefts of motor vehicle parts and accessories, shoplifting, purse-snatching, and pick-pocketing, among other offenses (see Figure 9.3). *Shoplifting* accounts for billions of dollars in losses to retail business each year. For some stores, the annual loss can be as high as 2 to 5 percent of the total value of inventory. Early criminologists found that shoplifters fell into three categories: the *snitch*—someone with no criminal record who systematically pilfers goods for personal use or to sell; the *booster* or *heel*—the professional criminal who steals goods to sell to fences or pawnshops; and the *kleptomaniac*—someone who steals for reasons other than monetary gain (e.g., for sexual arousal). Some contemporary shoplifters have become much more sophisticated and use the latest technology to avoid detection; others work in groups or rings to divert the attention of sales associates and security personnel from the shoplifters' actions.

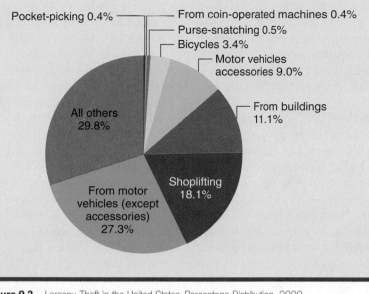

Figure 9.3   Larceny-Theft in the United States, Percentage Distribution, 2009

Note: Due to rounding, the percentages may not add to 100.

Source: FBI, 2010.

The average value of the property taken during larceny-thefts in 2009 was $864 per offense. Based on this average value, multiplied by the estimated number of larceny-thefts committed that year, the total loss to victims nationally in 2009 would be nearly $5.5 billion (FBI, 2010a). Larceny-theft arrests added up to 1,056,473 in 2009, and most offenders were white Americans (68 percent); however, African Americans were overrepresented in arrests (29 percent) when compared to the proportion of the total population that is African American. The arrest rates for females and males are closer on larceny-theft offenses than some other kinds of crime: Although males accounted for 56 percent of these offenses, females made up 44 percent of offenders who were arrested in 2009.

Burglary is the unlawful entry of a structure to commit a felony or theft. About 2 million burglaries were committed in 2009, accounting for 24 percent of the estimated number of property crimes in that year. Burglary is divided into three subcategories: forcible entry—61 percent of burglaries in 2009; unlawful entry (without force)—33 percent; and forcible entry attempts—6.5 percent. The average loss to victims is higher in burglaries than in the average larceny-theft. The average dollar loss per burglary offense in 2009 was $2,096, adding up to an estimated total of $4.6 billion

in lost property (FBI, 2010a). Based on arrest statistics, burglary is more a male crime than a female one: Men accounted for 85 percent of all burglary arrests while women accounted for only 15 percent in 2009. In regard to race-ethnicity, white Americans accounted for 67 percent of all arrests for burglary, while African Americans made up 32 percent of those arrested for this offense.

Motor vehicle theft is the theft or attempted theft of a motor vehicle. This crime includes a variety of motor vehicles, such as automobiles, SUVs, trucks, buses, motorcycles, all-terrain vehicles, and snowmobiles. However, this kind of theft does not include farm equipment, airplanes, motorboats, jet skis, and some other types of construction or recreational vehicles. Thefts of motor vehicles were estimated at 794,616 in 2009, which was a 17 percent decline over the previous year. The average dollar loss per stolen vehicle was $6,505, adding up to nearly $5.2 billion in motor vehicle thefts in 2009 (FBI, 2010a). In regard to arrests for motor vehicle theft, a total of 63,919 persons were arrested in 2009: 83 percent were male; 17 percent were female. White Americans accounted for 61 percent of all arrests, and African Americans accounted for 36 percent of arrests.

Statistics on auto theft are more accurate than those for many other crimes because insurance companies require claimants to report the theft to police.

Analysts have identified four basic motives for auto theft: (1) joyriding—the vehicle is stolen for the fun of riding around in it and perhaps showing off to friends; (2) transportation—the vehicle is stolen for personal use; (3) as an aid in the commission of another crime; and (4) profit—the vehicle is sold or taken to a "chop shop," where it is dismantled for parts, which are then sold separately.

The issue of income level and social class is particularly important when examining property crimes: Lower-income households experience higher rates of property crime than do higher-income households. The highest overall property crime rate is for households in the lowest-income category—less than $7,500 per year. This rate is about 1.6 times higher than the rate of property crime in households earning $75,000 or more per year. Similarly, households with six or more persons were about three times more likely to be victims of property crime than households make up of single persons (Truman and Rand, 2010).

The last type of nonviolent property crime that we will examine is *identity theft*—using another individual's personal information to commit fraud or theft. A lost or stolen wallet or purse can provide a potential offender with all the identification necessary—including bank and credit card information, driver's license, and Social Security number—to open up new charge accounts in the victim's name and run up large bills before the individual becomes aware of what has happened. Thieves can also obtain personal information by stealing mail, such as credit card and bank statements, or on the Internet by hacking into systems where they gain useful personal data. The Federal Trade Commission (2011) reported that identity theft was the number one consumer complaint for the eleventh year in a row in 2010. Identity theft is a serious and growing problem—both in the United States and around the world—because of vast amounts of personal information that is stored on computers, as well as the increasing sophistication of the criminals who obtain and misuse that information (see Box 9.1). Identity theft can be difficult on the victim. Sometimes, it takes several years for the victim to get his or her credit and finances back to normal.

Social Problems in Global Perspective

Box 9.1

Identity Theft: A Persistent Problem in the Global Village

Item: Journalist Nancy Trejos (2008) reports in the *Washington Post* that she has been the victim of identity theft: "It had been a pleasant Saturday afternoon until I got the dreadful cell phone call. The woman on the other end said she was from Bank of America. . . . 'Are you at a Pacers Running Store in Arlington trying to buy $812.18 worth of merchandise?' 'No,' I said. . . . Suddenly I was a personal-finance writer whose finances were a mess thanks to an identity thief."

Item: Online banking customers in South Africa were shocked when a perpetrator gained unauthorized access by means of spyware to the personal computer of an Absa [Bank] customer's banking particulars and used the identity of that customer to transfer money from the victim's account to his own account. . . . [The] Absa incident should [be] a wake-up call for all those who, in this electronic age, so carelessly assume that our identity is our own exclusive right and is immune from criminal abuse. (Watney, 2004:20)

As these news items suggest, identity theft is a concern not only in the United States (where about 10 million Americans are victimized annually) but in nations around the world (Javelin Strategy and Research, 2010). Newspapers and television reports inform us almost daily that hackers have stolen another million credit card numbers from an ill-protected database or that financial group insiders have hawked credit card and account information to outsiders who have committed a flurry of costly crimes. Instant computer communications and the Internet have made it easier for identity theft to occur on a large scale, and organized crime groups in eastern Europe, Nigeria, and Somalia are known to operate large identity theft divisions because the profits are so great and the risks are so low.

Businesses across the world lose $221 billion a year due to identity theft (spendonlife.com, 2011). Total annual reported fraud losses in the United States were $37 billion in 2010, down from $56 billion in 2009. However, individual victims lost more money on average than in the past: Out-of-pocket expenses went up to $631 from $387 (Javelin Strategy and Research, 2010). Compared with

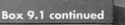

bank robberies and other kinds of garden-variety theft, the nature and extent of this problem is only now being fully understood. Hopefully, however, progress is being made in reducing this problem as we become more aware of its existence. Although efforts are just begin-ning, at least we are starting to look at this social problem from a global perspective rather than from the viewpoint that individuals who are not careful are the ones whose identities are stolen and that they have no one to blame but themselves.

Occupational (White-Collar) Crime

Occupational (white-collar) crime refers to illegal activities committed by people in the course of their employment or normal business activity. When soci-ologist Edwin H. Sutherland (1949) introduced the term *white-collar crime*, he was referring to acts such as employee theft, fraud (obtaining money or property under false pretenses), embezzlement (theft from an employer), and soliciting bribes or kickbacks. Today, the concept of white-collar crime may sound outdated because it referred to an era when men in well-paying careers wore white-collared shirts and neckties. However, in the twenty-first century, occupational or white-collar criminals wear all kinds of clothing and engage in a wide variety of illegal practices ranging from fraud and bribery to corruption, money laundering, and embezzlement. The behavior remains even if the terminology has shifted.

Although we hear more about property and violent crimes, occupational (white-collar) crimes are also an all-too-familiar occurrence in our nation. Bernard "Bernie" Madoff, shown here going to court, was convicted for his role in one of the largest financial frauds in U.S. history when he defrauded thousands of investors billions of dollars.

Some researchers have replaced the concept of white-collar crime with the term *occupational fraud—* the use of one's occupation for personal enrichment through the deliberate misuse or misappropriation of resources or assets that belong to the individual's employer. According to estimates by the Association of Certified Fraud Examiners (ACFE), the typical business worldwide loses 5 percent of its annual revenue to fraud. If we apply this percentage to the 2009 estimated Gross World Product of $58.07 trillion, we would find a total global fraud loss of more than $2.9 trillion. However, we should note that this is an estimate and is not based on specific data from all nations (Association of Certified Fraud Examiners [ACFE], 2010.) But, we do know that a median loss of $160,000 was caused by occupational fraud in 2010, and approximately 25 percent of all frauds committed in that year involved losses of $1 million or more. This cost is particularly high given the fact that small organizations are much more likely than larger corporations to be the victims of occupational fraud. Larger corporations typically have more antifraud con-trols in place as a deterrent to such activities. Banking/ financial services, manufacturing and government/pub-lic administration sectors are the most vulnerable to occupational crimes (ACFE, 2010).

ACFE (2010) has identified three major categories of occupational fraud: asset misappropriation, corrup-tion schemes, and financial statement fraud schemes. When the perpetration steals or misuses an organiza-tion's resources, the crime is referred to as *asset misap-propriation*. By contrast, *corruption schemes*—such as bribery, extortion, and conflict of interest—occur when employees use their influence in business transactions in a way that violates their duty to the employer for the purpose of obtaining benefits for themselves. *Finan-cial statement fraud* refers to schemes that involve the intentional misstatement or omission of relevant infor-mation in the organization's financial reports. Examples of financial statement fraud include recording revenues that have not been received, concealing liabilities or expenses that have been incurred, and artificially inflating reported assets (ACFE, 2010). In the United States, the first of these categories, asset misappropriation, accounts for nearly 90 percent of occupational frauds, followed by corruption (22 percent) and financial statement fraud (4 percent). These figures add up to more than 100 percent because some cases involve multiple schemes that fall into more than one category (ACFE, 2010).

Corporate Crime

Unlike occupational crimes that typically benefit *employees* at the expense of their employing organization, corporate crimes primarily benefit *corporations* and harm the *national and international financial community*. **Corporate crime refers to illegal acts committed by corporate employees on behalf of the corporation and with its support.** Examples include antitrust violations (seeking an illegal advantage over competitors); deceptive advertising; infringements on patents, copyrights, and trademarks; unlawful labor practices involving the exploitation or surveillance of employees; price fixing; and financial fraud, including securities fraud, tax evasion, and insider trading. These crimes arise from deliberate decisions by corporate personnel to profit at the expense of competitors, consumers, employees, and the general public.

Corporate crime involves a variety of activities, including corporate fraud, securities and commodities fraud, health care fraud, mortgage fraud, insurance fraud, mass marketing fraud, and money laundering. The majority of corporate fraud cases involve accounting schemes designed to deceive investors, auditors, and analysts about the true financial condition of a corporation. These activities are often done to keep investors in the dark about the true nature of the organization's financial affairs. Examples include the recent actions of some subprime lending institutions, hedge funds, and financial institutions that have contributed to trillions of dollars in losses and brought about immeasurable damage to the U.S. economy.

Securities and commodities fraud refers to activities such as Ponzi schemes and securities market manipulation by way of cyber intrusion. In one of the most highly publicized and costly ($64 billion) Ponzi schemes in recent decades, Bernard Madoff, a securities broker dealer and founder of an investment service,

provided his clients with monthly investment statements and trade confirmations for transactions that never actually occurred. Madoff got away with this scheme by using new client funds to pay profits and redemptions to existing clients. The victims of this kind of fraud are individual investors, financial institutions, public and private companies, government entities, and retirement funds.

Health care fraud occurs when health care programs, including private insurance plans and government-funded plans such as Medicare and Medicaid, are billed for excessive amounts, or when they are charged for health services that were not provided or for medically unnecessary services. An example is a corporation that bills Medicare for health services to residents of assisted living facilities when no such services were provided or even requested. In addition to the loss of billions of dollars annually from this type of crime, another major issue is the possibility that patient harm can come from these schemes (FBI, 2009).

Mortgage fraud involves misstatement, misrepresentation, or omission of relevant information regarding a property or potential borrower which is relied on by an underwriter or lender to fund, purchase, or insure a loan (FBI, 2009). Examples include inflated appraisals of how much a property is worth, using fictitious or stolen identities to secure mortgage loans, and providing false information on a loan application. A recent example is people who applied for a tax credit of up to $8,000 for qualified first-time homebuyers under the American Recovery and Reinvestment Act of 2009 but, since they were not actually first-time homebuyers, these individuals used the personal information of relatives or other individuals on their applications to qualify for the credit.

Insurance fraud involves misuse of some of the nearly $1 trillion in premiums that are collected each year by the insurance industry. Examples include staged auto accidents; property insurance fraud; insurance agents and brokers who divert policyholder premiums for their own benefit; insurance companies that use customers' premiums to pay corporate expenses; and disaster fraud—when organizations or individuals solicit contributions for disaster victims but keep the proceeds for their own use, or when people make false or exaggerated claims about the monetary damages they incurred as a result of the disaster.

Mass marketing fraud occurs through telemarketing, mass mailings and the Internet and involves such activities as the "Nigerian letter fraud" in which potential victims are informed that they have inherited or otherwise been given large sums of money that are being held for them in foreign accounts. To gain access to the promised money, persons must pay fees to receive their winnings. Obviously, the funds are never released regardless of the number of steps that victims go through and how much money they are willing to send in hopes of coming into a financial windfall. Numerous other lottery and sweepstakes schemes also come under this kind of fraud. These cases often involve elderly victims and people who have limited financial means or knowledge of how schemes such as this work.

Money laundering is the process by which criminals conceal or disguise the proceeds of their crimes or convert those proceeds into goods and services. In this way, criminals are able to take illegal money and infuse their illegal money into the stream of commerce and thus corrupt financial institutions and the money supply. Cases involving money laundering often include drug cartels and other organized crime groups. An example is the crime organization La Cosa Nostra that ran a multimillion-dollar Internet gambling operation out of Costa Rica and used this for money laundering as well as profit-making.

How much does corporate crime cost? Corporate crime has both direct and indirect economic effects. Direct economic losses from corporate crime are immense in comparison to the money lost in ordinary, street-level property crime. According to the FBI (2009), for corporate crime cases that have been successfully pursued (and this leaves out many that are either undetected or unsolved), in 2009 alone, corporate fraud netted $6.1 billion in restitution orders and $5.4 billion in recoveries; securities and commodities fraud netted $8.1 billion in restitution orders and $63.4 million in recoveries; health care fraud netted $1.6 billion in restitution orders and $853 million in recoveries; mortgage fraud netted $2.5 billion in restitution orders, and $7.5 million in recoveries; insurance fraud netted $22.9 million in restitution orders and $31.4 million in recoveries; and money laundering netted $81.9 million in restitution orders and $643,000 in recoveries. If you total all of the money recovered by the Justice Department for these corporate crimes and add to that the amount of the restitution orders—an order granting victims a money judgment against the defendant for the victim's losses—it is obvious how large the actual financial losses for corporate crime would be if we knew of, and pursued, all such offenses that are committed annually.

In addition to direct costs, the indirect costs of corporate crime include higher taxes for law-abiding individuals and legitimate businesses, increased cost for goods and services, higher insurance rates, massive losses by investors, and an overall loss of faith by the public in the economy. Loss of retirement benefits is also a key concern as a result of corporate crimes that contributed to the economic crisis associated with the Great Recession. This national and international economic meltdown was partly brought about by corporate officials who vastly increased their personal wealth without regard for the effect that their criminal actions had on employees, stockholders, and everyday citizens. Finally, although personal injury and loss of life are usually associated with homicides and conventional street crimes, deaths resulting from corporate crimes such as deliberately polluting the air and water, manufacturing defective products, or selling unsafe foods and drugs far exceed the number of homicides each year.

Organized Crime

Organized crime **is a business operation that supplies illegal goods and services for profit.** These illegal enterprises include drug trafficking, prostitution, gambling, loan-sharking, money laundering, and large-scale theft such as truck hijackings. In the past, most people thought of organized crime in the United States as being the Italian or Sicilian Mafioso as shown on television and in popular movies. However, this is no longer an accurate picture: According to the FBI (2011a), organized crime today includes people from around the world, including Russian mobsters, groups from African countries such as Nigeria that engage in drug trafficking and financial scams, members of the Chinese tongs, Japanese Boryokudan, and other Asian crime rings, and enterprises that are based on eastern European countries such as Hungary and Romania.

No single entity controls the entire range of corrupt and illegal enterprises in the United States. Instead, there are many groups—syndicated crime networks—that can thrive because there is great demand for illegal goods and services. For example, in the past two decades, the FBI has begun active prosecution of sports bribery to help colleges and professional sporting associations ensure the integrity of their sporting events. Organized crime groups have attempted to corrupt collegiate and professional athletes in regard to gambling, bribery, and drugs. In the past, La Cosa Nostra members have bribed college basketball players to "throw" games by shaving points so that mob figures will have large winnings from gambling on the games.

Sometimes organized crime syndicates form alliances with supposedly legitimate businesspeople, law enforcement officials, and politicians. Some law enforcement and government officials are corrupted through bribery, campaign contributions, and favors that are intended to buy them off. Known linkages between legitimate businesses and organized crime exist in banking, hotels and motels, real estate, garbage collection, vending machines, construction, delivery and long-distance hauling, garment manufacture, insurance, stocks and bonds, vacation resorts, and funeral parlors.

Syndicated crime networks operate at all levels of society and around the world. The FBI (2011a) estimates that global organized crime reaps illegal profits of around $1 trillion per year; however, it is impossible to know the actual amount of money made from organized criminal activity because of the depth and diversity of the activities included under organized crime. In an effort to combat organized crime, the FBI Organized Crime Section is divided into three units: La Cosa Nostra, Italian organized crime and racketeering; Eurasian–Middle Eastern organized crime; and Asian and African criminal enterprises. We periodically see newspaper headlines or news items on the Internet such as "La Cosa Nostra Bosses, Members Charged in Rico Case" (Kouri, 2011) or "Nearly 125 Arrested in Sweeping Mob Roundup" (Rashbaum, 2011) after officials have arrested mob bosses and members of organized crime families for racketeering, extortion, loan-sharking, money laundering, illegal gambling, witness tampering, and the like. In recent years, these arrests have contributed to a widely held public perception that organized crime is being wiped out in the United States; however, officials with the U.S. Department of Justice argue that these arrests and indictments represent only the tip of the iceberg regarding organized criminal activity in the United States and worldwide.

Juvenile Delinquency

Juvenile delinquency **involves a violation of law or the commission of a status offense by a young person under a specific age.** Persons under age eighteen are referred to as "juveniles" by the U.S. Department of Justice and other government officials. Many behaviors that are identified as juvenile delinquency are not criminal acts per se but *status offenses*—acts that are illegal because of the age of the offender—such as cutting school, buying and consuming alcoholic beverages, or running away from home. For this reason, when we look at FBI arrest statistics, we see that virtu-

ally all arrests for curfew violations and runaways are young people under age eighteen. In most states, the age range for juvenile delinquency is from seven to seventeen. Juveniles accused of status crimes go before a juvenile judge who determines a plan to improve their behavior, and this official may also impose some kind of punishment (such as paying a fine) or rehabilitation (such as performing community service). By contrast, older offenders are considered adults and are tried in a criminal court.

How prevalent is juvenile crime? This is a difficult question to answer because, once again, we must rely on arrest statistics. Moreover, victimization data are not particularly useful in determining the extent of juvenile crime because victims must *estimate* the age of perpetrators, with the exception of cases where the alleged perpetrator is personally known by the victim. In 2009, law enforcement agencies made an estimated 1.5 million arrests of persons younger than age eighteen. Juvenile arrests have continued to decrease over the past decade despite fears in the first decade of the 2000s that another juvenile crime wave was approaching. According to the latest available arrest records, individuals under age eighteen account for about 14 percent of all arrests in the United States. About 15 percent of all arrests for violent crime and 24 percent of all arrests for property crime were young people under the age of eighteen in 2009 (FBI, 2010a). The highest arrests rates for people under age eighteen are for such offenses as arson (44 percent), vandalism (34 percent), and burglary, robbery, and motor vehicle theft (25 percent each). In other words, juveniles were involved in about one in ten arrests for murder and about one in four arrests for robbery, burglary, larceny-theft, and motor vehicle theft. Females account for about 30 percent of juvenile arrests, and the arrests for young females decreased less than male arrests in most crime categories. Looking at the issue or race-ethnicity, although African American young people accounted for about 16 percent of the U.S. youth population between the ages of ten and seventeen in 2009, they accounted for about 52 percent of all juvenile arrests for violent crime and 33 percent of all juvenile property crime arrests (FBI, 2010a). The African American proportion of juvenile arrests was highest for robbery (67 percent), murder (58 percent), motor vehicle theft (45 percent), and aggravated assault (42 percent). Note that these arrest figures do not necessarily reflect the true nature and extent of juvenile crime among young people.

Juveniles who are apprehended are processed by the juvenile justice system, which is based on the assumption that young people can do better if they are placed in the right setting and receive guidance. Thus unlike adult offenders, whose cases are heard in criminal courts, most cases involving juveniles are heard in juvenile courts or by specially designated juvenile judges. In the juvenile justice system, proceedings are similar to those in adult courts; however, the juvenile system supposedly recognizes that children and young people may not always understand the consequences of their actions or comprehend that these actions are wrong, particularly if they have been influenced by other people. The term *diminished moral culpability* is sometimes used to refer to a juvenile who is still maturing as an individual and might benefit from rehabilitation, rather than punishment, as a response to the offense with which the young person has been charged. Juvenile courts have three major hearings: detention—to determine if the juvenile should be detained; adjudication—to determine whether the juvenile is guilty of the crime; dispositional—to determine what sentence the juvenile will be given by the judge (there are no juries in juvenile court). Possible sentences in juvenile court include detention, probation/supervision, community service, counseling and fines/restitution. Factors that often contribute to how the juvenile's case will be disposed of include the following: the severity of the offense; the juvenile's age, past record, and attitude; and whether the parents are involved in the young person's life and able to control his or her behavior.

BIOLOGICAL AND PSYCHOLOGICAL EXPLANATIONS OF CRIME

As with other social problems, crime and delinquency have been explained in biological, psychological, and sociological terms. Most biological and psychological explanations assume that criminal behavior is an inherent or acquired individual trait with genetic, biological, or psychological roots. Sociological perspectives, in contrast, focus on external factors.

Biological Explanations

One of the earliest biological explanations of criminality came from the *positivist school*, which created physical typologies that were used to classify and study criminals. The biological approach of Cesare Lombroso, a nineteenth-century Italian physicist, is probably the best known. Lombroso suggested that some people were born criminals or *atavists*—biological throwbacks to an earlier stage of evolution—and could be recognized by their low foreheads and smaller than normal human cranial capacities. A later theory, also based on physical traits, that received some attention for a time was proposed by physician William Sheldon (1949). According to Sheldon's *somatotype theory, mesomorphs*—people who are muscular, gregarious, aggressive, and assertive—are more prone to delinquency and criminal behavior than are *endomorphs*—people who are fat, soft, round, and extroverted—or *ectomorphs*—people who are thin, wiry, sensitive, and introverted.

Contemporary biological approaches based on genetics have attempted to link higher rates of aggression in men to levels of testosterone or chromosomal abnormality (an extra Y chromosome). But this research has produced no consistent findings, and social scientists argue that the differences in aggression could be due to gender-role socialization of men and women rather than to biological factors (Katz and Chambliss, 1995).

Other contemporary biological approaches suggest that violence is a natural and inevitable part of human behavior that can be controlled only by social organization. Some scientists, however, say that violence is neither natural nor inevitable but is the result of traumatic brain injury or some combination of brain injury and other factors. Although most people with brain injuries are not violent, injuries to certain parts of the brain or injuries in combination with an abusive childhood or psychotic symptoms (e.g., paranoia) can affect an individual's ability to conform to societal norms.

The cortex of the brain—particularly the frontal lobes—is most closely associated with violent behavior. It is the cortex that modifies impulses, allowing us to use good judgment, make decisions, and organize behavior; it also facilitates learning and adherence to rules of conduct. Using various neurological and psychiatric examinations, medical experts try to determine whether violent offenders have frontal-lobe impairment, were abused as children, or have any psychological disorders. These factors, especially in combination, make people prone to violent behavior because they have fewer inhibitions.

Since the Human Genome Project produced new information about the genetic makeup of the human species, more researchers have become interested in explaining criminal behavior from a genetic perspective. No one is arguing that there is a "crime gene" as such. Instead, the specific focus of most research has been on how genes might heighten the risk of a person committing a crime and whether such a trait can be inherited (Cohen, 2011). According to some researchers, as many as 100 studies have demonstrated that genes do play a role in crimes. However, most of these studies have emphasized that genes are ruled by the environment, which can either strengthen or weaken violent impulses. In other words, some persons with the same genetic tendency for aggression will never harm another individual, while others who do not have the same genetic tendency may become violent criminals. Various studies about the relationship between genetic makeup and crime have looked at characteristics such as self-control, callousness, and lack of empathy. Sociologists, criminologists, and scientists involved in genetic research do not agree on the biology–crime link, but most do acknowledge that further study of both genes and social context—such as living in a disadvantaged neighborhood or having delinquent friends—are important in gaining a better understanding of the causes and consequences of criminal behavior (Cohen, 2011).

Psychological Explanations

Like biological explanations of delinquency and crime, psychological explanations focus on individual characteristics. Some researchers have used personality inventories in hopes of identifying abnormal personality traits in individuals who have committed crimes or engaged in delinquent behavior. Other researchers have investigated the effects of social learning and positive reinforcement (e.g., rewards such as money or special attention) and negative reinforcement (e.g., the withdrawal of reward or lack of attention) on delinquent and criminal behavior.

The most enduring psychological explanations of delinquency and crime seem to be the ones that bridge the biological explanations by linking intelligence and crime. Since the introduction of IQ (intelligence quotient) tests in the early 1900s, some analysts have suggested that people with lower intelligence scores are more likely to commit crimes than are people with higher intelligence scores. However, both the validity of IQ tests and the assertion that low intelligence causes delinquency or crime have come under great scrutiny and much criticism (see Hirschi and Hindelang, 1977).

Of course, some social analysts do acknowledge the possibility of a relationship between low intelligence and delinquency or crime. These analysts note that low intelligence might indirectly promote delinquency because it affects school performance. Similarly, less intelligent offenders might commit more obvious crimes and be more likely to be apprehended by law enforcement officials (Vito and Holmes, 1994).

One psychological explanation of violent crime focuses on *aggression*—behavior that is intended to hurt someone, either physically or verbally—that results from frustration (Weiten and Lloyd, 1994). According to the *frustration-aggression hypothesis*, people who are frustrated in their efforts to achieve a highly desired goal become aggressive toward others (Dollard et al., 1939). The object of the aggression becomes a *scapegoat*, a substitute for the actual source of frustration who can be blamed, especially if that person or group is incapable of resisting the hostility or aggression.

Explaining violence in biological and/or psychological terms suggests responses that are based on some type of psychiatric or other medical intervention. After all, if violent behavior is associated with specific neurological problems, it can be diagnosed like any other neurological illness and treated with drugs, including, possibly, anticonvulsants, antidepressants, and antihypertensive medications that act on the cortex to moderate violent behavior.

SOCIOLOGICAL EXPLANATIONS OF CRIME

Unlike biological and psychological explanations that focus on individual behavior, sociological explanations focus on those aspects of society that might contribute to delinquent or criminal behavior.

The Functionalist Perspective

Although there are numerous functionalist perspectives on crime and delinquency, we will focus on two perspectives: strain theory and control theory as illustrated in social bond theory.

Functionalist explanations for why people commit crimes can be traced to Emile Durkheim, who believed that the macrolevel structure of a society produces social pressures that result in high rates of deviance and crime. Durkheim introduced the concept of *anomie* to describe a social condition that engenders feelings of futility in people because of weak, absent, or conflicting social norms. According to Durkheim (1964/1895), deviance and crime are most likely to occur when anomie is present in a society. On the basis of Durkheim's theory, sociologist Robert Merton (1938, 1968) developed strain theory to explain why some people conform to group norms while others do not. **Strain theory is the proposition that people feel strain when they are exposed to cultural goals that they cannot reach because they do not have access to a culturally approved means of achieving those goals.** When some people are denied legitimate access to cultural goals such as success, money, or other material possessions, they seek to acquire these things through deviant—and sometimes criminal—means.

Merton identified five ways in which people respond to cultural goals: conformity, innovation, ritualism, retreatism, and rebellion (see Table 9.2). *Conformity* occurs when people accept the culturally approved goals and pursue them through the approved means. People who choose conformity work hard and save their money to achieve success. Someone who is blocked from achieving a high level of education or a lucrative career typically conforms by taking a lower-paying job and attending school part time, joining the military, or trying alternative (but legal) avenues, such as playing the lottery. People who choose *innovation* accept society's goals but use illegitimate means to achieve them. Innovations for acquiring material possessions include shoplifting,

theft, burglary, cheating on income taxes, embezzling money, and other kinds of occupational crime. *Ritualism* occurs when people give up on societal goals but still adhere to socially approved means for achieving them. People who cannot obtain expensive material possessions or wealth seek to maintain the respect of others by being "hard workers" or "good citizens" to an extreme degree. *Retreatism* occurs when people abandon both the approved goals and the approved means of achieving them. Retreatists include hard-core drug addicts and some middle- or upper-income people who reject conventional trappings of success and the means to acquire them, choosing to "drop out" instead. *Rebellion* occurs when people reject both the approved goals and the approved means for achieving them and advocate an alternative set of goals and means. Rebels might use violence (such as vandalism or rioting) or nonviolent tactics (such as civil disobedience) to change society and its cultural beliefs, or they might withdraw from mainstream society, like the Amish, to live their own style of life.

Another functionalist perspective—control theory—seeks to answer the question "Why do people *not* engage in deviant behavior?" According to control theory, people are constantly pulled and pushed toward deviant behavior. Environmental factors (pulls)—such as adverse living conditions, poverty, and lack of educational opportunity—draw people toward

TABLE 9.2 Merton's Strain Theory

Mode of Adaptation	Method of Adaptation	Agrees with Cultural Goal	Follows Institutional Means
Conformity	Accepts culturally approved goals; pursues them through culturally approved means	Yes	Yes
Innovation	Accepts culturally approved goals; adopts disapproved means of achieving them	Yes	No
Ritualism	Abandons society's goals but continues to conform to approved means	No	Yes
Retreatism	Abandons both approved goals and the approved means to achieve them	No	No
Rebellion	Challenges both the approved goals and the approved means to achieve them	No—seeks to replace	No—seeks to replace

Source: Adapted from Merton (1968).

criminal behavior while at the same time internal pressures (pushes)—such as feelings of hostility or aggressiveness—make people not want to act according to dominant values and norms (Reckless, 1967). If this is true, why doesn't everyone who is poor or has a limited education commit crimes? According to control theorists, people who do not turn to crime or delinquent behavior have *outer containments*—supportive family and friends, reasonable social expectations, and supervision by others—or *inner containments*—self-control, a sense of responsibility, and resistance to diversions.

The best-known control theory is **social bond theory—the proposition that criminal behavior is most likely to occur when a person's ties to society are weakened or broken.** According to Travis Hirschi (1969), who proposed this theory, social bonding consists of (1) *attachment* to other people, (2) *commitment* to conformity, (3) *involvement* in conventional activities, and (4) *belief* in the legitimacy of conventional values and norms. When a person's social bonds are weak and when peers promote antisocial values and violent behavior, the probability of delinquency and crime increases (Massey and Krohn, 1986).

When analyzing violent crime, some functionalists believe that a sense of anomie is the root cause. Others believe that violence increases when social institutions such as the family, schools, and religious organizations weaken and the primary mechanisms of social control in people's everyday lives become external—law enforcement and the criminal justice system.

The *subculture of violence hypothesis* notes that violence is part of the normative expectations governing everyday behavior among young males in the lower classes (Wolfgang and Ferracuti, 1967). These violent subcultures are most likely to develop when young people, particularly males, have few legitimate opportunities available in their segment of society and when subcultural values accept and encourage violent behavior.

According to the *lifestyle-routine activity approach*, the patterns and timing of people's daily movements and activities as they go about obtaining the necessities of life—such as food, shelter, companionship, and entertainment—are the keys to understanding violent personal crimes and other types of crime in our society (Cohen and Felson, 1979). In other words, changes in social institutions, such as more families in which both parents (or the sole parent) work outside the home or shopping hours being extended into the night, put some people at greater risk of being victims of violent crime than others (Parker, 1995).

Functionalist explanations contribute to our understanding of crime by emphasizing that individuals who engage in such behavior are not biologically or psychologically impaired but are responding to social and economic conditions in society. However, functionalists are not without their critics. Strain theory might point out that people from low-income and poverty-level backgrounds are prevented from achieving success goals through legitimate channels, but it is still criticized for focusing almost exclusively on crimes committed by the lower classes and ignoring crimes committed by people in the middle and upper classes. Critics of social bond theory say that it is limited in its ability to explain more serious forms of delinquency and crime (Krohn, 2000).

The Conflict Perspective

Conflict theorists explain criminal behavior in terms of power differentials and/or economic inequality in society. One approach focuses on how authority and power relationships can contribute to some people—but not others—becoming criminals. According to Austin Turk (1966, 1971), crime is not a *behavior* but a *status* that is acquired when people with the authority to create and enforce legal rules apply those rules to others.

A second conflict approach focuses on the relationship between economic inequality and crime. Having roots in the work of Karl Marx, the *radical-critical conflict approach* argues that social institutions (such as law, politics, and education) create a superstructure that legitimizes the class structure and maintains capitalists' superior position. In fact, say these theorists, the crimes people commit are based on their class position. Thus, crimes committed by low-income people typically involve taking things by force or physical stealth, whereas white-collar crime usually involves nonphysical means such as paper transactions or computer fraud. Some critical theorists believe that affluent people commit crimes because they are greedy and continually want more than they have, whereas poor people commit street crimes such as robbery and theft to survive (Bonger, 1969/1916). Finally, some conflict explanations are based on feminist scholarship and focus on why women commit crimes or engage in delinquent behavior. Scholars who use a *liberal feminist* framework believe that women's delinquency or crime is a rational response to gender discrimination in society. They attribute crimes such as prostitution and shoplifting to women's lack of educational and job opportunities and stereotypical expectations about roles women should have in society (Daly and Chesney-Lind, 1988). Scholars who espouse radical feminism believe that patriarchy contributes to crimes such as prostitution, because, according to society's sexual double standard, it is acceptable for a man to pay for sex but unacceptable for a woman to accept money for such services. A third school of feminist thought, *socialist feminism*, believes that women are exploited by capitalism and patriarchy. Because most females have relatively low-wage jobs and few economic resources, crimes such as prostitution and shoplifting become a means of earning money and acquiring consumer products. Feminist scholars of color, however, point out that none of the feminist theories include race-ethnicity in their analyses. As a result, some recent studies have focused on the relationship between crime and the simultaneous effects of race, class, and gender (Arnold, 1990).

In sum, the conflict approach is useful for pointing out how inequalities of power, class, race, and gender can contribute to criminal or delinquent behavior. Nevertheless, critics say that conflict theorists have not shown that powerful political and economic elites manipulate law making and enforcement for their own benefit. Rather, say these critics, people of all classes share a consensus that acts such as murder, rape, and armed robbery are bad (Klockars, 1979).

The Symbolic Interactionist Perspective

Symbolic interactionists emphasize that criminal behavior is learned through everyday interaction with others. We will examine two major symbolic interactionist theories: differential association theory and labeling theory. ***Differential association theory* states that individuals have a greater tendency to deviate from societal norms when they frequently associate with people who tend toward deviance rather than conformity.** According to sociologist Edwin Sutherland (1939), who formulated this theory, people learn not only the techniques of deviant behavior from people with whom they associate but also the motives, drives, rationalizations, and attitudes. Former gang member Nathan McCall (1994:93–94) describes such a learning process in his own life:

> Sometimes I picked up hustling ideas at the 7 Eleven, which was like a criminal union hall: Crapshooters, shoplifters, stickup men, burglars,

everybody stopped off at the store from time to time. While hanging there one day, I ran into Holt. . . . He had a pocketful of cash, even though he had quit school and was unemployed. I asked him, "Yo, man, what you been into?" "Me and my partner kick in cribs and make a killin.' You oughta come go with us sometimes. . . . " I hooked school one day, went with them, and pulled my first B&E [breaking and entering]. . . . After I learned the ropes, Shell Shock [another gang member] and I branched out, doing B&Es on our own. We learned to get in and out of houses in no time flat.

As McCall's description indicates, criminal activity often occurs within the context of frequent, intense, and long-lasting interactions with people who violate the law. When more factors favor violating the law than not, the person is likely to become a criminal. Although differential association theory contributes to our knowledge of how deviant behavior reflects the individual's learned techniques, values, attitudes, motives, and rationalizations, critics note that many individuals who are regularly exposed to people who break the law still conform most of the time. Many critics think that the theory does not adequately take into account possible connections between social inequality and criminal behavior.

Labeling theory, which was mentioned briefly in Chapter 1, takes quite a different approach from differential association theory. According to **labeling theory, delinquents and criminals are people who have been successfully labeled as such by others.** No behavior is inherently delinquent or criminal; it is defined as such by a social audience (Erikson, 1962). According to sociologist Howard Becker (1963), labeling is often done by *moral entrepreneurs*—people who use their own views of right and wrong to establish rules and label others "deviant." Furthermore, the process of labeling is directly related to the power and status of the people who do the labeling and those who are being labeled. In support of this theory, one study of juvenile offenders has found that youths from lower-income families were more likely to be arrested and indicted than were middle-class juveniles who did the same things (Sampson, 1986). Sociologists have also noted that the criminal justice system generally considers such factors as the offender's family life, educational achievement (or lack thereof), and social class in determining how to deal with juvenile offenders. According to one study, the individuals who are most likely to be apprehended, labeled delinquent, and prosecuted are people of color

Many children around the world (including this young boy in Leicestershire, England) love to play with toy guns. How might functionalists, conflict theorists, and symbolic interactionists explain this social phenomenon?

who are young, male, unemployed, and undereducated and who live in urban high-crime areas.

Sociologist Edwin Lemert (1951) expanded labeling theory by distinguishing between primary and secondary deviance. **Primary deviance is the initial act of rule breaking** in which the individual does not internalize the delinquent or criminal self-concept. **Secondary deviance occurs when a person who has been labeled a deviant accepts that new identity and continues the deviant behavior.** The concept of secondary deviance is important to labeling theory because it suggests that when people accept a negative label or stigma that has been applied to them, the label can actually contribute to the behavior it was meant to control. In other words, secondary deviance occurs if a person is labeled a juvenile delinquent, accepts that label, and then continues to engage in delinquent behavior. Labeling theory is useful for making us aware of how social control and personal identity are intertwined. Critics, however, do not think that labeling theory explains what causes the original acts that constitute primary deviance, nor do they think that it adequately explains why some people accept deviant labels and others do not (Cavender, 1995).

Using functionalist, conflict, or symbolic interactionist perspectives, it is increasingly difficult to determine what types of criminal behavior may be learned through ideas that are set forth in video games, television programs, and movies. Scholars have begun to systematically study the popularity of video games, for example, that provide opportunities for seemingly law-abiding individuals to live vicariously by committing a series of crimes, including rape and murder within the context of the video game.

THE CRIMINAL JUSTICE SYSTEM

The term *criminal justice system* is misleading because it implies that law enforcement agencies and courts constitute one large, integrated system when actually they are a collection of somewhat interrelated, semiautonomous bureaucracies. The **criminal justice system is the network of organizations—including the police, courts, jails, and prisons—involved in law enforcement and the administration of justice.** Let's look at how these various entities are intertwined in dealing with crime in the United States.

The Police

Police are the most visible link in the criminal justice system because they determine how to apply the law to control crime and maintain order. Nearly 13,000 local or municipal police departments operate in the United States. Four factors seem to influence the occurrence of an arrest: (1) the nature of the alleged offense or problem; (2) the quality of available evidence; (3) the age, race, and sex of the alleged offender; and (4) the level of deference shown to police officers. Given these factors, law enforcement officials have fairly wide *discretion*—use of personal judgment regarding whether and how to proceed in a given situation—in deciding who will be stopped and searched and which homes and businesses will be entered and for what purposes. Because they must often make these decisions in a dangerous environment, sociologist Jerome Skolnick (1975) argues, police officers develop a sense of suspicion, social isolation, and solidarity. A New York City police officer describes this feeling:

> Guys… will eat you alive, even with the uniform on. They can sense fear, smell it like a dog smells it. Some of the mopes will come right out and tell you you're nothing, and you don't want that, oh no. If you're going to do this job, wear this uniform, you definitely don't want that. If it gets around that you're soft, that without your nightstick and gun you can't fight, that's bad. If you allow someone to smoke a joint in front of you or curse you out, word will spread throughout the neighborhood

like a disease. You're a beat cop, out here every day, alone, so you set standards right away. (Norman, 1993:64)

Most officers feel that they must demand respect on the streets, but they also know that they must answer to their superiors, who expect them to handle situations "by the book."

The problem of discretion is most acute in the decision to use deadly force. Generally, deadly force is allowed only when a suspect is engaged in a felony, is fleeing the scene of a felony, or is resisting arrest and has endangered someone's life. But police officers' lives are often on the line in confrontations with suspects, as it is a well-known fact that more than 1,600 law enforcement officers have died in the line of duty over the past ten years, with 116 killed in 2009 alone.

Historically, criminal justice personnel at all levels have been white and male. However, the composition in local police department is slowly changing. One in four officers was a racial or ethnic minority in 2007, as compared to one in six in 1987 (U.S. Bureau of Justice Statistics, 2010a). In regard to sex, one in eight local police officers was a woman in 2007, as compared to one in thirteen officers in 1987. In the past, women largely have been excluded from law enforcement work because of a stereotypical belief that they were not strong enough to do work. Today, women account for slightly more than 12 percent of all police officers (U.S. Bureau of Justice Statistics, 2010a).

How can police departments become more effective in reducing crime as a social problem? According to some analysts, police departments with entrenched problems must first reform their own agencies and win the respect of the communities they serve. One way to do this is to be sure that police departments reflect the racial and ethnic composition of the communities they serve. It is difficult for an all-white police force to build trust in a primarily African American neighborhood. Greater representation of women in police departments might reduce complaints that domestic violence, child abuse, and other family-related problems are sometimes minimized or ignored by police officers.

Some police departments have begun community policing as a way of reducing crime. Community policing involves integrating officers into the communities they serve—getting them out of their patrol cars and into a proactive role, recognizing problems, and working with neighborhood citizens to find solutions. In cities where community policing has been implemented, crime rates appear to have dropped; however, it should be noted that there has also been a general trend toward fewer crimes, especially violent crimes, in some cities where community policing is not employed.

The Courts

Criminal courts are responsible for determining the guilt or innocence of people who have been accused of committing a crime. In theory, justice is determined in an adversarial process: A prosecutor (an attorney who represents the state) argues that the accused is guilty, and a defense attorney argues that the accused is innocent. In reality, judges have a great deal of discretion. Working with prosecutors, they decide who will be

"My client pleads great wealth."

released, who will be held for further hearings, and—in many instances—what sentences will be imposed on people who are convicted.

Because courts have the capacity to try only a small fraction of criminal cases, prosecuting attorneys also have considerable discretion in deciding when to prosecute and when to negotiate a plea bargain with a defense attorney. About 90 percent of criminal cases are never tried in court; they are resolved by **plea bargaining—a process whereby the prosecution negotiates a reduced sentence in exchange for a guilty plea.** In other words, defendants (especially those who are poor and cannot afford to pay an attorney) plead guilty to a lesser crime in return for not being tried for the more serious crime for which they were arrested. As cases are sifted and sorted through the legal machinery, steady attrition occurs. At each stage, various officials determine what alternatives will be available for the cases that remain in the system. In the 1970s and 1980s, many jurisdictions established mandatory minimum sentencing guidelines, and offenders typically spent a longer time in prison. Some analyst believe that mandatory sentencing guidelines have removed some aspects of sentencing power from judges and juries and transferred it to prosecutors, who determine what charges will be brought against the defendant. Unless the defendant is found not guilty, the judge must sentence him or her according to the statutory prescription for the offense regardless of any facts that might have led a different prosecutor to charge differently or of any mitigating circumstances in the case.

Punishment and the Prisons

Punishment is any action designed to deprive a person of things of value (including liberty) because of an offense the person is thought to have committed. Punishment is seen as serving four functions:

1. *Retribution* imposes a penalty on the offender. Retribution is based on the premise that the punishment should fit the crime: The greater the degree of social harm, the more the offender should be punished. A person who commits a homicide, for example, should be punished more severely than one who steals an automobile.
2. *Social protection* results from restricting offenders so that they cannot continue to commit crimes.
3. *Rehabilitation* seeks to return offenders to the community as law-abiding citizens. However, the few rehabilitation programs that exist in prisons are seriously understaffed and underfunded. Often, the job skills (such as agricultural work) that are taught in prison do not transfer to the outside world, and offenders are not given help in finding work that fits the skills they might have once they are released.
4. *Deterrence* seeks to reduce criminal activity by instilling a fear of punishment. Criminologists debate, though, whether imprisonment has a deterrent effect, given that 30 to 50 percent of those who are released from prison commit further crimes.

In 2009, more than 7.2 million people were on probation, in jail or prison, or on parole. Among the nearly 2.3 million inmates held in custody in state or federal prisons or in local jails, about 205,000 were federal prisoners in publicly or privately operated facilities or in community correctional facilities. State prisoners accounted for 1.3 million inmates, and local jails held 767,620 inmates where they spent at least one night of

According to the text, punishment serves four functions: retribution, social protection, rehabilitation, and deterrence. Which of these functions is shown in this photo?

incarceration while awaiting trial or serving a sentence (U.S. Bureau of Justice Statistics, 2010b).

Although incarceration rates have declined in recent years, the rate for minorities (with the exception of Asian Americans, who are the least likely to be incarcerated) is disproportionately higher than for whites. Black males were incarcerated at a rate more than six times higher than white males and 2.6 times higher than Hispanic males. Black females were more than two times as likely as Hispanic females and over 3.6 times more likely than white females to be incarcerated in 2009. Overall, the rate of incarceration for African American males is 4,749 inmates per 100,000 U.S. residents, as compared to 1,822 Hispanic inmates per 100,000 U.S. residents, and 708 white inmates per 100,000 U.S. residents. Looking at incarceration by sex, the rate of incarceration for African American females is 333 per 100,000 population, as compared to 142 per 100,000 for Hispanic females, and 91 per 100,000 for white females (U.S. Bureau of Justice Statistics, 2010b).

Jail and prison conditions often do little to rehabilitate offenders. In fact, three out of four inmates are housed in such over-crowded facilities that two people often live in a space only slightly larger than a walk-in closet. Some inmates

Explore the Concept

Social Explorer Activity: Increases in Prison Populations on mysoclab.com

suffer physical abuse by prison officials or other inmates. Because of plea bargains, credit for "good time" served, and overcrowded prison conditions, most convicted criminals do not serve their full sentences. They are released on either probation (close supervision of their everyday lives in lieu of serving time) or parole (early release from prison). About 4.2 million people were on probation or parole in 2009 (U.S. Bureau of Justice Statistics, 2010b). If offenders violate the conditions of their probation or parole, they can be returned to prison to serve their full sentence. Some courts use shaming penalties—named for punishments that were used by the seventeenth-century Puritans—with probationers or as alternatives to incarceration. Shaming penalties typically take the form of a message to the community, just as the public stocks did in the seventeenth century. Drunk drivers might get special license plates; men who have been convicted of soliciting prostitutes might be identified in the media or on billboards; and shoplifters have been required to walk in front of the stores from which they stole, carrying signs admitting their guilt. Because these sentences are usually the result of a guilty

plea, they cannot be appealed except under very special circumstances.

In a study released in 2011, it was found that the annual cost of keeping someone imprisoned at a Federal Bureau of Prison facility in 2010 was $28,284.16. The annual cost of probation supervision was $3,938.35. Those figures work out to a daily cost of $77.49 for incarceration of a convicted criminal, and $10.79 for supervised release.

In recent years, a large increase in the number and power of private juvenile detention facilities and prisons has been an issue of concern as government spending on corrections has soared by 75 percent since the late 1990s and now costs in excess of $75 billion annually in what some analysts refer to as the "prison-industrial complex" (see Box 9.2).

The Death Penalty

In 2010, 46 persons were executed with many (7) being in Texas. These numbers were down slightly from 2009, when 52 persons were executed with 17 being in Texas. The latest year for which complete statistics on executions by race and Hispanic origin are available are 2009 when 24 white Americans, 21 African Americans, and 7 Hispanics were executed for a total of 52 persons (U.S. Bureau of Justice Statistics, 2010b).

About 4,800 people have been executed in the United States since 1930, when the federal government began collecting data on executions (U.S. Bureau of Justice Statistics, 2010b). The death penalty—or *capital punishment*—is a highly controversial issue. Removal—not just expulsion—from one's group is considered the ultimate form of punishment. In the United States, capital punishment is considered an appropriate and justifiable response to very serious crimes.

In 1972, the U.S. Supreme Court ruled (in *Furman v. Georgia*) that *arbitrary* application of the death penalty violates the Eighth Amendment to the Constitution but that the death penalty itself is not unconstitutional. In other words, determining who receives the death penalty and who receives a prison term for similar offenses should not be done on a lottery-like basis (Bowers, 1984). To be constitutional, the death penalty must be imposed for reasons other than the race-ethnicity, gender, and social class of the offender. Since the *Furman v. Georgia* ruling, various states have rewritten their criminal codes so that the death sentence was more narrowly defined. These codes generally have been upheld in subsequent Supreme Court cases, and in *Greg v. Georgia* (1976), the Court explicitly upheld the constitutionality of the death sentence.

Social Problems and Social Policy

Box 9.2

Crime Prevention or the Prison-Industrial Complex?

The demand for our facilities and services could be adversely affected by the relaxation of enforcement efforts, leniency in conviction or parole standards and sentencing practices or through the decriminalization of certain activities that are currently proscribed in our criminal laws. For instance, any changes with respect to drugs and controlled substances or illegal immigration could affect the number of persons arrested, convicted, and sentenced, thereby potentially reducing demands for correctional facilities to house them.

—*Corrections Corporation of America 2010 Annual Report (quoted in Ashton and Petteruti, 2011:2)*

As this statement suggests, private prison companies have something to gain by lobbying for "get tough on crime" laws and lengthy periods of incarceration for those who are convicted. Although some politicians and social analysts believe that building more prisons and giving long sentences to offenders is the way to reduce the crime problem in the United States, others think that we should spend our money and energy on crime prevention instead. According to *prevention ideology*, the best way to reduce delinquency and crime is early intervention and prevention (Bynum and Thompson, 1996). Prevention typically takes three avenues: (1) early childhood and youth socialization that contributes to law-abiding behavior; (2) attacking the roots of delinquency and crime—poverty, unemployment, racism, sexism, drug abuse, and other problems discussed in this book; and (3) specific programs or services that intervene before individuals who have already engaged in delinquent or criminal behavior become immersed in deviant subcultures.

However, current U.S. social policy is not based on prevention, but instead it consists of programs for hiring more law enforcement officers, strengthening and enforcing existing laws, and requiring lengthy sentences for convicted felons. This "war on crime" approach has been in place for several decades, contributing to the growth of a prison-industrial complex—a network of private companies, the government, and politicians—that greatly influ-

ences crime policy. In the past, most money spent on crime control went to public prisons. Today, many state and local governments contract with private companies to build and operate correctional facilities. This process generates large revenues for two major companies, Corrections Corporation of America (CCA) and GEO Group, of more than $2.9 billion annually (Ashton and Petteruti, 2011). Private prisons generally charge a daily rate per person incarcerated, and the rate depends on the facility, population, and security level. Recent studies have documented how the for-profit private prison industrial complex uses political strategies to influence legislators responsible for criminal justice policy to pass legislation and produce policies that benefit for-profit private prison companies (Ashton and Petteruti, 2011).

Other private enterprises also benefit from the prison-industrial complex, including investment houses that are underwriters of jail and prison construction and companies that provide food service, transportation, and health care for the facilities. Still other companies benefit from the sale of protective vests for guards, security systems, closed-circuit television systems, and other surveillance apparatus. Some analysts suggest that the prison-industrial complex, with its interlocking financial and political interests, has good reason to support the "war on crime" instead of developing social policies that prevent delinquency and crime before they happen.

Questions for Consideration

1. In 2009, 8 percent of the state and federal prison population was housed in private prisons. Do you see this as a trend for the future? Will for-profit private prisons eventually replace publicly funded and publicly run prison facilities? Why or why not?

2. Should there be limits on the amounts of money that corporations benefiting from the prison-industrial complex can give to politicians? Do you believe that corporate campaign contributions influence elected officials' decision making in regard to prisons or other areas of social policy and public spending?

Opponents of capital punishment argue that the death penalty is discriminatory because people of color, especially African Americans and poor people, are at greater risk of receiving a death sentence than are their white, more affluent counterparts (M. D. Smith, 2000). In fact, the former slave states are more likely to execute criminals than are other states, and African Americans are eight to ten times more likely to be sentenced to death for crimes such as homicidal rape than are whites (non-Latinos/as) who commit the same offense (Marquart, Ekland-Olson, and Sorensen, 1994).

People who have lost relatives and friends because of a crime often see the death penalty as justifiable compensation—"an eye for an eye." Others fear that innocent individuals will be executed for crimes they did not commit. However controversial the death penalty is, it is likely to remain in place well into the twenty-first century because many political leaders and U.S. Supreme Court justices have expressed support for it. One thing is clear: The existing criminal justice system cannot solve the crime problem. Is equal justice under the law possible? As long as racism, sexism, classism, and ageism exist in our society, equal justice under the law might not be possible for all people. However, that does not keep it from being a goal that citizens and the criminal justice system can strive to reach.

IS THERE A SOLUTION TO THE CRIME PROBLEM?

Since most efforts to reduce or eliminate crime in the United States rely at least partly on the political system and on law enforcement officials, many people look to elected officials and community volunteers for answers on how to deal with the crime problem.

Functionalist/Conservative Solutions

Some functionalist approaches suggest that it is important to identify the social pressures that result in high rates of deviance and crime if we are to reduce the number of crimes that are committed. According to this perspective, when there is a vast disparity between what people would like to have and what they think they can reasonably attain, there is a greater likelihood that crimes will be committed. Based on this approach, one way to reduce crime is through community policing, an organizational strategy among law enforcement agencies that focuses on addressing the causes of crime and reducing the fear of crime and social disorder by using problem-solving tactics and police–community partnerships (COPS, 2011). According to Herman Goldstein, a founder of the problem-oriented approach, more careful analysis of what's going on in communities and a better understanding of the types of crimes that are being committed will make it possible for law enforcement officials and community residents to implement new and more effective strategies for dealing with the problem. In sum, learning about current problems to prevent them from occurring again in the future is the key to this approach (COPS, 2011). However, some critics view this as a form of social control and surveillance by law enforcement officials, which they believe is wrongfully applied more often in low-income and minority neighborhoods than in urban enclaves and affluent suburbs.

Similar to functionalist approaches to reducing crime, conservative political analysts typically focus on how to strengthen neighborhoods, communities, and society through the maintenance of a moral order that is rooted in strong families, social and religious organizations, and other community networks. Some conservative analysts emphasize the importance of "get-tough" policies that result in more "law and order" as an effective means of reducing crime, and they suggest that laws must be enforced and criminal penalties imposed on those who violate the rules. Some conservative analysts support "three strikes" laws passed by various states that mandate that a person who receives a third conviction of a serious crime must be sentenced to life in prison without possibility of parole.

Conflict/Liberal Solutions

From a conflict approach, it would be necessary to reduce power differentials and/or economic inequality in society in order to solve the problem of crime. According to conflict theorists using a Marxist approach, although some consensus may exist across class lines that certain types of crime, such as murder, rape, and armed robbery, are bad, other crimes primarily may be viewed as a threat to members of the capitalist class who desire to maximize their wealth and power in society. In other words, people who have few opportunities to gain a good education or to get a job that pays a living wage are more likely to commit property crimes to help them get by than are those who have greater opportunities. Of course, this explanation does not deal satisfactorily with the issue of why some wealthy people commit property crimes or engage in fraudulent behavior within major corporations.

Some branches of conflict theorizing and liberal political analysis look at race as an important variable that must be addressed when we think about how to reduce crime. From this approach, if crime is to be reduced, racism must also be reduced. Members of racial and ethnic groups that have been the objects of prejudice and discrimination across generations have not had the same opportunities as dominant group members, and once they are accused of committing a crime, the criminal justice system becomes a revolving door that offers no legitimate exit because they have a "record" and few employers are willing to hire them.

In recent years, advocates using conflict and/or liberal assumptions about reducing crime have suggested that a start to solving the problem of the relationship between race and crime might be for the police, the courts, and other branches of the criminal justice system to treat people in different classes and racial-ethnic groups more fairly and more equally. For example, allegations against police officers pertaining to excessive injuries or brutality toward detainees have frequently been lodged against white officers who were in the process of investigating crimes where the alleged perpetrators were persons of color.

Liberal political analysts believe that an important way to eliminate crime in the United States is to empower people. They suggest doing this by greatly improving our public schools; having city, state, and national economic development programs that expand job opportunities for all people; and using public dollars to create better, safer housing where people do not feel threatened in their own homes. Critics of this approach point out that, particularly in tough economic times, suggestions such as these for reducing or eliminating crime have little chance of succeeding, first because there is no money for such programs, and second, because the private sector, not the government, should be responsible for the creation of jobs, housing, and other needed goods and services in society.

Symbolic Interactionist Solutions

As with the solution to other types of social problems, symbolic interactionists make us aware that any behavior that is learned, including criminal behavior, can be unlearned. As a result, the way to reduce crime is teach people the importance of law-abiding behavior and to engage in other endeavors that help to modify and eliminate criminal behavior in society. People who have frequent, intense, and long-lasting interactions with individuals who violate the law, for example, are more likely to violate the law themselves. Finding a means to keep children and young people away from individuals who commit crimes by getting them out of schools and neighborhoods known for high crime rates may help some individuals break out of a cycle of criminal behavior, incarceration, and more criminal behavior. However, applying this individualistic approach does little for solving the larger crime problem in society even if it helps some individuals avoid crime and gain new opportunities. Consider, for example, an elite private school in New York City or another large urban area that provides scholarships for promising low-income students, often from predominantly minority neighborhoods, so that they can get a good education and eventually enroll in a prestigious Ivy League university such as Harvard, Yale, or Princeton. Success stories such as these are frequently printed in major newspapers and posted on the Internet; however, some critics argue that this is elitism ("We know best for a few well-chosen individuals") rather than making a genuine effort to help disadvantaged youths achieve their American Dream.

Finally, symbolic interactionists who use a social constructionist approach point out that different people have different realities about what causes crime, and thus it is necessary to listen to diverse voices to find out how we might reduce or eliminate crime. Based on a social construction of reality approach, for example, the presence of guns is a key factor in why some crimes are committed. As a result, taking illegal handguns off the street has been identified as a viable way to reduce crime in cities such as New York and Boston where illegal firearms have widely been seized and destroyed. If the assumption is correct that guns contribute to crime rates, then the solution is to have far fewer guns in people's hands, particularly those individuals who have a prior criminal record. However, those who disagree with this perspective have their own social construction of reality viewpoint: "Guns don't kill people; people kill people."

With varying degrees of success, the U.S. government has attempted to balance the need to protect its citizens against violence and crime with its responsibility to protect individual rights. The government is responsible for upholding the democratic principle that any individual accused of a crime is "innocent until proven guilty." However, many are concerned that this principle is being violated and that what some people see as a *solution* to our crime problem, such as greater surveillance and social control, ultimately may not be a solution at all but instead may contribute to our crime *problem* as greater surveillance is placed on law-abiding citizens while individuals who perpetrate the most dangerous crimes largely remain undetected. Hopefully, we will gain a better grasp on how to reduce or solve crime in the future.

SUMMARY

■ **Why is it difficult to study crime and delinquency?**

Studying crime, criminals, and juvenile delinquency is difficult because it involves complex human behavior, and many criminals and victims hide their involvement. There also are problems inherent in using official sources of data such as the Uniform Crime Report because they reflect crimes that are reported rather than crimes that are committed and they do not provide detailed information about offenders.

■ **How does violent crime differ from property crime?**

Violent crime consists of actions involving force or the threat of force against others and includes murder, rape, robbery, and aggravated assault. Property crime consists of taking money or property from another without force, the threat of force, or the destruction of property.

■ **Why is rape as a violent crime not well understood, and how is this lack of understanding reflected in our social response to rape?**

Many people think that rape is a sexually motivated crime, but it is actually an act of violence in which sex is used as a weapon against a powerless victim. Moreover, statistics on rape are misleading at best because rape is often not reported. Many reasons keep victims from coming forward. Some victims may be so traumatized that they just want to forget about it. Others fear that their attacker will try to get even. Many also fear how they will be treated by the police and, in the event of a trial, by prosecutors and defense attorneys.

■ **What is occupational crime?**

Occupational (white-collar) crime refers to illegal activities committed by people in the course of their employment or normal business activity. Occupational crime includes computer and other high-tech crimes, as well as more traditional crimes such as employee theft, fraud (obtaining money or property under false pretenses), embezzlement (theft from an employer), soliciting bribes or kickbacks, and insider trading of securities.

■ **How does occupational crime differ from corporate crime?**

Occupational crimes are illegal activities committed by people in the course of their employment or normal business activity. Corporate crimes are illegal acts committed by corporate employees on behalf of the corporation and with its support.

■ **What is organized crime and why does it flourish in the United States?**

Organized crime is a business operation that supplies illegal goods and services for profit. These illegal enterprises include drug trafficking, prostitution, gambling, loan-sharking, money laundering, and large-scale theft. Organized crime thrives because there is great demand for illegal goods and services.

■ **How does juvenile delinquency differ from adult crime?**

Juvenile delinquency refers to a violation of law or the commission of a status offense by people who are younger than a specific age. Many behaviors that are identified as juvenile delinquency are not criminal acts per se but status offenses—acts that are illegal because of the age of the offender—such as cutting school or purchasing and consuming alcoholic beverages. Juvenile hearings take place in juvenile courts or before juvenile judges, whereas adult offenders are tried in criminal courts.

■ **How do functionalists explain crime?**

Functionalists use several theories to explain crime. According to strain theory, people are socialized to desire cultural goals, but many people do not have institutionalized means to achieve the goals and therefore engage in criminal activity. Control perspectives, such as social bond theory, suggest that delinquency and crime are most likely to occur when a person's ties to society are weakened or broken.

■ **How do conflict theorists explain crime?**

Conflict theorists explain criminal behavior in terms of power differentials and/or economic inequality in society. One approach focuses on the relationship between authority and power and crime; another focuses on the relationship between economic inequality and crime. Feminist approaches offer several explanations of why women commit crimes: gender discrimination, patriarchy, and a combination of capitalism and patriarchy.

■ **How do symbolic interactionists explain crime?**

Symbolic interactionists emphasize that criminal behavior is learned through everyday interaction with others. According to differential association theory, individuals have a greater tendency to deviate from societal norms when they frequently associate with people who are more likely to deviate than conform. Labeling theory says that delinquents and criminals are those people who have been successfully labeled by others as such.

■ **What are the components of the criminal justice system?**
The criminal justice system is a network of organizations involved in law enforcement, including the police, the courts, and the prisons. The police are the most visible link in the criminal justice system because they are responsible for initially arresting and jailing people. Criminal courts are responsible for determining the guilt or innocence of people who have been accused of committing a crime. Imprisonment, probation, and parole are mechanisms of punishment based on retribution, social protection, rehabilitation, and deterrence.

■ **Why is the death penalty controversial?**
The death penalty—or capital punishment—is a highly controversial issue because removal from the group is considered the ultimate punishment. Some people believe that it is an appropriate and justifiable response to very serious crimes; others view this practice as discriminatory because people of color—especially African Americans—and poor people are at greater risk of receiving a death sentence than are their white, more affluent counterparts.

KEY TERMS

acquaintance rape, p. 197
corporate crime, p. 204
criminal justice system, p. 212
differential association theory, p. 211
felony, p. 195
forcible rape, p. 197
juvenile delinquency, p. 206
labeling theory, p. 211

mass murder, p. 196
misdemeanor, p. 195
murder, p. 195
occupational (white-collar) crime, p. 203
organized crime, p. 205
plea bargaining, p. 214
primary deviance, p. 212

property crime, p. 200
punishment, p. 214
secondary deviance, p. 212
serial murder, p. 196
social bond theory, p. 210
statutory rape, p. 197
strain theory, p. 209
violent crime, p. 195

QUESTIONS FOR CRITICAL THINKING

1. Why doesn't the United States use all of its technological know-how to place known criminals and potential offenders under constant surveillance so that the crime rate can be really reduced?

2. If most of the crimes that are committed are property crimes, why do so many people fear that they will be the victims of violent crime?

3. Does the functionalist, conflict, or symbolic interactionist perspective best explain why people commit corporate crimes? Organized crimes? Explain your answer.

4. If money were no object, how would you reorganize the criminal justice system so that it would deal more equitably with all people in this country?

5. What approach do you believe might be most effective in reducing crime in the United States?

Succeed with MySocLab®   www.mysoclab.com

The new MySocLab delivers proven results in helping students succeed, provides engaging experiences that personalize learning, and comes from a trusted partner with educational expertise and a deep commitment to helping students and instructors achieve their goals.

Here are a few activities you will find for this chapter:

Watch on **mysoclab.com**

Core Concepts video clips feature sociologists in action, exploring important concepts in the study of Social Problems. Watch:
● Crips and Bloods: Clip 1

Explore on **mysoclab.com**

Social Explorer is an interactive application that allows you to explore Census data through interactive maps. Explore:
● Social Explorer Activity: Increases in Prison Populations

Read on **mysoclab.com**

MySocLibrary includes primary source readings from classic and contemporary sociologists. Read:
● Fraternities and Collegiate Rape Culture: Why Are Some Fraternities More Dangerous Places for Women?

10

Health Care: Problems of Physical and Mental Illness

THINKING SOCIOLOGICALLY

- What are some of the most pressing health problems in the United States and other high-income nations? In low-income nations?

- Why are people more likely to discuss a physical illness with others as compared with a mental illness?

- How is health care paid for in the United States? What effect does this have on the care people receive?

Web blogs and and social networking have opened up a new world of communication for individuals with chronic diseases such as Laurie Edwards (http://www.achronicdose.com/) who has maintained an blog in which she described what it was like to experience the joy of communicating with, and sometimes actually meeting face-to-face with, other individuals with PCD. People with PCD often have collapsed lungs and pneumonia at birth, *and they contract serious infections throughout childhood. They experience frequent hospitalization, and many of them have ongoing medical problems throughout life. As Laurie explained in her blog, being able to have cyberspace conversations and make friends with "real people" who have similar conditions and experiences is vital to people with rare diseases because it is so difficult for them to have a sense of community (see Edwards, 2011).*

For individuals such as Laurie, illness is a *personal problem* involving a single person. Laurie's illness, primary ciliary dyskinesia (PCD), is an inherited disorder of the structure and/or function of cilia—a minute, hairlike part of the cell that lines the surface of certain cells. People with PCD do not have functioning cilia and are unable to protect their respiratory system, resulting in frequent infections of the lungs, ears, throat, and sinuses. This condition is rare, with perhaps as many as 25,000 people in the United States being diagnosed with this disorder. As a result, persons such as Laurie feel even more alone and isolated than people with other illnesses. From this approach, it is common to look at such an illness as a personal problem. However, from a larger sociological perspective, Laurie's illness is also a *social problem* that requires the attention of the entire nation to provide appropriate treatment, to fund research for new drugs and treatments, and to create an environment that is open and welcoming to all persons with chronic illnesses, whether they are frequent in occurrence or very rare, as in Laurie's case. This chapter examines health care problems, including both physical and mental illness, and current problems in providing health services in this country.

> ### Did You Know
> - More than 50 million people are uninsured in the United States.
> - The United States has lower rates of life expectancy and higher infant mortality rates than many countries that spend far less on health care.
> - More than 1 million people are living with HIV in the United States.
> - Race, class, and gender are intertwine with health disparities around the world.

HEALTH CARE AS A SOCIAL PROBLEM

What does the term *health* mean to you? At one time, health was considered to be simply the absence of disease. However, the World Health Organization (2011) defines *health* as a state of complete physical, mental, and social well-being. According to this definition, health involves not only the absence of disease but also a positive sense of wellness. In other words, health is a multidimensional phenomenon: It includes physical, social, and psychological factors.

What is illness? Illness refers to an interference with health; like health, illness is socially defined and may change over time and between cultures. For example, in the United States and Canada, obesity is viewed as unhealthy, whereas in other times and places, obesity indicated that a person was prosperous and healthy.

What happens when a person is perceived to have an illness or disease? Healing involves both personal and institutional responses to perceived illness and disease. One aspect of institutional healing is health care and the health care delivery system in a society. *Health care* is any activity intended to improve health. When people experience illness, they often seek medical attention in hopes of having their health restored. A vital part of health care is *medicine*—an institutionalized system for the scientific diagnosis, treatment, and prevention of illness.

Many people think that there is a positive relationship between the amount of money a society spends on health care and the overall physical, mental, and social well-being of its people. After all, physical and mental health are intertwined: Physical illness can cause emotional problems; mental illness can produce physical symptoms. According to this belief, spending a great deal of money on health care should result in physical, mental, and social well-being. If this is true, however, people in the United States should be among the healthiest and fittest in the world. We spent $2.5 trillion—the equivalent of $8,086 per person—on health care in 2009 (Centers for Medicare and Medicaid Services [CMS], 2011). The health service industry accounts for more than 17 percent of U.S. gross domestic product, a proportion that has increased substantially since the 1960s (CMS, 2011).

Table 10.1 shows the increase in health service expenditures between 1990 and 2008, the last year for which detailed information was available.

However, although we, as individuals, pay more for health services than do people in other high-income nations, our expenditures do not translate into improved life expectancy for everyone. *Life expectancy* **is an estimate**

TABLE 10.1 National Health Expenditures, by Type: 1990–2009

Type of Expenditure*	1990	1995	2000	2009
Total	696.0	990.2	1,309.4	2,338.7
Annual percent change	11.8	5.7	7.1	4.4
Percent of gross domestic product	12.0	13.4	13.3	16.2
Private expenditures	413.5	533.6	714.9	1,232.0
Health services and supplies	401.9	521.1	697.3	1,138.1
Out-of-pocket payments	137.3	146.5	192.6	277.8
Insurance premiums	233.5	329.7	449.3	783.2
Other	31.1	44.9	55.3	77.2
Medical research	1.0	1.4	3.4	4.7
Public expenditures	282.5	456.6	594.6	1,106.7
Percent federal or public	68.2	70.6	70.0	73.8
Health services and supplies	267.7	436.5	564.2	1,043.1
Medicare	110.2	183.1	225.1	469.2
Public assistance medical payments	78.7	149.5	209.3	362.0
Temporary disability insurance	0.1	0.1	–	0.1
Workers' compensation (medical)	17.5	21.9	25.3	33.1
Defense Dept. hospital, medical	10.4	12.1	14.0	33.1
Maternal, child health programs	1.8	2.2	2.7	2.7
Public health activities	20.2	31.4	45.8	69.4
Veterans' hospital, medical care	11.3	15.4	19.1	38.1
Medical vocational rehabilitation	0.5	0.7	0.8	0.5
State and local hospitals	13.1	14.1	13.4	22.1
Other	3.8	6.0	8.8	12.8
Medical research	11.7	15.7	25.4	38.9
Medical structures and equipment	9.2	11.5	14.7	24.7

*In billions of dollars, except percentages; excludes Puerto Rico and island areas.

Source: U.S. Census Bureau, 2010.

of the average lifetime of people born in a specific year. During the past 100 years, overall life expectancy has increased in the United States. The life expectancy of individuals born in 2010, for example, is 78.3 years, compared to only 47.3 years for people born in 1900. It is important to note that life expectancy statistics vary by sex and race. Overall, females born in 2010 can expect to live about 80.8 years, compared to 75.7 years for males. African American males born in 2010, however, have a life expectancy of only 70.2 years, compared to 77.2 years for African American females. White males have an estimated life expectancy of 76.5 years as compared to 70.2 years for African American males. (U.S. Census Bureau, 2010).

In high-income nations, life expectancy has increased as a nation's infant mortality rate has decreased. The *infant mortality rate* **is the number of deaths of infants under one year of age per 1,000 live births in a given year**. The infant mortality rate is an important indication of a society's level of preventive (prenatal) medical care, maternal nutrition, childbirth procedures, and care for infants. For all our expenditures in health care, however, infant mortality in the United States is considerably higher (at 6 infants per 1,000 live births) than it is in a number of other high-income nations (see Table 10.2). Perhaps the single most important cause of infant mortality is lack of prenatal care. Drinking, smoking, taking drugs, and

TABLE 10.2 Infant Mortality Rates in Selected Countries (2011 Est.)

Country or Area	Rate	Country or Area	Rate
United States	6.1	Iraq	41.7
Afghanistan	149.2	Italy	3.4
Algeria	25.8	Japan	2.8
Argentina	10.8	Kenya	52.3
Australia	4.6	Korea, North	27.1
Bangladesh	50.3	Korea, South	4.2
Brazil	21.2	Mexico	17.3
Burma	49.2	Netherlands	4.6
Canada	4.9	Pakistan	63.3
Chile	7.3	Peru	22.2
China	16.1	Philippines	19.3
Colombia	16.4	Poland	6.5
Egypt	25.2	Russia	10.1
Ethiopia	77.1	Saudi Arabia	16.2
France	3.3	Spain	3.4
Germany	3.5	Syria	15.6
Guatemala	26.0	Taiwan	5.2
India	47.6	Thailand	16.4
Indonesia	28.0	United Kingdom	4.6
Iran	42.3		

Note: Numbers have been rounded. Rate = number of deaths of children under one year of age per 1,000 live births in a calendar year.

Source: CIA, 2011.

maternal malnutrition all contribute. Divergent infant mortality rates for African Americans and whites indicate another problem: unequal access to health care. Even with today's high-tech medicine, the infant mortality rate for African American infants is twice as high as the rate for white infants. In 2007, for example, the U.S. mortality rate for African American infants was 13.2 per 1,000 live births compared to 5.6 per 1,000 live births for white infants (National Center for Health Statistics [NCHS], 2010). Compare U.S. infant mortality rates of all racial and ethnic categories to these of infant mortality rates in low-income nations such as Afghanistan (where the rate is 149 infants per 1,000 live births), and a vast difference is apparent (Central Intelligence Agency [CIA], 2011). Some analysts estimate that two-thirds of infants in low-income nations who die during their first year of life die during the *first month* of life. There are many reasons for these differences in infant mortality. Many people in low-income countries have insufficient or contaminated food; lack access to pure, safe water; and do not have adequate sewage and refuse disposal. Added to these hazards is a lack of information about how to maintain good health. Many of these nations also lack qualified physicians and health care facilities with up-to-date equipment and medical procedures.

Acute and Chronic Diseases and Disability

Life expectancy in the United States and other developed nations has increased largely because vaccinations and improved nutrition, sanitation, and personal hygiene have virtually eliminated many acute diseases, including measles, polio, cholera, tetanus, typhoid, and malaria. **Acute diseases are illnesses that strike suddenly and cause dramatic incapacitation and sometimes death** (Weitz, 2010). Examples of acute illnesses range from coughs and cold to chicken pox and various strains of influenza.

With the overall decline in death from acute illnesses in high-income nations, however, has come a corresponding increase in **chronic diseases**, **illnesses that are long term or lifelong and that develop gradually or are present from birth** (Weitz, 2010). Chronic diseases are caused by various biological, social, and environmental factors. Worldwide, some of these factors are the same, and some are different (see Box 10.1 on page 229). According to some social analysts, we can attribute many chronic diseases in our society to the *manufacturers of illness*, groups that promote illness-causing behavior and social conditions, such as smoking (McKinlay, 1994). The effect of chronic diseases on life expectancy varies because some chronic diseases are progressive (e.g., emphysema worsens over time), whereas others are constant (e.g., paralysis after a stroke); also, some are fatal (lung cancer), but others are not (arthritis and sinusitis).

Some chronic diseases produce disabilities that significantly increase health care costs for individuals and for society. Disability can be defined in several ways. Medical professionals tend to define it in terms of organically based impairments—that is, the problem is entirely within the body. However, disability rights advocates believe that disability is a physical or health condition that stigmatizes or causes discrimination. ***Disability is a restricted or total lack of ability to perform certain activities as a result of physical limitations or the interplay of these limitations, social responses, and the social environment*** (Weitz, 2010). An estimated 54 million people in the United States have one or more physical or mental disabilities, and the number continues to increase for several reasons. First, with advances in medical technology, many people who in the past would have died from an accident or illness now survive with an impairment. Second, as people live longer, they are more likely to experience chronic diseases (such as arthritis) that can have disabling consequences. Third, people born with serious disabilities are more likely to survive infancy because of medical technology. (Estimates suggest that fewer than 15 percent of people with a disability today were born with it; accidents, disease, violence, and war account for most disabilities in this country.) For many people with chronic illness and disability, life takes on a different meaning. Knowing that they probably will not live out the full life expectancy for people in their age category, they come to treasure each moment. Today, some of the most tragic instances of life cut short occur because of AIDS.

The AIDS Crisis

By the early 1990s, AIDS—acquired immune deficiency syndrome—had reached crisis proportions in the United States and other nations. AIDS is caused by infection with a virus called human immunodeficiency virus (HIV), which is passed from one person to another through blood-to-blood and sexual contact.

How is AIDS transmitted? AIDS is transmitted primarily through bodily fluids, such as semen (through oral, anal, or vaginal sex with someone who is infected with HIV) or blood (usually by sharing drug needles and syringes with an infected person). It can also be transmitted by blood transfusions (although testing donated blood for the presence of HIV has made this rare in

Progress has been made in curbing the progression of HIV in some affected individuals. However, AIDS remains a pressing social problem that is largely addressed through the efforts of activists and protesters such as the ones shown here, who are participating in a rally outside New York's United Nations building on the twenty-fifth anniversary of the AIDS pandemic.

high-income nations) and by infected mothers before or during birth or while breast-feeding. AIDS is *not* transmitted by routine contact such as a handshake or hugging a person who has the disease or by using eating utensils that a person with AIDS has used.

How many people have been diagnosed with HIV/ AIDS in the United States? The Centers for Disease Control and Prevention (CDC) estimated in 2010 that more than one million persons in this country are living with HIV/AIDS. Each year, up to 56,300 new cases of HIV/ AIDS are diagnosed in adults, adolescents, and children. Males accounted for almost three-quarters (73 percent) of all new diagnoses among adolescents and adults in 2006, and the majority of these cases were attributed to male-to-male sexual contact. Especially jarring is the fact that, although African Americans make up about 12 percent of the population, they constitute about 45 percent of all new HIV/AIDS cases each year. Hispanic and Latino individuals are also disproportionately affected, representing 15 percent of the U.S. population but 17 percent of people living with HIV and 17 percent of new infections each year (CDC, 2010).

The CDC (2010) estimates that more than 576,000 people in the United States have died from AIDS-related complications since the epidemic began. Advances in treatments have slowed the progression of HIV infection to AIDS and significantly reduced the number of deaths among persons with AIDS. However, we should

note that people do not die of AIDS; they die because HIV gradually destroys their immune systems by attacking the white blood cells, making them vulnerable to diseases such as pneumonia, tuberculosis, yeast infection, Kaposi's sarcoma, and other forms of cancer. Thus far, there is no cure for AIDS. Although anti-HIV medications can be used to control the reproduction of the virus and slow the progression of HIV-related disease, these drugs are expensive and often have side effects.

Not all social scientists agree on how AIDS will ultimately affect life expectancy, mortality rates, or the health care industry in the United States. Treatment for AIDS-related illnesses, perhaps even more than that for other chronic diseases, is complex and costly and typically requires lengthy stays in a hospital or hospice. The incidence of AIDS, the number of AIDS patients, and the cost of caring for AIDS patients are highest and most concentrated in city centers, where clinics, hospitals, and other medical facilities are overcrowded, underfunded, and understaffed. Some analysts estimate that more people in the United States will die from AIDS-related illnesses in the future than have died in all the wars fought by this nation. Unfortunately, the AIDS problem in the United States is only a small part of the global picture of devastation caused by this disease.

MENTAL ILLNESS AS A SOCIAL PROBLEM

Mental illness is a social problem because of the number of people it affects, the difficulty of defining and identifying mental disorders, and the ways in which mental illness is treated. Although most social scientists use the terms *mental illness* and *mental disorder* interchangeably, many medical professionals distinguish between a *mental disorder*—a condition that makes it difficult or impossible for a person to cope with everyday life— and *mental illness*—a condition that requires extensive treatment with medication, psychotherapy, and sometimes hospitalization. The most widely accepted classification of mental disorders is the American Psychiatric Association's (2000) *Diagnostic and Statistical Manual of Mental Disorders IV (DSM–IV–TR)* (see Figure 10.1 on page 229). With each new edition of the *DSM*, its list of disorders has changed and grown. Listings change partly because of new scientific findings, which permit more precise descriptions that are more useful than are broad terms covering a wide range of

Explore the **Concept**

Social Explorer Activity: Mental Illness in the U.S. on mysoclab.com.

Social Problems in Global Perspective   Box 10.1 🌐

Global Enemies of Health: The Double Burden of Low-Income Nations

Recently, the World Health Organization (WHO) listed these top ten health risks and death rates for people living in low-income countries around the globe:

1. Childhood underweight = 2 million deaths
2. High blood pressure = 2 million deaths
3. Unsafe sex = 1.7 million deaths
4. Unsafe water, sanitation, hygiene = 1.6 million deaths
5. High blood glucose = 1.3 million deaths
6. Indoor smoke from solid fuels = 1.3 million deaths
7. Tobacco use = 1.0 million deaths
8. Physical inactivity = 1.0 million deaths
9. Suboptimal breastfeeding = 1.0 million deaths
10. High cholesterol = 0.9 million deaths

Although some items on this list (such as high blood pressure, high blood glucose, and high cholesterol) are also risk factors in high-income countries, some items listed are distinct to low-income nations. Children who are underweight, as opposed to people who are overweight or obese, is one stark example. Another is unsafe water, sanitation, and hygiene in low-income nations, as compared to occupational risks in high-income countries.

Some health-related problems in low-income nations are associated with poverty, such as being underweight. This problem is most prevalent among children who are five years of age or younger, and it is estimated that being underweight is a contributing factor in 60 percent of all child deaths in low-income nations. By contrast, other items on this list—such as high cholesterol, high blood pressure, and obesity—are typically associated with wealthy societies. WHO estimates that there are more than 1 billion adults worldwide who are overweight, of whom at least 300 million are "clinically obese." In North America and western Europe combined, for example, more than 500,000 people die annually from obesity-related diseases. Thus, obesity is a health problem because it can contribute to premature death, but it is even more likely to produce chronic disease and disability.

In recent years, obesity, diabetes, and heart disease have also become significant health problems in many lower-income nations. The dividing line between the health problems of people in high-income nations and those in low-income nations is not as clear as we might initially think. Although a significant number of people in some low-income nations are underweight and lack proper nutrition, many more people around the globe are consuming foods that contribute to health problems such as high blood pressure and high cholesterol. WHO attributes the problem of obesity to a change in global dietary patterns worldwide as more people are consuming larger amounts of industrially processed fatty, salty, and sugary foods. Some social analysts believe that a contributing factor to the growth in the rates of obesity is the global spread of processed (as compared to freshly produced) foods and the proliferation of fast-food restaurants.

Ironically, we are faced with dual and seemingly competing problems in regard to global nutrition: Some individuals are chronically underweight and in peril because of the lack of food, whereas others are chronically overweight and in peril because of either too much food intake or too much of the wrong kinds of foods. We cannot ignore this problem if, in fact, millions of the world's children under age six are overweight or obese.

Throughout the world, individuals, governments, and corporations will need to cooperate if we are to reduce the problems associated with being underweight or being obese. Similarly, prevention will be essential for reducing health risks, and education is the first step in that direction.

Questions for Consideration

1. Can you think of ways in which individuals, corporations, and governmental agencies might combat enemies of health around the world?
2. What part does food play in contributing to health problems?
3. Have U.S. corporations contributed to nutrition problems in other nations? Why or why not?

Independent Research

Visit the World Health Organization's website to learn more about global health risks: www.who.int/healthinfo/global_burden_disease/global_health_risks/en/index.html. You may wish to look at the ten leading risk factor causes of death that is broken down by the world, and by low-, middle-, and high-income countries. What factors can you identify that might contribute to tobacco use being the number one risk factor associated with death by income group in high-income countries? What differences do you see in risk factors based on income? Which risk factors are most closely associated with lifestyle choices and which are most closely related to conditions that are beyond the control of individuals?

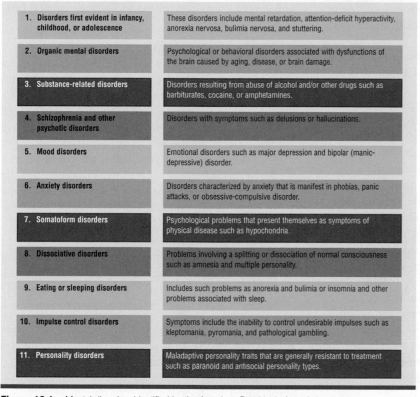

1. Disorders first evident in infancy, childhood, or adolescence	These disorders include mental retardation, attention-deficit hyperactivity, anorexia nervosa, bulimia nervosa, and stuttering.
2. Organic mental disorders	Psychological or behavioral disorders associated with dysfunctions of the brain caused by aging, disease, or brain damage.
3. Substance-related disorders	Disorders resulting from abuse of alcohol and/or other drugs such as barbiturates, cocaine, or amphetamines.
4. Schizophrenia and other psychotic disorders	Disorders with symptoms such as delusions or hallucinations.
5. Mood disorders	Emotional disorders such as major depression and bipolar (manic-depressive) disorder.
6. Anxiety disorders	Disorders characterized by anxiety that is manifest in phobias, panic attacks, or obsessive-compulsive disorder.
7. Somatoform disorders	Psychological problems that present themselves as symptoms of physical disease such as hypochondria.
8. Dissociative disorders	Problems involving a splitting or dissociation of normal consciousness such as amnesia and multiple personality.
9. Eating or sleeping disorders	Includes such problems as anorexia and bulimia or insomnia and other problems associated with sleep.
10. Impulse control disorders	Symptoms include the inability to control undesirable impulses such as kleptomania, pyromania, and pathological gambling.
11. Personality disorders	Maladaptive personality traits that are generally resistant to treatment such as paranoid and antisocial personality types.

Figure 10.1 Mental disorders identified by the American Psychiatric Association
Source: Based on information from the American Psychiatric Association, 2000.

behaviors, and partly because of changes in how we view mental disorders culturally. When the next edition (*DSM–V*) is published in 2012, the listings will probably differ somewhat from those found in Figure 10.1.

How many people are affected by mental disorders? About 57.7 million people, or one in four adults, in the United States suffer from a diagnosable mental disorder. Many of these illnesses began in childhood or adolescence, with the most common problems being anxiety disorder, mood disorders, impulse-control disorders, and substance abuse disorders. Even though mental disorders are widespread in the population, people who are suffering from a serious mental illness—such as schizophrenia, bipolar affective disorder, and major depression—accounted for about 4.5 percent of adults in the United States. The highest rate of serious mental illness among U.S. adults in 2008 was for persons between the ages of eighteen and twenty-five, and the rates for females were higher than those for males. Persons reporting two or more races had the highest prevalence of serious mental illness in that same year, followed by white Americans, and then American Indians (Native Americans)/Alaska Natives (National Institute of Mental Health [NIMH], 2010).

Mental disorders are very costly to the nation. Direct costs associated with mental disorders include the price of medication, clinic visits, and hospital visits. It is estimated that nearly $60 billion is spent for mental health services annually, with an average expenditure per person of approximately $1,600. However, there are many indirect costs as well. These include the lost earnings of individuals, the costs associated with homelessness and incarceration, and other indirect costs that exist but are difficult to document (NIMH, 2010).

Treatment for Mental Illness

Although statistics indicate that some people with mental disorders do not seek professional treatment, the leading cause of hospitalization for men between the ages of fifteen and forty-four and the second leading cause (after childbirth) for women in that age group is mental disorders, particularly disorders related to substance abuse (U.S. Census Bureau, 2010). Veterans returning from military service with posttraumatic stress disorder (PTSD)—a mental health problem that can occur after a person has been through a traumatic event—have added to

Mental illness is depicted in films such as *Black Swan*, in which actress Natalie Portman plays a schizophrenic dancer. Some films make us more aware of the actual problems associated with mental illness, but others sensationalize or trivialize this important social problem.

the number of individuals who have sought treatment for mental-health-related conditions in the past decade.

People who do seek professional help are treated with medication and psychotherapy to help them understand the underlying reasons for their problem. Sometimes they are treated on an outpatient basis or in psychiatric wards of local hospitals or in private psychiatric hospitals. Because medication is used so routinely today, we tend to forget that institutionalization used to be the most common treatment for severe mental illness. In fact, it was the development of psychoactive drugs that made possible the deinstitutionalization movement of the 1960s. **Deinstitutionalization is the practice of discharging patients from mental hospitals into the community**. Although deinstitutionalization was originally devised as a solution to the problem of warehousing patients with mental illness in large, prisonlike mental hospitals in the first half of the twentieth century, some medical practitioners and social scientists view deinstitutionalization as a problem because it has contributed to more patients not receiving the treatment they need and to other social problems such as homeless individuals with mental illness.

To understand how deinstitutionalization came to be viewed as both a solution and a problem, it is necessary to understand the state of mental health care in the United States in the 1950s and 1960s. Involuntary (i.e., without a patient's consent) commitment allowed many patients to be placed in state mental hospitals for extended periods of time with only minimal and sometimes abusive custodial care. According to sociologist Erving Goffman (1961), mental hospitals in that time were a classic example of a *total institution*—**a place where people are isolated from the rest of society for a period of time and come under the complete control of the officials who run the institution**. Patients are stripped of their individual identities—or depersonalized—by being required to wear institutional clothing and to follow a strict regimen of activities, meals, and sleeping hours. The deinstitutionalization movement sought to release patients from the hospitals so that they could live at home and go about their daily activities. Professionals believed that the patients' mental disorders could be controlled with medication and treatment through community-based mental health services. Other advocates hoped that deinstitutionalization would remove the stigma attached to hospitalization for mental illness. This stigma is described by Susanna Kaysen (1993:123–124), who, at

age eighteen, was committed to a private mental hospital for two years:

The hospital had an address, 115 Mill Street ....

In Massachusetts, 115 Mill Street is a famous address. Applying for a job, leasing an apartment, getting a driver's license: all problematic ....

"You're living at One fifteen Mill Street?" asked [one prospective employer].... "And how long have you been living there?"

"Oh, a while." I gestured at the past with one hand.

"And I guess you haven't been working for a while?" He leaned back, enjoying himself.

"No," I said. "I've been thinking things over."

I didn't get the job.

As I left the shop my glance met his, and he gave me a look of such terrible intimacy that I cringed. I know what you are, said his look.... In the world's terms ... all of us [at the hospital] were tainted.

Although deinstitutionalization had worthwhile goals (protection of civil rights and more humane and less costly treatment), in too many cases it simply moved people out of mental hospitals into the streets and jails. Many social analysts believe that the movement was actually triggered by changes in public health insurance. With the introduction of Medicare and Medicaid in 1965, states were more than willing to move patients from state-funded mental hospitals to private facilities that would be paid for largely by federal government funding. In the 1950s, there were about 650,000 hospital beds for patients with mental illness; today, the number is between 25,000 and 45,000 (Jerrard, 2007). Critics of deinstitutionalization argue that it further intensified long-term problems associated with treating mental illness. The drastic reduction in state psychiatric facilities and extensive state budget cuts across the United States have brought about mass closings of public psychiatric facilities over the past forty years, leaving many persons with mental illness among the homeless in states such as California and New York. Psychiatric care has become a class-based issue: Those with wealth are able to find an abundance of mental health services and practitioners; those with little or no financial resources must largely do without.

If schizophrenia and other serious mental illnesses do not lead to jail, they often result in homelessness. On a given night in 2008, a study of sheltered homeless individuals showed that 26 percent had severe mental illness (HUD, 2009). However, it is difficult to determine which came first—the mental disorder or homelessness. If you or I were homeless, for instance, what are the chances that we might develop mental health problems if we tried to survive on the streets or in and out of shelters and city jails?

Race, Class, Gender, and Mental Disorders

Studies of race-, class-, and gender-based differences in mental disorders show that some of these factors are more important than others. Although there are no significant differences in diagnosable mental illness between African Americans and white Americans (the two groups that are most often compared), studies of racism show interesting implications for mental health. For example, in a study of the effects of racism on the everyday lives of middle-class African Americans, social scientists Joe R. Feagin and Melvin P. Sikes (1994) found that repeated personal encounters with racial hostility deeply affect the psychological well-being of most African Americans, regardless of their level of education or social class. In a subsequent study, Feagin and Hernán Vera (1995) found that white Americans also pay a high psychic cost for the prevalence of racism because it contradicts deeply held beliefs about the American dream and equality under the law. In earlier work on the effects of discrimination on mental well-being, social psychologist Thomas Pettigrew (1981) suggested that about 15 percent of whites have such high levels of racial prejudice that they tend to exhibit symptoms of serious mental illness. According to Pettigrew, racism in all its forms constitutes a "mentally unhealthy" situation in which people do not achieve their full potential.

Researchers are now focusing on mental disorders among diverse racial-ethnic groups. Among immigrant populations, for example, age at immigration is a key factor in mental health. One study of Asian Americans found that age at immigration was associated with the onset of mental disorders: Asian immigrants who arrived in the United States at age twelve or younger had a greater risk for psychiatric disorders during childhood than their U.S.-born counterparts. Similarly, among Latinos/as, the later the age of immigration, the later the onset of any psychiatric disorders. In most studies of the relationship between mental illness and immigration status, key factors included the presence or absence of extended (intergenerational) family networks, coping strategies based on religious and social beliefs, and strength of feelings about a sense of community.

Most researchers agree that social class is related to mental illness. However, researchers do not agree on whether lower social class status causes mental illness or mental illness causes lower social class status (Weitz,

2010). Analysts using the *social stress framework* to examine schizophrenia—the disorder that is most consistently linked to class—believe that stresses associated with lower-class life lead to greater mental disorders. In contrast, analysts using the *social drift framework* argue that mental disorders cause people to drift downward in class position. To support their argument, they note that individuals who are diagnosed with schizophrenia typically hold lower-class jobs, that is, lower than would be expected on the basis of their family backgrounds (Weitz, 2010).

Gender also appears to be a factor in mental illness. Researchers have consistently found that the rate of diagnosable depression is about twice as high for women as for men, that this gender difference typically emerges in puberty, and that the incident rate rises as women and men enter adulthood and live out their unequal statuses. Although women have higher rates of minor depression and other disorders that cause psychological distress, men have higher rates of personality disorders (for example, compulsive gambling or drinking) as well as higher rates of maladaptive personality traits such as antisocial behavior. Some analysts suggest that the difference in types of mental disorders is linked to gender-role socialization, which instills aggressiveness in men and learned helplessness in women. According to the *learned helplessness theory*, people become depressed when they think they have no control over their lives (Seligman, 1975). Because this theory emphasizes that people think they have no control, it assumes a *subjective perception* and therefore implies that women contribute to their own helplessness. But feminist analysts argue that the powerlessness in many women's lives is an *objective condition* (Jack, 1993). Support for the feminist view comes from numerous studies indicating that women in high-income, high-status jobs usually have higher levels of psychological well-being and fewer symptoms of mental disorders regardless of their marital status (Horowitz, 1982; Angel and Angel, 1993).

THE CRISIS IN U.S. HEALTH CARE

Much has been happening in recent years in U.S. health care: The costs continue to rise dramatically at the same time as a new law to make health care more accessible for all citizens is being implemented. In the past, the United States was the only high-income nations that did not have some form of universal health coverage. Although no

Robotic surgery, which can filter out a doctor's tiny hand tremor, is an example of contemporary high-tech medicine. However, the high cost of some medical equipment is a factor in the crisis in health care in the United States today.

system of health care in the world fully meets the medical needs of all residents living in a country, health care in the United States has been especially criticized because its costs are far higher than in any other advanced nation regardless of whether we measure these costs in regard to the total dollars that are spent on health care, what percentage health care costs are of the total economy, or on a per capita basis.

What is being done to change this situation? In 2010 the U.S. Congress passed a sweeping health care reform bill, the Patient Protection and Affordable Care Act (usually referred to as the Affordable Care Act), which was signed into law and is gradually bringing about changes in how health care is delivered and funded. Let's look first at the new health reform legislation and then compare its provisions with current methods of funding of health care in the United States.

The Affordable Care Act

Although individuals already covered by employer-based insurance or Medicare are unlikely to see major changes in their health coverage, the law will bring about changes in the future as it is implemented over a multiyear timetable. One of the central tenets in the law is the creation of a new insurance marketplace that lets individuals and families without coverage and small business owners pool their resources to increase their buying power to make health insurance more affordable. Private insurance companies will complete for their business based on cost and quality. Advocates of the new law believe that it is a first step in curbing abuses in the insurance industry.

Health care reform under the Affordable Care Act was scheduled to occur in the following stages:

- **2010:** Adults who had been unable to get coverage because of a preexisting condition could join a high-risk insurance pool (as a stop-gap measure until the competitive health insurance marketplace begins in 2014). Insurance companies were required to cover children with preexisting conditions. Policies could not be revoked when people got sick. Preventive services were fully covered without copays or deductibles. Dependent children could remain on their parents' insurance plans until they reached the age of twenty-six.
- **2011:** Medicare recipients would have access to free annual wellness visits with no cost for preventive care, and those recipients who had to pay out of pocket for prescription drugs would receive substantial discounts.
- **2012:** The federal government would provide additional money for primary care services, and new incentives would be offered to encourage doctors to join together in accountability care organizations. Hospitals with high readmission rates would face stiff penalties.
- **2013:** Households with incomes above $250,000 would be subject to higher taxes to help pay for health care reform. Medicare would launch "payment bundling" so that hospitals, doctors, and other health care providers are paid on the basis of patient outcome, not services provided.
- **2014:** Most people would be required to buy health insurance or pay a penalty for not having it. Insurance companies could not deny a policy to anyone based on health status, nor could they refuse to pay for treatment on the basis of preexisting health conditions. Annual limits on health care coverage would be abolished. Each state would be required to open a health insurance exchange, or marketplace, so that individuals and small businesses without coverage could comparatively shop for health packages. Tax credits would make insurance and health care more affordable for those who earned too much to qualify for Medicaid.
- **2018:** Insurance companies and plan administrators would pay a 40 percent excise tax on all family plans costing more than $27,500 a year.
- **2019:** Health reform law should have reduced the number of uninsured people by 32 million, leaving about 23 million uninsured. About one-third of the uninsured will be immigrants residing in the country without legal documentation.

These are a few of the highlights of the plan, which is a document of more than 2,000 pages in length. Some medical analysts believe this reform measure will provide more cost control, such as competitive insurance exchanges that are supposed to lower premiums, and increase the quality of health care. Critics of the plan believe that it will bankrupt the nation while leaving many individuals without the health services that they need. How health care should be paid for is an issue not only in the United States but for many other

nations around the world (see Box 10.2). Although we can examine the strengths and limitations of how health care systems are funded and operate in nations such as Sweden, Britain, and Canada, it is important to realize that accurate comparisons are difficult to make because the social policies and populations of these countries vary widely.

Social Problems and Social Policy

Box 10.2

Paying for Health Care: Can We Learn from Canada, the United Kingdom, and Sweden?

We often hear complaints about health care in the United States, where it is a well-known fact that we spend more on health care than any other high-income nation. However, despite that expenditure, we have a lower life expectancy and higher infant mortality rates than countries that spend half as much, and we have many people who go without health care because it is too expensive.

Who should pay for health care? Some people believe that it is not up to a nation to take care of everyone, but others believe health care should be available for all. In other words, they advocate a *universal health care system* like those found in Canada, the United Kingdom, and Sweden. In Canada's single-payer system, for example, citizens never see a medical bill or an insurance form or pay for a prescription because the national health insurance system pays all medical costs directly. Hospitals get a yearly budget, and doctors bill the provincial governments (equivalent to our state governments), which administer the health care system, on a fee-for-service basis. Fees are negotiated annually between doctors and the provincial government. Individuals choose any primary care doctor they wish, but they need a referral to a specialist. Overall, Canadians have better access to health care than U.S. citizens do and, as a result, they make more visits to the doctor, are hospitalized more often and for longer periods of time, and have higher immunization rates. By international standards, Canadians are healthier, have longer life expectancies, and a lower infant mortality rate than do U.S. citizens.

Is there any fly in this ointment? Well, two. The cost of health care is skyrocketing, and Canada—like the United States—must find ways to control costs. Efforts continue to find ways to reduce spending for hospitals, drugs, and doctors' services, which account for the bulk of health spending. Because Canada has a dual system in which doctors also may operate a private practice where they offer patients medical care on a fee-for-service basis, one way to reduce costs would be to encourage more patients to go the private insurance route. The second problem: Lengthy

waits, particularly in hospital emergency departments and for diagnostic scans such as MRIs and CTs, which keep patients in limbo for longer periods of time than seems reasonable to some observers (see MacQueen, 2011).

The United Kingdom (Britain) also has a dual system, but most patients are covered through the National Health System (NHS), which is funded by general taxation and national insurance contributions. NHS pays for hospital stays, physicians' services, and prescription drugs, but this system has been extensively criticized because of its heavy backlog, including long waiting times for appointments, doctor visits, emergency services, and surgery partly brought about by lack of sufficient doctors and nurses and inadequate medical facilities. In 2000, the British government launched a ten-year reform program to overhaul the health system. However, this program apparently failed to reduce the system's major problems, and a new health care reform bill was introduced into the Parliament of the United Kingdom in 2011 to significantly reform the nation's health care system in regard to massive costs and lack of quality performance (Rahn, 2011). In the second decade of the twenty-first century, the NHS cost the nation about $160 billion (U.S. dollars) a year.

The central component of the Health and Social Care Bill of 2011 is to shift control of the annual health care budget from a centralized bureaucracy to physicians at the local level. General practitioners would be given between $100 billion to $125 billion a year to buy services from hospitals and other health care providers (Lyall, 2010). The idea behind this approach is to reduce the governmental bureaucracy that has handled the finances associated with the NHS and reallocate these funds so that they contribute to the direct health care services for patients. Currently, the new health plan would involve only England because other parts of Britain have separate health care systems. At the time of this writing, the British government is engaging in a "listening exercise" to provide people with an opportunity to respond to the new plan, which has already received extensive praise and criticism.

Sweden, our final country for comparison, has a health care system that covers all residents of Sweden regardless of nationality. National health insurance is financed through taxes, and county councils own and operate hospitals, employ physicians, and run the majority of general practices and outpatient facilities. Although most physicians are salaried employees of the government, some work in private practice and are paid by the counties on a fee-for-service basis. Like other countries, Sweden faces numerous problems with its health care system, including how to motivate doctors who are paid the same amount regardless of how many patients they see and how to deal with sharply rising costs as the country's population ages and as more people are diagnosed with chronic problems such as allergies, obesity, and psychosomatic problems. The most frequent complaints about the Swedish system include lack of services in emergency departments, having to pay multiple copayments as the patient is moved from physician to physician or department to department in a hospital, and general apathy of some health care providers. Although some believe that the level of health in Sweden is generally better than in other nations for what the services cost, other analysts believe that Sweden will be unable to provide even the current level of coverage in the future.

As we look at other nations, we see that the lessons we might learn from these countries are mixed because they have similar problems to ours when it comes to the organization and financing of health care. As the United States moves toward a more nationalized system of health care, nations such as Britain are moving toward decentralizing health care. The Canadian system, which has often been used as a possible model for reforming the U.S. health care system, is now the object of harsh criticism by some analysts about the timeliness and quality of care in that country. Having a high quality of health care available for all people in the United States is clearly an important long-term goal; however, in the short term, we must also ask how we are spending money. The phrase "follow the money" has become a popular rallying cry for many groups; perhaps health care is also a social problem where this approach might be useful. Will the Affordable Care Act pave the way for high-quality medical care in the United States that will not bankrupt the nation in the process? This is a question you may wish to examine in greater detail.

Questions for Consideration

1. Many countries with national health plans have a dual system of medical service for both "public" and "private" patients. What does the presence of this dual system tell us about social inequality generally, and in health care specifically, in those nations?

2. Thinking about your own experiences with doctors, hospitals, and other medically related settings, what are you learning in this sociology course that might help you evaluate the treatment (from a nonmedical standpoint) that you and others you know receive in U.S. health care?

3. When people in the United States are trying to reduce or solve a social problem, what might we gain by analyzing how other countries deal with a similar problem? What are the limitations of such an approach?

Health Care Organization, Rising Costs, and Unequal Access

How has health care been organized and paid for prior to implementation of the Affordable Care Act? For many years, medical care in the United States has been provided on a fee-for-service basis: Patients are billed individually for each service they receive, including treatment by doctors, laboratory work, hospital visits, prescriptions, and other health-related services. Fee-for-service is an expensive way of delivering health care because there are few restrictions on the fees charged by doctors, hospitals, and other medical providers. Because the United States is a wealthy nation, we have been willing to spend more on health care than other nations. According to a report in the *New York Times* (2007:WK9), for example:

> We are richer than other countries and so willing to spend more. But authoritative analyses have found that we spend well above what mere wealth would predict. This is mostly because we pay hospitals and doctors more than most other countries do. We rely more on costly specialists, who overuse advanced technologies, like CT scans and M.R.I. machines, and who resort to costly surgical or medical procedures a lot more than doctors in other countries do.

Another problem in regard to overspending is the manner in which incentives from some insurance plans may encourage patients and doctors to overutilize expensive medical services and procedures.

Private Health Insurance

Costly to begin with, fee-for-service health care became even more so with the development of the health insurance industry. During the Great Depression of the 1930s, the American Hospital Association, fearing that

👁 Watch on **mysoclab.com**
Managed Care on **mysoclab .com**

many hospitals would go bankrupt because patients could not pay their hospital bills, founded Blue Cross— which at the time was a nonprofit company—to sell health insurance to people so that they could pay their hospital bills. Shortly thereafter, the American Medical Association established Blue Shield to provide coverage for physicians' bills. Under Blue Cross/Blue Shield and other private insurance programs, patients do not pay doctors and hospitals directly. Instead, they pay premiums into a fund that in turn pays doctors and hospitals for each treatment a patient receives as long as the services are covered and the patient has paid the annual deductible.

Some believe that a third-party fee-for-service approach is the best and most cost-efficient method of delivering medical care. Others argue that fee-for-service is outrageously expensive and a very cost-ineffective way in which to provide for the medical needs of people in this country, particularly those who are without health insurance coverage. According to medical sociologist Paul Starr (1982), the main reason for medical inflation in this country is third-party fee-for-service because it gives doctors and hospitals an incentive to increase provision of medical services. That is, the more services they provide, the more fees they charge and the more money they make. At the same time, patients have no incentive to limit their visits to doctors or hospitals because they have already paid their premiums and feel entitled to medical care (Starr, 1982). Although Starr extensively studied these issues in the 1980s, the problems have only intensified in the three decades that have followed. Health care costs began to spiral with the expansion of medical insurance programs in the 1960s. At that time, third-party providers (public and private insurers) began picking up large portions of doctor and hospital bills for insured patients.

In the twenty-first century, private health insurance premiums have continued to increase by about 6 percent per year, after a peak of 10.7 percent in 2002. Between 2002 and 2007, benefit payments slowed, from 9.4 percent to 6.6 percent, largely due to a decline in private health insurance spending growth on prescription drugs. During the same period, out-of-pocket spending (spending not reimbursed by a health insurance plan) increased by 5.3 percent because of increased out-of-pocket payments for prescription drugs, nursing home services, and nondurable medical supplies (Fritze, 2010).

Like other private insurance plans, HMOs emerged during the Great Depression as a means of providing workers with health coverage at a reasonable rate by keeping costs down. A *health maintenance organization (HMO)* **provides, for a fixed monthly fee, total heath care with an emphasis on prevention to avoid costly treatment later.** The doctors do not work on a fee-for-service basis, and patients are encouraged to get regular checkups and to practice good health habits (exercise and eat right). As long as patients use only the doctors and hospitals that are affiliated with their HMO, they pay no fees, or only small copayments, beyond their insurance premium. Recent concerns about physicians being used as gatekeepers who might prevent some patients from obtaining referrals to specialists or from getting needed treatment have resulted in changes in the policies of some HMOs, which now allow patients to visit health care providers outside an HMO's network or to receive other previously unauthorized services by paying a higher copayment. However, critics charge that those HMOs whose primary care physicians are paid on a capitation basis—meaning that they receive only a fixed amount per patient whom they see, regardless of how long they spend with that patient—in effect encourage doctors to undertreat patients.

Another approach to controlling health care costs is known as *managed care*—**any system of cost containment that closely monitors and controls health care providers' decisions about medical procedures, diagnostic tests, and other services that should be provided to patients.** One type of managed care in the United States is a *preferred provider organization (PPO)*, which is an organization of medical doctors, hospitals, and other health care providers who enter into a contract with an insurer or a third-party administrator to provide health care at a reduced rate to patients who are covered under specific insurance plans. In most managed care programs, patients choose a primary care physician from a list of participating doctors. Unlike many of the HMOs, when a patient covered under a PPO plan needs medical services, he or she may contact any one of a number of primary care physicians or specialists who are "in-network" providers. Like HMOs, most

PPO plans do contain a precertification requirement in which scheduled (nonemergency) hospital admissions and certain kinds of procedures must be approved in advance. Through measures such as this, these insurance plans have sought unsuccessfully to curb the rapidly increasing costs of medical care and to reduce the extensive paperwork and bureaucracy involved in the typical medical visit.

Not only are physicians' revenues reduced under managed care, but so are revenues to hospitals, many of which can no longer afford to treat uninsured patients. In the past, hospitals passed on much of the cost of treating uninsured patients to paying patients, but managed care has cut out any margin for doing this. Finally, despite cost-containment measures, health care continues to be a significant expenditure in the United States because of the for-profit structure of much medical care, the fragmented health care provided by government-funded insurance programs, and the spiraling cost of high-tech medicine. In recent years, new medical technologies have added millions of dollars to hospital budgets even as the basic health care needs of many people have not been met.

For the foreseeable future, HMOs and PPOs are supposed to remain somewhat the same. After the passage of the health care reform measure, the Obama administration issued a statement that people in HMO and PPO plans would not be affected by the new law. Rather, they would have assurance that they could get health care coverage even if they lost their job, changed jobs, moved out of state, got divorced, or were diagnosed with a serious illness. Of course, how implementation of the Affordable Care Act really affects other payment methods remains to be seen, particularly given the legal challenge that the new health care law faces in the in the U.S. Supreme Court.

Public Health Insurance

Although private health insurance companies were well established by the 1950s and almost all working people and their immediate families had hospitalization insurance, those who did not work—individuals who were elderly or poor—were often uninsured. Federal legislation extending health care coverage to these individuals and was not passed until the 1960s. From its inception, federally funded health care assistance was a two-tiered system: a medical entitlement program for older people (Medicare) and a medical welfare system for low-income individuals (Medicaid). Medicare is a program that covers most people age sixty-five and over. Workers pay a Medicare tax, similar to the Social Security tax, and Medicare patients pay a monthly premium to help cover their benefits. Medicare Part A is a hospital insurance program that provides coverage for some inpatient hospital expenses, including critical care hospitals and skilled nursing facilities. Part B (a supplementary medical insurance program) helps cover costs for doctors' services and outpatient care. It covers some of the services of physical and occupational therapists, and some home health care. Most people pay a monthly premium for Part B. Beginning in 2006, Medicare prescription drug coverage became available to everyone covered under Medicare. Private companies provide the coverage, and beneficiaries choose the drug plan and pay a monthly premium.

Medicaid is a health care program for persons who are low income or disabled and certain groups of seniors in nursing homes. Medicaid is jointly funded by federal, state, and local funds. Income and other economic resources are taken into account, as well as a person's citizenships status, in determining eligibility. Rules for eligibility differ from state to state, and some provide time limits on coverage. Medicaid provides medical, hospital, and long-term care for people who are poor and either aged, blind, disabled, or pregnant. As such, Medicaid fills in the gaps for elderly Medicare patients whose income is below the poverty level. Whereas Medicare is largely funded by workers' payments into the system throughout their working lives, Medicaid is funded by federal and state governments. As a result, many people view Medicaid as a welfare program and Medicare as an entitlement program—people are assumed to have earned medical coverage through years of hard work and paying into the system. Both Medicare and Medicaid, like other forms of health insurance, dramatically expand the resources for supplying and financing medical services, especially for people with chronic disabling illnesses that extend over months or years. Analysts therefore suggest that these programs are extremely costly to the public because they provide no incentive for keeping down costs or managing resources. Some physicians abuse the system by operating "Medicaid mills" that charge excessive fees for unnecessary tests and treatments. As discussed in Chapter 9, fraudulent billing practices by some unscrupulous health care providers also have driven up the cost of medical care in this country.

When the health care reform law was passed in 2010, both Medicaid and Medicare were in financial difficulty, as these programs had grown more rapidly than the U.S. economy and the revenues used to finance them. Medicare and Medicaid accounted for 25 percent of all federal spending and cost more than $760 billion annually at that time. Under the new Affordable Care law, eligibility for "free" Medicaid coverage is set up expand significantly, so it will be difficult to reduce costs in this area. By contrast, it is assumed that focusing on preventive health services will improve the quality of care provided and reduce costs. This remains to be seen and is a topic of great debate, particularly by organizations that are opposed to so-called Obama Care.

The Uninsured

Despite public and private insurance programs, the percentage of people without health insurance has been increasing in recent years. This problem has intensified because some provisions of the Affordable Care law have not gone into effect, leaving large number of individuals without health insurance coverage. The U.S. financial crisis of 2007–2008 and the slow recovery in the aftermath of this Great Recession have contributed to a higher unemployment rate and less job creation, leaving millions of people without employment-based insurance. In 2009, the percentage of people in the United States without health insurance increased to almost 17 percent, up from 15 percent in 2008. Overall, 50.7 million people were uninsured in 2009, as compared to 46.3 million in 2008 (DeNavas-Walt et al., 2010). The problem of being uninsured cuts across income lines (see Box 10.3 on page 238). About 10 percent of children under age eighteen, or 7.5 million, were uninsured in 2009. For children living in poverty, the percentage of uninsured was even higher: About 15 percent of children in homes below the official poverty line were without health insurance of any kind (DeNavas-Walt et al., 2010).

Race-ethnicity and age are important variables in examining the uninsured rate. Among Latinos/as

Read the Document
The Medically Uninsured: Will They Always Be With Us? on mysoclab.com

(Hispanic Americans), the uninsured rate was 32.4 percent (15.8 million) in 2009, followed by African Americans at 21 percent (8.1 million), Asian Americans at 17.2 percent (2.4 million), and white (non-Hispanic) Americans at 12 percent (23.7 million). Looking at age across racial and ethnic groups, the highest rates of uninsured are between eighteen and forty-four years of age: Those in this age category (30 percent) have the highest rate of uninsured persons, followed by the twenty-five to thirty-four years of age bracket (29 percent), and thirty-five to forty-four years category (22 percent). Because of programs such as Medicare and Medicaid, persons age sixty-five and older have an uninsured rate of only 1.8 percent (DeNavas-Walt et al., 2010). Similarly, the uninsured rate for children under age eighteen is only 10 percent because of a State Children's Health Insurance Program (CHIP) that was stated in 1997 and reauthorized in 2009 to provide health care to millions of children across the United States. This program helps states expand health care coverage to uninsured children and is jointly funded by the federal and state governments and is administered by the states.

Although lack of insurance contributes to many serious health problems, one of the greatest is that people either delay or do not receive needed medical care because of cost. Often delay or lack of medical care means the difference between life and death for patients with diseases such as cancer. Through early detection of breast, colon, and prostate cancers, for example, patients can receive appropriate treatments, such as surgery, radiation, and chemotherapy, which help them survive a life-threatening disease. The prognosis (potential outcome) for late-stage detection of cancer and other diseases is much more limited and may result in the patient having only weeks or months to live. Lack of insurance is an important factor in why some people between the ages of eighteen and sixty-four do not seek medical care or delay seeking such care (see Figure 10.2 on page 238).

Race, Class, Gender, and Health Care

Just as deinstitutionalization was initially seen as the solution to mental health care and is now viewed by many as the problem, health insurance plans were initially considered a solution but have now become a problem, especially when they perpetuate unequal access to health care because of race, class, or gender. According to some analysts, even when people are covered by Medicare or Medicaid, the care they receive

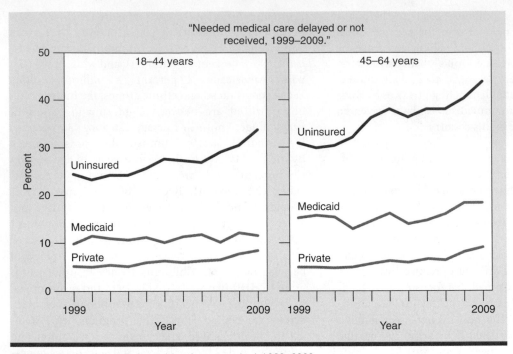

Figure 10.2 Needed medical care delayed or not received, 1999–2009
Source: CDC, 2010.

Social Problems and Statistics   Box 10.3

Families without Health Insurance

Uninsured Americans—including those with incomes well above the poverty line—leave hospitals with unpaid tabs of up to $49 billion a year. . . . On average, uninsured families can pay only about 12% of their hospital bills in full. Families with incomes above 400% of the poverty level, or about $88,000 a year for a family of four, pay about 37% of their hospital bills in full.

—A USA Today analysis of government statistics from a Department of Health and Human Services study shows that uninsured persons in various income categories have difficulty paying for all, or part, of their hospital care (Kennedy, 2011).

Sometimes, it is easy to get confused when the media report on statistics released by organizations such as the Department of Health and Human Services because it is not clear what the statistics actually represent.

What is health insurance coverage? The Census Bureau classifies health insurance coverage as private coverage or government coverage. Private health insurance is provided through an employer or a union or purchased by an individual from a private company. Government health insurance includes federal programs such as Medicare, Medicaid, and military health insurance, as well as the state Children's Health Insurance Program (CHIP) and individual state health plans. By contrast, individuals are considered to be uninsured if they were not covered by any type of health insurance *at any time* during the given calendar year in which the data were reported.

What does it mean when the media recently reported that nearly 17 percent of households were without health insurance in 2009 (the latest year for which data were available)? Does this mean that the problem of lack of insurance is evenly distributed across the nation? No, we must have additional data to determine the distribution of households without health insurance in the United States. For example, the percentage of households without health insurance varies widely based on family income: The likelihood of being covered by health insurance rises with income. Consider the following difference statistics: Among families with incomes of $75,000 or more, about 9 percent were without health insurance at any time during 2009 while slightly less than 27 percent of people in families with incomes of $25,000 or less were

Social Problems and Statistics

Box 10.3 continued

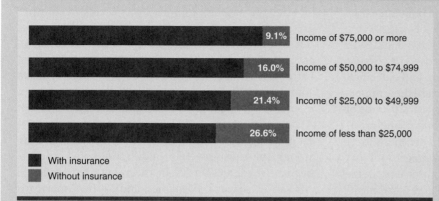

9.1% Income of $75,000 or more

16.0% Income of $50,000 to $74,999

21.4% Income of $25,000 to $49,999

26.6% Income of less than $25,000

■ With insurance
■ Without insurance

Figure 10.3 Percentages of households without health insurance, 2009, by income
Source: DeNavas-Walt et al., 2010.

without health insurance. Figure 10.3 shows the percentage of households within an income bracket that were without health insurance.

Regardless of how you view the statistics, the lack of health insurance is a social problem, since 17 percent of all households in the United States in 2009 were not covered by any type of health insurance for some period of time in that year. The number of households without health insurance increased to 50.7 million people in 2009, up from 47 million people who were uninsured in 2006. Because of the high costs of medical care, particularly for those who are uninsured and often charged higher fees because they are not part of an insurance plan that has negotiated with the health care providers for a set fee, even individuals and families with higher incomes are unable to pay the full bills that they receive from physicians and hospitals. Once again, we reach the same question: Will the new health care law be able to gradually reduce the number of uninsured people in the United States?

Questions for Consideration

1. What do you think should be done to reduce the health insurance problem in the United States?

2. Should we assume that people have better health and receive better quality health care because they have a higher income? Why or why not?

Source: Based on DeNavas-Walt et al., 2010.

and their overall life expectancies are influenced by their race and income. Among other things, people of color across class lines and low-income whites typically receive less preventive care and less optimal management of chronic diseases than others. Under Medicaid, the poorest people sometimes receive the fewest services because of limitations placed on eligibility and the way in which payment of fees to doctors is structured. Regardless of the kind of health insurance coverage, if any, that individuals have, a recent report by the Centers for Disease Control and Prevention (CDC) concluded that wide health disparities—differences in health outcomes between groups that reflect social inequalities—exist across lines of race-ethnicity and class (CDC Morbidity and Mortality Weekly Report, 2011). Higher rates of HIV, untreated hypertension, diabetes, coronary artery disease, and numerous other illness and conditions are found among African Americans and Latinos/as than among white (non-Hispanic) Americans and

Inequalities in health care based on race, class, and gender are often very evident in settings such as this dental clinic, which was set up in a school to provide temporary health services to disadvantaged people. How might we better meet the medical and dental needs of all people in this country?

Asian Americans. Studies indicate that lower-income residents report fewer average healthy days per year and, as previously discussed, life expectancy and infant mortality rates vary by racial-ethnic and income categories (CDC Morbidity and Mortality Weekly Report, 2011).

Gender is intertwined with race-ethnicity and class in examining health care. Numerous researchers have found pervasive gender inequality in healthcare and outcomes, particularly as gender intersects with racial-ethnic minority status, in the United States. In recent years, the rate of women being screened for colorectal, breast, and cervical cancer has improved, and women were more likely than in the past to receive complete treatment for heart attacks, respiratory diseases, and similar problems. In the past, research showed that physicians and other medical personnel took men's health-related complains and symptoms more seriously than those of women, sometimes putting their health in jeopardy by not running sufficient tests to diagnose the condition or releasing them from a medical facility before their condition had been adequately treated. However, the percentage of female patients who received potentially inappropriate medications was significantly higher than for male patients (18.1 percent compared to 11.8 percent). Overall, between 2002 and 2007, females were more likely than males to be unable to get, or were delayed in getting, needed medical care, dental care, or prescription medicines (Agency for Healthcare Research and Quality, 2011).

The long-term exclusion of women from medicine has had a detrimental effect on health care in this country, but things are slowly changing. In regard to medical schools, more men than women apply to medical school each year, partly because the so-called pipeline of pre-med and science majors has a higher percentage of males than females. Although women were expected to be awarded slightly more than 57 percent of all bachelor's degrees nationwide in 2009–2010, for example, only 2.2 percent of all female college graduates (as compared to 3.2 percent of all male college graduates) applied to medical school from that cohort. However, the total number of women entering U.S. medical schools has increased every year since the late 1960, and women's share of the entering class has increased also. Almost half of all medical school graduates (48.3 percent) were women in 2009–2010, and women represented 46.9 percent of persons enrolling in medical school in 2010–2011 (Association of American Medical Colleges, 2010). In examining residency applications for 2010, we find that higher percentages of women apply for specialty programs in fields such as family medicine, internal medicine, obstetrics and gynecology, and pediatrics than

areas such as orthopedic surgery, radiology, and urology, where female doctors remain underrepresented (Association of American Medical Colleges, 2010).

An increase in minority physicians is another pressing concern for medical schools and the practice of medicine now and in the future. Referred to as "underrepresented minorities," African Americans, Latinos/as (Hispanics), and American Indians/Alaska Natives have not had proportional representation in medicine throughout U.S. medical history. Although African Americans and Hispanics are among the fastest growing segments of the U.S. population, they are among the most severely underrepresented minorities in the medical field. In the twenty-first century, African Americans, Hispanics, and Native Americans combined make up 25 percent of the U.S. population, but constitute only 6 percent of practicing physicians in this country (AspiringDocs.org, 2011). The medical school pipeline of minority applicants is not growing fast enough to bridge the gap between the actual number of minority physicians and the rapidly growing minority population in the United States. African American medical school enrollment grew by slightly less than 3 percent in 2010; however, total Hispanic enrollment rose by 9 percent, with men accounting for most of the increase. (Enrollment for Hispanic men increased by 17 percent, as compared to 1.6 percent for Hispanic women.) American Indian (Native American) medical school enrollment has remained about the same, with just 191 first-year students in 2010 out of the total medical school enrollment (all years) of slightly more than 79,000 students (Association of American Medical Colleges, 2010). Asian Americans are not considered to be underrepresented minorities in medical school, however. They constituted 22 percent of applicants and 23 percent of new first year students in 2010–2011.

Although the more equitable racial-ethnic and gender enrollments in medical schools are welcome and long overdue, there is still a white, male-centered focus on some aspects of human health and health care delivery in both medical school and medical practice. Funding for research on minority and women's health issues and diseases is lacking, and some people of color and all women have been excluded from experimental drugs trials, which are conducted to determine the positive and negative effects that a specific drug has on a given category of patients. According to medical sociologists, all physicians and other health care personnel need to focus on diversity in relation to health-related problems so that they can treat the majority of the U.S. population even more effectively.

SOCIOLOGICAL EXPLANATIONS AND SOLUTIONS

What are the primary causes of health care problems in the United States? How can health care problems be reduced or eliminated? The answers that social scientists give to these questions depend on their theoretical framework. Analysts approaching these questions from a functionalist perspective focus on how illness affects the smooth operation of society and on the functions medicine serves as a social institution. Some sociologists using a conflict perspective focus on how a capitalist economy affects health and health care delivery; others look at inequalities of race, class, and gender. Finally, sociologists who use a symbolic interactionist framework look at the social and cultural factors affecting communication between doctors and patients.

The Functionalist Perspective

The functionalist perspective views illness as a threat to a smoothly functioning society because it is necessary for all people to fulfill their appropriate social roles. According to this view, when people become ill, they cannot fulfill their everyday responsibilities to family, employer, or the larger society and instead adopt the *sick role*—patterns of behavior expected from individuals who are ill. Sociologist Talcott Parsons (1951) identified four role expectations of the sick role: (1) sick people are not responsible for their incapacity, (2) they are exempted from their usual role and task obligations, (3) they must want to leave the sick role and get well, and (4) they are obligated to seek and comply with the advice of a medical professional. In other words, illness is a form of deviance that must be controlled. According to Parsons, physicians are the logical agents of social control. By certifying that a person is physically or mentally ill and by specifying how the ill person should behave, doctors use their professional authority to monitor people with illnesses, thereby granting them only a temporary reprieve from their usual social roles and responsibilities. Today, however, the dramatic increase in chronic illness and the disorganization in the delivery system for medical services mean that many people have less access to doctors and doctors have less control over those aspects of patients' lives that can increase their chances of becoming ill. Patients thus end up incurring large medical bills and being unproductive in society.

Functionalists believe that the problems in U.S. health care are due to macrolevel changes, such as the development of high-tech medicine, overspecialization

of doctors, erosion of health-insurance coverage, and increased demand for health care by consumers. Since World War II, functionalists say, the rapid growth of medical knowledge has produced a glut of information, new technologies, and greatly improved surgical techniques. To remain competitive in the face of this new technology and the demand for it, hospitals operating in the same city have often purchased the same extremely expensive equipment. The costs of the equipment are passed on to consumers in the form of higher medical bills and insurance premiums. In the same way that hospitals believe they must have all the latest technology, most medical students have come to believe that they have to specialize—rather than enter general or family practice—to build a large patient base and thereby increase their income and prestige. Thus, both doctors and hospitals have begun to view health care as a commodity and to provide a far wider array of services (treatment for substance abuse, day care for individuals who are mentally ill, and elective procedures such as cosmetic surgery) to sell to consumers (potential patients). At the same time, most individuals have come to view health care as a right to which they are entitled. As both the supply of and demand for medical treatment have grown, lobbying organizations such as the American Medical Association and the American Hospital Association and business, labor, and consumer (especially elderly) groups have entered into battle with Congress and the Obama administration over the extent to which federal and state government should regulate health care and how it should be funded.

What solutions might emerge from a functionalist approach to problems associated with health care? Although functionalists agree that the high cost of health care and disorganization in the U.S. health care industry are clearly dysfunctional for both individuals and society, they do not agree on what should be done. Some believe that the health care system should be reorganized and national programs such as the one set forth in the Affordable Health Care Act should be implemented. However, some conservative analysts have suggested that national-level solutions to this problem constitute nothing more than "Big Government" interfering in the lives of ordinary people who will see little or no change in skyrocketing health costs and insurance premiums. From this perspective, reforms now in the process of being implemented will fundamentally change nearly every aspect of health care, from insurance to final delivery of health care, while creating even greater dysfunctions in an already overburdened and debt-ridden system

The Conflict Perspective

The conflict approach is based on the assumption that problems in health care delivery are rooted in the capitalist economy, which views medicine as a commodity that is produced and sold by the medical-industrial complex. The *medical-industrial complex* **encompasses both physicians and hospitals as well as global health-related industries such as the pharmaceutical and medical supply companies that deliver health care today**. Although wealthy patients and patients with good insurance might receive high-quality care in the medical-industrial complex structure, low-income and poverty-level people often do without. In this view, physicians hold a legal monopoly over medicine and benefit from the existing structure because they can charge inflated fees. Similarly, hospitals, clinics, and other medical facilities control how health care is delivered and what various services will cost patients.

Three factors will inevitably perpetuate inequalities of U.S. health care: (1) high health care costs due to advanced medical services and the use of expensive medications and technology; (2) abuse of existing systems by some health care professionals, particularly those who overcharge patients, provide unnecessary services, or charge for expensive services that were never rendered; and (3) the aging population that will continue to increase sharply and place greater strain on Medicare, Medicaid, and other health resources.

What solutions might arise if we apply a conflict/liberal approach to analyzing health care issues? As strange as it may seen, some conflict/liberal thinkers agree with the functionalist/conservative analysts who believe that managed care and other cost-containment strategies might be helpful in solving some health care problems. However, conflict/liberal theorists focus primary on managed care and other cost-containment methods as ways of reducing the control of physicians over patients and others in the medical-industrial complex, such as nurses, medical technicians, or other hospital and clinical personnel.

Conflict theorists are quick to point out that cost-containment efforts such as managed care are nothing more than a bandage being placed on the hemorrhaging cost of health care. This approach, say conflict theorists, does not deal with the larger systemic problem of how health care is delivered in a capitalist economy where medical care is a commodity like a pair of shoes or other items and services an individual might purchase in the marketplace.

For this reason, some conflict theorists believe that problems in health care will be reduced in the United States only when large-scale race-, class-, and gender-based inequalities in this nation are adequately addressed and reduced. As long as societal conditions—environmental pollution, lack of affordable housing, high levels of stress associated with working conditions or unemployment, inadequate nutrition, and lack of early diagnosis for diseases such as breast cancer and heart disease—affect people differentially based on their race, class, and gender, health care will be unequal. Most conflict theorists believe that short of a dramatic change in the nation's political economy, the primary way to deal with health care is to treat it as a common good that should be provided and regulated by the government just as highways, schools, courts, and national defense are. From this approach, the Affordable Care Act is a beginning for changing how health care is delivered in the United States and for providing services to a larger proportion of the population.

The Symbolic Interactionist Perspective

Symbolic interactionists believe that many problems pertaining to health and illness in our society are linked to social and cultural factors that influence how people define physical illness and mental illness. According to symbolic interactionists, we socially construct "health" and "illness" and how both should be treated. As a result, both medical and nonmedical "experts" play a role in determining what constitutes physical and mental illnesses and how these illnesses should be treated by society. For example, in 1997, under the Americans with Disabilities Act, the Equal Employment Opportunity Commission established guidelines requiring that employers take "reasonable steps" to accommodate employees with mental illnesses—the same requirement that previously applied only to people with physical disabilities (Stolberg, 1997). What exactly does "reasonable steps" mean? According to one analyst, "That could mean anything from a flexible

In the twenty-first century, health care delivery takes place in large medical complexes such as the one shown here. According to conflict theorists, medical centers are only one component of the much larger medical-industrial complex that generates billions of dollars in revenue annually.

schedule for an anxious person, to a desk near a window for a person who grows depressed with too little light, to a quiet work space for a schizophrenic" (Stolberg, 1997:E1).

Symbolic interactionists also examine how doctors and patients interact in health care settings. For example, medical schools provide future doctors with knowledge and skills that laypeople do not have. Given this competence gap, some physicians do not think that it is necessary—or possible—to communicate certain kinds of medical information to patients. Some hesitate to communicate the diagnosis of a fatal illness or, more often, might simply not explain why they are prescribing certain medications or what side effects or drug interactions could occur.

One way to solve this communication problem, according to symbolic interactionists, is to increase the number of family practice doctors, because these doctors usually focus on patient care and communication, not just the scientific and technological aspects of health care. Another way is to emphasize prevention and work with patients on behaviors to practice and avoid if they want to stay healthy. A third way to change health care is to limit the bureaucracies in mental hospitals where individuals are labeled by their diagnosis and not viewed as people with specific emotional and physical needs to be met. Finally, symbolic interactionists say, more public health campaigns are needed to make people aware of issues in health care and health care reform, and perhaps those campaigns need to emphasize what it is like to be unable to afford necessary health care. This approach has been extensively used by proponents of the Affordable Care Act, but some critics argue that these messages are not public service announcements but instead biased, and sometimes manipulative efforts, to shift public opinion and individual voters' views on certain social policy issues.

In a nutshell, what are some symbolic interactionist solutions to the health care problem? As previously stated, some analysts who use a symbolic interactionist approach focus on the doctor–patient relationship as being problematic. According to these analysts, the doctor–patient relationship should be demystified so that the physician does not have all of the social power in the encounter. Then better communication must be encouraged between health care providers and the patients who are the recipients of their services. These theorists argue that if patients were given the information and resources they need for prevention, self-treatment, and home care, the need and demand for expensive medical care would be greatly reduced (Stewart, 1995). For example, if patients received more information and encouragement from their doctors in regard to preventive measures that might improve their health, patients might become more concerned about weight control, exercise, going to a physician for regular checkups, and eliminating

habits such as smoking and excessive alcohol consumption that are potentially detrimental to their health.

Because of the emphasis on interpersonal communications in many symbolic interactionist approaches to health care, some other solutions deal with disease management after a patient has been diagnosed with a chronic condition such as heart disease, diabetes, or cancer. Those patients who believe that they can successfully communicate with their physicians and other health care providers are more likely to comply with health-related directives they have been given regarding a treatment regime, taking proper dosages of medications in a timely fashion, and routinely scheduling physical exams and other tests as needed or recommended. By contrast, those patients who do not have a good understanding of what their doctors have told them to do, or who receive an inadequate explanation about the importance of following a medical regime, will more often fail to follow the doctor's directions.

Symbolic interactionist views on the doctor–patient relationship are faced with a different set of challenges today because of newer technologies. Some physicians and nurses now routinely interact with established patients through text messages, e-mail communications, and social networking sites as a personal solution to larger, potential communication problems, particularly as doctors and other members of their medical staff typically see more patients per hour and per day than in the past: Patients can text or e-mail the doctor's office to get a prescription refilled, to ask a question, or to report such medical information as their blood pressure or glucose level if requested by the physician. However, there are new problems built into using newer forms of communication between doctors and patients because it sometimes is crucial for the doctor, nurse, or another health care professional to see the patient in order to diagnose a condition, prescribe the most appropriate medication, or determine if other health-related problems are present.

In the past, most patients relied primarily on doctors for health-related information. Today, many people receive medical information from the media and the Internet. Thousands of websites are devoted to health and medical information, ranging from potentially life-saving research in top medical journals to alternative therapies such as herbal preparations and colonic irrigation. Many computer bulletin boards, chat rooms, and Usenet newsgroups have emerged to support people with diseases such as AIDS and multiple sclerosis (Kantrowitz, 1993). Whether this proliferation of information helps demystify doctor–patient relationships remains to be seen, and as has been previously discussed, applying symbolic interactionist perspectives to problems does not address larger, systemic problems in the larger system of health care in the United States.

What is the future of health care in the United States? The answer to this question partly depends on the future of the Affordable Care Act as it is either implemented or challenged before the U.S. Supreme Court. Thus far, a Florida federal judge has ruled that Congress did not have the authority to pass this act because of its unique use of the commerce clause of the U.S. Constitution to mandate that all Americans must enter into a commercial relationship with a private (insurance) company because they will be required by law to carry health insurance coverage. Some legal attacks have focused only on this dimension of the law, but others seek to strike down the entire law. As some legal analysts have suggested, if the Supreme Court does hear this case and agrees with the Florida judge, the health care bill will be undone and the government will lose some of its power to use legislation to solve problems (Lindenberger, 2011). On the other hand, if the Affordable Care Act is fully implemented, health insurance and health care delivery will look quite different in the future than they have in the past. It remains to be seen what will happen and when it will occur.

SUMMARY

✓•⸢ **Study** and **Review** on **mysoclab.com**

■ **Why is health care a social problem?**

Health care is a social problem because, according to the World Health Organization, health is a state of complete physical, mental, and social well-being. In other words, health is a social issue. Although people in the United States pay more for health services than people in other high-income nations, our expenditures do not translate into improved life expectancy for everyone.

■ **What kinds of health problems cause most of today's high health care costs?**

Because acute illnesses (e.g., measles, polio) are largely under control with vaccinations and improved public health practices, most health problems today are chronic diseases (e.g., arthritis, diabetes, heart disease) or disabilities (e.g., back injuries, hearing or vision problems, mental retardation), which require long-term treatment. Medical advances mean that many people who are born with serious disabilities survive, as do many who would have died from acute illnesses or accidents in earlier times. As more people survive and live longer, more are likely to experience chronic illnesses and disabilities.

■ **Why is AIDS considered a health crisis in the United States and other nations?**

First, the number of cases is rising annually. Second, many people infected worldwide are infected through heterosexual intercourse; it is not a disease that is restricted to any single group. Third, there is no cure; once HIV develops into AIDS, it is fatal. Fourth, treatment is complex and costly and typically requires lengthy stays in a hospital or hospice. Finally, numerous ethical issues (e.g., issues relating to testing) have yet to be resolved.

■ **Why is mental illness a social problem?**

Mental illness is a social problem because of the number of people it affects, the difficulty in defining and identifying mental disorders, and the ways in which it is treated. Deinstitutionalization—discharging mental patients from hospitals into the community—was considered a solution to the problem of warehousing patients, but it has created new problems.

■ **Historically, what kinds of health care have been available in the United States?**

Originally, there was fee-for-service care in which patients paid directly for treatment they received from doctors and hospitals. The Great Depression brought about third-party fee-for-service care: Patients pay premiums to private or public health insurance companies that in turn pay the doctors and hospitals. Both of these health care structures are expensive because there are few restrictions on fees charged by health care providers.

■ **What other types of private health care insurance are available in the United States?**

Some insurance companies now offer preferred provider organizations (PPOs) in which doctors contract to treat insured patients for set fees; these fees may be higher or lower than the fees for other patients who are not enrolled in the PPO. For a set monthly fee a health maintenance organization (HMO) provides total care with an emphasis on prevention; patients must use the doctors and hospitals affiliated with the HMO. Managed care refers to any system of cost containment that closely monitors and controls health care providers' decisions about what medical tests, procedures, and other services should be provided to patients. Private insurance will look much different in if the Affordable Care Act is fully implemented in the future.

■ **What is the difference between Medicare and Medicaid?**

Medicare is public health insurance for people age sixty-five and over that is funded by Medicare payments. Medicaid is public health insurance for people who are poor and either aged, blind, disabled, or pregnant; it is funded by federal and state governments. Both programs are considered costly to the public because there are no incentives to keep down costs.

- **How do race, class, and gender affect health care?**
  Research shows that people of color across class lines and low-income whites typically receive less preventive care and less optimal management of chronic diseases than others do. Women have been underrepresented in the medical profession (though that is changing); medical training, practice, and research are male-centered; and women have received differential treatment for certain kinds of medical problems.

- **What are the sociological explanations for health care problems?**
  Functionalists consider the sick role a form of deviance that medicine as an institution controlled until recently. Today, however, the supply of and demand for health care means that patients incur large medical bills and are unproductive to society. Some functionalists believe that the whole health system must be reorganized; others think that managed care is the best answer. Some conflict theorists believe that our health problems are rooted in capitalism and the medical-industrial complex; others believe that only when race-, class-, and gender-based inequalities are reduced will inequalities in health care be reduced. Symbolic interactionists believe that communication problems between doctors and patients create many of our health problems and that people must, among other things, become more involved in health care issues and health care reform.

KEY TERMS

acute diseases, p. 226
chronic diseases, p. 226
deinstitutionalization, p. 230
disability, p. 226

health maintenance organization
(HMO), p. 235
infant mortality rate, p. 225
life expectancy, p. 224

managed care, p. 235
medical-industrial complex, p. 242
total institution, p. 230

QUESTIONS FOR CRITICAL THINKING

1. Because the United States takes pride in its technological and social standing in the world, people are usually surprised to learn that our infant mortality rate is higher than the rates in most other high-income countries. Why is it and what do you think individuals can do at the community level to save these young lives?

2. In what ways are race, class, and gender intertwined with mental disorders? Consider causes and treatments.

3. Will the Affordable Health Care Act help reduce costs and increase medical services, especially for the uninsured, in the United States? Based on what you have heard and read, what do you think will be the future of health care in this country?

Succeed with MySocLab® www.mysoclab.com

The new MySocLab delivers proven results in helping students succeed, provides engaging experiences that personalize learning, and comes from a trusted partner with educational expertise and a deep commitment to helping students and instructors achieve their goals.

Here are a few activities you will find for this chapter:

Watch on **mysoclab.com**   **Core Concepts** video clips feature sociologists in action, exploring important concepts in the study of Social Problems. Watch:
- Managed Care

Explore on **mysoclab.com**   **Social Explorer** is an interactive application that allows you to explore Census data through interactive maps. Explore:
- Social Explorer Activity: Mental Illness in the U.S.

Read on **mysoclab.com**   **MySocLibrary** includes primary source readings from classic and contemporary sociologists. Read:
- The Medically Uninsured: Will They Always Be With Us?

The Changing Family

THINKING SOCIOLOGICALLY

- Why do some people believe that the family as a social institution is in a state of decline?

- How are family problems linked to larger issues of social inequality in society?

- Does extensive media coverage of high-profile domestic violence cases make us more aware of the causes and consequences of this pressing social problem?

Being a single parent right now is very tough. It's a lot of extra work, which I don't mind doing, but I still think what bothers me is that I think that my children are being short-changed. They don't get the mother side of it. I'm not a woman. I never have been. I try to nurture my children as much as I can, but I'm still a guy, and these are two girls. And I feel like sometimes they get short-changed, and I feel bad for that. But there's nothing I can do to help that at this point.

—A working-class Latino (Hispanic), single father of two tells a researcher why he worries about what his daughters might be missing without a mother present in their household (quoted in Nelson, 2010:102).

[The greatest difficulty is] knowing when to step in and when to let her be on her own. . . . I think my parents were parents who didn't ask questions that much, so I don't know if they ever really knew what I was thinking about. I didn't find myself confiding in them and sharing, but I think [my daughter and I] have a different form of communication where she can share if she needs to. And I'm not sure my parents would have been ready to share.

—Jeff Wright, a widowed father of a teenage daughter, describes his concern about guiding his daughter through adolescence while at the same time helping her cope with the recent death of her mother (quoted in Nelson, 2010:93).

Many people experience family-related problems similar to those described by these two fathers who are rearing their children alone: How to nurture children and be there for them without hovering over them or encroaching on their personal space. However, there is something unique about the lived experiences quoted: When we hear the term *single-parent families,* the first image that comes to mind for many of us is a single woman who resides with one or more of her own children under the age of eighteen. But, today single-parent families—like other kinds of families—come in many varieties and reflect differences in parenting styles. Although the economic hardships associated with single parenthood and divorce are particularly problematic for women, single-parenting for men is a difficult task also because of societal perceptions about the appropriate roles for mothers and fathers in the lives of their children. Thinking about these issues from a sociological perspective, we may conclude that family-related problems are a challenge not only for individuals such as the ones described but also to our entire society. Let's take a closer look at contemporary families and some problems many of them face.

THE NATURE OF FAMILIES

What is a family? For many years, this question has generated heated debate. Although some analysts using a functionalist/conservative approach typically state that any definition of the family must emphasize tradition and stability, other analysts argue that any useful definition of families must take into account diversity and social change. Traditionally, family has been defined as a group of people who are related to one another by blood, marriage, or adoption and who live together, form an economic unit, and bear and raise children. According to this definition, families are created through childbearing, and it is the parent–child relationship that links generations. Today, however, the traditional definition of family is often modified to incorporate diverse living arrangements and relationships such as single-parent households, cohabiting unmarried couples, domestic partnerships of lesbian or gay couples, and several generations of family members (grandparent, parent, and child) living under the same roof. To encompass these arrangements, we will use the following definition as we look at family-related social problems: **Families are relationships in which people live together with commitment, form an economic unit and care for any young, and consider the group critical to their identity** (Lamanna and Riedmann, 2012).

DID YOU KNOW

- Less than one-quarter (21 percent) of U.S. families are made up of married couples with children under age eighteen.

- Heterosexual cohabitation has become an increasingly popular alternative to marriage for unemployed males.

- The estimated U.S. rate of maltreatment for children between the ages of zero and seventeen is 10 per 1,000 children in the same age category.

Changing Family Structure and Patterns

The basis of the traditional family structure is **kinship**, **a social network of people based on common ancestry, marriage, or adoption.** Kinship is very important in preindustrial societies because it serves as an efficient means of producing and distributing food and goods (e.g., clothing, materials for building shelter) and transferring property and power from one generation to the next. In many preindustrial societies the primary kinship unit is the **extended family—a family unit composed of relatives in addition to parents and children, all of whom live in the same household or in close proximity.** Extended families typically include grandparents, uncles, aunts, and/or other relatives in addition to parents and children. When the growing and harvesting of crops are the basis of economic production, extended families mean that large numbers of people participate in food production, which can be essential to survival. Living together also enables family members to share other resources, such as shelter and transportation. Though

Read the **Document**
The Way We Weren't: The Myth and the Reality of the "Traditional" Family on **mysoclab.com**

extended families are not common in the United States, they are in some countries in Latin America, Africa, Asia, and parts of eastern and southern Europe. Often relatives who are part of extended families help each other out in ways that contribute to the economic survival of the entire family grouping, such as grandparents or other relatives who care for the children of migrant workers who leave their kids behind to work abroad and send money home to support the family back home (see Box 11.1).

With industrialization, other social institutions begin to fulfill kinship system functions. The production and distribution of goods and services, for example, largely shifts to the economic sector. The form of kinship that is most typical in industrialized nations is the **nuclear family—a family unit composed of one or two parents and their dependent children that lives apart from other relatives.** The nuclear family in an industrialized society functions primarily to regulate sexual activity, socialize children, and provide family members with affection and companionship. Although many people view the two-parent nuclear family as the ideal family, today, married couples with children under age eighteen now constitute only 21 percent of U.S. families (U.S. Census Bureau, 2010). This is a significant decrease since 1970, when two out of five families (40 percent) were

Social Problems in Global Perspective

Motherhood from Afar: Parenting Other People's Children to Give One's Own Children a Better Future

When Maridel Sagum left her twin daughters in the Philippines to work as a nanny in France, they were 8 years old.... Twelve years [later] ... the twins are young women with colleges degrees and Ms. Sagum, 47, ... will soon see them again for the first time since 1998.

—Journalist Katrin Bennhold (2011) describes a situation that is not uncommon: Many women around the world take care of other people's children in hopes of giving their own children a better life.

Since I have been at [the Time 100 Gala], I have given birth to two boys and I've left Saturday Night Live and I started my own TV show, and it's been a crazy couple of years, and I thought who ... [has] influenced me? And it was the women who helped me take care of my children: It is Jackie Johnson from Trinidad and it is Dawa Chodon from Tibet, who come to my house and help me raise my children.

—Actress Amy Poehler thanks her children's nannies for their importance in her life when she gave an award acceptance speech (quoted in Belkin, 2011).

Both of these excerpts call our attention to the significant role that women around the world play as nannies who rear other people's children, even when these nannies have children of their own that they leave behind to become "undocumented" or "illegal" workers on other nations.

According to journalist Katrin Bennhold (2011), undocumented women workers are willing to sacrifice so that their children can have opportunities they otherwise would not have. These women often work six-day weeks, send most of their earnings home for the children, and know that they cannot leave the country where they are employed to visit their families. Some of the undocumented nannies have the luxury of talking to their children by way of Skype or by text messaging, but others do not see their children for lengthy periods of time. Recent statistics from the

two-parent households; and a steep drop since 2000, when the figure was 24 percent. Sociologists attribute the decrease to a greater number of births among unmarried women, a trend toward postponing or forgoing marriage and childbearing, and a relatively high rate of separation and divorce. It is also possible that marriage with children has become the province of people who are college educated and affluent, while the working class and poor have steered away from marriage and opted to live together and raise children without being married. Does this mean that the future of the U.S. family is in doubt? We turn to that issue now.

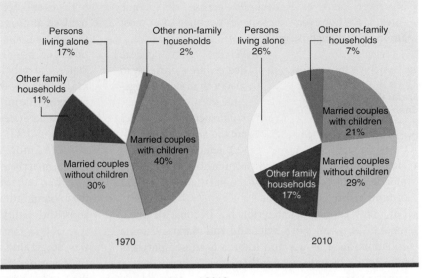

Figure 11.1 U.S. Household by type, 1970 and 2010
Source: U.S. Census Bureau, 2010

Are U.S. Families in Decline?

Will the family as a social institution disappear in the future? Families are not necessarily in decline, but some new patterns have emerged:

- Compared with previous decades, fewer people are currently married. In 2010, slightly less than half (49 percent) of U.S. households contained a married couple. By contrast, about 71 percent of households in 1970 contained a married couple (see Figure 11.1).

World Bank suggest that nannies sending money home to their families account for remittances in the amount of $325 billion each year. Unlike migration in the past where women moved as dependents of male migrants, if they migrated at all, many more women are now moving on their own to work in other nations. Increasingly, women are the primary (or only) breadwinners in their families.

In a cost–benefit analysis, migrant nannies benefit financially by moving from a lower-income nation to a higher-income nation. They also benefit by knowing that their own children will have more economic resources because of hard work. On the other hand, the costs are also high: The women do not get to spend time with their children or see them do basic things such as take their first step or speak their first word. Instead, the nannies see other people's children go through these important life stages.

Sociologist Arlie Hochschild has suggested that the situation of migrant nannies and other international household workers could be made easier if the rich nations that rely on the women's work would introduce legislation to help the women obtain work permits, bring their children with them, or at least have an opportunity to return home

to see the children regularly. Because most of the women are undocumented workers in the United States illegally, the nannies fear that if they return home to visit their children they will not be allowed to return to this country, which is where their livelihood—and to them, the future prospects of their children—are located.

Questions for Consideration

1. What larger societal factors in the United States have contributed to the large number of undocumented women immigrants who work as nannies and other household workers in this country?

2. According to journalist Katrin Bennhold, who wrote the article, the story of women's undocumented work is one of both "emotional hardship" and "female empowerment." How do you think the work of the nannies described here might contribute to female empowerment on a global basis?

3. The women discussed in this feature came from the Philippines, Trinidad, and Tibet. What other countries can you name that make a significant contribution to the number of undocumented women (and men) workers in the United States?

- Marriage rates have declined across all income categories; however, rates have declined the most among lower-income individuals.

✻ Explore the Concept on mysoclab.com
Social Explorer Activity: Changing Household Size Between 1970 and 2000 on mysoclab.com

- People with college degrees are more likely to marry than non-college-educated individuals. Dual-income families are the norm among college-educated persons.

- However, college-educated women often postpone marriage, choosing to live with a partner for a period of time before marriage.

- For many people, cohabitation has become an intermediate step between singlehood and marriage. Some cohabitation is by gay and lesbian domestic partners who reside in states where they are not permitted by law to marry.

- More people are living alone today because they either never married or experienced divorce or the death of a spouse.

- There are more single-parent households than in the past. One of the largest increases has been in the number of single-father households.

If we examine these trends in marriage and family relations, it does not necessarily mean that the family as a social institution is declining: It is simply changing. For example, 55 percent of all people age fifteen and older in 2009 had been married once, 12 percent had been married twice, and 3 percent had been married more times. More than half (55 percent) of currently married couples had been married for at least fifteen years, and 35 percent of currently married couples had reached their twenty-fifth anniversary (census.gov, 2011). As these figures show, marriage and family arrangements may be more complex and diverse, but they are not necessarily in a state of decline. In the 1990s, sociologist Andrew Cherlin predicted that the family would last as a social institution precisely because it can adapt to social change and modify its form. So far, his prediction has held true. And, the United States is not alone in seeing family structure undergo profound change: Around the world, in both rich and poor nations, new patterns are emerging in regard to single-parent households, divorce rates, and other factors that affect families (see Box 11.1 on page 248–249).

Changing Views on Marriage and Families

Are our views relatively consistent regarding marriage and families over time? The answer to this question is both yes and no. The term *marriage* refers to a legally recognized and/or socially approved arrangement between two individuals that carries certain rights and obligations and usually involves sexual activity. In the United States, the only legal form of marriage is **monogamy—a marriage between one woman and one man.** The marriage rate (number of marriages per 1,000 population) in the United States was 10.6 percent in 2008, as compared to 12.5 in 2000 and 14.9 in 1990 (U.S. Census Bureau, 2010). As more states have changed their laws to allow for the marriage of same sex couples, law at the federal level has not been changed despite announcements by the Obama administration that it will not defend the constitutionality of the Defense of Marriage Act.

Getting married was once a cultural imperative. There was "something wrong" with a person who didn't marry. But since the 1970s, people's attitudes toward marriage and the family have changed as other aspects of society have changed. Cultural guidelines on marriage and childbearing have changed as our society has experienced a broader cultural shift toward autonomy and personal growth. In the 1970s, according to Cherlin (1992:127), "Family life became a matter of personal choice in which individuals made decisions based on a calculus of self-interest and self-fulfillment. Marriage was still desirable, but no one any longer had to be married to be a proper member of society." Marriage also became much less of an economic necessity for women in the 1970s because of new job opportunities and rising incomes. Today, our perspectives have greatly changed on women in the workplace, and their earnings are often crucial to the economic well-being of the family.

Of course, we cannot discuss marriage without also taking into consideration the high rate of divorce in the United States. Over the past century and beyond, the U.S. divorce rate (the number of divorces per 1,000 population) shifted from a low of 0.7 in 1900 to an all-time high of 5.3 in 1981. In 2005, the divorce rate leveled off at 3.6 per 1,000 population ages fifteen to sixty-four years but then moved upward to 5.2 in 2008 (U.S. Census Bureau, 2010). Though many people believe that marriage should last "until death do us part," others feel that marriage is a commitment "for as long as love allows." Through a pattern of marriage, divorce, and remarriage, many people reaffirm their commitment to the institution of marriage but not to the individual they initially married. This pattern of successive marriages, in which a person has several spouses over a lifetime but is legally married to only one partner at a time, is referred to as *serial monogamy.* Some social analysts consider serial monogamy a natural adaptation to other social changes in society; others think that it is detrimental to individuals and to society and serves as further evidence of deeply embedded problems in the family as a social institution. One thing is certain, however: Much greater diversity exists in intimate relationships and families in this nation.

DIVERSITY IN INTIMATE RELATIONSHIPS AND FAMILIES

Greater diversity in intimate relationships and families in the United States has come about because of dramatic increases in (1) singlehood, (2) postponing marriage, (3) living together without marriage (cohabitation and domestic partnerships), (4) dual-earner marriages, and (5) one-parent families.

Singlehood

Although most will eventually marry, there are about 74 million adults (40.2 million men and 34.0 million women) in the United States who have never been married (U.S. Census Bureau, 2010). The proportion of the U.S. population that has never been married has continued to grow since the 1960s. By 2009, 30 percent of all people age fifteen and older had never been married. Some people choose singlehood over marriage because it means greater freedom from commitments to another person. Others choose it because of more career opportunities (especially for women), the availability of sexual partners without marriage, the belief that the single lifestyle is full of excitement, and the desire for self-sufficiency and freedom to change and experiment.

Some people are single because they have not found an acceptable partner or out of necessity. Because of macrolevel factors such as war, recession, and high rates of unemployment, many young people cannot afford to marry and set up their own households. Indeed, even some college graduates have found that they cannot earn enough money to set up households separate from those of their parents, and more people in their twenties and thirties are now returning to live, at least for a period of time, with their parents.

Although the unmarried population has increased across racial and ethnic categories, African Americans and Latinos are more likely to have never married than are white (non-Hispanic) Americans. Among males age fifteen and over, about 47 percent of African Americans have never been married, compared to about 38.7 percent of Latinos and 26.1 percent of whites. Among women age fifteen and over, about 45.5 percent of African Americans have never married,

Singlehood is an important period in the life of many people. Being single is often idealized by the media, as in the HBO series *Entourage*, where these characters are shown going out together for a night on the town.

compared to 33.7 percent of Latinas and 22.7 percent of whites (U.S. Census Bureau, 2010). If these figures seem to be unusually high, the U.S. Census Bureau has changed the way in which such data are compiled, now using age fifteen, rather than age eighteen, when calculating data for never-married persons. However, still striking is the lower marriage rate among African Americans when compared to Latinos/as, and whites (non-Hispanic). Trends that may contribute to these rates include:

1. Young African American men have higher rates of mortality than young African American women do.
2. More African American women are college educated and tend to make more money than African American men do.
3. Some African American men have less to offer to potential female partners in a marriage because they have experienced discrimination, have had limited educational opportunities, and now have few job prospects.
4. Reported rates of homosexuality are higher among African American men than those in other racial-ethnic categories. Homosexuality rates among African American men are also higher than for women.
5. More African American men than African American women marry members of other racial-ethnic groups.

The numbers of singles have also increased among Latinos/as because a larger proportion of this population is made up of younger people than are non-Latino (non-Hispanic) populations. In other words, many Latinos/as have not reached the age when marriage is considered to be appropriate among family and friends.

Among older singles who want to marry for the first time or to remarry after divorce or widowhood, men have an advantage over women because men are more likely to marry women who are younger than themselves, particularly in second and subsequent marriages. Moreover, because women live longer than men, the pool of eligible persons seeking marriage contains more women than men, and this imbalance becomes more pronounced in the older age categories.

Postponing Marriage

Young people today are less eager to get married than they were two decades ago; many are remaining single into their late twenties. The median age at which men first get married is 28.2 years, and the median age for women is 26.1 years (U.S. Census Bureau, 2010). Although the age at which people marry for the first time has been rising steadily since the 1950s, it has accelerated since the 1970s. Over the past forty years, the proportion of women aged twenty-five to twenty-nine who have never married has more than tripled.

Why are more people postponing first marriages or choosing not to marry at all? Although some reasons are the same as those for staying single, sociologists suggest four key factors: (1) economic uncertainty, (2) women's increasing participation in the labor force, (3) sexual relationships outside marriage having become more socially acceptable and contraception having become more effective, and (4) as a result of rising divorce rates, less eagerness to get married and thus risk getting divorced. Likewise, a significant increase in cohabitation and domestic partnerships contributes to the percentage of people who are counted as single or postponing marriage.

Cohabitation, Domestic Partnerships, and Same-Sex Marriages

Cohabitation **is two adults living together in a sexual relationship without being legally married.** It is not known how many people actually cohabit because the U.S. Census Bureau refers to couples who live together simply as "unmarried couple households" and does not ask about emotional or sexual involvement. According to Census Bureau data, heterosexual couples who are most likely to cohabit are under age forty-five and are not in school. Divorced individuals are also choosing cohabitation as an alternative to marriage (Sassler, 2010). In newly formed cohabiting couples in 2010, the partners were younger, less likely to be white (non-Hispanic)

Americans, and were more likely to live in the South (Kreider, 2010).

Between 2009 and 2010, the number of opposite sex couples who were cohabiting increased by 13 percent. Economic conditions nationwide and the partners' employment statuses are key factors that contributed to a decision to cohabit, particularly among couples who began cohabiting more recently (within a year prior to the study). Both partners were employed in only 39 percent of newly formed couples, as compared to 50 percent of couples in longer-term relationships. Living together, rather than separately, reduces how much each individual must pay in rent or mortgage payments, as well as other household expenses. Apparently men who have lost jobs, or who are otherwise unemployed, tend to benefit from cohabitation: In 2010, nearly one-fourth (24 percent) of all men in newly formed cohabiting couples had not been employed in the last year as compared to 14 percent of men in newly formed couples in 2009 (Kreider, 2010). This change reflects not only the increasing popularity of cohabitation among unemployed men but also the difficulty that many people have experienced in the job market during the Great Recession and the slow recovery in its aftermath. With the U.S. unemployment rate hovering between 9.0 and 9.2 percent nationwide, cohabitation may become an even more viable option for men.

Does cohabitation lead to marriage? For some couples, cohabitation is a form of trial marriage and constitutes an intermediate stage between dating and marriage. For others, cohabitation is an end in itself, and the issue of cohabitation leading to marriage does not appear to be important. Examples include divorced persons who do not wish to remarry and older individuals nearing retirement age who do not want to comingle their financial resources because of their children's inheritance, or those who are reliance on a former spouse's pension, or those who want a chance to do what they would like without concerning themselves with someone else's wishes (Sassler, 2010). According to the results of one national survey, many cohabiting relationships do not last for extended periods of time: Only 13 percent of cohabitations remain intact after five years if partners do not make the transition into marriage (Sassler, 2010).

However, for gay and lesbian couples not living in states where same-sex marriage is legal, cohabitation or domestic partnerships have been the only choices in many years. Because laws in most states have not allowed same-sex couples to marry legally, they have established *domestic partnerships* (see Chapter 6). **Domestic partnerships are household partnerships in which an unmarried couple lives together in a committed, sexually intimate** relationship and is granted the same rights and benefits as those accorded to married heterosexual couples. In some states with limited protection for domestic partnerships, some employers offer full benefits to domestic partners; however, many do not. Over the past decade, bitter controversy has emerged over the legal status of gay and lesbian couples, particularly those who seek to make their relationship a legally binding commitment through marriage. As of July 2011, same-sex marriage licenses are granted in Connecticut, Iowa, Massachusetts, New Hampshire, New York, Vermont, Washington, DC, and the Coquille Indian Tribe in Oregon, but a recent, major change at the federal level may bring about additional changes by the time you read this. For a number of years, same-sex marriage was recognized only at the state level because—for the purposes of federal law—the 1996 Defense of Marriage Act explicitly defines marriage as the union of one man and one woman. As a result, no act or agency of the federal government recognized same-sex marriage until President Obama's 2011 pronouncement that the Defense of Marriage Act is unconstitutional and his order that the U.S. Justice Department stop defending this law in court. This highly controversial decision was applauded by gay and lesbian rights advocates but sharply denounced by conservative political leaders. This decision raises many new questions about whether gay couples living in the eight states that already have legally recognized same-sex marriage may be discriminated against by the federal government, and it also brings to the forefront the more basic question about whether same-sex couples should have a legal right to marry. The status of same-sex marriages no doubt will remain in the public eye and before the courts for a number of years to come.

Dual-Earner Marriages and Women as Breadwinners

In the past thirty years, two major shifts in family life have occurred because more women are in the paid workforce than ever before. More women with children now hold down full-time employment, and some women are their family's primary source of income, even if a husband is present in the household. In 1975, only two out of every five mothers with a child under age six held a paid job; however, almost 64 percent of women in this category were employed in 2007 (NACCRRA.org, 2011).

Dual-earner marriages—**marriages in which both spouses are in the labor force**—account for about 57 percent of all marriages in the United States. For families with children under age five with employed mothers and income less than $18,000 a year, the mother's income typically accounts for 95 percent of all household income. By contrast, in families with income between $36,000 and $60,000, the mother's income usually makes up slightly more than half (53 percent) of all household income (NACCRRA.org, 2011). A central problem facing couples in dual-earner marriages is how to have sufficient time for both family and work. By the end of the workday, some people are too tired to spend much time with family members. Other people are employed in jobs that require their attention 24/7 (twenty-four hours a day, seven days a week), particularly jobs where the company's employees and clients are scattered around the world or where it is assumed that a person will always be available for work-related communications.

Many married women who are employed outside the household face hours of domestic work and child care when they arrive at home. In the past, studies found that men were less likely to participate in domestic work. (In some households this remains true in the 2010s.) In a 1989 study, sociologist Arlie Hochschild coined the term *second shift*—**the domestic work that many employed women perform at home after completing their work day on the job**—to describe the differential effect that being employed outside the household had on women as compared to men. According to Hochschild, the unpaid housework that women do on the second shift amounts to an extra month of work each year. In households with small children or many children, the amount of housework increases. Although many things have changed since Hochschild's study, the key

> ◉──Watch on **mysoclab.com**
> *Women in the Workplace* on **mysoclab.com**

This is an increasingly familiar sight in many U.S. neighborhoods where both parents are employed outside the household and have child-care responsibilities at home as well. How might our nation be more responsive to the needs of parents in dual-earner marriages and their children?

issue of women's domestic work, combined with their paid employment, remains a compelling issue in many American households. There are only so many hours in the day, and someone must do the housework and child care if family life is to function smoothly. On the other hand, workplace demands, particularly in the increasingly 24/7 technology-driven economy, add a burden on women (as well as men) that may reduce the amount of their physical and emotional well-being.

In many families in the 2010s, more husbands share household and child-care responsibilities. Couples with more egalitarian ideas about women's and men's roles tend to share more equally in food preparation, housework, and child care. An *egalitarian family* is one in which the partners share power and authority equally. As women have gained new educational and employment opportunities, a trend toward more egalitarian relationships has become evident in the United States. According to some research, family life has changed significantly in terms of the work–family balancing that women and men do. For example, men's absolute and proportionate contributions to household tasks have increased substantially over the past three decades. Child care has been the area of family life in which men's contribution has increased most significantly. Some studies show that men have tripled the amount of time they spend in child care, and researchers believe that men's involvement in family work will continue to grow rather than stall, as some originally predicted. If these assumptions are correct, dual-earner couples and other families where women are the primary breadwinners will continue to work out mutually satisfying arrangements about how men and women can share the responsibilities of breadwinning and family care without one partner bearing more of the burden than the other and without family discord which is dysfunctional for everyone in the family (Sullivan, 2008). However, problems associated with providing economic support for the family and rearing children are even more pressing in many one-parent households.

Comparing Two-Parent and One-Parent Households

When the mother and father in a two-parent household truly share parenting, children have the benefit of two primary caregivers. Some researchers have found that when fathers take an active part in raising the children, the effect is beneficial for all family members. Fathers find increased contact with their children provides more opportunities for personal and emotional gratification (Coltrane, 2004).

However, living in a two-parent family does not guarantee children a happy childhood. Children whose parents argue constantly, are alcoholics, or abuse them have a worse family experience than do children in a single-parent family where there is a supportive environment. Women who are employed full-time and are single parents probably have the greatest burden of all. These women must fulfill their paid employment duties and meet the needs of their children and the household, often with little help from ex-husbands or relatives.

How prevalent are one-parent households? There were 19.8 million one-parent families in 2010, and single mothers headed 17.3 million of those, as compared with 2.5 million single-father families. In that same year, 26 percent of children lived with one-parent only. Twenty-three percent of children between the ages of zero and seventeen lived with only their mothers, 3 percent lived with only their fathers (U.S. Census Bureau, 2010).

What effect does a one-parent household have on children? According to some studies, children who grow up in a single-parent household headed by the mother are at risk for problems such as poor academic achievement, dropping out of school, drug and alcohol abuse, teen pregnancy, early marriage, and divorce. However, other studies reach different conclusions: There are benefits to growing up in a one-parent family because children develop a sense of responsibility and learn how to deal with independence at an earlier age. Some analysts emphasize that the socioeconomic status of the family is an important variable in assessing the experiences of children in one-parenthouseholds headed by women. Poverty, unemployment, crowded and unsafe housing and neighborhoods, gangs, and high crime rates are factors that can negatively influence a child's life much more than living with one parent only.

What about the fathers of children in one-parent households headed by women? Although many fathers remain involved in their children's lives, others become "Disneyland daddies"—occasionally taking their children out for recreational activities or buying them presents on birthdays and holidays. Personal choice, workplace demands on time and energy, location of the ex-wife's residence, and limitations placed on visitation by custody arrangements are all factors that affect how often absentee fathers visit their children. Many parents receive joint custody of their children, and it appears that this legal arrangement can minimize the disruption of divorce in a child's life if the ex-spouses cooperate with each other and live in relatively close geographic proximity. Ex-spouses who constantly argue or live far away from each other can create serious problems for children.

CHILD-RELATED FAMILY ISSUES

One of the major issues facing many individuals and families today is reproductive freedom, a term that implies both the desire of individuals to have a child and the desire *not to have* one. As sociologists Leslie King and Madonna Harrington Meyer (1997:8) explain,

> The average woman is fertile, and therefore must attempt to control her reproductivity, for one-half of her life. For most women, it is the preoccupation with preventing births that consumes their health-care dollars and energies; for a small minority, it is the preoccupation with achieving a birth that dominates. The ability to control fertility is, to a great extent, linked to access to various forms of reproductive health services, including contraceptives and infertility treatments. Yet, in the United States, insurance coverage of contraceptive and infertility treatments is fragmented.

Reproductive Freedom, Contraception, and Abortion

Reproductive freedom has been a controversial issue throughout much of U.S. history. In the nineteenth century, the government instituted formal, legal policies to ensure that some people would not produce children. By incarcerating "wayward girls" and limiting their right to marry and by passing laws that permitted the sterilization of individuals who were poor, criminal, or "feebleminded," political leaders attempted to prevent people who were thought to be "unfit" from reproducing (Luker, 1996). Today, say some researchers, the government discourages births among the poor by mandating the coverage of contraceptives for women on Medicaid (King and Harrington Meyer, 1997).

Contraceptive devices such as condoms and diaphragms were widely available and relatively technologically sophisticated in the first half of the nineteenth century. By the 1850s, however, the government had begun to establish policies limiting their availability to prevent a drop in the birthrate among white Americans (Luker, 1996). Abortion became illegal in most states by 1900. Physicians—among others—had begun to crusade against abortion in the 1800s because most procedures

were done by people (such as barbers) who had no medical training. Some physicians apparently believed that if these abortionists could be stopped, physicians would become the arbiters of whether or not women should have abortions. The ban on abortion and the limited availability of contraceptives did not prevent wealthy women from practicing birth control or procuring an abortion (Luker, 1996).

It was not until the introduction of the birth control pill in 1960 that women gained almost complete control of their fertility. The "Pill" quickly became the most popular contraceptive among married women in the United States. During this time and into the early 1970s, public opinion about women's reproductive freedom began to change somewhat. In 1971, the U.S. Supreme Court upheld women's right to privacy in reproductive matters in *Griswold v. Connecticut*. The Court ruled that laws prohibiting the use of contraception by married couples violated the constitutional right to privacy. In subsequent cases, the Court included unmarried adults and minors in this protection.

Many U.S. women spend about 90 percent of their fertile years trying to avoid pregnancy. An estimated 98 percent of all women who have ever had sexual intercourse have used one or more contraceptive methods (CDC, 2010). Unplanned pregnancies are usually the result of not using contraceptives or using contraceptives that do not work or are not used as intended. By the age of forty-five, at least half of American women will experience an unintended pregnancy. About half of all pregnancies in the United States each year are unintended, and approximately four in ten of these are terminated by abortion (Guttmacher Institute, 2011). About 40 percent of pregnancies among white (non-Hispanic) American women are unintended, as compared to 70 percent among African American women, and slightly more than half (54 percent) among Latinas (Hispanics).

In the 2010s, poor women are getting pregnant unintentionally at considerably higher rates than they were in the mid-1990s; consequently they are giving birth to more unplanned children and having more abortions. By contrast, unplanned pregnancies among middle- and upper-income women have declined substantially. Sociologists attribute this change to the fact that state and federal reproductive health programs have been cut back substantially and that those programs that still exist have more restrictions placed on the kinds of services they may provide to clients. For example, many programs now focus on abstinence rather than contraception, and many clients are unwilling to accept

Planned Parenthood facilities throughout the nation have experienced opposition and sometimes defunding even as advocates have pointed out that these organizations provide the only affordable health care option available for many low-income women.

this restriction on their sexual conduct (Guttmacher Institute, 2011).

Since the 1960s, the roles that government, religious organizations, physicians, and the legal establishment should play in reproductive decisions continue to be highly controversial in this country. Perhaps the most significant legal action involving reproductive rights was the Supreme Court decision in *Roe v. Wade* (1973) that women have a constitutionally protected right to choose abortion, and the state cannot unduly interfere with or prohibit that right. The Court distinguished among trimesters of pregnancy in its ruling. During the first three months, decisions about the pregnancy are strictly private—made by women in consultation with their physicians; in the second trimester, the state may impose some restrictions but only to safeguard women's health; in the third trimester, the state may prohibit abortion—because of the fetus's viability (ability to survive outside a woman's womb)—except when necessary to preserve the woman's life or health.

Although the Court has not overturned *Roe v. Wade,* subsequent laws and decisions have eroded some of women's reproductive rights and made abortions more difficult to obtain, particularly for poor women and unmarried pregnant teenagers. For example, in 1993, the Supreme Court ruled that requiring a minor to get written permission from both parents for an abortion did not constitute an "undue burden" for a fourteen-or fifteen-year-old girl. And in 2003, Congress enacted a law banning partial birth (late term) abortions. Various states have further limited access to abortion services by placing requirements on pregnant women, such as proposed laws that women must view an ultrasound of the fetus before an abortion can be performed or placing waiting periods on the time between a Planned Parenthood consultation appointment and the time when an abortion can be performed.

Opposition to abortion has resulted in violence against physicians and the personnel of clinics where abortions are performed, which has caused a number of facilities to close. In response, in 1993, Congress passed the Freedom of Access to Clinic Entrances Act, making it a federal offense to attack an abortion clinic or obstruct clients from going to one. Nevertheless, antiabortion activists continue to try to make it difficult for women to have abortions. Some social analysts fear that if abortion is restricted, women will once again seek abortions in "back rooms," as they did in the era of illegal abortions (see Miller, 1993; Messer and May, 1994).

In recent years, the abortion pill *mifepristone* (originally known as RU-486), which was approved in 2000 for use in the United States by the Food and Drug Administration, has become an increasingly popular alternative to abortions. The pill allows women to make abortion-related decisions in private, as compared to the necessity of visiting public clinics where they may be confronted by protesters. It is estimated that about one-fifth of all abortions are medically induced using such pharmaceuticals. This procedure is effective in early-term abortions, whereas surgical abortions in the first twelve weeks of pregnancy use the suction-aspiration or vacuum method. Abortion procedures are not without risk to women and controversy continues over public funding for Planned Parenthood Clinics that perform such procedures.

At the microlevel, abortion is a solution for some pregnant women and their families but a problem for others, particularly when they face religious or family opposition. At the macrolevel, abortion is both a problem and a solution when activists try to influence the making and enforcement of laws pertaining to women's reproductive rights and the control of new reproductive technologies.

Infertility and New Reproductive Technologies

Infertility is defined as an inability to conceive after a year of unprotected sexual relations. Today, infertility affects more than 7.3 million U.S. couples, or one in eight couples in which the wife is between the ages of fifteen and forty-four. In 40 percent of the cases, the woman is infertile, and in another 40 percent it is the man; 20 percent of the time, the cause is impossible to determine.

About 50 percent of infertile couples who seek treatment can be helped by conventional, relatively low-tech treatments such as fertility drugs, artificial insemination, and surgery to unblock fallopian tubes. The other 50 percent require advanced technology, sometimes called assisted reproductive technology (ART). Many middle- and upper-income couples, for example, receive in vitro fertilization (IVF), which costs between $10,000 and $15,000 per cycle (see Table 11.1). Often the first attempt is unsuccessful, and couples may pay for second and third cycles of the drug before pregnancy occurs or they become discouraged and terminate the treatments. Despite the popularity of such treatments and the growth of fertility clinics, some couples are still unable to become parents. This is especially difficult for young couples who are constantly bombarded by questions from family, acquaintances, and even Facebook friends who want to know when they are going to become parents (see Box 11.2 on page 258). Many couples finally decide to remain childless, but some adopt one or more children.

Adoption

Adoption is a legal process through which the rights and duties of parenting are transferred from a child's biological and/or legal parents to new legal parents. The adopted child has all the rights of a biological child. In most adoptions, a new birth certificate is issued, and the child has no further contact with the biological parents.

During the first decade of the twenty-first century, 1.1 percent of women and 2.3 percent of men between the ages of eighteen and forty-four had adopted a child. Although this is a very small number, it reflects an interesting change in how data are gathered. This was the first time that never-married women and men were counted, as compared to previous studies that had reported only on the experience of married women. One of the possible reasons why men may have a higher rate of adoption than women is that when parents divorce, children are more likely to live in households with their biological mothers than with their biological fathers. When these single parents remarry, the new husbands have greater opportunities to adopt these stepchildren than the new wives. Women between the ages of thirty-five and thirty-nine are the largest category of individuals actively seeking to adopt a child (U.S. Department of Health and Human Services [HHS], 2010).

TABLE 11.1 Forms of Assisted Reproductive Technology

Name	Description
In vitro fertilization (IVF)	Eggs that were produced as a result of administering fertility drugs are removed from the woman's body and fertilized by sperm in a laboratory dish. The embryos that result from this process are transferred to the woman's uterus.
Gamete intrafallopian transfer (GIFT)	The woman is given hormones to stimulate the production of multiple eggs. Unfertilized eggs and sperm are placed into the woman's fallopian tube(s) using laparoscopy, a microsurgical procedure. Fertilization occurs in the fallopian tubes before the embryo implants in the uterine wall.
Zygote intrafallopian transfer (ZIFT) and tubal embryo transfer (TET)	Eggs are removed from the woman and fertilized in a lab before being transferred by laparoscopy to the fallopian tube rather than the uterus.
Intracytoplasmic sperm injection (ICSI)	A single sperm is injected directly into a mature egg. The embryo is then transferred to the woman's uterus or fallopian tube.

Box 11.2

Social Media in the Twenty-First Century: Posting One's Fertility (or Infertility) on Facebook

"We've told our immediate family, and are so excited to tell you! We're pregnant!"

"[Name of pregnant woman] has a bun in the oven."

"Wondering what the future holds for the class of 2029? . . ."

—Rachel Carpenter (2010) suggests ways that pregnant women can inform their friends and family of the happy news of impending parenthood.

I know it's not meant to hurt, but you feel like you're getting kicked every time you see these. I have to unfriend people for a while. If I was smart, I wouldn't go on Facebook anymore, but I'd completely lose connections with family and friends.

—Diane Colling, an occupational therapist and fertility patient, explains why scrolling through her Facebook page is so difficult when she sees postings by friends about their pregnancy.

Like some other women between the ages of fifteen and forty-four, Diane Colling has been unable to become pregnant, and she is constantly reminded of her situation when she receives exuberant messages on her Facebook page about a friend's pregnancy.

In the past, people like Diane could limit their exposure to other people's happy announcements by avoiding them for a period of time. However, in today's always-connected and always-communicating era, it is virtually impossible to miss such broadcasts from friends and acquaintances on social media websites. According to a report in the *Washington Post*, personnel in some infertility clinics report that many patients talk about "Facebook envy" (because their friends have announced their own pregnancies) when they come in for fertility treatments or consultations (Shapira, 2010). In the words of one counselor, "Some people can't disengage from it, although it makes them miserable. I tell them 'Go on a diet from Facebook for a week'" (quoted in Shapira, 2010).

Stories such as these show how the nature of interpersonal communication has been drastically changed in a short period of time. In the past, people received information about pregnancies or other family matters by word of mouth or a written announcement. Today, we receive personal information through relatively impersonal technologies to which we log on and correspond without actually seeing or talking to another person.

In regard to "Facebook envy" on the part of infertile couples, it appears that one of the most stressful features of some social media is the ability to see photos and video recordings that have been posted. Apparently, people with fertility issues are less harmed psychologically by postings about pregnancies on Twitter because no pictures are shown. By contrast, postings on Facebook and other social media sites provide sonograms of a friend's baby or show a friend with a "baby bump."

More women are learning to use the "Hide" feature on Facebook to avoid baby announcements; still others admit that if their infertility treatments are successful and they become pregnant, they will quickly lose their angst about posting pregnancy announcements on Facebook and will proudly proclaim their own pregnancy and pending parenthood (Shapira, 2010). In the meantime, persons like Rachel Carpenter (2010), who provide advice on how to announce one's pregnancy on Facebook, have become sensitized to the problems of infertile friends and make online suggestions such as this: "If you have a close friend or family member who is currently experiencing infertility, please tell them first before posting the news. Try to be as sensitive as possible."

Questions for Consideration

1. What social factors in the United States contribute to how infertile couples feel about learning of the pregnancy of one of their friends?

2. How do social networking websites make it easier for people to learn news and communicate quickly with other individuals?

3. What are the strengths and limitations of social media as compared to interpersonal communication and/or traditional media in informing us about other people's major life events?

Independent Research

Search newspapers and social networking sites for announcements of major life events, such as engagements, marriages, births, and deaths. Compare the social media announcements with print announcements. Can you identify ways in which personal information is different when we receive it by Internet or social media as compared with personal conversation or print media?

Matching children who are available for adoption with prospective adoptive parents can be difficult. The available children have specific needs, and the prospective parents often set specifications on the type of child they want to adopt. Some adoptions are by relatives of the child; others are by infertile couples (although many fertile couples also adopt). Increasing numbers of gays, lesbians, and people who are single are adopting children. Although thousands of children are available for adoption each year in the United States, many prospective parents seek out children in developing nations such as Romania, South Korea, and India. The primary reason is that the available children in the United States are thought to be "unsuitable." They may have disabilities, or they may be sick, nonwhite (most of the prospective parents are white), or too old. In addition, fewer infants are available for adoption today than in the past because better means of contraception exist, abortion is more readily available, and more unmarried teenage parents decide to keep their babies.

Teen Pregnancies and Unmarried Motherhood

Although the U.S. teen pregnancy rate has gone down in recent years, this remains an issue of great concern because of the economic, social, and health costs on teen parents and their families. When compared to other high-income nations, the U.S. teen birthrate is nearly nine times higher than in the majority of other developed countries. In 2009, about 410,000 teenage girls in the United States between the ages of fifteen and nineteen gave birth—a 37 percent decrease from the number of teen birthrate in 1991. This means that the teen birthrate dropped to 39.1 births per 1,000 females in 2009 from 61.8 births per 1,000 females in 1991.

What are the primary reasons for the relatively high rates of teenage pregnancy? At the microlevel, several issues are most important: (1) Many sexually active teenagers do not use contraceptives; (2) teenagers—especially those from some low-income families and/or subordinate racial and ethnic groups—may receive little accurate information about the use of, and problems associated with, contraception; (3) some teenage males (due to a double standard based on the myth that sexual promiscuity is acceptable among males but not females) believe that females should be responsible for contraception; and (4) some teenagers view pregnancy as a sign of male prowess or as a way to gain adult status. At the macrolevel, structural factors also contribute to teenage pregnancy rates. Lack of education and employment opportunities in some central-city and rural areas may discourage young people's thoughts of upward mobility. Likewise, religious and political opposition has resulted in issues relating to reproductive responsibility not being dealt with as openly in the United States as in some other nations. Finally, advertising, films, television programming, magazines, music, and other forms of media often flaunt the idea of being sexually active without showing the possible consequences of such behavior.

According to social analysts, the outcome of teen pregnancies is problematic because teenage mothers are typically unskilled at parenting, are likely to drop out of school, and have no social support other than relatives. Family support is extremely important to unmarried pregnant teens because emotional and financial support from the fathers of their children is often lacking. Without this support, teen mothers rely on their own mothers and grandmothers to help with childrearing. As a result, many unmarried teenage mothers do not make the same transition from the family of orientation to the family of procreation that most people make when they become parents. The ***family of orientation* is the family into which a person is born and in which early socialization takes place.** When teenage mothers and their children live with their grandmothers or other relatives, they do not establish the separate family unit known as a ***family of procreation*—the family that a person forms by having or adopting children, which married couples with young children create.**

The picture for the children of teenage mothers without parental support is especially bleak because few of these mothers have adequate parenting skills or knowledge of child development. Children of unwed teenage mothers tend to have severely limited educational and employment opportunities and a high likelihood of living in poverty. Statistics also suggest that 43 percent of young women who first gave birth between the ages of fifteen and nineteen will have a second child within three years (Children's Defense Fund, 2008). As shown in Figure 11.2 on page 260, birth rates vary based on race and ethnicity as well as age.

Teenagers are not the only ones having children without getting married these days. Nearly four in ten U.S. births (to mothers between the ages of fifteen and forty-five) were to unmarried women in 2007. In that same year, the birthrate was 52.3 per 1,000 unmarried girls and women (never-married, widowed, and divorced), up from a rate of 44 per 1,000 unmarried females in 2000. The rate for African American females was slightly less than 73 per 1,000; for Latinas, 108 per 1,000; and for white (non-Hispanic) Americans, 48 per

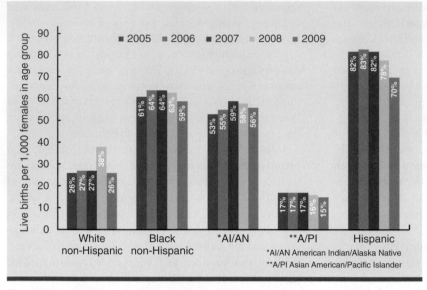

Figure 11.2 U.S. Birthrate for Women Aged 15-19 Years by Race/Ethnicity 2005-2009
Source: Centers for Disease Control and Prevention, 2010

1,000 unmarried females (U.S. Census Bureau, 2010). Some analysts believe that the rising birthrates among unmarried females are a reflection of the declining significance of marriage. Other analysts focus on women's rising employment rates and greater empowerment, leading more females who desire a child to decide that they can "go it alone" or cohabiting with partner rather than marrying a spouse. Still others focus on the number of same-sex female partners who become parents without being counted in official marriage statistics. Finally, with less stigma attached to unmarried pregnancy than in the past, fewer women may seek abortions and decide instead to raise the child themselves whether the pregnancy was planned or not.

DIVORCE AND REMARRIAGE

Divorce is the legal process of dissolving a marriage that allows former spouses to remarry if they so choose. Most divorces today are granted on the grounds of *irreconcilable differences,* meaning that there has been a breakdown of the marital relationship for which neither partner is specifically blamed. Prior to the passage of more-lenient divorce laws, many states required that the partner seeking the divorce prove misconduct on the part of the other spouse. Under *no-fault divorce laws,* however, proof of "blameworthiness" is generally no longer necessary.

Over the past 100 years, the U.S. divorce rate (number of divorces per 1,000 population) has varied from a low of 0.7 in 1900 to 7.9 in 1980; by 2008, it had decreased

to 5.2 per 1,000 population between the ages of fifteen and sixty-four (U.S. Census Bureau, 2010). Although many people believe that marriage should last for a lifetime, others believe that marriage is a commitment that may change over time.

One study found that 43 percent of first marriages end in separation or divorce within fifteen years; however, other analysts have disputed that percentage on the grounds that about one in ten of those who married between 1985 to 1989 had not reached their fifteenth anniversary by the time the 2004 survey was conducted. For those married at least fifteen years, only 33.4 percent of first marriages ended before their fifteenth anniversary (35.7 percent for women and 31.2 percent for men). Moreover, some couples did not reach their fifteenth anniversary because of death rather than divorce (Wolfers, 2008).

Why do divorces occur? Existing research has identified a number of factors at both the macrolevel and microlevel that make some couples more or less likely to divorce. At the macrolevel, societal factors contributing to higher rates of divorce include changes in social institutions, such as religion and family. Some religions have taken a more lenient attitude toward divorce, and the social stigma associated with divorce has lessened. Likewise, the family has undergone major changes that have resulted in less economic and emotional dependency among family members—thus reducing a barrier to divorce.

Ending a marriage produces stress not only on spouses but on other family members as well. If divorce is such a stressful process, why does the U.S. have such a high rate of divorce?

At the microlevel, a number of factors contribute to a couple's "statistical" likelihood of divorcing. Here are some of the primary social characteristics of those most likely to get divorced:

- Marriage at an early age (59 percent of marriages to brides under eighteen end in separation or divorce within fifteen years)
- A short acquaintanceship before marriage
- Disapproval of the marriage by relatives and friends
- Limited economic resources and low wages
- A high school education or less (although deferring marriage to attend college may be more of a factor than education per se)
- Parents who are divorced or have unhappy marriages
- The presence of children (depending on their gender and age) at the start of the marriage

The interrelationship of these and other factors is complicated. For example, the effect of age is intertwined with economic resources; persons from families at the low end of the income scale tend to marry earlier than those at more affluent income levels. Thus, the question becomes whether age itself is a factor or whether economic resources are more closely associated with divorce.

The relationship between divorce and factors such as race, class, and religion is another complex issue. Although African Americans are more likely than white (non-Hispanic) Americans to get a divorce, other factors—such as income level and discrimination in society—must also be taken into account. Latinos/as share some of the problems faced by African Americans, but their divorce rate is only slightly higher than that of whites of European ancestry. Religion may affect the divorce rate of some people, including many Latinos/as who are Roman Catholic. However, despite the Catholic doctrine that discourages divorce, the rate of Catholic divorces is now approximately equal to that of Protestant divorces.

Divorce may have a dramatic economic and emotional impact on family members. An estimated 60 percent of divorcing couples have one or more children. By age sixteen, about one out of every three white children and two out of every three African American children will experience divorce within their families. As a result, most of them will remain with their mothers and live in a single-parent household for a period of time. In recent years, there has been a debate over whether children who live with their same-sex parent after divorce are better off than their peers who live with an opposite-sex parent. However, sociologists have found virtually no evidence to support the belief that children are better off living with a same-sex parent.

Divorce also changes relationships not only for the couple and children involved, but also for other relatives. Some grandparents feel that they are the big losers. Grandparents who wish to see their grandchildren have to keep in touch with the parent who has custody, but if the grandparents are in-laws, they are less likely to be welcomed and might be seen as taking the "other side" simply because they are the parents of the ex-spouse. Recently, some grandparents have sued for custody of minor grandchildren. For the most part, these suits have not been successful except when there has been some question about the emotional stability of the biological parents or the suitability of a foster-care arrangement.

But divorce does not have to be negative. For some people, divorce may be an opportunity to terminate destructive relationships. For others, it may represent a means to achieve personal growth by managing their lives and social relationships and establishing their own social identity. Still others choose to remarry one or more times.

Divorce and remarriage often creates complex family relationships. **Blended families are families that consist of a husband and wife, children from previous marriages, and children (if any) from the new marriage.** At least initially, stress in blended families may be fairly high because of rivalry among the children and hostilities directed toward stepparents or babies born into the family. In some cases, when parents divorce and marry other partners, the children become part of a *binuclear family*, living with one biological parent and a stepparent part of the time and with the other biological parent and another stepparent the rest of the time.

The norms governing divorce and remarriage are ambiguous, so people must make decisions about family life (such as who should be invited to a birthday celebration or a wedding) on the basis of their own feelings about the people involved. But in spite of the problems, many blended families succeed.

DOMESTIC VIOLENCE

The term *domestic violence* obscures the fact that most victims of domestic violence are women and children. Women are more likely to be assaulted, injured, or raped by their male partners than by any other type of assailant. Children are extremely vulnerable to abuse and violence because of their age and their economic and social dependence on their parents or other adult caregivers.

Child Maltreatment

Although all child maltreatment does not occur within families, a surprising proportion of cases involve parents or other relatives who engage in child abuse, neglect, and sometimes sexual abuse of children. *Child abuse and neglect* is the physical or mental injury, sexual abuse, or negligent treatment of a child under the age of eighteen by a person who is responsible for the child's welfare. Most of us, when we hear the words *child abuse,* think in terms of physical injury or sexual abuse, but the most frequent form of child maltreatment is *child neglect*—not meeting a child's basic needs for emotional warmth and security, adequate shelter, food, health care, education, clothing, and protection. We will focus primarily on physical injury and sexual abuse because these actions are classified as violent personal crimes.

In the past, children in the United States were considered the property of their parents and could be punished or ignored as the parents wished. With passage of the Social Security Act in the 1930s, however, children became legally protected even from their own parents. Still, many physical injuries to children are intentionally inflicted by parents and other caregivers. Parental violence can, in fact, lead to the *battered child syndrome,* a psychological disorder in which a child experiences low self-esteem and sometimes clinical depression associated with former or current abuse perpetrated by a biological or custodial parent (Kempe et al., 1962).

The physical abuse of children in the United States is a serious social problem that remains largely hidden unless an incident results in the death or serious injury of a child. Each year, state and local child protective services agencies receive more than 3 million reports of children being abused or neglected. Approximately 10 per 1,000 children between the ages of zero and seventeen are victims of child maltreatment in any given year (Forum on Child and Family Statistics, 2010). Younger children typically are the most vulnerable to maltreatment, with many victims being younger than four years of age. Children less than one year of age had the highest rate of victimization at 20.6 per 1,000 children in the population of the same age (HHS, 2010). Slightly more than half (51.1 percent) of all victimization involved girls, while boys accounted for 48.2 percent of all victims (the rest had unknown sex). Three racial-ethnic categories—African Americans (22.3 percent), Hispanics (20.7 percent), and white (non-Hispanic) Americans (44 percent)—made up 87 percent of all children victimized. However, some children had higher rates of victimization: The rate of victimization for African American children is slightly less than 17 percent

per 1,000 children; for American Indian or Alaska Native, 14 percent per 1,000 children; and for multiracial children, 14 percent per 1,000 children (CDC, 2010). Most child victims of maltreatment were neglected (78.3 percent), nearly 18 percent were physically abused, and 10 percent were sexually abused (HHS, 2010).

Younger children are more vulnerable to death as a result of child abuse and neglect. Between 1,700 and 2,000 children ages zero to seventeen die each year from abuse and neglect. Approximately 80 percent of all child fatalities were younger than four years old; 10 percent among four- to seven-year-olds, 4 percent among eight- to eleven-year-olds, 4 percent among twelve- to fourteen-year-olds, and 2 percent among sixteen- to seventeen-year-olds. Of all child-abuse-related fatalities, 46 percent were younger than one year old. The rate of deaths from child abuse and neglect for children younger than one year of age is 18 per 100,000 children younger than one year in the U.S. population. Boys are slightly more likely to be the victims of child fatalities than girls, and 80 percent of child fatalities were made up of white (non-Hispanic) Americans (39 percent), followed by African Americans (29 percent) and 17 percent Hispanic (HHS, 2010).

In all child maltreatment cases combined, mothers had the highest percentage of abuse at 38 percent; fathers constituted 19 percent of abusers; and mothers and fathers together made up 18 percent of abusers. Among nonparent abusers, the highest percentages were other male relatives (2.8 percent) or the male partner of a parent (2.2 percent). Some researchers have found that children are most likely to be assaulted in their own homes if their parents were abused, neglected, or deprived as children and if their parents are socially isolated as adults.

The signs of physical abuse include bruises, particularly on the back of the legs, upper arms and chest, neck, head, or genitals. Fractures in infants less than one year old are a strong indication of abuse, as are head injuries and burns, especially cigarette burns. Most physicians and emergency room personnel are trained to identify signs of child abuse so that parents or guardians can be reported to the appropriate authorities. In fact, reporting of suspected child abuse has improved significantly in recent years because of increased training, awareness, and legislation, including the Federal Child Abuse Prevention and Treatment Act of 1974, which established that reports of suspected abuse would be investigated promptly and fully. In the past, even when physicians suspected abuse, they often chose to treat the child but not to report the incident, believing that abuse would be too difficult to prove (Tower, 1996).

One of the most disturbing forms of physical abuse of children is *sexual abuse*—inappropriately exposing or subjecting the child to sexual contact, activity, or behavior. Sexual abuse includes oral, anal, genital, buttock, and breast contact. It also involves the use of objects for vaginal or anal penetration, fondling, or sexual stimulation. At all ages, females are more likely than males to be victims of sexual abuse as well as *incest*—sexual relations between individuals who are so closely related that they are forbidden to marry by law. However, the rate of sexual abuse for males is also significant in that estimates suggest that boys and men account for 25 to 35 percent of child sexual abuse victims. Males are more likely to be victimized by other males who are known to the victim. Boys and young men are more likely to experience assault in public places by strangers or nonrelatives; girls are more likely to experience long-term victimization by relatives or family acquaintances in their own home.

Sexual abuse contributes to a wide variety of problems for children who experience this harmful occurrence. Some are too frightened to tell anyone, and many have untreated medical conditions (such as bleeding, pain, swelling, and other physical and mental symptoms). Behavioral problems are common, including loss of appetite, eating disorder, withdrawal, and aggressiveness. Sexual abuse, like other kinds of child maltreatment, all too often occurs in the home and negatively changes the relationships between children, parents, and other relatives.

Intimate Partner Violence

From the days of early Rome to current times, spouse abuse has been acknowledged to exist, but until recently, it was largely ignored or tolerated. Today, it is estimated that about 4.8 million women experience intimate partner-related physical assaults and rapes. Men are the victims of about 2.9 million intimate partner related physical assaults. Intimate partner violence includes physical violence, sexual violence, threats of physical or sexual violence, and emotional abuse. More than 2,300 deaths a year are the result of intimate partner violence, and 70 percent of these deaths are females, as compared to 30 percent for males. When women kill their spouses, it is often because they have been physically and sexually abused over a long period of time and see themselves as hopelessly trapped in a dangerous relationship. Even for those who experience less severe forms of intimate partner violence, the costs are great in psychological effects on the victim, medical care, mental health services, and lost productivity at work. Injuries sustained by victims of spouse abuse are as serious as, or more serious than, the injuries incurred in 90 percent of all rapes, robberies, and other aggravated assaults. Spouse abuse ranges in intensity from slapping, kicking, and hitting with a closed fist to inflicting critical injuries or death. Spouse abuse occurs across lines of race, class, region, religion, and other factors.

Related to the issue of spouse abuse is marital rape. In *marital rape*, a husband forces sexual intercourse on his resisting wife. The federal criminal code and most state laws now identify marital rape as a crime. Analysts have identified three types of marital rape: (1) battering rape, in which sexual violence is part of a larger pattern of abuse; (2) nonbattering rape, in which the husband and wife do not agree over when, where, and whether or not to have sex; and (3) obsessive rape, which involves male sexual obsessions, sometimes related to use of pornography or force to become aroused (Finkelhor and Yllo, 1985). Many victims of spouse abuse and/or marital rape fear that if they try to leave the abusive spouse, they will endanger themselves and their children. However, many women do take such measures, particularly if they are able to obtain the services of a "safe house" or other community residential services where they can remain safe from their abusive partner while trying to find another place to live.

Social Responses to Intimate Partner Violence

High-profile cases of domestic violence, often involving celebrities or professional athletes, call our attention to the problem of domestic abuse, but on a day-to-day basis many people who are aware of such violence do not report it because they do not want to become involved in what they see as a "private matter."

Historically, in the United States, an *ideology of nonintervention*—a strong reluctance on the part of outsiders to interfere in family matters—has led people and police officers to ignore or tolerate domestic violence. Unfortunately, the pattern of violence that ultimately results in a homicide is eerily similar in many cases of domestic abuse, and in most of those cases, death might have been prevented by earlier intervention. Positive changes are now being made in how law enforcement officials handle domestic violence calls—changes that are long overdue. As with other social problems we have examined, the causes, effects, and possible solutions for domestic violence and other family-related problems depend on the theoretical framework the analyst uses.

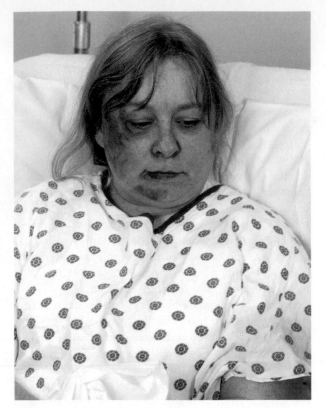

Domestic violence is a hidden problem in some families. Although the woman pictured here is receiving medical attention for her injuries, many victims do not come forward to report abuse because they fear that they may be battered again or be blamed by others for their problem.

SOCIOLOGICAL EXPLANATIONS AND SOLUTIONS

What purposes do families serve in contemporary societies? Do families create problems for society or solve them? How can we reduce family-related social problems in the twenty-first century? Different theoretical perspectives provide us with divergent answers and solutions. Functionalists believe that the family fulfills important functions for individuals at the microlevel and for the entire society at the macrolevel. Conflict and feminist theorists, on the other hand, consider families to be a primary source of inequality—and sometimes abuse and violence—in society. Taking a microlevel approach, symbolic interactionists analyze family-related social problems in terms of socialization and social interactions among family members.

Functionalist Perspectives

Functionalists emphasize the importance of the family in maintaining the stability of society and the well-being of individuals. According to Emile Durkheim, marriage is a microcosmic replica of the larger society; both marriage and society involve a mental and moral fusion of physically distinct individuals (Lehmann, 1994). Durkheim also believed that a division of labor contributed to greater efficiency in marriage and families (and all areas of life). In his study of family life in the United States, Talcott Parsons (1955) also viewed a division of labor as important. He saw the husband in an ideal nuclear family as fulfilling an instrumental role—meeting the family's economic needs, making important decisions, and providing leadership—and the wife as fulfilling an expressive role—running the household, caring for children, and meeting family members' emotional needs.

Using Durkheim's and Parsons's work as a basis for their model of the family, contemporary functionalists believe that a division of labor makes it possible for families to fulfill a number of functions that no other social institution in high-income nations can perform as efficiently and effectively:

1. *Regulating sexual behavior and reproduction.* Families are expected to regulate the sexual activity of their members and thus control reproduction so that it occurs within specific boundaries. Sexual regulation of family members by the family is supposed to protect the principle of legitimacy—the belief that all children should have a socially and legally recognized father (Malinowski, 1964).
2. *Socializing and educating children.* Parents and other relatives are responsible for teaching children the values and norms of their culture.
3. *Providing economic and psychological support.* Families are responsible for providing for their members' physical (food, shelter) and emotional needs.
4. *Providing social status.* Families confer social status on their members, including ascribed statuses such as race, ethnicity, nationality, class, and religious affiliation, although some of these statuses can change later in life.

Considering their view of the family, functionalists believe that problems in the family are a social crisis. The functional family provides both social order and economic stability by providing for the survival and development of children; the physical and emotional health of adults; and the care of the sick, injured, elderly, and disabled. The family is also the front line for reinforcing society's norms and values. Functionalists consider the family to be part of the solution to many problems faced by people in contemporary societies. In this view, dysfunctions in families are problems that threaten the well-being of individuals, groups, and nations.

Functionalists believe that changes in other social institutions, such as the economy, religion, education, law, medicine, and the government, contribute to family-related problems. For example, some functionalists think that changing the law to recognize no-fault divorce contributes to higher rates of divorce and dramatically increases the number of single-parent households, which do not provide children with the nurturance and guidance they get in a two-parent home (Popenoe, 1996).

Functionalist/Conservative Solutions

Based on a functionalist/conservative approach, a central way to reduce or eliminate family problems is through strengthening relationships and family ties, not reducing or diminishing them through practices such as cohabitation or divorce. Some functionalists and individuals applying a conservative political perspective suggest that marriage is protective, particularly for women because it provide the necessary stability and pledge of endurance that is required to maintain a healthy intimate relationship. Marriage, from this approach, should be seen as a lifelong commitment in which both partners meet their responsibilities to each other and seek to uphold the stability and protective nature of the family.

Conservative political solutions to reducing family problems include making divorces more difficult to obtain by revisiting state laws such as "no-fault divorce" that make it relatively easy for either partner to dissolve a marriage. Similarly, parents should be held accountable through laws that protect children by making parents responsible for their financial, social, and moral well-being. So-called deadbeat dads who do not pay child support payments should be more harshly dealt with so that all parents realize that they must take care of the children they produce.

In sum, functionalist/conservative perspectives on family problems emphasize the importance of keeping families together and reducing the ills that are created by domestic violence, abortion, and divorce. According to some analysts using this approach, divorce contributes to other social problems such as poverty, depression and mental illness, and poor health. Therefore, it is important to reinforce families so that we may reduce or eliminate other social problems in society.

Conflict and Feminist Perspectives

Most conflict and feminist analysts believe that functionalist views on family problems are idealized and inadequate. Rather than operating harmoniously and for the benefit of all members, families are sources of social inequality and conflict over values, goals, and access to resources and power.

Conflict theorists who focus on class relations in capitalist economies compare family members to workers in a factory. Women are dominated by men in the home just as workers are dominated by managers and capitalists in factories (Engels, 1972). As wives and mothers, women contribute to capitalism by producing the next generation of workers and providing the existing labor force with food, clean clothes, and emotional support. Not only does women's work in the family benefit the capitalist class, it also reinforces women's subordination because the work is unpaid and often devalued. In support of this view, conflict theorists note that women who work solely in their own homes for many years usually do not have health insurance or a retirement plan apart from sharing in their husbands' employment benefits.

Many feminist theorists, however, think that male dominance and female subordination began long before capitalism and the private ownership of property arose as an economic system. They see women's subordination as being rooted in patriarchy, particularly in men's control over women's labor power. At that time, women's labor in the home was directed by men and it was undervalued, which made it possible for men to benefit from their status as the family breadwinner (Firestone, 1970; Goode, 1982).

Conflict and Feminist Solutions

Both conflict and feminist theorists think that family problems derive from inequality—not just within the family, but in the political, social, and economic arenas of the larger society as well. According to these theorists, domestic violence may be a conscious strategy that men use to control women and perpetuate gender inequality. About one-third of all female murder victims are killed by current or former husbands or boyfriends, whereas only a very small percentage (ranging from 3 to 5 percent) of all male murder victims are killed by current or former wives or girlfriends.

In sum, family problems can be reduced or eliminated from a conflict or feminist perspective if we become aware of the true roots of oppression and do something about them. Laws must be strengthened not so much to maintain the strength of family ties but rather to aggressively pursue individuals who take advantage of or harm those with whom they share close domestic partnerships or marital ties. Problems associated with unplanned pregnancies and births among unmarried teenagers must be addressed head on, for example, by providing current and non-threatening information about the most effective means of contraception rather than trying to persuade hormone-driven teens that abstinence is the only way. Using this approach, people are empowered to make their own decisions about partnerships, marriage, family planning, and other issues that may produce problems in families and intimate relationships.

Symbolic Interactionist Perspectives

Some symbolic interactionists view the family communication process as integral to understanding the diverse roles that family members play; therefore these analysts examine how husbands, wives, and children act out their roles and react to the parts played by others. Although societies differ widely on the rules and norms that shape family and kin relationships, people are socialized to accept their society's form of the family as the acceptable norm. According to sociologists Peter Berger and Hansfried Kellner (1964), marital partners develop a shared reality through their interactions with each other. Although newlyweds bring separate identities to a marriage, over time they construct a shared reality as a couple. In the process, the partners redefine their past identities to be consistent with their new realities. Symbolic interactionists say that the process of developing a shared reality is continuous and occurs not only in the family, but also in any group in which the couple participates together. In cases of separation and divorce, the process is reversed: Couples may start with a shared reality but once again become individuals with separate realities in the process of uncoupling their relationship.

How do symbolic interactionists explain problems in a family? Some look at the subjective meanings and interpretations people give to their everyday lives. According to sociologist Jessie Bernard (1982), women and men experience marriage differently. While the husband might see his marriage very positively, the wife might feel less positive about her marriage. The reverse can also be true. Evidence for the different realities of marriage comes from research that shows that husbands and wives often give very different accounts of the same event (Safilios-Rothschild, 1969).

Still other symbolic interactionists view family problems in terms of partners' unrealistic expectations about love and marriage, which can lead to marital dissatisfaction and sometimes divorce. These

analysts note that our culture emphasizes romantic love—a deep and vital emotion based on significant need satisfaction, caring for and acceptance of another person, and the development of an intimate relationship (Lamanna and Riedmann, 2012). Indeed, most couples in the United States get married because they are in love, but being a "nation of lovers" doesn't mean that men and women have the same ideas about what constitutes romantic love. According to sociologist Francesca Cancian (1990), women tend to express their feelings verbally, whereas men tend to express their love through nonverbal actions such as fixing dinner or doing household repairs. Women might not always interpret these actions as signs of love. One man complained (L. B. Rubin, 1976:146), "What does she want? Proof? She's got it, hasn't she? Would I be knocking myself out to get things for her—like to keep up this house—if I didn't love her? Why does a man do things like that if not because he loves his wife and kids? I swear, I can't figure what she wants." His wife replied, "It's not enough that he supports us and takes care of us. I appreciate that, but I want him to share things with me. I need for him to tell me his feelings."

Symbolic Interactionist Solutions

Families and intimate relationships have changed dramatically during the past one hundred years as other interaction patterns in society have also changed. Some analysts believe that we expect too much of the family and our intimate relationships with others: We expect people to make us happy rather than realizing that we too must work at happiness in the relationship. According to symbolic interactionists, problems in marriages may be reduced if people become aware of the different realities they have about marriage and family life. Through better communication with each other, family members can work toward making the home a more positive place in which to live.

Dealing with negative communication patterns must be coupled with reducing partners' unrealistic expectations about love and marriage. Many of these expectations are fostered by media representations of "ideal love," "dream weddings," and "the perfect life." However, if problems in families are to be reduced at the macrolevel of society, symbolic interactionists believe that we must start at the microlevel to bring about this change. Through modifying people's everyday perceptions about intimate relationships and family life, we can begin to change larger patterns of belief in society about what is realistic and what is not in dealing with the dilemmas that face families today, ranging from interpersonal communication problems and work dilemmas to economic hardships and lack of time for family life in a more constructive manner. However, one thing is certain: We must be willing to accept change, but many changes continue to occur in individual families and in the family as a social institution in the United States and other nations.

As we have seen in this chapter, because of these changes, some people believe that the family as we know it is doomed. Some analysts think that returning to traditional family values can save this important social institution and create a more stable society. Another point of view, however, comes from sociologist Lillian Rubin (1994), who suggests that clinging to a traditional image of families is hypocritical in light of our society's failure to support the family, whether through family allowances or decent public-sponsored child-care facilities (see Box 11.3).

Social Problems and Social Policy  Box 11.3

Child Care: A Necessity That May Cost as Much as Public University Tuition?

Facts:

- Nearly three-fourths of women with children are employed in the United States.
- Three out of four working mothers work more than thirty hours a week.
- Over 90 percent of families with working mothers use some kind of child care.
- A national study found that the cost of child care in a center is more than the cost of public university tuition in a majority of U.S. states. (Belkin, 2010)

Child care has become a necessity for contemporary parents who must work to provide for themselves and their children. However, the question remains: "Who should pay for child care?" Some people believe that it should be the parents' responsibility—that parents should not have children whom they cannot afford to raise. Other people believe that paying for child care should be the responsibility of the government. According to this perspective, it is important for parents to be able to work so that they can earn a livelihood, pay taxes, boost consumer spending, and generally be contributing members of society. However, the U.S. government does not compare favorably with other high-income nations in regard to helping provide child care. At most, our government provides 25 to 30 percent of the cost of child care for three- to six-year-olds. By contrast, in most other high-income nations, the government provides most of the child-care costs for children above two years of age—France provides 100 percent, for example, and Denmark, Finland, and Sweden provide about 80 percent of the cost (The Future of Children, 2011). In the United States, child care ranges in cost from more than $4,500 per year for infant care to a high of more than $20,000. Although infant care is more expensive than the cost of care for children in their toddler and preschool years, costs remain high for center-based, quality child care. In Massachusetts, for example, the yearly infant-care cost of approximately $18,750 in 2010 was $9,533 more than the yearly cost of college tuition and fees at a public university (Belkin, 2010).

Does society have a responsibility to the children who represent that nation's future? For our government to contribute more to the cost of child care, we as a people would need to view child care as a national concern. But we don't view it as a national concern, especially compared with the federal deficit, funding security- and war-related activities, and other endeavors that have been prioritized about our nation's children.

Some analysts believe that employers should be the ones to pay the cost of child care because they benefit the most from the hours that their workers spend on the job. From this standpoint, subsidizing child care for employees' children is a good investment: Without safe, reliable, affordable care for their children, employees find it more difficult to be productive workers, and the cost of quality child care is a concern not only for families in low-income brackets, but also for many middle-class families who are feeling the squeeze of high gas prices, food costs, and rent or home mortgage payments. However, it appears that few employers are willing or able to provide real help with child care in the twenty-first century. Many employers complain of sharply rising health care costs for their employees and believe that global competition is cutting into their earnings, thus making funding of child care for their employees a luxury that the employers simply cannot afford.

In other words, we have not as yet embraced the concept that child care is a critical support for working families and that the government should be involved in financing this endeavor. We have not, as a nation, accepted the fact that we all have a responsibility to the children who represent this nation's future.

Social Problems and Social Policy

Box 11.3 continued

Why is high-quality, affordable day care a pressing problem in our society? How can we more effectively meet the needs of both children and their parents?

Questions for Consideration

1. Are financial constraints at various levels of government and in corporate America so great that these social institutions simply cannot afford to invest in the nation's future by putting more money into child care? Are we spending money for things that are less important than our children to the future of the nation?

2. Even if we have no children of our own, do we have a responsibility to the nation's children? Or are children the sole responsibility of their families, regardless of the parents' ability to pay for proper care and education for the children? What do you think?

Although many people demonstrate their faith in the future of the family as a social institution by their own choices, a macrolevel societal commitment to the family is also needed, as sociologist Demie Kurz (1995:232) stated about a decade ago, and her assertions remain valid today:

As a society we should make a commitment to helping all families—traditional nuclear families, two-parent, two-earner families, and single-parent families—and to providing adequately for their members, particularly their children. To help families we must reduce female and male poverty, making special efforts to end institutionalized discrimination against minorities. We must also promote equality between men and women in the family. This includes creating new conceptions of what it means to be a father and what it means to be a partner in a marriage and share family life and household work. It also means taking decisive steps to end violence toward women and children. Although the costs of creating humane and just social policies are high, the cost of failing to promote the welfare of family members is far higher.

SUMMARY

✓—Study and Review on mysoclab.com

■ **What is a family?**

A family is a relationship in which people live together with commitment, form an economic unit, care for any young, and consider the group critical to their identity. This definition modifies the traditional definition to account for today's greater diversity in living arrangements and relationships in families.

■ **Are U.S. families in decline?**

Not at all, say analysts who take a social change perspective. Families are becoming more complex and diverse, adapting to other changes in society. For one thing, marriage is no longer a cultural imperative; for another, many people reaffirm their belief in the institution through serial monogamy, a succession of marriages over a lifetime.

■ **What are the sociological perspectives on family-related problems?**

Functionalists believe that the family provides social order and economic stability; the family is the solution to many societal problems, and dysfunctional families threaten the well-being of individuals and the whole of society. Conflict and feminist theorists see the family as a problem in society, not a solution; they believe that the family is a major source of inequality in society. Symbolic interactionists view the family first in terms of socialization. Some speak of the shared reality of marriage; some view family problems in terms of the subjective meanings that people give to their everyday lives; and some cite partners' unrealistic expectations about love and marriage.

■ **What characterizes singlehood in the United States today?**

The proportion of the U.S. population that has never married has continued to grow since the 1960s. Some people remain single by choice, others by necessity; many working-class young people cannot afford to marry and set up a household.

■ **Why do young people postpone marriage today?**

Four factors are important: The changing job structure in the United States leads to economic uncertainty; more women are in the labor force; sexual relationships outside marriage are more socially acceptable than before; and young people observing the rising divorce rate may be cautious about jumping into marriage.

■ **Does cohabitation usually lead to a successful marriage? What is a domestic partnership?**

According to one recent study, only about 50 percent of cohabiting couples marry, and evidence on whether those marriages succeed is mixed. Some studies show little or no effect; others show that partners who cohabit are more likely to divorce than partners who do not. A domestic partnership is a household partnership in which an unmarried couple lives together in a committed, sexually intimate relationship and is granted the same rights and benefits as married heterosexual couples.

■ **What does research show about dual-earner marriages?**

More than 50 percent of all marriages in the United States are dual-earner marriages, that is, marriages in which both spouses are in the labor force. Many women in these marriages do the domestic work at home after completing their workday jobs, though there seems to be a trend toward more egalitarian families.

■ **Is a two-parent family always preferable to a one-parent family?**

If the parents argue constantly, are alcoholics, or abuse the children, a supportive single-parent family would be preferable. However, growing up in a single-parent household poses serious risks to a child that are complicated by other factors, such as poverty, discrimination, unsafe neighborhoods, and high crime rates.

■ **Why is reproductive freedom such a controversial issue?**

Reproductive freedom implies the desire to have or not to have a child, and the roles that religious organizations, physicians, and the legal establishment should play in controlling a woman's fertility continue to be debated. Contraception, abortion, and the new reproductive technologies all raise personal and—when activists on either side get involved—societal issues.

■ **Are teen pregnancies increasing or declining?**

Teen pregnancies have decreased over the past thirty years, but the teenage birthrate is higher in the United States than in any other high-income nation. Recently, there has been an increase in births among unwed teenage mothers, particularly among African American teens.

■ **Who gets divorced, and do most people remarry?**

Many factors affect who gets divorced (e.g., marrying during the teen years or having limited economic resources), and these factors are interrelated with class, race, and age, so it is very difficult to determine any kind of statistical likelihood of divorce. Most people do remarry, and divorce and remarriage leads to complex family relationships, such as blended families.

KEY TERMS

blended family, p. 261
cohabitation, p. 252
domestic partnership, p. 252
dual-earner marriages, p. 253
extended family, p. 248
families, p. 247
family of orientation, p. 259
family of procreation, p. 259
kinship, p. 248
monogamy, p. 250
nuclear family, p. 248
second shift, p. 253

QUESTIONS FOR CRITICAL THINKING

1. Sociologist Andrew Cherlin says that the family is a highly adaptable social institution, but we can minimize the costs of change in the family unit by modifying other social institutions of daily life, such as the economy and workplace. What specific suggestions can you give for modifications in these and other areas?

2. What suggestions can you offer to help offset the potentially detrimental effects of single-parent households, especially when the parent is a woman who is employed fulltime?

3. How can problems of family abuse and violence be successfully addressed by our nation? Do all social policies require large sums of money to implement? Why or why not?

4. How do you think changing trends in American families will affect families and intimate relationships in the future?

Succeed with MySocLab® www.mysoclab.com

The new MySocLab delivers proven results in helping students succeed, provides engaging experiences that personalize learning, and comes from a trusted partner with educational expertise and a deep commitment to helping students and instructors achieve their goals.

Here are a few activities you will find for this chapter:

Watch on **mysoclab.com**

Core Concepts video clips feature sociologists in action, exploring important concepts in the study of Social Problems. Watch:
• Women in the Workplace

Explore on **mysoclab.com**

Social Explorer is an interactive application that allows you to explore Census data through interactive maps. Explore:
• Social Explorer Activity: Changing Household Size Between 1970 and 2000

Read on **mysoclab.com**

MySocLibrary includes primary source readings from classic and contemporary sociologists. Read:
• The Way We Weren't: The Myth and Reality of the "Traditional" Family

Problems in Education

Thinking Sociologically

- What factors have contributed to your success in school? Have you also experienced problems that caused you to fall short of some of your objectives?

- Major sociological perspectives differ on problems related to education. What are the major causes, effects, and possible solutions for problems in today's schools according to each of these approaches?

- How do race, class, and gender affect people's educational opportunities?

When we were in junior high school, my friend Rich and I made a map of the school lunch tables according to popularity. This was easy to do, because kids only ate lunch with others of about the same popularity. We graded them from A to E. "A" tables were full of football players and cheerleaders and so on. "E" tables contained the kinds with mild cases of Down's syndrome, which in the language of the time we called "retards."

We sat at a "D" table, as low as you could get without looking physically different. We were not being especially candid to grade ourselves as D. . . . Everyone in the school knew exactly how popular everyone else was, including us. . . . I know a lot of people who were nerds in school, and they all tell the same story: there is a strong correlation between being smart and being a nerd, and an even stronger inverse correlation between being a nerd and being popular. Being smart seems to

make you unpopular. . . . And that, I think, is the root of the problem. Nerds serve two masters. They want to be popular, certainly, but they want even more to be smart. And popularity is not something you can do in your spare time, not in the fiercely competitive environment of an American secondary [middle and high] school. . . . Merely understanding the situation [nerds are in] should make it less painful. Nerds aren't losers. They're just playing a different game, and a game much closer to the one played in the real world.

—Paul Graham (PhD in computer science from Harvard, designer of ARC language, and creator of Yahoo Store) describes in his recent book, Hackers & Painters: Big Ideas from the Computer Age *(2004), how he and other "nerds" have become successful as adults, an accomplishment that he does not attribute to American public schools.*

Most of us have memories about our junior high and high school years that include where we thought we fit in to the student pecking order. Often this hierarchy or pecking order was symbolized by the people we ate with and where we sat at lunch because this was one brief period in the school day when we were allowed to make personal choices about our interactions with other people. Individuals like Paul Graham remember the school hierarchy as being based on athletic ability, personal appearance, and one's general popularity while others remember their cafeteria as having enclaves where students "chose" to sit with others from their own racial or ethnic category (see Tatum, 2003). At the individual level (microlevel), some people realize that their school's social environment did not mesh with their personal interests and aptitudes while others describe their school years as being among the best in their lives. At the societal level (macrolevel), sociologists who study *education*—**the social institution responsible for transmitting knowledge, skills, and cultural values in a formally organized structure**—are particularly interested in factors that contribute to the success of schools and problems that cause them to fall short of their ideals and objectives. Today, we have a wide gap between the ideals of U.S. education and the realities of daily life in many schools. As a result, many business and political leaders, parents, teachers, students, and other concerned citizens identify a number of problems with U.S. education. In this chapter, we examine contemporary problems in education and assess how these problems are intertwined with other social problems in the United States and worldwide. We'll begin with an overview of sociological perspectives on problems in education.

DID YOU KNOW

- Fourteen percent of U.S. adults (about 30 million people) do not read well enough to fill out a job application.

- A higher percentage of secondary school teachers are threatened with injury by students, but a higher percentage of elementary school teachers are actually physically attached by students.

- The average cost of center-based child care is higher than the average cost of public university tuition in a majority of U.S. states.

- Parents' level of education is a stronger predictor of students' standardized test scores than the amount of public money spent on education.

SOCIOLOGICAL PERSPECTIVES ON EDUCATION

The way in which a sociologist studies education depends on the theoretical perspective he or she takes. Functionalists, for example, believe that schools should promote good citizenship and upward mobility and that problems in education are related to social disorganization, rapid social change, and the organizational structure of schools. Conflict theorists believe that schools perpetuate inequality and that problems in education are the result of bias based on race, class, and gender. Meanwhile, interactionists focus on microlevel problems in schools, such as how communication and teachers' expectations affect students' levels of achievement and dropout rates.

Functionalist Perspectives

Functionalists believe that education is one of the most important social institutions because it contributes to the smooth functioning of society and provides individuals with opportunities for personal fulfillment and upward social mobility. According to functionalists, when problems occur, they can usually be traced to the failure of educational institutions—schools, colleges, universities—to fulfill one of their manifest functions. **Manifest functions are open, stated, and intended goals or consequences of activities within an organization or institution.** Although the most obvious manifest function of education is the teaching of academic subjects (reading, writing, mathematics, science, and history), education has at least five major manifest functions in society:

Socialization. From kindergarten through college, schools teach students the student role, specific academic subjects, and political socialization. In kindergarten, children learn the appropriate attitudes and behavior for the student role (Ballantine and Hammack, 2009). In primary and secondary schools, students are taught specific subject matter that is appropriate to their age, skill level, and previous educational experience. At the college level, students expand their knowledge and seek out new areas of study. Throughout, students learn the democratic process.

Transmission of culture. Schools transmit cultural norms and values to each new generation and play a major role in assimilation, the process whereby recent immigrants learn dominant cultural values, attitudes, and behavior so that they can be productive members of society.

Social control. Although controversy exists over whose values should be taught, schools are responsible for teaching values such as discipline, respect, obedience, punctuality, and perseverance. Schools teach conformity by encouraging young people to be good students, conscientious future workers, and law-abiding citizens.

Social placement. Schools are responsible for identifying the most qualified people to fill available positions in society. Students are often channeled into programs on the basis of their individual ability and academic achievement. Graduates receive the appropriate credentials for entering the paid labor force

Change and innovation. Schools are a source of change and innovation. To meet the needs of student populations at particular times, new programs—such as HIV/AIDS education, computer education, and multicultural studies—are created. College and university faculty members are expected to conduct research and publish new knowledge that benefits the overall society. A major goal of change and innovation in education is to reduce social problems.

In addition to these manifest functions, education fulfills a number of **latent functions—hidden, unstated, and sometimes unintended consequences of activities in an organization or institution.** Consider, for example, these latent functions of education: Compulsory school attendance keeps children and teenagers off the streets (and, by implication, out of trouble) and out of the full-time job market for a number of years (controlling the flow of workers). High schools and colleges serve as matchmaking institutions where people often meet future marriage partners. By bringing people of similar ages, racial and ethnic groups, and social class backgrounds together, schools establish social networks.

Functionalists acknowledge many dysfunctions in education, but one seems overriding today: Our public schools are not adequately preparing students for jobs and global competition. In comparative rankings of students across countries on standardized reading, mathematics, and science tests, U.S. students are lagging. However, the current state of the U.S. economy, including high rates of unemployment and low levels of job creation, also contribute to this problem in many regions of the country.

Functionalist and conservative efforts to improve education were introduced during the first term of the Bush administration. To reform education, President George W. Bush signed into law the No Child Left Behind (NCLB) Act of 2001. Proponents of this law hoped to improve education for the nation's children by changing the federal government's role in kindergarten through twelfth grade and by asking schools to be accountable for students' learning. Several critical steps were set forth to produce a more "accountable" education system:

- States created a set of standards—beginning with math and reading—for what all children should know at the end of each grade in school; other standards would be developed over a period of time.
- States were required to test every student's progress toward meeting those standards.
- States, individual school districts, and individual schools are all expected to make yearly progress toward meeting the standards.
- School districts must report results regarding the progress of individual schools toward meeting these standards.
- Schools and districts that do not make adequate progress are to be held accountable and could lose funding and pupils; in some cases, parents can move their children from low-performing schools to schools that are meeting the standards.

After the 2008 presidential election, NCLB was subsequently opposed by the Obama administration; however, the end products of this act remain in effect in the nation's schools. During the NCLB era, some improvements were made in fourth- and eighth-grade reading and math scores nationwide, particularly among African American and Hispanic students. However, critics believed that NCLB did not accurately address the main problems facing U.S. education—lack of money and lack of incentives for teaching and learning, not more testing of students and teachers.

In 2010, the Obama administration issued "A Blueprint for Reform" in an effort to reauthorize the Elementary and Secondary Education Act, an initiative that had been in place prior to the NCLB era. Four major priorities were included in this blueprint:

1. Improving teacher and principal effectiveness to ensure that every classroom has a great teacher and every school has a great leader
2. Providing information to families to help them evaluate and improve their children's schools, and to educators to help them improve their students' learning

3. Implementing college- and career-ready standards and developing improved assessments aligned with those standards
4. Improving student learning and achievement in America's lowest-performing schools by providing intensive support and effective interventions (U.S. Department of Education, 2010)

Overall, the plan's purpose is to produce greater equity and opportunity for all students. A "Race to the Top" in education, built on the American Recovery and Reinvestment Act of 2009, was supposed to provide additional competitive grants to expand innovations in education, support effective charter schools, promote public school choice, and provide assistance to magnet schools. However, with the United States facing financial crises at home and international problems abroad, the national political climate has not been conducive to adding more money to overburdened state and local school budgets. Consequently, even with those with a functionalist/conservative perspective highlighting the importance of education, it remains difficult to determine if progress will be made in improving schools through the Obama plan or similar proposals in the future. Critics claim such plans cannot be adequately funded in difficult economic times and that these blueprints for change are usually too ambitious.

Conflict Perspectives

Sociologists using a conflict framework for analyzing problems in education believe that schools—which are supposed to reduce social inequalities in society—actually perpetuate inequalities based on class, race, and gender (Apple, 1982). In fact, conflict theorists such as Pierre Bourdieu argue that education *reproduces* existing class relationships (see Bourdieu and Passeron, 1990). According to Bourdieu, students have differing amounts of *cultural capital* that they learn at home and bring with them to the classroom (see Chapter 2). Children from middle- and upper-income homes have considerable cultural capital because their parents have taught them about books, art, music, and other forms of culture. According to Bourdieu, children from low-income and poverty-level families have not had the same opportunities to acquire cultural capital. Some social analysts believe that it is students' cultural capital, rather than their "natural" intelligence or aptitude, that is measured on the standardized tests used for tracking. Thus, test results unfairly limit some students' academic choices and career opportunities (Oakes, 1985).

Other sociologists using the conflict framework focus on problems associated with the hidden curriculum, a term coined by sociologist John C. Holt (1964) in his study of why children fail. The **hidden curriculum refers to how certain cultural values and attitudes, such as conformity and obedience to authority, are transmitted through implied demands in the everyday rules and routines of schools** (B. R. Snyder, 1971). These conflict theorists suggest that elites use a hidden curriculum that teaches students to be obedient and patriotic—values that uphold the status quo in society and turn students into compliant workers—to manipulate the masses and maintain their power in society.

Although students from all social classes experience the hidden curriculum to some degree, studies in the past have shown that working-class and poverty-level students are the most adversely affected (Ballantine and Hammack, 2009). According to these studies, when middle-class teachers teach students from lower-class backgrounds, the classrooms are more structured, and teachers have lower expectations of students. Studies have also shown that schools that primarily serve upper-middle and upper-class families primarily focus on developing students' analytical powers and critical thinking skills, such as teaching them how to apply abstract principles to problem solving. These schools also emphasize creative activities so that students can express their own ideas and apply them to different areas of study. By contrast, schools for children from working-class and poverty-level families tend to spend much more time each day on disciplinary procedures and remedial programs to help students catch up and make higher scores on standardized tests. From the conflict approach, the hidden curriculum teaches working-class and poverty-level students that they are expected to arrive on time, follow bureaucratic rules, take orders from others, and to endure boredom without complaining (Ballantine and Hammack, 2009). The limitations on what and how these students are taught mean that many of them do not get any higher education and therefore never receive the credentials to enter high-paying professions. Our society emphasizes *credentialism*—a process of social selection that gives class advantage and social status to people who possess academic qualifications (R. Collins, 1979).

Credentialism is closely related to *meritocracy*—a social system in which status is assumed to be acquired through individual ability and effort (Young, 1994). People who acquire the appropriate credentials for a job are assumed to have gained the position through what they know, not who they are or who they know. According to conflict theorists, however, the hidden curriculum determines in advance that credentials will stay in the hands of the elites, so the United States is not a meritocracy even if it calls itself one.

Symbolic Interactionist Perspectives

Whereas functionalists examine the relationship between the functions of education and problems in schools and conflict theorists focus on how education perpetuates inequality, symbolic interactionists study classroom dynamics and how practices such as labeling affect students' self-concept and aspirations.

Symbolic interactionists believe that education is an integral part of the socialization process. Through the formal structure of schools and interpersonal relationships with peers and teachers, students develop a concept of self that lasts long beyond their schooling. Overall, social interactions in school can be either positive or negative. When students learn, develop, and function effectively, their experience is positive. For many students, however, the school environment and peer group interactions leave them discouraged and unhappy. When students who might do better with some assistance from teachers and peers are instead labeled "losers," they might come to view themselves as losers and thus set the stage for *self-fulfilling* prophecies. As was noted in Chapter 1, a self-fulfilling prophecy occurs when an unsubstantiated belief or prediction results in behavior that makes the original false belief come true. Past studies have shown that teachers who distinguish among children based on perceived levels of intelligence do create self-fulfilling prophecies in children who typically perform according to how the teacher has treated them: The allegedly "bright" children do extremely well and become successes, and the other children are labeled as underachievers or failures.

Standardized tests can also lead to labeling, self-fulfilling prophecies, and low self-esteem. In fact, say symbolic interactionists, standardized tests such as IQ (intelligence quotient) tests particularly disadvantage racial, ethnic, and language minorities in the United States. IQ testing first became an issue in the United States in the early 1900s when immigrants from countries such as Italy, Poland, and Russia typically scored lower than immigrants from northern Europe did. As a result, teachers did not expect them to do as well as children from families with northern European backgrounds and therefore did not encourage them or help them overcome educational obstacles (Feagin, Baker, and Feagin, 2006). In time, these ethnic groups became stigmatized as less intelligent.

Today, the debate over intelligence continues, but the focus has shifted to African Americans. In their highly controversial book *The Bell Curve: Intelligence and Class Structure in American Life*, Richard J. Herrnstein and Charles Murray (1994) argue that intelligence is genetically inherited and people cannot be "smarter" than they are born to be, regardless of their environment or education. According to Herrnstein and Murray, certain racial-ethnic groups differ in average IQ and are likely to differ in "intelligence genes" as well. To bolster their arguments, Herrnstein and Murray point out that on average, people living in Asia score higher on IQ tests than white Americans and that African Americans score 15 points lower on average than white Americans.

Watch on **mysoclab.com**
Inequities in Education
on **mysoclab.com**

Many scholars have refuted Herrnstein and Murray's conclusions, but the idea of inherited mental superiority and inferiority tends to take on a life of its own when some people want to believe that such differences exist (Duster, 1995; Hauser, 1995; H. F. Taylor, 1995). In 2008, the British psychologist Richard Lynn's *The Global Bell Curve: Race, IQ, and Inequality Worldwide*, expanded the ideas of Herrnstein and Murray to include the nations of the world. According to Lynn, in multiracial nations, people of Jewish and east Asian ancestry have the highest average IQ scores and socioeconomic positions, followed by whites, south Asians, Hispanics, and people of African descent. Lynn attributes people's positions in the socioeconomic hierarchy to differences in intelligence on the basis of race-ethnicity. Today, so-called IQ fundamentalists continue to label students and others on the basis of IQ tests, claiming that these tests measure some identifiable trait that predicts the quality of people's thinking and their ability to perform. By contrast, critics of IQ tests argue that these exams measure a number of factors—including motivation, home environment, type of socialization at home, and quality of schooling—not intelligence alone (Yong, 2011). But, perhaps the most important criticism of IQ testing is how this practice can lead to the self-fulfilling prophecy for individuals. According to symbolic interactionists, labels about intelligence and other innate characteristics stigmatize

students and *marginalize* them—put people at the lower or outer limits of a group—in their interactions with parents, teachers, and other students, and lead to self-fulfilling prophecies. Likewise, students who are labeled as having above-average intellectual ability, academic aptitude, creative or productive thinking, or leadership skills may achieve at a higher level because of the label.

PROBLEMS IN U.S. EDUCATION

Although we have already identified a variety of problems in education, other issues must be addressed in planning for the future of this country. These issues include the problem of illiteracy; the impact of high rates of immigration on educational systems; race, class, and gender inequalities in educational opportunities; and growing concerns about violence in schools.

Functional Illiteracy

In her memoir *Life Is Not a Fairy Tale*, Fantasia Barrino, a popular U.S. singer and former *American Idol* winner, explained that she is functionally illiterate and that she had to fake her way through portions of the televised talent show that required her to read lines. The story of her life was dictated to a freelance writer, but she committed herself to learning how to read because she wants to be able to read to her daughter. Moreover, Fantasia Barrino's situation is not an isolated case. People were shocked with a recent study by the National Institute for Literacy found that about 47 percent of adults in Detroit, Michigan, are **functionally illiterate— unable to read and/or write at the skill level necessary for carrying out everyday tasks**. Although similar studies have not been conducted throughout the United States in recent years, functional illiteracy remains a problem in many cities.

It is estimated that as many as 30 million people over age sixteen (which would be 14 percent of the U.S. adult population) do not read well enough to fill out a job application or understand a newspaper story with an eighth-grade reading level (ProLiteracy.org, 2010). Higher rates of functional illiteracy typically are found in areas with higher percentages of minority and immigrant populations. This may be partly due to larger, underlying social problems, such as high rates of poverty and lack of available resources to help people gain a better education. Especially telling is the fact that more than 60 percent of inmates in state and federal correctional facilities can barely read and write (ProLiteracy.org, 2010).

Illiteracy is a social problem that we may be able to reduce with adequate time and resources. Various organizations seek to reduce illiteracy by offering classes to help children and adults learn how to read and write.

Some social analysts believe that illiteracy will not be as big a problem in the future because new technologies will make reading and writing as we know it obsolete. These analysts note that the information age increasingly depends on communication by computers and other smart machines, not on basic reading and math computation skills. Still other educators and community leaders believe that illiteracy can be overcome through televised instruction in basic skills and courses on the Internet. However, not all social analysts believe that technology is the answer: Knowing how to read the printed word remains the access route to every other form of intellectual information. People need basic literacy skills before they can benefit from computers and other information technologies. Business and industry are now playing a role in solving the problem. Some critics say that the illiteracy problem is largely an

immigration problem. Recent immigrants to this country continue to speak their own languages rather than learn English. However, high rates of illiteracy should not necessarily be blamed on U.S. immigration policies because many persons who have lived in this country since birth have this problem.

Immigration and Increasing Diversity in Schools

Debates over the role of schools in educating immigrants for life in the United States are not new. In fact, high rates of immigration—along with the rapid growth of industrial capitalism and the factory system during the Industrial Revolution—brought about the free public school movement in the second half of the nineteenth century. Many immigrants arriving in U.S. cities during this time spoke no English and could neither read nor write. Because of the belief that democracy requires an educated citizenry, schools were charged with the responsibility of "Americanizing" immigrants and their children. Workers needed basic reading, writing, and arithmetic skills to get jobs in factories and offices. Initially, an eighth-grade education was considered sufficient for many jobs, but soon a high school diploma became a prerequisite for most jobs above the level of the manual laborer. Schooling during this era was designed primarily to give people the means to become self-supporting. Educational systems were supposed to turn out workers who had the knowledge and skills needed to enter the labor market and produce profits for managers and owners.

In the second half of the twentieth century, this country again experienced high rates of immigration from many nations around the world, and many of the newcomers were school-age children. In the twenty-first century, some recent groups of immigrants are well educated, but most have limited formal education and few job skills. Today, about 20 percent of U.S. residents age five and older speak a language other than English at home (see Table 12.1 on page 278). Because we use language to communicate with others, develop a sense of personal identity, and acquire knowledge and skills necessary for survival, schools must cope with language differences among students.

Although most recent immigrants rely on public schools to educate their children, some supplement school efforts with additional educational opportunities. For example, some Asian and Pacific American parents have established weekend cram schools, which are similar to the *juku* in Japan, *buxiban* in the People's Republic of China, and *hagwon* in Republic of Korea, also known as South Korea (see Box 12.1). Students spend a full day on subjects such as math and English and get specialized help in building study skills and learning test-taking strategies. Their parents are willing to pay for these classes so that the children will not experience language and cultural barriers that limit opportunities.

How best to educate children of recent immigrants with lower levels of education and income is a pressing problem in states that have high levels of immigration, such as California, New York, Florida, Texas, and New Jersey. Some school districts establish transitional programs for newcomers, six months to four years of classes taught in English and in the student's native language. Some schools offer bilingual education in as many as ten languages in major subjects such as math, science, and social studies.

Educational Opportunities and Race, Class, and Gender

Most research on access to educational opportunities for minority students has focused on how racially segregated schools affect student performance and self-esteem. Indeed, more than fifty years after the 1954 Supreme Court ruling in *Brown v. The Board of Education of Topeka, Kansas*, which stated that "separate but equal" schools are unconstitutional because they are inherently unequal, racial segregation or resegregation appears to be increasing in education rather than decreasing. Progress in bringing about racial *desegregation* (the abolition of legally sanctioned racial-ethnic segregation) and *integration*, which, for schools, involves taking specific action to change the racial or class composition of the student body, has been extremely slow for African Americans because segregated schools mirror race- and class-based residential segregation. Today, students of color make up the vast majority of the student body in some urban school districts, whereas middle- and upper-class white students make up the majority of the student body in private urban schools or suburban public schools. According to sociologists, schools in which racial and ethnic minorities are in the majority typically have high teacher–student ratios (more students per teacher), inexperienced teachers who are sometimes less qualified, lower expectations of students, and high dropout rates (Feagin et al., 2006).

Read the Document

Detours on the Road to Equality: Women, Work and Higher Education on mysoclab.com

TABLE 12.1 Principal Languages Spoken at Home (United States)

Language Used at Home	Persons Five Years Old and Over Who Speak It
English only	227,366,000
Spanish	34,560,000
Chinese	2,466,000
Tagalog	1,488,000
French	1,333,000
German	1,122,000
Korean	1,052,000
Russian	864,000
Arabic	786,000
Italian	782,000
Portuguese	661,000
French Creole	646,000
Polish	620,000
Hindi	560,000
Japanese	440,000
Persian	379,000
Urdu	353,000
Greek	337,000
Gujarathi	333,000
Serbo-Croatian	274,000
Armenian	231,000
Hebrew	213,000
Mon-Khmer (Cambodian)	183,000
Navaho	171,000
Yiddish	169,000
Other Native North American languages	193,000

Source: U.S. Census Bureau, 2010.

How segregated are U.S. schools? Here are a few facts: More than half of all African American public school students in Illinois, Michigan, and New York

Cramming for Success in Japan and South Korea

It's no secret that the Japanese have long been obsessed with education. Students flock to shrines to write prayers on wooden tablets asking for good grades. The lure of top schools is so strong that even kindergartners sometimes study for months before entrance exams, and students who fail college entrance tests are known to spend a year or two polishing their skills for another shot. For years that obsession has paid off in global leadership in innovation and design for Japan. These days, though, the country is losing its edge.

—*Business journalists Ian Rowley and Hiroko Tashiro (2005) describe the emphasis placed on education in Japan as a prelude to explaining why cram schools have become a billion-dollar industry.*

The students here were forsaking all the pleasures of teenage life. No cell phones allowed, no fashion magazines, no television, no Internet. No dating, no concerts, no earrings, no manicures—no acting their age. All these are mere distractions from an overriding goal . . . to clear the fearsome hurdle that can decide their future—the national college entrance examination.

—*Journalist Choe Sang-Hun (2008) of the* New York Times *explains the "boot camp" atmosphere of a cram school in Yongin, South Korea (also known as Republic of Korea), to show how much importance parents and students place on getting high marks on the exam that determines whether students will be admitted to a top-notch university.*

Cram schools, or *juku, buxibani*, and *hagwon*, have been around for many years in nations such as Japan, People's Republic of China, and Republic of Korea (South Korea); however, they are growing in popularity as the need to excel on standardized entrance examinations for college has become increasingly important to many families. What are cram schools? These schools are afternoon, evening, and weekend tutoring schools where students receive additional instruction in academic subjects, while specifically focusing on how to score high on standardized exams. At Jongro Yongin Campus, students are miles away from any kind of transportation and they do nothing but cram from 6:30 A.M. to past midnight, seven days a week. To attend a cram school, major family commitments are required: Money from parents and time from young people. In Japan, for example, Atsuki Yamamoto's parents pay $9,200 a year for him to attend Nichinoken four evenings a week from 5 to 9 P.M. and take exams every Sunday to prepare for entrance exams at elite junior high schools. The Yamamotos hope that if Atsuki is admitted to an elite private junior high school, he will later be accepted at a top high school and, eventually, a prestigious university (Rowley and Tashiro, 2005). In South Korea, Park Hong-ki spends $1,936 a month for his son's tuition at Jongro and admits that "It's a big financial burden for me" (Sang-Hun, 2008). The Yamamotos in Japan and the Hong-kis in South Korea are not alone in their hopes and aspirations for their children, as evidenced by the popularity of cram schools in these Southeast Asian nations.

In Japan, the People's Republic of China, and South Korea, education is everything to many people: The job you get depends on the university you attended, which depends on the high school you went to, which in turn depends on your elementary school, which, finally, depends on where you went to preschool. Thus, the sooner a child begins cramming, the better: Three- and four-year-olds prepare for preschool entrance exams by sitting at little desks in a ninety-minute class designed to improve performance on IQ tests. Even at this young age, the competition to attend the better schools is so strong that children may see each other as rivals rather than as classmates. In cities such as Hong Kong, the top cram school teachers are thought of as educational "stars," and students compete to get the best teachers in these "tutorial schools."

Cram schools have increased in popularity not only with parents but also with business investors. Many of the *juku* in Japan, for example, are owned by national corporations that advertise extensively and earn profits in the billions each year. According to business journalists, "Japan's new insecurity over its age-old obsession [education], it seems, is good for business" (Rowley and Tashiro, 2005). As long as the future of so many students hangs on scores from one major exam, the future of top tutors and cram schools is probably secure in many nations.

Questions for Consideration

1. How does the emphasis on high test scores and educational achievement in Japan and South Korea compare with the major educational concerns in U.S. education?

2. Do children in nations such as Japan, China, and South Korea pay too high a price for educational achievement? Why or why not?

3. What might students in the United States gain from intensive educational tutoring in cram school? What problems might U.S. students face in such a high-pressure environment?

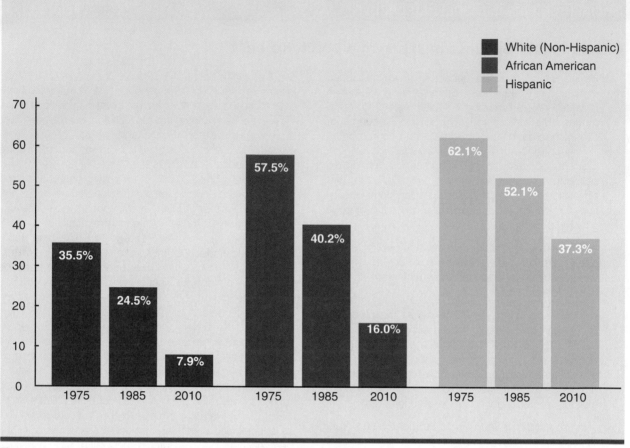

Figure 12.1 Percentage of persons 25 years and over not completing high school by race and Hispanic origin, 1975, 1985, and 2010
Source: U.S. Census Bureau, 2010.

Urban high schools face many challenges today. One pressing concern is how to provide the best educational opportunities for a highly diverse group of students.

state attend predominately black schools. In Maryland, Alabama, Mississippi, Tennessee, Georgia, and Texas, approximately 30 percent of African American public school students attend schools that have at least a 95 percent African American population. Children of color now constitute more than half of public school students in a number of states because White (non-Hispanic) children are more often enrolled in charter schools, suburban school districts, or private schools with a high percentage of white students (Dewan, 2010). Even more problematic is the high percentage of Latinos/as (Hispanics) who have dropped out of school or otherwise not completed high school (see Figure 12.1).

Why are dropout rates so high for Latino/a students? One explanation for the

Report Card Framing: Does Education Get an A or an F?

Some *New York Times* headlines read:

- "U.S. Students Remain Poor at History, Tests Show" (Dillon, 2011b)
- "Failing Grades on Civics Exam Called a 'Crisis'" (Dillon, 2011a)
- "12th-Grade Reading and Math Scores Rise Slightly After a Historic Low in 2005" (Dillon, 2010)

The scores go up slightly; the scores go down slightly; or they remain "poor" or "failing." What's going on in U.S. schools when it comes to test scores as reported in the media? Media reports showing the latest results of national exams given to students in U.S. schools are routinely found in newspapers, on Internet websites, and on television news broadcasts. In most cases, bad test scores receive more attention than good scores in media accounts. In fact, the media often use test scores to "grade" students and schools in much the same way that educators use report cards to inform students and their parents about how students are doing in school.

Some sociologists who study the media use the terminology *report card framing* to refer to this type of coverage. As previously discussed, media framing refers to the manner in which reporters and other journalists organize information before they present it to an audience. For reporters on the "education beat," for example, part of that organization involves determining how to report on nationwide student testing and what slant to give the story regarding the positive or negative evaluation of those grades. As a result, *report card framing* refers to how the media give students, teachers, and schools "passing" or "failing" grades based on the results of standardized test scores. This type of framing assumes that such scores are a good measure of the academic achievements of students and the quality of teachers and schools. This framing does not take into account students' diverse family backgrounds in regard to class, race-ethnicity, nationality,

region, and urban, suburban, or rural residential location. It also does not consider whether standardized exams may be biased against students who come from backgrounds that are different from those who prepare the questions on standardized exams. Similarly, report card framing assumes that tests are the best way to determine how well teachers teach and how well the educational system in our country functions.

In the past decade, major national newspapers such as the *New York Times* have expanded their coverage of students' test scores to include issues such as how student populations vary on the basis of race-ethnicity and country of origin in test scores. Other media sources, such as television and Internet news sites, use catchy "zippers" across the bottom of the TV screen or "pop-ups" on computer screens to get users' attention, and these sources typically do not have in-depth analysis of education statistics for fear of losing their audience. Catchy banners such as "Have U.S. students lost the competitive edge in the global economy?" are more likely to be the framing approach of this type of news coverage, leaving media audiences with little to go on except the "Pass–Fail" perspective on how students and schools are doing in the twenty-first century.

Questions for Consideration

1. Should journalists and other members of the media expand their reporting on education to cover a wider array of issues than just the results of standardized examinations?

2. To what extent do standardized test scores capture what is really happening in the classroom? Do they show what is most important in the learning process for students?

3. What other issues do you believe might be equally, or more, important for the media to cover in regard to schools and problems in education today?

high dropout rate comes from a comprehensive study of Latino/a high school graduates in Texas. Researchers found that high dropout rates were more closely linked to practices in schools and attitudes within the community than to individual or family problems (Romo and Falbo, 1996). Across lines of race and ethnicity, students from poor families are three to four times more likely to become school dropouts than are students from affluent families.

Another explanation for high dropout rates among all students of color, is that students may be "pushed out" of school because low-achieving students are viewed as bringing down standardized test scores, which are used to evaluate not only students but also teachers and administrators. Media reports may further contribute to the emphasis placed on standardized tests as a means of "passing" or "failing" students, teachers, and schools (see Box 12.2).

Even racially integrated schools often recreate segregation in the classroom when tracking or ability grouping is used. *Tracking* **is the practice of assigning students to specific courses and educational programs on the basis of their test scores, previous grades, or both.** Lower-level courses and special education classes are disproportionately filled with children of color, while gifted-and-talented programs and honors courses are more likely to be filled with white and Asian and Pacific American students.

Does gender bias in schools negatively affect female students? An extensive national survey on gender and self-esteem by the American Association of University Women (1992) found that girls were shortchanged in schools at that time. For example, reading materials, classroom activities, and treatment by teachers and peers often contributed to a feeling among many girls and young women that they were less important than male students. The accepted wisdom was that, over time, differential treatment undermines females' self-esteem and discourages them from taking certain courses, such as math and science, which have been dominated by male teachers and students. The *AAUW Report: How Schools Shortchange Girls* highlighted inequalities in women's education and started a national debate on gender equity. However, since this report was published, improvements have occurred in girls' educational achievement, as females have attended and graduated from high school and college at a higher rate than their male peers. More females have enrolled in advanced placement or honors courses and in academic areas, such as math and science, where they had previously lagged (AAUW, 2008). After many years of discussion about how schools disadvantaged female students, the emphasis has shifted to the issue of whether girls' increasing accomplishments have come at the expense of males. However, this assumption is false, according to the AAUW (2008:2): "Educational achievement is not a zero-sum game, in which a gain for one group results in a corresponding loss for the other. If girls' success comes at the expense of boys, one would expect to see boys' scores decline as girls' scores rise, but this has not been the case."

Although changes have occurred in regard to race, class, and gender and educational opportunities, differences still remain: White (non-Hispanic) American children are more likely to graduate from high school and college than are their African American and Hispanic peers. Likewise, children from higher-income families are more likely to graduate from high school than children from lower-income families who are also less likely

to attend college. Females may be gaining in certain areas, but they have a long way to go in others (AAUW, 2008). Schools increasingly have been encouraged to foster the development of all students regardless of their gender, race, or class; however, many factors—including lack of adequate funding and other resources—make it difficult for this already hard-pressed social institution to meet the needs and demands of highly diverse student populations.

School Safety and Violence

School officials are increasingly focusing on how to improve safety at schools and how to reduce or eliminate violence. In many schools, teachers and counselors are instructed in anger management and peer mediation, and they are encouraged to develop classroom instruction that teaches values such as respect and responsibility (National Center for Education Statistics [NCES], 2010a). Some schools create partnerships with local law enforcement agencies and social service organizations to link issues of school safety to larger concerns about safety in the community and the nation.

Clearly, some efforts to make schools a safe haven for students and teachers are paying off. Statistics related to school safety continue to show that U.S. schools are among the safest places for young people. According to "Indicators of School Crime and Safety," jointly released by the National Center for Education Statistics (NCES) and the U.S. Department of Justice's Bureau of Justice Statistics, young people are more likely to be victims of violent crime at or near their home, on the streets, at commercial establishments, or at parks than they are at school (NCES, 2010a). However, these statistics do not keep many people from believing that schools are becoming more dangerous with each passing year and that all schools should have high-tech surveillance equipment to help maintain a safe environment.

Even with all of these safety measures in place, violence and fear of violence continue to be pressing problems in schools throughout the United States. This concern extends from kindergarten through grade twelve because violent acts have resulted in deaths in communities such as Jonesboro, Arkansas; Springfield, Oregon; Littleton, Colorado; Santee, California; Red Lake, Minnesota; and an Amish schoolhouse in rural Pennsylvania.

About fifteen students are murdered at U.S. schools each year, but fortunately, this number is lower late in the second decade of the twenty-first century than it

Prison, airport, or school? Security guards and metal detectors have become an increasingly visible scene in many social institutions, including schools, throughout the United States. Do such measures deter school violence? Why or why not?

was in the 1990s. In collecting data on school violence, the CDC includes killings that occur at elementary, middle, or high schools, on school-sponsored trips, or while students are on their way to or from school. Even though the numbers and rates are somewhat lower than in the past, violence and the threat of violence remain a serious problem in many schools. Today, some school buildings look like fortresses or prisons with high fences, bright spotlights at night, and armed security guards. Many schools have installed metal detectors at entrances, and some search students for weapons, drugs, and other contraband as they enter. However, most educational analysts acknowledge that technology alone will not rid schools of violence and crime. Organizations such as the American Federation of Teachers have called for enhancing safety in schools by requiring higher student standards of conduct and achievement and giving teachers and administrators the authority to remove disruptive students. Some school districts require students to wear uniforms in an effort to reduce violence and crime because it was assumed that, if all students are required to dress alike, young people are less likely to be killed for their sneakers, jewelry, or designer clothes.

In 2008 (the latest year for which statistics were available), students between the ages of twelve and eighteen were victims of about 1.2 million nonfatal crimes (such as theft) at school. Although the rates of at-school crimes were lower than previously, many students still feel concern about safety at school. The total crime victimization rate of students ages twelve to eighteen at school declined from 57 victimizations per

1,000 students in 2007 to 47 victimizations per 1,000 students in 2008 (NCES, 2010a).

Teachers, too, may be the victims of bullying or violence on school premises. During the 2007–2008 school year, 10 percent of teachers in city schools reported that they had been threatened with injury. This was a slightly higher percentage than for teachers in smaller communities (7 percent) or suburban or rural schools (6 percent each). Although a greater percentage of secondary school teachers (8 percent) reported that they had been threatened with injury by a student than elementary school teachers (7 percent), elementary school teachers were actually the victims of physical attach (6 percent) more often than teachers in secondary schools (2 percent) (NCES, 2010a). Providing safety at school for students and teachers alike is only one crisis facing school districts that are burdened with shrinking budgets, decaying buildings, and heightened demands for services.

PROBLEMS IN SCHOOL FINANCING

Because financing affects all other aspects of schooling, perhaps it is the biggest problem in education today. Most educational funds come from state legislative appropriations and local property taxes: State sources contribute less than half of public elementary–secondary school system revenue, and the rest comes from local sources and the federal government. In 2008–2009, for example, states contributed slightly less than 47 percent of total public school revenue, as compared to nearly

Teacher layoffs are one of many signs of problems in today's schools where budget shortfalls are limiting students' learning opportunities.

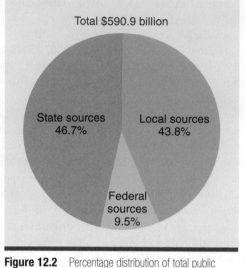

Total $590.9 billion

State sources
46.7%

Local sources
43.8%

Federal
sources
9.5%

Figure 12.2 Percentage distribution of total public elementary–secondary school system revenue, 2008–2009

Note: Percentages may not add up to 100.

Source: Blumerman, 2011.

44 percent from local sources, and 9.5 percent from the federal government (Blumerman, 2011). The total amount of public elementary and secondary school system revenues in that same year was $590.9 billion (see Figure 12.2). Much of the money from federal sources is earmarked for special programs for students who are disadvantaged (e.g., the Head Start program) or who have a disability.

School funding is in crisis in many areas of the nation because of a declining property tax base. Housing foreclosures mean that families are not paying property taxes on their residences. Similarly, as small businesses and major corporations have gone out of business or relocated to other areas, local school districts have been drained of much-needed revenue for operating expenses and maintenance of facilities. The problem of erosion of local property tax revenues is further compounded by the fiscal crises of states that are unable to provide even previously promised funds to school districts. Without the funds from property taxes, schools cannot purchase the textbooks and latest computer technology for educating today's students. At the same time that educational funds are drying up, a record number of students are enrolled in the nation's schools: 76 million in 2008. In addition to meeting the daily needs of today's students and teachers, many schools are in need of major repairs or replacement because of the physical condition of these outdated structures.

Voucher Programs

Is there a way to resolve problems of unequal funding among the states, among school districts within states, and among schools within school districts? Most proposals to improve educational funding have been limited in scope and seem to benefit some groups at the expense of others. For example, some groups encourage what they refer to as "school choice," which usually means some kind of school voucher programs in which public funds (tax dollars) are provided to parents so that they can pay their child's tuition at a private school of their choice. The original idea for school choice was to provide a voucher (equal in value to the average amount spent per student by the local school district) to the family of any student who left the public schools to attend a private school. The private school could exchange the voucher for that amount of money and apply it to the student's tuition at the private school; the school district would save an equivalent amount of money as a result of the student not enrolling in the public schools. Between the origins of vouchers in 1955 and today, variations have been proposed, such as allowing vouchers to be used for transfers between public schools in the same school district, transfers from one public school district to another, transfers only to schools with no religious connections, and vouchers for use only by students from low-income families.

Many parents praise the voucher system because it provides them with options for schooling their children. Some political leaders applaud vouchers and other school choice policies for improving public school performance. However, voucher programs are controversial: Some critics believe that giving taxpayer money to parents so that they can spend it at private (often religious) schools violates some state's constitutions in regard to separation of church and state. The U.S. Supreme Court previously ruled in *Zelman v. Simmons-Harris*, a case involving a Cleveland, Ohio, school district, that voucher policies are constitutional because parents have a choice and are not required to send their children to religious-affiliated schools. Other critics claim that voucher programs are less effective in educating children than public schools. According to studies of the District of Columbia, Milwaukee, and Cleveland, public school students outperformed voucher students in both reading and math on state proficiency tests; however, neither group reached state proficiency requirements (Ott, 2011). In sum, advocates like the choice-factor in voucher programs while critics believe that vouchers undermine public education, lack accountability, and may contribute to the collapse of the public school system.

Charter Schools and For-Profit Schools

Some social analyst and political leaders believe that charter schools and for-profit schools are a more efficient way to educate children and that these schools solve some of the problems of underfunding in public education. Charter schools are primary or secondary schools that receive public money but are free from some of the day-to-day bureaucracy of a larger school district that may limit classroom performance. These schools operate under a charter contract negotiated by the school's organizers (often parents or teachers) and a sponsor (usually a local school board, a state board of education, or a university) that oversees the provisions of the contract. Some school districts "contract out" by hiring for-profit companies on a contract basis to manage charter schools, but the schools themselves are nonprofit. Among the largest educational management organizations are Imagine Schools, National Heritage Academies, The Leona Group, EdisonLearning, White Hat Management, and Mosaica Education (Molnar, Miron, and Urschel, 2010).

Charter schools provide more autonomy for individual students and teachers, and many serve an important function in education: A large number of minority students receive a higher-quality education than they would in the public schools (see J. Hardy, 2010; Winters, 2010). Charter schools attempt to maintain an organizational culture that motivates students and encourages achievement rather than having a negative school environment where minority students are ridiculed for "acting white" or making good grades. Some charter schools offer college preparatory curriculums and help students of color achieve their goal of enrolling in the college or university of their choice (J. Hardy, 2010). However, it is debatable whether charter schools save money and reduce the larger fiscal crises facing large urban school districts that are costly to operate. And, for-profit schools, as the name suggests, have as their goal making money for large corporations more than providing the highest-quality education at the lowest possible cost to students and their families.

On a final note: Some analysts believe that the economic problem of schools might be solved by significantly reducing expenditures for administration and other noninstructional activities and using that money in the classroom. More than one-third of every dollar spent on public education goes for support services rather than education. Expenses for support services include such things as the cost of administration, libraries, buses, sporting events, and repairs to buildings. However, problems in education are not limited to the elementary and secondary levels; higher education has its problems, too.

PROBLEMS IN HIGHER EDUCATION

Higher education serves several important functions in society: the transmission of specialized knowledge and skills, production of new information and technologies, and preparation of the next generation of professionals and scholars. Over the past decade, however, many public colleges and universities have come under increasing financial pressure as appropriations by state legislatures and federal funding have been cut. In response, some schools have intensified their fund-raising efforts, pursuing corporations, nonprofit foundations, and alumni. To remain solvent, many of these schools have also had to increase tuition and student fees.

Explore the Concept

Social Explorer Activity:
Higher Education in America
on mysoclab.com

The Soaring Cost of a College Education

One of the fastest-growing areas of U.S. higher education today is the community college, and one of the greatest challenges facing community colleges today is money. Community colleges educate about half of the nation's undergraduates. The 1,167 community colleges (including public, private and tribal colleges) in the United States enroll about 12.4 million students in credit and noncredit courses. Community college enrollment accounts for 44 percent of all U.S. undergraduate students. Women make up more than half (58 percent) of community college students. Community colleges are also important for underrepresented minority student enrollment: Fifty-five percent of all Native American college students attend a community college, as do 52 percent of all Hispanic students, 44 percent of African American students, and 45 percent of Asian American/Pacific Islanders (American Association of Community Colleges, 2011). However, across the nation, state and local governments struggling to balance their budgets have slashed funding for community colleges. In a number of regions, these cuts have been so severe that schools have been seriously limited in their ability to meet the needs of their students. In some cases, colleges have terminated programs, slashed course offerings, reduced the number of faculty, and eliminated essential student services.

At four-year colleges, increases in average yearly tuition continue to be higher than the rate of inflation. More than 12 million students attend public or private four-year colleges or universities in the United States. Although state colleges and universities typically have lower tuition rates than private colleges because they are funded primarily by tax dollars, some have grown too expensive for students from lower-income families, particularly with the decline in scholarship funds and grants. Many students must take out student loans and go into debt to attend college. Although some students find part-time jobs, their earnings make only a small dent in the cost of tuition and books.

What does a college education cost? According to the *Chronicle of Higher Education* (2010), the average tuition and fees per year at a public four-year institution are $6,319, as compared to $22,449 at a private four-year institution. Average tuition and fees per year at a public two-year institution are $2,137.

Some social analysts believe that a college education is a bargain; however, others argue that the high cost of a college education reproduces the existing class system: Students who lack money may be denied access to higher education, and those who are able to attend college receive different types of education based on their ability to pay. For example, a community college student who receives an associate's degree or completes a certificate program may be prepared for a position in the middle of the occupational status range, such as a dental assistant, computer programmer, or auto mechanic. In contrast, university graduates with four-year degrees are more likely to find initial employment with firms where they stand a chance of being promoted to high-level management and executive positions. In other words, higher educational attainment is associated with positions that offer higher earnings on average. In 2009, high school graduates had average earnings of $31,283, while those with a bachelor's degree earned about $58,613. Median earnings for a worker with a high school diploma alone were about 53 percent of the median earnings of a worker with a bachelor's degree. Average earnings for those with an advanced degree totaled $83,144 (U.S. Census Bureau, 2010).

Given the necessity of getting a college education, is any financial assistance on the way? In 2010 the Obama administration passed a student-loan bill to aid colleges and students. The legislation is designed to "cut out the middle person" by ending the bank-based system of distributing federally subsidized student loans and instead have the Department of Education give loan money directly to colleges and their students. With the savings from this approach, more money is to be put into the Pell Grant program. Unlike a loan, a federal Pell Grant does not have to be repaid. The maximum award for 2011–2012 was $5,500, but not all students were eligible for this amount. Some legislation also provides for additional assistance to historically black colleges in an effort to help more low-income students enroll and succeed in college (Basken, 2010). Many questions remain about student loans and possible long-term effects of high student debt on individuals after they complete their college education.

The Continuing Debate over Affirmative Action

For many years, affirmative action programs in higher education—programs that take race, ethnicity, and gender into consideration for admissions, financial aid, scholarships, fellowships, and faculty hiring—have been the subject of debate among academics and non-academics alike. The legal battle over affirmative action heated up with the 1978 U.S. Supreme Court decision in *Bakke v. The University of California at Davis*. In that case, Allan Bakke, a white male, sued the University of California at Davis, claiming that its policy of allocating 16 of 100 places in the first-year class to members of underrepresented minority groups was discriminatory. Bakke claimed that he had been denied admission to the university's medical school even though his grade point average and Medical College Admissions Test score were higher than those of some minority applicants who were admitted under the university's affirmative action program. Although the Court ruled that Bakke should be admitted to the medical school, it left the door open for schools to increase diversity in their student population.

The affirmative action controversy intensified in the 1990s. In 1995, the regents of the University of California adopted a policy discontinuing any special consideration of "race, religion, sex, color, ethnicity, or national origin" in admissions criteria, and voters in California passed Proposition 209, which is a sweeping prohibition of affirmative action. Proposition 209 amended the California State Constitution to prohibit public institutions from considering race, sex, or ethnicity in admissions policies or other procedures. In 1996, the U.S. Fifth Circuit Court of Appeals ruled in *Hopwood v. State of Texas* that affirmative action programs in public education—even if they were intended to achieve a more diverse student body or to eliminate the present effects of past discrimination—unconstitutionally discriminated against whites. As a result of these and other similar events, it appeared that programs designed to increase subordinate-enrollment at institutions of higher education might become a thing of the past.

In 2003, however, the U.S. Supreme Court ruled in *Grutter v. Bollinger* (involving admissions policies of the University of Michigan's law school) and *Gratz v. Bollinger* (involving the undergraduate admissions policies of the same university) that race can be a factor for universities in shaping their admissions programs, as long as it is within carefully defined limits. Among these limits are that affirmative action plans must not involve quotas (a set number of students from a specific racial or ethnic background *must* be admitted each year, for example) or carry predetermined weight in decisions.

But this was not the end of this contentious issue. In the second decade of the twenty-first century, the University of California once again banned racial affirmative action in public university admissions. A federal lawsuit was filed challenging the constitutionality of California's ban on racial affirmative action. At the time of this writing, California Governor Jerry Brown had filed a legal opinion supporting the lawsuit and speaking out against the ban. It remains to be seen what happens next in the long battle over affirmative (or nonaffirmative) action policies in various states and throughout the nation.

In the twenty-first century, organizations such as the American Association of University Women continue to be advocates for continuing and expanding affirmative action programs in the belief that equity is still an issue. According to affirmative action advocates, greater opportunities in education and the workplace are still very important for women and people of color because discriminatory policies and covert practices often work against them. From this approach, having affirmative action programs in place also serves as a preventive measure: Making people aware that it is important to be committed to equal opportunity for all people and to diversity in education and jobs may help reduce or eliminate potential problems of bias before they occur.

Racial and Ethnic Minorities: Underrepresentation and Discrimination

One of the reasons many social analysts argue for affirmative action is that some racial and ethnic minority categories are underrepresented in higher education. How does college enrollment differ by race and ethnicity? White Americans made up slightly more than 63 percent of all college students as compared to African American enrollment at 13.5 percent and Hispanic/Latina/o enrollment at almost 12 percent (*Chronicle of Higher Education*, 2010). Native American/Alaska Native enrollment rates have remained stagnant at about 1.0 percent; however, tribal colleges on reservations have experienced growth in student enrollment. Founded to overcome racism experienced by Native American students in traditional four-year colleges and to shrink the high dropout rate among Native American college students, 37 colleges are now chartered and run by the Native American nations (American Association of Community Colleges, 2011). Unlike other community colleges, the tribal colleges receive no funding from state and local governments and, as a result, are often short of funds to fulfill their academic mission.

The proportionately low number of people of color enrolled in colleges and universities is reflected in the educational achievement of people age 25 and over, as shown in the "Census Profiles" feature. If we focus on persons who receive doctorate degrees, the underrepresentation of persons of color is even more striking. According to the *Chronicle of Higher Education* (2010), of the 84,960 doctoral degrees conferred in the 2007–2008 academic year, African Americans earned slightly less than 6 percent (4,766 degrees), Hispanics earned slightly less than 4 percent (3,199, and Native Americans/American Indians earned 0.005 percent (432). By contrast, whites (non-Hispanic) earned 47,246 PhDs, or 57 percent of the total number of degrees awarded.

Underrepresentation is not the only problem faced by students of color: Problems of prejudice and discrimination continue on some college campuses. Some problems are overt and highly visible; others are more covert and hidden from public view. Examples of overt racism include mocking Black History Month or a Latino celebration on campuses, referring to individuals by derogatory names, tying nooses on door knobs of dorm rooms or faculty offices, and having "parties" where guests dress in outfits that ridicule people from different cultures or nations.

A study by the sociologists Leslie Houts Picca and Joe R. Feagin (2007) found that many blatant racist events, ranging from private jokes and conversations to violent incidents, occurred in the presence of 600 white students at twenty-eight colleges and universities who were asked to keep diaries and record any racial events they observed. In addition to overt patterns of discrimination, other signs of racism included numerous conversations that took place "back stage" (in white-only spaces where no person of color was present) and involved derogatory comments, skits, or jokes about persons of color. According to Picca and Feagin, most of the racial events were directed at African Americans, but Latinos/as and Asian Americans were also objects of some negative comments.

ARE THERE SOLUTIONS TO EDUCATIONAL PROBLEMS?

During the twenty-first century, we must not underestimate the importance of education as a social institution. It is a powerful and influential force that imparts the values, beliefs, and knowledge that are necessary for the social reproduction of individual personalities and entire cultures (Bourdieu and Passeron, 1990). But in what direction should this tremendous social force move? As a nation, we have learned that spending more money on education does not guarantee that the many pressing problems facing this social institution will be solved (see Box 12.3). On the other hand, it is essential that schools be funded at a level where they can meet the

---

Social Problems and Statistics

Does Spending More Money Guarantee a Better Education?

When political leaders and other policy makers debate problems in education, they often use statistics to back up their arguments. Statistics show that some problems—such as large class size or inadequate school facilities—might be reduced if more money were spent on education. However, statistics also show that simply spending more money does not guarantee better outcomes for children's education. Figure 12.3 shows, for example, that although federal discretionary spending on education more than doubled between 1990 and 2009, this additional expenditure has not improved reading scores overall. Consider the following facts regarding education in the United States:

- Gains in reading and other subject areas occur in some testing years but do not always continue across years and at all levels (testing is done at grades 4, 8, and 12).

- The gap in reading scores across racial and ethnic categories remains. White (non-Hispanic) students continue to score higher than African American and Hispanic (Latino/a) students.

- Researchers presume the scores of Hispanic students remain lower than those of White (non-Hispanic) Americans because of language barriers.

- In subject areas other than reading, such as history, American students score poorly. Only 20 percent of fourth graders, 17 percent of eighth graders, and 12 percent of twelfth graders showing proficiency on recent history exams given by the National Assessment of Educational Progress (NAEP).

- On the civics exam, less than half of all U.S. eighth graders knew the purpose of the Bill of Rights, and 75 percent of twelfth graders could not name a power granted to Congress by the U.S. Constitution.

On the basis of these data, should we assume that less money should be spent on education? Definitely not! However, statistics do show that money alone isn't always the answer to pressing social problems in our nation. Source: Based on NCES, 2010b.

Questions for Consideration

1. If some studies show a stronger relationship between parents' income and students' academic achievement, should the United States be more concerned about addressing income inequality in this nation rather than pouring more money into schools or trying other approaches (such as "teaching to the test") to increase students' scores on standardized examinations?

2. What other factors contribute to low scores on reading, history, and civics exams? How might some of these problems be reduced or eliminated?

Independent Research

If you want to know how U.S. students score on national tests in arts, civics, economics, mathematics, reading, science, and writing, go to "The Nation's Report Card," a U.S. Government website (http://nationsreportcard.gov). These reports provide test results, sample questions, and state-by-state information about student scores. If you are writing a research paper for your social problems class (or another course), you will find useful data in these "Report Cards" that might help with your study.

needs of growing and increasingly diverse student populations. Equally important to funding issues are factors such as the quality of instruction received by students, the safety of the school environment, and the opportunity for each student to reach his or her academic and social potential. Various theoretical approaches and political perspectives provide different solutions to the educational problems that we face today.

Functionalist/Conservative Solutions

Functionalist approaches emphasize the importance of the manifest functions of education and making certain that these functions are fulfilled in contemporary schools. From this approach, greater emphasis should be placed on teaching students the basics and making certain that they have the job skills that will make it possible for them to become contributing members of the U.S. workforce. Problems such as functional illiteracy, school violence, unprepared or ineffective teachers, and school discipline issues must be dealt with so that test scores are improved and a higher percentage of students not only graduate from high school but also attend college. Functionalists typically believe that when dysfunctions exist in the nation's educational system, improvements will occur only when more stringent academic requirements are implemented for students. To make this possible, teachers must receive more rigorous training and evaluation, and high expectations must be

Box 12.3

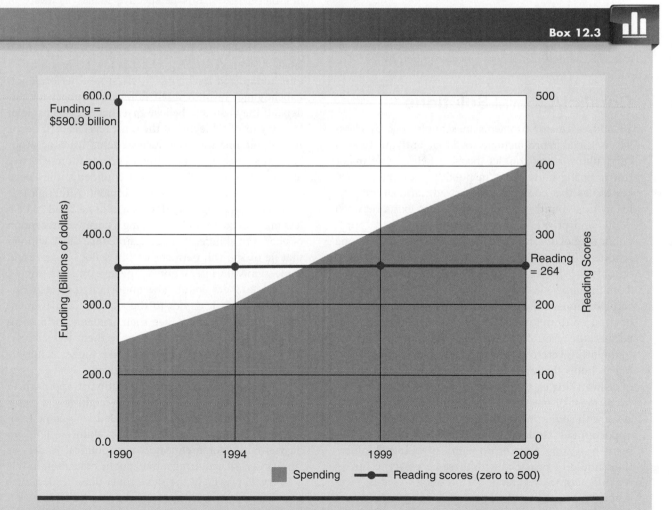

Figure 12.3   Education spending and reading scores, 1990–2009

Note: Reading scores are for thirteen-year-olds.

Source: Organization for Economic Cooperation and Development, 2010.

held for all students to help them reach grade-level or above achievement in all subjects they are studying.

Conservative political leaders in various states have emphasized that one possible solution to educational problems is to increase support for struggling students and underperforming schools by requiring school districts to use federal funds that have been set aside for tutoring and school choice. At the national level, there has been much discussion about rewarding the best teachers and encouraging them to take jobs in underperforming schools by providing them with additional pay and other incentives for assuming these positions. At the bottom line, the focus of functionalist/conservative approaches to solving educational problems in the United States is to make schools more competitive and to ensure that students graduate from high school prepared for jobs in the twenty-first century global marketplace. Strengthening math and science education, for example, is a key way in which political leaders believe that U.S. schools can become more competitive.

Conflict/Liberal Solutions

To address major problems in schools such as class-based social reproduction, tracking, and the hidden curriculum, many conflict theorists believe that major restructuring must occur in public education. In fact, key issues that contribute to vast educational inequality in this country are the divide that exists between public and private schools, between "rich" and "poor" public school districts, and inequalities that exist among schools within one district. Although exclusive private schools provide an outstanding education for children from the upper classes to prepare them for future leadership positions, these schools often serve to the detriment of children from low-income and poverty-level families because the resources of the affluent do not flow into the frequently overcrowded, outdated, and "underachieving" schools that are attended by children of members of the working class and the poor. In public school districts, great disparities in school funding must be done away with so that students have more equal educational opportunities. Students who would benefit from enrichment programs, special programs, or bilingual education should be provided with these necessary resources regardless of their parents' socioeconomic status, race-ethnicity, or country of origin.

Liberal political leaders typically believe that legislation must be passed or continually reaffirmed to fight race discrimination and gender and sexual inequality in schools. These are viewed as continuing problems that are not solved simply by the passage of one measure, such as Title IX of the Educational Amendments of 1972, but instead require continued vigilance across the decades. The same is true in regard to the funding of education: Increased government funding for public schools is crucial if we are to produce greater equality and more opportunity for students in the public schools of this nation. Head Start and bilingual education programs are vital to the success of students from lower-income families and those who reside in families where English is not the primary language spoken.

Symbolic Interactionist Solutions

Since symbolic interactionist approaches focus on microlevel issues, this perspective makes us aware of the importance of how we deal with individuals and small groups of people in educational settings. Problems in schools may be created or perpetuated when we label children and young adults as low achievers based on standardized test scores or classroom performance. Labeling may result in a self-fulfilling prophecy for students if they come to believe that they are incapable of learning or of achieving at the same level as their peers. As a result, one way to reduce students' learning problems in schools is to help them become more effective learners and to develop the self-confidence they need to reach greater educational attainment. Although fear of failure alone typically does not cause a child to be a less than adequate student, having a negative perception of one's own abilities certainly can reduce the likelihood that he or she will perform well in school. As a result, some symbolic interactionists believe that we should educate teachers about how important their expectations are when it comes to the student's achievement level. If teachers encourage their students, help them become higher achievers, and make them feel successful, those students often will act like higher achievers and come to expect more of themselves.

Applying the symbolic interactionist approach to viewing problems in education, we might take a closer look at how some children are labeled who come from recent immigrant families. These children tend to be viewed by some educators and political leaders as "unworthy" of acquiring a free, public education in this country. However, at the same time, these leaders suggest that education is the key to the future of this nation in the global economy. Perhaps changing our perspective on students who differ from the so-called norm of the white, middle- and upper-middle class student population that historically has been considered to be the most successful and the most popular grouping in many schools might be a starting place for reducing social divisions that become insurmountable as students progress through the educational system or decide to drop out because they perceive that school is largely unrelated to their life.

In the final analysis, schools will continue to play a key role in the future of this nation, and changes are inevitable. Other social, economic and political changes over which we have little or no control are occurring, including globalization of the marketplace and workforce, new technologies that will continually revolutionize how we work and play, and the day-to-day reality of other social problems—such as high levels of stress and bullying, peer pressure, family problems, drugs, and crime—being present in and around the schools of our nation. Unlike some social problems, analysts applying virtually all sociological and political perspectives to the problems found in schools believe that change must occur. They simply disagree on what those changes should be.

SUMMARY

✔•⌐Study and Review on mysoclab.com

■ **What is education?**
Education is the social institution responsible for transmitting knowledge, skills, and cultural values in a formally organized structure.

■ **What is the functionalist perspective on education?**
Functionalists believe that education contributes to the smooth functioning of society when it fulfills its manifest functions—the open, stated, and intended goals or consequences of its activities. Education has at least five major manifest functions: socialization, transmission of culture, social control, social placement, and change and innovation. Schools also fulfill a number of latent functions—hidden, unstated, and sometimes unintended consequences of its activities.

■ **What is the conflict perspective on education?**
Conflict theorists believe that schools, which are supposed to reduce inequality in society, actually perpetuate inequalities based on class, race, and gender. The sociologist Pierre Bourdieu, for example, says that children from low-income and poverty-level families come to school with less cultural capital (values, beliefs, attitudes, and competencies in language and culture) than middle- and upper-income children have. Conflict theorists also think that elites manipulate the masses and maintain their power in society through a hidden curriculum that teaches students to be obedient and patriotic and thus perpetuates the status quo in society.

■ **What is the symbolic interactionist perspective on education?**
Symbolic interactionists study classroom dynamics and how practices such as labeling affect students' self-concept and aspirations. If students are labeled "learning disabled" for example, the label might become a self-fulfilling prophecy, that is, an unsubstantiated belief or prediction that results in behavior that makes the false belief come true. A student who is erroneously labeled "learning disabled" might stop trying, and teachers might lower their expectations, with the result that the student doesn't succeed in the long run.

■ **What is functional illiteracy and what can be done about it?**
Functional illiteracy is being unable to read and/or write at the skill level necessary for carrying out everyday tasks. When the economic climate of the nation is better, leaders in business and industry are more likely to establish programs to educate functionally illiterate workers; however, their efforts are more limited in difficult economic times. Volunteer organizations that teach basic reading skills to young people and adults have been successful in helping more people learn to read, write, and engage in such important daily activities as balancing a checkbook.

■ **Why is immigration a problem for U.S. schools?**
Though some immigrants are well educated, most have limited formal education and few job skills. Also, many immigrants are children, so schools must cope with language differences among students. Some school districts offer transitional newcomer programs with bilingual instruction, but critics say that these programs are a form of segregation.

■ **How do race, class, and gender affect educational opportunities?**
The Supreme Court outlawed segregation in 1954, but segregated schools still exist because segregated schools mirror race- and class-based residential segregation. Schools in which racial and ethnic minorities are in the majority typically have high teacher–student ratios, less-qualified teachers, lower expectations of students, and high dropout rates.

■ **How has violence affected our schools?**
Many schools now look like fortresses and use metal detectors and security guards to screen entering students. To lessen the possibility of students being killed for shoes, jewelry, or designer clothes, some school districts now require students to wear uniforms.

■ **What is the crisis in school financing?**
Most educational funds come from state legislative appropriations and local property taxes, but the eroding tax base in city centers leaves schools underfunded. At the same time, record numbers of students are entering the public school system, and many schools are overcrowded and need major repairs. One proposed solution is the voucher system, whereby families are given vouchers to "buy" education at the school of their choice. Critics say that this plan would offer better opportunities to only a limited number of students and wouldn't solve the funding problem.

■ **What are the major problems in higher education?**
The soaring cost of a college education is a major problem because, say conflict theorists, it reproduces the existing class system: Those who attend college are stratified according to their ability to pay. There is also the question of affirmative action. Should race, ethnicity, and gender be taken into consideration for admissions, financial aid, scholarships, and faculty hiring?

■ **What are the urgent educational problems of the twenty-first century?**
To compete in the global economy, we must come to terms with illiteracy in our adult population and we must provide all children with a safe, high-quality education. Some experts say that the best way to achieve both goals is through holding schools and school districts accountable for the education their students receive. Others believe that we will have to tackle many other societal problems, including poverty, racism, and family discord, before we can meet our educational goals.

KEY TERMS

education, p. 272
functionally illiterate, p. 276

hidden curriculum, p. 275
latent functions, p. 273

manifest functions, p. 273
tracking, p. 282

QUESTIONS FOR CRITICAL THINKING

1. How do peer networks and school environment affect students' learning and their overall educational opportunities? Why are problems such as harassment and bullying so persistent in many schools? What can be done to reduce these concerns?

2. What creative solutions can you propose for the school financial crisis? That is, if the federal government doesn't increase its contribution and voters resist increased taxes, where can state legislatures find more money for education?

3. Should we think of more innovative ways to educate students who come from diverse family backgrounds and other nations of the world? Or should students be expected to quickly accept the language and cultural patterns that are prevalent in their school?

Succeed with MySocLab®   www.mysoclab.com

The new MySocLab delivers proven results in helping students succeed, provides engaging experiences that personalize learning, and comes from a trusted partner with educational expertise and a deep commitment to helping students and instructors achieve their goals.

Here are a few activities you will find for this chapter:

Watch on **mysoclab.com** — **Core Concepts** video clips feature sociologists in action, exploring important concepts in the study of Social Problems. Watch:
• Inequities in Education

Explore on **mysoclab.com** — **Social Explorer** is an interactive application that allows you to explore Census data through interactive maps. Explore:
• Social Explorer Activity: Higher Education in America

Read on **mysoclab.com** — **MySocLibrary** includes primary source readings from classic and contemporary sociologists. Read:
• Detours on the Road to Equality: Women, Work and Higher Education

CHAPTER

13

Problems in Politics and the Global Economy

THINKING SOCIOLOGICALLY

- Do the rich actually get richer while the poor get poorer? What part does the political economy play in the distribution of wealth in the United States?

- How is uneven economic development related to problems in the global economy?

- "Politics is a rich man's game." Based on this chapter, do you agree or disagree with this statement?

Mrs. Parry is a woman battered by events that were outside her control. I met her in the centre of Ashington, a 27,000-strong community about seventeen miles north of Newcastle. It was the world's biggest mining village until the local pit closed in 1986, just a year after the defeat of the Miners' Strike. Thousands were thrown out of work; the community has never recovered.

When I asked Mrs. Parry what impact the pit's closure had on the community, she interrupted me before I had even finished the question. "We died!" she responded with a combination of grief and conviction. "Once all the mines closed, all the community had gone. It's just been a big depression ever since, just struggling to survive, that's all." Both her father and her then-husband were miners. They split up the year he lost his job. "We owed not just our livelihoods, but our lives to the pits as well. My dad retired, and then he died. My marriage broke up."

—Owen Jones (2011), author of Chavs: The Demonization of the Working Class, *describes the long-term effects that closing all the mines in Ashington (England) had on*

the community and on Mrs. Parry's family. This is one of many examples of how numerous villages in Great Britain were devastated by the collapse of mining and other local industries, as well as the lack of a governmental response to such economic conditions.

Even if we had depressing issues before [in Detroit, Michigan], the decline [in population] makes it so much harder to deal with. Yes, the city feels empty physically, empty of people, empty of ambition, drive. It feels empty.

—Samantha Howell, a Detroit resident, explains to journalist Katharine Q. Seelye (2011) how it feels to live in Detroit, which saw the largest percentage loss (25 percent) of any American city with more than 100,000 residents (other than New Orleans) between 2000 and 2010. Deindustrialization and loss of automobile manufacturing plants devastated this urban area and caused many residents to flee to the suburbs and elsewhere.

Whether in Great Britain or the United States, stories such as these are being told by ordinary citizens and journalists who want to describe the effects that changes in the economy have had on people, communities, and the larger society. Coupled with these stories is the question of what, if anything, should governments do about job loss, unemployment, and rising inequality. In most high-income nations, many people see their economic fate as being intricately linked not only to local, national, and global economic conditions but also to decisions made by political leaders that affect their livelihood and overall economic situation. In this chapter we examine politics and the economy together because they are deeply interrelated.

Politics **is the social institution through which power is acquired and exercised by certain individuals and groups.** Although political decisions typically are made on a nation-by-nation basis, many of these decisions affect the lives and economic status of people in other nations as well. The *economy* **is the social institution that ensures that a society will be maintained through its production, distribution, and consumption of goods and services.** Because of the extent to which politics and the economy are related in high-income, industrialized nations such as the United States, some sociologists believe that it is more accurate to refer to the "political economy" as one entity—a combined social institution where the players, rules, and games often overlap. The *political economy* **refers to the interdependent workings and interests**

DID YOU KNOW

- Many people who make money from the underground economy have legitimate jobs and are thought of as "law-abiding" citizens.

- Some individual transnational corporations have more financial clout than entire nations.

- If we divided all of the personal debt in the United States among all citizens, each person would owe at least $52,000.

of political and economic systems. To gain a better understanding of how the political economy works, it is important to take a closer look at various types of economic systems, the global economy, and the role of governments and corporations in shaping economic conditions around the world.

MODERN ECONOMIC SYSTEMS AND THE UNDERGROUND ECONOMY

There are three major modern economic systems: capitalism, socialism, and mixed economies. Of course, there is no such thing as "pure" capitalism or "pure" socialism, but each is characterized by several key tenets that distinguish it as an approach to producing and distributing goods and services in a society. In addition to these three "legitimate" economies, the underground ("illegal") economy is also growing around the world.

Capitalism

Capitalism **is an economic system characterized by private ownership of the means of production, from which personal profits can be derived through market** **competition and without government intervention.** There are four distinctive features of "ideal" capitalism: private ownership of the means of production, pursuit of personal profit, competition, and lack of government intervention.

Read the **Document**
Asceticism and the Spirit of Capitalism on mysoclab.com

First, capitalism is based on the right of individuals to own various kinds of property, including those that produce income (e.g., factories and businesses). In a capitalist economy, individuals and corporations not only own income-producing property, but they also have the right to "buy" people's labor.

Second, capitalism is based on the belief that people should be able to maximize their individual gain through personal profit, which is supposed to benefit everyone, not just the capitalists. The idea that "rising tides lift all boats" is central to the pursuit of personal profit being a major tenet of capitalism: the belief is that, if some businesses have high profits, these profits will benefit not only the capitalists who own those businesses, but also their workers and the general public, which will benefit from increased public expenditures for things that everyone uses, such as roads and schools.

Third, capitalism is based on competition, which is supposed to prevent any one business from making excessive profits. For example, when companies are competing for customers, they must offer innovative goods and services at competitive prices. The need to do this, it is argued, prevents excessive profits. One twenty-first century economic problem is the extent to which competition has been reduced or eliminated in many economic sectors by the business practices of major corporations.

Finally, capitalism is based on a lack of government intervention in the marketplace. According to this *laissez-faire* (meaning "leave alone") policy, also called *free enterprise*, competition in a free marketplace should be the force that regulates prices and establishes workers' wages, rather than the government doing so.

Socialism

As compared to capitalism, *socialism* **is characterized by public ownership of the means of production, the pursuit of collective goals, and centralized decision making.** Under socialism, there are governmental limits on the right of individuals and corporations to own productive property. In a truly socialist economy, the means of production are owned and controlled by a collectivity or by the state, not by private individuals or corporations. Unlike capitalist economies, in which the primary motivation for economic activity is personal profit, the primary motivation in a socialist economy is supposed to be the collective good of all citizens. Although socialist economies typically have less economic inequality than the United States, there has been a move in many nations toward *privatization*, a process in which resources are converted from state ownership to private ownership, and the government maintains an active role in developing, recognizing, and protecting private property rights. Privatization continues today in formerly socialist countries such as the Republic of Turkey, where the nations iron and steel industry has been privatized so that it could compete with similar businesses in the rest of the world. Through privatization of the steel maker, political leaders hoped to realize a profit that would help pay down the country's budget deficit and attract foreign investors (Presidency of the Republic of Turkey, 2010). As socialist countries continue to develop a capitalist model of economic production and distribution, it is important to reflect on how

Karl Marx viewed socialism as an answer to the problems produced by capitalism.

Highly critical of the growing economic inequality that emerged as capitalism flourished in the 1800s, the early economist and social thinker Karl Marx argued that socialism could serve as an intermediate stage on the way to an ideal communist society in which the means of production and all goods would be owned by everyone. Under communism, Marx said, people would contribute according to their abilities and receive according to their needs. Moreover, government would no longer be necessary, since government existed only to serve the interests of the capitalist class. However, in actual practice, problems of economic and political instability, low standards of living, and other internal issues plagued the former Soviet Union as well as Cuba, the Republic of China, and other nations that have tried to establish socialist and communist economic systems.

Mixed Economies

No economy is purely capitalist or purely socialist; most are mixtures of both. A **mixed economy combines elements of both capitalism (a market economy) and socialism (a command economy)**. In one type of mixed economy, *state capitalism*, the government is involved in the dealings of privately owned companies, including having a strong role in setting the rules, policies, and objectives of the businesses. Countries such as Japan and Singapore in Asia and Saudi Arabia in the Middle East are examples of state capitalism; however, the outcomes are quite different. In Asia, greater government involvement may have resulted in greater good for more individuals, but in Saudi Arabia, it appears to have only made a few people extremely wealthy.

Some western European nations, including Sweden, Britain, and France, have an economic and political system known as *democratic socialism*, in which private ownership of some of the means of production is combined with governmental distribution of some essential goods and services and free elections. In these nations, the government is heavily involved in providing services such as medical care, child care, and transportation for all residents. For this reason, some analysts refer to these economies as *welfare capitalism* to highlight the fact that privately owned companies coexist with extensive governmental programs that provide certain essential services to everyone without cost or at a greatly reduced cost.

The Underground (Informal) Economy

As compared to the legitimate economy in which taxes are paid on income and people have licenses or credentials that allow them to perform the work they do, the *underground economy* is made up of money-making activities that people do not report to the government and for jobs they may not have the licenses or credentials to perform (such as the "gypsy" cabs in New York City that do not have proper medallions, or permits, to operate as taxis for hire). Sometimes referred to as the "informal" or "shadow economy," one segment of the underground economy is made up of workers who are paid "off the books," which means that they are paid in cash, their earnings are not reported, and no taxes are paid. Lawful jobs, such as nannies, construction workers, and landscape/yard workers in the United States, are often part of the shadow economy because workers and bosses make under-the-table deals so that both can gain through the transaction: Employers pay less for workers' services, and workers have more money to take home than if they paid taxes on their earnings.

The underground economy also involves trade in lawful goods that are sold "off the books" so that no taxes are paid and unlawful goods, such as the worldwide sale of "designer alternative fashion" products that are counterfeit ("knockoff") merchandise. Demand for such products is strong at all times but frequently improves in difficult economic times because many people retain a desire for luxury goods, particularly those that are widely discussed and publicized by the media even when individuals have fewer resources to allocate to luxury purchases (Box 13.1).

According to one way of thinking, operating a business in the underground economy reveals capitalism at its best because it shows how the "free market" might work if there were no government intervention. However, from another perspective, selling goods or services in the underground economy borders on—or moves into—criminal behavior. For some individuals, the underground economy offers the only means for purchasing certain goods or for overcoming unemployment, particularly in low-income and poverty areas where people may feel alienated from the wider world and believe that using shady means is the only way to survive (Venkatesh, 2006). The underground economy operates on a global basis. Labor and products easily flow across national borders despite the efforts of law enforcement officials to curb such practices.

The Media and the Underground Economy

While some people love their [knockoff] Chanel bags (I spot those fakes all over campus!), others would rather rock Target than fake designer anything. . . . Personally, I'm not 100% against knockoffs—they make design affordable for everyone. . . . On the other hand, I'd never carry a faux Chanel bag—it would be sacrilegious! I don't think I could live with myself if I pretend a fake Chanel was real. Every time I wore it (which would be almost every day), I'd know I was lying to myself and the world. I'd rather save up and earn the real thing or not have one at all.

—One woman expresses the ambivalence some women feel about buying "knockoff" or illegal "designer alternative" handbags, but this does not keep millions of people around the world from purchasing such merchandise (Zephyr, 2009).

We are pretty use[d] to seeing stories about fake Apple products that stream out of China but it seems that some bootleggers have decided to raise the bar and have opened up "Apple Stores" in some Chinese cities. According to one American couple who came across one in the city of Kunming, several hundred miles from the nearest official Apple Store. . . . [It takes] careful observation to spot the fake stores [because they] are faithful reproductions of the Apple Store theme. The really amazing things is that the employees in these stores believe that they are actually working for Apple, blue t-shirts and all.

—Steve Hodson (2011) posted this sighting (with photos) of a fake "Apple Store" that sells fake "Apple" products in China on The Inquisitr website.

From ads to "celebrity sightings" of media stars wearing designer handbags to using their Apple iPads, iPhones, and iPods, everyday people are bombarded with images of the rich and famous carrying or wearing the latest name-brand products. Media framing of stories about luxury merchandise (legally or illegally produced) typically uses a "price-tag framing" approach. *Price-tag framing* occurs when the cost and "exclusivity" of a luxury item is a key feature in a media story or blog. This type of framing focuses on *how much*? and encourages potential consumers to focus on the cost of a luxury item and on the high-profile status of people who own similar goods (Kendall, 2011). A second type of framing also comes into play in heightening consumers' desire for Apple products or other communications technology: *Show-off framing* is the use of a name-brand product to make a person feel important, in-the-know, and on the cutting edge of technology. For example, to have an iPhone 3 when iPhone 4 came out was to be unimportant, out-of-the-loop with

other people, and not on the cutting edge. Real and fake products are used to fill this need in people and the image of the company—real or fake—is used to lure customers.

Consumers' desires for trendy and luxury products are fulfilled in the underground economy because manufacturers make look-alike products that are sometimes offered for lower prices. These products typically are made by low-wage workers who use less expensive materials and shoddy workmanship. Then unscrupulous—or unsuspecting, in the case of the Apple store in China—salespersons hawk the goods on the streets, in fake stores, or the Internet. In the underground economy, knockoff products are sold at global tourist attractions such as the Eiffel Tower in Paris and streets bordering the Venice canals to "Counterfeit Triangle" along Canal Street in New York City and Internet websites.

Why do people purchase fake merchandise? How do the media become involved in this charade? Although full equality does not exist in any society, consumers around the world tend to view themselves as having an "equal right" to purchase items that will make them equal to others regardless of their position in the economic hierarchy. If luxury merchandise that they want comes from the underground economy, so be it, at least from their perspective. The media become involved through endless ads and journalistic descriptions about the intangible aspects of clothing, handbags, cell phones, and other smart technologies that suggest that consumption of certain products defines who we are and elevates us in the eyes of other people, and apparently this approach works despite the origins of the merchandise.

Questions for Consideration

1. What effect does the underground economy have on the legitimate economy in high-income nations such as the United States? What about low-income nations?

2. How does media framing influence consumer desires even in difficult economic times?

3. To what extent do political leaders encourage (or discourage) the growth of an underground economy in their country?

Independent Research

If you are interested in doing further research on this topic, find websites that offer fashion knockoffs or other high-demand merchandise for sale. Analyze these ads or blurbs to see what claims are being made and how these claims compare with "legitimate" advertising and media stories about the same products. Discuss ways in which the underground economy makes it possible for individuals to purchase products they otherwise might not have. Identify problems the underground economy causes for the legitimate economy in a nation.

PROBLEMS IN THE GLOBAL ECONOMY

The global financial crisis that began in 2007–2008—and has not been fully resolved—demonstrates how closely connected problems in the U.S economy are with those of other nations. When U.S. financial institutions were in crisis, the economic well-being of many other nations was also in question because it was widely assumed that high-income nations with advanced economic development would continue to set the pace of global economies.

◉ Watch on **mysoclab.com**
Globalization on **mysoclab.com**

Not all nations are at the same stage of economic development, however, and this creates a widely stratified global economy in which some countries are very wealthy, some are much less wealthy, and still others are very poor. As we discussed in Chapter 2, we refer to these as high-income, middle-income, and low-income nations. How these nations are classified is related to their level of economic development and the amount of national and personal income in the country. This development can be traced back to the economic organization of societies in the past.

Inequality Based on Uneven Economic Development

Depending on the major type of economic production, a society can be classified as having a preindustrial, industrial, or postindustrial economy. In preindustrial economies, most workers engage in *primary-sector production*—**the extraction of raw materials and natural resources from the environment**. In this type of economy, materials and resources are used without much processing. Today, extracting gold and silver from mines in Indonesia is an example of primary-sector production.

By comparison with preindustrial economies, most workers in industrial economies are engaged in *secondary-sector production*—**the processing of raw materials (from the primary sector) into finished products**. Work in industrial economies is much more specialized, repetitive, and bureaucratically organized than in preindustrial economies. Assembly-line work, now done on a global basis, is an example. Here is Ben Hamper's (1991:88–89) description of his first day working on the rivet line at a truck and bus manufacturing plant here in the United States:

The Rivet Line was the starting point for all that went on during the three-day snake trail needed to assemble a truck. The complex birth procedure began right here. It started with a couple of long black rails. As the rails were hoisted onto crawling pedestals, the workers began riveting them together and affixing them with various attachments. There weren't any screws or bolts to be seen. Just rivets. Thousands upon thousands of dull gray rivets. They resembled mushrooms. . . . I looked around at [other workers] who would soon be my neighbors. I'd seen happier faces on burn victims.

Although Hamper's discussion about assembly-line work is more than two decades old, the basic description of how factories work remains largely unchanged with the exception of additional technology and robotics in some industrial settings. In other countries where secondary-sector production is moving from the United States, even greater abuses of workers are often found. In China, for example, workers in grim factories have high rates of suicide and job turnover because they cannot stand the working conditions. After a number of suicides at Foxconn Technology in Shenzhen, China, journalist David Barboza (2010) wrote about factory life as follows:

[Ma Xiangqian, who committed suicide, hated his job which included] . . . an 11-hour overnight shift, seven nights a week, forging plastic and metal into electronic parts amid fumes and dust. Or at least that was Mr. Ma's job until, after a run-in with his supervisor, he was demoted to cleaning toilets. Mr. Ma's pay stub shows that he worked 286 hours in the month before he died, including 112 hours of overtime, about three times the legal limit. For all of that, even with extra pay for overtime, he earned the equivalent of $1 an hour.

Although computers and other technology have changed the nature of the production process in some settings, the kinds of factory work described previously are often repetitive, heavily supervised, and full of rules for workers to follow, whether these assembly plants are located in the United States, China, or other nations in today's global economy.

Unlike preindustrial and industrial economies, postindustrial economies are characterized by *tertiary-sector production*, which means that **workers provide services rather than goods as their primary source of livelihood**. Tertiary-sector production includes work in such areas as food service, transportation, communication, education, real estate, advertising, sports,

Industrial and postindustrial economies often blend in the twenty-first century workplace. Shown here is a clean room (a factory-type setting) at a computer hard-drive manufacturing plant where products are made for use in the communication and information technology sectors.

and entertainment. Inequality typically increases in postindustrial economies where people in high-tech, high-wage jobs often thrive financially and have business connections throughout the world while, at the same time, workers in low-tech, low-wage jobs in the service sector (such as fast-food servers or hotel cleaning personnel) may have a hard time paying their basic bills and may feel very isolated from the economic mainstream of their own society. Today, manufacturing and production accounts for slightly more than 10 percent of U.S. economic output, and the service sector is the most rapidly growing component. For this reason, some sociologists refer to the United States as an advanced industrial society, which is characterized by greater dependence on an international division of labor (R. Hodson and Sullivan, 2008). In the United States, corporations rely on workers throughout the

world to produce goods and services for paying customers in this country and elsewhere.

At one end of the international division of labor is low-wage labor. For example, along the U.S.–Mexican border, some U.S. corporations run *maquiladora* plants—factories in Mexico where components manufactured in the United States are assembled into finished goods and shipped back to the United States for sale. In countries such as Mexico, where the economy has been less robust, it was possible to find workers who are willing to work for lower wages and fewer benefits than the typical worker in a high-income nation. Recently, employment opportunities have expanded in Mexico, and average family income has increased more than 45 percent since 2000. At the other end of the international division of labor are workers in countries such as Ireland and India, where U.S. corporations are able to find well-educated workers who view jobs in fields such as insurance claims processing, reading of certain types of medical tests, and filling out tax returns for U.S. workers to be a source of economic stability and upward mobility. As a result, what may be viewed as a problem in the global economy for some in the United States, namely the shifting of jobs from this country to other nations, may be viewed as a solution in those countries where young workers see their employment opportunities expanding and no longer feel a need to move elsewhere to work. Transnational corporations headquartered in high-income nations have had a major influence on economies and governments worldwide.

Transnational Corporations and the Lack of Accountability

Today, the most important corporate structure is the **transnational corporation—a large-scale business organization that is headquartered in one country but operates in many countries, which has the legal power (separate from individual owners or shareholders) to enter into contracts, buy and sell property, and engage in other business activity**. Some transnational corporations constitute a type of international monopoly capitalism that transcends the boundaries and legal controls of any one nation. The largest transnationals are headquartered in the United States, Japan, Korea, other industrializing Asian nations, and Germany. Currently, transnational corporations account for more than half of total world production. The shareholders in transnational corporations live throughout the world. Although corporate executives often own a great number of shares, most shareholders have little control over where plants

The Malling of Dubai: Transnational Corporations in the Midst of Affluence and Poverty

The Dubai Mall is the world's largest shopping mall based on total area and fifth largest by gross leasable area. Located in Dubai, United Arab Emirates, it is part of the 20-billion-dollar Burj Khalifa complex, and includes 1,200 shops. . . . The Dubai Mall has 10–15 distinct 'malls-within-a-mall.' . . . It also has a 250-room luxury hotel, 22 cinema screens plus 120 restaurants and cafes.

In addition to the features described in this listing for the Dubai Mall, the center includes an indoor theme park with 150 amusement games, an aquarium, a discovery center, and an Olympic-sized ice rink that can host up to 2,000 guests.

With transnational corporations and shops such as Galeries Lafayette (France), Bloomingdale's (the United States), and others from around the world backing this massive enterprise, how might the Mall of Dubai possibly be viewed as a problem for anyone? According to some social analysts who closely examined the issue of wealth and poverty in Dubai, the building of the world's tallest building (Burj Khalifa) and the malling of Dubai have a hidden, "dark side" that is unknown to outsiders.

What tourists and other outsiders do not see are the shantytown conditions where workers live when they are not building the gleaming new towers and luxury hotels and residences in Dubai. Labor violations in Dubai have attracted the attention of human rights organizations. Many workers live eight to a room and send most of the money they make home to their family in another country.

Labor camps are often gated and guarded, and some of the workers live in dirty conditions, such as the smell of raw sewage) and ride on roads that are full of garbage.

In the aftermath of the worldwide economic crisis in 2007–2008, some of the migrant workers were let go. Some have returned to their countries of origin; others have remained in the low-paid workforce in Dubai where service workers in general have low wages and few opportunities for advancement. Some of the migrant workers came to Dubai in hopes of a better life for themselves and their families back home, but they have found instead problems of poverty and not being able to afford a flight home.

Descriptions of the lifestyles of the rich and affluent in Dubai and other major world cities stand in stark contrast to the poverty and lack of opportunity of many of the people who help make such opulence possible for those at the top of the hierarchy. What unique problems do nations face if their economy is largely based on tourism and trade?

Questions for Consideration

1. Do you believe that global consumerism is a problem? If so, are corporations responsible for the problem?
2. What is the relationship between consumerism and the demand for cheap labor?
3. How does the glamour of Dubai and some cities in the United States, such as Las Vegas, hide the poverty that exists in high-profile, luxury-oriented areas?

are located, how much employees are paid, or how the environment is protected.

Because transnational corporations are big and powerful, they play a significant role in the economies and governments of many countries. At the same time, by their very nature, they lack accountability to any government or any regulatory agency. Because of this lack of accountability, some major corporations offshore their profits in countries such as the Cayman Islands to avoid paying taxes. Transnational corporations do not depend on any one country for labor, capital, or technology, and they can locate their operations in countries where political and business leaders accept their practices and few other employment opportunities exist. Although many workers in low-income nations earn less than a living wage from

transnational corporations, the products they make are often sold for hundreds of times the cost of raw materials and labor. Designer clothing and athletic shoes are two examples of this kind of exploitation.

Still another concern is that transnational corporations foster global consumerism that inevitably changes local cultures and encourages a "shop till you drop" mentality through extensive advertising and strategic placement of their business operations around the world. McDonald's golden arches and Coca-Cola signs can be seen from Times Square in New York to Red Square in Moscow, and the malls in Dubai might be mistaken for those located anywhere except that they are much larger and they had the darker side of a poverty and an immigrant work force in that nation (see Box 13.2).

Traditional and ultramodern are often found in close proximity in the global economy.

PROBLEMS IN THE U.S. ECONOMY

Although an economic boom occurred late in the twentieth century, corporate wealth became increasingly concentrated. Economic concentration refers to the extent to which a few individuals or corporations control the vast majority of all economic resources in a country. Concentration of wealth is a social problem when it works to society's detriment, particularly when people are unable to use the democratic process to control the actions of the corporations.

Concentration of Wealth

The concentration of wealth in the United States can be traced through several stages. In the earliest stage (1850–1890), most investment capital was individually owned. Before the Civil War, about 200 families controlled all major trade and financial organizations. By the 1890s, even fewer—including such notables as Andrew Carnegie, Cornelius Vanderbilt, and John D. Rockefeller—controlled most of the investment capital in this country (Feagin et al., 2006).

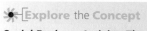

Explore the Concept

Social Explorer Activity: The Nation's Wealthiest [report] on **mysoclab.com**

In early monopoly capitalism (1890–1940), ownership and control of capital shifted from individuals to corporations. As monopoly capitalism grew, a few corporations gained control over major U.S. industries, including the oil, sugar, and grain industries. A ***monopoly*** **exists when a single firm controls an industry and accounts for all sales in a specific market**. In early monopoly capitalism, some stockholders derived massive profits from such companies as American Tobacco Company, F. W. Woolworth, and Sears, which held near-monopolies on specific goods and services (Hodson and Sullivan, 2008).

In advanced monopoly capitalism (between 1940 and the present), ownership and control of major industrial and business sectors became increasingly concentrated. After World War II, there was a dramatic increase in ***oligopoly***—**a situation in which a small number of companies or suppliers control an entire industry or service**. Today, a few large corporations use their economic resources—through campaign contributions, PACs, and lobbying—to influence the outcome of government decisions that affect their operations. Smaller corporations have only limited power and resources to bring about political change or keep the largest corporations from dominating the economy.

Today, mergers often occur across industries. In this way, corporations gain near-monopoly control over all aspects of the production and distribution of a product because they acquire both the companies that supply the raw materials and the companies that are the outlets for the product. For example, an oil company might hold leases on the land where the oil is pumped out of the ground, own the refineries that convert the oil into gasoline, and own the individual gasoline stations that sell the product to the public. Corporations that have control both within and across industries and are formed by a series of mergers and acquisitions across industries are referred to as conglomerates—combinations of businesses in different commercial areas, all of which are owned by one holding company. Media ownership is a case in point (see Chapter 14).

Concentration of wealth and excessive consumer spending have reached new highs among an elite few in the United States and other high income nations.

Further complicating corporate structures are *interlocking corporate directorates*—members of the board of directors of one corporation who also sit on the board of one or more other corporations. Although the Clayton Antitrust Act of 1914 made it illegal for a person to sit on the boards of directors of two corporations that are in direct competition with each other at the same time, a person may serve simultaneously on the board of a financial institution (a bank, for example) and the board of a commercial corporation (a computer manufacturing company or a furniture store chain, for example) that borrows money from the bank. Directors of competing corporations also may serve together on the board of a third corporation that is not in direct competition with the other two. The problem with such interlocking directorates is that they diminish competition by producing interdependence. People serving on multiple boards are in a position to forge cooperative arrangements that benefit their corporations but not necessarily the general public. When several corporations are controlled by the same financial interests, they are more likely to cooperate with one another than to compete. The directors of some of these corporations are highly paid for their services: Annual compensation for board members of some top corporations is well over a million dollars per person with stock and stock options. Many directors serve on the boards of several companies, receiving lucrative salaries and benefits from each of them.

Corporate Welfare

Corporate welfare occurs when the government helps industries and private corporations in their economic pursuits. Corporate welfare refers to financial aid, such as a subsidy or tax break, that the government provides to corporations or other businesses. Some analysts prefer the more neutral term, corporate subsidies, for this practice, because they argue that "corporate welfare" implies that the aid is wasteful or unjust. Corporate welfare is not new in the United States. Between 1850 and 1900, corporations received government assistance in the form of public subsidies and protection from competition. To encourage westward expansion, the federal government gave large tracts of land to privately owned railroads. Antitrust laws that were originally intended to break up monopolies were used against labor unions that supported workers' interests. Tariffs, patents, and trademarks all serve to protect corporations from competition. Today, government intervention includes billions of dollars in subsidies to farmers through crop subsidy programs, tax credits for

corporations, and large subsidies or loan guarantees to auto makers, aircraft companies, railroads, and others. In 2009, the federal government spent $11 trillion in an effort to stable the financial and housing markets in the United States. Overall, most financial institutions and other corporations have gained much more than they have lost as a result of government involvement in the economy. Obviously, they do not refer to these programs as corporate welfare or corporate handouts, but rather by names that make the programs sound more deserving. The words used can be very important in the political process (see Box 13.3).

The National Debt and Consumer Debt

The national debt—the U.S. total public debt—is a major concern in the twenty-first century. The national debt is the amount of money owed by the federal government to creditors who hold U.S. debt instruments. In other words, the national debt consists of the total amount of money the federal government has borrowed over the years from U.S. citizens and foreign lenders to finance overspending. As of July 2011, the total U.S. federal debt was approximately $14.5 trillion, or about $46,544 per U.S. resident. This figure does not include other promises that the government will disburse future funds for Social Security, Medicare, and Medicaid.

Throughout U.S. history, this nation has had public debt, and for many years, this debt has continued to grow. However, after decades of the federal government spending more money each year than it was making, in the late 1990s, a period of economic expansion occurred and slower growth in some spending areas made it possible for the government to produce a surplus of more than $100 billion a year (between 1999 and 2001). But, as the nation entered the twenty-first century, a combination of tax cuts and increased spending as a result of terrorism and war (among other factors) resulted in a growing budget deficit—which is excess of spending over income over a particular period of time. When a budget deficit is accumulated by the federal government, this deficit must be financed by the issuance of Treasury bonds. The federal deficit increased from $318 billion in 2005 to approximately $1.4 trillion in 2010.

National debt and the budget deficit are only two of the major problems we face; another is the amount of consumer debt in this country. Like the federal government, many individuals and families in this country are deeply in debt. Consumer debt has grown significantly since the 1980s, and in 2008, it had reached more than $2.52 trillion. In July 2011, consumer debt was $2.44 trillion for the

Critical Thinking and You

Box 13.3

Are You a Conservative or a Liberal? The Language of the Political Economy

The American Heritage Dictionary of the English Language (2011) defines *conservatism* and *liberalism* as follows:

Conservatism

1. The inclination, especially in politics, to maintain the existing or traditional order
2. A political philosophy or attitude emphasizing respect for traditional institutions (such as family, education, and religion), distrust of too much government involvement in business and everyday life, and opposition to sudden change in the established order

A conservative is one who favors traditional views and values. A conservative is a supporter of political conservatism.

Liberalism

1. The state or quality of being liberal
2. A political theory founded on the natural goodness of humans and the autonomy of the individual and favoring civil and political liberties, government by law with the consent of the governed, and protection from arbitrary authority

A liberal is one who is open to new ideas for progress, favors proposals for reform, and is tolerant of the ideas and behavior of others.

This sounds simple enough, doesn't it? However, politicians, scholars, and everyday people constantly argue about the meaning of these words as they seek to determine where individuals fit on the political spectrum, a continuum that represents the wide range of political attitudes. Linguistics scholar George Lakoff (2002) raises a number of interesting points that might assist us in our critical thinking about our views on the political economy. According to Lakoff, conservatives and liberals not only choose different topics on which to focus their attention, but they also use different words to discuss these topics:

Here are some words and phrases used over and over in conservative discourse: character, virtue, discipline, tough it out, get tough, tough love, strong, self-reliance, individual responsibility, backbone, standards, authority, heritage, competition, earn, hard work, enterprise, property rights, rewards, freedom,

intrusion, interference, meddling, punishment, human nature, traditional, common sense, dependency, self-indulgent, elite, quotas, breakdown, corrupt, decay, rot, degenerate, deviant, lifestyle.

Lakoff asks us to think about the following questions: What unifies this collection of words? Why do conservatives choose the words they do? What do these words mean to conservatives? Now, let's look at Lakoff's list of words that are favorites among liberals:

Liberals talk about: social forces, social responsibility, free expression, human rights, equal rights, concern, care, help, health, safety, nutrition, basic human dignity, oppression, diversity, deprivation, alienation, big corporations, corporate welfare, ecology, ecosystem, biodiversity, pollution, and so on.

Obviously, we cannot easily sort everyone into either the conservative or liberal school of thought based on their choice of words. In fact, people move around somewhat on the political spectrum: Individuals may have more liberal attitudes on some social issues and more conservative attitudes on others.

Where does this discussion leave you? Do you most often use the language of liberalism or of conservatism? Are you a middle-of-the-road type of person when it comes to political issues? What words do you most often use in discussing political and economic issues? Think about your attitudes on the following topics and state what, if anything, you believe the government should do about the following: abortion; death penalty; government funds for victims of floods, earthquakes, fires, and other natural disasters; health care as a commodity; health care as a right; increasing/decreasing budgets for the military, prisons, and homeland security; increasing/decreasing spending for regulatory agencies that control businesses and seek to protect the environment; and welfare for individuals who are chronically poor and homeless. These are only a few of the social concerns that face our nation today. Listen to local, state, and national political leaders: What language do they use? Do their actions reveal attitudes that are conservative, liberal, or somewhere in between as they confront social problems and seek to reduce or eliminate them? Where would you place the Tea Party movement in this regard?

---

first nine months of the year and some analysts suggested that consumer spending was decreasing because of major concerns about the U.S. economy and the high unemployment rate (Bater, 2011). Even more worrisome to analysts

was the fact that the ratio of consumer debt to income has increased. Two factors contribute to high rates of consumer debt. The first is the instability of economic life in modern society; unemployment and underemployment are commonplace. The second factor is the availability of credit and the extent to which credit card companies and other lenders extend credit beyond people's ability to repay. Recent increases in consumer debt have largely been attributed to heavier use of revolving credit, primarily credit cards, in which consumers, at best, paid only their minimum balance rather than the total amount owed on a card in a given month. Some people run up credit card charges that are greatly out of proportion to their income; others cannot pay off the charges they initially believed they could afford when their income is interrupted or drops. Having a high level of consumer debt is a personal problem for individuals, but it is also a public issue, particularly when credit card issuers give fifth, sixth, or seventh credit cards to people who are already so far in debt that they cannot pay the interest, much less the principal, on their cards.

In recent years, many homeowners who have been having trouble juggling their credit card debts have turned to home equity loans as a means of reducing their bills. Home equity loans consist of borrowing money from a mortgage company and pledging the equity in your home (the difference between what you previously owed and the value of the residence) as collateral for the new debt. For a number of years, large numbers of U.S. homeowners refinanced their residential mortgages only to see the housing boom in their region of the country become a national housing bust, or to have other unexpected events occur (such as loss of a job or a medical emergency), which resulted in foreclosure on their home. Federal National Mortgage Association (FNMA or "Fannie Mae") and Federal Home Loan Mortgage Corporation (FHLMC or "Freddie Mac") are stockholder-owned corporations that were originally set up as government entities in the 1930s and 1970s, respectively. As buyers of home mortgages, they have been a critical part of the nation's housing finance system for decades, owning or guaranteeing more than half of all home mortgages outstanding. However, in 2008, Fannie Mae and Freddie Mac were placed under federal control as the U.S. government took over these massive corporations because they recorded combined losses of about $14 billion and had a history of accounting scandals, questionable management practices, and maintaining inadequate capital reserves. The bailout and recapitalization of Fannie Mae and Freddie Mac was only the beginning of what became a major financial crisis: The U.S. housing market continued to experience a meltdown with homeowners seeing the value of their residences decline sharply in some areas of the country. In addition, the financial market lost confidence in government-sponsored mortgage entities, and numerous mortgage companies and banks were either bought out by other financial institutions or were bailed out by the federal government. This institutional crisis then spread around the globe and to individuals in this country who were heavily in debt. Many of these persons have filed for bankruptcy and lost their homes to foreclosure. When this major economic crisis will end is unknown at this time, even though the decline has leveled off in some areas of the country and housing values have risen somewhat. A full recovery appears to be a long way off at this time.

Unemployment

There are three major types of unemployment—cyclical, seasonal, and structural. *Cyclical unemployment* occurs as a result of lower rates of production during recessions in the business cycle; a recession is a decline in an economy's total production that lasts at least six months. Although massive layoffs initially occur, some of the workers will eventually be rehired, largely depending on the length and severity of the recession. *Seasonal unemployment* results from shifts in the demand for workers based on conditions such as the weather (in agriculture, the construction industry, and tourism) or the season (holidays and summer vacations). Both of these types of unemployment tend to be relatively temporary.

By contrast, structural unemployment may be permanent. *Structural unemployment* arises because the skills demanded by employers do not match the skills of the unemployed or because the unemployed do not live where the jobs are located. This type of unemployment often occurs when a number of plants in the same industry are closed or when new technology makes certain jobs obsolete. Structural unemployment often results from capital flight—the investment of capital in foreign facilities, as previously discussed. Today, many workers fear losing their jobs, exhausting their unemployment benefits (if any), and still not being able to find another job.

The **unemployment rate** **is the percentage of unemployed persons in the labor force actively seeking jobs.** The second decade of the twenty-first century has seen a significant increase in unemployment. By contrast, the U.S. unemployment rate in 2000 was 4.0 percent. By 2011 the overall rate hovered around 9 percent with some people no longer actively seeking work and thus not being counted as "unemployed." In 2011, the unemployment rate for adult men was 8.7 percent, as compared to 8.0 percent for adult women. However, the breakdown for unemployment across racial-ethnic and age categories tells a more complete story: Teenagers of all racial-ethnic categories had a 23.9 percent unemployment rate. African Americans of all ages had a 15.3 percent unemployment rate; Hispanics (Latinos/as) had an 11.6 percent rate, as compared to a rate for whites (non-Hispanics) of 8.0 percent and for Asian Americans of 6.8 percent (U.S. Bureau of Labor Statistics, 2011a). However, individuals who become discouraged in their attempt to find work and no longer actively seek employment are not counted as unemployed. According to a Bureau of Labor Statistics (2011a) report, 1 million "discouraged workers" are not currently looking for work because they believe that no jobs are available for them. Another 8.3 million people report that they are employed part time because they cannot find full-time employment. Both in the United States and other nations of the world, the linkage between the economy, levels of employment, and how people view government and politics are closely linked together.

PROBLEMS IN POLITICAL PARTICIPATION AROUND THE WORLD

Social scientists distinguish between politics and government: *Politics*, as previously defined, is the social institution through which power is acquired and exercised by some people and groups. The essential component of politics is *power*—the ability of people to achieve their goals despite opposition from others (see Chapter 2). People who hold positions of power achieve their goals because they have control over other people; those who lack power carry out the wishes of others. Powerful people get others to acquiesce to their demands by using persuasion, authority, or force.

In contemporary societies, the primary political system is *government*—**a formal organization that has legal and political authority to regulate relationships among people in a society and between the society and others outside its borders**. The government (sometimes called the state) includes all levels of bureaucratized political activity such as executive, central, and local administrations; the legislature; the courts; and the armed forces and police.

Political participation varies widely because political freedom is uneven worldwide. Although people in the United States might take elections as a given and decide not to participate even when they have the freedom to do so, people in many other nations do not have the opportunity to participate in free and fair elections. As a result, issues pertaining to political participation remain a concern both in the United States and around the world.

PROBLEMS IN U.S. POLITICS

The United States is a *democracy*, **a political system in which the people hold the ruling power either directly or through elected representatives**. In a *direct participatory democracy*, citizens meet regularly to debate and decide issues of the day. Ancient Athens was a direct democracy, as was colonial New England with its town meetings. Even today, many New England towns use the town meeting. However, even in its beginnings as a nation, the United States was not a direct democracy. The framers of the Constitution believed that decisions should be made by representatives of the people. To ensure that no single group could control the government, they established a *separation of powers* among the legislative, executive, and judicial branches of government and a *system of checks and balances*, giving each branch some degree of involvement in the activities of the others.

In countries that have some form of *representative democracy,* such as the United States, citizens elect representatives who are responsible for conveying the concerns and interests of those they represent. If these representatives are not responsive to the wishes of the people, voters can unseat them through elections. This is not to say that representative democracy is equally accessible to all people in a nation. The framers of the U.S. Constitution, for example, gave the right to vote only to white males who owned property. Eventually, nonlandowners were given the vote, then African American men, and finally, in 1920, women. Today, democratic participation is at least theoretically available to all U.S. citizens age eighteen and over.

Political Parties, Elections, and Public Discontent

A *political party* **is an organization whose purpose is to gain and hold legitimate control of government**. Persons who make up a specific political party typically have similar attitudes, interests, and socioeconomic status. In the democratic process, political parties are supposed to develop and articulate policy positions, educate voters about issues and simplify the choices for them, and recruit and support candidates for public office. To accomplish these goals, political parties create a *platform*, a formal statement of the party's political positions on various social and economic issues. Since the Civil War, the Democratic and Republican Parties have dominated the U.S. political system. Although one party may control the presidency for several terms, at some point the voters elect the other party's nominee, and control shifts. Although both parties have been successful in getting their candidates elected, these parties are dominated by active elites who hold views further from the center of the political spectrum than the views of a majority of party members. As a result, voters in primary elections (in which the nominees of political parties for most offices other than president and vice president are chosen) may select nominees whose views are closer to the center of the political spectrum and further away from the party's own platform. Overall, party loyalties appear to be declining among voters, who may vote in one party's primary but then cast their ballot in general elections without total loyalty to that party, or cast a "split-ticket" ballot (voting for one party's candidate in one race and another party's candidate in the next one).

Although most individuals identify themselves as Republicans or Democrats, a growing number of people have expressed discontent with the existing U.S. political parties. In 2009 a movement emerged to support more constitutionally limited government and to oppose various stimulus and bailout programs that require the use of federal monies. These protesters have referred to themselves as the "Tea Party" movement, based on the 1773 Boston Tea Party, a protest by American colonists against "taxation without representation" by the British government because the colonists were not represented in the British Parliament but were required to pay taxes to that government. According to a *New York Times*/CBS News poll, Tea Party supporters are "wealthier and more well-educated than the general public, and are no more or less afraid of falling into a lower socioeconomic class" (Zernike and Thee-Brenan, 2010:A1). A demographic analysis reveals that the typical Tea Party supporter is white, male, married, and over forty-five years of age. Most are registered Republicans, but they disagree with party leadership about various issues. Although some movement members have been accused of being racist and homophobic, others have applauded the movement for opening up new arenas for political debate when few other options have existed in the U.S. two-party system. Clearly, Tea Party activists are pessimistic about the direction that the United States is going and want to do something about it (Zernike and Thee-Brenan, 2010).

What will become of the Tea Party movement? Will it take a place alongside other, more established political parties, or will it disappear? At the time of this writing, the Tea Party movement does not have a formal organizational structure, and the majority of the group's participants surveyed in the recent *New York Times*/CBS poll stated that they did not want a third party and would still vote Republican. Regardless of how formally organized the group becomes, it appears that participants will remain vocal on a number of issues, including protection of the Constitution, demand for a balanced budget and tax reform, an end to "runaway spending," and other measures that emphasize fiscal restraint and limited government and deemphasize putting government money into social issues (Zernike and Thee Brenan, 2010). Those who participate in the Tea Party movement are engaged in a form of political activism; however, many people in the United States respond in a different manner to current political parties and social issues: They simply do not participate and, as a result, contribute to high levels of voter apathy in many elections. Unfortunately, today voter apathy and influence-buying through campaign contributions threaten to undermine the principles on which our government is based.

Voter Apathy and the Gender Gap

Since democracy in the United States is defined as a government "of the people, by the people, and for the people," we would assume that citizens would participate in their government at any or all of four levels: (1) voting, (2) attending and taking part in political meetings, (3) actively participating in political campaigns, and (4) running for and/or holding political office. At most, about 10 percent of the voting-age population in this country participates at a level higher than simply voting, and over the past forty years, less than half of the voting-age population has voted in nonpresidential elections. Even in presidential elections, voter turnout often is relatively low. In the 2008 presidential election, about 62 percent of the 208.3 million eligible voters cast ballots, compared with 60.6 percent in the 2004 presidential election. The number of ballots cast in 2008 was the highest in history because about 6.5 million more people were registered to vote in 2008. The larger turnout in 2008 was partly a result of significant increases in voting by younger people, Latinos/as, and African American voters. Women's votes were also a significant factor in the election of Barack Obama because women strongly preferred Obama (56 percent) to John McCain (43 percent), whereas men split their votes almost evenly between Obama (49 percent) and McCain (48 percent). State-by-state differences in voting preferences are also highly visible in what political analysts refer to as the "red states" and the "blue states."

Why is it that so many eligible voters in this country stay away from the polls? During any election, millions of voting-age persons do not go to the polls due to illness, disability, lack of transportation, nonregistration, or absenteeism. However, these explanations do not account for why many other people do not vote. According to some conservative analysts, people may not vote because they are satisfied with the status quo or because they are apathetic and uninformed—they lack an understanding of both public issues and the basic processes of government.

By contrast, liberals argue that people stay away from the polls because they feel alienated from politics at all levels of government—federal, state, and local—due to political corruption and influence peddling by special interests and large corporations. Participation in politics is influenced by gender, age, race-ethnicity, and, especially, socioeconomic status (SES). One explanation for the higher rates of political participation at higher SES levels is that advanced levels of education may give people a better understanding of government processes, a belief that they have more at stake in the political process, and greater economic resources to contribute to the process. Some studies suggest that during their college years, many people develop assumptions about political participation that continue throughout their lives.

In the 2010 midterm election, when candidates ran for governor in some states and the U.S. Senate and House of Representatives, approximately 40 percent of eligible voters participated in the election. More people vote in presidential election years than in midterm elections, but the overall percentage of voters is not dramatically higher. In the 2000 and 2004 presidential elections, for example, slightly over 50 percent of the voting-age population (age eighteen and older) voted. The 2004 election was one in which the winning candidate (George W. Bush) received only slightly more than one-half of all votes cast.

When elections can be that close, what causes voter apathy? According to studies by the Pew Research Center for the People and the Press, many people do not vote because they see no reason for change, others are turned off by excessive polling by media and other groups (people see no point to voting if the outcomes are predictable), and still others either disagree with negative advertising by candidates and parties or believe that the issues raised by the candidates are not important or will have no effect on their personal economic situation.

Along with voter apathy, the emergence and persistence of the *gender gap*—**the difference between a candidate's number of votes from women and men**—is a dominant feature of U.S. politics today. Political analysts first noticed a gender gap in the early 1980s, but the gap grew wider and more apparent in subsequent elections. In 1980, the gender gap was about eight points (men were 8 percent more likely than women to support Ronald Reagan for president). In 2004, the gap increased to eleven points (women were 11 percent more likely than men to vote for John Kerry than for George W. Bush). In 2008, a sizable gender gap was evident in the presidential election results. Women strongly preferred Obama (56 percent) to McCain (43 percent) while men split their votes about evenly, with Obama receiving 49 percent of the votes to 48 percent for McCain. The gender gap for 2008 was 7 percentage points, which was virtually identical to the seven-point gap in 2004.

Gender gaps in voting were even more evident in the 2010 races for governor and the U.S. Senate than in previous elections. In races where a gender gap was evident, women were much more likely than men to a support Democratic candidate, and less likely to support the Republican contender. According to the Center for American Women and Politics (2010), "Gender gaps of 4 to 19 percentage points were evident in 17 or 18 gubernatorial races where exit polls were conducted. Similarly, among the 26 U.S. Senate races with exit polls, gender gaps of 4 to 17 points were evident in 15." In the past, gender gaps might have been evident in about two-thirds of statewide races, but in 2010, gender gaps existed in virtually all of the political races.

Why is there a gender gap? Most analysts agree that the gap is rooted in how women and men view economic and social issues, such as welfare reform, abortion, child care, and education, and what they believe the nation's priorities should be. Voter apathy and an increase in the gender gap have received substantial attention in recent years but nothing like the scrutiny given to allegations of political influence-buying by large campaign contributors.

Politics and Money in Political Campaigns

Presidential and congressional candidates and their supporters raise and spend millions of dollars every two years on the elections for national political positions.

Where does all the money go? The cost of running for political office has skyrocketed. The costs of advertising and media time, staff, direct-mail operations, telephone banks, computers, consultants, travel expenses, office rentals, and many other campaign expenses have increased dramatically over the past two decades. Unless a candidate has private resources, contributions can determine the success or failure of his or her bid for election or reelection.

In the past certain kinds of campaign contributions were specifically prohibited by law: Corporate contributions to presidential and congressional candidates have been illegal since 1907, and contributions from labor unions were outlawed in 1943. In 1974, Congress passed a law limiting an individual's total contribution to federal candidates to $25,000 a year and no more than $1,000 per candidate. In 2002, these limits were raised to $2,000 per candidate and no more than $95,000 in any two-year period. However, these individual limits have been sidestepped by bundling, which occurs when a donor collects contributions from family members, business associates, and others and then "bundles" them together and sends them to a candidate. For example, during the 2000 presidential election, supporters of Republican candidate George W. Bush included a group of volunteer fundraisers referred to as the "pioneers," each of whom pledged to raise at least $100,000 which would be bundled as hard money contributions and given to Bush's campaign for use in getting him elected (Nyhart, 2001).

Federal law also limits individual contributions to a political action committee to a maximum of $5,000. *Political action committees (PACs)* **are special-interest groups that fund campaigns to help elect (or defeat) candidates based on their positions on specific issues**. PACs were originally organized by unions to get around the laws that prohibited union gifts. Today, there are thousands of PACs representing businesses, labor unions, and various single-issue groups (such as gays and lesbians and environmental groups).

Finally, federal law limits contributions made to political parties for campaigning to $28,500, but until 2002, there was no limit on contributions made for the purpose of party-building, such as distributing "vote Democratic" or "vote Republican" bumper stickers or organizing get-out-the-vote drives. However, both the Democratic and Republican parties used these contributions to pay for administrative expenses and overhead, thus freeing up other party money to support candidates. This *soft-money loophole*—contributing to a political party instead of to a specific candidate—became a

TABLE 13.1 Top Ten Corporate Campaign Contributors, 2010	
AT&T	$45.6 million
Goldman Sachs	$36.7 million
Citigroup	$27.5 million
United Parcel Service	$24.9 million
Altria (formerly Philip Morris)	$24.3 million
Microsoft	$21.0 million
J. P. Morgan	$20.3 million
Time Warner	$20.0 million
Morgan Stanley	$19.8 million
Lockheed Martin	$19.3 million

Source: Based on data from The 10 Biggest Corporate Campaign Contributors in U.S. Politics at http://www.dailyfinance.com/2010/10/13/the-10-biggest-corporate-campaign-contributors-in-u-s-politics/

major issue, and the same law that increased contribution limits in 2002 allegedly closed this loophole.

But the most controversial recent change occurred in 2010 when the U.S. Supreme Court ruled that corporations can spend unlimited money on behalf of political candidates. Now, corporations can legally pay for extensive political advertising on behalf of candidates and causes, and they will not be required to disclose these contributions (Palmer, 2010). By donating anonymously to nonprofit civic leagues and trade associations, corporations and labor unions can in essence donate to candidates' campaigns (see Table 13.1).

What agency monitors campaign contributions and how effective has this agency been? The Federal Election Commission—the enforcement agency that monitors campaign contributions—is considered "one of the most toothless agencies in Washington" (Cohn, 1997). Violations, when discovered, are typically not punished until some time after an election is over. As a result, a very small percentage of the U.S. population is contributing extraordinarily large amounts to get their candidates elected. Is this sort of influence-buying a recent phenomenon? According to journalist Kevin Phillips (1995), influence-buying has been going on for some time in this country, and most political candidates and elected officials do not refuse such contributions.

Although the general public realizes that special-interest groups and lobbyists often have undue influence on political decisions and the outcome of elections, most people believe that they are powerless to do anything about it. When respondents in a 1990s Gallup Poll survey were asked "Would you say the government is pretty much run by a few big interests looking out for themselves or that it is run for the benefit of all the people?" 76 percent said that they believed big interests ran the country, only 18 percent believed the government operates for the benefit of all, and 6 percent had no opinion (Golay and Rollyson, 1996). Do you think that their answer would be different today? How might the percentages have changed in the meantime?

Government by Special-Interest Groups

What happens when special-interest groups have a major influence on how the government is run? Some special-interest groups exert their influence on single issues such as the environment, gun ownership, abortion, or legislation that affects a particular occupation (e.g., the American Medical Association) or business (e.g., the National Restaurant Association).

Other special-interest groups represent specific occupations and industries and make contributions to candidates who will protect their interests and profits. Lawyers and law firms were among the top contributors in the 2008 presidential election with the American Association for Justice and a number of nationwide law firms contributing in the range of $100,000 to $300,000 to both presidential candidates. Other industries that engage in heavy lobbying efforts are health professionals, securities and investment firms, real estate groups, and public sector unions that want to be heard in regard to such matters as health care and pension plans. Another highly effective lobby is AARP (American Association of Retired Persons), which spent $21 million lobbying, particularly for candidates who were seen as friendly toward the issues that affect older persons, such as Social Security and Medicare.

Government by Bureaucracy

Special-interest groups wield tremendous political power, but so does the federal bureaucracy. The federal bureaucracy, or **permanent government, refers to the top-tier civil service bureaucrats who have a strong power base and play a major role in developing and implementing government policies and procedures**.

The federal government played a relatively limited role in everyday life in the nineteenth century, but its role grew during the Great Depression in the 1930s. When faced with high rates of unemployment and persistent poverty, people demanded that the government do something. Under a series of "New Deal" initiatives, security markets were regulated, federal jobs and relief programs were instituted, and labor-management relations were regulated. In the ensuing decades, as voters continued to demand that the government "do something" about the problems facing society, government has continued to grow. In fact, since 1960, the federal government has grown faster than any other segment of the U.S. economy. Today, slightly more than 2.1 million people are employed by the federal bureaucracy, in which much of the actual functioning of the government takes place.

Sociologists point out that bureaucratic power in any sphere tends to take on a life of its own over time, and this is evident in the U.S. government. Despite efforts by presidents, White House staffs, and various presidential cabinets, neither Republican nor Democratic administrations have been able to establish control over the federal bureaucracy (Dye, Zeigler, and Schubert, 2012). In fact, many federal bureaucrats have seen a number of presidents come and go. The vast majority of top-echelon positions have been held by white men for many years. Rising to the top of the bureaucracy can take as long as twenty years, and few white women and people of color have reached these positions.

The government bureaucracy is able to perpetuate itself and expand because many of its employees possess highly specialized knowledge and skills and cannot easily be replaced. As the issues facing the United States have grown in number and complexity, offices and agencies have been established to create rules, policies, and procedures for dealing with such things as nuclear power, environmental protection, and drug safety. These government bureaucracies announce about twenty rules or regulations for every one law passed by Congress (Dye, Zeiger, and Schubert, 2012). Today, public policy is increasingly made by agencies rather than elected officials. The agencies receive little direction from Congress or the president, and although their actions are subject to challenge in the courts, most agencies are highly autonomous.

The federal budget is the central ingredient in the bureaucracy. Preparing the annual federal budget is a major undertaking for the president and the Office of Management and Budget, one of the most important agencies in Washington. Getting the budget approved by Congress is an even more monumental task. However, as Dye, Zeigler, and Schubert, (2012) point out, even with the highly publicized wrangling over the budget by the president and Congress, the final congressional appropriations usually are within 2 to 3 percent of the budget that the president originally proposed. In the difficult economic and political climate of 2011, however, there is no guarantee that these percentages will hold as budget negotiations move forward.

As powerful as the federal bureaucracy has become, it is not immune to special-interest groups. Special-interest groups can help an agency get more operating money. Although the president has budgetary authority over the bureaucracy, any agency that believes that it did not get its fair share can raise a public outcry by contacting friendly interest groups and congressional subcommittees. This outcry can force the president to restore funding to the agency or prod Congress into appropriating money that was not requested by the president, who might go along with the appropriation to avoid a confrontation. Special-interest groups also influence the bureaucracy through the military-industrial complex.

The Military-Industrial Complex

The term *military-industrial complex* **refers to the interdependence of the military establishment and private military contractors**. The complex is actually a three-way arrangement involving one or more private interest groups (usually corporations that manufacture weapons or other military-related goods), members of Congress who serve on congressional committees or subcommittees that appropriate money for military programs, and a bureaucratic agency (such as the Defense Department). Often, a revolving door of money, influence, and jobs is involved: Military contractors who receive contracts from the Defense Department also serve on advisory committees that recommend what weapons should be ordered. Many people move from job to job, serving in the military, then in the Defense Department, then in military industries (Feagin et al., 2006).

In the 1970s, sociologist C. Wright Mills (1976) stated that the relationship between the military and private industry was problematic and could result in a "permanent war economy" or "military economy" in this country. But economist John Kenneth Galbraith (1985) argued that government expenditures for weapons and jet fighters stimulate the private sector of the economy, creating jobs and encouraging spending. In other words, military spending by Congress is not an economic burden but a source of economic development. It also enriches those corporations that build jet fighters and other warplanes, such as Boeing and Lockheed Martin. According to one executive who spent much of his career

Corporations in the military-industrial complex produce weapons systems such as the F-22 Raptors shown here. What are the benefits of spending billions of dollars on advanced military equipment such as this? What are the economic and noneconomic costs?

involved in building jet fighters for the U.S. military, getting a $1 trillion Pentagon contract for a new generation of jet fighters was of utmost importance to his company: "It's the Super Bowl. It's winner takes all. It's the huge plum. It's the airplane program of the century. If you don't win this program, you're a has-been in tactical aircraft" (quoted in Shenon, 1996:A1).

The 2011 fiscal year budget provides $553 billion for the base budget of the Department of Defense, an increase of $22 billion above the 2010 appropriation. Many believe that the United States will always have an active military-industrial complex because of our emphasis on *militarism*—a societal focus on military ideals and an aggressive preparedness for war. The belief in militarism is maintained and reinforced by values such as patriotism, courage, reverence, loyalty, obedience, and faith in authority, as sociologist Cynthia H. Enloe (1987:542–543) explains:

Military expenditures, militaristic values, and military authority now influence the flow of foreign trade and determine which countries will or will not receive agricultural assistance. They shape the design and marketing of children's toys and games and of adult fashions and entertainment. Military definitions of progress and security dominate the economic fate of entire geographic regions. The military's ways of doing business open or shut access to information and technology for entire social groups. Finally, military mythologies of valor and safety influence the sense of self-esteem and well-being of millions of people.

SOCIOLOGICAL PERSPECTIVES ON THE POLITICAL ECONOMY

Politics and the economy are so intertwined in the United States that many social scientists speak of the two as a single entity: the political economy. At issue for most social scientists is whether political and economic power are concentrated in the hands of the few or distributed among the many in this country. Functionalists adopt a pluralistic model of power, whereas conflict theorists adopt an elitist model.

The Functionalist Perspective

Pluralism is rooted in the functionalist perspective, which assumes that people generally agree on the most important societal concerns—freedom and security—and that government fulfills important functions in these two regards that no other institution can fulfill. According to the early functionalists, government serves to socialize people to be good citizens, to regulate the economy so that it operates effectively, and to provide necessary services for citizens (Durkheim, 1933/1893). Contemporary functionalists identify four similar functions: A government maintains law and order, plans society and coordinates other institutions, meets social needs, and handles international relations, including warfare.

But what happens when people do not agree on specific issues or concerns? Functionalists say that divergent viewpoints lead to political pluralism; that is, when competing interests or viewpoints arise, government arbitrates. Thus, according to the ***pluralist model*, power is widely dispersed throughout many competing interest groups in our political system** (Dahl, 1961). In the pluralist model, (1) political leaders make decisions on behalf of the people through a process of bargaining, accommodation, and compromise; (2) leadership groups (such as business, labor, law, and consumer organizations) serve as watchdogs to protect ordinary people from the abuses of any one group; (3) ordinary people influence public policy through voting and participating in special-interest groups; (4) power is widely dispersed in society (the same groups aren't equally influential in all arenas); and (5) public policy reflects a balance among competing interest groups, not the majority-group's view (Dye, Zeigler, and Schubert, 2012).

How might a social analyst who uses a functionalist framework address problems in politics and the economy? Such an analyst might begin by saying that since dysfunctions are inevitable in any social institution, it is important to sort out and remedy the specific elements of the system that are creating the problems. It should not be necessary to restructure or replace the entire system. Consider, for example, government regulations: Some regulations are good, and some are bad. The trick, functionalists say, is to keep the good ones and get rid of the bad. Too often, the U.S. government moves between two extremes: overregulation of business and society or seeking to end most, if not all, regulation. As social analysts Donald L. Barlett and James B. Steele (1996:214) suggest, "We must preserve the rules that assure the quality of American life: the food you eat, the medicines you take, the air you breathe and the water you drink. They have evolved over a century." Barlett and Steele also state, however, that demanding that U.S.-owned companies comply with regulations that are not required of their competitors in foreign countries creates an uneven playing field. Hence, a tariff should be imposed on imported products equal to the amount of money that U.S. businesses must spend to comply with government regulations (Barlett and Steele, 1996). This perspective is based on the belief that a certain amount of government intervention in the economy is appropriate but that too much—or the wrong kind—is detrimental. Since the time when Barlett and Steele made these comments, the national and international playing field in regard to business and regulation has become much more, not less, complicated and has many more players involved.

The Conflict Perspective

Most conflict theorists believe that democracy is an ideal, not a reality, in our society today because the government primarily benefits the wealthy and the politically powerful, especially business elites. In fact, according to conflict theorists, economic and political elites use the powers of the government to impose their will on the masses. According to the ***elite model*, power in political systems is concentrated in the hands of a small group, whereas the masses are relatively powerless**. In the elite model, (1) elites possess the greatest wealth, education, status, and other resources and make the most important decisions in society; (2) elites generally agree on the basic values and goals for the society; (3) power is highly concentrated at the top of a pyramid-shaped social hierarchy, and those at the top set public policy for everyone; (4) public policy reflects the values and preferences of the elite, not of ordinary people; and (5) elites use the media to shape the political attitudes of ordinary people (Dye, Zeigler, and Schubert, 2012).

According to sociologist C. Wright Mills (1959a), the United States is ruled by a ***power elite*, which at the**

top is composed of business leaders, the executive branch of the federal government, and the military (especially the "top brass" at the Pentagon). The corporate rich—the highest-paid CEOs of major corporations—are the most powerful because they have the unique ability to parlay their vast economic resources into political power. The next most powerful level is occupied by Congress, special-interest groups, and local opinion leaders. The lowest (and widest) level of the pyramid is occupied by ordinary people, the unorganized masses who are relatively powerless and vulnerable to economic and political exploitation.

Individuals in the power elite have similar class backgrounds and interests and interact on a regular basis. Through a revolving door of influence, they tend to shift back and forth between and among business, government, and military sectors. It is not unusual for people who have served in the president's cabinet to become directors of major corporations that do business with the government, for powerful businesspeople to serve in the cabinet, or for former military leaders to become important businesspeople. Through such political and economic alliances, people in the power elite can influence many important decisions, including how federal tax money will be spent and to whom lucrative subsidies and government contracts are awarded.

In his lengthy analysis of the political economy over many decades, sociologist G. William Domhoff (1978) has identified a ruling class, which is made up of the corporate rich, a relatively fixed group of privileged people who wield power over political processes and serve capitalist interests. The corporate rich influence the political process in three ways: (1) by financing campaigns of candidates who favor their causes; (2) by using PACs and loophole contributions to obtain favors, tax breaks, and favorable regulatory rulings; and (3) by gaining appointment to governmental advisory committees, presidential commissions, and other governmental positions. For example, some members of the ruling class influence international politics through their involvement in banking, business services, and law firms that have a strong interest in overseas sales, investments, or raw materials extraction (Domhoff, 1990).

Some analysts who take a conflict perspective say that the only way to overcome problems in politics and the economy is to change the entire system. Our present system exploits poor whites, people of color, women of all colors, people with disabilities, and others who consider themselves disenfranchised from the political and economic mainstream of society. Other conflict theorists think that we can solve many

problems by curbing the abuses of capitalism and the market economy and thereby reducing the power of political and economic elites. Political scientist Benjamin R. Barber (1996:242) believes that we cannot rely on the capitalist (market) economy to look after common interests:

> It is the job of civil society and democratic government and not of the market to look after common interests and make sure that those who profit from the common planet pay its common proprietors their fair share. When governments abdicate in favor of markets, they are declaring nolo contendere [no contest] in an arena in which they are supposed to be primary challengers, bartering away the rights of their people along the way. . . . Markets simply are not designed to do the things democratic polities do. They enjoin private rather than public modes of discourse, allowing us as consumers to speak via our currencies of consumption to producers of material goods, but ignoring us as citizens speaking to one another about such things as the social consequences of our private market choices. . . . They advance individualistic rather than social goals. . . . Having created the conditions that make markets possible, democracy must also do all the things that markets undo or cannot do. It must educate citizens so that they can use their markets wisely and contain market abuses well.

ARE THERE SOLUTIONS TO PROBLEMS IN POLITICS AND THE ECONOMY?

A number of key factors will establish the future course of politics, both in the United States and in other nations. The level of economic growth will have a significant effect on the amount of money that high-income nations will be able to invest in domestic programs (such as education, the environment, health care, and elder care) and in alleviating international problems (such as growing economic inequality within and among nations, the spread of HIV/AIDS and other diseases, and political upheavals and wars). However, political decisions also will be crucial in determining where money is spent and how much is allocated for war, international programs, and domestic programs.

In the United States, the future of our well-being is, at least to some extent, in the hands of our political leaders, whom—at least in most instances—we have elected.

Our future is also in the hands of powerful economic leaders, such as corporate decision makers whom we did not elect. Some political leaders and corporate officers appear to seek the common good; however, others have proven themselves to be unworthy of our trust, as revealed in numerous media headlines and articles. As discussed in the next chapter, the media provide us with most of the information we have about the current political and economic issues that confront us today and in the future.

SUMMARY

✓•⎯ **Study** and **Review** on **mysoclab.com**

▪ **What kind of economic system does the United States have?**

The United States has a capitalist economy. Ideally, capitalism is characterized by private ownership of the means of production, pursuit of personal profit, competition, and lack of government intervention.

▪ **How are societies classified by their predominant type of work?**

Societies are classified as preindustrial, industrial, or postindustrial. Preindustrial societies engage in primary-sector production—the extraction of raw materials and natural resources from the environment. Industrial societies engage in secondary-sector production—the processing of raw materials (from the primary sector). Postindustrial societies engage in tertiary-sector production—providing services rather than goods.

▪ **What are transnational corporations, and why do they pose social problems?**

Transnational corporations are large-scale business organizations that are headquartered in one country but operate in many countries. Transnationals lack accountability to any government or regulatory agency. They are not dependent on any one country for labor, capital, or technology. They can play important roles in the economies and governments of countries that need them as employers and accept their practices.

▪ **Why is the national debt a serious problem? How is consumer debt a public issue?**

When we increase the national debt, we are borrowing from future generations, which will leave them with higher taxes, fewer benefits, and a lower rate of economic growth. Consumer debt becomes a public issue when people cannot repay their credit card loans.

▪ **What is corporate welfare?**

Corporate welfare occurs when the government helps industries and private corporations in their economic pursuits. Many subsidies that were originally put in place to help stabilize the economy continue unnecessarily because of labor union and PAC lobbying and campaign contributions.

▪ **Why is voter apathy a problem? What is the gender gap?**

Voter apathy undermines the basis on which representative democracy is built; if large numbers of people don't vote, the interests of only a few are represented. The gender gap is the difference between a candidate's number of votes from women and men. More than ever today, women and men seem to view economic and social issues differently.

▪ **Why have campaign contributions been an issue in recent elections?**

Campaign contributions are regulated, but individuals, unions, and corporations have circumvented the law through the soft-money loophole—contributing to a political party instead of to a specific candidate—and through political action committees. Political action committees (PACs) are special-interest groups that fund campaigns to help elect (or defeat) candidates on the basis of their positions on specific issues. Because running for office is expensive, contributions can make the difference between a candidate's success or defeat. A recent Supreme Court decision has made it possible for corporations to make unlimited contributions in political elections. It remains to be seen what effect this will have on funding of elections and the overall political process.

▪ **What is the military-industrial complex?**

The military-industrial complex refers to the interdependence of the military establishment and private military contractors. The military-industrial complex can be a revolving door of money, influence, and jobs.

▪ **What are the sociological perspectives on the political economy?**

The functionalists use a pluralist model, believing that power is widely dispersed through many competing interest groups in our political system. Functionalists therefore believe that problems can be solved by identifying dysfunctional elements and correcting them. Conflict theorists use an elite model, believing that power in political systems is concentrated in the hands of a small group, whereas the masses are relatively powerless. Sociologist C. Wright Mills used the term *power elite* for this small group of top business leaders, the executive branch of the federal government, and the "top brass" of the military.

KEY TERMS

capitalism, p. 295
democracy, p. 305
economy, p. 294
elite model, p. 311
gender gap, p. 307
government, p. 305
military-industrial complex, p. 310
mixed economy, p. 296

monopoly, p. 301
oligopoly, p. 301
permanent government, p. 309
pluralist model, p. 311
political action committees (PACs),
p. 308
political economy, p. 294
political party, p. 305

politics, p. 294
power elite, p. 311
primary-sector production, p. 298
secondary-sector production, p. 298
socialism, p. 295
tertiary-sector production, p. 298
transnational corporation, p. 299
unemployment rate, p. 304

QUESTIONS FOR CRITICAL THINKING

1. Imagine that you are given unlimited funds and resources to reverse the trend in voter apathy. What would you do at the local level? What would you do at the state and national levels to bring about change?

2. How would you respond to the Gallup Poll survey question, "Would you say the government is pretty much run by a few big interests looking out for themselves or that it is run for the benefit of all the people?" Explain your answer.

3. What do you think should be done to reduce unemployment in the United States? Should employers be given a financial incentive or tax credit for creating additional jobs? Should a compulsory retirement age be reestablished for older workers? Should the government start new public works projects similar to those used in the Great Depression to reduce unemployment? What solutions would you suggest?

Succeed with MySocLab® www.mysoclab.com

The new MySocLab delivers proven results in helping students succeed, provides engaging experiences that personalize learning, and comes from a trusted partner with educational expertise and a deep commitment to helping students and instructors achieve their goals.

Here are a few activities you will find for this chapter:

Watch on **mysoclab.com**

Core Concepts video clips feature sociologists in action, exploring important concepts in the study of Social Problems. Watch:
• Globalization

Explore on **mysoclab.com**

Social Explorer is an interactive application that allows you to explore Census data through interactive maps. Explore:
• Social Explorer Activity: The Nation's Wealthiest [report]

Read on **mysoclab.com**

MySocLibrary includes primary source readings from classic and contemporary sociologists. Read:
• Asceticism and the Spirit of Capitalism

Problems in the Media

THINKING SOCIOLOGICALLY

○ How do new technologies continue to make the media more important in all aspects of contemporary life?

○ Why are today's media industries known as "Big Media"?

○ Do the media—either intentionally or unintentionally—perpetuate race, class, and gender stereotypes that may influence our thinking about people outside our own social groupings?

United States:

Dear readers,

While I was at the beach, I realized that I, Amanda Hirsch, am an Internet Addict.... It started out innocently enough. I thought I wanted a tech holiday.... But there I was, surrounded by ocean and sand, and a little voice inside me said, darkly, "give me my blogs." (I wanted to check the dozen or so blogs I read on a regular basis—a subset of the longer list of blogs to which I subscribe.)

My inner dialogue proceeded as follows:

"No! You're at the beach. You should relax."

"But—"

"No. Don't open that can of worms. You'll get sucked in and miss this beautiful day."

"But what if I really want to read blogs? Why is that so different than reading a novel? It's not like I'll be surfing aimlessly."...

Then, approximately 15 minutes later:

"Oh, it was so much fun to read my blogs, I think I'll read a little email...."

"I know, I know, it sounds bad. But I won't check work messages—just emails from friends."

And so it began....

—Amanda Hirsch (2008), a freelance Web consultant, explains how reading blogs and e-mails and surfing the Internet had become a difficult habit for her to break, even when she allegedly was taking a day off for leisure activities.

F ew forms of mass media have become so widely used and popular as quickly as the Internet with its vast amounts of information, communication options, and games to play. The Internet provides us with a vast invisible community, and it sometimes provides us with an opportunity to become a part of what is going on, not just to sit by as a passive observer as when we are watching television. According to psychologist Kimberly Young, the Internet is so popular and habit-forming because it "allows us to create new personalities and use them to fulfill unmet psychological needs" (quoted in Heffernan, 2011). As this statement suggests, despite all that the Internet has to offer as a form of media, it also has a potentially addictive effect on people. Whether spending large amounts of time on the Internet should or should not be considered an addiction in the medical usage of the term is a topic of widespread debate, but some medical experts believe that addiction to the Internet is a common disorder that should be included among the psychiatric disorders listed in the American Psychiatric Association's *DSM–V* classification (Block, 2008). Although individuals who "withdraw" from Internet use are not going to have physical symptoms as do those who cease to use alcohol or tobacco, some heavy Internet users believe that they would experience severe psychological effects from being disconnected from information, communications, and entertainment on the World Wide Web.

Today, the Internet is only one of a myriad of media sources that vie for our time and attention and garner billions of dollars for some of the owners of global media conglomerates. In this chapter, we examine social problems related to the political economy of media industries, potential effects the media might have on viewers and readers, and how sociological perspectives inform our thinking on media-related problems.

DID YOU KNOW

- The top six media conglomerates have revenues totaling more than $276 billion annually.

- On average, each person spends more than 3,500 hours using various forms of media each year.

- Most top-earning movies worldwide are produced by U.S.-owned film production companies.

THE IMPORTANCE OF THE MEDIA IN CONTEMPORARY LIFE

The media play a vital role in the daily lives of many people. Whether we realize their existence or try to ignore their influence, various forms of the media are with us constantly. What constitutes the media? *Media* is the plural of *medium*, which refers to any device that transmits a message. Thus, as we noted in Chapter 4, the media include newspapers, magazines, television, and movies among other things. When sociologists refer to the media (or mass media), however, they are usually speaking of the **media industries—major businesses that own or own interests in radio and television production and broadcasting; motion pictures, movie theaters, and music companies; newspaper, periodical (magazine), and book publishing; and Internet services and content providers that influence people and cultures worldwide.** To understand how pervasive media industries are in our daily lives, consider one day in the life of Scott Schatzkamer, a college student who reported that one morning he awakened to the sound of an AM/FM adult-contemporary radio station and, during the day and evening, watched ESPN's *SportsCenter* (owned by Disney), read part of Time Warner's *Sports Illustrated*, listened to a radio station owned by Disney, played Electronic Arts' *Madden NFL 2000* on his fraternity's Sony PlayStation, checked his e-mail several times on AOL, logged on to ESPN.com for sports scores, read assignments in *General Chemistry* (published by Cengage) and *Psychology in Perspective* (published by Pearson), and watched a baseball game on News Corporation's FOX Network (updated from Heilbrunn, 2000).

During the course of Scott's day, he was under the influence of numerous forms of media provided by a number of media outlets, some of which share corporate ownership at the top. Recent estimates show that the average person in the United States spends more than one-half of his or her waking hours in some media-related activity. Indeed, today many people spend more time in media-related activities (see Table 14.1) than they do in any other single endeavor, including sleeping, working, eating, or talking with friends and family (Biagi, 2012).

Is this time well spent? Most analysts and media scholars agree that the media industries that first emerged in the twentieth century and have now flourished in the twenty-first century are one of the most significant social institutions at work in the United States and many other nations. They facilitate human communication and provide news and entertainment

TABLE 14.1 How Much Time Do People Spend with Media?

It is estimated that the average U.S. adult age eighteen and older spent the following number of hours with various forms of media in 2009.

Type of Media	Number of Hours
Television (including pay cable)	1,721
Broadcast and satellite radio	716
Recorded music	165
Consumer-online Internet services	184
Daily newspapers	158
Video games	121
Books	106
Magazines	126
Home video	59

Source: U.S. Census Bureau, 2010.

while having a powerful influence on all other social institutions, including education, health care delivery, religion, families, and politics. Some aspects of this influence are positive, but other aspects might be negative. Some critics who are concerned about possible negative influences note that we are experiencing a media glut and increasing commercialization of all aspects of life. It has been suggested, for example, that mobile media in the form of cell phones or smartphones that we carry with us at all times are the fastest-growing media (Biagi, 2012). One of the most pressing issues in regard to media is the concentration of ownership. From this perspective, it is important for audiences to know who owns the media and how to assess the quality of information that is being disseminated.

THE POLITICAL ECONOMY OF MEDIA INDUSTRIES

How did the contemporary media industries come to be known as "Big Media"? The answer seems to lie in one word: *technology*. Technology, in the form of motion pictures, radio, and television, increased competition and broadened markets in the twentieth century. Before that, newspapers and books had been the primary means of disseminating information and entertainment to large numbers of people simultaneously. The companies that were involved in these forms of media were usually small and focused on a single output: Newspapers were produced by companies whose only business was newspapers, and books were published by companies whose only business was books (Biagi, 2012). However, at least two factors limited the market for the information and entertainment provided by the newspaper and publishing industries: the length of time it took to get the product to consumers and the consumers' literacy.

Radio, by contrast, offered consumers immediate access to information and entertainment from coast to coast. Introduced in 1920, radio promptly became a competitor to the newspaper and publishing industries. Simply by turning a knob, consumers could listen to the latest news (sometimes even as it happened), hear the latest song, laugh with their favorite comedian, or thrill to the adventures of their favorite detective. Consumers and corporate executives alike believed that radio's dominance in the media industries could not be shaken.

However, in the 1950s, a new technology emerged to threaten the newspaper and radio industries: television. Television had all the advantages of radio and one more: moving images. Now consumers could not only listen to the world around them, they could also watch it. Although older-media forms such as newspapers, magazines, radio, and television have continued to have distinct audiences, the most sweeping form of audience gathering and keeping occurs on the Internet where people increasingly rely on "faceless" journalists, bloggers, posters, and Wikipedia "experts" for information and entertainment of all kinds.

Media Ownership and Control

Just as technology played a significant role in the development of the media industries, it has played a significant role in the changes that have occurred within these industries.

Consider, for a moment, the effects that fiber-optic cable, broadcast satellites, and computers have had on these industries. The introduction of cable television, for example, brought about a significant shift in media ownership. The development of more sophisticated space satellites in the 1970s made it possible for cable television systems to become interconnected throughout the United States and contributed to the success of cable networks such as Home Box Office (HBO) and Cable News Network (CNN), for which viewers pay a monthly fee. Having a variety of cable channels to watch increased the number of cable TV subscribers, resulting in more broadcast stations being built and the creation of additional cable channels. At the same time, the dramatic increase in cable television viewers drastically reduced the audience share previously held by the "Big Three" television networks—NBC, CBS, and ABC—and led to rapid changes in the ownership and control of these networks. Within a few months in the mid-1980s, the three major networks, which had seemed indomitable, all changed ownership through purchases, takeovers, and mergers.

In the 2010s, NBC, CBS, and ABC are now part of what is known as "The Big Six," which refers to massive corporations that, through an elaborate series of mergers and acquisitions, have come to control the news and entertainment industry and much more. Let's take a closer look at the Big Six. *General Electric* is a partial owner (holding a 49 percent ownership stake), along with Comcast, of NBCUniversal, which owns NBC and numerous other holdings as shown in Figure 14.1. Comcast is the country's largest cable and Internet provider, as well has owning various cable channels. *Walt Disney Company* owns ABC. CBS Corporation owns CBS. *News Corp.* owns FOX Broadcasting Company. *Time Warner* is the largest media conglomerate in the world; and *VIACOM* owns cable networks and film studios.

Looking at the holdings of the Big Six, it is apparent that media ownership has become highly concentrated in a few megacorporations that own and control most of the media industry. The Big Six control all aspects of the television industry, from program production to distribution to the audience. In their never-ending search for profit, these corporations also consolidated their holdings in other sectors of the media, ranging from film and music production to books and magazine publishing and to the Internet. Analysts describe these types of mergers in the media industries as *convergence*, meaning that a melding of the communications, computer, and electronics industries has occurred. Convergence in the media industry has led to media concentration. **Media concentration refers to the tendency of the media industries to cluster together in groups with the goal of enhancing profitability** (Biagi, 2012).

As this definition suggests, profit is the driving force in media concentration. According to media scholar Shirley Biagi (2012), media companies are owned by people who want to make money. Since profits in this sector are high compared with profits in the manufacturing sector, businesspeople view investments in

NEWS CORPORATION	TIME WARNER	NBCUNIVERSAL*	WALT DISNEY	VIACOM
Filmed Entertainment Fox Filmed Entertainment Twentieth Century Fox Film Corporation Fox Searchlight Pictures Twentieth Century Fox Television **Television** FOX Broadcasting Company MyNetworkTV FOXSports.com Fox Television Stations **Cable Network Programming** FOX News Channel FOX Business Network FOX Cable Networks FX Fox Movie Channel SPEED FSN National Geographic Channel **Newspapers and Information Services** The Wall Street Journal Dow Jones Newswires Barrons MarketWatch New York Post Community Newspaper Group **Book Publishing** HarperCollins Publishers **Other** News Corp. Digital Media Group MySpace IGN Entertainment Fox Mobile Group Hulu (32%)	**Home Box Office (HBO)** **Turner Broadcasting System** Adult Swim Boomerang Cartoon Network CNN Fashion TV HTV HLN NASCAR.com PGA.com TBS TNT Turner Classic Movies **Warner Bros. Entertain- ment DC Entertainment** New Line Cinema Warner Bros. Home Entertainment Group Warner Bros. Pictures Group Warner Bros. Television Group **Time, Inc.** Entertainment Weekly Fortune Golf Magazine Health InStyle Money People Sports Illustrated Southern Living Sunset Time Magazine **Time Warner Investments Group**	**National Broadcasting Company** NBC Network Television Stations NBC Entertainment NBC News **NBCUniversal Sports & Olympics** **NBCUniversal Television Group** **NBCUniversal Cable** A&E Television Networks A&E (co-owned with Disney) History Channel (co-owned with Disney) Lifetime Military History Channel **Bravo** **CNBC** MSNBC SyFy USA Network The Weather Channel **Telemundo Stations** **Universal Studios** Universal Pictures Universal Parks & Resorts	**Television** ABC-Owned Television Stations Group Disney ABC Television Group ABC Television Network ABC Family A&E Television (co-owned with NBC) Disney Channel History (co-owned with NBC) Lifetime (co-owned with NBC) SOAPnet **ESPN** Radio Stations Film and Theater Disney Theatrical Productions Hollywood Pictures Miramax Films Touchstone Pictures Walt Disney Pictures Walt Disney Studios Home Entertainment **Music** Disney Music Group Walt Disney Records **Publishing** Disney Publishing Worldwide **Parks and Resorts** Disney Cruise Line Disneyland Walt Disney World Resort	**Cable Networks** Atom Entertainment BET Networks CMT Comedy Central MTV Nick at Nite Nickelodeon Spike TV TV Land VH1 **Film** Paramount Pictures Corporation **Viacom Digital**

*Comcast owned 51 percent of NBCUniversal as of January 28, 2012.

Figure 14.1 Selected U.S. holdings of Big Media conglomerates, 2011

the media industries positively. Thus far, corporate megamergers have led to the following changes in the media industries (based on Biagi, 2012):

1. *Concentration of ownership within one industry.* Book publishing and newspapers are two examples. In book publishing, companies were bought and sold until only a few giant companies remain, and they control the market in areas such as trade books and textbooks. Similarly, newspapers buy out other newspapers and typically stop their presses, leaving cities with only one major newspaper and, in recent years, its Web-version available online.

2. *Cross-media ownership.* Cross-media ownership occurs when media companies own more than one type of media property. Today, a single giant media corporation might own newspapers, magazines, radio, television stations, and numerous cable television channels. Even among smaller media corporations, cross-media ownership is common.

3. *Conglomerate ownership.* Conglomerates occur when a single corporation owns companies that operate in different business sectors. As stated, General Electric, one of the leading electronics and manufacturing firms in the United States, owns 49 percent of

the stock of NBCUniversal, a media conglomerate that owns NBC Television Network, NBC Studios, more than a dozen local NBC television stations, and MSNBC.

4. *Vertical integration.* Vertical integration occurs when the corporations that make the media content also control the distribution channels. Walt Disney Company, for example, owns film and television production companies (Miramax Films and ABC Entertainment Television Group), which supply programming for its television network (ABC), which helps promote cable channels that are owned in part by Disney (ESPN, Lifetime TV and E! Entertainment TV). These in turn have ties with the Disney book publishing unit that features book-length stories about Disney characters and similar popular themes.

Supporters of convergence believe that much can be gained by these corporate strategies and speak of synergy. The term *synergy* is often used to describe the process that is used in capitalizing on a product to make all the profit possible. Media analysts believe that synergy is created, for example, when a corporation acquires ownership of both a production studio and a television network. Theoretically, the products that are made by one branch of the company may be distributed and sold by the other branch of the company in a more efficient and profitable manner than they would if separate companies were involved.

Problems Associated with Convergence

Clearly, concentration and conglomeration are profitable for owners, investors and media executives. Table 14.2 lists ten of the top media moguls who have made portions of their wealth through media ownership and control. According to *Forbes* (2010), nineteen of the top fifty on the *Forbes* 400 list of richest people in the United States had a source of their wealth based in the media industry. However, convergence is not necessarily positive for media audiences. Many analysts believe that convergence has reduced the amount of *message pluralism*, the broad and diverse representation of opinion and culture that is available to the public (Biagi, 2012). Dire warnings about problems associated with convergence and the lack of message pluralism have been issued for more than a decade and are similar to comments by this media scholar:

[As a result of convergence], media fare is even more closely linked to the needs and concerns of a handful of enormous and powerful corporations, with annual revenues approaching the [gross domestic product] of a small nation. These firms are run by wealthy managers and billionaires with clear stakes in the outcome of the most fundamental political issues, and their interests are often distinct from those of the vast majority of humanity. By any

TABLE 14.2 Selected Media Moguls and Their Wealth, 2010

Name	Key Media Business	Estimated Wealth
Michael Bloomberg	Bloomberg	$18.0 billion
Ann Cox Chambers	Cox Enterprises	$12.5 billion
Rupert Murdoch	News Corp.	$6.2 billion
Samuel Newhouse, Jr.	Publishing	$6.2 billion
James Kennedy	Cox Enterprises	$6.2 billion
Blair Parry-Okedon	Cox Enterprises	$6.2 billion
Donald Newhouse	Publishing	$5.4 billion
David Geffen	Movies, music	$5.0 billion
Haim Saban	TV, film	$3.4 million
Sumner Redstone	Viacom	$2.8 billion

Source: Forbes, 2010.

known theory of democracy, such a concentration of economic, cultural, and political power into so few hands—and mostly unaccountable hands at that—is absurd and unacceptable. On the other hand, media fare is subjected to an ever-greater commercialization as the dominant firms use their market power to squeeze the greatest possible profit from their products. (McChesney, 1999:29–30)

Convergence has contributed to commercialization and branding on the Internet. Although the Internet originally was hailed as a newer source of news and entertainment that was relatively free from corporate constraints, in recent years, the Internet and social media have experienced criticisms similar to those leveled at more established forms of media in the past (see Box 14.1).

Social Problems in the Media   Box 14.1

Where Does Your News Come From? Should You Care?

Mainstream media is the term often used to describe the collective group of big TV, radio, and newspapers in the United States. Mainstream implies that the news being produced is for the benefit and enlightenment of the mainstream population—the majority of people living in the U.S. . . . However, mainstream media no longer produce news for the mainstream population—nor should we consider the media as plural. Instead it is more accurate to speak of big media in the U.S. today as the corporate media and to use the term in the singular tense—as it refers to the singular monolithic top-down power structure of self-interested news giants.

—Peter Phillips (2011), a sociology professor and former director of Project Censored, explains why he does not trust large media corporations to bring him the most important news.

As the corporate media industries have become increasingly concentrated, some people have grown outraged at what they consider to be centralized control over information resources. They believe that Big Media's control over news, entertainment, and some Internet websites results in a variety of problems, including unverified information, media bias hidden under the cloak of objectivity, and a narrowing of the voices, ideas, and opinions that are available to the general public.

As a result, watchdog groups and alternative media outlets provide divergent perspectives on issues such as terrorism, war, the global financial crisis, and problems in the U.S. government. Two (of many) media watchdog organizations are Fairness and Accuracy in Reporting (FAIR) at www.fair.org and FreePress at www.freepress .net/. Another accessible source for alternative perspectives on the media is Project Censored, which creates an annual list of the most underreported stories in the United States. These stories are then reported on the Project Censored website and in an annual book, *Censored: The*

News That Didn't Make the News. Many students and faculty members at Sonoma State University, along with experts in various fields, read thousands of news stories and choose the top twenty-five stories. In 2009–2010, topics of these stories ranged from global plans to replace the dollar and how the U.S. Department of Defense is the worst polluter on the planet to topics such as Internet privacy. (To view all twenty-five top censored stories, visit Project Censored at www.projectcensored.org.)

This brings us to a larger question: What role should the media play in keeping us informed? The media are sometimes referred to as the "Fourth Estate" or the "Fourth Branch of the Government" because journalists are supposed to provide people with relevant information on important topics regarding how the government operates in a democratic society. This information can then be used by citizens to decide how they will vote on candidates and issues presented for their approval or disapproval on the election ballot. And, as previously discussed, the media are one of the prime ways that we learn about pressing social problems, and what (if any) efforts are being made to reduce or solve them in our society.

Questions for Consideration

1. Is it possible for each individual to become a "media watchdog"? Can we become more analytical about the news than we currently are?

2. Do print media advertisements and commercials on radio and television influence our thinking about social problems? For example, do you see any relationship between the typical motor vehicle ad on television and our nation's problem with excessive gasoline consumption and high rates of highway accidents and deaths?

3. Have you paid attention to the language of mainstream media newscasts? What do television journalists and reporters say and what do they mean? How does this language compare with that of alternative media and blogs on the Internet?

How many product placements do you see in this scene from the film *Talladega Nights: The Ballad of Ricky Bobby*? Why are corporations willing to pay large amounts of money for such product placements?

Among the problems that analysts believe have been brought about by convergence are (1) the decline of ethics in journalism, (2) constant pressure for all journalistic endeavors to be immediately profitable and not merely a public service, (3) a significant decrease in the quantity and quality of international news available to U.S. audiences, (4) the quashing of public debate about the power of the media industries and how they deal with important social issues, and (5) a dramatic increase in the influence of powerful Washington lobbyists who represent the interests of the media conglomerates. Because the reach of the media industries is worldwide, these concerns are not limited to the United States.

GLOBAL MEDIA ISSUES

Although a number of global media concerns are significant in the 2010s, the central issues are (1) the role that large media conglomerates play in disseminating information and entertainment worldwide, and (2) the role that state-run media and/or government censorship play in distorting or repressing news and information in nations such as Cuba, North Korea, and Iraq.

In the past, information traveled slowly in many regions of the world, but globalization and the technological revolution have changed that in many nations. The proliferation of cell phones, satellite television, and Internet access has increased instant communications and access to information, particularly among middle- and upper-income persons in many regions. The Internet and social media have provided people with more opportunities to speak out, giving their opinions about what is happening in their nation and around the world.

In high-income, more highly development nations, access to newer information technologies has increased dramatically in a relatively short time. However, in low-income, less-developed nations, the process has been much slower and is nonexistent in some countries.

To understand the effect that transnational media corporations may have on other nations of the world, we must recall that the Big Six, which is comprised of General Electric, Walt Disney Company, CBS Corporation, News Corp., Time Warner, and VIACOM, operates globally and has a vast influence on news reporting and entertainment. All in all, the global information industry has proved profitable for media conglomerates, many of which are headquartered in the United States. Using News Corporation (News Corp.) as a case study, let's look briefly at its "Annual Report: 2010" (2010:8):

> From our vibrant news businesses to our newest digital initiatives, our strategy once again paid off in 2010, with double digit segment operating income growth at the majority of our businesses. Our content channels have never been stronger, our video production business continues to thrive, and our newspapers are expanding their brands through new technologies.

The scope of News Corp. alone is seen in the operations of this diversified global media company that operates in six industry segments: cable network programming, filmed entertainment, television, direct broadcast satellite television, publishing, and miscellaneous media interests. Although the interests and activities of News Corp. are primarily in the United States, the corporation also operates throughout Continental Europe, the United Kingdom, Australia and New Zealand, Asia, and Latin America. In the United States, News Corp. owns FOX Broadcasting Company and FOXSports.com, as well as at least thirty FOX television stations in major media markets, including two stations in New York City, Los Angeles, Chicago, Dallas, Washington, DC, Houston, Phoenix, Minneapolis, Orlando, and one station in numerous other cities. The purpose of this discussion about News Corp. is to demonstrate the breadth and depth of information and entertainment coverage that only one (of several) media giants has in the world market. As of March 2011, News Corp. had assets of approximately $60 billion (U.S. dollars) and total annual revenues of about $33 billion (U.S. dollars). However, News Corp. has been under investigation for some of its journalist practices, an issue which may be the beginning of addition investigations on media excess in the twenty-first century (see Box 14.2).

Journalism Ethics 101: The Media and the People They Cover

The Guardian, **London, July 2011:**

"Milly Dowler Phone Hacking: Family Shocked by NoW Revelations"

Washington Post, **July 2011**

"Tabloid Accused of Hacking Slain Teen's Phone"

As simple as these headlines sound, these accusations of phone hacking were the beginning of an international uproar regarding the journalism ethics of the worldwide news media. Especially in the spotlight were the actions of News Corp., under the ownership of Rupert Murdoch, the world's most powerful media mogul. Although accusations had been made for more than a decade that News Corp.'s *News of the World*, Britain's top Sunday tabloid, was hacking the phones of celebrities, politicians, British royalty, and members of Parliament, these accusations became headline news only when the British parliament held hearings in which it was revealed that this tabloid often hired "investigators" to hack into other people's voicemails so that the tabloid could use information gathered for its own enrichment. In the case of Milly Dowler, a teenage girl reported missing in 2002 and found murdered six months later, *News of the World* officials admitted that their "investigators" had hacked her voicemail repeatedly during the period that she was listed as "missing." Little did law enforcement officials or her family know that her voicemail was being hacked by investigators who were deleting some messages, including ones left by family members, to free up additional space for new messages. The tabloid wanted to "scoop" other media in its coverage of the Dowler case and listen to the parent's desperate pleas to their daughter. However, in addition to the privacy issue, the tabloid's actions could have jeopardized the police investigation by making authorities believe that the victim was alive. When the hackers deleted messages from Dowler's voicemail, her family was also given false hope that she was listening to her phone messages, but this was not the case. Had this been the only case, it might not have received so much attention. But, it was soon learned that numerous cases of hacking by News Corp. personnel had allegedly occurred, including one in which *News of the World* had offered to pay New York Police officers to hack into the phone messages of victims of the September 11, 2001, terrorist attacks in the United States.

Several key questions emerge as a result of media hacking cases: What has happened to ethics in journalism? What about the international concept of *breach of privacy*—intrusion into the personal life of another individual, without just cause, that gives the person whose

privacy has been invaded a right to bring a lawsuit for damages against the person or entity that intruded? According to law professor Richard T. Karcher (2009:783), journalism ethics is "a system of moral principles and values, or a set of principles governing righteous conduct, recognized and understood within the culture of journalism." In a nutshell, journalists have an "ethnical obligation to 'seek the truth,' avoid sensationalism and trivia, and protect individual privacy interests" (Karcher, 2009:781). In the case of media coverage of sensationalized crime stories or of stories about celebrities, sports figures, and other high-profile individuals, the media's ethical obligations are routinely discounted. Because members of the media are largely self-regulating in regard to journalism ethics, when violations do occur, few external enforcement mechanisms exist apart from judgments in lawsuits filed by aggrieved individuals (Karcher, 2009). Whether in Great Britain, the United States, or other nations, the issue of privacy is a key concern in journalism ethics. Now, more than ever, so many communications devices and software technologies exist for "hacking" and other illegitimate access to supposedly private information: E-mail, voicemail, social media sites such as Facebook and Twitter, and smartphones containing vast amounts of personal data and individual preferences are all potentially available to hackers who desire to use our personal information in ways we have not approved.

What will be the outcome of the News Corp.–Dowler hacking scandal? Will it change anything? In the aftermath of the 2011 scandal, Rupert Murdoch promised to usher in a new era of ethics in journalism by issuing an updated and revised code of behavior for all News Corp. employees. Similarly, the Associated Press updated and reissued its guidelines on how reporters should use social media. Previously, the *New York Times* made substantial revisions to its ethical policies after that corporation was embroiled in a 2003 scandal over plagiarism and fabrication. It seems like most alleged change occurs after a scandal. Is this just a smoke screen, or will new or updates sets of journalism codes of ethics make a difference in news and social media industries? Only time will tell, of course, but in the meantime, it remains for each of us to be vigilant in separating out the "tabloidization" of life from what is actually newsworthy information we need to know. It is also important to identify valid journalistic methods and sources of information as opposed to relying on tidbits picked up by hackers and those who spy through illegal and/or unethical "keyholes" to see what unsavory information they can gather about people for their own financial gain. In the words of law professor Karcher (2009:821):

Social Problems and Social Policy   Box 4.3 continued

[T]he social values journalism ethics codes seek to promote simply cannot survive in today's economic and technological environment in which media outlets are vigorously competing with one another in print, cable television, internet, and real time platforms amounting to thousands of available new sources. For the first time in history, society is actually confused about basic questions concerning what constitutes "news" and who are the legitimate sources of the news. To be a viable enterprise in the twenty-first century's media environment, the press is focused on how to best "grab the audience's attention," which comprises journalism ethics principles.

Questions for Consideration

1. What limits should be placed on the news media in terms of how journalists and other media employees go about gathering information about supposedly newsworthy individuals?

2. Will it be possible to protect the privacy of individuals in the future, given rapid advances in information technologies (such as in medical environments) and the proliferation of handheld communications devices such as iPads and cell phones?

Independent Research

If you would like to know more about the issue of journalism ethics, visit various media websites and compare the organizations' policies on this issue. Here are a couple of suggestions to get you started:

New York Times Company Policy on Ethics in Journalism: www.nytco.com/press/ethics.html

Ethics Codes of various news organizations: www.journalism.org/resources/ethics_codes

---

A second important global media issue is the effect of state-run media and/or government control on information in some nations. *Government-controlled media* refers to media that operate in a government-controlled environment. Some of the most dominant forms of government-controlled media have existed in nations where the media are controlled and directed by the Community Party; however, the strength of this kind of censorship or propaganda has been diminished over the past two decades with the introduction of the Internet and social

media, which have made it more difficult for governmental authorities to maintain control over information that is disseminated in, and about, a country. China's state-run media are a contemporary example of the influence of the Communist Party on news. The *People's Daily* newspaper, which includes People's Daily Online Co., Ltd. (www.People.com/cn), is published by the Community Party and has largely published information at the pleasure of the party in the past. However, in the 2010s, there has been more discussion about state-run media in China going public and selling shares to private shareholders who agree to invest money into reinvigorating these official news organizations (Bloomberg News, 2011).

Cuba and North Korea are two other countries in which the media are closely controlled by the government. Human Rights Watch (2011) reports that Cuba represses virtually all political dissent, and many journalists have been incarcerated for trying to get out information about human rights abuses and other problems in that nation. According to Human Rights Watch (2011), "The government maintains a media monopoly on the island, ensuring that freedom of expression is virtually nonexistent." Some journalists have been arbitrarily detailed, interrogated, and threatened by authorities; others have been jailed for extended periods of time. In North Korea as well, there are no free media, and torture and inhumane treatment of people often goes unreported. Human Rights Watch (2011) reports on North Korea state:

The parents and sister of murder victim Milly Dowler appeared with their lawyer outside the British Prime Minister's residence after the News Corp. phone hacking investigation was made public.

The government uses fear-generated mainly by threats of forced labor and public executions—to prevent dissent, and imposes harsh restrictions on freedom of information, association, assembly, and travel. . . . All media and publications are state-controlled, and unauthorized access to non-state radio or TV broadcasts is severely punished.

These are only a few of the nations in which state-run and/or state-controlled media limit people's access to news and information. An organization known as Reporters without Borders seeks to defend journalists and other media personnel who have been imprisoned or persecuted for doing their job. This organization has sought to expose the mistreatment and torture that have been directed toward persons associated with the media who are simply trying to inform others about conditions in a country and human rights violations that are perpetrated against citizens. To find out more about global media concerns or the work of Reporters without Borders, visit Human Rights Watch (www.hrw.org) and Reporters without Borders (www.rsf.org).

POTENTIAL MEDIA EFFECTS ON AUDIENCES

Today, as we have said, the global media industries are the primary source of news and entertainment for many people. Although these industries probably have greater influence over some people than others, media analysts suggest that all of us are more profoundly—and often negatively—influenced by media messages than we realize. In at least two areas—the portrayal of aggression and violence and the presentation of race, class, and gender stereotypes—the influence might be negative.

Watch on **mysoclab.com**

Motherhood Manifesto: Clip 1 on **mysoclab.com**

Aggression, Violence, and the Media

Should we be concerned about how—and the extent to which—the media depict aggressive and/or violent behavior? A number of media analysts assert that the need of media industries to capture public interest and thus increase the size of their markets has contributed to the use of violence or incidences of violence as a means of selling newspapers, television programs, movies, heavy metal and rap music, and other media-related commodities. According to an extensive study that was conducted by the Center for Communications and Social Policy at the University of California at Santa Barbara, violent television shows made up 60 percent of all television programming during the three years of the study. Moreover, that percentage continued to increase over the course of the study (Stern, 1998). Today, the amount of violence shown, and the severity of violence, is even greater if we primarily look at portrayals of crime, terrorism, and criminal investigations. To capture younger, male audiences, many shows focus on the depiction of brutal crimes, horrendous crime scenes, and violent encounters among ordinary citizens, criminals, and law enforcement officials. Aggression and violence are more often found in programming on cable channels and subscription movie channels such as HBO and Showtime.

Some analysts have suggested that violent fare is intricately related to commercial broadcasting because bloody, violent encounters and sex are what sells. Although some television executives claim that their programs reflect audience desires, it is also true that high ratings encourage corporations to spend millions on advertising their products. Not all highly rated series have violence, particularly in the age of reality television, but franchises such as *CSI*, *NCIS*, *Criminal Minds*, and their successors are rooted in a culture of aggression and violence.

What effect does the depiction of violence have on audiences? There is no definitive answer to this question. Most media scholars do not believe that media portrayals alone *cause* aggressive behavior in people. Some studies have shown a relationship between at least short-term aggressive behavior and media depictions of violence. Other studies have found that the media may prevent acts of violence by providing people with an outlet for pent-up feelings and emotions. According to the *cathartic effect hypothesis*, the media offer people a vicarious outlet for feelings of aggression and may reduce violence by the media consumer. However, other analysts argue that the cathartic effect hypothesis has been disproven, meaning that continual depictions of violence actually desensitize viewers and create attitudes that contribute to aggressive behavior and reinforce feelings of fear and frustration (Gerbner, 1995). Over time, as people become more desensitized to portrayals of violence, it is necessary for films and television series to become even more violent in order to attract the audience's attention. This theory might help explain the recent popularity of animal documentaries showing "kill sequences" and

Explore the Concept on **mysoclab.com**

Social Explorer Activity: Adolescent Violence and Social Conditions on **mysoclab.com**

blood fights among animals, such as on Animal Planet and the Discovery Channel, as opposed to earlier programming that focused on topics such as cute puppies and how animals seek to communicate with humans.

In sum, at a minimum, constant exposure to violence-laden media content might contribute to an individual's feelings of fear and a need for greater security and protection in everyday life. As studies continue on the relationship between violence in the media and in everyday life, we will no doubt learn more about the causes and consequences of extensive media violence in society.

Racial and Ethnic Stereotyping

Although a growing number of media consumers are not members of the dominant racial or ethnic groups or of the privileged classes, some media may reinforce existing racial, ethnic, and gender stereotypes and even create new ones. As defined previously, a stereotype is an overgeneralization about the appearance, behavior, or other characteristics of all members of a group.

Numerous media scholars have documented the long history of stereotyping of racial and ethnic subordinate groups in film, television programming, and other media forms. Studies have examined the effects

Children and young people often watch violent scenes such as this on television. Social scientists are interested in how such images influence a person's attitudes about violence throughout life.

of stereotyping on people's perceptions of groups ranging from Italian Americans and Jewish Americans to African Americans, Latinos/Latinas, Asian and Pacific Americans, and Arab Americans.

No matter which racial or ethnic group is depicted, stereotyping often involves one or more of the following:

1. *Perpetuating images that appear to be positive in nature and thus flattering to members of a specific racial or ethnic group but which convey a negative undertone.* For example, some stereotypes attribute a superior trait or ability, such as being "naturally" better at activities such as music and sports or mathematics and science, to members of one racial or ethnic category. Exaggerating African Americans' proficiency at sports or Asian Americans' ability to do math are among the continuing one-dimensional characterizations of many films and television shows, including several recent reality series.

2. *Exaggerating the physical appearance of subordinate-group members or suggesting that all people in a specific category "look alike" or "act alike."* Statements by subordinate-group characters in various forms of media entertainment, such as "Well, you know how all of us _____s are!" supposedly are inoffensive because they are spoken by a person from that racial or ethnic category, and some analysts see nothing wrong with this, believing that such comments are not meant to be taken seriously. However, constant repetition of the same "humorous" comments may influence our perceptions about people.

3. *Creating racial or ethnic characters who have undesirable attributes, ranging from laziness and unwillingness to work to a lack of education or intelligence and lower class attitudes and behavior.* Italian American media-watch groups such as the National Italian American Foundation have argued that shows such as *The Sopranos* (a fictionalized TV entertainment show now in syndication) reinforce negative stereotypes by portraying Italian Americans as criminals or bigots. Similarly, members of the white working class have been stereotyped as "trailer park trash" or as lacking the refinement of the middle and upper classes. Overall, however, far more stereotyping has occurred regarding Latinos/Latinas and African Americans.

4. *Using statements and visual images that link subordinate racial or ethnic group members to illegal actions, such as terrorism, gang or organized crime activity, prostitution, and drug dealing.* In the aftermath of the 9/11 (2001) terrorist attacks in the United States and the 7/7 (2005) attacks in London, Arab, and Muslim

stereotypes have been considered "fair game" by many television comedians and entertainment writers. However, this is not an entirely new occurrence: For many years Hollywood films—many of which are now shown on classic movie cable channels—have portrayed Arabs in a negative manner, often as violent, religious fanatics or as outlandish sheiks or seductive belly dancers, leaving audiences to think of Arabs as being "all alike" even though persons in this category come from some two dozen different countries.

Why does racial and ethnic stereotyping persist in the entertainment media? Negative stereotyping continues to exist in shows and films for several reasons. Offensive material, including the use of negative stereotypes, offensive language, and inappropriate behavior, often produces controversy, which brings more media coverage and sometimes turns an average or mediocre

television show or film into an overnight success. Similarly, racial stereotyping is frequently used for comic effect or to create stock characters. Media entertainment writers, editors, and producers heavily rely on readily recognizable stock characters who make it possible for audiences to give little thought to who the person is or what he or she is really like so that the plot on a sitcom or the "games" on a reality TV show can begin. In reality television, conflict among the contenders (such as to become Donald Trump's next apprentice or to win the big prize after numerous ordeals on *Survivor*) is heavily edited before the programs are aired. By selecting contestants with divergent attributes, such as race-ethnicity, age, gender, or education level, and by emphasizing those differences during filming, it is easier to incite conflict among the contenders that can be further edited to create greater controversy and generate audience interest. Reality TV is discussed in Box 14.3.

Critical Thinking and You   Box 14.3

Is Reality TV Important to You?

These shows depict ordinary people competing in everything from singing and dancing to losing weight, or just living their lives. . . . Most people believe that the reality these shows portray is authentic, but they are being misled.

—A statement in a recent SAT test question about reality TV shows (quoted in Steinberg, 2011).

This is one of those moments when I wish I actually watched TV. I ended up talking about Jacob Riis and how any form of media cannot capture reality objectively. I kinda want to cry right now.

— "littlepenguin," an SAT test-taker, explained on the website College Confidential why he had been taken aback that this important college-entry exam had asked a question about reality TV on some versions of the 2011 test (quoted in Steinberg, 2011).

Some high school students who took the SAT exam in summer 2011 were confronted with a question of their own: "Is it necessary to watch reality TV shows in order to write about them on a college-admissions exam?" First, what exactly do we mean by "reality TV"? The term *reality TV* refers to two types of television programming: (1) series that supposedly show unscripted situations involving ordinary people who engage in contests or compete in events where a prize is awarded (such as *Big Brother*, *Survivor*, *American Idol*, *The X Factor*, and *America's Got Talent*),

and (2) shows that document some aspect of social life (such as what it is like to live with strangers in the same house—*The Real World*—or to be a "real housewife" in Beverly Hills, New York, Atlanta, or other cities). Second, what happened after the reality TV question appeared on some SAT exams? After completing this exam, numerous test-takers discussed their answers on the website *College Confidential*. Some test-takers believed that the question was unfair because they do not watch reality shows. Others argued that it did not matter whether you had watched reality shows if you simply responded to this comment in the question: "Most people believe that the reality these shows portray is authentic, but they are being misled." From this approach, reality shows inherently are misleading and are a betrayal of their audiences because they do not reflect "real" life. How would you answer a question such as this if you had been taking the exam? What sociological insights would you apply in an analysis of reality TV?

Questions for Consideration

1. Why do some people like to watch reality TV shows? Do they want a realistic experience? Or do they desire a simulation of reality in which they live vicariously but have no personal commitment or cost?

2. How authentic can reality TV shows be when producers design challenges for the participants and then editors alter filmed scenes? What do you think?

Obviously, stereotypes sometimes are unintentional. However, when media creators and producers become aware of the negative effects that stereotypical depictions may have on subordinate-group members, particularly children, will they continue to perpetuate these images? Perhaps as the media industries and those who use them to advertise their goods begin to view nonwhite racial and ethnic groups around the globe as viable consumers of their products, greater concern will be shown over stereotypical images.

Gender Stereotyping

According to scholars who have conducted studies of gender stereotypes in the contemporary media, such stereotyping may result, at least in part, from the underrepresentation of women as producers, directors, and executives in the largest media industries. Regardless of the cause, some studies of television and film have shown the following gender stereotypes of women:

1. *The intertwining of gender and age bias as it uniquely affects women.* Gender-specific age bias is apparent in the casting of many female characters. Older men and significantly younger women are often cast in leading roles in films, causing some women actors to ask "where are the roles for older women in Hollywood?"

2. *The perpetuation of traditional roles for women and the maintenance of cultural stereotypes about the importance of beauty, thinness, and femininity for getting and keeping a man.* Female characters who do not live up to the gendered expectations associated with femininity are overtly or subtly punished for their conduct. ABC's *Desperate Housewives* is both a satiric portrayal of housewives living in suburbia and a reaffirmation of beliefs about how white, affluent women should look and behave, particularly if they want to get and keep a husband.

3. *Impulsive conduct by women holding professional positions.* When television shows portray professional women, the women are often shown as engaging in compulsive behavior such as constantly purchasing very expensive designer shoes, smoking or drinking alcohol excessively, and having other bizarre habits. Men are not exempted from such portrayals, but they are more likely to be shown as displaying professional competence in the workplace.

4. *Women in positions of power as abusing their positions.* Prior to the 1990s, most female characters were depicted in lower-status occupations or in roles that were clearly subordinate to those of men. Although more female characters on prime-time television shows and in film today are lawyers or judges than in the past, these characters are often shown as "seducers, harassers, and wimps in black robes" (Goodman, 1999:AR 47). When female characters are not seducing men, they are often depicted as "bitches" or "bimbos." On *Judge Judy*, Judy Sheindlin, a former family court judge in New York, berates and demeans people appearing in her court (Goodman, 1999).

5. *Women overwhelmed by their work or seemingly having few job responsibilities even when they are employed full time.* The imbalance between the portrayal of female characters as either having so much work to do that they cannot complete it all or the depiction of them as having an important occupation but spending little time actually doing the work tends to convey the message that women are less than adequate in many careers and occupations. Examples include *Grey's Anatomy* where female surgical interns are more often shown in romantic liaisons than in hospital work, and attorney and police shows where female characters primarily focus on interpersonal relationships, especially with men, rather than getting their job done.

Although "Judge Judy" Sheindlin's remarks are sometimes tempered with humor, she often berates the people who appear in her TV courtroom. Why are "outspoken women" often evaluated more harshly than "firm, decisive men"?

Although the depiction of women characters in television programs, films, and other forms of media has improved significantly in recent decades, much remains to be done if women are to be shown in the wide diversity of occupations and endeavors in which real-life women participate on a daily basis.

It should be noted that, although the nature of male stereotypes is somewhat different, men have not been exempt from gender stereotyping in the media. Among the most frequently employed stereotypes of male characters are men depicted primarily as jokers, jocks, strong silent types, big shots, action heroes, or buffoons. For example, working-class men frequently are portrayed as buffoons who are dumb, immature, irresponsible, or lacking in common sense. These male characters are the object of jokes and are often shown as being sloppy in appearance, ignorant, and sometimes racist (Kendall, 2011).

SOCIOLOGICAL PERSPECTIVES ON MEDIA-RELATED PROBLEMS

Just as they do in regard to other social issues, symbolic interactionist, functionalist, and conflict approaches to media-related problems start with differing assumptions about these problems.

The Symbolic Interactionist Perspective

Perhaps the earliest symbolic interactionist theory concerning the media's effect on individuals and groups was the *hypodermic needle theory*, which suggested that audiences were made up of passive individuals who were equally susceptible to the messages of the media. However, a World War II study of military personnel who were shown movies that were designed to portray the enemy as evil and to increase morale among soldiers concluded that most of the subjects showed little change in their morale level. On the basis of these findings, researchers suggested an alternative explanation: the theory of limited effects. The **theory of limited effects states that the media have a minimal effect on the attitudes and perceptions of individuals**. According to this theory, people are not always selective about what they watch or read, but they gather different messages from the media, and many people carefully evaluate the information they gain. This theory notes that when people are interested in and informed about an issue,

they are less likely to be influenced by what members of the media report. Those who are poorly informed or have no personal information about a particular topic or issue are likely to be affected by what other people, including reporters and journalists, say about the social concern.

A similar theory, known as *use and gratification theory*, suggests that people are active audience participants who make conscious decisions about what they will watch, listen to, and read and where they will surf on the Internet. However, this theory assumes that people using different media have specific wishes or desires and will choose media sources that gratify their desires. In other words, people use the media to entertain and inform themselves but are aware of the limitations the media have in their coverage of topics and the forms of entertainment.

Another symbolic interactionist theory, mentioned in previous chapters, is **social learning theory, which is based on the assumption that people are likely to act out the behavior they see in role models and media sources**. To support this theory, social psychologist Albert Bandura conducted a series of experiments on aggression in children (Bandura and Walters, 1977). For the experiment, children were divided into four groups. One group watched a film of a man attacking and beating a large, inflatable doll and being rewarded for his behavior. The second group saw a similar film, except that in this version the man was punished for attacking the doll. The third group was shown a version in which the man was neither rewarded nor punished for his behavior. The final group was not shown any film. Before the experiment, researchers believed that the children who saw the man rewarded for hitting the doll would be the most likely to show aggressive behavior toward the doll. However, this did not prove to be true. Regardless of which version of the film they saw, children who were prone to aggression before the film tended to act aggressively toward the doll, but other children did not. As a result, the researchers concluded that many factors other than the media influenced aggressive behavior in children, including their relationship with their parents, how much formal education their parents possessed, and the personality of the children.

More recent theories have sought to explain the effects of media on individuals by emphasizing the part that viewers, listeners, and readers play in shaping the media. According to the *audience relations approach*, people use their own cultural understandings to interpret what they hear and see in the media. Factors involved in the audience relations approach include how much previous knowledge individuals have about a topic and the availability of other sources of information. This viewpoint is somewhat in keeping with functionalist approaches, which highlight the important contemporary functions of the media.

The Functionalist Perspective

Functionalist approaches to examining the media often focus on the functional—and sometimes dysfunctional—effects the media have on society. Functionalists point out that the media serve several important functions in contemporary societies.

- First, the media provide news and information, including warnings about potential disasters such as an approaching hurricane.
- Second, the media facilitate public discourse regarding social issues and policies such as welfare reform.
- Third, the media pass on cultural traditions and historical perspectives, particularly to recent immigrants and children (Lasswell, 1969).
- Fourth, the media are a source of entertainment, providing people with leisure-time activities (Biagi, 2012).
- Finally, the media confer status on individuals and organizations by frequently reporting on their actions or showing their faces and mentioning their names. According to sociologist Joshua Gamson (1994:186), becoming a media celebrity is a means of gaining power, privilege, and mobility: "Audiences recognize this when they seek brushes with it and when they fantasize about the freedom of fame and its riches and about the distinction of popularity and attention."

As Gamson notes, some people become celebrities because the media confer that status on them. In other words, as the popular saying goes, "Some people are famous for being famous." For example, most people in the United States knew nothing about the Kardashian family until the American reality-based television series *Keeping Up With the Kardashians* was introduced on E! The daily ups and downs of the Kardashian/Jenner family constituted the entire storyline for this continuing series until several spin-offs, including *Kourtney & Khloe Take Miami* and *Kourtney & Kim Take New York*, were introduced.

Although the media are a source of entertainment for many, functionalist theorists state that the media are dysfunctional when they contribute to a reduction in social stability or weaken other social institutions such as the family, education, politics, and religion. For example, the Internet, social media, video games, and

television have brought about significant changes in family interaction patterns. In regard to television, one media scholar stated:

> The most pervasive effect of television—aside from its content—may be its very existence, its readily available, commanding, and often addictive presence in our homes, its ability to reduce hundreds of millions of citizens to passive spectators for major portions of their waking hours. Television minimizes interactions between persons within families and communities. (Parenti, 1998:188)

Over time, not only television but also the Internet, social media, and video games have changed how people interact with each other and how they see the world. Consider this familiar sight: A family goes out to dinner together and is sitting at the same table, but each person in the group is engaged in some individual, media-related activity that does not include anyone else at the table. The younger children are playing video games; the older children are texting their friends; and the parents are reading e-mail from work or friends. From a

Most of the world would not have heard of the Kardashians if they had not starred in E! Television Network's reality series *Keeping Up With the Kardashians*. Shown here are the mother and stepfather, Kris and Bruce Jenner, and the Kardashian sisters, Khloe, Kourtney, and Kim. Do you think the comment "Famous for being famous" might apply here? Why or why not?

functionalist approach, overemphasis on media and spending only limited amounts of face-time with people who are physically present is dysfunctional because it contributes to a lack of social stability in families and weakens the larger social institution of family. When dysfunctions in families occur, the problems should be addressed for the benefit of individuals, families, and the larger society.

The Conflict Perspective

Conflict theorists typically link the media industries with the capitalist economy. In this approach, members of the capitalist class own and control the media, which, along with other dominant social institutions, instruct people in the values, beliefs, and attitudes that they should have (Curran, Gurevitch, and Woollacott, 1982). According to this perspective, the *process of legitimization* takes place as media consumers are continually provided with information that supports the validity of existing class relations. As a result, members of the working class are lulled into a sense of complacency in which they focus more on entertainment and consumption than on questioning existing economic and social relations. This perspective is sometimes referred to as *hegemony theory*—**the view that the media are instruments of social control and are used by members of the ruling classes to create "false consciousness" in the working classes.** Although there are various conflict approaches, most view ownership and economic control of the media as a key factor in determining what kinds of messages are disseminated around the globe. Media analysts such as Michael Parenti (1998:149) believe that media bias is inevitable as transnational media industries become concentrated in the hands of a few megacorporations:

> Media bias usually does not occur in random fashion; rather, it moves in the same overall direction again and again, favoring management over labor, corporations over corporate critics, affluent whites over inner-city poor, officialdom over protestors, the two-party monopoly over leftist third parties, privatization and free-market "reforms" over public-sector development, U.S. domination of the Third World over revolutionary or populist social change, investor globalization over nation-state democracy, national security policy over critics of that policy, and conservative commentators and columnists . . . over progressive or populist ones.

According to Parenti, the built-in biases of the media reflect the dominant ideology that supports the privileged position of members of the capitalist class. Parenti (1998) lists a number of ways in which media manipulation occurs: (1) Sponsors control broadcasting decisions; (2) information might be suppressed by omitting certain details of a story or the entire story, particularly if the story could have a negative effect on a person or organization to whom members of the media feel beholden; (3) a story might be attacked or the reporting may not present a balanced view of the diverse viewpoints involved; (4) negative labels that subsume a large number of people, for example, "Islamic terrorists," "inner-city gangs," might be used; and (5) stories might be framed to convey positive or negative connotations through the use of visual effects, placement, and other means. Like other conflict theorists, Parenti (1998:157) believes that the media tell people what to think before they have had a chance to think about an issue for themselves: "When we understand that news selectivity is likely to favor those who have power, position, and wealth, we move from a liberal complaint about the press's sloppy performance to a radical analysis of how the media serve the ruling circles all too well with much skill and craft."

In an era marked by increased concentration of all forms of media, including the Internet and websites, conflict perspectives on media ownership and control raise important questions in the United States and around the world. Although people who are engaged in social activism, such as the Go-Green movement, have been able to marshal the media on their behalf, the media often implicitly support the status quo because of their own corporate interests and the need to maintain and enhance advertising revenues. Of course, it is another matter when products can be sold through the media, and money can be made by promoting "Living Green" through the purchase of products ranging from garbage bags to more energy-efficient motor vehicles.

Regardless of which theoretical perspective on the media industries most closely resembles our own thinking, each of us should take a closer look at the ideas, images, and advertisements that bombard us daily. Although most of us may believe that we are not affected by the constant stream of advertisements that we encounter, we should realize some of the power of advertising is linked to the fact that many of us believe that what we see and hear by way of the media does not affect us. Although individuals alone cannot solve the problems associated with the media industries, they can become more aware of the pervasive impact of television, films, newspapers, the Internet, social media and other forms of mass communication.

ARE THERE SOLUTIONS TO MEDIA-RELATED PROBLEMS?

Problems associated with the media will continue well into this century, and many of the issues will probably become even more complex. For example, it has been suggested that the Internet and e-commerce will affect all aspects of life, particularly in high-income nations such as the United States. Some analysts have suggested that U.S. cities will lose more of their tax base to untaxed Internet commerce, bringing about a need to restructure relations between cities, states, and the federal government (Friedman, 2000). Indeed, the ability of a single government to control the activities of transnational media industries may be weakened as globalization continues to occur. Thus, according to journalist Thomas L. Friedman (2000:A31), a world of global communications means that many issues that were once considered the domain of individual nations and governments will have to be rethought:

Issues such as freedom of speech and libel are going to have to be rethought as the Internet makes everyone a potential publisher in cyberspace—but with no censor or editor in charge. Privacy protection is going to have to be rethought in a world where for $39 web sites will search out anyone's assets and home address for you. And our safety nets are going to have to be rethought in a world in which access to the Internet is going to be viewed as a human right, essential for basic survival—especially as governments move more services to the web.

In the years to come, new communication technology will undoubtedly continue to change our lives. Although new forms of media offer many potential benefits, they also raise serious concerns about social life as many of us know it.

SUMMARY

✓•⌐ **Study** and **Review** on **mysoclab.com**

■ **What are the media industries? How much time do individuals spend in media-related activities?**

According to social scientists, the media industries are media businesses that influence people and cultures worldwide and own interests in radio and television production and broadcasting; motion pictures, movie theaters, and music companies; newspaper, periodical (magazine), and book publishing; and Internet services and content providers. Today, many people spend more time in media-related activities than they do in any other single endeavor, including sleeping, working, eating, or talking with friends and family; therefore some analysts believe that the media have a major influence on how people think, feel, and act.

■ **What part does technology play in how various media industries change over time?**

For many years, newspapers were the primary source of news. However, new technologies brought about radio as the media phenomenon of the 1920s and television as the phenomenon of the 1950s. With the introduction of communications technologies such as computers, fiber-optic cable, and broadcast satellites, the media industries continue to change rapidly. One of the most compelling recent changes has been smartphones and other handheld technology that makes it possible for audiences to take their media devices wherever they go and to use them whenever they wish by downloading a wide variety of apps.

■ **How has media ownership changed?**

Although there once were a variety of independent companies that produced books, records, television programs, and films, there are now large corporate conglomerates that own most of the media business.

■ **What is convergence? How does it relate to media concentration?**

Convergence refers to a melding of the communications, computer, and electronics industries that gives a few huge corporations control over an increasing proportion of all media sources. Convergence contributes to greater concentration in the media. Media concentration refers to the tendency of the media industries to cluster together in groups.

■ **What forms can media concentration take?**

Media concentration can take several forms: (1) within one industry (such as newspaper chains); (2) cross-media ownership, in which media companies own more than one type of media property (such as newspaper chains and television stations); (3) conglomerate ownership, in which corporations own media properties but also own other businesses; and (4) vertical integration, in which the corporations that make the media content also control the distribution channels (such as film and television production companies, television networks, and movie theaters).

Why do some people favor media convergence whereas others do not?

Supporters believe that much can be gained from the synergy created by media convergence because it makes it possible to take a media brand and capitalize on it. This process is clearly profitable for investors and media executives; however, media critics believe that convergence limits the news and entertainment that the public receives by reducing message pluralism. Other problems include (1) the decline of ethics in journalism, (2) constant pressure for all journalistic endeavors to be immediately profitable and the inability to view journalism as a public service, (3) a significant decrease in the quantity and quality of international news available to U.S. audiences, (4) the quashing of public debate about the power of the media industries and how they deal with important social issues, and (5) a dramatic increase in the influence of powerful Washington lobbyists representing the interests of the media giants.

What potential problems are associated with global media concentration?

A few large media conglomerates are rapidly gaining control over most of the publishing, recording, television, film, and mega–theme park business worldwide. One major problem is the extent to which a few media giants have almost complete control over the world's information. Some people in other nations have been critical of how the media conglomerates depict nations around the globe and the influence, often negative, that they have on the politics and culture of other nations.

Why are some media critics concerned about depictions of violence in the media?

Although most scholars do not believe that the media cause aggressive behavior in people, a number of media analysts assert that the media's need to capture public interest has contributed to the gratuitous use of violence as a means of selling newspapers, television programming, movie tickets, heavy metal and rap music, and other media-related commodities. Some studies have shown a relationship between short-term aggressive behavior and media depictions of violence; however, others have suggested that the media may prevent acts of violence by providing people with an outlet for pent-up feelings and emotions.

What is a stereotype and how can the media perpetuate stereotypes about racial and ethnic groups?

A stereotype is an overgeneralization about the appearance, behavior, or other characteristics of all members of a group. The media can perpetuate stereotypes by casting some groups as having superior traits such as being "naturally" better at music and sports or mathematics and science and then using the "model minority" image to question why some people succeed while others do not. Other media stereotyping includes exaggerating people's physical appearance, suggesting that all people in a specific category "look alike," creating racial or ethnic characters who have undesirable attributes, and using statements and visual images that continually link subordinate racial or ethnic group members to illegal actions.

Why is gender stereotyping pervasive in the media? What major forms does this problem take?

Underrepresentation of women among producers, directors, and executives in the largest media industries might be a factor in the more limited range of roles available to women in television programs and films. First, gender-specific age bias is apparent in the casting of many female characters. Second, television shows and films often perpetuate traditional roles for women and maintain cultural stereotypes of femininity.

How do symbolic interactionists explain the influence of the media on individuals?

According to the theory of limited effects, the media have a minimal effect on individuals' attitudes and perceptions. The use and gratification theory suggests that people are active audience participants who make conscious decisions about what they will watch, listen to, and read and where they will surf on the Internet. However, social learning theory is based on the assumption that people are likely to act out the behavior they see in role models and media sources. The audience relations approach states that people interpret what they hear and see in the media by using their own cultural understandings as a mental filtering device.

How do functionalist and conflict perspectives on the media differ?

According to some functionalist analysts, the media fulfill several important functions in contemporary societies, including providing news and information, facilitating public discourse on social issues and policies, passing on cultural traditions and historical perspectives, and entertaining people. In contrast, conflict theorists assert that members of the capitalist class (either intentionally or unintentionally) use the media to provide information that supports the validity of existing class relations. Hegemony theory states that the media are instruments of social control that are used by members of the ruling classes to create false consciousness in the working classes.

KEY TERMS

hegemony theory, p. 331
media concentration, p. 318

media industries, p. 317
social learning theory, p. 329

theory of limited effects, p. 329

QUESTIONS FOR CRITICAL THINKING

1. Why is media concentration a potentially greater social problem than concentration in other industries?

2. If you were an owner or large shareholder in a major media company, how might you view synergy? What negative effects might synergy have on those who are in your reading, listening, viewing, and/or Internet audiences?

3. Is continued consolidation in the media a serious threat to democracy? Should we be concerned about the ability of some companies to "buy" political influence? Why or why not?

Succeed with MyFamilyLab®   www.myfamilylab.com

The New MyFamilyLab is designed just for you. Each chapter features a pre-test and post-test to help you learn and review key concepts and terms. Experience Marriages and Families in action with dynamic visual activities, videos, and readings to enhance your learning experience.

Here are a few activities you will find for this chapter.

Watch on **mysoclab.com**

Core Concepts video clips feature sociologists in action, exploring important concepts in the study of Social Problems. Watch:
• Motherhood Manifesto: Clip 1

Explore on **mysoclab.com**

Social Explorer is an interactive application that allows you to explore Census data through interactive maps. Explore:
• Social Explorer Activity: Adolescent Violence and Social Conditions

Read on **mysoclab.com**

MyFamilyLab includes primary source readings from classic and contemporary sociologists. Read:
• Media Magic: Making Class Invisible

Population, Global Inequality, and the Environmental Crisis

THINKING SOCIOLOGICALLY

○ If fertility and mortality also affect population growth, why is immigration typically described as *the* driving force behind changes in the size, composition, and distribution of the U.S. population?

○ How are wealth and material comfort in high-income nations related to depletion of the earth's resources and pollution of the environment?

○ What does the environmental justice framework add to our knowledge of contemporary environmental problems? Would functionalists typically agree with this perspective?

America has a problem and the world has a problem. America's problem is that it has lost its way in recent years—partly because of 9/11 and partly because of the bad habits that we have let build up over the last three decades, bad habits that have weakened our society's ability and willingness to take on big challenges.

The world also has a problem: It is getting hot, flat, and crowded. *That is, global warming, the stunning rise of middle classes all over the world, and rapid population growth have converged in a way that could make our planet dangerously unstable. . . .*

I am convinced that the best way for America to solve its big problem—the best way for America to get its "groove" back—is for us to take the lead in solving the world's big

problem. In a world that is getting hot, flat, and crowded, the task of creating the tools, systems, energy sources, and ethics that will allow the planet to grow in cleaner, more sustainable ways is going to be the biggest challenge of our lifetime.

But this challenge is actually an opportunity for America. If we take it on, it will revive America at home, reconnect America abroad, and retool America for tomorrow.

—*In his book,* Hot, Flat, and Crowded, *journalist Thomas L. Friedman (2008:5–6) calls for people in the United States to lead the way in a worldwide effort to replace wasteful, inefficient energy practices with a strategy for clean energy, energy efficiency, and conservation that he refers to as Code Green.*

Clearly, many individuals share Thomas Friedman's (2008:11) concerns about the future given current worldwide patterns of rapid population growth; the massive number of new consumers who walk onto "the global economic playing field with their own versions of the America dream" and create a massive demand for "things" that devour energy, natural resources, land, and water while emitting climate-changing greenhouse gases; and global warming. In this chapter, we will look first at the problem of global overpopulation as it is influenced by fertility, mortality, and immigration. Then we turn to the relationship between population and the environment, focusing on the environmental crisis of the twenty-first century.

GLOBAL OVERPOPULATION

The world's population has more than doubled since the 1950s, growing from 2.5 billion in 1950 to over 6.9 billion by 2011. Estimates suggest that the world's population will hit more than 9 billion by 2050. As a result of rapid population growth and other pressing social problems around the world, more than 1 billion of the world's people do not have enough food and lack basic health care. Will the earth's resources be able to support such a population? This is an urgent question and one for which we need answers.

▶️┤ **Read** the **Document**
Sixteen Impacts of Population Growth on **mysoclab.com**

Population Growth

Growth rates vary among nations; high-income nations (for example, the United States) have a lower population growth rate than low-income nations do, especially those in Africa, Asia, and Latin America. A *population* is all the people living in a specified geographic area. In some nations, the population growth rate is negative; that is, fewer people are added to the population through birth and immigration than are lost through death and emigration. Current estimates suggest that countries such as Italy, Romania, Russia, and Spain will shrink in population over the next fifty years.

***Demography* is the study of the size, composition, and distribution of populations.** Global population changes are important because they have a powerful influence on social, economic, and political structures both within societies and between societies. For example, the population growth imbalance between high-income and middle- and low-income nations is a potential source of global conflict, particularly if world hunger and environmental destruction increase. Three primary factors affect the rate of population growth in any nation or area: fertility (births), mortality (deaths), and migration (movement between geographic areas). We can see how population growth occurs by looking at estimates of these factors. In the United States there is:

- One birth every 7 seconds
- One death every 13 seconds
- One international migration (net) every 45 seconds
- Net gain of 1 person every 12 seconds (as of July 2011)

Let's look specifically at how each of these factors affects our nation and world.

Fertility

***Fertility* refers to the number of children born to an individual or a population.** The most basic measure of fertility is the *crude birth rate*—the number of live births per 1,000 people in a population in a given year. The most basic measure of fertility is the **crude birth rate—the number of live births per 1,000 people in a population in a given year.** In 2010, the crude birth rate in the United States was almost 14.0 (13.83) per 1,000, as compared with an all-time high rate of 27 per 1,000 in 1947 (following World War II). This measure is referred to as a "crude" birth rate because it is based on the entire population and is not "refined" to incorporate significant variables affecting fertility, such as age, marital status, religion, and race-ethnicity.

In most areas of the world, women are having fewer children. Women who have six or seven children tend to live in agricultural regions of the world, where children's labor is essential to the family's economic survival and child mortality rates are very high. For example, Uganda has a crude birth rate of almost 48.0 (47.5) per 1,000, as compared with 14 per 1,000 in the United States (U.S. Census Bureau, 2010). However, in Uganda and some other African nations, families need to have many children to ensure that one or two will live to adulthood due to high rates of poverty, malnutrition, and disease.

The level of fertility in a society is associated with social, as well as biological, factors. For example, countries that have high rates of infant and child mortality often have high birth rates. By having many children, parents in these nations are more likely to see some of them survive to adulthood. In nations without social security systems to provide old-age insurance, parents often view children as an "insurance plan" for their old age. In patriarchal societies, having many children—especially sons—is proof of manliness. Finally, in cultures in which religion dictates that children are God-given and family planning is forbidden because it "interferes with God's will," many more children are usually born.

Although men obviously are important in the reproductive process, the measure of fertility focuses on women because pregnancy and childbirth are more easily quantified than biological fatherhood. One factor in determining how many children will be born in a given year is the number of women of childbearing age (usually between the ages of fifteen and forty-five) who live in the society. Other biological factors that affect fertility include the general health and nutrition level of women of childbearing age. If biological capability were the only factor to consider, it would be possible for most women to produce twenty or more children during their childbearing years. However, in industrialized nations, the majority of people limit their biological reproductive capabilities by practicing abstinence, refraining from sexual intercourse before a certain age, using contraceptives, being sterilized, or having one or more abortions over the course of their reproductive years. Fertility rates also are affected by the number of partners who are available for sex and/or marriage, the number of women of childbearing age in the workforce, and government policies regarding families.

Mortality

Birth rates are one factor in population growth; another is a decline in ***mortality*—the number of deaths that occur in a specific population.** The simplest measure of mortality is the *crude death rate*—the number of deaths per 1,000 people in a population in a given year. In 2010, the U.S. crude death rate was about 8.4 (8.38) per 1,000 (U.S. Census Bureau, 2010). In high-income, developed nations, mortality rates have declined dramatically as diseases such as malaria, polio, cholera, tetanus, typhoid, and measles have been virtually eliminated by vaccinations and improved sanitation and personal hygiene. Just as smallpox appeared to be eradicated, however, HIV/AIDS rapidly rose to surpass the 30 percent fatality rate of smallpox. In low-income, less-developed nations, infectious diseases remain the leading cause of death; in some areas, mortality rates are rapidly increasing as a result of HIV/AIDS. Children under age fifteen constitute a growing number of those who are infected with HIV (Weeks, 2012).

In addition to measuring the crude death rate, demographers often measure the *infant mortality rate*— the number of deaths of infants under one year of age per 1,000 live births in a given year. In general, infant mortality has declined worldwide over the past two decades because many major childhood and communicable diseases are now under control. Still, infant mortality rates vary widely between nations. As discussed in Chapter 10, the infant mortality rate is an important reflection of a society's level of preventive (prenatal) medical care, maternal nutrition, childbirth procedures, and neonatal care for infants. Countries with the highest infant mortality rates are Angola with almost 176 deaths per 1,000 live births, Afghanistan with 149 per 1,000, and Niger with 112 per 1,000 (CIA, 2011). By contrast, the lowest death rates are in nations such as Japan (2.78 per 1,000), Sweden (2.74 per 1,000), Singapore (2.32 per 1,000), and Monaco (1.79 per 1,000). The United States has an infant death rate of approximately 6.06 per 1,000 live births each year; however, this figure varies for males and females. The rate for infant males is 6.72 deaths per 1,000 live births while the rate for female infants is 5.37 per 1,000 live births (CIA, 2011).

Differential levels of access to prenatal care and newborn services are reflected in the divergent infant mortality rates for African Americans and White Americans: White infants had a mortality rate of 5.67 per 1,000 live births, as compared with 13.3 per 1,000 live births for African American infants (CIA, 2011).

Demographers also study *life expectancy,* the estimated average lifetime of people born in a specific year. For persons born in the United States in 2009, for example, life expectancy at birth was 78.2 years, as compared with 82.2 years in Japan and 50 years or less in the African nations of Nigeria, Somalia, and South Africa (U.S. Census Bureau, 2010). Life expectancy varies by race and sex; for instance, white females born in the United States in 2009 could expect to live almost 81 years as compared with 76.2 years for white males. By contrast, life expectancy for African American females born in 2009 is estimated at 77.4 as compared with 70.9 for African American males (National Vital Statistics System, 2011).

Migration

Migration **is the movement of people from one geographic area to another for the purpose of changing residency.** Migration takes two forms: *immigration*—the movement of people *into* a geographic area to take up residency—and *emigration*—the movement of people *out of* a geographic area to take up residency elsewhere.

Today, more than 214 million people in the world live outside their countries of origin (International Organization for Migration, 2011). Many nations face the challenges and opportunities offered by the migration of people worldwide (see Box 15.1).

About 1.1 million people legally immigrate to the United States each year. Between 1990 and 2010, the number of foreign-born U.S. residents almost doubled from 20 to 40 million. In recent decades, the majority of immigrants have been Hispanic or Asian. If these trends continue until 2050, the white (non-Hispanic) proportion of U.S. residents will decline to about 50 percent while the share of Hispanics (Latinos/as) and Asian Americans taken together will rise to about one-third (33 percent) of the overall population (P. Martin and Midgley, 2010).

To determine the effects of immigration and emigration, demographers compute the *crude net migration rate*—the net number of migrants (total in-migrants minus total out-migrants) per 1,000 people in a population in a given year. To determine the net migration in a geographic area, the number of people leaving that area to take up permanent or semipermanent residence elsewhere (emigrants) is subtracted from the number of people entering that area to take up residence there (immigrants), unless more people are moving out of the area than into it, in which case the mathematical process is reversed. It is estimated that net immigration rate in the United States is about 4.31 migrants per 1,000 population (CIA, 2011).

In regard to immigration data, it should be noted that official immigration statistics do not reflect the actual number of immigrants who arrive in this country. The U.S. Citizenship and Immigration Service records only legal immigration based on entry visas and change-of-immigration-status forms. Some individuals enter the country as temporary visitors, coming for pleasure or business, as students, or as temporary workers or trainees. However, some of these individuals do not leave when their stated purpose has been achieved or their permit expires. At this point, they are considered to be in the United States illegally and are subject to deportation. Immigration in the United States and its effects will be discussed later in the chapter.

The Effects of Population Composition and Growth

What is population composition and how does it affect social life? *Population composition* **refers to the biological and social characteristics of a population,**

International Migration: Problem or Solution?

"We cannot bear all the misery in the world!" This simple slogan has long been proclaimed in most industrialized countries. The misery to which they refer is that endured by the millions of people who come knocking on the doors of the richest countries to obtain a small piece of the development cake to which they have hitherto been denied. However, while misery is a very sad reality, the spectre of invasions en masse by foreign nationals seeking to grab nations' riches is no more than a deceptive fantasy blithely dreamt up by reactionary forces and extremists bent on stirring up the xenophobic sentiments which they have long cashed in on at the ballot box. . . .

The fact that migrant workers are used as scapegoats remains a sad reality. As soon as economic or political crises are upon us . . . the spotlight unfailingly shines on immigrant workers.

—*Manuel Simón Velasco (2002), director of the International Labor Organization (an agency of the United Nations) Bureau for Workers' Activities, explains how the world's political leaders often use the issue of international migration to stir up voters' sentiments and to provide a ready scapegoat for current social problems.*

The point Manuel Velasco made in 2002 remains true in the second decade of the twenty-first century: When tough times come to a nation, migrant workers are among the first to be blamed for the country's problems. For years, many nations have strictly limited immigration; however, anti-immigrant sentiment does not bode well in the future for nations that have aging populations and declining birth rates. According to the United Nations, migrants follow the flow of jobs, and in countries with severely shrunken labor forces and increasing ranks of older retirees, immigrants may be part of the solution to population concerns rather than part of the "problem" as they have been perceived in the past.

Today, many European countries (as well as the United States, Canada, and Japan) are faced with populations that will have more persons who are older and fewer babies than ever before. If these nations want to maintain the social services and economic structures that many residents have become accustomed to, some analysts argue that it will be necessary for these countries to "lower their borders" and accept even more change in the racial and ethnic composition of their populations.

As the pressure from overpopulation builds in some nations, and the United States, Canada, and some European countries have increasingly "aging" populations, demographers believe that the flow of migrant workers, both "legal" and "illegal," will increase dramatically around the world. Many immigration-related challenges remain, however, and perhaps the greatest of these is the perpetual threat of terrorism, which is typically attributed first to immigrants whether this is true or not. Recent terrorist threats in the United States and violence in Norway have deep roots in race, religion, nationality, and anti-immigration sentiment.

While some nations continue to look to the past to determine what should be done about immigration in the future, spokespersons for organizations such as the International Organization for Migration (2010) believe that political leaders and citizens must acknowledge that their countries face either a declining and aging population or a future that is built by immigrants.

Questions for Consideration

1. To what extent is it possible for a nation to control its borders? What part does geography play in border control? What part does politics play?

2. How might functionalist and conflict theorists differ in their explanations of the causes and consequences of international migration?

3. What do you think will be the future of immigration in the United States? Will our concerns about terrorism overshadow the ever-present demand for low-wage workers in this country?

including such attributes as age, sex, race, marital status, education, occupation, income, and size of household. Population composition affects many aspects of life in a nation. In the United States, for example, children make up less of the country's population than ever before, and in the future, this younger generation will pay the nation's bills and support the expanding elderly population. According to 2010 Census data, the share of children in the overall population is decreasing at the same time

Watch on **mysoclab.com**
Population Growth and Decline on **mysoclab.com**

that the older population is growing. The percentage of the population made up of children under age eighteen hit a new low in the second decade of the twenty-first century when children made up 24 percent of the U.S. population, down from 26 percent in 1990, and the percentage is projected to slip to 23 percent by 2050. By contrast, people sixty-five and older made up 13 percent of the U.S. population in 2010, but estimates suggest that this figure will jump to about 20 percent by 2050, when one in five people in the United States will be sixty-five or older (U.S. Census Bureau, 2010). How do changes in the age distribution of the population affect individuals, communities, and the nation as a whole? The age distribution of the population is associated with the demand for community resources such as elementary and secondary schools, libraries, health care and recreational facilities, employment opportunities, and age-appropriate housing.

What are the consequences of global population growth? Not all social analysts agree on the answer to this question. As you will discover in the sections that follow, some analysts warn that the earth is a finite system that cannot support its rapidly growing population. Others believe that capitalism—if freed from government intervention—will develop innovative solutions to such problems as hunger and pollution. Still others argue that capitalism is part of the problem, not part of the solution.

The Malthusian Perspective

Rapid population growth and overpopulation are not new problems. Causes and solutions have been debated for more than two centuries. In 1798, for example, Thomas Malthus, an English clergyman and economist, published *An Essay on Population*. Malthus (1965/1798) argued that the global population, if left unchecked, would exceed the available food supply. The population would increase in a geometric (exponential) progression (2, 4, 8, 16, . . .), but the food supply would increase only by an arithmetic progression (1, 2, 3, 4, . . .). Thus, the population would surpass the food supply, ending population growth and perhaps eliminating the world population (Weeks, 2012). Disaster, according to Malthus, could be averted only by positive checks (e.g., famine, disease, and war) or preventive checks (e.g., sexual abstinence before marriage and postponement of marriage for as long as possible) to limit people's fertility. However, the ideas of Malthus were attached by a variety of critics who disagreed with various assertions or estimates that he made.

The Marxist Perspective

Among those who attacked the ideas of Malthus were Karl Marx and Frederick Engels. According to Marx and Engels, the food supply is not threatened by overpopulation; technologically, it is possible to produce the food and other goods needed to meet the demands of a growing population. Marx and Engels viewed poverty as a consequence of the exploitation of workers by the owners of the means of production. For example, they argued that England had poverty because the capitalists skimmed off some of the workers' wages as profits. The labor of the working classes was used by capitalists to earn profits, which, in turn, were used to purchase machinery that could replace the workers rather than supply food for all. From this perspective, overpopulation occurs because capitalists desire to have a surplus of workers (an industrial reserve army) so as to suppress wages and force workers concerned about losing their livelihoods to be more productive.

According to some contemporary economists, the greatest crisis today facing low-income nations is capital shortage, not food shortage. Through technological advances, agricultural production has reached the level at which it can meet the food needs of the world if food is distributed efficiently. Capital shortage refers to the lack of adequate money or property to maintain a business; it is a problem because the physical capital of the past no longer meets the needs of modern economic development.

Marx and Engels made a significant contribution to the study of demography by suggesting that poverty, not overpopulation, is the most important issue with regard to food supply in a capitalist economy. Although Marx and Engels offer an interesting counterpoint to Malthus, some scholars argue that the Marxist perspective is self-limiting because it attributes the population problem solely to capitalism. In actuality, nations with socialist economies also have demographic trends similar to those in capitalist societies.

The Neo-Malthusian Perspective

More recently, *neo-Malthusians* (or "new Malthusians") have reemphasized the dangers of overpopulation. To neo-Malthusians, the earth is "a dying planet" with too many people and too little food, compounded by environmental degradation and overconsumption. Publication of Paul R. Ehrlich's *The Population Bomb* in 1968 launched a worldwide discussion about the effects of overpopulation and rapid population growth. *The Population Bomb Revisited,* published forty years later, reasserted the growing importance of the demographic element in the human predicament: "The Earth's finite capacity to sustain human civilization" (Ehrlich and Ehrlich, 2009:63). In other words, overpopulation and rapid population growth result in global environmental problems, ranging from global warming and rain-forest destruction to famine and vulnerability to epidemics (Ehrlich and Ehrlich, 2009). Unless significant changes are made, including improving the status of women, reducing racism and religious prejudice, reforming the agriculture system, and shrinking the growing gap between rich and poor, the consequences will be dire (Ehrlich and Ehrlich, 2009).

Early neo-Malthusians published birth control handbooks, and widespread acceptance of birth control eventually reduced the connection between people's sexual conduct and fertility (Weeks, 2012). Later neo-Malthusians have encouraged people to be part of the solution to the problem of overpopulation by having fewer children (Weeks, 2012).

Demographic Transition Theory

Some scholars who disagree with the neo-Malthusian viewpoint suggest that the theory of demographic transition offers a more accurate picture of future population growth. According to **demographic transition theory, some societies move from high birth and death rates to relatively low birth and death rates as a result of technological development.** The demographic transition takes place in four stages. The *preindustrial stage* is characterized by little population growth: High birth rates are offset by high death rates. This period is followed by the *transitional* or *early industrial stage,* which is characterized by significant population growth as the birth rate remains high but the death rate declines because of new technologies that improve health, sanitation, and nutrition. Today, large parts of Africa, Asia, and Latin America are in this second stage. The third stage is *advanced industrialization and urbanization:* The birth rate declines as people control their fertility with various forms of contraception, and the death rate declines as medicine and other health care technologies control acute and chronic diseases. Finally, in the *postindustrial stage,* the population grows very slowly, if at all. In this stage, a decreasing birth rate is coupled with a stable death rate.

Proponents of demographic transition theory believe that technology can overcome the dire predictions of Malthus and the neo-Malthusians. Critics point out that not all nations go through all the stages or in the manner outlined. They think that demographic transition theory explains development in Western societies but not necessarily that in others.

Other Perspectives on Population Change

Scholars continue to develop theories about population growth. Some have focused on the process of *secularization*—the decline in the significance of the sacred in daily life—and how a change from believing that otherworldly powers are responsible for one's life to a sense of responsibility for one's own well-being is linked to a decline in fertility. This approach is based on the assumption that people have fewer children as societies industrialize and gain economic strength. When this occurs, people rely less on higher powers such as a God or gods to help them make decisions in their everyday lives, and their rates of reproduction decline. Simply put, an increase in industrialization and economic development in society contributes to secularization, which, in turn, is associated with a decline in fertility rates.

Looking at the same issue from a microlevel approach, education and social psychological factors are important in determining how people decide to have children. Family planning information is more readily available to people with more years of formal education and may cause them to engage in decision making in accord with *rational choice theory*. According to rational choice theory, people make decisions based on a calculated cost–benefit analysis ("What do I gain and/or lose from a specific action?"). In low-income countries or other settings in which children are identified as an economic resource for their parents throughout life, fertility rates are higher than in higher-income countries. However, as modernization and urbanization occur in societies, the positive economic effects of having more children are typically offset by how much it costs to care for children and the lowered economic advantage that one might gain from having a child or children in an industrialized nation.

As demographers have reformulated the demographic transition theory, they have highlighted additional factors that are likely to be causes of fertility decline, and they have suggested that demographic transition is not just one process, but rather a set of intertwined transitions. One is the *epidemiological transition*—the shift from deaths at younger ages due to acute, communicable diseases. Another is the *fertility transition*—the shift from natural fertility to controlled fertility, resulting in a decrease in the fertility rate. Other transitions include the *migration transition*, the *urban transition*, the *age transition*, and the *family and household transition*, which occur as a result of lower fertility, longer life, an older age structure, and predominantly urban residence.

Regardless of how we explain population growth, it is evident that rapid, unchecked growth does contribute to numerous problems in nations, particularly low-income, less-developed countries where people and governments can least afford the costs that are associated with having children. World hunger is a persistent problem associated with large populations, although this clearly is not the only factor that intensifies the problem of hunger around the globe.

World Hunger and Malnutrition

Food shortages, chronic hunger, and malnutrition are the consequences of rapid population growth and increasing economic inequality and geopolitical power struggles. According to the World Health Organization, *malnutrition* is a cellular imbalance between the supply of nutrients and energy and the body's demand for them to ensure growth, maintenance, and specific functions. Women and young children are the most likely to experience malnutrition, which contributes to people being underweight and chronically hungry. Malnutrition is the most important risk factor for illness and death, contributing to more than half of deaths in children in low-income, developing nations.

Among adults and children alike, life expectancies are strongly affected by hunger and malnutrition. It is estimated that people in the United States spend more than $60 billion each year on weight loss products (Wapner, 2011), whereas the world's poorest people suffer from chronic malnutrition, and many die each year from hunger-related diseases. Inadequate nutrition affects people's ability to work and to earn the income necessary for a minimum standard of living. In pregnant women, malnutrition increases the risk of anemia, infection, birth complications, and lack of breast milk (see Figure 15.1). Although some gains have been made in reducing the rate of malnourishment in some lower-income nations, about 1 billion people around the world are malnourished, and 63 percent of these are in Asian and the Pacific, 26 percent in sub-Saharan Africa, and 1 percent in developed countries (United Nations Development Programme, 2010).

What efforts are being made to reduce global food shortages and world hunger? Organizations such as the United Nations, the World Health Organization,

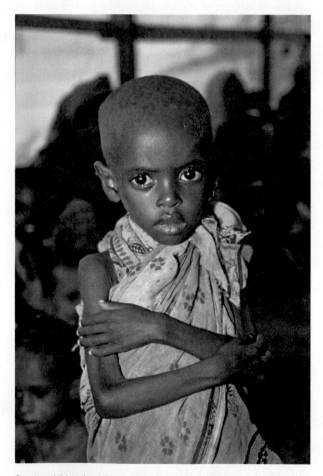

Starving children in nations such as Somalia raise important questions about Malthusian and neo-Malthusian perspectives. Is world hunger primarily a consequence of overpopulation or are other political and economic factors also important?

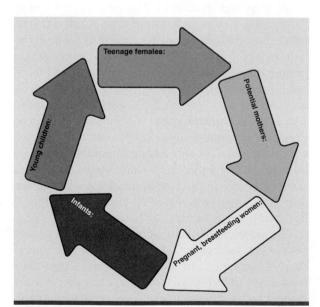

Figure 15.1 The circle of malnutrition

Source: Based on United Nations, 1995.

and the International Red Cross have programs in place, but the most far-reaching initiatives are known as the green revolution and the biotechnological revolution.

The Green Revolution

The *green revolution* refers to dramatic increases in agricultural production that have been made possible by high-yield "miracle" crops. In the 1940s, researchers at the International Maize and Wheat Improvement Center started the green revolution by developing high-yield varieties of wheat, which increased world grain production. The new dwarf-type wheat, which produces more stalks, has dramatically increased the wheat yield in countries such as India and Pakistan since the 1960s. Researchers have also developed a high-yield dwarf rice with twice as many grains per plant, greatly improving the rice output in India, Pakistan, the Philippines, Indonesia, and Vietnam (Weeks, 2012).

How successful has the green revolution been in reducing world hunger? During the 1970s, the green revolution helped increase the global food supply at a somewhat faster pace than the global population grew, but in the 1980s and 1990s, agricultural production slowed considerably. In the twenty-first century, food production still has not increased at the rate that earlier advocates of the green revolution had hoped. Various reasons have been given for lack of success in this regard. For one thing, the fertilizers, pesticides, and irrigation systems that are needed to produce crops are very costly and are beyond the budgets of most middle- and low-income nations. These fertilizers and pesticides may also constitute health hazards and become a source of surface water and groundwater pollution (Weeks, 2012). Moreover, for the green revolution to eliminate hunger and malnutrition, the social organization of life in many middle- and low-income nations would have to change significantly. People would have to adopt the Western methods of farming on which the green revolution was built, and they would have to be willing to produce a single crop in very high volume. But reliance on a single crop can lead to nutritional deficiencies if other varieties of food are not available. Even with these drawbacks, however, the green revolution continues. Researchers have developed high-yield sorghum, yams, and other crops that can be grown successfully in the nations of Africa where some of the greatest food shortages exist (Weeks, 2012). One of the major drawbacks to the green revolution has been substantial cutbacks in funding of agricultural research which has greatly reduced the ability of farmers in low-income nations to generate sufficient crops to feed growing populations. Some analysts attribute this problem to the fact that money was diverted from agricultural research to environmental projects, leaving persistent problems of malnutrition and hunger that remained unresolved (Tierney, 2008). More emphasis has been placed on going green because of global warming concerns and influential political figures and celebrities advocating greater awareness of environmental issues. Although go-green activities such as recycling, reusing, eating locally, conserving water, and finding different energy sources are very important in developed, high-income nations, these activities are of less concern in nations with too little to eat and vast economic inequality.

The Biotechnological Revolution

A second approach to reducing global food shortages, known as the *biotechnological revolution,* encompasses any technique for improving plants or animals or using microorganisms in innovative ways. Scientists have explored ways to genetically alter the reproductive cells of fish, poultry, sheep, and pigs to speed up conventional breeding times. Scientists have already genetically altered microorganisms in several ways. Researchers have found, for example, that it is possible to spray frost-sensitive plants, such as strawberries, with a strain of bacteria that will protect the plants against up to 80 percent of frost damage.

Some scientists believe that the biotechnological revolution can close the gap between worldwide food production and rapid population growth, but the new technology is not without problems. First, giving growth hormones to animals can make their meat unfit for human consumption. Hogs that get growth hormones are prone to gastric ulcers, arthritis, dermatitis, and other diseases. As a result, porcine growth hormones are not approved by the Food and Drug Administration for commercial use in food animals. Second, the cost of biotechnological innovations is beyond the budget of most middle- and low-income nations. Third, the biotechnologies are developed for use with conventional (Western) farming methods and are not always easily adapted to other regions. Fourth, genetic erosion (by breeding or gene manipulation) might eventually make the people of the world reliant on only a few varieties of plants and animals for their entire food supply and thus vulnerable to famine as the result of a single pest or disease. Finally, environmental accidents, such as the unintentional release of genetically manipulated microorganisms, pose a potential hazard.

Increasing the food supply is one way of coping with a rapidly growing world population—but hardly the only way. Some analysts believe that other problems must be addressed, such as the maldistribution of food and corporate monopolization of the food industry. Much food is lost through inadequate transportation and storage facilities, which contribute to a 35 to 40 percent loss of harvests. Much of the food that makes it to consumers sits on supermarket shelves or in the home pantries of families in high-income nations. In other words, food shortages cannot be solved by the biotech revolution or similar means when poverty remains such a persistent problem. In the global food marketplace, both production and distribution of food are tied to corporate profits (globalissues.org, 2011). When the problem is looked at from this approach, the most important factors in improving the global food supply are sustainable farming techniques, better education about food and nutrition for all people, and creation of infrastructures that nurture farmers around the world. It will take a variety of innovative approaches to help make the food supply come closer to matching the world's needs. However, other analysts argue for another method to curb hunger and malnutrition—control fertility.

CONTROLLING FERTILITY

The global population increase since 1900 has been unprecedented, and an additional three billion young people will soon enter their reproductive years. Although demographers know that limiting fertility is the best way to slow down population growth, they also know that the issue is fraught with controversy. More than forty years ago, demographer Ansley Coale (1973) identified three conditions he believed are necessary before there can be a sustained decline in a society's fertility:

- *People must accept calculated choice as a valid element in marital fertility.* If people believe that a supernatural power controls human reproduction, it is unlikely that they will risk offending that deity by trying to limit fertility. On the other hand, the more worldwise people are, the more likely they are to believe they have the right to control reproduction.
- *People must see advantages to reduced fertility.* People must have some reason to want to limit fertility. Otherwise, natural attraction will lead to unprotected sexual intercourse and perhaps numerous children.
- *People must know about and master effective techniques of birth control.* The means for limiting family size must be available, and people must know how to use them successfully.

Although Coale argued that all three preconditions must be met to limit fertility effectively, most government policies focus only on the third: family planning measures (Weeks, 2012).

Family Planning

Family planning programs provide birth control information, contraceptive devices, sometimes sterilization and abortion procedures, and health services. The earliest programs were based on the assumption that women have large families because they do not know how to prevent pregnancy or they lack access to birth control devices. Though we know today that other issues are involved, most programs are still based on this assumption. They do little, for example, to influence a couple's desire to have children and appear not to realize that in some middle- and low-income nations, women are not free to make their own decisions about reproduction. There is overwhelming evidence that women want only the number of children that they can care for adequately (Population Institute, 2010).

Recent research has pointed out how family planning increases survival and improves the health of millions of people, as well as reducing rapid population growth. In the poorest nations, family planning can help people in a number of ways. It is estimated that family planning could prevent as many as one in every three maternal deaths because women could delay motherhood, space births of children, and avoid unintended pregnancies and abortions. Spacing of children helps women determine what size family they want and can afford; leaving at least two years between pregnancies also helps reduce the rates of newborn, infant, and child deaths. For teenagers, family planning can help reduce health risks associated with pregnancy and childbearing during this high-risk time. Family planning helps reduce deaths from AIDS if people are instructed on how to consistently and correctly use condoms and such birth control devices are readily available (Population Reference Bureau, 2009).

Critics of family planning programs argue that most policies are developed by political leaders in high-income nations who are motivated by race and class issues rather than by a genuine concern about world hunger or overpopulation. They say that high-income nations—such as England, France, and the United States—encourage births among middle- and upper-income white women in their own countries but advocate depopulation policies in low-income regions such as sub-Saharan Africa, where most residents are people of color (O'Connell, 1994). For example, the French

Organizations such as Planned Parenthood work to make people aware of the importance of limiting the number of children that they have. What factors contribute to people's choices in regard to controlling fertility?

government is promoting larger families because of a rapidly aging population, a low fertility rate, and a national concern that the country is losing its identity because of high immigration rates (Weeks, 2012).

Zero Population Growth

With *zero population growth,* **there is a totally stable population, one that neither grows nor decreases from year to year because births, deaths, and migration are in perfect balance** (Weeks, 2012). For example, the population growth rate would be zero if a nation had no immigration or emigration and the birth rate and the death rate were the same (Ehrlich and Ehrlich, 2009).

The United States is nearing zero population growth because of several factors: (1) A high proportion of women and men in the labor force find satisfaction and rewards outside of family life; (2) birth control is inexpensive and readily available; (3) the trend is toward later marriage (see Chapter 11); (4) the cost of raising a child from birth to adulthood is rising rapidly; and (5) schools and public service campaigns make teenagers more aware of how to control fertility (United Nations Development Programme, 2002). Near-zero population growth is one characteristic of the U.S. population; another is a rapidly changing population.

IMMIGRATION AND ITS CONSEQUENCES

Immigration is an important issue in the United States and other developed nations where millions of people have sought entry in hopes of improving their life chances and opportunities. In 2010, a total of 1,042,575 persons were admitted to the United States as legal permanent residents. A *legal permanent resident* or "green card" holder is a person who has been granted lawful permanent residence in the United States. Permanent residents may live and work permanently anywhere in the United States, own property, and attend public schools, colleges, and universities. Individuals in this category also are able to apply for U.S. citizenship if they meet certain eligibility requirement.

A second category of people allowed to enter the United States legally are refugees and asylees. *Refugees* and *asylees* are persons who have been persecuted or have a well-founded fear of persecution based on their race, religion, nationality, membership in a particular social group, or political opinion. The number of refugees worldwide ranges from 14 to 15.2 million. In the United States, about 73,000 refugees were admitted to the country in 2010, with the largest percentage coming from Iraq, Burma, and Bhutan. The difference between being a refugee and an asylee is location. For example, those seeking refugee status in the United States typically are outside of this country when they apply for legal entry, while applicants seeking asylum status are already in the United States or are in the process of arriving at a U.S. port of entry. In 2010, slightly more than 21,000 individuals were granted asylum, and most of these were from China, Ethiopia, and Haiti (Homeland Security, 2011).

Immigrants in the previous categories typically generate little public attention or media coverage; however, those in "illegal" and "undocumented" status have been the topic of continual political debate and extensive media coverage. The legal immigrant process is governed by the Immigration and Nationality Act and other laws and administrative guidelines that specify certain details, such as who will receive preference in the immigration process. For example, preference is given to immigrants who have a close family relationship with a U.S. citizen or legal resident, and to individuals with marketable job skills that are in short supply in this country (Homeland Security, 2011).

Although it is virtually impossible to get an accurate count on illegal immigration, government officials estimate that between 8 and 10 million people enter this country illegally each year (U.S. Census Bureau, 2010). Of course, it is not known how many of these individuals return to their countries of origin, or how many people enter, leave, and reenter, as is frequently the case of undocumented workers who come and go between the United States and Mexico or Canada. Many illegal immigrants come to the United States for better job opportunities and freedom from the political, religious, sexual, or racial-ethnic oppression of their home countries. According to immigration authorities, many recent immigrants have come from Mexico, El Salvador, Guatemala, Poland, Haiti, the Bahamas, and Nicaragua (U.S. Census Bureau, 2010). However, the Great Recession of 2008–2009 and slow economic recovery and lack of new job creation have reduced the flow of immigrants who might have previously considered coming to the United States. Stricter U.S. immigration enforcement by U.S. Immigration and Customs Enforcement, combined with new job opportunities in countries such as Mexico, has stemmed the massive flood of immigrants that arrived when the U.S. economy was rising.

What are the central consequences of immigration and how are they measured? Securing a nation's borders is one central concern about immigration: Who comes in and what do they do after they arrive? A second concern involves the demographic characteristics (such as age, education level, nationality and race-ethnicity) of those who enter. A third factor is the effect newly arrived immigrants and their children and grandchildren will have on population growth and its composition now and in the future.

In recent decades, most new arrivals have been illegal (undocumented) immigrants rather those entering the country as legal permanent residents. As a result, immigration policy has shifted from a focus on people desiring to enter as legal permanent residents to those who are entering the country illegally. Consequently, efforts to reduce illegal immigration and to deport those who are already in the country illegally have became the emphasis of congressional initiatives, including authorization for the construction of more than 700 miles of border fences to keep out those without proper documentation and stepped-up deportation if undocumented immigrants, particularly those who have committed drug crimes or were caught driving drunk. After federal legislation to further control immigration failed, states such as Arizona and Georgia adopted their own laws to reduce illegal immigrants' access to driver's licenses and public benefits. It is estimated that between 350,000 and 400,000 people have been deported annually.

In the second decade of the twenty-first century, the Obama administration has generally enforced strict immigration policies, including negative sanctions against employers who hire undocumented workers and implementing efforts to verify workers' immigration status. States such as Arizona have attempted to pass stricter immigration laws that called for actions such as police officers being required to ask that all persons being stopped for even routine traffic violations show documentation that they were in the United States legally. Because of challenges in the lower courts regarding the constitutionality of laws such as these, many legal analysts believe that challenges to the Arizona anti-immigration law will eventually be heard by the U.S. Supreme Court.

On a global basis, immigration and internal migration are causing urban populations to grow faster than the total population (see Map 15.1). Because most cities do not have the capacity to deal with existing residents, much less significant increases in the number of those residents—especially those with limited education and economic wherewithal, immigration, and internal migration—often lead to patterns of urban squalor and high levels of stress in daily living.

Map 15.1   Urban population as a percent of total national population
Source: U.S. Census Bureau, 2010.

What are the consequences of high rates of immigration to the United States? Not all social analysts agree on the answer to this question. Some economists believe that the entry of large numbers of immigrant workers into the country provides a great benefit to everyone because existing land, capital, and technology can be used more efficiently, and the standard of living can rise for many people. These economists also argue that, rather than being a drain on the U.S. economy, immigrant workers add to this nation's coffers by paying property taxes, sales taxes, Social Security taxes, and income taxes. This argument particularly has been made for well-educated immigrants in high-paying occupations (Camarota, 2006). In sharp contrast, however, other economists conclude that immigrant workers who have little education and low incomes are a liability because they use public services, such as public education, government assistance, and fire and police protection, far in excess of what they pay in taxes (Camarota, 2006). For example, the Center for Immigration Studies estimated that an immigrant without a high school diploma created a net lifetime burden of $89,000 on the United States, as compared with an immigrant with education

beyond high school is a fiscal benefit of $105,000 to the country (Camarota, 2006).

Any discussion of the costs and benefits of immigration should distinguish between legal and illegal immigration. From this perspective, illegal immigration differs from legal immigration because illegal immigrants are more likely to have low job skill levels, which means that they are typically employed in agriculture, construction, household work, lawn mowing and landscaping, fast-food and hotel service, and lower-level manufacturing jobs. Because of the nature of these jobs and the relationships between employers and recent illegal immigrants, those who benefit the most from the presence of illegal immigrants are the employers who hire these workers and the consumers who use their services.

Members of the media have played an active role in disseminating information, as well as generating controversy, on problems associated with international immigration (see Box 15.2). But stemming the flow of immigrants appears to be a virtually impossible task for any one nation, as does alleviating the problem of environmental degradation.

Social Problems in the Media

Box 15.2

"Run! Hide!" Media Framing of the Illegal Border-Crossing Experience

My group's hike began outside a white stucco church, where we huddled around Poncho and another masked guide, Luís Santiago. About 10 Hñahñus accompanied us on the walk, playing the role of fellow immigrants. The men explained they were heading north to look for work. A woman carrying a two-year-old girl slung in a shawl said she was seeking her boyfriend.

After unfurling the Mexican flag and singing the national anthem, the guides organized us, telling us to walk in a file, strongest in the back, weakest and slowest in front. "In the night, everyone is equal," Poncho said. "Here, everyone wins, not just the fastest or smartest. If we make it, we all make it; if they catch us, they catch us all."

—*New York Times* journalist Patrick O'Gilfoil Healy (2007) describes his participation in a *Caminata Nochturna* (Night Hike), a three-hour simulation of the Mexican border crossing, which is held in a park about 400 miles from the U.S.–Mexico border.

According to media sources, the Mexican government sponsors *Caminata* to help raise money to compensate for the loss to the local farm economy from crops of tomatoes, corn, and chilies in that region (Johnson, 2008). However, there is another reason for the simulation: Officials want tourists to understand what it is like to be an illegal immigrant trying to cross the border while the Border Patrol systematically tracks them down and threatens to send them back to Mexico or to prison.

How do the U.S. media frame stories about illegal immigration? A number of stories focus on the relative increase or decrease in the number of known illegal immigrants during a specific period of time. Other stories emphasize the vile nature of immigrant smuggling rings and how their activities frequently end in death for some individuals trying to get into the United States illegally. But, media stories about the simulated border-crossing experience described here are relatively new and bring new issues to light: Should journalists and other members of the media participate in activities such as the Night Hike so that they can report on it for their readers or television audiences? Clearly, many journalists believe this is an important topic to cover, and they typically frame their stories relatively simply: It isn't worth the cost! If you do not have documents to legally enter the United States, the best way not to get caught is to not try at all: Stay away from the border! Moreover, they imply, any benefits that might be gained by illegally entering the country are not worth the price (both in money and life) people often have to pay. As described by journalists who participated in the simulated border crossing, participants are told to run as quickly as they can, but they often slip and fall on the muddy riverbanks and stumble over rocks while the guides continually yell "¡Vamos! ¡Vamos! ¡Más rápido!" (Let's go! Let's go! Faster!").

Although some analysts believe that media framing of stories about the illegal border-crossing experience serve to reduce the number of illegal immigrants (along with more stringent border-crossing policies of the U.S. government), other analysts suggest that describing the

Caminata may be an advertisement for it because some Mexicans and Central Americans may use the Night Hike as a "kind of boot camp" to learn how to sneak into Brownsville, Texas, or San Diego, California.

Questions for Consideration

1. How might media framing of stories about "illegal" and "legal" immigration influence our thinking about this important social issue?

2. Do you think that journalists frame their stories about immigration differently if they personally participate in a simulation of an illegal border crossing or ride along with authorities when they break up an illegal smuggling ring or go into a business and arrest undocumented workers? Explain.

3. Besides the one discussed here, what other ways might media messages about immigration be framed?

POPULATION AND THE ENVIRONMENT

Although it is popularly believed that most environmental problems arise from rapid growth in middle- and low-income nations, this isn't the case. Many scientists believe that high-income nations present a much greater threat to the earth's ecosystems. An *ecosystem* is "all the populations of plants and animal species that live and interact in a given area at a particular time, as well as the chemical and physical factors that make up the nonliving environment" (Cable and Cable, 1995:124). Thus, an ocean is an ecosystem; a tropical rain forest is an ecosystem; and on a much smaller scale, a house on a lot is an ecosystem. When all of the earth's ecosystems are put together, they make up the *biosphere.*

Ecosystems do not have an infinite ability to support population growth or environmental depletion or destruction. In fact, some scientists believe that many of the world's ecosystems have already exceeded their *carrying capacity*—the maximum population that an ecosystem can support without eventually being degraded or destroyed. According to biologists Paul Ehrlich and Anne H. Ehrlich (1991), a baby born in the United States will have twice the destructive impact on the earth's ecosystems and services as a baby born in

Sweden, 140 times the impact of a baby born in Bangladesh or Kenya, and 280 times the impact of a baby born in Chad, Rwanda, Haiti, or Nepal. How did the Ehrlichs reach such a conclusion? They developed a formula for determining the impact that human beings have on their environment: $I = P \times A \times T$, or Impact = Population × Affluence × Technology. Thus, the size of the population, its level of affluence, and the technology available in the society are major contributing factors to *environmental degradation*—**disruptions to the environment that have negative consequences for ecosystems** (Cable and Cable, 1995). Environmental degradation involves both removing natural resources from the environment and adding to environmental problems through pollution.

In the United States, environmental degradation increases as people try to maintain the high levels of wealth and material comfort to which they have become accustomed. They consume the earth's resources and pollute its environment with automobiles, airplanes, speedboats, computers, television sets, year-round air conditioning and heating, and other amenities that are far beyond the grasp of most of the world's people. Although these products are made possible by high levels of industrial production and economic growth, economic growth often depletes and destroys the environment.

Economic Growth and Environmental Degradation

During most of the twentieth century, economic growth in the United States was based on increased output in the manufacturing sector. The environment is affected at all phases of the manufacturing process, from mining and transportation to manufacturing and waste disposal. As you will recall from Chapter 13, industrial production involves extracting raw materials—natural resources—from the environment, usually through mining. Mining depletes mineral resources and fossil fuel reserves—coal, oil, and natural gas. Mining also disturbs ecosystems, particularly surface mining, which strips bare the land, destroying natural vegetation and wildlife habitats. Other problems typically follow, including erosion of the land by wind and water and runoff of acids, silt, and toxic substances into nearby surface water and groundwater, which leads to the pollution of rivers and streams with toxic compounds that kill fish and other aquatic life.

The environmental impact of mining doesn't stop when the raw materials have been mined. Now the raw materials must be transported to a plant or factory, where workers will transform them into manufactured products. Transporting requires the use of energy, particularly the burning of fossil fuels, which contributes to air pollution because motor vehicles produce carbon monoxide, nitrogen oxides, and photochemical pollutants. Each of these pollutants is associated with various illnesses, including heart and respiratory disease and cancer. The manufacturing process further depletes fossil fuels and contributes to air pollution. People who work in or live near facilities that pollute the environment are often harmed by the manufacturing process because of the solid or toxic wastes.

Many analysts believe that we cannot continue this pattern of environmental degradation. Future economic development—in the United States and globally—will require drastic changes in the structure of industry, especially in the energy, transportation, chemical, and agricultural sectors of the economy. If we don't make changes, environmental degradation constitutes a major threat to the well-being of all human beings and ecosystems on the earth. Let's look now at some specific kinds of environmental degradation: air pollution; problems with water, soil, and forests; and solid, toxic, and nuclear waste.

Air Pollution

Nature performs many *ecosystem services*–valuable, practical functions that help preserve ecosystems. For example, if the atmosphere is not overburdened, it can maintain a proper balance between carbon dioxide and oxygen, as well as providing ozone for protection against ultraviolet radiation (see Table 15.1 on page 350). However, air pollution interferes with many ecosystem services. The carbon dioxide that pollutes the air we breathe keeps the sun's heat from radiating back into space, thereby causing the earth to heat up (the greenhouse effect, discussed in the next section). Other air pollutants deplete the upper atmosphere ozone layer— a gaseous layer thirty miles above the earth's surface— that shields the earth from ultraviolet radiation. Ozone depletion can make life unsustainable by killing the organic life that produces food and oxygen.

The drastic increase in air pollution that began in the twentieth century and has continued largely unabated in some areas has placed an undue burden on the atmosphere's ecosystem services. Beginning with the Industrial Revolution in the late nineteenth and early twentieth centuries, more and more pollutants have been emitted into the atmosphere by households, industries, and automobile traffic. The result is constantly increasing amounts of carbon dioxide, carbon monoxide, nitrogen oxide, and sulfur oxide, as well as heavy metals such as lead, zinc, and copper in our air. Today, 85 percent of the air pollution in urban areas can be attributed to the internal combustion engines that are used in automobiles and other vehicles (U.S. Census Bureau, 2010). Although laws have reduced the amount of pollution from automobiles and industries in the United States,

"I'm rather fortunate. I have no parents, so Medicare is no problem, and I have no children, so the environment is no problem."

TABLE 15.1 What the Natural World Does for Us (If We Don't Mess It Up Too Much)

Food production	Produces fish, game, and crops—even without our help.
Raw materials	Produces (without our help) the raw materials from which humans create things.
Genetic resources	On its own, creates the ability for crops, vegetation, and animals to survive.
Pollination	Without our help, plants and animals naturally reproduce.
Biological control	Somehow, most species of plants and animals survive for millions of years without our help.
Climate regulation	Unless we mess it up, nature has created an ozone layer that protects all plant and animal life from the sun's ultraviolet radiation.
Water regulation	If we don't mess with it, the world's water supply keeps reproducing and distributing itself.
Gas regulation	If we don't mess it up too badly, nature keeps carbon dioxide and oxygen in balance—a balance that is necessary for life.
Recreation	Just think of the wonderful sights and recreation that nature has created.

Source: Stevens, 1997.

many residents live in areas where air pollutants exceed acceptable levels.

Air pollution affects all life and ecosystems on the planet. Air pollution in the form of acid rain destroys forests, streams and lakes, and other ecosystems. *Acid rain is rainfall containing large concentrations of sulfuric and nitric acids (primarily from the burning of fuel and car and truck exhausts).* In Germany, for example, acid rain is believed to have damaged more than half the trees—up to 80 percent in some regions (Hauchler and Kennedy, 1994). Efforts to reduce acid rain in the United States have been blocked by the automobile industry; companies that mine, haul, and sell high-sulfur coal; and coal miners. Fortunately, new industries are less dependent on burning coal than are older factories in the industrial Northeast and Midwest.

In the past, air pollution in middle- and low-income nations was attributed primarily to the fight for survival and economic development, whereas most air pollution in high-income nations was attributed to relatively luxurious lifestyles. However, distinctions between air pollution in high-income and middle- and low-income nations are growing weaker. Automobile ownership, once considered a luxury, is rising rapidly in urban centers in middle-income nations such as Mexico, Brazil, Taiwan, Indonesia, and China. Cities such as Bombay, Lagos,

Shanghai, and Jakarta have also seen significant increases in the number of automobiles, bringing corresponding rises in air pollution and traffic problems.

Some efforts are being made to curb fossil fuel pollution. In the United States, antipollution laws have brought about changes in how automobiles are made and the fuels they consume. Cars are now equipped with catalytic converters and other antipollution devices, and leaded gasoline (a major offender) has been phased out. However, although some middle-income nations are requiring antipollution devices on new vehicles, many leaded gas-burning cars—often used cars from the United States—are still a significant source of air pollution.

Industrial air pollution has been reduced in some regions of the United States, but pollution controls are often expensive, and many corporations try to find ways to avoid making costly plant conversions. Some move their plants to middle- and low-income nations that have less stringent environmental regulations; others try to avoid antipollution guidelines through government waivers, sometimes known as pollution credits. The federal Clean Air Act Amendments of 1990 created these credits to reward state agencies and companies that kept their emissions below federal governmental limits. However, some environmental groups have emphasized that the

Air pollution is a pressing problem in many nations, but nowhere more so than in Mexico City, where daylight hours often look like this photo. How is air pollution related to people's health and life expectancy?

Environmental Protection Agency (EPA) has not set and enforced environmentally based goals in an effective manner, and that rewards to state agencies and companies simply have not worked quickly or effectively. For the Clean Air Act to fulfill its purpose, more regulation will be required. For example, emissions in new vehicles would have to be reduced significantly, and the amount of lead in gasoline would have to be regulated. Greater regulation would also be required of acid-rain-causing emissions from power plants and for stratospheric-ozone-destroying chemicals. The goal of stepped-up enforcement is to cut pollution at a faster pace and provide better controls for conventional pollutants (Schoenbrod and Witte, 2011).

In the past, one of the key policies for dealing with climate change was known as *cap and trade*, which is a regulatory system in which the government sets a limit on overall emissions of pollutants, and then lets market forces take care of the rest. In other words, utilities, manufacturers, and others who create emissions that might damage the environment work out trades on pollution permits, or allowances, among themselves and within the guidelines set forth by governmental agencies. This type of approach was not a form of direct government regulation, and potential polluters were free to negotiate among themselves. Although industrial leaders and some environmental activist groups initially supported this approach, widespread disagreement erupted by 2010 about whether this policy would effectively reduce pollution and slow down global warming (Broder, 2010). Two major concerns limit the ability of the U.S. government to improve the climate: money and discord. Budget cuts in the more austere financial times of the 2010s, combined with lack of agreement about such matters as whether or not the "greenhouse effect" actually exists, have made it more difficult to gain any consensus about how to deal with environmental problems. In 2011, alone the budget of the EPA was cut $1.6 billion, which amounts to 16 percent of the agency's total budget. Disagreements among elected officials from the Republican and Democratic Parties have created an impasse on the U.S. national debt and government spending to the extent that efforts to combat climate change have taken a backseat. Among the programs affected are those which are supposed to deal with greenhouse gases (K. Galbraith, 2011).

The Greenhouse Effect

Emissions from traffic and industry not only add to general air pollution but also contribute to the *greenhouse effect*—an environmental condition caused by excessive quantities of carbon dioxide, water vapor, methane, and nitrous oxide in the atmosphere. When carbon dioxide molecules build up in the earth's atmosphere, they act like the glass roof of a greenhouse, allowing sunlight to reach the earth's surface but preventing the escape of solar infrared radiation (heat) back into space. The heat that cannot escape is reflected, causing the earth's surface temperature to rise. Some scientists believe that the earth will have a temperature increase of as much as five degrees over the next 100 years. In fact, if current rates of emission into the atmosphere remain unchanged, temperature increases might eventually bring about catastrophic consequences.

One consequence could be significant changes in weather patterns and climate. Changes in weather patterns could bring increased evaporation, creating new deserts and decreasing regional water reserves. Changes in air circulation and climatic conditions could result

> **Explore the Concept**
> *Social Explorer Activity:*
> *Carbon Emissions and*
> *Global Warming* on
> mysoclab.com

in more frequent hurricanes, flooding, tidal waves, and droughts. Vegetation zones could shift, and forests in the Northern Hemisphere might die off.

Not all scientists believe that the greenhouse effect exists or that its effects will be this disastrous. However, studies show a marked retreat of glaciers and the beginning of a shift in vegetation, and one possible cause is the greenhouse effect. Moreover, the more intense these conditions become, the more it is like putting a lid on a pot of boiling water on the stove. The lid does not heat the water, but it certainly makes the effects of the heat generated from the stove more intense after the lid is placed on the pot.

To reduce greenhouse gases, political and economic leaders in high-income nations want middle- and low-income nations to lower their birth rates so that the total number of people contributing to the problem does not rise. But leaders in these nations think that high-income nations should institute stringent restrictions on consumption and pollution in their own countries and use some of their resources to help other countries with economic development. Then, they say, it may be possible to significantly reduce their birth rates.

Depletion of the Ozone Layer

The ozone layer is the thin atmospheric band that protects the earth and its inhabitants from the sun's harmful ultraviolet rays. Ozone is vital to life on earth because it is the only gas in the atmosphere that can absorb the sun's radiation. As a result, it was cause for great concern when, in 1992, a hole the size of North America was reported in the ozone layer over Antarctica. A thinning ozone layer increases risk of skin cancer, damages marine life, and lowers crop yields. To reduce this problem, the Montreal Protocol on Substances That Deplete the Ozone Layer was adopted in 1987 and fully implemented by 1989. Since adoption of the Montreal Protocol, fewer ozone-depleting substances have been found in the atmosphere, and authorities believe that efforts to control the emissions of these substances have been successful so far and that a return to pre-1980 levels of ozone might be accomplished about 2050 if people continue to adhere to the Montreal Protocol in the future (National Oceanic and Atmospheric Administration, 2011).

Problems with Water, Soil, and Forests

Water, soil, and forests (vegetation) are interdependent crucial resources that face increasing degradation or destruction because of pollution. As a result of climate changes, waste, pollution, and rapid depletion, the earth's drinking water is endangered, and its fertile land is being lost.

Water Shortages and Pollution

Water depletion and pollution are serious problems. Although approximately 70 percent of the earth's surface is covered by water, most water is not drinkable: 97 percent is saltwater, 2 percent is in ice caps and glaciers, and less than 1 percent is usable freshwater supply for ecosystems and humans (unwater.org, 2011). The primary sources of water for use and consumption are rainfall, streams, lakes, rivers, and aquifers. About half of the world's rivers are seriously depleted and polluted, and aquifer depletion is also a pressing problem. An *aquifer* is an accessible underground water supply, such as a wet underground layer of permeable rock or gravel, sand, or silt which contains groundwater that can be extracted using a water well. In recent decades, the people worldwide have pumped dry vast underground stores of water. Excessive pumping of groundwater and depletion of aquifers seriously jeopardizes people, agricultural products, farm animals, and many other components of the ecosystem.

Because of the current rate of world population growth and existing climatic conditions, water scarcity is increasing throughout the world. About eighty countries, comprising 40 percent of the world's population, are suffering serious water shortages. If the greenhouse effect brings about changes in the climate, many countries in Africa may experience serious water shortages that will be further exacerbated by the growing problem of water pollution.

Where does the water go? The largest amount (about 70 percent) is used for crop irrigation; in some African and Asian countries, as much as 85 percent of the available water is used in agriculture. The second largest use of water is in industry (23 to 25 percent). Industrial use of water depends on the level of development in a country and the structure of its economy. For example, high-income nations use as much as 60 percent of their water for industry, whereas a middle- or low-income nation might use less than 10 percent. A mere 8 percent of all available water is used for domestic or private household use. Affluent people in high-income nations use far more water (up to 1,000 quarts per person per day) than do families living in African villages, where water must often be carried several miles. Diseases related to the lack of safe drinking water cause over 4 million deaths annually (United Nations Environmental Program, 2002).

Water pollution seriously diminishes the available supply of water. Water can be polluted in a variety of ways. Most often, the cause is unpurified or insufficiently treated sewage from households and industry discharged into groundwater or surface water or pesticides and mineral fertilizers leached from farmland. The pollutants range from nitrates and phosphates to metals, salts, and pathogenic microorganisms.

Agriculture, especially as practiced by transnational corporations that are engaged in agribusiness, pollutes water. Fertilizers and pesticides containing hazardous toxic chemicals that seriously impair water quality are used extensively and often leach into water supplies.

Soil Depletion and Desertification

About 11 percent of the earth's surface is used for growing crops, 31 percent is forest, and 24 percent is used to graze animals. Each year, however, many acres of usable land are lost through erosion and contamination. *Deforestation*—excessive removal of trees—usually results in serious erosion. Since the 1992 Earth Summit in Rio de Janeiro, high-income nations have made an effort to protect forests. Unfortunately, prior industrialization in the United States and other high-income nations has already taken a serious toll on forests, and the pattern is continuing in some middle- and low-income nations as they become more industrialized. In the United States, logging in the national forest system, especially in the Pacific Northwest, is an issue. Environmentalists say that logging increases landslides, floods, and changes in rivers and streams, which devastate fish stocks. Furthermore, when road building, which is necessary to get to the trees in the forest, is combined with cutting all the timber in an area (clear-cutting), the damage is even greater. More water flows down slopes, and when roads wash out, rocks and soil fall onto lower slopes and into streambeds.

Today, many regions are losing an increasing amount of useable land as a result of *desertification—* **the process by which usable land is turned into desert because of overgrazing, harmful agricultural practices, or deforestation.** It is estimated that desertification destroys as many as 15 million acres of land a year. An additional 50 million acres of crop and pasture land become inefficient each year because of excessive application of herbicides and pesticides, insufficient crop rotation, and intensified agricultural production.

Although desertification takes place in high-income as well as middle- and low-income nations, its effects are particularly devastating in middle- and low-income nations. When a country is already hard-hit by rapid population growth, virtually any loss of land or crops is potentially devastating to large numbers of people. The United Nations and other international organizations have therefore tried to make protection of the environment an integral part of all economic development policy. However, environmental protection specialists say that to translate policy into action, conservation programs must be supported by the people and the major sources of the problem must also be addressed: overpopulation and poverty.

Solid, Toxic, and Nuclear Wastes

Even with a rapidly growing world population and ongoing economic development in industrialized nations, the planet might be able to sustain life for a long time if it weren't for all the solid and toxic chemical waste that is dumped into the environment.

Solid Waste

In the United States and some other high-income nations, people consume a vast array of products and—in these *disposable societies*—throw away huge quantities of paper, plastic, metal, and other materials. U.S. residences, businesses, and institutions produce more than 243 million tons of trash each year (Environmental Protection Agency [EPA], 2010). *Solid waste* is any and all unwanted and discarded materials that are not liquids or gases, including sewage solids. Between 1980 and 2009, solid waste generation has increased from 3.66 pounds to 4.34 pounds per person per day in the United States (EPA, 2010). According to the EPA (2010), however, the good news is that the recycling rate has also increased.

Recycling refers to reusing resources that would otherwise be discarded. About 61 million tons of municipal solid waste (including packaging, food scraps, grass clippings, furniture, computers, tires, and appliances) were recycled in 2009. About 21 million tons of waste was recovered through composting. If we subtract what is recycled or composted, then each person discarded only about 2.9 pounds of waste per person per day. But even this amount is far too high in a rapidly growing nation and world.

Toxic Waste

At the same time that technology has brought about improvements in the quality and length of life, it has created the potential for new disasters. One source of a potential disaster is *toxic waste,* the hazardous chemical by-products of industrial processes. Perhaps the most widely known U.S. case of toxic waste is Love Canal.

In travel brochures, Mexico is known for its beautiful, unlittered beaches; however, as the trash piled on this Acapulco beach shows, some formerly pristine areas are now endangered by environmental pollution.

In the late 1970s, residents of Niagara Falls, New York, learned that their children were attending a school that had been built on top of a toxic landfill (Gibbs, 1982). After large numbers of children became ill and the smell and appearance of the chemicals permeated the entire area, many people mobilized against Hooker Chemical Company, which had dumped tons of chemicals there (Gibbs, 1982). Eventually, the federal government bought many of the houses, moved the residents out, and removed as much of the toxic waste as possible. Today, families again live in the area, but they have a highly visible neighbor: a forty-acre grassy landfill, thirty feet high at the center, with an eight-foot-high chain-link fence surrounding it. The landfill contains 21,000 tons of toxic chemical waste and the remains of 239 contaminated houses (Hoffman, 1994).

Today, the U.S. government regulates the disposal of toxic wastes, but some hazardous wastes are not covered by regulations, and some corporations avoid the regulations by locating their factories in other countries.

In addition, there is often nowhere to safely dispose of the chemicals. Many people take a "not in my backyard" attitude toward toxic chemical waste dumps (Dunlap, 1992; Freudenberg and Steinsapir, 1992).

What is it like to discover that your neighborhood is being polluted by toxic waste? A resident of the East Swallow Road neighborhood in Fort Collins, Colorado, describes the uncertainty and worry caused by pools of petroleum leaking out of a service station's underground tanks (Erikson, 1994:115):

> [Y]ou just sort of live your life on hold. I'm always saying, "God, will it ever end so we can get on with our lives?" You can't really make any plans, you just sort of live your life in limbo. Sometimes it's almost unbearable. It's like you really don't live, you just sort of exist, and you wait and you wait and you wait for it to end. But it doesn't, so you just struggle through each day and you worry. You know, it's really, really a pretty sad way to have to live.

Nuclear Waste

Nuclear, or radioactive, wastes are the most dangerous of all toxic wastes. Radioactive waste comes primarily from manufacturers of nuclear weapons and nuclear power plants, although small amounts of waste are by-products of certain medical procedures. Weapons manufacturing plants in Washington, South Carolina, and Colorado store huge amounts of radioactive waste and chemicals in underground tanks. Inspectors have found that some of the older tanks leak and others are empty. When tanks leak, they contaminate groundwater and thousands of cubic feet of soil. Nuclear waste remains deadly for prolonged periods of time. For example, uranium waste from nuclear power plants (an estimated 50,000 tons by the early 2000s) will remain dangerously radioactive for the next 10,000 years, and plutonium waste will be radioactive for the next 240,000 years (Petersen, 1994).

Technological Disasters

Technological disasters, such as the Deepwater Horizon Gulf of Mexico oil spill in 2010, and the 2011 Fukushima Daiichi nuclear plant disaster in Japan, which occurred in the aftermath of a massive tsunami, have increased global awareness of problems associated with technological disasters. The Deepwater Horizon oil spill, also known as the BP oil spill because British Petroleum (BP) was the principal developer of the oil field where the accident occurred, was the largest marine oil spill in history. This disaster was caused by an explosion on an offshore oil platform, which then sank into the water causing crude oil to gush out of the 5,000-foot pipe that connected the well at the ocean floor to the drilling platform on the surface. Eventually, BP was able to cap the well and stop the flow of oil into the Gulf of Mexico. However, by then massive damage had been done to wildlife and the overall environment, to the economy in the communities along the Gulf where the accident occurred and elsewhere, and to areas below the water's surface that still have not been adequately assessed.

Like the aftermath of the oil spill, the nuclear disaster at Fukushima Daiichi remains on the minds of many people because of the extensive damage caused by both of these technological disasters and the fear that we live in a world more, rather than less, prone to have similar or worse disasters in the future. The nuclear power plant disaster was caused by a massive 9.0 magnitude earthquake and tsunami that hit a region of Japan in 2011. The disaster involved a series of equipment failures, nuclear meltdowns, and the release of radioactive materials into the atmosphere. This crisis continued for days as various reactors experienced full meltdown, multiple fires broke out, and fuel rods began to overheat. Radiation exposure for workers and those living within a range of the nuclear plant was of great concern. Eventually, workers were able to bring the crisis under control; however, the effects on humans, food, and the environment will not be fully known for generations to come. The level of this crisis was eventually placed at a seven, which is the maximum value an international nuclear event can be given for its devastating effects that will take many years and perhaps even decades to clean up and decommission the plant.

These are only two of many technological disasters we could examine in detail; however, the nature and scope of all such crises are monumental and the adverse outcomes are far more than we can actually predict at the time of their occurrence and the immediate aftermath. In the words of sociologist Kai Erikson (1991:15), technological disasters constitute a "new species of trouble":

> [Environmental problems] contaminate rather than merely damage.... They pollute, befoul, taint, rather than just create wreckage.... They penetrate human tissue indirectly rather than just wound the surfaces by assaults of a more straightforward kind.... And the evidence is growing that they scare human beings in new and special ways, that they elicit an uncanny fear in us.

Erikson (1994:141) describes *technological disasters* as "everything that can go wrong when systems fail, humans err, designs prove faulty, engines misfire, and so on." Previous technological disasters that meet this definition include the 1986 meltdown and radiation leak at the Chernobyl nuclear power plant in the Ukraine, the leakage of lethal gasses at a pesticide plant in Bhopal, India, in 1984, and a radiation leak at the Three Mile Island nuclear power plant in Pennsylvania in 1979, among others. In the worst-case scenario, technological disasters kill tens of thousands of people; in the best-case scenario, they place tremendous stress on the world's ecosystems, give people an additional reason to fear for their health and lives, and greatly diminish the quality of life for everyone.

SOCIOLOGICAL PERSPECTIVES AND SOLUTIONS FOR POPULATION AND ENVIRONMENTAL PROBLEMS

As sociologists have examined how human behavior affects population and environmental problems, the subdiscipline of environmental sociology has emerged (see Box 15.3 on page 356). According to Cable and Cable (1995:5), "*environmental sociology* examines people's beliefs about their environment, their behavior toward it, and the ways in which the structure of society influences them and contributes to the persistent abuse of the environment." Like all sociologists, environmental sociologists—as well as demographers—approach their study from one or another perspective.

The Functionalist Perspective

Some functionalists focus on the relationship between social structure, technological change, and environmental problems. On the one hand, they say, technological innovation serves important functions in society. For example, automation and mass production have made a wide array of goods—from automobiles and computers to McDonald's burgers—available to many people. On the other hand, technological innovation has latent dysfunctions; automation and mass production, for example, create air pollution, overuse and depletion of natural resources, and excessive solid waste. From this point of view, some environmental problems are the price a society pays for technological progress. If this is true, the best way to alleviate the problem is to develop new technologies. This is what happened, some functionalists

Critical Thinking and You   Box 15.3

Do We Have a Problem or Not? Learning from Environmental Sociology

- "I take care of the environment. I recycle my paper and soft drink cans, and I don't throw stuff out the window when I'm driving."

- "My sorority participated in Clean Up Day last year. We cleared out brush and trash at an old person's house and made it look a lot better."

- "With gas prices what they are now, I'll probably walk the rest of my life. That'll probably help the environment." (author's files)

Comments such as these by college students are typical expressions of how many of us think about our relationship to the environment. We think of ourselves as "good" or "bad" based on how our actions might affect the environment. And, indeed, sociologists who specialize in environmental sociology believe that reciprocal interactions between the physical environment, social organization, and social behavior are an extremely important topic to study. So, on the one hand, what we do as individuals is important. However, on the other hand, what corporations, governmental agencies, and political leaders do at the macrolevel is also important.

Some members of Congress have been slow to acknowledge that the climate is changing and that human activity is a major contributing factor; others have suggested that the nation is faced with more pressing issues than environmental degradation, global warming, and similar concerns. Ordinary citizens have become concerned and vocal advocates for environmental controls and changes that will help, not harm, the planet. Many Internet websites and social media outlets are full of advice about what we should do to save the planet and thus to save ourselves and our loved ones. Are our political leaders among the last to notice problems such as global warming, environmental pollution, and other deteriorating conditions that contribute to a diminished quality of life on planet Earth? Of course, these leaders might say that it is not so much a matter of acknowledging that the environment is a major international problem as it is determining how we might reduce or solve the problem. Some analysts believe that economic growth and the introduction of new technologies and alternative forms of energy can bring about vast improvements in the environment. Other analysts believe that without significant changes in national and global laws and policies, the environment that is problematic now will be largely unsustainable in future generations.

Questions for Consideration

1. One school of thought suggests that there is a positive relationship between economic growth and the environment. In your own community, can you give examples of situations in which economic growth contributed to the quality of the environment? How about situations in which economic growth contributed to environmental problems?

2. We often hear people being criticized for driving "gas-guzzling" vehicles or eating at fast-food restaurants that dispense millions of sacks, wrappers, cups, and other disposable products, some of which eventually litter the nation's roadways and dump sites. Do you think that our individual choices—such as the vehicle we own or where we eat our food—really affect the quality of our environment? Or are environmental problems beyond our control because they are caused by natural causes or decisions of large corporations and governmental agencies over which we have no control?

3. The United States uses more than one-quarter of the entire world's energy, and some scientists believe we are experiencing global warming because of this vast energy consumption. Is global warming a national issue? An international issue? Can you think of ways in which we might make an aggressive effort to deal with environmental problems now and in the future?

Independent Research

Go to www.govtrack.us and look up legislation on the environment being discussed in congressional committees such as the Senate Committee on Environment and Public Works. Based on the pressing environmental issues we have examined in this chapter, can you identify specific legislation that might address those problems? What chance do you think these bills have of becoming law? What social, economic, and political factors might contribute to the bills becoming law? What factors might hinder the bills from becoming law?

note, when the catalytic converter and other antipollution devices were developed for automobiles.

Other functionalists take a neo-Malthusian perspective and believe that to reduce food shortages and environmental problems, population must be controlled. In other words, the more people there are alive, the greater are the overuse of finite resources and degradation of soil, water, and land.

No matter which view functionalist environmental sociologists take, they believe that solutions to overpopulation and environmental degradation lie in social institutions such as education and the government. Educators can encourage population control by teaching people about the limits to agriculture and the difficulty of feeding rapidly increasing populations. Government leaders and international organizations such as the United Nations can cooperate to find far-reaching and innovative solutions and develop understandings about more equitable use of the world's resources.

The Conflict Perspective

Analysts using a conflict framework believe that population and environmental problems have less to do with overpopulation and shortages of resources than they have to do with power differentials in societies and in the larger global economy. For example, early conflict theorists, such as Karl Marx and Friedrich Engels (1976/1848), did not think that the food supply was threatened by overpopulation because agricultural technology (even in their era) could meet the food needs of the growing world population if it were not for poverty. According to Marx and Engels (1976/1848), poverty exists because workers are exploited by capitalists. They argued, for example, that poverty existed in England because the capitalists skimmed off some of the workers' wages as profits. Thus, the labor of the working classes was used by capitalists to earn profits, which, in turn, were used to purchase machinery that could replace the workers rather than supply food. From this classical Marxist point of view, population growth is encouraged by capitalists who use unemployed workers (the industrial reserve army) to keep other workers from demanding higher wages or better working conditions.

According to contemporary conflict theorists, corporations and the government are the two main power institutions in society. As a result, when economic decisions made by members of the capitalist class and elite political leaders lead to environmental problems, the costs are externalized, or passed along to the people (Cable and Cable, 1995:13):

> [The externalization of environmental costs of production] . . . means that the costs of production's negative impact on the environment (for example, the expense of cleaning polluted water to make it suitable for drinking) are not included in the price of the product. The company neither pays for the privilege of polluting the water nor cleans it; it saves the cost of proper waste disposal and makes environmentally conscious competition impossible. Not even the consumer of the product pays the environmental costs of production directly. Rather, the public at large essentially subsidizes the company, by either paying for the cleanup of the environment or enduring degraded environmental quality.

Although most conflict approaches to studying the environment focus on the relationship between members of the capitalist class and political elites, there is also an approach known as *ecofeminism*—the belief that patriarchy is a root cause of environmental problems. According to ecofeminists, patriarchy results in not only the domination of women by men but also the belief that nature is to be possessed and dominated rather than treated as a partner (Ortner, 1974; Merchant, 1983, 1992; Mies and Shiva, 1993).

Another conflict approach uses an *environmental justice framework*—examining how race and class intersect in the struggle for scarce environmental resources. Of particular interest to these theorists is **environmental racism—the intentional or unintentional enactment of a policy or regulation that has a negative effect on the living conditions of low-income individuals and/or persons of color as compared to those of people from more affluent communities.** One of the earliest manifestations of environmental racism identified by social scientists was the placing of a disproportionate number of hazardous facilities in areas populated primarily by poor people and people of color. Hazardous facilities include waste disposal and treatment plants and chemical plants. A 1987 study by the Commission for Racial Justice concluded, "Race was the most potent variable in predicting the location of uncontrolled (abandoned) and commercial toxic waste sites in the United States" (Bullard and Wright, 1992:41). One sociological study conducted about two decades ago examined the Carver Terrace housing subdivision in Texarkana, Texas, which was composed of 100 African American households and was built over an area that had been previously contaminated by a creosote wood treatment facility (Capek, 1993). The federal government eventually bought out some of the homeowners and relocated the subdivision, but not until a number of years after it was determined that toxins in the neighborhood had caused the deaths of twenty-six people and the illnesses of many others (Capek, 1993).

More recently, environmental racism has been identified in the treatment of low-income, minority persons during and following the Hurricane Katrina crisis, which destroyed large sections of New Orleans and the Mississippi coastline and inland areas. Many of the people heavily affected by Hurricane Katrina and the flooding that occurred in its aftermath were low-income African Americans whose residences were located in the low-lying areas of New Orleans, where infrastructure problems had been ignored for years. By contrast, more affluent, white American residents lived on higher ground in the city and had less worry that they and their property would wash away if the levees on Lake Pontchartrain failed. After all of these failures occurred and the city was flooded with water, rescue workers were extremely slow in coming to the low-income areas of the community. In the years that have followed, advocates for environmental justice have spoken out for the rights of Katrina survivors, particularly those most hard hit by the crisis, but many analysts believe that the losses and devastation have never been thoroughly addressed and that they never will be because the nation has moved on to newer natural disasters and other environmental crises.

The Symbolic Interactionist Perspective

Since symbolic interactionists take a microlevel approach, viewing society as the sum of all people's interactions, they look at environmental problems in terms of individuals. Specifically, they think environmental problems are exacerbated by people's subjective assessment of reality. They point out that children learn core values that are considered important in the United States through socialization, but some of these values can be detrimental to the environment. Consider the following widely held beliefs (Cable and Cable, 1995:11–12):

- *A free-market system provides the greatest good for the greatest number of people:* Economic decision making works best in private hands.

- *The natural world is inexhaustible:* There will always be more natural resources.
- *Faith in technology:* Any challenge can be met through technology.
- *The growth ethic:* Growth equals progress; bigger is better.
- *Materialism:* Success can be measured in terms of consumption.
- *Individualism:* Individual rights and personal achievement are most important.
- *An anthropocentric worldview:* Human beings are at the center of the world, and humans are superior to other species. Standing *apart from* nature rather than recognizing that we are *part of* nature, we attempt to conquer and subdue the environment.

It might be, however, that as people become aware of the effects of environmental degradation, concern for the environment will emerge as a core value in the United States. To eliminate the global problems posed by overpopulation and environmental degradation, all societies must make the following changes (based on Petersen, 1994:109):

- Reduce the use of energy.
- Shift from fossil fuels to solar-based energy systems or other energy-efficient systems such as water power, wind power, or geothermal energy.
- Develop new transportation networks and city designs that reduce automobile use.
- Work for redistribution of land and wealth so that the poor in all nations can make a positive contribution.
- Push for equality between women and men in all nations, emphasizing literacy training, educational opportunities, and health care (including reproduction and contraception information) for women.
- Effect a rapid transition to smaller families.
- Cooperate internationally to reduce the consumption of resources by the wealthy nations and bring higher living standards to poorer nations.

Are these changes likely to occur? Some social analysts think that it will take a threatening event—a drastic change in the earth's weather patterns or a sudden increase in natural disasters—to capture the attention of enough of the earth's people and to convince political leaders that a serious change in direction is required if the planet is to continue to support human life. We can only hope that people will not wait until it is too late.

SUMMARY

✓•⌐[Study and Review on mysoclab.com

■ **What is the global population and why is population growth a problem?**

The world's population has now reached 7 billion, and it continues to grow rapidly. The concern is whether the earth's resources can support this rapid population growth.

■ **What are the primary factors that affect population growth?**

Three factors affect population growth: fertility, the actual number of children born to an individual or a population; mortality, the number of deaths that occur in a specific population; and migration, the movement of people from one geographic area to another for the purpose of changing residency.

■ **How does population growth affect a society?**

Population growth affects population composition, the biological and social characteristics of a population, including such attributes as age, sex, race, marital status, education, occupation, income, and size of household. In the United States, for example, the age distribution of the population affects the need for schools, employment opportunities, health care, and age-appropriate housing.

■ **What are the major theoretical perspectives on overpopulation?**

According to the Malthusian perspective, population expands geometrically while the food supply increases arithmetically; disaster can be averted through positive checks (e.g., famine, disease, war) or preventive checks (e.g., sexual abstinence, delayed marriage). The neo-Malthusians believe that the earth is a ticking bomb because population problems exacerbate environmental problems. The third perspective is more hopeful. According to demographic transition theory, societies move from high birth and death rates to low birth and death rates as a result of technological development. However, critics say that demographic transition theory applies chiefly to Western societies.

■ **What solutions do we have to world hunger?**

Two of the most far-reaching initiatives have been the green revolution (the growing of high-yield "miracle" crops) and the biotechnological revolution, which involves "improving" plants or animals or using microorganisms in innovative ways. However, some social analysts believe that the solution is not to produce more food but to control fertility.

■ **How is immigration changing the population composition of the United States?**

Today, the proportion of U.S. immigrants in the population is the highest it has been since 1940. If immigration continues at the present rate, it will account for two-thirds of the expected population growth in the next fifty years. (The United States is otherwise almost at zero population growth—a stable population.) Immigration leads to higher taxes, but it also brings substantial economic benefits.

■ **What is environmental degradation and what are its causes?**

Environmental degradation is caused by disruptions to the environment that have negative consequences for ecosystems. Human beings, particularly as they pursue economic development and growth, cause environmental degradation.

■ **What is the major source of air pollution and what are its effects?**

The major source is fossil fuel pollution, especially from vehicles but also from industry. One of the most serious consequences of air pollution is the greenhouse effect, an environmental condition caused by excessive quantities of carbon dioxide, water vapor, methane, and nitrous oxide in the atmosphere leading to global warming.

■ **What water, soil, and forest problems do we face?**

Water scarcity is increasing around the world, and water pollution further diminishes the available water supply. One of the major water polluters in the United States is the paper manufacturing industry. About 15 million acres of soil are lost each year to desertification (the process by which usable land is turned into desert because of overgrazing and harmful agricultural practices) and deforestation (excessive removal of trees). Desertification is greatest in middle- and low-income nations.

■ **Why are solid, toxic, and nuclear wastes a problem?**

High-income nations are running out of space for the amount of solid waste produced by their "disposable societies." Toxic waste (hazardous chemical by-products of industry) causes death and disease if it is not disposed of properly. Nuclear, or radioactive, waste is a problem because of the length of time it remains deadly.

■ **What is the functionalist perspective on population and the environment?**

On the subject of environment, functionalists say that the latent dysfunctions of technology cause problems but that new technologies can solve these problems. Most functionalists take a neo-Malthusian perspective on population but believe that social institutions, especially education and the government, can cooperate to solve population and environmental problems.

■ **What is the conflict perspective on population and the environment?**

In the classical Marxist view, there would be enough food for all people if poverty were alleviated, and poverty exists because capitalists skim workers' wages for profits. Contemporary conflict theorists believe that the two main power institutions in society—corporations and the government—make economic decisions that result in environmental problems. An approach known as ecofeminism says that patriarchy is a root cause of environmental problems: Nature is viewed as something to be possessed and dominated. The environmental justice approach examines how race and class intersect in the struggle for scarce environmental resources.

■ **What is the symbolic interactionist perspective on population and environment?**
Symbolic interactionists see population and environment problems in microlevel—individual—terms. Through

socialization, children learn core values that are often detrimental to the environment. However, there is some indication that concern for the environment is becoming a core value in the United States.

KEY TERMS

acid rain, p. 350
crude birth rate, p. 337
demographic transition theory, p. 341
demography, p. 337

desertification, p. 353
environmental degradation, p. 348
environmental racism, p. 357
fertility, p. 337
greenhouse effect, p. 351

migration, p. 338
mortality, p. 337
population composition, p. 338
zero population growth, p. 345

QUESTIONS FOR CRITICAL THINKING

1. Which perspective on population growth seems to best apply to the twenty-first century?

2. How do political leaders describe the "immigration problem" in the United States? Are these biased or unbiased views? Explain.

3. If you had to focus on a single aspect of environmental degradation—air pollution; water, soil, or forest problems; solid, toxic, or nuclear waste disposal—which would it be and why? What would you do to make people aware of the seriousness of the problem? What new solutions could you propose?

Succeed with MySocLab® www.mysoclab.com

Watch. Explore. Read. The New MyFamilyLab is designed just for you. Each chapter features a pre-test and post-test to help you learn and review key concepts and terms. Experience Marriages and Families in action with dynamic visual activities, videos, and readings to enhance your learning experience.

Here are a few activities you will find for this chapter.

Watch on **mysoclab.com**
Core Concepts video clips feature sociologists in action, exploring important concepts in the study of Social Problems. Watch:
• Population Growth and Decline

Explore on **mysoclab.com**
Social Explorer is an interactive application that allows you to explore Census data through interactive maps. Explore the Social Explorer Activity:
• Social Explorer Activity: Carbon Emissions and Global Warming

Read on **mysoclab.com**
MyFamilyLab includes primary source readings from classic and contemporary sociologists from around the world. Read:
• Sixteen Impacts of Population Growth

Urban Problems

THINKING SOCIOLOGICALLY

- Why do people living in the same city often have divergent perspectives on and experiences in that city?

- Can contemporary urban problems such as fiscal crises, housing shortages, and high rates of homelessness be traced to growth and development patterns of the past?

- How does globalization influence urban and rural areas around the world?

"Take a fresh look at the city around you. Make a personal—or secret—map, of where you go that other people at school might not go or even know about." I gave this instruction to my students and asked them to report back to the sociology class about their findings. I think many were surprised to learn that their "secret maps" revealed shadow places that other students did not know existed. Some students discussed driving on unpaved streets and seeing substandard houses within a few miles of our campus that other students had never seen. Other students described the "Church under the Bridge" that meets each Sunday in an open-air setting under an Interstate highway. Still other students talked about volunteering at a soup kitchen, a women's shelter, and a home for abused children that are "off-the-map" for other students. Why don't you draw your own personal map to see what your city looks like using your own sociological perspective?

What is life like in the city? People living in the same city have very divergent perspectives and experiences because of their positions in the social structure and particularly as their position is affected by race, class, gender, and age. Although the rich and the poor may live near one another in many cities, they are worlds apart in lifestyles and life chances. At the individual, microlevel, each of us has a secret map of the city in which we live. These secret maps are subjective: "We leave out some parts of the original map, and we add our own embellishments" (Kazemi, 2005). As social science research shows, differences in lifestyle and life chances can be attributed partly to the fact that most U.S. cities are enclaves of geographic, socioeconomic, and racial-ethnic isolation.

In this chapter, we examine how people *experience* urban life as well as looking at some of the most pressing urban problems in the United States and other nations. Many social problems discussed in this book—including the wide gap between the rich and the poor, racial and ethnic strife, inadequate educational opportunities, and homelessness—are found in rural areas, but, of course, they are much more pronounced in densely populated urban areas. For example, crime rates typically are higher in urban areas, and schools tend to be dilapidated. As a framework for examining urban problems today, let's briefly look at the changes in U.S. cities that have led to these problems.

DID YOU KNOW

- U.S. cities may have a collective budget shortfall of $60 billion or more.

- Housing shortages have existed in the United States for more than fifty years.

- U.S. homeownership reached almost 70 percent before the 2006 housing crash.

- Tokyo, Japan, is the world's largest urban agglomeration.

CHANGES IN U.S. CITIES

Urban problems in the United States are closely associated with the profound socioeconomic, political, and spatial changes that have taken place since the Industrial Revolution. Two hundred years ago,

👁─ **Watch** on **mysoclab.com**
Challenges Facing Cities
on **mysoclab.com**

most people (about 94 out of 100) lived in sparsely populated rural areas, where they farmed. In the twenty-first century, about 80 percent of the U.S. population lives in urban areas, and many of these people live in cities that did not exist 200 years ago (U.S. Census Bureau, 2010).

Early Urban Growth and Social Problems

Industrialization and urbanization bring about profound changes in societies and frequently spawn new social problems, such as housing shortages, overcrowding, unsanitary living and working conditions, environmental pollution, and crime (see Chapter 1). By definition, a city involves population density. According to sociologists, a city is a relatively dense and permanent settlement of people who secure their livelihood primarily through nonagricultural activities (Weeks, 2012). Although cities existed long before the Industrial Revolution, the birth of the factory system brought about rapid *urbanization*, which we defined in Chapter 1 as the process by which an increasing proportion of a population lives in cities rather than in rural areas. For example, the population of New York City swelled by 500 percent between 1870 and 1910 as rural dwellers and immigrants from Ireland, Italy, Germany, Poland, and other nations arrived in massive numbers, seeking jobs in factories and offices.

Early cities were a composite of commercial, residential, and manufacturing activities located in close proximity. But even then, rapidly growing cities such as New York had a few blocks (e.g., Upper Fifth Avenue) of houses where the wealthy lived. These residences were located near the center of the city, and their addresses were considered a sign of social and economic success. With the introduction of horse-drawn streetcar lines in the 1850s and electric streetcars in the 1880s, people were able to move more easily from place to place within the core city and to commute between the core city and outlying suburban areas. As a result, many middle-class families moved out of the central areas.

City leaders established municipal governments for building and repairing streets, fire protection, crime control, sewage disposal, lighting, and other general needs. In the late nineteenth and early in the twentieth century, improved transportation and new technologies for supplying water and disposing of waste enabled cities to grow even faster. However, municipal governments had trouble keeping pace with the negative side effects of "progress," including urban slums, traffic congestion, and high crime rates. Despite these problems, people continued to move to northeastern and midwestern cities in unprecedented numbers, looking for jobs, educational opportunities, and such new amenities as big department stores, parks, libraries, and theaters.

Contemporary Urban Growth

The growth of suburbs and outlying areas forever changed the nature of city life in this country. Suburban areas existed immediately adjacent to many city centers as early as the nineteenth century, but in the 1920s, these communities began to grow in earnest because of the automobile. They were referred to as "bedroom communities" because most of the residents were there on nights and weekends but went into the city for jobs, entertainment, and major shopping. During the 1930s, about 17 million people lived in suburban areas (Palen, 2012). With the exception of a few cities that built subways or other forms of mass transit—New York and Chicago, for example—most suburban dwellers drove to work each day, establishing a pattern that would result, decades later, in traffic congestion and air pollution, problems that have drastically worsened in the past two decades.

Between the end of World War II (1945) and 1970, suburbanization brought about a dramatic shift in the distribution of the U.S. population. During the war, construction of apartments and single-family dwellings had halted as industry produced war-related goods. When the war ended, many veterans returned home, married, and had children (the "baby boom" generation). Consequently, in the late 1940s, as many as 6 million families were unable to find housing; many had to live with relatives or friends until they could find a place of their own (Palen, 2012).

To reduce the housing shortage, the federal government subsidized what became a mass exodus from the city to outlying suburbs. Congress passed the Housing Act of 1949, which gave incentives to builders to develop affordable housing. In addition, federal agencies such as the Veterans Administration (VA) and the Federal Housing Administration (FHA) established lenient lending policies so that war veterans could qualify to buy homes for their families. Other factors also contributed to the postwar suburban boom, including the availability of inexpensive land, low-cost mass construction methods for building tract houses, new federally financed freeway systems, inexpensive gasoline, racial tension in city centers, and consumers' pent-up demands for single-family homes on individually owned lots. The most widely known and perhaps the most successful suburban developer of this era was Abraham Levitt and Sons, the company that developed Levittown (on Long Island, New York). Levittown was the first large-scale, mass-produced housing development in this country (see Map 16.1 on page 364).

Eventually, more than 17,000 single-family residences—occupied by more than 82,000 people—were located in Levittown. Sometimes referred to as "cracker boxes" because of their simple, square construction, Levitt houses were typically two-bedroom, one-bath Cape Cod–style homes built on concrete slabs. Driveways were unpaved, and each home had its own small lawn with a couple of small bushes (Nieves, 1995).

Although early suburbanization provided many families with affordable housing, good schools and parks, and other amenities not found in the city, the shift away from city centers set up an economic and racial division of interests between cities and suburbs that remains in place even today. Although many people in the suburbs still rely on the city centers for employment, entertainment, or other services, they pay taxes to their local governments and school districts. As a result, suburban police and fire departments, schools, libraries, and recreational facilities are usually well funded and well staffed, with up-to-date facilities. Suburbs also have newer infrastructures (such as roads, sewers, and water treatment plants) and money to maintain them. In contrast, many cities have aging, dilapidated schools and lack funds for essential government services.

Since 1970, cities in the South, Southwest, and West have been considered postindustrial cities because their economic production largely consists of information-processing or service jobs (Orum, 1995). Whereas cities in the Northeast and Midwest grew up around heavy manufacturing, the newer Sunbelt cities have grown through light industry (e.g., computer software manufacturing), information-processing services (e.g., airline and hotel reservation services), educational complexes, medical centers, convention and entertainment centers, and retail trade centers and shopping malls. In these postindustrial cities, most families do not live near the central business district.

In the 1980s and 1990s, edge cities emerged beyond existing cities and suburbs. An *edge city* **is a middle- to upper-middle-class area that has complete living, working, shopping, and leisure activities so that it is not dependent on the central city or other suburbs** (Garreau, 1991). When this concept was originally introduced, the Massachusetts Turnpike Corridor, west of Boston, and the Perimeter Area, north of Atlanta, were edge cities in the United States. These edge cities began as residential areas; then retail establishments and office parks moved into the adjacent area, and created an unincorporated edge city. Automobiles are the primary source of transportation in many edge cities, and pedestrian traffic is discouraged—and even dangerous—because streets are laid out to facilitate high-volume automobile traffic, not walkers or bicyclists. Some edge cities do not have a governing body, so they drain taxes from cities and

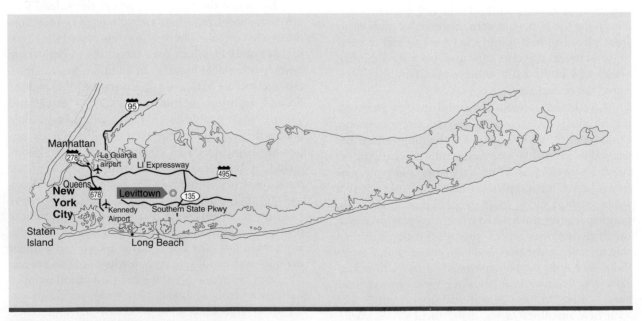

Map 16.1   Levittown, New York.

older suburbs. Many businesses and industries move their physical plants—and tax dollars—to these areas because land is cheaper, workers have more years of formal education, and utility rates and property taxes are lower than those in the city. As a result, many businesses and the jobs associated with them move away from poor neighborhoods and low-income workers in central cities, intensifying the problem of long-term, structural unemployment.

Some analysts believe that the era of the edge city has passed in the United States as urban sprawl has consumed some of these areas and made them no longer identifiable. However, in developing nations of the world where automobile ownership and international investment have increased, edge cities have more recently sprung up in China, India, and the United Arab Emirates. These edge cities are located on the outskirts of cities such as Bangalore (India) and Dubai (United Arab Emirates). Like the earlier U.S. edge cities, residential, business, and commercial properties have sprung up to meet the needs of individuals who do not need to be connected, either for work or social ties, to the central urban center or its immediate suburbs for their daily activities.

Over time, large-scale metropolitan growth produces a *megalopolis*—**a continuous concentration of two or more cities and their suburbs that have grown until they form an interconnected urban area.** The Northeast Corridor, for example, is a megalopolis, with Boston, Providence, Hartford, and their suburbs merging into New York City and its suburbs, which in turn, merge southward into Newark, Philadelphia, Baltimore, and Washington, DC, and their suburbs. It is almost impossible to tell where one metropolitan area ends and another begins. When metropolitan areas merge into a megalopolis, there are big population changes that can bring about or exacerbate social problems and inequalities based on race, class, and gender.

URBAN PROBLEMS IN THE UNITED STATES

Even the most optimistic of observers tends to agree that cities in the United States have problems brought on by years of neglect and deterioration. As we saw in previous chapters, poverty, crime, racism, homelessness, inadequate public school systems, alcoholism and other drug abuse, and other social problems are most visible and acute in urban settings. Intertwined with and exacerbating these problems in many older cities are periodic fiscal crises.

Fiscal Crises in Cities

The largest cities in the United States have faced periodic fiscal crises for many years, and some have teetered on the brink of bankruptcy. New York City was on the edge of financial collapse in 1975 until the federal government provided an elaborate bailout plan; Cleveland went into financial default in 1978. When federal aid to cities was slashed during the recession of the early 1980s, some state governments provided additional monies to cities, but most did not have the financial resources to do so. As a result, the governments of Detroit, Boston, and New York had to drastically reduce services; they closed some public hospitals and other facilities, laid off employees, significantly cut public transit, and all but stopped maintaining the cities' infrastructures. Finding a solution to the fiscal crises of the 1980s was a real dilemma that only got better when the U.S. economy started to thrive. However, in the 2010s, the situation hasn't gotten much better and some believe that it has even gotten worse because of the larger size of populations and the greater complexity of the social problems cities face.

In the 2010s, cities of all sizes are experiencing financial problems partially linked to a major downturn in national and international economic trends. It is estimated that U.S. cities will soon experience a collective budget shortfall of approximately $60 billion. Economic recoveries in cities take a number of years longer than a national recovery, which means that financial problems brought about by the Great Recession may last for years to come.

Why have national and international economic downturns hurt U.S. cities so drastically? What are cities doing about it? Cities have experienced extensive shortfalls in revenue because states have reduced the amount of money that they provide for cities, and the cities have had decreased revenue from sales taxes, corporate taxes, and personal income taxes. Funds from the federal government to states and cities have also been limited and are often earmarked for specific projects rather than for use in the general operating budget. These budget crises have forced states to cut funding to already cash-strapped cities. Vital services, including police, firefighting, and public works, have been cut drastically, and some analysts believe that the slashing of city budgets and programs will continue for some time in the future. As cities lose revenue, officials must decide to lay off or furlough employees, charge higher fees for services, and cancel major projects such as street repairs or infrastructure improvements (building a new water treatment facility, for example).

City officials continue to urge leaders at the state and federal levels to create new programs that will help cities meet their residents' needs. Demands specifically are being made for more federal aid through job creation programs and other economic stimulus packages. Some analysts believe that inaction at the state and federal levels may create even greater financial chaos by forcing some cities into bankruptcy. Local officials emphasize that the state of America's cities continues to threaten the long-term national economic recovery (National League of Cities, 2010). It remains to be seen what the eventual effects of these continuing fiscal crises will be on various cities throughout the nation.

Although some cities are able to retain existing residents and attract new ones, the larger national picture shows that many middle- and upper-income people reside in the suburbs or in incorporated cities located within or adjacent to the larger city. The suburbs and incorporated cities within a city have their own tax base, fire and law enforcement, city government and other services where residents neither contribute to, nor expect assistance from, the larger, urban center they are near. Consequently, central cities have been left with greatly reduced sources of revenue, and a higher proportion of the population that is poor, unemployed, or older people who are living on fixed incomes and have over-age-sixty-five tax exemptions on property they own. Low-income individuals living in the central city cannot afford additional taxes but still need city services such as hospitals, police and fire departments, and public transportation. By contrast, the wealthier residents who reside in the city proper typically send their children to private schools and live in security-conscious residences where they perceive that they are safe and untouched by the problems of poor and homeless individuals nearby.

Long-term unemployment and the low wages of those fortunate enough to find work diminish the tax base in cities and create tremendous social dislocation. To understand the extent of job loss and its impact on many cities, consider this now-classical description by sociologist William J. Wilson (1996:34–35) of the predominantly African American community of North Lawndale in Chicago:

> After more than a quarter century of continuous deterioration, North Lawndale resembles a war zone. . . . Two large factories anchored the economy of this West Side neighborhood in its good days— the Hawthorne plant of Western Electric, which employed over 43,000 workers and an International Harvester plant with 14,000 workers. The world

headquarters for Sears, Roebuck and Company was located there, providing another 10,000 jobs. The neighborhood also had a Copenhagen snuff plant, a Sunbeam factory, and a Zenith factory, a Dell Farm food market, an Alden's catalog store, and a U.S. Post Office bulk station. But conditions rapidly changed. Harvester closed its doors in the late 1960s. Sears moved most of its offices to the Loop in downtown Chicago in 1973; a catalogue distribution center with a workforce of 3,000 initially remained in the neighborhood but was relocated outside the state of Illinois in 1987. The Hawthorne plant gradually phased out its operations and finally shut down in 1984. The departure of the big plants triggered the demise or exodus of the smaller stores, the banks, and other businesses that relied on the wages paid by the large employers. . . . In 1986, North Lawndale, with a population of over 66,000, had only one bank and one supermarket; but it was also home to forty-eight state lottery agencies, fifty currency exchanges, and ninety-nine licensed liquor stores and bars.

But things are looking a little better in North Lawndale now. In the twenty-first century, efforts have been made by community-based organizations to revitalize North Lawndale and improve the quality of life there. Economic development, affordable and mixed-income housing, and education have all been part of the revitalization plan. The latest study available on this revitalization project shows that some progress has been made; however, much more redevelopment is needed because the community continues to have high rates of poverty, unemployment, and crime and low rates of education and commercial activity. North Lawndale remains disproportionately African American (94.2 percent) but has seen an increase in the Latino/a population, which now accounts for 4.5 percent of the community (Lane et al., 2004). The future of North Lawndale, as with many other areas like it throughout the country, depends on the commercial development, an adequate supply of affordable and mixed-income housing, and improved academic performance and educational opportunities in local schools. As of 2011, it appears that community members are continuing their efforts to make their neighborhood a better place to live and work. Various websites keep people in the community posted about neighborhood concerns and social events of interest to them.

Given the acute shortage of funds in many cities, community groups and neighborhood associations will increasingly have to work together to solve problems in their area: They will be unable to rely on local, state or national funds for assistance. Many cities have also experienced natural disasters such as floods, brushfires, earthquakes, hurricanes, or tornados—all of which add to the cities' financial burdens by creating new infrastructure problems at the same time that relief must be provided for the hardest-hit residents.

What will be the future of U.S. cities? Part of the answer to this question lies in what happens to real estate markets, which have been slow to recover from the massive downturn of 2008–2009. When the real estate market is slow and properties are not selling, or are selling for much less than in previous years, then the city's property tax revenues are also down. It is difficult, if not impossible, for cities to make up for these revenues, and most budget decisions become a matter of which services to reduce, which jobs to slash, and how to survive the fiscal crisis until conditions get better in the future (Muro and Hoene, 2009). Another part of the answer is related to the history of various cities: In the past some suffered frequent financial problems with others had very few. What is unusual and deeply concerning about the fiscal crisis of cities this time is that cities that previously had been able to stay afloat even in rough economic times have faced economic hardship this time around because they have experienced a decline in all three major general tax sources for cities—property, income, and sales (Saulny, 2008). It appears that the global and U.S. economies will have to improve before there is much hope that city and state budgets will look much better.

The Crisis in Health Care

As we have seen in Chapter 10, health care is a growing problem throughout the United States and federal efforts to reduce the problem are only in the beginning stages where they face widespread disagreement from many sectors.

The growing problems in health care are most evident in the nation's largest cities. Although hospitals and other medical facilities are subject to cutbacks and closings because of economic problems, poor people who live in central cities are more likely to become ill or injured than are people in more affluent suburbs. Poverty is associated with many medical problems, including certain diseases (such as tuberculosis) and problems associated with inadequate nutrition and lack of preventive care (many children are not immunized against the basic childhood diseases). Moreover, drug-related problems and HIV/AIDS place tremendous financial burdens on already underfunded community clinics,

hospitals, and other medical facilities. According to the Centers for Disease Control and Prevention (CDC) in Atlanta, both the number of AIDS patients and the costs of caring for AIDS patients are highest in cities.

Because lack of funding has caused many community clinics and publicly financed hospitals to close, finding affordable health care is a major problem for city residents. Essential services have been cut back in many metropolitan hospitals. Furthermore, as managed care plans and large hospital chains have taken over the ownership of privately funded hospitals, some private hospitals now claim that they cannot afford to provide uncompensated care, and some refuse to admit uninsured patients except in life-threatening circumstances. As a result, although public hospitals cannot legally deny emergency medical care because of the 1986 Emergency Medical Treatment and Active Labor Act, a patient might have to wait hours (sometimes even days) to see a physician or other medical personnel, who must deal with one life-and-death medical emergency after another. Today, many poor people use emergency rooms for all medical services because they do not have—and cannot afford to pay—a private physician. Consequently, the cost of providing medical services is driven higher at a time when public hospitals have greatly diminished resources. The growing homeless population in major urban areas has added to the cost of providing health care.

Despite the problems that urban dwellers face in regard to health care access, some rural Americans have an even greater problem. A recent study found that people residing in rural areas of the United States are more likely to suffer from chronic health conditions such as diabetes, heart problems, and cancer. They are also likely to face greater difficulty in trying to get quality health care (Reuters, 2011). In cities, there are about 105 primary care physicians per 100,000 residents (varying from one city to another). However, only 65 primary care physicians exist for each 100,000 rural residents, creating an acute shortage in some regions. Whether in rural or urban areas, our nation has much remaining to do about problems of access to health care, both in terms of the number and kinds of physicians and other health care providers that are available to see patients and in how people will pay for the services they receive.

Housing Problems

Many regions in the United States lack affordable housing for low-income individuals and families (see Chapter 2). Homelessness is an ever-present problem in the United States that has only grown worse with high rates of current unemployment, more long-term unemployment, subprime mortgages and excessive defaults. Each year, we are made aware of the plight of homeless people through extensive media coverage during the Thanksgiving to Christmas holiday season. During the rest of the year, many view homeless people with less compassion (see Box 16.1).

Social Problems in the Media

Box 16.1

Media Framing of Stories about Homelessness and the Holidays

In a *Doonesbury* comic strip, cartoonist Gary Trudeau shows a homeless man standing in line waiting for his free meal on Thanksgiving Day. A journalist walks up and talks to the homeless man: "You're getting a free meal today . . . but afterwards . . . what do you hope for?" The homeless man replies, "Seconds." The journalist counters: "No, no . . . I mean in the long term." The homeless man replies, "Dessert . . . definitely dessert."

Kendall, 2011:112

As this cartoon shows, the homeless man and the journalist are operating under different assumptions about life and what the future should hold for people. In four quick cartoon frames, Trudeau captures the essence of much media reporting about holiday assistance to the poor by showing how out of place most reporters are when they try to impose their own thinking on the homeless people they are interviewing.

In a study I conducted on how the media frame stories about the poor and homeless, I identified two central frames that often are used in the news—thematic framing and episodic framing (Kendall, 2011). *Thematic framing* is used in news stories that emphasize statistics and trends in homelessness over the experiences of homeless persons, meaning that journalists primarily write about *facts* regarding homelessness, such as changes in rates of homelessness, hunger, and poverty. Thematic framing also focuses on how the government defines poverty and homelessness and what changes have occurred over a specific period of time in regard to these statistics. By contrast, *episodic framing* in news stories examines homelessness and poverty in terms of personal experience, particularly how these conditions affect an individual or family. This type of framing provides a human face for homelessness or poverty, but it often ignores the larger structural factors (such as high rates of unemployment) that contribute to the problem.

One of the most benevolent media messages contained in episodic framing is that the poor are down on their luck and just need a helping hand. This type of framing is especially popular in news stories published near holidays such as Thanksgiving or Christmas, asking readers for assistance in temporarily meeting some of the needs of the poor. Reporting of this type gradually increases in the fall of each year, reaches its height during the Thanksgiving and Christmas holiday season and the cold weather months, and then drops sharply from late winter to early spring. During the peak period of these human interest stories, members of the press barrage service providers at soup kitchens and homeless shelters for interviews, and volunteers are shown serving turkey dinners to the poor at Thanksgiving and preparing baskets of food for indigent families at Christmas. An example of this type of media coverage is found in an annual series, "The Neediest Cases," published in the *New York Times*. One article, "Offering a Hand, and Hope, in a Year of Record Homelessness in New York," describes the problems of Gloria Hernandez, a homeless woman residing in New York City:

> Gloria Hernandez tries to be strong for her five children, but strength, like privacy or full stomachs, does not come easily when you and your family live in a shelter for the homeless. "The children say, 'Mommy, when are we going to get out of here?'" Ms. Hernandez, forty, said softly, her eyes downcast. "You see it in their faces: they don't speak, but they show it. They say it's your fault." (Bovino, 2003:A25)

The photo accompanying the article shows Hernandez, looking depressed, standing with her nine-year-old son, whose arm is protectively wrapped around her neck.

Although one important function of the media is to make the public aware of social problems, why do the media increase coverage at *this* time of year—during the holidays? Part of the explanation may come from sociologist Lewis A. Coser, who says "we have only so much emotional energy and yet we live in a world filled with inhumanity and suffering" (1969:104). Thus, sympathy for the afflicted in a society fluctuates over time. Otherwise, we would be emotionally overwhelmed. Another reason comes from Emile Durkheim, who points to the holidays as the time that most people express sympathy for the homeless: Holidays are times of ritual, opportunities to affirm shared values. In the United States, where individualism is highly valued but people believe that they are responsive to social problems, the holidays reassert community solidarity by redistributing goods in the community (Barnett, 1954). What have you observed in the media's coverage of homelessness? Can you identify other framing devices used by journalists and television entertainment writers to convey certain messages to media audiences about homelessness and poverty?

Questions for Consideration

1. Are news reports and the story lines of television entertainment shows a reflection of readers' and viewers' interests and preferences in content material, or are these reports and story lines a reflection of the corporate interests that own the media?

2. What, if anything, do transnational media giants gain by providing coverage of the poor and homeless in their publications, broadcasts, and websites?

Independent Research

Examine a number of scripted television series and allegedly "unscripted" reality TV shows to find occasions where people are helping other people, supposedly for no benefit of their own. Try to record the programs so that you can carefully observe the expressions on the "givers" and the "receivers" faces as well as their body language. What kinds of messages are being conveyed by their words and actions? Do you think these might have been orchestrated or "framed" by the shows' producers? Also, see if you can find examples of the framing devices discussed previously that typically happen during the holiday season. What other types of framing can you identify that are not covered in this box?

The Shortage of Affordable Housing

When people speak of "the housing shortage," they typically are referring to the availability of affordable or relatively low-cost housing. Throughout the United States, millions of apartments and houses in a wide variety of price ranges are available to rent, lease, or purchase. However, the presence of these housing units does not mean that there is adequate housing available in all price ranges and locations throughout the nation.

Since the 1980s, the number of low-cost (affordable) housing units has continued to decrease in the United States. Some of these units became more expensive apartments or condominiums that were no longer within the price range of individuals who might have previously lived in properties located at that site. Millions of other low-cost units have been abandoned. Although it might seem surprising that landlords will abandon rental property that they own, inexpensive apartments for lower-income residents sometimes become so great an economic liability that landlords simply abandon the properties. Landlords are most likely to give up their property when they find themselves caught between increasing property taxes, demands from the city to maintain or upgrade the property to comply with safety standards or building codes, and tenants who demand services but do not pay their rent or severely damage the units.

Abandoned buildings increase fear and isolation in the residents of adjoining properties. The empty buildings often become hiding places for drug dealers or fugitives, and some are dangerous places for children to play. In some cities, however, *urban squatters*—people who occupy land or property without any legal title to it—have moved into abandoned apartment buildings and fixed them up. As people take up unofficial residence in the buildings, they create a sense of community by watching out for each other's possessions. However, most of these projects have been short-lived. Developers who recognize potential in the area demand that the buildings be razed to make way for new hotels and office towers.

Beginning in the 1970s, some lower-income people were displaced in large urban centers when more middle- and upper-middle-class families reentered city areas and gentrified properties. **Gentrification is the process by which people renovate or restore properties in cities.** Centrally located, naturally attractive areas are the most likely candidates for gentrification. Although gentrification contributed to the revitalize of some cities, it further depleted the stock of affordable housing for the poor and pushed many low-income people out of the area where they had previously lived.

As a result of housing shortages, some cities have instituted programs to provide low-cost owner-occupied housing. However, some social analysts believe that these programs promote the interests of the housing industry and protect property values more than they actually help people to acquire housing. One federal government housing initiative was designed to allow low-income families to purchase—for a nominal fee—abandoned properties.

Efforts to reduce the problem of homelessness are addressed by volunteers with organizations such as this Habitat for Humanity project in New Orleans. How might a combination of public and private initiatives be used to provide homes for a larger percentage of the U.S. population?

In return, the purchasers had to agree to live in the property and make improvements to it for a period of time, after which the property could be sold. Unfortunately, it appears that the government did not provide sufficient housing units in a given area to meet the demand and offset the urban deterioration. In addition, in the 1990s, the Federal Housing Administration (FHA) flooded central city neighborhoods with federally insured loans that were attractive to lenders and real estate agents, who often arranged for families to purchase homes that they were then unable to maintain when repairs became necessary. As a result, massive foreclosures occurred, causing people to lose their homes, bringing about further deterioration of city neighborhoods.

The Housing Meltdown of the Twenty-First Century

The massive foreclosures that took place as people defaulted on their mortgages near the end of the twentieth century were a foreshadowing of an even larger housing meltdown in the 2000s. Early in the twenty-first century, it became possible for millions of people to purchase houses by taking out mortgages that were more than they could repay. One of the first indicators of the extent to which the United States and other nations around the world were entering a financial crisis was the subprime mortgage crisis in the United States. Like the name suggests, *subprime* mortgages were made available to many people who did not have sufficient financial resources to purchase a residential

property and make monthly payments on it. About 80 percent of U.S. mortgages issued to subprime borrowers were adjustable-rate mortgages, which meant that after an initial time period set out in the loan, the interest rates were reset at a higher rate, causing delinquencies to increase and foreclosures to soar.

Historically, banks made and held home loans with money from local deposits. However, in the 1980s, banks and other lenders began to sell these mortgages to investors in the bond market. During the economic boom of the early 2000s, institutional investors (such as insurance companies, labor union funds, and pension systems) poured trillions of dollars into mortgage securities. Initially, housing prices soared, and homeownership reached a high of almost 70 percent in the United States. However, following the peak of U.S. house sales prices in 2006, prices began a steep decline, and subprime mortgages and securities backed with mortgages lost most of their value. This was the beginning of the U.S. and global economic crisis and also the beginning of a downward spiral for homeownership and a sharp uptick in defaults on loans, foreclosures, and bankruptcies. In the fallout from the housing crisis, Fannie Mae and Freddie Mac, government-financed mortgage companies, collapsed, leaving many potential borrowers with no place to secure a loan to purchase a house. Fannie Mae refers to the Federal National Mortgage Association which was started by Congress in 1938 to fund mortgages and make home ownership affordable for more people. Unlike Fannie Mae, which purchased FHA-backed mortgages from lenders, Freddie Mac (the Federal Home Loan Mortgage Corporation founded in 1970) purchased large bundles of mortgages from financial institutions. Some of these mortgages were sound but others were not, based on the ability of the persons who took out the mortgages to repay their loans.

Although these two organizations were established by Congress to foster the American dream of homeownership, both Fannie Mae and Freddie Mac became more concerned with deriving profits from their partners, such as Countywide Financial, the subprime mortgage lender that Bank of America bought in 2008 when the mortgage boom collapsed (Morgenson, 2010). Not only were the mortgagors in trouble, but also Fannie Mae and Freddie Mac, which were taken over by the U.S. Treasury Department in 2008 as part of the deal for the federal

This all-too-familiar sight in an urban neighborhood is one of many signs that the U.S. housing crisis is far from over.

government pumping billions of dollars into them to avert an even-greater housing meltdown and financial crisis in the United States.

Throughout the years, the federal government's involvement in housing has been criticized on several fronts. Some critics believe that federal housing aid, which is supposed to provide decent housing for the poor, has done a better job of providing housing for more affluent people. Federally funded urban renewal projects started in the 1950s were supposed to replace housing units in slums with better quality, affordable housing for the poor. However, some analysts say that once the slums were cleared, more expensive housing or commercial properties were built (J. Jacobs, 1961). Moreover, they say, sometimes the worst, most dilapidated housing units were not chosen for redevelopment because they were not in strategic locations for economic development. Because the power of *eminent domain* gives government officials the authority to condemn certain properties, individual owners' wishes regarding their property were not always taken into consideration. The most successful recent initiatives for replacing substandard housing and building lower-cost housing for poor and lower-income families have come from community groups and volunteer organizations. One of the best known of these is Habitat for Humanity, which has received extensive press coverage because of former President Jimmy Carter's participation.

A second major criticism of federal housing initiatives has been directed at public housing. Most federal and state housing projects have been huge, high-rise constructions that have intensified many problems and created new ones. Most urban sociologists agree that public housing works best when it is situated in less densely populated areas with a small number of families in any

one housing project. In Charleston, South Carolina, for example, one public housing project is located in a neighborhood of historic residences that tourists visit on horse-drawn carriage tours. Tour guides even point to the housing unit as a sign that their community has overcome housing segregation. But when some communities place federally funded housing projects in neighborhoods of middle-income apartments and housing, adjoining property owners object, fearing that the value of their property and their personal safety will be diminished.

What role should the federal government play in housing? Should the government promote affordable homeownership through tax policy, such as granting people special tax deductions for purchasing a home? Contemporary political discussions typically focus on the debt ceiling, the health care crisis, and other issues rather than attacking the problem of affordable housing and homelessness.

Homelessness

Accurate data about the actual number of homeless people in the United States is unavailable. The total is probably somewhere between 500,000 and the 3.5 million estimated by advocates for the homeless. It is extremely difficult to count the number of homeless people because most avoid interviews with census takers and social scientists.

Each year, however, the U.S. Conference of Mayors conducts a survey on urban homelessness in twenty-seven cities, and some consistent patterns have emerged. Among households with children, unemployment was the top factor contributing to homelessness. Lack of affordable housing, poverty, low-paying jobs, and domestic violence were other factors closely associated with homelessness. Among the homeless, people of color are overrepresented; African Americans make up the largest part of the homeless population, when compared to white Americans, Latinas/os, Native Americans, and Asian Americans (U.S. Conference of Mayors, 2010). Single men comprise 51 percent of the homeless population, families with children 30 percent, single women 17 percent, and unaccompanied youth 2 percent (U.S. Conference of Mayors, 2010).

Families and children are the fastest-growing segment of the homeless population in both urban and rural areas of this country. Today, infants, preschoolers, and school-age children and their parents account for almost half of the homeless. Many people think that "the homeless" are all alike, but homeless people come from all walks of life and include Vietnam War veterans;

people with mental illnesses, physical disabilities, or AIDS; elderly individuals; runaway children and teenagers; alcoholics and other substance abusers; recent immigrants; and families with young children (U.S. Conference of Mayors, 2010). Some recent efforts by government agencies to reduce homelessness have focused on individuals with specific problems such as chronic alcoholism or HIV/AIDS, in addition to being without a domicile (see Box 16.2).

Some perspectives on homelessness look at larger structural issues in society, such as lack of educational opportunities and jobs, which contribute to this problem. However, other perspectives are rooted in the assumption that homelessness is primarily a problem of individuals and how they live their lives. According to social scientists, studies that focus exclusively on personal problems of the homeless, such as mental illness or substance abuse, may result in *specialism*— the assumption that individual characteristics of poor people cause their homeless condition and that, therefore, the only way to alleviate homelessness is to cure the individual's personal problems (Wagner, 1993). This approach downplays the significance of structural factors such as the unavailability of low-income housing and of mental health care, which are the most important determinants of homelessness. According to sociologists Marta Elliott and Lauren J. Krivo (1991:128), any solution to the problem of homelessness must take into account these two structural factors:

> Attempts to lower levels of homelessness in U.S. metropolitan areas must address the structural conditions which underlie this phenomenon. More specifically, mental health-care services for the indigent mentally ill must be made more available

In the 2010s, homeless shelters are serving growing numbers of women and families.

to those who are or would become homeless without them. Furthermore, the structure of the housing market must be altered in order to have the greatest effects on reducing homelessness. This means that more low-cost rental housing needs to be made available to reach the most marginal and disadvantaged members of society. Such a restructuring of the housing market is unquestionably one of the primary means by which people will avoid or overcome homelessness. Without this basic resource of cheap housing in an area, some individuals fall out of the housing market completely, a problem exacerbated by an economic environment with proportionately higher numbers of unskilled jobs. Stable well-paid employment must replace this segment of the economy to reduce current levels of homelessness.

Racial and Ethnic Segregation

Problems in housing are closely intertwined with racial and ethnic segregation in the United States. Despite passage of the Federal Fair Housing Act in 1968, segregation of African Americans and whites in major metropolitan areas declined only slightly since 1970. According to sociologists Douglas S. Massey and Nancy A. Denton (1992), no other racial or ethnic group in the history of this country has ever experienced the sustained high levels of residential segregation that African Americans have experienced in central cities. Moreover, residential segregation not only affects living conditions but is also associated with other problems (Massey and Denton, 1992:2):

Read the Document
Use of Black English and Racial Discrimination in Urban Housing Markets on mysoclab.com

> Residential segregation is not a neutral fact; it systematically undermines the social and economic well-being of blacks in the United States. Because of racial segregation, a significant share of black America is condemned to experience a social environment where poverty and joblessness are the norm, where a majority of children are born out of wedlock, where most families are on welfare, where educational failure prevails, and where social and physical deterioration abound. Through prolonged exposure to such an environment, black chances for social and economic success are drastically reduced.

A Kind Heart and Government Funding: Providing a Stable Home for Persons with HIV/AIDS

To the Editor:

The encouraging medical advances in the fight against AIDS will not bare its full impact if infected individuals fall victim to yet another killer: homelessness. . . . With an estimated 500,000 people (in 2001) with HIV or AIDS in the United States lacking suitable housing, it is simply impossible for most of them to find access to health care and adhere to strict treatment regimes. While we have made progress toward addressing the treatment of AIDS, we still have a long way to go toward eradicating conditions like homelessness that are significant barriers to long-term survival of people living with AIDS.

—Regina Quattrochi (2001), executive director, Bailey House, New York

A decade after Regina Quattrochi wrote this letter to the editor of the *New York Times*, she continues her work as executive director of Bailey House, Inc. where she sees firsthand how difficult it is for low-income people living with HIV/AIDS to find long-term housing and acquire other services they need. In New York City, Bailey House helps people meet this need, and its efforts go further because of funding the nonprofit organization receives from the U.S. Department of Housing and Urban Development (HUD) through the Housing Opportunities for Persons with AIDS (HOPWA) Program. In 2011, for example, Bailey House was awarded a HOPWA permanent supportive housing renewal grant of $1.3 million to continue providing permanent housing and supportive services to homeless or marginally housed youth living with HIV/AIDS in the Bronx. The program, titled Success Through Accessing Rental Assistance and Support (STARS), leases twenty scattered site units for young adults ages eighteen to twenty-four, including those aging out of foster care with a history of or current substance abuse and mental illness issues. Supportive services such as mental health and substance abuse counseling and vocational/educational life skills services are also provided for people in the program.

Housing assistance and related services are vital to the overall care system needed by individuals living with HIV or AIDS. Having a place to call home is critical for low-income persons who are managing complex drug therapies and dealing potential side effects from HIV/AIDS treatments. Bailey House and other HOPWA Program recipients have developed and implemented integrated modes of housing, client services, vocational training, rehabilitation, and job placement for persons living with HIV or AIDS and their families.

Should the federal government do more to provide funding for organizations such as Bailey House that seek to meet the housing needs of low-income people living with HIV/AIDS? How about funding for homes and other services for people who experience chronic homelessness? Those who are opposed to "government handouts for the poor" typically argue that providing funding for homeless shelters and for agencies that assist homeless people does not accomplish the goal of getting them off the streets and out of a cycle of dependency. By contrast, those who believe the government should be doing more to help the homeless argue that more money is needed for all low-income people with a variety of issues and concerns. Overall, HUD made available a record $334 million in HOPWA funds in 2011. However, much concern exists about how massive federal deficits and a slow economic recovery will affect future funding for significant projects such as the ones funded by these grants. Some analysts believe that if we as a nation are truly committed to ending homelessness and helping people with HIV/AIDS remain stably housed, political leaders and ordinary citizens alike must be concerned about how little money is being spent or allocated for major tasks such as these and how much money is being spent for endeavors that do not improve the quality of life for all people in the United States.

Questions for Consideration

1. What are the strengths of public grants that provide money for organizations that serve a specific category of individuals, such as people living with HIV/AIDS or those experiencing chronic homelessness, rather than providing larger sums for general "homeless" programs? What are the limitations of a targeted approach?

2. Another HUD program (Housing for People Who Are Homeless and Addicted to Alcohol Program) provides money to assist homeless persons who also struggle with chronic alcoholism. What are the strengths of having a funding program specifically directed at agencies that "serve those in the grips of alcoholism who perpetually call the streets or emergency shelters their home," as HUD states? What are the limitations of this approach?

3. Do government funding programs targeting homeless persons living with HIV/AIDS or those who are addicted to alcohol have the potential to negatively stereotype *all* homeless people as being seriously ill or addicted? What do you think?

After reaching its highest point in the 1960s, racial segregation in housing has decreased slightly in subsequent decades; however, the pace of change has been slow, particularly in the persistence of African American–white American segregated patterns (National Public Radio [NPR], 2011a). In a recent study of public life in an American city, sociologist Elijah Anderson finds that city dwellers are often able to move beyond racial and ethnic issues and interact across racial, ethnic, and social borders because of the unique quality that cities possess (see Box 16.3).

Critical Thinking and You   Box 16.3

The "Cosmopolitan Canopy": Civility for Persons of Color in the City?

Under the cosmopolitan canopy, city dwellers learn new ways of interacting with people they do not know who are visibly different from their own group. They become more comfortable with diversity and discover new ways that people express themselves in public. These experiences may lead people to question and modify their negative presuppositions about others. Even if they do not want to know those others intimately, they practice getting along with everyone. The canopy offers a taste of how inclusive and civil social relationships could become. That people find such pleasure in diversity is a positive sign of the possibilities of urban life in the twenty-first century.

—*Sociologist Elijah Anderson (2011:281–282) describes patterns of social interaction and behavior among racial and ethnically diverse persons whom he has observed while conducting his urban ethnographic research in Philadelphia.*

As Elijah Anderson suggests, it is possible for diverse people to get along with one another in settings where racial and ethnic boundaries are deemphasized, and individuals have a chance to encounter one another in a relaxed context. One Philadelphia location that Anderson identifies as a cosmopolitan canopy is the Reading Terminal Market, which is composed of shops, restaurants, and kiosks that sell goods and provide services. According to Anderson (2011:31), "In this highly diverse setting all kinds of people shop, eat, and stroll." Another location is Rittenhouse Square, a public park that takes up a square city block downtown and is covered by a canopy of trees, providing people with a comfortable place to sit, eat or walk through the square. Other public areas also exist in Philadelphia (and other cities) where people can, at least temporarily, set aside racism and classism and enjoy interacting in a civil manner with a wide diversity of people. As Anderson points out, however, it is also possible for the opposite effect to occur: People from diverse backgrounds may become defensive, or start checking each other out. They also may hold the other person accountable for any perceived racist slur or discriminatory action.

What keeps people from diverse ethnic and racial backgrounds coming back to cosmopolitan canopies to share time with each other? According to Anderson (2011:273), "The simple provocations, revelations, and pleasures diverse people find in one another's company induce them to return to the cosmopolitan canopy again and again. It is through such ongoing activity, the goings-on of everyday life in public, that the canopy renews itself." The cosmopolitan canopy is important because people from many racial and ethnic backgrounds can feel free to go there. As cities become more densely populated and diverse, it is important to have cosmopolitan canopies that give people a chance to stretch ourselves mentally, emotionally, and socially by interacting with people who are different from themselves (E. Anderson, 2011). It is true that segregation is persistent and that prejudice and discrimination are still directed toward individuals and groups based on their race, ethnicity, nationality, religion, gender, age, perceived social class location, physical appearance, and a myriad of other characteristics and attributes, but the way in which cities are laid out and the social interactions that they allow may help us develop a more civil society if we heed the advice of Elijah Anderson to move beyond the past, ease racial tensions, and promote interracial harmony.

Questions for Consideration

1. Do you believe that the concept of the "cosmopolitan canopy" is a useful tool in helping us overcome segregation and discrimination in this country? Why or why not?

2. Why does urban segregation remain so difficult to eradicate after six decades of legislation directed at reducing or eliminating this type of social injustice?

Although racial segregation persists in some suburban areas of our nation, other suburbs have become more diverse. These neighbors are having a friendly conversation that offers hope for positive social encounters across racial and ethnic lines in the future.

As a result of continued "white flight," which is now less overt and inflammatory than it was in the past, some white Americans still flee from a neighborhood if the racial and ethnic composition changes sufficiently that whites will become a minority. By contrast, neighborhoods are still becoming more diverse. If Asian Americans and/or Latinos have already settled in a neighborhood, white Americans appear to be less concerned when African Americans move into the area. But, as Logan suggests, "There is not much pioneering by whites into minority neighborhoods, at all" (quoted on NPR, 2011a).

Although African Americans have experienced the longest and most harmful effects of housing segregation in the United States, other groups have also suffered from housing discrimination (Santiago and Wilder, 1991; Menchaca, 1995; Santiago and Galster, 1995). A number of studies have documented a history of restrictive covenants that have prohibited Mexican Americans from living in white (Anglo) areas. These covenants were frequently supported by racial harassment and violence (see Menchaca, 1995). In some cases, local custom has dictated residential segregation patterns that continue into the present. In one study of Mexican American segregation, one woman recalls that Twelfth Street was the dividing line between the white (Anglo) American and Mexican American neighborhoods in Santa Paula, California (Menchaca, 1995:27):

La calle doce was the main division. The ranchers owned the homes in the northeast, and that was for the people whose parents worked in agriculture—

which would be the lemon or the orange. . . . If you worked for them in the packing house or picking lemons, that's where you would live. . . . They used to tell us, You live in that side and we live in this side. . . . The rednecks used to tell us that.

Vestiges of similar patterns of residential segregation based on race or ethnicity remain in many cities. In Austin, Texas, the historic geographic and political divide between Mexican Americans and white (Anglo) Americans has been an interstate highway. In other communities, the divide is a river or some other geographic or social boundary that is well known to local residents, whether or not they acknowledge its existence. Although there is less overt discrimination, and courts have ruled that racial and ethnic restrictive covenants on property are unenforceable, housing segregation continues through custom.

Since the 1980s, the level of Latino and Asian American segregation as remained relatively constant. In the past, both were concentrated in their own ethnic neighborhoods, and many of these remain today. Although earlier residents may have moved to suburban areas or other locales, later-arriving immigrants have found "home" in those enclaves because of readily available people and schools where their language is spoken, grocery stores and restaurants that sell familiar foods, and churches and other social support networks that are unavailable elsewhere.

Racial isolation in housing is closely linked to poverty. Economically poor neighborhoods primarily occupied by persons of color restrict opportunities for schooling and employment that cripple the changes of young people and expose children to high rates of crime and violence.

Some analysts argue that residence is a personal choice and that people voluntarily segregate themselves on the basis of whom they want to live near. But many people are involuntarily segregated because of certain attributes—such as race, religion, age, or disability—that others devalue. Some landlords, homeowners, and white realtors perpetuate residential segregation through a discriminatory practice known as *steering*—guiding people of color to different neighborhoods than those shown to their white counterparts. Banks sometimes engage in a discriminatory (and illegal) practice known as *redlining*—refusing loans to people of color for properties in certain areas or requiring a larger down payment. In sum, discrimination in housing can occur through steering, redlining, exclusionary zoning laws and land use practices, and many other ways in which purchasing a property is made more difficult for persons of color (particularly those with fewer economic resources) than for white American house hunters.

The continual influx of immigrants into urban areas is changing the population composition in many of the nation's largest cities, including Los Angeles, Houston, Miami, Chicago, and New York. The 2010 Census shows that minorities have experienced a higher percentage of growth in the nation's suburbs than in its cities. The persistence of racial segregation in suburban areas is closely intertwined with growing economic inequality in the United States. Some of the "first" suburbs—those developed earliest and located closest to the older city—have increasingly become the home for high concentrations of low-income persons, recent immigrants, and older individuals who live on small, fixed incomes. Cities that are becoming gentrified, along with some fast-growing outer suburbs, now have significantly more affluent populations, newer facilities, and fewer urban problems than these first suburbs.

PROBLEMS IN GLOBAL CITIES

Although cities have existed for thousands of years, the time has arrived when more people worldwide (50.5 percent) are living in cities rather than in rural areas. In 1900, only one person out of ten lived in a city; today, one out of every two lives in a city (United Nations Population Division, 2010). Northern America, Latin America and the Caribbean, Europe, and Oceania are highly urbanized, and their level of urbanization is expected to rise. Northern America is 82 percent urban, for example. By contrast, Africa and Asian are mostly rural. Only forty percent of people living in Africa and 42 percent of persons in Asia live in urban areas. Although they are projected to reach a proportion of urban of more than 60 percent by 2050, they will be remain far below the 84 percent projected for northern America, Latina America and the Caribbean, Europe, and Oceania (United Nations Population Division, 2010).

Today, twenty-one urban agglomerations account for almost 10 percent of the world urban population. An *urban agglomeration* is the population contained within a large central city and suburbs that are linked to it by a continuous urban growth. Asia has the largest number of urban agglomerations, including Delhi, Mumbai (Bombay), and Kolkata (Calcutta), India; Dhaka, Bangladesh; and Shanghai, China. It is estimated that by 2025, only one U.S. urban agglomeration

Some cities in core nations, such as Shanghai, China, are referred to as "global" cities. They are also considered "postindustrial" cities because their economic base has shifted from heavy manufacturing to information technologies and services.

will be among the ten most populous in the world (see Table 16.1).

As rural populations decline and millions of people move into urban areas around the world, the existing problems of global cities will increase. Rapid population growth produces a wide variety of urban problems, including overcrowding, environmental pollution, and the disappearance of farmland. In fact, many cities in middle- and low-income nations are quickly reaching the point at which food, housing, and basic public services are available to only a limited segment of the population. With rapidly growing urban populations, cities face an increased burden on their water supply. Many regions are using water at unsustainable rates, and urban residents are among the heaviest users of water. Some of the

TABLE 16.1 Populations of the World's Ten Largest Urban Agglomerations (in millions, estimated)

1996		2025	
Tokyo, Japan	26.8	Tokyo, Japan	37.1
São Paulo, Brazil	16.4	Delhi, India	28.6
New York City, USA	16.3	Mumbai (Bombay), India	25.8
Mexico City, Mexico	15.6	São Paulo, Brazil	21.7
Bombay, India	15.1	Dhaka, Bangladesh	20.9
Shanghai, China	15.1	Mexico City, Mexico	20.7
Los Angeles, USA	12.4	New York–Newark	20.6
Beijing, China	12.4	Kolkata (Calcutta), India	20.1
Calcutta, India	11.7	Shanghai, China	20.0
Seoul, South Korea	11.6	Karachi, Pakistan	18.7

Source: *New York Times*, 1996a; United Nations Population Division, 2010.

world's largest cities were already short on water before they suffered drought emergencies, which now have brought them to a virtual crisis stage. Among these are Melbourne, Australia; Barcelona, Spain; and Mexico City (Prud'Homme, 2011). For two decades, Mexico City has suffered from a chronic water shortage that is only growing worse with extreme heat and drought conditions. What does this mean for the future of cities? It may mean a great deal. In the words of one journalist, "Consider Perth, Australia: Its population has surpassed 1.7 million while precipitation has decreased. City planners worry that unless drastic action is taken, Perth could become the world's first 'ghost city'—a modern metropolis abandoned for lack of water" (Prud'Homme, 2011).

Natural increases in population (higher birth rates than death rates) account for two-thirds of new urban growth, and rural-to-urban migration accounts for the rest. Some people move from rural areas to urban areas because they have been displaced from their land. Others move because they are looking for a better life. No matter what the reason, migration has caused rapid growth in cities in sub-Saharan Africa, India, Algeria, and Egypt. At the same time that the population is growing rapidly, the amount of farmland that is available for growing crops to feed people is decreasing. Some analysts believe

that the United Nations should encourage governments to concentrate on rural development; otherwise, acute food shortages brought about by unchecked rural-to-urban migration may lead to riots.

As global urbanization has increased over the past four decades, differences in urban areas based on economic development at the national level have become apparent. According to sociologist Immanuel Wallerstein (1984), nations occupy one of three positions in the global economy: core, semiperipheral, and peripheral. **Core nations are dominant capitalist centers characterized by high levels of industrialization and urbanization.** The United States, Japan, and Germany, among others, are core nations. Some cities in core nations are referred to as *global cities*—interconnected urban areas that are centers of political, economic, and cultural activity. New York, Tokyo, and London are generally considered the largest global cities. They are also considered postindustrial cities because their economic base has shifted largely from heavy manufacturing to information technologies and services such as accounting, marketing, finance, mergers and acquisitions, telecommunications, and other highly specialized fields. Global cities are the sites of new and innovative product development and marketing, and they often are the "command posts" for the world economy. But economic prosperity is not shared equally by all people in the core nation global cities. Growing numbers of poor people work in low-wage service sector jobs or in assembly production, in which they are paid by the item (piecework) for what they produce, but they have no employment benefits or job security. Sometimes the living conditions of these workers more closely resemble the living conditions of workers in semiperipheral nations than those of middle-class workers in their own country.

Most African countries and many countries in South America and the Caribbean are *peripheral nations*—**nations that depend on core nations for capital, have little or no industrialization (other than what may be brought in by core nations), and have uneven patterns of urbanization.** According to Wallerstein (1984), the wealthy in peripheral nations support the exploitation of poor workers by core nation capitalists in return for maintaining their own wealth and position. Poverty is thus perpetuated, and the problems worsen because of the unprecedented population growth in these countries.

Between the core and the peripheral nations are the *semiperipheral nations*, **which are more developed than peripheral nations but less developed than core nations.** Global cities located in semiperipheral nations include São Paulo, Brazil, the center of the Brazilian economy, and Singapore, the economic center for a multicountry region in Southeast Asia. Like peripheral nations, semiperipheral nations—such as India, Iran, and Mexico—are confronted with unprecedented population growth. In addition, a steady flow of rural migrants to large cities is creating enormous urban problems. Semiperipheral nations exploit peripheral nations, just as the core nations exploit both the semiperipheral and the peripheral nations.

According to Wallerstein (1984), it is very difficult—if not impossible—for peripheral and semiperipheral nations to ever occupy anything but their marginal positions in the classlike structure of the world economy because of their exploitation by the core nations. Capital investment by core nations results in uneven economic growth, and in the process, the disparity between the rich and the poor in the major cities increases. Such economic disparity and urban growth is obvious at the U.S.–Mexican border, where transnational corporations have built *maquiladora plants*—factories where goods are assembled by low-wage workers to keep production costs down—on the Mexican side. The demand for workers in these plants caused thousands of people to move from the rural areas of Mexico to urban areas along the border in hope of earning higher wages. The influx has pushed already overcrowded cities far beyond their capacity. Because their wages are low and affordable housing is nonexistent, many people live in city slums or at the edge of cities in *shantytowns*, where houses are made from discarded materials, or squatter settlements. Many of these areas lack roads, sewers, electricity, and a clean water source, thus making living conditions even more hazardous.

Social analysts are just beginning to develop comprehensive perspectives on the position of cities in the contemporary world economy, and not all analysts agree with Wallerstein's hierarchy (1984). However, most scholars acknowledge that nations throughout the world are influenced by a relatively small number of cities (e.g., New York) and transnational corporations that have brought about a shift from an international to a more global economy (see Knox and Taylor, 1995; D. Wilson, 1997). In middle- and low-income nations, all social problems are "incubated and magnified in cities" (Crossette, 1996:A3).

SOCIOLOGICAL PERSPECTIVES AND SOLUTIONS TO URBAN PROBLEMS

For more than 100 years, sociologists have analyzed urban problems to determine the causes and consequences of rapid industrialization and urbanization on people's daily lives and the structure of society. The conclusions they reach about the underlying problems and possible solutions depend on the framework they apply.

The Functionalist Perspective

In examining urban problems, most functionalists focus on three processes that have contributed to social disorganization and the disruption of social institutions. First, mass migration from rural areas to urban areas during the Industrial Revolution contributed to social disorganization by weakening personal ties in the family, religion, education, and other institutions. Second, large-scale immigration in the late nineteenth and early twentieth centuries was more than most cities could absorb, and many individuals were never fully

Explore the Concept

Social Explorer Activity: The Industrial Revolution and Urbanization on mysoclab.com

assimilated into the cultural mainstream. With larger numbers of strangers living close together in central cities, symptoms of social disorganization, such as high rates of crime, mental illness, and suicide, grew more pronounced. According to Emile Durkheim (1933/1893), urban life changes people's relationships. Rural areas are characterized by *mechanical solidarity*—**social bonds based on shared religious beliefs and a simple division of labor**—but these bonds are changed with urbanization. Urban areas are characterized by *organic solidarity*—**social bonds based on interdependence and an elaborate division of labor (specialization).** Although Durkheim was optimistic that urbanization could be positive, he also thought that some things were lost in the process. Third, mass suburbanization created additional social disorganization, and most cities have been unable to reach equilibrium since the mass exodus to the suburbs following World War II. According to urban ecologist Amos Hawley (1950, 1981), new technologies, such as commuter railways and automobiles, have led to the decentralization of city life and the movement of industry from the central city to the suburbs, with disastrous results for some people. Although urbanization, mass immigration, and suburbanization have had functional consequences—including U.S. citizenship, job opportunities, and home ownership—for many people, they have also created problems, particularly for people who are left behind in rapidly declining central cities and people who experienced discrimination.

How do functionalists suggest that urban problems may be reduced? When confronted with the fiscal crisis facing cities and level the inequality in services provided in cities and suburbs in the 1990s, sociologist Anthony M. Orum (1995) suggested establishing metropolitan or regional governments. Problems such as water supply, pollution, and traffic congestion, which are not confined to one geographic area, could be dealt with more effectively through metropolitan or regional planning. However, as Orum acknowledged, it was unlikely that officials of cities and suburban municipalities would willingly give up some of their power, and people living in the more affluent suburbs would be unlikely to take on the problems of the cities. This prediction has come true as we enter yet another fiscal crisis of the cities in the 2010s.

Another option for alleviating urban problems was expanding the urban tax base by creating urban enterprise zones. Cities could offer tax incentives for industries to open plants in cities and provide job training for workers, so a match could be made between jobs and workers. Critics of enterprise zones argued that business tax incentives alone would not improve conditions in cities. In the tight economic times of the 2010s, states such as New Jersey are scrapping thirty-year-old Urban Enterprise Zone Programs that allowed for reduced sales tax on merchandise sold in distressed commercial districts so that more money can supposedly come into the state's coffers.

Finally, functionalist approaches to solving urban problems often emphasize slashing spending and keeping the cost of government low. Increased taxation is discouraged because this supposedly harms wealthier residents, leaving the primary way in which to overcome debt being to reduce spending. Cutting spending constitutes a difficult problem for cities that are already on the edge of bankruptcy and facing massive infrastructure problems, such as outdated roads with gaping potholes, traffic lights that do not work, parks that are unattended, and other physical conditions that are harmful for people.

The Conflict Perspective

Conflict analysts do not believe that cities grow or decline by chance. Members of the capitalist class and political elites make far-reaching decisions about land use and urban development that benefit some people at the expense of others (Castells, 1977; Feagin and Parker, 1990). According to conflict theorists, the upper classes have successfully maintained class-based and sometimes racially based segregation through political control and legal strategies such as municipal incorporation, defensive annexation, restrictive covenants, and zoning regulations. But where do these practices leave everyone else? Karl Marx suggested that cities are the arenas in which the intertwined processes of class conflict and capital accumulation take place; class consciousness and worker revolt are more likely to develop when workers are concentrated in urban areas.

Conflict theorists Joe R. Feagin and Robert Parker (1990) speak of a *political economy model*, believing that both economic *and* political factors affect patterns of urban growth and decline. Urban growth, they say, is influenced by capital investment decisions, power and resource inequality, class and class conflict, and government subsidy programs. Members of the capitalist class choose corporate locations, decide on sites for shopping centers and factories, and spread the population that can afford to purchase homes into sprawling suburbs located exactly where the capitalists think they should be located (Feagin and Parker, 1990). In this view, a few hundred financial institutions and developers finance and construct most major and many smaller urban development projects, including skyscrapers, shopping malls, and suburban housing projects. These decision makers can make housing more affordable or totally unaffordable for many people. Ultimately, their motivation rests not in benefiting the community, but rather in making a profit, and the cities they produce reflect this mindset (Feagin and Parker, 1990).

The concept of *uneven development*—the tendency of some neighborhoods, cities, or regions to grow and prosper while others stagnate and decline—is a by-product of the political economy model of urban development (Perry and Watkins, 1977). Conflict theorists argue that uneven development reflects inequalities of wealth and power in society. Uneven development not only affects areas in decline, but also produces external costs that are paid by the entire community. Among these costs are increased pollution, traffic congestion, and rising rates of crime and violence. According to sociologist Mark Gottdiener (1985:214), these costs are "intrinsic to the very core of capitalism, and those who profit the most from development are not called upon to remedy its side effects." One advantage of the political economy framework is that it can be used to study cities in middle- and low-income nations as well as high-income nations (see Jaffee, 1990; Knox and Taylor, 1995; D. Wilson, 1997). Short of major changes in the political economy, most analysts who take a conflict perspective believe that urban problems can be reduced only through political activism and organized resistance to oppressive conditions. Some believe that central cities are powder kegs of urban unrest that periodically threaten to explode because of massive job loss and economic hardship, racial tensions, allegations of police brutality, controversial court cases, and similar issues.

The Symbolic Interactionist Perspective

Symbolic interactionists examine urban problems from the standpoint of people's experience of urban life and how they subjectively define the reality of city living. How does city life affect the people who live in a city? According to early German sociologist Georg Simmel (1950), urban life is so highly stimulating that people have no choice but to become somewhat insensitive to events and individuals around them. Urban residents generally avoid emotional involvement with one another and try to ignore the events—including violence and crime—that take place nearby. They are wary of other people, looking at others as strangers; some

people act reserved to cloak deeper feelings of distrust or dislike toward others. At the same time, Simmel thought that urban living could be liberating because it gives people opportunities for individualism and autonomy.

On the basis of Simmel's observations of social relations in the city, early University of Chicago sociologist Louis Wirth (1938) suggested that urbanism is a "way of life" that increases the incidence of both social and personality disorders in individuals. *Urbanism* refers to the distinctive social and psychological patterns of life that are typically found in the city. According to Wirth, the size, density, and heterogeneity of urban populations result in an elaborate division of labor and in spatial segregation of people by race-ethnicity, social class, religion, and/or lifestyle. The division of labor and spatial segregation produce feelings of alienation, powerlessness, and loneliness.

In contrast to Wirth's gloomy analysis of urban life, sociologist Herbert Gans (1982/1962) believed that not everyone experiences the city in the same way. On the basis of research in the West End of Boston in the late 1950s, Gans concluded that many residents develop strong loyalties and a sense of community in city areas that outsiders often view negatively. According to Gans, personal behavior is shaped by the type of neighborhood a person lives in within the larger urban area. For example, *cosmopolites*—students, artists, writers, musicians, entertainers, and professionals—view the city as a place where they can be close to cultural facilities and people with whom they share common interests. *Unmarried people and childless couples* live in the city because they want to be close to work and entertainment. *Ethnic villagers* live in ethnically segregated neighborhoods because they feel most comfortable within their own group. The *deprived* and the *trapped* live in the city because they believe they have no other alternatives. Gans concluded that the city is a pleasure and a challenge for some urban dwellers and an urban nightmare for others.

According to symbolic interactionists, the deprived and the trapped contribute to a social construction of reality that stereotypes city dwellers as poor, down-and-out, and sometimes dangerous, whereas many city dwellers are not this way at all. Because movies, television shows, and, particularly, extensive media coverage of crime or racial unrest in the nation's largest metropolitan areas present a very negative image of cities, an antiurban bias remains strong among many nonurban dwellers.

Cities typically have large numbers of people living, working, and playing in close proximity to each other. In New York City, urban street life is further intensified by the presence of large numbers of pedestrians and heavy traffic.

To reduce problems of loneliness and alienation in city life, some symbolic interactionists propose that people who live in large metropolitan areas develop subcultural ties to help them feel a sense of community and identity. A *subculture* **is a group of people who share a distinctive set of cultural beliefs and behaviors that set them apart from the larger society.** Joining an interest group—from bowling with friends from the office to volunteering in a literacy program— is one way of feeling connected. Ethnic neighborhoods are an example of subcultures; some are tightly knit, whereas others have little influence on residents' daily lives. Interactionists note that members of subcultures, especially those based on race, ethnicity, or religion, sometimes come into conflict with each other. These conflicts can result in verbal exchanges, hate crimes, or other physical violence, or they can cause the individuals to withdraw almost entirely from the larger community and become more intensely involved with the subculture.

However, some cause for hope is found in the recent studies of two scholars who claim that cities are far from dead because of the many benefits they offer people. According to urban economist Edward Glaeser (2011), the future of nations and the world relies on cities that bring people together in a setting which is "healthier, greener, and richer" than urban myths would have us believe. From this perspective, incomes are higher in metropolitan areas; cities are more energy efficient than suburban areas where people commute great distances, often in heavy traffic congestion with stop-and-go traffic, between work and home. Cities are also centers of consumption; however, this benefit primarily accrues to the wealthy. By contrast, the poor in urban areas fare better than many think because they have inexpensive mass transit, the ability to "cram into small apartments in the outer boroughs," and "plenty of entry-level service-sector jobs with wages that beat those in Ghana or Guatemala" (Glaeser, 2011). People in the middle-income category often have a harder time because of the costs of housing in good neighborhoods and a quality education for their children, but overall, cities offer people a unique setting in which to connect with one another and to gain from face-to-face collaboration even in an age of new technologies that make it less necessary to physically be in the presence of another human being (Glaeser, 2011).

A second perspective on the future of cities has been offered by John D. Kasarda, who believes that a new kind of city and a new kind of social interaction are emerging. An *aerotropolis* is a combination of giant airport, planned city, shipping facility, and business hub. In other words, the *aerotropolis* is an urban pattern in which cities are built around airports rather than airports being built around cities. According to this approach, the pattern of the twentieth century was city in the center, airport on the periphery. However, this pattern has shifted with the airport now in the center, and the city on the periphery because of extensive growth in jet travel, 24/7 workdays, overnight shipping and global business networks (Kasarda and Lindsay, 2011). Aerotropoli are now found in Seoul, Amsterdam, Dallas, Memphis, Washington, DC, and other cities where globalization has forever changed the nature of urban life. But, as these changes continue to occur, our social bonds in the "Instant Age" will become even stronger as we "invent new ways to find each other, follow each other, and come together" (Kasarda and Lindsay, 2011:414).

In the twenty-first century, the problems of cities are both global and local. In nations around the globe, the wealthiest people establish enclaves in which they enjoy safety and prosperity while the poorest people live in areas where neither safety nor prosperity is available. Urban change that will benefit the greatest number of people will require a revised way of looking at our social world. Fixing a pothole in the street or opening a shelter for the homeless, although a worthy activity, will not solve the problems of our cities. Larger structural changes in how we conduct business and how political decisions are made—and who benefits from that business and those decisions—must also occur.

SUMMARY

■ **How did urbanization come about?**

Urbanization—the process by which an increasing proportion of a population lives in cities rather than rural areas—began with industrialization. Before the Industrial Revolution, most people lived in sparsely populated rural areas, where they farmed. Industrialization led to the growth of cities, and urbanization brought about profound changes in societies and spawned new social problems such as housing shortages, overcrowding, unsanitary conditions, environmental pollution, and crime.

■ **How did mass suburbanization occur and what were the results?**

Mass suburbanization began with government efforts to correct the housing shortage that followed World War II. The Housing Act of 1949 gave incentives to builders to develop affordable housing, while government agencies made it possible for returning veterans to qualify for home mortgages. Other factors included the availability of inexpensive land, low-cost mass construction methods, new federally financed highway systems, inexpensive gasoline, racial tension in cities, and consumers' pent-up demands for single-family homes on individually owned lots. Mass suburbanization brought about a dramatic shift in the distribution of the U.S. population and set up an ongoing economic and racial division of interests between cities and suburbs.

■ **Why are many cities in fiscal crisis?**

In the past, large numbers of middle- and upper-income people moved out of the central cities to the suburbs, and retail businesses and corporations followed them to the suburbs or moved their operations abroad. The shrinking central cities were left with reduced sources of revenue. Many remaining central city residents were poor, unemployed, or older people living on fixed incomes who could not afford higher taxes. The global economic crisis in 2008–2009 contributed to the existing problems of cities, and the federal debt crisis of 2011 brought with it even more reduction in funding for local and state services and programs.

■ **Why is health care a crisis in U.S. cities?**

Health care is a problem in big cities because hospitals and other medical facilities are subject to cutbacks and closings when cities face economic problems. Also, people in impoverished sections of cities are more likely to become ill or injured because poverty is associated with many medical problems. Drug-related problems and HIV/AIDS put an added burden on facilities.

■ **Why is there a housing crisis in the United States and what is being done about it?**

When city agencies demand that a landlord comply with safety standards and building codes, many landlords abandon their buildings rather than make the investment.

A bigger reason, however, is that the United States has yet to find a way to provide safe, livable, low-income housing. The urban homesteading program, for example, has been criticized for promoting the interests of the building industry instead of actually helping people to get good housing. Federal housing projects have characteristically been monolithic high rises that intensify many problems and create new ones. In recent years, high rates of mortgage foreclosures and long-term unemployment have contributed to the housing crisis. Fewer people are able to own their own home, and the nation is still trying to dig out of the deep hole created by the subprime mortgage debacle.

■ **How great a problem is homelessness? Are there any solutions?**

Accurate data on the actual number of the homeless are extremely difficult to get because homeless people avoid interviews with census takers and social researchers. Annual surveys conducted by the U.S. Conference of Mayors continue to show that low-income individuals and persons of color are overrepresented in the homeless population, and the fastest-growing segment of the homeless population is families and children. Most experts agree that any long-term, successful solution to homelessness must take structural factors into account, especially low-income housing and mental health care.

■ **Why does residential segregation exist even if it is illegal?**

In some cases, housing segregation continues through custom. Sometimes landlords, homeowners, and white realtors perpetuate residential segregation through steering—guiding people of color to different neighborhoods than those shown to their white counterparts. Unequal property taxation is another kind of residential segregation problem. In the 2010s, demographers have suggested that residential segregation continues to exist because many white Americans are unwilling to live in neighborhoods that have a 40, 50, or 60 percent African American population.

■ **What are the major problems in global cities?**

Almost one out of every two people in the world today lives in a city. Rapid urban growth brings a wide variety of problems, including overcrowding, environmental pollution, and the disappearance of farmland. The exploitation of semi-peripheral nations by core nations and of peripheral nations by both semiperipheral and core nations serves to increase the urban problems in these nations. Core nations are dominant capitalist centers that are characterized by high levels of industrialization and urbanization. Peripheral nations depend on core nations for capital, have little or no industrialization (other than what is brought in by core nations), and have uneven patterns of urbanization. Semi-peripheral nations are more developed than peripheral nations but less developed than core nations.

■ **What are the functionalist and conflict perspectives on urban problems?**

Functionalists believe that today's urban problems are the result of mass migration from rural areas during the Industrial Revolution, large-scale immigration in the late nineteenth and early twentieth centuries, and mass suburbanization. One solution is to create metropolitan governments. Conflict theorists believe that cities grow or decline according to decisions made by capitalists and the political elite. In other words, conflict theorists use a political economy model. Urban problems can be reduced through political activism and organized resistance to oppressive conditions.

■ **What is the symbolic interactionist perspective on urban problems?**

Symbolic interactionists look at how people subjectively experience urban life. According to German sociologist Georg Simmel, urban life is so stimulating that people have no choice but to become somewhat insensitive to people and events around them. On the other hand, urban living gives people opportunities for individualism and autonomy. Sociologist Louis Wirth expanded on Simmel's ideas, saying that urbanism produces feelings of alienation and powerlessness. Herbert Gans concluded from his research that city life is a pleasure for some and a nightmare for others. The way to avoid alienation is to develop subcultural ties.

KEY TERMS

core nations, p. 377
edge city, p. 364
gentrification, p. 369

mechanical solidarity, p. 379
megalopolis, p. 365
organic solidarity, p. 379

peripheral nations, p. 378
semiperipheral nations, p. 378
subculture, p. 381

QUESTIONS FOR CRITICAL THINKING

1. Where do you live: in the core central city, an edge city, a suburb, a rural area, a megalopolis? What examples from your everyday life can you give that relate to the problems described in this chapter? Which sociological perspective do you think best explains the urban problems you observe?

2. The government has so far failed to provide adequate low-income and poverty-level housing. What new initiatives can you suggest?

3. Why do you think families with children are the fastest-growing segment of the homeless population in both urban and rural areas of this country? What can be done about the problem?

Succeed with MySocLab® www.mysoclab.com

The new MySocLab delivers proven results in helping students succeed, provides engaging experiences that personalize learning, and comes from a trusted partner with educational expertise and a deep commitment to helping students and instructors achieve their goals.

Here are a few activities you will find for this chapter:

Watch on **mysoclab.com**   **Core Concepts** video clips feature sociologists in action, exploring important concepts in the study of Social Problems. Watch:
- Challenges Facing Cities

Explore on **mysoclab.com**   **Social Explorer** is an interactive application that allows you to explore Census data through interactive maps. Explore:
- Social Explorer Activity: The Industrial Revolution and Urbanization

Read on **mysoclab.com**   **MySocLibrary** includes primary source readings from classic and contemporary sociologists. Read:
- Use of Black English and Racial Discrimination in Urban Housing Markets

17

Global Social Problems: War and Terrorism

THINKING SOCIOLOGICALLY

- Why do some people see war as a *problem* while others see war as a *solution* to certain social problems?

- What are the major types of international and domestic terrorism?

- Has the "war on terror" affected individual rights and liberties in the United States?

What does terrorism mean in the lives of people? Individuals going about their everyday activities . . . at work in New York, Washington, London, Oslo, or elsewhere in the world . . . when they hear a loud explosion and see billows of smoke in the sky that suddenly forebodes ill, casting a deep shadow over their life and that of millions of other people now and in the future. That is what a terrorist attack feels like in the life of an ordinary person . . . that life somehow may never be quite the same again!

I live near a military town. Some people try not to read the death notices in the newspaper. "It's too sad," they say,

"Even if you don't know the people . . . . 'Oh no, here's another one.'" This one was an honor student and a star athlete who played on a state high school championship football team. He always made his friends and family smile, and now he's dead—killed in combat operations in Afghanistan. But, his heroism it doesn't make it easier for his relatives, and even a stranger reading the paper, to absorb the loss that his death from war brings to the nation. What might have been?

Reading descriptions of terrorist attacks and death notices of people killed in war is difficult for many people. Terrorism and war are anguishing situations of great concern to individuals and to society. At national and international levels, terrorism and war are among the most pressing social problems of our times. Through sporadic and random acts of violence, terrorism creates widespread fear and injures or kills victims from all walks of life. In Oslo, two sequential terrorist attacks against civilians occurred in 2011 within a three- or four-hour time span: First, the car bomb exploded in the government quarter of Oslo, killing eight people and critically injuring or wounding about twenty-six. Then, a thirty-two-year-old gunman, Anders Behring Breivik—disguised as a police officer and using the bomb as a diversion—moved to another location, an island youth camp organized by the ruling Norwegian Labor Party, and killed sixty-nine camp participants in the deadliest attack in history by a lone gunman. Terrorist attacks such as this take a serious toll on human life and create billions of dollars in property losses, some of which—such as government office buildings, hospitals, schools, and residences—primarily serve a civilian population. Moreover, war is a major social problem because it causes loss of life. War also creates a massive economic burden on nations: Billions of dollars are spent in the war effort that could be used for domestic and international spending that might have benefited people and improved their quality of life.

Sometimes, war—or the threat of military action—is viewed as the way to remedy social problems such as terrorism, religious or ethnic conflicts, or nations encroaching on the territory of other nations. However, many believe that war is the *problem,* not the *solution* to many social ills of our time. In this chapter, we examine the sociological implications of war, terrorism, and future prospects for peace.

WAR AS A SOCIAL PROBLEM

What is war? *War* **is organized, armed conflict between nations or distinct political factions.** Although many people think of war as being between two nations (general warfare) or between rival factions located within a specific geographic area of a country (regional warfare), sociologists define war more broadly to include not only *declared* wars between nations or parties but also *undeclared* wars, civil and guerrilla wars, covert operations, and some forms of terrorism. Social scientists also say that societies that remain prepared at all times for war possess a *war system*—components of social institutions (e.g., the economy, government, and education) and cultural beliefs and practices that promote the development of warriors, weapons, and war as a normal part of the society and its foreign policy (Cancian and Gibson, 1990).

How, then, do social scientists define *peace*? Although some sociologists simply refer to peace as the absence of violent conflict, others, including the sociologists Francesca M. Cancian and James William Gibson (1990), argue that peace is a less clearly defined concept than war. According to Cancian and Gibson, most people agree that peace is highly desirable but often have different ideas of what constitutes peace. Some equate peace with harmonious relations in a world where there is no bloodshed between groups; but sometimes nations equate peace with prevailing in battle (Gibson and Cancian, 1990). Despite the problems associated with distinguishing between war and peace, we can conclude that both consist of actions and beliefs held by people like ourselves and that these actions and beliefs have serious consequences for individuals, groups, and nations.

The Nature of War

First and foremost, war is an institution that involves *violence*—behavior that is intended to bring pain, physical injury, and/or psychological stress to people or to harm or destroy property. As we have seen, violence is a component of many social problems, particularly violent crime and domestic violence. Both of these forms of *interpersonal violence* typically involve a relatively small number of people who are responding to a particular situation or pursuing their own personal goals. In contrast, war is a form of **collective violence that involves organized violence by people seeking to promote their cause or resist social policies or practices that they consider oppressive.**

Except for media coverage and for those who go into combat or are friends or relatives of those who go, war is only a concept to most people in the United States. Early in our country's history, during the Civil War or the war with Mexico, for example, just the opposite was true: War took place at home or close to home. But in the twentieth century, the nature of U.S. military action was transformed. First, wars were fought on foreign soil; second, vastly more U.S. military personnel were involved. In World War I, for example, about 5 million people served in the U.S. armed forces, and more than 16 million men and women served in World War II (Ehrenreich, 1997).

The two world wars were different from each other in a very significant way. In World War I, killing civilians was considered unduly violent, but in World War II, civilians were killed intentionally. The targeting of civilians during World War II added a new dimension to war (Hynes, 1997).

In 2001, terrorists with ties to al Qaeda used a different form of "air power"—hijacked commercial airplanes—to bring war and terror back to U.S. soil, intentionally killing thousands of civilians in the process. However, when the United States launched the so-called War on Terror, first in Afghanistan and then in Iraq, major combat again took place in nations other than the United States.

One of the most significant characteristics of war is its persistence. According to Ehrenreich (1997), World War II not only provided the United States with the opportunity to declare itself the "leader of the free world," but also gave political and economic leaders the impetus to perpetuate this nation's position as a world military superpower. Accordingly, Congress established defense spending as a national priority, and the U.S. military-industrial complex that had emerged during World War II became a massive industrial infrastructure that today produces an array of war-related goods such as uniforms, tanks, airplanes, and warships. The military-industrial complex flourished during the 1950s, when the international arms race brought about what became known as the *Cold War*—a conflict between nations based on military preparedness and the threat of war but not actual warfare. Between 1950 and the mid-1990s, the U.S. government responded to the perceived Soviet threat by spending approximately $10.2 trillion for its arms buildup. In 1991 alone, the defense industry received more than $121 billion in government contracts, giving some corporations a virtual monopoly over an entire market in which there was only one buyer (the U.S. government) and very few (if any) competitors.

The Consequences of War

The direct effects of war are loss of human life and serious physical and psychological effects on survivors. It is impossible to determine how many human lives have been lost in wars throughout human history. Were we to attempt to do so, we would need a more precise definition of what constitutes war, and we would have to assume that there would always be survivors available to count the dead (Hynes, 1997).

> **Explore the Concept**
> *Social Explorer Activity:*
> *War Veterans in Mississippi*
> on mysoclab.com

Despite these difficulties, social analyst Ruth Sivard (1991, 1993) tackled the problem in a limited way. She determined that 589 wars were fought by 142 countries between 1500 and 1990 and that approximately 142 million lives were lost. But according to Sivard, more lives were lost in wars during the twentieth century than in all of the other centuries combined. World War I took the lives of approximately 8 million combatants and 1 million civilians. The toll was much higher in World War II: More than 50 million people (17 million combatants and 35 million civilians) lost their lives. During World War II, U.S. casualties alone totaled almost 300,000, and more than 600,000 Americans were wounded.

If we look at the approximate number of deaths of U.S. military personnel alone in subsequent wars, these numbers are jarring: 34,000 in the Korean conflict and 47,000 in the Vietnam War. As of early August 2011, the total number of U.S. military fatalities in Operation Iraqi Freedom is 4,474, and in Operation Enduring Freedom (primarily Afghanistan) the total is 1,684. If we add to these the number of military personnel wounded in these two military operations, we have an additional 45,000 U.S troops injured in these conflicts (see Table 17.1).

Like troop casualties, civilian war deaths are another negative consequence of war. Because contemporary military strategy calls for deploying bombs and long-range missiles to eliminate the enemy's weapons production plants and supply centers, civilians are more likely to be killed than in the past because many plants are located in major cities. Civilian war casualties have grown in middle- and low-income nations because these countries are the primary sites for today's warfare.

TABLE 17.1 U.S. Armed Forces Personnel Casualties in Wars		
War	Battle Deaths (in thousands)	Wounds, Not Mortal (in thousands)
Spanish-American War	a	2
World War I	53	204
World War II	292	671
Korean conflict	34	103
Vietnam War	47	153
Operation Iraqi Freedom[b]	4.4	32
Operation Enduring Freedom (Afghanistan)[b]	1.7	13

[a] Fewer than 500 total deaths.
[b] Through August 2, 2011 (rounded).

Source: U.S. Census Bureau, 2008b; iCasualties .org, 2011

The trend toward more civilian casualties began in World War II and has continued in subsequent wars. Some analysts believe that civilians accounted for 75 percent of all war-related deaths in the 1980s and nearly 90 percent in the 1990s (Renner, 1993). Other social analysts disagree. In their book *The Future of War* (1996), George Friedman and Meredith Friedman argue that the use of precision-guided munitions ("smart weapons") in Operation Desert Storm (the military name for the 1991 Gulf War) made it possible for the United States to strike specific parts of particular buildings without striking noncombatants, hence keeping the civilian death count low. However, a demographer employed by the U.S. Census Bureau calculated that 40,000 Iraqi soldiers were killed during that war, but more than 80,000 Iraqi civilians, mostly women and children, were killed in air strikes—13,000 in "precision" bombing and 70,000 as a result of disease associated with the systematic destruction of water purification and sewage treatment systems in their country (Colhoun, 1992). Moreover,

This all-too-common scene of war reflects only a small part of the continuing devastation from our nation's lengthy and troubling wars. What do you think are the most important consequences of war?

many hospitals were damaged or destroyed. In some cases, when nearby power plants were hit, hospitals could no longer operate basic equipment or provide emergency medical care to people who had been injured by bombs (Burleigh, 1991).

Overall, the consequences of conventional war pales when compared to the consequences of an all-out nuclear war. The devastation would be beyond description. Although the development of nuclear weapons might have contributed to peace among the major world powers since the late 1940s, we can see the potentially destructive effects of nuclear war in the U.S. attacks on Hiroshima and Nagasaki, Japan. In an effort to end World War II, a U.S. aircraft dropped a 1.5-kiloton atomic bomb on Hiroshima, killing 130,000 people either instantly or over the next few months as a result of the deadly radiation that rained on the city (Erikson, 1994). Today, some nuclear warheads held by governments throughout the world are more than 4,000 times as powerful as the bombs that were dropped on Japan. In fact, scientists estimate that a nuclear war would kill more than 160 million people outright and that more than 1 billion people would die in the first few hours as a result of radiation poisoning, environmental contamination and destruction, and massive social unrest.

Even though an international treaty bans underground nuclear tests, it is believed that a number of nations are developing and stockpiling nuclear weapons. In the case of the 2003 U.S.-led invasion of Iraq, for example, the Bush administration claimed that the regime of the late Iraqi President Saddam Hussein was in possession of *weapons of mass destruction (WMDs)—* **nuclear, biological, chemical, or radiological weapons that can kill thousands of people and destroy vast amounts of property at one time**—and had to be overthrown as a preemptive measure to protect the United States and other nations. When no WMDs were found in Iraq, extensive public debate and much criticism of the Bush administration followed for having inaccurately represented the scope and immediacy of the threat posed (Moeller, 2004). Media coverage of the WMD debate is one example of how the media have framed stories about war (see Box 17.1).

Although concerns about weapons of mass destruction come and go in the United States, the FBI's assistant director of the Weapons of Mass Destruction Directorate has repeatedly stated that the probability the United States will be hit with a weapon of mass destruction attack at some point is 100 percent (Bilirakis and Lundgren, 2011). Moreover, he and other security analysts believe

Social Problems in the Media

Box 17.1

Political Spin and Media Framing of Wars: From "Going In Because of Weapons of Mass Destruction" to "Let Us Out! Let Us Out!"

March 17, 2003: Intelligence gathered by this and other governments leaves no doubt that the Iraq regime continues to possess and conceal some of the most lethal weapons ever devised.... [We] cannot live under the threat of blackmail. The terrorist threat to America and the world will be diminished the moment that Saddam Hussein is disarmed.

—Former President George W. Bush (2003b) in an address to the nation

March 19, 2003: The people of the United States and our friends and allies will not live at the mercy of an outlaw regime that threatens the peace with weapons of mass murder.

—Former President George W. Bush (2003a) in an address to the nation

June 25, 2008: What I do know is that war should only be waged when necessary, and the Iraq war was not necessary.

—Scott McClellan (2008), former White House press secretary, explaining that he had been mislead about the necessity of war with Iraq. He also stated that he unintentionally misinformed the media about the alleged importance of the war to spread democracy in the Middle East.

June 22, 2011: Tonight, I can tell you that we are fulfilling that commitment [in Afghanistan]. Thanks to our extraordinary men and women in uniform, our civilian personnel, and our many coalition partners, we are meeting our goals. As a result, starting next month, we will be able to remove 10,000 of our

Social Problems in the Media

Box 17.1 continued

troops from Afghanistan by the end of this year, and we will bring home a total of 33,000 troops by next summer, fully recovering the surge I announced at West Point. After this initial reduction, our troops will continue coming home at a steady pace as Afghan security forces move into the lead. Our mission will change from combat to support. By 2014, this process of transition will be complete, and the Afghan people will be responsible for their own security. . . . America, it is time to focus on nation building here at home.

—President Barack Obama (2011), describing the U.S. plan to leave Afghanistan as soon as possible and to focus on nation building at home instead

These statements by a former official in the Bush administration, by former President George W. Bush, and by President Barack Obama are about the wars in Iraq and Afghanistan. Looking first at media framing of Operation Iraqi Freedom, during the weeks before the 2003 U.S. invasion of Iraq, then-President George W. Bush conveyed the message to journalists and the general public that he believed an invasion of Iraq, with the subsequent removal of president Saddam Hussein from office and the establishment of a new government, were necessary to protect vital security interests of the United States and other nations. Through extensive media coverage of the president's comments on weapons of mass destruction and the imminent threat posed by Saddam Hussein, the War on Terror was launched, making Iraq the "big" international news story and overshadowing coverage of the U.S. military's then-unsuccessful search in Afghanistan for Osama bin Laden (see discussion of bin Laden's eventual death in this chapter).

Many news reporters and television anchors quickly embraced the language of war, including terms such as *weapons of mass destruction (WMDs)* and *War on Terror.* And, although he now apparently regrets his decision, Scott McClellan helped publicize this perspective to the world as the president's press secretary. However, in this case, *political spin* by McClellan and others was incorporated into *media framing* of news stories about war. *Spin* is the act of selectively describing or deliberately shading an event in a way that favors one partisan response over another or that attempts to control a negative political reaction before it fully emerges and becomes detrimental to the spinners' interests (based on Safire, 1993).

Unlike the extensive media coverage of the Iraq War, Operation Enduring Freedom in Afghanistan has received less coverage. According to one study by the Pew Research Center Project for Excellence in Journalism

(2011), the war in Afghanistan has been featured primarily in the media when something happens in Washington—such as a change in policy—not in Afghanistan. In other words, media framing of stories about the war in Afghanistan has focused on U.S. policy more than what is going on in that nation. In fact, the previous time the conflict in Afghanistan was among the top news stories was when *Rolling Stone* contained an article about how U.S. soldiers in an Army platoon allegedly killed innocent civilians. Since that time, the war in Afghanistan accounted for only 2 percent of all news reported in the U.S. mainstream media. When President Obama made his 2011 speech about troop withdrawal, media framing of the story primarily focused on U.S. policy in Afghanistan rather than violence or events on the ground. Some journalists framed the story in terms of "getting out of Afghanistan" and if this declaration was designed to improve the president's reelection bid. In the words of one blogger, "President Obama gave a speech tonight that was aimed at re-election—not victory in Afghanistan. In doing so, he made clear that he doesn't much care whether we accomplish our mission (making certain Afghanistan is not a safe haven for terrorists): *his* mission is ending a war so we can spend more money domestically" (Rubin, 2011).

From a sociological perspective, political spin and media framing are important concerns because these ideological activities may influence our beliefs on war, terrorism, and many other social problems.

Questions for Consideration

1. Should we be concerned if we think that political leaders and journalists are not providing us with the information we need to make informed judgments about what we think our country should do in regard to domestic and international problems?

2. What part does national security play in the kind of information we receive from the government and the media? Is national security a more pressing priority today than the right of individuals to know what is going on in their nation? What do you think?

Independent Research

Search various media sources and the Internet to find other examples of political leaders' statements (direct quotes) on a social issue and identify what kinds of media framing you believe journalists used to convey this message or, if relevant, to shift the focus of the message to reflect the ideological perspective of the journalist and/or the publication that he or she represents.

that the weapons employed are more likely to be chemical, biological, or radiological rather than nuclear. The FBI investigates more than a dozen U.S. cases each year where investigators conclude that the alleged perpetrator did have intent to use WMDs. Although a WMD attack might be perpetrated by a group of terrorists, analysts and law enforcement officials with the FBI and Homeland Security believe that the lone wolf who does not need other people is the one we should fear the most. Individuals such as this can sneak around and wreak havoc on other people's lives, leaving a path of deadly destruction much like the work of the Oslo bomber (see Box 17.2). According to the FBI, planning a nuclear attack is more difficult than other kinds of mass destruction:

A terrorist bent on detonating a nuclear weapon would have to successfully negotiate a series of steps. He would have to find an expert with the right knowledge. He would have to find the right material. He would have to bring the device into the country, and he would have to evade detection programs. (Kessler, 2011)

Patriotism—supporting "our troops" and "our cause"—is another consequence of war. In this way, war is functional because it provides an external enemy for people to hate. A dysfunctional aspect of war, however, is that the enemy is dehumanized—that is, seen as an object to obliterate rather than as another human being. According to sociologist Tamotsu Shibutani (1970), prolonged conflicts such as wars tend to be turned into a struggle between good and evil; one's own side is, of course, righteous and just, while the other side has no redeeming social or moral value.

In 2009, more than $35.3 billion were paid to U.S. veterans who were receiving compensation from the government for service-connected disabilities (meaning injuries they sustained in war-related activities) (U.S. Census Bureau, 2010). However, not all injuries that are sustained in wars are physical. We have no accurate count of the soldiers and civilians—of all nations involved—who experience psychological trauma that affects them the remainder of their lives. According to a RAND Corporation study, about one in five service members returning from deployment are thought to have symptoms of

Social Problems in Global Perspective

Anti-Muslim Blogs That Travel around the World

In July 2011, the media reported that Anders Behring Breivik, a thirty-two-year-old man accused of the bombing of a government office complex and the killing of scores of young people at a summer camp in Norway, was deeply influenced by a small group of American bloggers who have warned people about the threat from Islam. Breivik reportedly included numerous quotations from these blogs in the 1,500-page manifesto that was made public after his arrest.

As is true of all acts of violence and terrorism, many disturbing issues emerged in the aftermath of one of the worst rampages in the history of Oslo, Norway. One fact in the Oslo case is the role that online forums and blogs may have played in reinforcing Breivik's anti-Muslim thoughts.

Throughout his planning of these horrendous acts that killed about 77 people and injured more than 150 others, Breivik outlined his beliefs in a manifesto that eventually grew to more than 1,500 pages and urged Europeans to engage in modern-day crusades against Islam. In the manifesto, he quoted from anti-Islamic Internet posts written by European and U.S. bloggers such as Robert

Spencer, who maintains the Jihad Watch website and portrays Islam as a pronounced threat to the West (Shane, 2011). Breivik also quotes from blogs known as Atlas Shrugs and Gates of Vienna (named for the 1683 siege of Vienna by Muslim fighters). Both were full of anti-Islamist commentary until Gates of Vienna was shut down following the 2011 Norway killings (Shane, 2011). Specifically, the commonality between these websites and Breivik's own anti-Muslim ideology is the belief that immigration from Muslim countries to Scandinavia and the rest of Europe poses a grave threat to Western culture and that something must be done to end this plague.

In addition to blogs and websites, Breivik allegedly was influenced by the manifesto of the so-called Unabomber, a U.S.-based domestic terrorist named Ted Kaczynski, who sent bombs and bomb threats to universities and airlines between 1978 and 1995. The Unabomber's manifesto was published in the *New York Times* and the *Washington Post* in a highly unusual agreement with Kaczynski. Newspaper editors reached an agreement with the Unabomber that his manifesto would be published in the papers if he

posttraumatic stress disorder (PTSD) or major depression. The symptoms of PTSD include difficulty sleeping and concentrating; anxiety; and recurring flashbacks or nightmares, many of which are triggered by loud, sudden noises such as thunder, automobiles backfiring, or other things that sound like gunshots or explosions. When some stimulus triggers a flashback, the individual reexperiences the horror of some deeply traumatic event. Some medical specialists link high rates of drug abuse and suicide among returning veterans with PTSD.

Problems with PTSD have been pronounced among Vietnam veterans, and an older congressional study found that more than 475,000 of the 3.5 million Vietnam veterans had severe symptoms of PTSD, and another 350,000 had moderate symptoms (Witteman, 1991). It is too soon to estimate how many veterans of Operation Iraqi Freedom and Operation Enduring Freedom (Afghanistan) will suffer from the potentially long-term effects of this disorder. Early estimates of Iraq veterans seeking treatment of PTSD are as high as 35 percent, particularly because of the higher rate of deployment cycles in the Iraq War as compared with any other war

since World War II (ScienceDaily, 2009). Some public finance experts estimate that the total cost of health care and disability compensation to veterans of the Iraq and Afghanistan wars combined will total as much as $1 trillion over the next forty years (Dao, 2011).

Although we cannot put a price tag on loss of life, physical disability, or psychological trauma associated with war, we know that the direct economic costs of war are astronomical. Consider, for example, that the 2011 federal budget allocated $712 billion for the Department of Defense, which includes, among other things, $549 billion in discretionary funding, $4 billion in mandatory funding, and $159 billion for military operations in Iraq and Afghanistan (Harrison, 2011).

DID YOU KNOW

$700 billion in defense spending would pay for:

- Tuition for 5.4 million students at a public university.
- Rebuilding New Orleans and the Gulf Coast after Hurricane Katrina.
- 2,000 McDonald's apple pies for every single American.

Box 17.2

would desist in his terrorist activities. In the 2010s, counterterrorism analysts now claim that Kaczynski's writings, coupled with many anti-Muslim screeds on the Internet, further fueled Breivik's militant, right-wing extremist worldview to the extent that he committed these deadly acts. Website owners and bloggers such as Robert Spence argue otherwise, claiming that their sites and blogs have been unfairly blamed for influencing Breivik.

At this time, much more is *not* known about what happened in Norway or why it happened than about what *did* happen. However, regardless of the outcome, this case points out how small the world is with newer communications technologies and blogs that can provide others with our most personal feelings and beliefs, even when these perceptions run afoul of the rules for a civil society and world and instead move into the realm of Muslim-bashing (or any other kind of bashing, for that matter) and that deaths of other human beings or martyrdom for oneself is a worthy cause in the fight to save one's own culture and way of life from such evils as multiculturalism and religious diversity. For persons such as Breivik who want to reverse

the "Arabization" of Europe, terrorist acts are the way to become a part of history and make people aware of what is going on in the world around them.

Questions for Consideration

1. Why are sociologists concerned about the terrorism on a global basis? What can we learn from terrorism in other nations?

2. To what extent might counterterrorism efforts in countries such as the United States contribute to anti-Muslim and anti-Islamic sentiment in this country and around the world?

3. What, if any, balance can we strike between establishing policies that protecting our nation and those policies and ideologies that reinforce anti-Muslim and anti-Arab sentiments in the United States and Europe?

4. To what extent might Islamophobia (fear, hatred, and/or violent acts against persons who are Muslim or Islamic) be used to justify laws and policies in many nations?

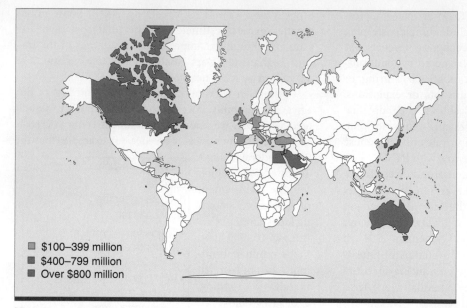

Map 17.1   U.S. military sales to foreign governments, 2008 (in millions of dollars)
Source: U.S. Census Bureau, 2010.

$100–399 million
$400–799 million
Over $800 million

Today, more middle- and low-income nations around the world are involved in defense buildups. Map 17.1 shows the nations that purchase military equipment and supplies from the United States. In 2010, these nations spent about $2.15 trillion on military-related purchases (GlobalSecurity.org, 2011).

MILITARY TECHNOLOGY AND WAR

War is conducted on the basis of the technology that is available in given societies at a specific point in time. However, wars are not necessarily won or lost on the basis of military technology alone. In the Vietnam War, for example, many factors contributed to the inability of the United States to declare a victory. Among these factors were conflicting ideologies and war strategies set forth by government officials and the fact that U.S. troops could not readily distinguish the Viet Cong ("the enemy") from the South Vietnamese ("the ally") (Hynes, 1997). Similarly, efforts by the U.S. government in the 2010s to complete the military mission this country began when the George W. Bush administration ordered U.S. troops to Iraq to find weapons of mass destruction and remove Sadam Hussain from power have been slowed by "frequent bombings, assassinations and a resurgence in violence by Shiite militias" (Jakes, 2011).

In fact, recent reports suggest that Iraq was more dangerous in 2011 than it was in the previous year, suggesting that efforts to leave Iraq in a better position than when U.S. troops arrived and war commenced may be a difficult, if not impossible, task (Jakes, 2011). Withdrawal at the end of 2011, ordered by the Obama administration, appeared to be less certain at the time of this writing given the increased terrorism and warfare that is occurring on some fronts in Iraq. Like Viet Nam before it, the Iraq War (officially referred to as Operation Iraqi Freedom) had vague, ill-defined beginnings, and it appears that the ending may be similar.

The most significant military technology is referred to as the **weapons system, which comprises a weapons platform (e.g., a ship, aircraft, or tank), a weapon (e.g., a gun, missile, or torpedo), and the means of command and communication** (Kaldor, 1981). The importance of the weapons system is pointed out by George Friedman and Meredith Friedman (1996:25): "The rise and fall of strategically significant weapons systems is the history of the rise and fall of nations and epochs. The **strategically significant weapon is the one that brings force to bear in such a way that it decisively erodes the war-making capability of the enemy."** According to Friedman and Friedman (1996:25–26), the use of strategically significant weapons determines the "winners" and "losers" in war:

Let us assume that the greatest threat presented by the enemy is the ability to move weapons platforms around quickly, and that by destroying his petrochemical production facilities we could impede his mobility. Strategically significant weapons would be those that would destroy petrochemical plants. So, in World War II, bombers with the range to reach these targets were such weapons. In Vietnam, the enemy's war-making ability could not be decisively crippled by the same sort of long-range bombers. There, the strategic weapon was North Vietnamese infantry, able to move stealthily and impose a rate of attrition on American troops that was politically unacceptable to the United States. The failure to recognize strategically decisive weapons is catastrophic. The Soviet Union's illusion that intercontinental ballistic missiles and swarms of tanks were strategically decisive led it to disaster.

In other words, though factors other than military technology may determine a nation's ability to win or lose a war, military technology is a dominant factor.

For example, in the fourteenth century, Europeans used a simple new technology—black powder, an explosive made from charcoal, sulfur, and saltpeter—to overwhelm larger armies. Black powder could destroy the enemy's walls and other fortifications. When it was discovered that black powder could be exploded at the base of a metal tube and propel a projectile to a target, the gun became the basis of European and Western military power. Gunpowder made it possible for a small number of troops to overwhelm a much larger army that had only nonexplosive weapons (G. Friedman and Friedman, 1996).

Although black powder weapons remained the primary type of weaponry for many years, the platform that was used for carrying the weapons changed over time. With the development of such weapons platforms as coal-powered ships, petroleum-driven ships, and railroad locomotives, it became possible to move explosive-based technology virtually anywhere to destroy enemy forces. From the early 1900s to the end of World War II, the battleship, the tank, and the bomber were the primary weapons platforms. Today, the battleship has been replaced by the aircraft carrier, but the tank and the bomber continue to be important sources of weapons transportation.

As the U.S. military sought to enhance traditional weapons platforms to deal with enemy threats, new precision-guided munitions were developed, rendering many of the older ideologies and technologies obsolete, including the concept of the battlefield. No longer do foot soldiers have to engage in skirmishes for war to take place; missiles can be fired from sites located 10,000 miles from the target (G. Friedman and Friedman, 1996). Unfortunately, the same technology that makes possible the expanded battlefield brings with it a new system of intelligence that makes global warfare possible. According to Friedman and Friedman (1996:37–38), sensors, guidance systems, satellite communications, and other technologies that make it possible to hit a target 10,000 miles away also make it possible for weapons fired from one continent to guide themselves to targets on other continents very quickly and relatively inexpensively:

> The hyperintelligent, hypersonic, long-range projectile. . . . will destroy the old way of making war, while securing the new geopolitical system for generations. Where guns were inaccurate, these projectiles are extraordinarily precise. Where guns must travel to within miles of a target before firing, precision munitions can devastate an enemy from any distance. Where gun/petrochemical technology requires total commitment of resources and mass production, precision munitions require technical skill. The new weaponry places inherent limits on war, both in terms of scope and in terms of damage to unintended targets. The age of total war is at an end and a more limited type of war is at hand.

Clearly, the nature of warfare has changed dramatically over the past century as older technologies have become obsolete, and newer weaponry, such as hyperintelligent projectiles with extraordinary precision, has been introduced. As the nature of warfare continues to evolve in the twenty-first century, even newer technologies, such as unmanned aerial vehicles (UAVs) or drones—pilotless aircraft operated by remote control—have been increasingly employed by the U.S. government to track down suspected militants and terrorists in remote, unreachable areas, as well as to strike enemy leaders, troops, and infrastructure. Some drones are unarmed and used primarily for surveillance; others are armed predator drones that hunt down a target and get it. Drones have a unique ability to fly lower and get better visibility on targets than other kinds of aircraft, and they are uniquely suited for use in high-density, urban areas (Defensetech.org, 2011). UAVs have been employed in nations such as Iraq, Afghanistan, Pakistan, Yemen, Somalia, and Libya.

As drone technology becomes more affordable and accessible, the popularity of drones will probably increase because of their stealth nature, the lack of need for human pilots who may be injured or killed, and the drone's unique ability to stalk an enemy and bring it down before the enemy knows what has happened. For example, the high-flying Global Hawk jet, which is designed to slip through the air at 60,000 feet and carry cameras and eavesdropping gear, costs a whopping $218 million for each plane, compared with $28 million for the Reaper, the Air Force's largest armed drone (Drew, 2011). The Reaper will also be replacing the older

U-2 spy planes that were created in the 1950s to monitor nuclear sites in what was then the Soviet Union. Some of these planes are still used for surveillance in North Korea and Iran from outsider the borders of those nations (Drew, 2011).

Although drones are changing the nature of warfare because they can be remotely piloted, they are not without their critics. Some analysts believe that drones have the potential to invade people's privacy, including U.S. citizens who might be observed without being aware that they are under surveillance. Another second major criticism involves the deadly effects of armed, predator drones, which may kill only militants and terrorists but also produce extensive "collateral damage," a term that refers to civilian casualties and destruction of non-combat-related locations such as private homes, hospitals, schools, and other public property.

According to some experts, the "drone race" is just starting with about fifty countries using surveillance drones. However, few countries are using armed drones in the same way that the United States does. The involvement of other nations in the drone buildup opens up a new world for warfare and potential terrorism. Many countries have developed and deployed various kinds of unmanned aerial vehicles. In the future drones will be even more accessible to various nations because the components are now more available than they have been in the past. If we look at recent technology that we use daily, such as smart phones, laptops, and tablets, we can see how many components for equipment used in surveillance and warfare may be no farther away than the local electronics store. This creates new concerns because it places potentially dangerous technology in the hands of terrorists or others who operate outside of the control of any governmental regulatory body, or in the hands of governmental officials in a nation whose interests do not mesh with those of the United States.

Although high-technology weaponry used in warfare has been the topic of widespread political debate and extensive media coverage, less attention has been paid to the potential significance of poison gas manufacturing and the use of chemical and biological toxic agents by domestic and international terrorists.

GLOBAL TERRORISM

Terrorism is the use of calculated, unlawful physical force or threats of violence against a government, organization, or individual to gain some political, religious, economic, or social objective. Terrorist

Terrorist events, like the attacks in Mumbai in November 2008, exact a high toll on people and social life around the world.

tactics include bombing, kidnapping, hostage taking, hijacking, assassination, and extortion. Although terrorists sometimes attack government officials and members of the military, they more often target civilians as a way of pressuring the government.

As collective violence, terrorism shares certain commonalities with war. Both terrorism and war are major threats to world stability and domestic safety. Terrorism and war also extract a massive toll on individuals and societies by producing rampant fear, widespread loss of human life, and extensive destruction of property.

One form of terrorism—political terrorism—is actually considered a form of unconventional warfare. *Political terrorism* uses intimidation, coercion, threats of harm, and other violent attempts to bring about a significant change in or overthrow of an existing government. There are three types of political terrorism: revolutionary terrorism, repressive terrorism, and state-sponsored terrorism.

***Revolutionary terrorism* refers to acts of violence against civilians that are carried out by enemies of a government who want to bring about political change.** Some dissident groups believe that if they perpetrate enough random acts of terrorism, they will achieve a political goal. Modern terrorism is not always based in a single country, as we learned from efforts to apprehend Osama bin Laden and the al Qaeda network, who have been accused of planning the September 11, 2001, terrorist attacks on the United States, as well as attacks at other sites associated with U.S. interests and citizens. In fact, it was some of the newer technology previously discussed that eventually helped the United States bring down Osama bin Laden on May 1, 2011. On that date, two MH-60 Black Hawk helicopters left Jalalabad Air Field in eastern Afghanistan and flew into Pakistan on a covert mission to kill bin Laden. At that time, Pakistan had all their air defenses focused on India, making it possible for the helicopters to slip in unnoticed and arrive at a compound where bin Laden had been living. A team of Navy SEALS known as the Naval Special Warfare Development Group then raided the house and shot Osama bin Laden after killing his adult son and several guards armed with AK-47s. So, nine years, seven months, and twenty days after the September 11 terrorist attacks, Osama bin Laden was no longer one of the world's revolutionary terrorists, and on May 6, al Qaeda confirmed his death, promising Americans that "their joy will turn to sorrow and their tears will mix with blood" (see Schmidle, 2011).

How do officials find terrorists? Money usually is a crucial ingredient in terrorism, and following the so-called money trail has been a key way in which law enforcement agencies have sought to apprehend those accused of violent terrorist attacks and of financing terrorism. Underground economic activities that allegedly support terrorism in the United States have been traced to seemingly innocent religious organizations and a variety of other groups in this country and elsewhere.

Unlike revolutionary terrorism, *repressive terrorism* **is conducted by a government against its own citizens for the purpose of protecting an existing political order.** Repressive terrorism characterized many of the uprisings in the "Arab spring" of 2011; government forces fired weapons on their own people in the streets and were accused of abductions, rapes, and torture in Tunisia, Iran, Egypt, Libya, Syria, and Bahrain, among others.

In the third type of political terrorism, *state-sponsored terrorism,* **a government provides financial resources, weapons, and training for terrorists who conduct their activities in other nations.** Nations that use terrorism as a means of political expression have been of concern to the United States for many years. Throughout the first two decades of the twenty-first century, countries such as Iran, Iraq, Syria, Libya, Cuba, North Korea, and Sudan have remained on a list of what the U.S. Department of State considers to be state sponsors of international terrorism. Returning to Libya and Muammar Qaddafi, for example, this dictator provided money and training for terrorist groups such as the Arab National Youth Organization. This group was responsible for skyjacking a Lufthansa airplane over Turkey and forcing the Bonn government to free the surviving members of Black September, a terrorist group that was responsible for killing Israeli Olympic athletes in the 1970s. Since that time, Qaddafi has been accused of many acts of state-sponsored terrorism, particularly in recent years in the North African country of Misrata.

In 2011, the United Nations sanctioned Qaddafi and the United States recognized the Transitional National Council as the legitimate government of Libya, not Muammar Qaddafi. In the 2010s, state-sponsored terrorism is a concern around the world. India has demanded that Pakistan not allow territory under its control to be used for terrorism directed against India. Similar concerns are shared by other nations, including the United States, which alleged that Pakistan had been harboring Osama bin Laden for several years prior to his death.

Cyberattacks have also been officially recognized as a new form of state-sponsored terrorism. In 2011, the Pentagon announced that computer sabotage coming from another country can be considered an act of war and that traditional military force may be used in responding to such an act when it is perpetrated against the United States (Gorman and Barnes, 2011). In the words of one Pentagon official, "If you shut down our power grid, maybe we will put a missile down one of your smokestacks" (quoted in Gorman and Barnes, 2011). And this issue will remain relevant throughout the 2010s because there is strong evidence that a number of acts of cyberhacking by other countries has occurred in the United States. A computer security firm's analysis of computer hacking drew international attention when researchers announced that, in the more than seventy cases of hacking of corporate or U.S. government computers they examined, the hacker was a "nation-state." Their conclusion led to numerous allegations against other countries, including China and Russia, which were believed to be responsible for some of the hacker attacks. In 2011, both the Pentagon and Lockheed Martin, a major military contractor, were the victims of infiltration of their computer systems, raising new concerns that U.S. defense secrets were now known by potential adversaries.

Further contributing to the possibility of state-sponsored terrorism in the form of cyberhacking is the era of cloud computing, in which important information is stored on servers that are accessible to a wider array of "online pickpockets" (Boudreau, 2011). Cyberterrorism is possible when hackers are able to steal government files, such U.S. Department of Defense files that were hacked. Although analysts state that many governments are involved in cyberespionage, how these governments use the data is a pressing social problem because it could affect human life, national security, and the nation's infrastructure. According to Secretary of Defense Leon Panetta, the United States faces the possibility of a "digital Pearl Harbor" that could disrupt U.S. electric power grids, banks and transportation networks (Boudreau, 2011). A major problem with cracking down on cyber-terrorism in its many forms is how difficult the attacks are to track and trace back to their origins, often making it impossible to determine who is behind them (Pilkington, 2011). However, it is important that nations persist in identifying the persons and countries responsible for cyberattacks because officials for the CIA's Counter Terrorism Center believe that al Qaeda will focus on cyber-space in their global jihad because it is "comparatively remote, comparatively safer than strapping on a bomb" (quoted in Ferran, 2011). One of the cyberattacks that awakened security experts to the dangerous of cyberter-rorism was the 2010 Stuxnet computer worm that alleg-edly attacked and damaged an Iranian nuclear facility.

Although many terrorist attacks in recent years have been attributed to people from other nations, our country also has a history of domestic terrorism.

TERRORISM IN THE UNITED STATES

Scholars have identified four types of terrorism that offer the greatest potential threat to U.S. citizens:

1. *Foreign-sponsored terrorism on U.S. soil.* Because of their unprecedented magnitude and destruction, the terrorist attacks in 2001 garnered more media cover-age—both in this country and abroad—than virtually any other event in U.S. history. Since the date of those attacks, for which responsibility was claimed by al Qaeda, a multinational terrorist organization led by Osama bin Laden, terrorism and/or potential terror-ist attacks have routinely captured newspaper head-lines and top billing on other media sources such as television and the Internet.

2. *Domestic-sponsored terrorism.* Although less atten-tion has been paid to "home-grown" terrorists since 2001, the FBI and other federal agencies remain con-cerned about domestic groups that could engage in acts of terrorism for political and religious reasons such as violent protests against abortion clinics. The worst act of domestic terrorism in the United States took place in 1995 when a bomb destroyed the Alfred P. Murrah Federal Building in Oklahoma City, tak-ing 168 lives and injuring 850 other people. The lon-gest series of terrorist acts in the United States was carried out by the "Unabomber," later identified as Theodore Kaczynski, who allegedly mailed sixteen bombs that caused three deaths and twenty-two

injuries. Primary targets for the self-described anar-chist's bombs were business executives and univer-sity researchers. It is believed that likely targets of internal terrorist groups today (such as radical envi-ronmental organizations) might include academic research facilities, government facilities, and differ-ent components of the infrastructure such as water plants, power stations, and pipelines.

3. *Terrorism in other nations that might affect U.S. citi-zens who are residing or traveling in other countries.* The U.S. Department of State and media outlets worldwide continually issue travel advisories for U.S. citizens abroad for fear that some terrorist group might attack tourist sites or other public accommo-dations that are frequently visited by U.S. citizens. The government also is concerned that U.S. embassies in other countries might be attacked by terrorists, and from time to time the media report on temporary embassy closings or extra precautions that are being taken to protect certain embassies.

4. *Cyberwarfare and information terrorism—aggressive assaults on a government's computers and IT infra-structure that lead to the copying or destruction of records and/or computer systems.* Terrorist-sponsored computer hackers could bring down entire educa-tional, economic, and governmental information networks if information terrorists are able to bypass built-in safeguards. By widening laws governing armed conflict to include cyberwarfare and allow-ing the United States to respond with force to any such threats to national security, Pentagon officials believe that this will send a message to hackers that they will be prosecuted and punished if they attack this country's nuclear reactors, pipelines, or public networks such as mass transport systems (Pilkington, 2011). As of this writing, many people believe that the United States is particularly vulnerable to state-sponsored cyberattacks, particularly from China and Russia.

What is the best way to let people know of a potential terrorist attack? Different agencies of the U.S. government have grappled with this problem, and in 2002 the Department of Homeland Security announced a color-coded system displaying five levels of alert: severe, high, elevated, guarded, and low. For the most part, the nation stayed in the elevated to high categories for a number of years to show the potential for an act of terrorism at any time or place. Although all of us want to be informed by governmental authorities and the media when our lives or homes may be in danger, the more frequently we are reminded of possible terrorism and bombarded by daily coverage of this sort, the more difficult it is to put fear out of our minds. As a result, Homeland Security decided to scrap the color-coded terror alerts in 2009. Is there a middle ground in times such as these? This question will remain a concern as communications technologies make it possible for news—whether fact or fiction—to reach us instantaneously and without filters from persons who may (or may not) have accurate information about possible threats. Recall, however, that terrorists—as well as the general public—have access to media sources, and widespread coverage of terrorist activities might encourage terrorists to act or might provide them with helpful information for circumventing existing safeguards against such attacks.

EXPLANATIONS OF WAR AND TERRORISM

What causes collective violence such as war and terrorism? Can war and acts of terrorism be reduced? Despite centuries of war and terrorism, we still know little about the origins of violence or how to reduce such acts (Turpin and Kurtz, 1997). In Chapter 9 we discussed biological, psychological, and sociological explanations for violence. We will now examine these approaches as they relate to war and terrorism.

Biological Perspectives

Analysts who use a biological framework for explaining war and terrorism emphasize that people inherit a tendency (or predisposition) toward aggressive behavior, which can culminate in warfare or terrorist acts. Contemporary policy makers who trace violent behavior to chemical or physical abnormalities such as a brain lesion, brain dysfunction, endocrine disorder, hormonal imbalance, or other genetic factors are taking such an approach (Turpin and Kurtz, 1997).

Perhaps the most widely known advocate for biological explanations of war and terrorism is anthropologist Konrad Lorenz (1966:261), who stated, "To the humble seeker of biological truth there cannot be the slightest doubt that human militant enthusiasm evolved out of a communal defense response of our prehuman ancestors." According to Lorenz, just as our hominid ancestors confronted and repelled predatory animals, we have an almost instinctive desire to protect ourselves from our perceived enemies. Therefore, people engage in terrorism or fight wars when stimuli trigger

Do human beings have biological predispositions toward aggressive behavior? How do analysts using a biological perspective differ in their answers to this question as compared to those using a sociological perspective?

their predisposition toward aggression. Lorenz believes that although the predisposition toward violence was functional at one time because it ensured survival of the "fittest," this instinct is a problem in contemporary societies. Philosopher William James suggested that the kind of courage and altruism people bring to war could be better directed toward some more worthy enterprise (cited in Ehrenreich, 1997).

Some scholars have sought to identify genetic influences on violence and warfare. Among the earliest was sociobiologist Edward O. Wilson (1975), who believed that aggressive tendencies are part of human nature but that people can learn not to engage in violent behavior. More recently, anthropologists Richard Wrangham and Dale Peterson, who study aggression in animals and humans, published their findings in *Demonic Males: Apes and the Origins of Human Violence* (1996). According to Wrangham and Peterson, both human and nonhuman animals, such as chimpanzees, have the inherent capacity to commit premeditated assaults. Premeditated violence is used by humans (especially males) and lower animals to intimidate enemies, beat them up, and destroy their ability to bring future challenges. Wrangham and Peterson believe that female chimps and humans are less apt to murder or take part in war. Women were deliberately excluded from participating in war-related activities in fifty-eight of the sixty-seven human societies that Wrangham and Peterson studied (Wheeler, 1997). But this brings up another question: Do women not participate in war by choice, or are they categorically excluded by social norms and customs? More research is needed to answer this and other questions about a biological origin for warfare and terrorism. Thus far, no scientific evidence conclusively demonstrates than humans are innately violent or that biological factors are more important than social factors in producing violent behavior (Turpin and Kurtz, 1997).

Psychological Perspectives

Psychologists have provided significant insights into violence, but they do not focus on collective violence in the form of war and terrorism. In fact, most psychological explanations emphasize individualistic sources of violence, resulting from such causes as abnormal psychological development. For example, Sigmund Freud contended that violent behavior occurs when the three aspects of the human personality come into conflict with one another. If the individual's *id* (unconscious drives and instincts) conflicts with the *superego* (internalized social values), and the *ego* (the mediator between the id and superego) is unable to resolve the conflict, violent behavior might ensue, particularly if the individual has an overdeveloped id, which contains the aggressive drive, or an underdeveloped superego (Turpin and Kurtz, 1997).

Contemporary social psychologists generally believe that both individual and cultural factors must be considered in explaining why people go to war or engage in terrorism. Some social psychologists focus primarily on the processes by which cultural influences make some individuals, but not others, behave violently. From these studies, they conclude that it is easier to harm enemies when they have been depersonalized (Milgram, 1974). People also are more likely to behave violently when they are placed in positions in which they have a great deal of power and authority over others (Haney, Banks, and Zimbardo, 1984).

An interesting insight into the psychological processes that are involved in violence comes from the work of Robert Jay Lifton (1997), who studied violence inflicted by Nazi doctors at Auschwitz. According to Lifton, these doctors—who had previously been committed to saving lives—were able to commit horrible atrocities because of the psychological principle of *doubling*—"the division of the self into two functioning wholes, so that a part-self acts as an entire self" (Lifton, 1997:30). Through the process of doubling, the doctors

could embrace evil without restraint, remorse, or guilt and, at the same time, be loving parents and normal members of society. According to Lifton (1997), not only can doubling save the life of a soldier in combat who is confronted with the enemy, but it also can contribute to extreme wartime brutalities and the embracing of evil.

If social psychologists are correct in believing that individual personality factors contribute to war and terrorism, then how can such behavior be reduced? The answer is to emphasize social and cultural factors that head off violence and deadly conflict. In other words, societies should deemphasize violence and encourage peaceful behavior in daily life. However, social critic Barbara Ehrenreich (1997:76) believes that our impulse to make war resides in a deep ancestral memory of our role as prey and that we live in a society that still glorifies such impulses:

> Why . . . would human beings want to reenact . . . the terror of predation? Probably for the same reason that "civilized" people today pay to see movies in which their fellow humans are stalked and devoured by flesh-eating ghouls, vampires, and extraterrestrial monsters. Nothing gets our attention like the prospect of being ripped apart, sucked dry, and transformed into another creature's meal.

Although she concedes that people enjoy such fictional encounters because they are "fun," Ehrenreich also thinks that today's films and television programming pose interesting questions about why many people enjoy watching acts of violence and terrorism.

Ehrenreich's analysis brings up a larger question: Why are many people relatively positive about war, and why do they seemingly condone the violence associated with war? According to sociologists Jennifer Turpin and Lester R. Kurtz (1997:1), many people are deeply ambivalent about war because they believe that the only way to fight violence is with more violence:

> Since most people believe they can be secure only by repelling violence with violence, they simultaneously deplore and condone it. The use of violence is considered taboo almost universally in modern society except under certain conditions. It is widely abhorred yet widely used to promote social control in settings ranging from the household to the global socioeconomic order. Because of that ambivalence, elaborate social mechanisms have been institutionalized to distinguish between legitimate and illegitimate violence. Not only are individuals threatened by violence, but so are whole

societies, and now—in the nuclear age—the species itself. Ironically, the very structures supposedly created to provide security against violence instead threaten everyone.

Sociological Explanations

Sociological explanations for war and terrorism use a functionalist, conflict, or interactionist perspective. We'll look at all three, starting with the functionalist.

The Functionalist Perspective

Some functionalist explanations focus on the relationship between social disorganization and warfare or terrorism. According to these explanations, disorganization in social institutions, for example, the government, contributes to overall political instability. Militia members believe that the U.S. government no longer serves the purpose for which it was intended, namely, to protect the individual's rights and freedom. In their eyes, the U.S. government has become dysfunctional, and they engage in acts of terrorism to undermine the government so that it will change radically or be abolished.

Other functionalists focus on the functions that war serves. Looked at from this perspective, war can settle disputes between nations. However, in the age of nuclear weaponry, many nations seek other means to deal with their disagreements. Among these means are *economic sanctions,* cutting off all trade. In some instances, the United States has imposed economic sanctions, rather than engaging in war or military action, against countries engaging in terrorism, environmental violations, abuse of workers' rights, regional strife, drug trafficking, human and political rights abuses, and nuclear proliferation (Myers, 1997). However, some political analysts argue that the United States is cutting off its nose to spite its face when it imposes economic sanctions against other governments: Economic sanctions are dysfunctional for another social institution—the economy. Also, even though the United States has used sanctions against other nations from its earliest days, corporations are concerned that the sanctions deny them access to the world's markets and the profits in those markets (Myers, 1997).

Some functionalists believe that we will always have wars because of other important functions that they serve in societies. First, war demonstrates that one nation or group has power over another. Historically, conquering forces acquire the "spoils of war," including

more territory and material possessions. Second, war functions as a means of punishment in much the same manner that the U.S. government uses sanctions to force other nations to comply with our viewpoint on certain issues. Third, war is a way to disseminate ideologies, usually political or religious. For example, under the slogan "making the world safe for democracy," the United States has fought its largest wars in defense of a democratic form of government (Crossette, 1997). According to sociologist Seymour Martin Lipset, "We are a revolutionary country with a revolutionary tradition. We want everyone to be democrats" (cited in Crossette, 1997:E3). But not all democracies are friends of the United States. Larry Diamond, a scholar who has examined new democracies in other nations, explains (cited in Crossette, 1997:E3):

> Political freedom has deteriorated in several of the longest-surviving democracies of the developing world, including India, Sri Lanka, Colombia, and Venezuela. . . . It isn't enough to have elections. . . . Democracy is not something that is simply present or absent. It's not like a light switch that you flip on or off. It emerges in different fragments in different sequences in different countries and in different historical periods.

Finally, many functionalists point out the economic function of war. War benefits society because it stimulates the economy through increased war-related production and provides jobs for civilians who otherwise might not be able to find employment. In 2002, for example, the United States sold more than $10.4 billion in military equipment and supplies to other countries (refer back to Map 17.1 on page 392). Conflict analysts also see an economic side to war, but they are not so optimistic.

The Conflict and Symbolic Interactionist Perspectives

Conflict theorists view war from the standpoint of how militarism and aggressive preparedness for war contribute to the economic well-being of some, but not all, people in a society. According to sociologist Cynthia Enloe (1987:527), people who consider capitalism the moving force behind the military's influence "believe that government officials enhance the status, resources, and authority of the military in order to protect the interests of private enterprises at home and overseas." In other words, the origins of war can be traced to corporate boardrooms, not to the U.S. government's war room. Those who view war from this standpoint note that workers come to rely on military spending for jobs. Labor unions, for example, support defense spending because it provides well-paid, stable employment for union members.

A second conflict explanation focuses on the role of the nation and its inclination toward coercion in response to perceived threats. From this perspective, nations inevitably use force to ensure compliance within their societies and to protect themselves from outside attacks.

A third conflict explanation is based on patriarchy and the relationship between militarism and masculinity. Across cultures and over time, the military has been a male institution, and the "meanings attached to masculinity appear to be so firmly linked to compliance with military roles that it is often impossible to disentangle the two" (Enloe, 1987:531).

Symbolic interactionists would call this last perspective the *social construction of masculinity*. That is, certain assumptions, teachings, and expectations that serve as the standard for appropriate male behavior—in this case, values of dominance, power, aggression, and violence—are created and recreated presumably through gender socialization, particularly in military training. Historically, the development of manhood and male superiority has been linked to militarism and combat—the ultimate test of a man's masculinity (Enloe, 1987; Cock, 1994).

SOLUTIONS TO WAR AND TERRORISM

What will happen as we move further into the twenty-first century? How will nations deal with the prolif-

Military training often involves a lengthy socialization process that teaches recruits how to dispense and cope with aggressive behavior.

Watch on **mysoclab.com**
Defining Social Movements on **mysoclab.com**

eration of arms and nuclear weapons? Will the United States continue to be a nation at war? No easy answers are forthcoming, as Ehrenreich explains (1997:239):

> War . . . is a more formidable adversary than it has ever been. . . . [W]ar has dug itself into economic systems, where it offers a livelihood to millions. . . . It has lodged in our souls as a kind of religion, a quick tonic for political malaise and a bracing antidote to the moral torpor of consumerist, market-driven cultures. In addition, our incestuous fixation on combat with our own kind has left us ill-prepared to face many of the larger perils of the situation in which we find ourselves: the possibility

of drastic climatic changes, the depletion of natural resources, and the relentless predations of the microbial world. The wealth that flows ceaselessly to the project of war is wealth lost, for the most part, to the battle against these threats.

But Ehrenreich, like most other social analysts, is not totally pessimistic about the future. She believes that human resistance to war can provide a means to spare this nation and the world from future calamities. According to Ehrenreich, the antiwar movements of the late twentieth century show that "the passions we bring to war can be brought just as well to the struggle *against* war." But, she notes, people must be willing to educate, inspire, and rally others to the cause. Like other forms of warfare, the people who are fighting for peace must be willing to continue the struggle even when the odds seem hopeless. Ehrenreich's point is supported by sociologists James William Gibson and Francesca

M. Cancian (1990:9), who believe that making peace can be more difficult than making war:

> [M]aking peace requires democratic relationships: soldiers who refuse to fight in a war they do not support; citizens who claim the right to participate in making decisions instead of accepting rule by elites who make decisions in secret; newspaper reporters, magazine editors, movie makers, and others in the mass media who question the necessity of casting another nation as an "enemy" and instead look for ways to communicate with other human beings who are potentially our friends.

What about the future of terrorism in the United States and other nations? One thing appears certain: Countries that have experienced terrorist attacks on their own soil will be forever changed in how they deal with security and surveillance of citizens and of those seeking to enter these countries. In the United States, for example, the security procedures we go through before boarding an airplane or attending public gatherings, including sporting events, political conventions, and concerts, have increased significantly in the post-9/11 era. Likewise, passage of the USA PATRIOT Act greatly expanded the powers of law enforcement officials in this country and intelligence agencies working abroad to track and intercept communications and to crack down on activities that in any way may be linked to terrorist operations. Some people may view this law as infringing on their rights and privacy (see Box 17.3).

Why do we end our discussion of social problems with war and terrorism? They are the ultimate category of social problems. When class, race, ethnicity, or any of the other dominant–subordinate categories discussed in this book escalate to a level of "doing something about it" regardless of the consequences, terrorism or war can be the result. The international society—the community of all the nations of the world—must work to alleviate inequalities and create a better—peaceful—world for future generations. What role will you and I play during the years to come? Will we be part of the problem or part of the solution? The answer is up to us.

Social Problems and Social Policy   Box 17.3

(Mis)Understandings about the USA PATRIOT Act and Your Library

QUIZ FOR LIBRARIANS:

1. Which kind of information about a [library] patron deserves no privacy/confidentiality protection?
   a. Staff knowledge of illegal computer activity
   b. The titles of materials used
   c. The subject of reference questions
   d. Interlibrary loan requests
2. True/False. Everyone who greets the public should be prepared to follow a court order for library records, which is delivered by a law enforcement officer.
3. True/False. A library staff member's response to the USA PATRIOT Act should not differ from the general guidelines given to protect privacy and confidentiality. (Libraries Linking Idaho, n.d.)

You may be wondering what questions like these have to do with being a librarian. The answer is simple: Librarians must know the requirements of the USA PATRIOT Act (an acronym for United and Strengthening America by Providing Appropriate Tools Required to Intercept and Obstruct Terrorism) so that they can respond if a law enforcement official asks for certain kinds of information about persons who use their library resources.

What is the PATRIOT Act anyway? Congress passed the PATRIOT Act shortly after the September 11, 2001, terrorist attacks, and in 2011 extended the law for four more years so that it will be in effect until 2015 at least. The USA PATRIOT Act amended over fifteen federal statutes, including the laws governing criminal procedure, computer fraud and abuse, foreign intelligence, wiretapping, immigration, and the laws governing the privacy of student records in order to expand the authority of the FBI and other law enforcement agencies to gain access to suspected terrorists' business records, medical records, educational records, and library records, including stored electronic data and communications. This act also expanded the laws governing use of telephone wiretaps and "trap and trace" devices to Internet and electronic communications (American Library Association, 2011).

When this law was passed, libraries throughout the nation were concerned about the effect that enhanced surveillance procedures might have on privacy and confidentiality in the library. Under Section 215, "Access to

> **Read the Document**
> *We Are All Suspects Now: Untold Stories from Immigrant Communities after 9/11* on **mysoclab.com**

Social Problems and Social Policy

Box 17.3 Continued

Records Under Foreign Intelligence Security Act," the FBI is permitted to obtain a search warrant for "any tangible thing," including books, records, papers, floppy disks, data tapes, and computers with hard drives. The FBI can also demand to see library circulation records, Internet use records, and registration information stored in any medium. FBI agents do not have to demonstrate "probable cause" (the existence of specific facts to support the belief that a crime has been committed or that the items sought are evidence of a crime) to gain access to this information. The agents only need to claim a belief that the records they are seeking are related to an ongoing investigation pertaining to terrorism or intelligence activities. Librarians and libraries are prohibited from informing a patron that his or her records were given to the FBI or that he or she is the subject of an FBI investigation. When the PATRIOT Act was reauthorized in 2006, it contained a section addressing the issue of privacy protection for library patrons, making most library records beyond the need of national security as long as the library did not operate as an electronic communication service to provide users with the ability to send or receive wire or electronic communications.

Although public concern about the USA PATRIOT Act has been more subdued in recent years, each time this law comes up for reauthorization, critics attack it for its potentially negative effect on library patrons. Over time, librarians and library patrons have been encouraged to understand that there has to be a legal balance between the protection of freedom of expression and the protection of national security. For some, however, what is threatened is the freedom to read and to gather whatever information a person in a free society might wish to obtain.

Now, back to those questions posed to librarians at the beginning of this discussion. The answer to question 1 is *a* because the information listed under letters *b* through *d* should remain confidential and be known only to those staff members who are directly involved. In regard to question 2, the correct answer is *False:* The person greeting the law enforcement officer should refer him or her to library personnel who are specifically designated to receive, and respond to, such a request. Finally, the answer to question 3 is *True* because each library is responsible for having policies and procedures in place for handling all requests from law enforcement agencies. In regard to the quiz and the issue of libraries and national security, as some social pundits have suggested, a law degree is handy for virtually any career today, and apparently that includes librarians.

Questions for Consideration

1. In your opinion, does the USA PATRIOT Act constitute a threat to intellectual freedom and civil liberties? Why or why not?

2. Since the terrorist attacks on September 11, 2001, how has life in the United States changed in regard to security and surveillance of individuals? For example, through reading you have done, interviews, and/or personal experiences, compare how airport security operates today with what it was like prior to the 2001 attack.

3. Are you concerned that law enforcement officials might gather personal data about you from bookstores, libraries, or online accounts such as Amazon.com or BarnesandNoble.com? Why or why not?

SUMMARY

✓•─ **Study** and **Review** on **mysoclab.com**

■ **How do social scientists define war?**
Social scientists define war broadly. The term *war* includes armed conflict between two countries, undeclared wars, civil and guerrilla wars, covert operations, and some forms of terrorism. War is a form of collective violence that involves organized violence by people seeking to promote their cause or resist social policies or practices that they consider oppressive.

■ **What are the consequences of war?**
The most direct effect of war is loss of human life. In World War I and before, it was mostly military personnel who lost their lives, but in World War II and thereafter, war was waged against civilians. If a nuclear war were to take place, the devastation would be beyond description. Other consequences for both military personnel and civilians are physical and psychological damage, including posttraumatic stress disorder. Finally, the economic costs of war and war preparedness are astronomical.

■ **How important is military technology to winning a war?**
Military technology is a dominant factor, as military history shows. In the fourteenth century, smaller European and Western armies defeated bigger armies by using the newly discovered black powder. Today, precision-guided munitions

render old technologies obsolete and global warfare possible. But wars can be won on the basis of factors other than military technology, too, as the U.S. experience in Vietnam shows.

What is terrorism?
Terrorism is the use of calculated unlawful physical force or threats of violence against a government, organization, or individual to gain some political, religious, economic, or social objective. Tactics include bombing, kidnapping, hostage taking, hijacking, assassination, and extortion.

What are the three types of political terrorism?
Revolutionary terrorism involves acts of violence against civilians that are carried out by enemies of the government who want to bring about political change. Repressive terrorism is conducted by a government against its own citizens for the purpose of protecting an existing political order. In state-sponsored terrorism, a government provides financial resources, weapons, and training for terrorists who conduct their activities in other nations.

What forms of terrorism represent the greatest potential threat to U.S. citizens?
Some analysts identify the following as forms of terrorism that offer the greatest potential threat to U.S. citizens: (1) foreign-sponsored terrorism on U.S. soil such as the 9/11 terrorist attacks; (2) domestic-sponsored terrorism with political or religious motivations such as violent protests against abortion clinics; (3) terrorism in other nations such as attacks at tourist sites or other public accommodations that are frequently visited by U.S. citizens; and (4) cyberterrorism or information terrorism—the destruction of computer systems and records or hacking into systems to gain valuable information and data.

What are the biological perspectives on war and terrorism?
Some biological proponents say that humans, especially males, are innately violent, but there is no conclusive scientific evidence to support this view or the view that biological factors are more important than social factors.

What are the psychological perspectives on war and terrorism?
Most strictly psychological perspectives focus on individualistic sources of violence, but social psychologists take both individual and cultural factors into account. Their research findings show that it is easier to harm enemies when they are depersonalized and that people are more likely to act violently when they are in positions of power. Some individuals can commit horrible atrocities without feeling guilt through the process of doubling. Social psychologists say that, to reduce war and terrorism, society must emphasize peace, not glorify violent impulses.

What is the functionalist perspective on war and terrorism?
Some functionalists focus on the relationship between social disorganization and warfare or terrorism. Examining the growth of militias, they note that disorganization in social institutions contributes to overall political instability. Other functionalists say that war serves certain functions: It settles disputes; demonstrates that one nation or group has power over another; punishes; is one way to disseminate religious and political ideologies; and, finally, stimulates the economy.

What are the conflict and interactionist perspectives on war and terrorism?
Some conflict theorists say that militarism and preparedness for war contribute to the economic well-being of some—not all—people. Another conflict perspective says that nations inevitably use force to ensure compliance within their society and to protect themselves from outside attacks. A third conflict perspective is based in patriarchy: Across cultures and over time, the military has been a male institution; it is almost impossible to untangle masculinity from militarism. Interactionists call this last perspective the *social construction of masculinity*—the connection between manhood and militarism is historically created and recreated through gender socialization.

KEY TERMS

collective violence, p. 386
repressive terrorism, p. 395
revolutionary terrorism, p. 394
state-sponsored terrorism, p. 395

strategically significant weapon, p. 392
terrorism, p. 394
war, p. 385
war system, p. 385

weapons of mass destruction
(WMDs), p. 388
weapons system, p. 392

QUESTIONS FOR CRITICAL THINKING

1. How has war changed in the age of drones and computers from the World War II era in which military personnel have been directly involved in all aspects of warfare? Given the technology that is available, how can we safeguard service personnel and civilians alike?

2. What do you believe is the biggest threat to national security in the United States today? How might we guard against this problem?

3. Consider the question posed in the last paragraph of this chapter: What can you yourself do to make the world a better—peaceful—place in the future?

Succeed with MySocLab® www.mysoclab.com

The new MySocLab delivers proven results in helping students succeed, provides engaging experiences that personalize learning, and comes from a trusted partner with educational expertise and a deep commitment to helping students and instructors achieve their goals.

Here are a few activities you will find for this chapter:

Watch on **mysoclab.com**

Core Concepts video clips feature sociologists in action, exploring important concepts in the study of Social Problems. Watch:
- Defining Social Movements

Explore on **mysoclab.com**

Social Explorer is an interactive application that allows you to explore Census data through interactive maps. Explore:
- Social Explorer Activity: War Veterans in Mississippi

Read on **mysoclab.com**

MySocLibrary includes primary source readings from classic and contemporary sociologists. Read:
- We Are All Suspects Now: Untold Stories from Immigrant Communities after 9/11

Can Social Problems Be Solved?

CHAPTER 18

THINKING SOCIOLOGICALLY

- What shocking lessons did we learn from the 2001 terrorist attacks, the 2005 Hurricane Katrina disaster, and the passive BP oil spill in 2010 about the importance of prevention and/or preparedness in dealing with major emergencies and massive social problems?

- When do macrolevel efforts work better than midrange or microlevel attempts to deal with social problems?

- What do social movements and special-interest groups have in common in their ideologies and efforts to influence politicians and other influential people? How do they differ in their goals and methods?

405

Before 9/11 the Federal Emergency Management Agency listed the three most likely catastrophic disasters facing America: a terrorist attack on New York, a major earthquake in San Francisco, and a hurricane strike in New Orleans. "The New Orleans hurricane scenario," The Houston Chronicle wrote in December 2001, "may be the deadliest of all." It described a potential catastrophe

very much like the one [that occurred in August, 2005]. So why were New Orleans and the nation so unprepared?

—Paul Krugman (2005a), a Nobel laureate economist, Princeton University professor, and columnist for the New York Times, criticizing the slow response by the federal government to Hurricane Katrina's devastation

Described by many as one of the worst natural disaster in U.S. history, Hurricane Katrina in 2005 not only left a wide path of death and destruction in its wake but also raised many serious questions about emergency preparedness and how we deal with social problems in this country. Some analysts suggest that local, state, and federal governments were not adequately prepared for unprecedented emergencies such as this devastating hurricane on the Gulf Coast (Shane and Lipton, 2005). Lack of adequate funding, resulting in part from federal income tax cuts and shifting national priorities after the 2001 terrorist attacks coupled with the continuing conflict in Afghanistan and Iraq, had left many emergency programs in a "bare-bones" condition. Funding problems and lack of long-range planning may also contribute to failures in components of the infrastructure at a time when it is most needed. **Infrastructure refers to a framework of support systems, such as transportation and utilities, that makes it possible to have specific land uses** (commercial, residential, and recreational, for example) **and a built environment** (buildings, houses, highways, and such) **that facilitate people's daily activities and the nation's economy.** Problems with the infrastructure create major crises, such as when transportation systems malfunction, utilities fail or are inadequate, and *infrastructural capital* (including bridges, dams, and levees) is unable to fulfill its purpose. Infrastructure failure contributed to existing problems in New Orleans when, in the aftermath of Hurricane Katrina, water pumps and several levees on Lake Pontchartrain were breached, spilling millions of gallons of polluted water onto the city's already-flooded streets, forcing residents from their homes, and leaving thousands of people homeless. Many Gulf Coast communities in Louisiana and Mississippi were also hard-hit by this hurricane, and some of these areas once again experienced extensive environmental degradation and social harm from the Deepwater Horizon (BP) oil spill in 2010. Both of these crises, which involved elements of natural and technological disasters, received extensive media coverage, but the nature and extent of news reporting in each was different (see Box 18.1).

✳—|Explore the Concept
Social Explorer Activity: Transportation and Social Status on mysoclab.com

The tragedy in New Orleans also reflects social problems experienced by many people but seldom seriously discussed in this country, including the high rate of poverty (28 percent) among African Americans living in that city, which was more than double the national poverty rate for all U.S. citizens (Whitesides, 2005). Many people across a variety of political spectrums, lifestyles and economic conditions, and racial-ethnic categories were extremely critical of the length of time that it took for political leaders, the military, and other governmental agencies to mobilize and help rescue victims, care for the ill and dying, and bring some order to the city.

Although Hurricane Katrina was a *natural disaster* (which includes floods, hurricanes, tornadoes, and earthquakes), from a sociological perspective it also was a *social disaster*. If Hurricane Katrina's first wave was the storm itself, the second wave of this hurricane was a *manmade disaster* because large numbers of injuries, deaths, and property damage may have resulted not from the devastating effects of the hurricane itself but rather from earlier decisions about priorities, allocation of funds, and the importance of certain kinds of preparedness. In essence, Hurricane Katrina revealed that our nation may have "penny pinched" in the wrong places, ignoring deep divisions of race, class, gender, and age

Covering Hurricane Katrina and the BP Oil Spill: Similar Location but Different Issues

More than 1,800 people lost their lives. There was more than $81 billion in damage. Eighty percent of New Orleans was submerged. Thousands of victims were forced to rooftops, and hundreds of thousand scattered to shelters around the country. . . . The hurricanes of 2005 destroyed or severely damaged approximately 350,000 homes within 90,000 square miles from southeastern Texas to the Florida Keys— an area the size of Great Britain. They were the costliest hurricanes in U.S. history.

—An American Red Cross (2010) report describing the loss of life and destruction that resulted from Hurricane Katrina

Dear Fellow Shareholder:
2010 was a profoundly painful and testing year. In April, a tragic accident on the Deepwater Horizon rig claimed the lives of 11 men and injured others. . . . The accident should never have happened. We are shocked and saddened that it did. The spill that resulted caused widespread pollution. Our response has been unprecedented in scale, and we are determined to live up to our commitments in the Gulf.

—Brief excerpts from a letter written by Carl-Henric Svanberg, chair of BP, explaining to the company's shareholders about the tragic gulf oil spill and vowing that the company would do everything necessary to clean up the disaster and ensure that similar disasters did not occur again (quoted in BP, 2010)

Images of destruction, death, and desperation such as the ones described have become an all-too-common sight on our television screens, computer monitors, smartphones, iPads and other tablets, and daily newspapers. Through photos, audio and video clips, and journalists' accounts we have witnessed numerous acts of terrorism, wars, earthquakes, tsunamis, bombings, and other horrendous occurrences. But all of the coverage has not been identical. It has depended on answers to journalists' questions of who?, what?, when?, where?, how?, and why?

Based on research about coverage of the BP oil spill and cleanup by the Pew Research Centers Project for Excellence in Journalism (www.journalism.org), let's briefly compare media framing of Katrina coverage with that of the BP oil spill. Obviously, both disasters were tragic and had a strong human interest angle: Many people were harmed, either directly or indirectly, by both tragic events. In Katrina, many journalists on the scene at least briefly lost their pro-

fessional detachment when they saw the magnitude of the disaster and the desperate plight of helpless victims. Images of death and despair that media audiences saw from afar were close and personal for reporters, some of whom temporarily left behind their dispassionate, journalistic demeanor and began to tell the story with a tone of advocacy, making demands on political leaders and relief workers to explain why help for the victims was so slow in arriving.

Although the deaths of eleven workers on the BP oil rig were devastating to family, friends, and coworkers, less media attention was paid to individual workers or their families, and most of the focus was on stopping the flow of oil into the Gulf of Mexico and expert opinions about what happened and why it occurred. Reporters and television crews spent extensive amounts of time interviewing experts about how to stop the flow and minimize the problem. According to the Pew study, the oil spill was by far the dominant story in all mainstream media coverage in the 100-day period after the explosion. At first the story lines focused on the explosion and the missing workers. Then the emphasis shifted to the size of the spill and who was responsible for the disaster. Finally, the story line moved to the environmental and economic effects of the spill (Journalism.org, 2011). At that time, paid workers and volunteers cleaning up the gulf water and along the shoreline were interviewed with regularity, and dead or dying birds, fish, and other animals were key props in heartrending stories about the short-term and long-term effects of the oil spill. Fisherman and other people who make money from tourism were extensively interviewed to learn how they planned to get by without the money they usually made from fishing or tourism.

If nature was identified as the antagonist in the Katrina story, the adversary in the oil spill story was BP and its CEO, who was characterized as not having control over the situation and not doing enough about the problem. In media coverage of both the Katrina aftermath and the BP oil spill, the U.S. government came out with mixed to negative media reviews. Katrina coverage focused on the ineptitude of the Bush administration in getting help to various disaster sites, the many problems associated with FEMA and disaster preparedness, and what was perceived to be the apathy of then-President George W. Bush about this tragic occurrence. Similarly, the Obama administration initially received mixed media reviews about its role in the oil spill saga, but this perspective generally diminished, except for a few cable news channels and in the blogosphere.

Social Problems in the Media

Box 18.1 continued

Finally, the Katrina and BP stories will not be exhausted for many years to come because they provide a near-perfect story line for television, social media, and the Internet. Disaster stories start with an initial burst of event-driven coverage and are followed by postmortems, extensive follow-ups, and commentary. Then, a slower trickle of related stories comes out in the years following the tragedy. In 2011, for example, media coverage of Katrina focused on the trial and conviction on civil rights violations and obstruction charges of local police officers who were accused of killing unarmed citizens on a New Orleans bridge in the hours following the flooding of portions of the city. In 2011, media coverage also discussed how some of Katrina's low-income victims reached a legal settlement in a civil rights lawsuit over Louisiana's Road Home program, which had failed to distribute aid to persons trying to rebuild homes after they were destroyed by Hurricane Katrina. Fewer stories have focused on the many unresolved problems in New Orleans, including the lack of low-income housing, problems in rebuilding and improving public schools, and inadequate hospitals and medical services partly as a result of Katrina's devastation. In 2011, coverage of the BP oil spill looked at how the affected areas had been restored to a higher level of cleanliness, particularly the water and beaches. Stories also emphasized that fish caught in the Gulf were now safe to eat, and that life had nearly returned to normal in the area. Of course, some media critics argue that some positive reporting resulted by spin placed on the coverage by public relations firms hired by BP to ensure that its side of the cleanup story was fairly told by the media.

In sum, the media coverage of Hurricane Katrina and the BP oil spill were similar in some significant ways because both crises involved disasters beyond the imagination of most people. However, each disaster had its own unique story, and various media sources took different approaches to framing those stories. What the Pew study concluded about media coverage of the BP oil spill might be changed slightly to reflect a truth

about coverage of both Katrina and BP: "The BP oil spill in the Gulf of Mexico [and Hurricane Katrina and its aftermath] proved to be a complex, technical and long-running saga that taxed the media's resources and attention span." And, perhaps, media coverage of these two tragedies had the same effect on media audiences and bloggers as well.

Questions for Consideration

1. Throughout this text, we have looked at how the media frame stories about social problems. We have also examined media representations of race, class, gender, age, and other ascribed characteristics. Do you think that issues such as race and class may have affected media coverage of stories such as Hurricane Katrina and its aftermath? How about the BP oil spill coverage? Did it make any difference that a massive transnational corporation was seeking to control the spin on stories about this disaster? Why or why not?

2. How do you think various kinds of media will cover disasters in the future? How might social media influence people's perceptions about the causes, effects, and possible solutions to social problems?

Independent Research

Hopefully, other major natural or technological disasters have not occurred since the time this box was written, but if they have, you might wish to gather information from newspapers, electronic media, websites, and social media about the disaster and identify key recurring themes or issues that are presented in various sources. How are the issues in the data you found similar to the ones highlighted in the Katrina and/or BP oil spill media coverage? How do they differ?

If you are unable to find information on newer disasters, how about revisiting the aftermath of Katrina and/or BP oil spill at "x" number of years later (the year in which you are conducting your research) to see which, if any, of the issues discussed in this box have been resolved and which remain as ongoing problems for people and for the environment.

that we usually do not examine or seek to remedy except when faced with massive disaster such as terrorist attacks or natural disasters of great magnitude.

Following in the aftermath of Hurricane Katrina was the *technological disaster* of the Deepwater Horizon (BP) oil spill in 2010, which also extensively damaged the coastline and gulf waters in some of the same areas that Hurricane Katrina had already damaged. As discussed in Chapter 15, the Deepwater Horizon oil spill,

also known as the BP oil spill, was the largest marine oil spill in history with crude oil gushing out of a 5,000-foot pipe that connected the well at the ocean floor to the drilling platform on the surface. Although BP was eventually able to cap the well and stop the flow of oil into the Gulf of Mexico, massive damage had been done to the environment, the economy, and other areas below the water's surface. Unlike the cleanup from Katrina, which was the responsibility of the government and voluntary relief organizations such as the Red Cross, the cleanup of the Deepwater Horizon oil spill was the responsibility of one of the world's largest oil companies. Although both events constituted major social problems in the United States, outlines for their solution were different in that the resolution in the Katrina disaster focused on money, personnel, and other resources from the government. By contrast, resolution in the BP disaster focused primarily on the role of private corporations in reducing the problem with the government playing a secondary, legalistic, oversight role in which certain timetables and demands had to be met in cleaning up the disaster and its fallout, such as the harm caused to water, beaches, the fishing industry, tourism, and a myriad of other things that were damaged or killed by the disaster.

In this chapter we look at the role of the U.S. government, voluntary organizations, and corporations in preventing and/or reducing social problems. However, persistent underlying social problems, such as the growing gap between the rich and the poor and the continuing significance of racial inequality in the United States, also rise to the surface for analysis in times of national crisis. In this chapter, we look at what might be done to reduce or eliminate social problems. Thinking sociologically about the causes and effects of, and possible solutions for, problems such as natural disasters like Hurricane Katrina and technological disasters such as the BP oil spill helps focus our attention on what needs to be done to reduce social problems.

DID YOU KNOW

- Preventive measures are less costly and time-consuming than after-the-fact measures when it comes to dealing with social problems.

- Individual solutions to personal problems are generally ineffective because many problems require collective action to bring about change.

- Sociological insights on social problems are used in various fields to help people understand issues and improve social conditions around the world.

THE PROBLEM WITH TACKLING SOCIAL PROBLEMS

Solving social problems is a far more complex undertaking than simply identifying them and pinpointing their social locations. It is much easier for us to call attention to a problem than it is to carry out a solution.

Designing and implementing programs to solve social problems may take years while the needs of individuals and groups are immediate. According to some analysts, programs to bring about positive social change face "innumerable obstacles, delays, and frustrations," and require that we have "immense dedication and perseverance" (Weinberg, Rubington, and Hammersmith, 1981:6).

Ideal versus Practical Solutions

Perhaps the first obstacle that we face in trying to reduce or solve social problems is in dealing with the difference between *ideal* solutions and *practical* solutions. As the sociologists Martin S. Weinberg, Earl Rubington, and Sue Kiefer Hammersmith (1981:6) state, "There is usually considerable conflict between what the *ideal* solution would be and what a *workable* solution might be." Sometimes the ideal solution to a problem entails prohibitive costs. In regard to natural disasters, for example, there is no ideal solution (given the fact that we cannot stop most natural disasters) but we can do far better than we have in regard to advance warnings about a potential disaster, evacuation of individuals regardless of who they are or their ability to pay, immediate help for those who must remain behind, and better fortification against naturally occurring hazards to protect communities and infrastructure.

Preventive measures such as these are costly and time-consuming, which means that they typically are allocated only a small percentage of the money and resources actually needed or they are entirely swept off the table in political discussions by being labeled as "prohibitive" in cost or "impractical" in view of other seemingly more urgent budget demands. Consequently, rather than employing preventive measures to deal with social problems, we frequently rely on *after-the-fact measures* (such as trying to remedy a problem or reduce its effects after it has occurred) to deal with issues and crises. In the case of Hurricane Katrina, for example, engineers, members of the media, and many others had long asserted that money for storm protection needed to be spent to protect New Orleans from massive flooding. The Louisiana congressional delegation had also asked for money for storm protection in the past but had received only a small portion of the amount they requested.

Although the exact cause of the explosion and fire on Deepwater Horizon rig that caused the massive Gulf of Mexico oil spill may never be fully known, the subsea blowout in deep water was what Bob Dudley, group chief executive of BP, referred to as a "very, very low-probability event, by BP and the entire industry—but it happened" (BP, 2010). Whether adequate resources were put into maintaining a safe drilling operation in the gulf will be a point of debate for years to come; however, the focus of the discussion about this disaster became not what had been spent in the past, but how much money BP was going to spend on resolving the problem and making restitution to those individuals and organizations that had experienced physical and/or monetary damage as a result of this crisis. Latest figures in 2011 estimated that more than $40 billion is the pricetag for cleanup, government fines, lawsuits, legal fees, and damage claims resulting from this oil spill (gulfspilloil.com, 2011).

Spending tens of billions of dollars after a disaster such as the BP oil spill, rather than a few billion in advance to prevent a technological disaster from occurring, or, in the case of Katrina, spending money for flood protection and for improving the infrastructure, are examples of an after-the-fact approach to dealing with social problems. Unfortunately, this approach is often used in problems associated with education, crime, and health care. When leaders do not allocate necessary funds for schools and juvenile prevention programs, they later have to spend much more money on programs that deal with school dropouts, juvenile offenders, and others who are left behind (or left out) in the existing system. Similar situations occur in health care when patients do not receive preventive care that might reduce their risk for certain illnesses or disease (such as cardiovascular accidents, diabetes, and cancer) but instead receive expensive "high-tech" medical treatment after the onset of their medical condition—if they are among the fortunate ones who have money, insurance, or a social welfare program (such as Medicare or Medicaid) that partly covers the cost of their treatment.

Defining the Problem versus Fixing It

Sometimes there is no agreement about what the problem *is* and what efforts should be made to reduce or eliminate it. After all, the people and organizations involved in the problem-*defining* stage of a social problem generally are not the same people and organizations involved in the problem-*solving* stage of a social problem. Social problems are often identified and defined by political or social activists, journalists, social scientists, and religious leaders. In contrast, the problem-solving stage usually involves elected officials and/or people working in agencies and governmental bureaucracies. Moreover, sometimes a proposed solution to a problem may only give rise to a whole new set of problems. For example, the Affordable Health Care law passed in 2010 was intended to expand health insurance coverage for all Americans, which would help reduce the problem of obtaining medical care for uninsured people. However, full implementation of this law means that the current health care system may be further swamped because it is already overburdened, particularly in low-income, central cities and in rural areas where physicians and other health care professionals are in short supply. As you can see, fixing a social problem is no easy matter because it often involves new laws or other kinds of social change, which makes many people uncomfortable because they believe that things could indeed get worse rather than better when individuals and groups start to tinker with the status quo (things as they currently are).

SOCIAL CHANGE AND REDUCING SOCIAL PROBLEMS

It should be clear from the preceding discussion that the concept of social change is an important factor in any attempt to reduce social problems. **Social change is the alternation, modification, or transformation of public policy, culture, or social institutions over time.** Notice that this definition states that social change occurs "over time." Thus, social change has temporal dimensions. Some efforts to deal with social problems are *short-term* strategies, whereas others are *middle-term* remedies, and still others constitute *long-term* efforts to alleviate the root causes of a social problem. In other words, efforts to alleviate individual unemployment or reduce unemployment rates in a community have a different temporal dimension than efforts to change the political economy in such a manner that high levels of employment and greater wage equity are brought about throughout a nation or nations. Clearly, efforts to alleviate individual unemployment are a short-term solution to the problem of unemployment, while efforts to reduce unemployment in a community or to change the political economy are middle-term and long-term solutions. Sometimes discussions of social change sound idealistic or utopian because they are middle-term or long-term strategies that attempt to target the root causes of a social problem. For many social problems, however, a combination of strategies is required to reduce social problems.

MICROLEVEL ATTEMPTS TO SOLVE SOCIAL PROBLEMS

In Chapter 1, we described sociologist C. Wright Mills's (1959b) belief that we should apply the sociological imagination to gain a better understanding of social problems. According to Mills, the sociological imagination is the ability to see the relationship between individual experiences and the larger society. For Mills, social problems cannot be solved at the individual level alone: These problems are more than personal troubles or private problems. Consequently, solutions must be found through social institutions such as the economy, politics, and education. However, sometimes social institutions cannot deal with a problem effectively, and political and business leaders are unwilling or unable to allocate the resources that are necessary to reduce a problem. In these situations, we have no choice but to try to deal with a problem in our own way.

Seeking Individual Solutions to Personal Problems

Microlevel solutions to social problems focus on how individuals operate within small groups to try to remedy a problem that affects them, their family, or friends. Usually, when individuals have personal problems, they turn to their *primary groups*—**small, less specialized groups in which members engage in face-to-face, emotion-based interactions over an extended period of time.** Primary groups include one's family, close friends, and other peers with whom one routinely shares the more personal experiences in life.

How can participation in primary groups help us reduce personal problems? According to sociologists, members of our primary groups usually support us even when others do not. For example, some analysts believe that we have many more people who are without a domicile (technically homeless) than current statistics suggest but that, whenever possible, these people live with relatives or friends, many of whom may already live in overcrowded and sometimes substandard housing. Most people who seek individualized solutions to personal troubles believe the situation will be temporary. However, if the problem is widespread or embedded in the larger society, it might stretch out for months or years without resolution. At best, individualized efforts to reduce a problem are short-term measures that some critics refer as the "Band-Aid approach" to a problem because these efforts do not eliminate the causes of the problem.

Some microlevel approaches to reducing social problems focus on how individuals can do something about the problems they face. For example, a person who is unemployed or among the "working poor" because of low wages, seasonal employment, or other factors might be urged to get more education or training and work experience in order to find a "better" job and have the opportunity for upward mobility. Individuals who appear to have eliminated problems in their own lives through such efforts are applauded for their determination, and they are often used (sometimes unwillingly or unknowingly) as examples that others are supposed to follow.

An example of this approach is columnist John Tierney's assessment of Hurricane Katrina and his encouragement to readers to "fight floods like fires, without the feds." According to Tierney, urbanites in cities such as New York have learned to protect themselves from fire losses by purchasing insurance, and the people of New Orleans and along the Gulf Coast should do likewise:

> Here's the bargain I'd offer New Orleans: the feds will spend the billions for your new levees, but then you're on your own. You and others along the coast have to buy flood insurance the same way we all buy fire insurance—from private companies with more at stake than Washington bureaucrats. . . . If Americans had to pay premiums for living in risky areas, they'd think twice about building oceanfront villas. Voters and insurance companies would put pressure on local politicians to take care of the levees, prepare for the worst—and stop waiting for that bumbling white knight from Washington. (Tierney, 2005:A29)

Although Tierney raises an interesting point, his approach does not take into account the fact that many who experienced devastating losses in this disaster were individuals and families with the fewest material possessions and little or no hope of ever affording an oceanfront villa, much less the insurance to protect it from fire and hurricanes.

Limitations of the Microlevel Solutions Approach

Although individuals must certainly be responsible for their own behavior and must make decisions that help solve their own problems, there are serious limitations to the assumption that social problems can be solved one person at a time. When we focus on individualistic solutions to reducing social problems, we are not taking into account the fact that secondary groups and societal institutions play a significant part in creating, maintaining, and exacerbating many social problems. *Secondary groups* **are larger, more** specialized groups in which members engage in impersonal, goal-oriented relationships for a limited period of time. Without the involvement of these large-scale organizations, which include government agencies and transnational corporations, it is virtually impossible to reduce large-scale social problems. Consider, for example, the problem of air pollution:

If I live in a city with excessive amounts of air pollution, I can decide to stay inside all the time, or, if I can afford it, I could move to a low-density suburb with lots of trees where I will not have to inhale the polluted air, but this is only an individual solution that does not solve the greater problem of air pollution in the United States and around the world. My individualistic approach also does not address the role of others (vehicle manufacturers, gasoline producers, and consumers) in the creation of air pollution. With the excessively high price of gasoline and other fuels due to factors such as wars in the Middle East, damage to oil-producing facilities, and disruptions in oil production due to disasters like the Deepwater Horizon spill, people may seek out more fuel-efficient vehicles as an economic survival strategy. At the bottom line, however, personal choices alone cannot do much to reduce most national and global problems. Given this fact, what typically happens is a political mandate to reduce the level of pollution in the environment or to establish a new standard of fuel efficiency that vehicle manufacturers must follow for cases sold in the United States. Such a measure was announced in 2011 by the Obama administration when major automakers agreed to increase fuel economy in cars and light-duty trucks by 2025 (EPA, 2010). Social problems such as environmental pollution and excessive fuel usage require larger-scale solutions such as this because, if one person decides to reduce fuel usage for a day or a year, the environment continues to be contaminated, and the air quality for future generations comes more and more into question. However, if a larger group of people banded together in a grassroots effort to deal with a social problem, the effects of their efforts might be more widespread.

MIDRANGE ATTEMPTS TO SOLVE SOCIAL PROBLEMS

Midrange solutions to social problems focus on how secondary groups and formal organizations can deal with problems or assist individuals in overcoming problems such as drug addiction or domestic violence. Some groups help people cope with their own problems, and some groups attempt to bring about community change.

Groups That Help People Cope with Their Problems

Most midrange solutions to social problems are based on two assumptions: (1) that some social problems can best be reduced by reaching one person at a time and (2) that prevention and intervention are most effective at the personal and community levels. Groups that attempt to reduce a social problem by helping individuals cope with it or by eliminating it from their own lives are commonplace in our society (see Table 18.1). Among the best known are Alcoholics Anonymous (AA) and Narcotics Anonymous (NA); however, a wide range of "self-help" organizations exist in most communities. Typically, self-help groups bring together individuals who have experienced the same problem and have the same goal: quitting the behavior that has caused the problem, which can be anything from abuse of alcohol, tobacco, and other drugs to overeating, gambling, or chronic worrying. Volunteers who have had similar problems (and believe that they are on the road to overcoming them) act as role models for newer members. For example, AA and NA are operated by alcoholics and/or other substance abusers who try to provide new members with the support they need to overcome alcohol addiction or drug dependency. According to some analysts, AA is a subculture with distinct rules and values that alcoholics learn through their face-to-face encounters with other AA members. Social interaction is viewed as central for individual success in the programs. Confessing one's behavioral problems to others in an organizational setting is believed to have therapeutic value to those who are seeking help. Like other midrange approaches, organizations such as AA and NA may bring changes in the individual's life; however, they do not systematically address the structural factors (such as unemployment, work-related stress, and aggressive advertising campaigns) that might contribute to substance abuse problems. For example, AA typically does not lobby for more stringent laws pertaining to drunk driving or the sale and consumption of alcoholic beverages. As a result, larger, societal intervention is necessary to reduce the problems that contribute to individual behavior.

Read the Document
Community Building: Steps Toward a Good Society on mysoclab.com

Grassroots Groups That Work for Community-Based Change

Some grassroots organizations focus on bringing about a change that may reduce or eliminate a social problem in a

TABLE 18.1 A Brief List of the Best-Known Self-Help Groups	
Alcoholics Anonymous www.aa.org/?Media=PlayFlash	Gamblers Anonymous www.gamblersanonymous.org/
Al-Anon and Alateen www.al-anon.alateen.org/	Narcotics Anonymous www.na.org/
Alzheimer's Support Group www.alz.org/index.asp	National Coalition for the Homeless www.nationalhomeless.org/
Breast Cancer Support Group www.komen.org/	Overeaters Anonymous www.oa.org/
Bulimia, Anorexia Self-Help www.nationaleatingdisorders.org/	Parents Without Partners www.parentswithoutpartners.org/
Cocaine Anonymous www.ca.org/	People with a Lesbian, Gay, Bisexual, Transgender, or Queer Parent www.colage.org/
Co-Dependents Anonymous www.coda.org/	Step-Families Association of America www.stepfamilies.info/
Diabetes Support Group www.diabetes.org/	United Fathers of America www.unitedfathers.org/

specific community or region. *Grassroots groups* **are organizations started by ordinary people who work in concert to change a perceived wrong in their neighborhood, city, state, or nation.** Using this approach, people learn how to empower themselves against local and state government officials, corporate executives, and media figures who determine what constitutes the news in their area:

> By their nature, grassroots groups emerge to challenge individuals, corporations, government agencies, academia, or a combination of these when people discover they share a grievance. In their search for redress, they have encountered unresponsive, negative public agencies, self-serving private businesses, or recalcitrant individuals and groups. The answer for them is to select specific issues and find like-minded others. (Adams, 1991:9)

A central concern of those who attempt to reduce a social problem through grassroots groups is the extent to which other people are apathetic about the problem. Some analysts suggest that even when people are aware of problems, they do not think that they can do anything to change them or do not know how to work with other people to alleviate them:

> The biggest problem facing Americans is not those issues that bombard us daily, from homelessness

and failing schools to environmental devastation and the federal deficit. Underlying each is a deeper crisis. Some see that deeper problem in the form of obstacles that block problem solving: the tightening concentration of wealth, the influence of money in politics, discrimination, and bureaucratic rigidity, to name a few. These *are* powerful barriers. But for us the crisis is deeper still. The crisis is that *we as a people don't know how to come together to solve these problems.* We lack the capacities to address the issues or remove the obstacles that stand in the way of public deliberation. Too many Americans feel powerless. (Lappé and Du Bois, 1994:9)

According to social analysts, more community dialogue is needed on social issues, and more people need to become involved in grassroots social movements. A *social movement* **is an organized group that acts collectively to promote or resist change through collective action.** Because social movements when they begin are not institutionalized and are outside the political mainstream, they empower outsiders by offering them an opportunity to have their voices heard. For example, when residents near Love Canal, located in Niagara Falls, New York, came to believe that toxic chemicals were damaging the health of their children, they banded together to bring about change in government regulations concerning the disposal of

TABLE 18.2 Selected Organizations That Seek to Address a Social Problem

Category	Organization	Website Address
Environment	Earth First!	www.earthfirst.org/
	Sierra Club	www.sierraclub.org/
	Slow Food USA	www.slowfoodusa.org/
Driving While Drinking	Mothers Against Drunk Driving	www.madd.org/
Wages and Working Conditions	American Rights at Work	www.americanrightsatwork.org/
	Industrial Workers of the World	www.iww.org/
Neighborhoods/Poverty	National Low Income Housing Coalition	www.nlihc.org/template/index.cfm
	National Urban League	www.nul.org/
Homelessness Violence and War	National Coalition for the Homeless	http://nationalhomeless.org/
	Food Not Bombs	www.foodnotbombs.net/
	International Fellowship of Reconciliation	www.ifor.org/
	The Nonviolence Web	www.nonviolence.org/

toxic wastes. Indeed, Love Canal was the birthplace of the environmental movement against dumping toxic waste. Social movements such as Mothers Against Drunk Driving (MADD), Earth First!, People for the Ethical Treatment of Animals (PETA), and the National Federation of Parents for Drug Free Youth began as community-based grassroots efforts. Over time, many midrange organizations evolve into national organizations; however, their organization and focus often change in the process. Table 18.2 provides examples of activist organizations that seek to reduce specific social problems in communities.

Grassroots organizations and other local structures are crucial to national social movements because national social movements must recruit members and gain the economic resources necessary for nationwide or global social activism. Numerous sociological studies have shown that the local level constitutes a necessary microfoundation for larger-scale social movement activism (Buechler, 2000). According to social movement scholar Steve M. Buechler (2000:149),

> [S]ome forms of activism not only require such microfoundations but also thematize local structures themselves as the sources of grievances, the site of resistance, or the goal of change. By consciously identifying local structures as the appropriate areas of contention, such movements comprise a distinct

subset of the larger family of movements that all rely on microfoundations but do not all thematize local structures in this way.

To understand how grassroots organizations aid national social movements, consider the problem of environmental degradation. Leaders of national environmental organizations often make use of social media,

Midrange attempts to solve social problems typically focus on how secondary groups and formal organizations deal with problems or seek to assist individuals in overcoming problems. An example is this grassroots social movement, whose members are protesting the placement of a low-level radioactive dumping site in their neighborhood.

particularly Facebook and Twitter, to get other people involved in rallies, protests, and e-mail campaigns, particularly when politicians are making decisions that environmentalists believe will have a negative effect on the environment. By working with local and regional activists and seeking to influence local and regional power structures—city councils, statewide planning commissions, and legislatures—national organizations assert the need for their existence and attempt to garner additional supporters and revenue for their efforts nationwide or around the globe. By intertwining local, regional, and national organizational structures, these groups create a powerful voice for social change regarding some issue.

Limitations of the Midlevel Solutions Approach

Although local efforts to reduce problems affecting individuals and collectivities in a specific city or region bring about many improvements, they typically lack the sustained capacity to produce the larger, systemic changes at the national or international levels that are necessary to actually reduce or eliminate the problem. For example, organizations that represent the homeless often challenge the attempts of various cities to remove homeless persons and their personal belongings from city sidewalks or public parks. Although it is important for powerless people to have organizations that advocate for their rights, efforts such as these typically do not address the larger, structural factors that cause, or at least contribute to, the problem of homelessness. Examples include lack of affordable housing, few job opportunities, and dollar-strapped social service agencies that cannot help all of the individuals who need assistance.

Many people who are involved in midrange organizations see themselves primarily as local activists. Some display a bumper sticker saying, "Think globally, act locally" (Shaw, 1999). Many activists believe that in the absence of any sustained national agenda, national problems such as child poverty, low wages, and lack of affordable housing can be reduced by community-based organizations; but some analysts now believe that local activists must demand large-scale political and economic support to bring about necessary changes.

According to Randy Shaw (1999:2–3), the director of the Tenderloin Housing Clinic in San Francisco, California, and the founder of Housing America, a national mobilization campaign to increase federal housing funds,

> America's corporate and political elite has succeeded in controlling the national agenda because citizen activists and organizations are not fully participating

in the struggles shaping national political life. As the constituencies central to reclaiming America's progressive ideas bypass national fights to pursue local issues, their adversaries have faced surprisingly little opposition in dismantling federal programs achieved by six decades of national grassroots struggle. Citizen activities and organizations have steadfastly maintained their local focus even as national policy making drastically cut the resources flowing to communities. From 1979 to 1997, for example, federal aid to local communities for job training, housing, mass transit, environmental protection, and economic development fell by almost one trillion real dollars.

As this statement suggests, those working in grassroots organizations might be fighting a losing battle because the loss of federal aid can only diminish their future efforts. Accordingly, in the 1990s some grassroots activists changed their motto to "think locally and act globally" (Brecher and Costello, 1998), and began to work at the macrolevel, attempting to educate national leaders and corporate executives about the part that governments and transnational corporations must play if social problems are to be reduced or solved.

MACROLEVEL ATTEMPTS TO SOLVE SOCIAL PROBLEMS

Macrolevel solutions to social problems focus on how large-scale social institutions such as the government and the media can be persuaded to become involved in remedying social problems. Sometimes individuals who view themselves as individually powerless bind together in organizations to make demands on those who make decisions at the national or global level. As one social analyst explains,

> Most individuals are largely powerless in the face of economic forces beyond their control. But because millions of other people are affected in the same way, they have a chance to influence their conditions through collective action. To do so, people must grasp that the common interest is also their own personal interest. This happens whenever individuals join a movement, a union, a party, or any organization pursuing a common goal. It happens when people push for a social objective—say universal health care or human rights—which benefits them by benefiting all those similarly situated. It underlies the development of an environmental movement which seeks to preserve the environment on which all depend. (Brecher and Costello, 1998:107)

For example, when groups such as AARP (the American Association of Retired Persons) and the American Medical Association (AMA) support new health care legislation their efforts are more likely to culminate in passage of laws such as the 2010 Affordable Care Act, even though the individual interests of retired persons are more on the protection of Medicare and the individual interests of physicians who are members of the AMA may be on protecting the rights and income of physicians and guarding the viability of the doctor–patient relationship. In fact, most social analysts would place AARP and AMA in the following category—special-interest groups—that work for political change.

Working through Special-Interest Groups for Political Change

At the national level, those seeking macrolevel solutions to social problems may become members of a *special-interest group*—a political coalition composed of individuals or groups sharing a specific interest they wish to protect or advance with the help of the political system. Examples of special-interest groups include Common Cause, the League of Women Voters, and other organizations that advocate for specific issues such as the environment, gun control, educational reform, or thousands of other single- or multiple-issue concerns.

Through special-interest groups, which are sometimes called *pressure groups* or *lobbies*, people can seek to remedy social problems by exerting pressure on political leaders. These groups can be categorized on the basis of these factors:

1. *Issues.* Some groups focus on *single issues*, such as abortion, gun control, or school prayer; others focus on *multiple issues*, such as equal access to education, employment, and health care.
2. *View of the present system of wealth and power.* Some groups make *radical demands* that would involve the end of patriarchy, capitalism, governmental bureaucracy, or other existing power structures; others do not attack the legitimacy of the present system of wealth and power but insist on specific social reforms.
3. *Beliefs about elites.* Some groups want to *influence* elites or incorporate movement leaders into the elite; others want to *replace* existing elites with people whom they believe share their own interests and concerns.

Since the 1980s, an increasing number of more special-interest groups have been single-issue groups that focus on electing and supporting politicians who support their views. There might be more than one single-interest group working to reduce or eliminate a specific social problem. Usually, however, these groups do not agree on the nature and extent of the problem or on proposed solutions to the problem. For this reason, competing single-interest groups aggressively place their demands in front of elected officials and bureaucratic policy makers (see Chapter 13).

Working through National and International Social Movements to Reduce Problems

Collective behavior and national social movements are significant ways in which people seek to resolve social problems. *Collective behavior* is voluntary, often spontaneous, activity that is engaged in by a large number of people and typically violates dominant-group norms and values. Everything ranging from public protests and riots to flash mobs that are brought together on the spur of the moment by text messaging and social media, such as Facebook and Twitter, are examples of collective behavior. Since the civil rights movement in the 1960s, one popular form of public demonstration has been *civil disobedience—nonviolent action that seeks to change a policy or law by refusing to comply with it.* People often use civil disobedience in the form of sit-ins, marches, boycotts, and strikes to bring about change. When people refuse to abide by a policy or law and challenge authorities to do something about it, they are demanding social change with some sense of urgency. Recent examples include small-scale protester-on-legislator action where advocates backing specific legislation, such as demands for a universal health care system before the Affordable Care Act was passed. In 2009, advocates briefly occupied the offices of public officials, such as Senator Joe Lieberman, to make their wishes known.

> ◉—**Watch on mysoclab.com**
> *Grievances, Anger, and Hope*
> on **mysoclab.com**

Groups that engage in activities that they hope will achieve specific political goals are sometimes referred to as *protest crowds*. In 2011, protests in other nations, including Greece and Eqypt, made headlines around the world. In the United States, we have had fewer organized protests in recent years than might be expected with high rates of unemployment, a sluggish economy, and political turmoil among members of Congress in the nation's capital. However, at the time of this writing, we have to look back to the 2008 Republican National Convention to find a good example of a situation in which at least 10,000 protesters came forward to publicize an issue. At that time, more than 10,000 protesters marched in St. Paul, Minnesota, to show their opposition to the Iraqi War and call for the return of American troops to the United States. A second group of about 2,000 people marched on behalf of the homeless and the poor and to call attention to injustices they believed were perpetuated and exacerbated by government policies. Among those in the protest crowds were members of Veterans for Peace, Iraq Veterans Against the War, Military Families Speak Out, the Teamsters, Code Pink, the American Indian Movement, and the Poor People's Economic Human Rights Campaign.

What types of national and international social movements can be used to reduce social problems? National social movements can be divided into five major categories: reform, revolutionary, religious, alternative, and resistance movements. *Reform movements* seek to improve society by changing some specific aspect of the social structure. Environmental groups and disability rights groups are examples of groups that seek to change (reform) some specific aspect of the social structure. Reform movements typically seek to bring about change by working within the existing organizational structures of society, whereas *revolutionary movements* seek to bring about a total change in society. Examples of revolutionary movements include utopian groups and radical terrorist groups that use fear tactics to intimidate and gain—at least briefly—concessions from those with whom they disagree ideologically. Some radical terrorists kill many people in their pursuit of a society that more closely conforms to their own worldview.

Religious movements (also referred to as expressive movements) seek to renovate or renew people through inner change. Because these groups emphasize inner change, religious movements are often linked to local and regional organizations that seek to bring about changes in the individual's life. National religious movements often seek to persuade political officials to enact laws that will reduce or eliminate what they perceive to be a social problem. For example, some national religious movements view abortion as a problem and therefore lobby for a ban on abortions. In contrast, *alternative movements* seek limited change in some aspects of people's behavior. An example is MADD—Mothers Against Drunk Driving—an organization that specifically targets drunk driving and those who engage in such harmful behavior. Advocates from MADD often show up at court hearings when a person is being tried for a drunken driving offense to call attention to this pressing social problem and to call for justice to be done in this specific case.

Finally, *resistance movements* seek to prevent change or undo change that has already occurred. In public debates over social policies, most social movements advocating change face resistance from reactive movements, which hold opposing viewpoints and want social policy to reflect their own beliefs and values. An example of a resistance movement is an anti-immigrant organization that seeks to close U.S. borders to outsiders or to place harsher demands on employers who hire illegal immigrant workers.

Can national activism and social movements bring about the changes that are necessary to reduce social problems? Some analysts believe that certain social problems can be reduced through sustained efforts by organizations committed to change. According to social activist Randy Shaw (1999), efforts by Public Interest Research Groups and the Sierra Club, the nation's two largest grassroots environmental groups, were successful in stimulating a new national environmental activism in the 1990s. Wanting to strengthen the Clean Air Act of 1967, these two organizations engaged in affirmative national environmental activism, mobilizing people who had previously been disconnected from national environmental debates (Shaw, 1999). As a result, a strong working relationship developed between grassroots activists at the local level and the leaders of the national movement. In previous decades, national groups had believed that their national leaders knew what was best for the environmental movement and had relied solely on their leadership's relationship with lawmakers to bring about change (Shaw, 1999). However, this belief changed as activists sought to strengthen the Clean Air Act:

> The Clean Air Act standards became a battle over framing the issue. If the public saw the new standards as a health issue environmentalists would

The Raging Grannies is a group of activists who promote peace, justice, and social and economic equality through song and humor. Do you believe that activism will increase in the future? Why or why not?

prevail. Industry would win if, as in the health care debate [of the 1990s], it could define its campaign as trying to stop Big Government from hampering the private sector's ability to improve people's lives. The campaign would revisit the philosophical battleground where corporate America had increasingly prevailed in the past decade. Whether environmentalists' new emphasis on national grassroots mobilizing would change this would soon be seen. (Shaw, 1999:157)

Eventually, supporters declared that the clean air campaign had been a success and vowed that they would continue to demand changes that they believed would benefit the environment and improve the quality of life (Shaw, 1999).

What about global activism? Once again, we turn to the environmental movement for an example. In a 2000 *New York Times* article, Jared Diamond, a physiology professor and a board member of the World Wildlife Fund, observed that some transnational corporations were becoming aware that they have a responsibility for the environment. Diamond (2000) described a new attitude taking hold of corporations such as Chevron and Home Depot, both of which claimed to realize that it is better to have a clean operation than to have costly industrial disasters. Of course, consumers also demanded that corporations become more accountable for their actions: "Behind this trend lies consumers' growing awareness of the risks that environmental problems pose for the health, economies, and political stability of their own world and their children's world" (Diamond, 2000:A31). At that time, it was hoped that growing consumer awareness would lead companies that buy and retail forest products to no longer sell wood products from environmentally sensitive areas of the world and instead give preference to certified wood—that is, lumber that has been derived from forests where guidelines for environmentally sound logging practices have been met (Diamond, 2000). However, this belief has proven to be unduly optimistic, coming as it did, before the terrorist attacks of 2001 and eight years of the Bush administration when corporate power grew and government regulations and enforcement were weakened, if not crippled, in some cases.

Other analysts have argued that what is needed is "globalization-from-below" (Brecher and Costello, 1998). In other words, people cannot rely on corporations to solve environmental problems. Indeed, it is necessary to develop a human agenda that will offset the corporate agenda that has produced many of the problems in the first place. Social activists Jeremy Brecher and Tim Costello (1998) suggest these criteria for any proposed human agenda:

- It should improve the lives of the great majority of the world's people over the long run.
- It should correspond to widely held common interests and should integrate the interests of people around the world.
- It should provide handles for action at a variety of levels.
- It should include elements that can be at least partially implemented independently but that are compatible or mutually reinforcing.
- It should make it easier, not harder, to solve noneconomic problems such as protection of the environment and reduction of war.
- It should grow organically out of social movements and coalitions that have developed in response to the needs of diverse peoples.

On the basis of these guidelines, the only way in which a major global social problem, such as environmental degradation or world poverty, can be reduced is through a drastic redirection of our energies, as Brecher and Costello (1998:184) explain:

The energies now directed to the race to the bottom need to be redirected to the rebuilding of the global economy on a humanly and environmentally sound basis. Such an approach requires limits to growth—in some spheres, sharp reduction—in the material demands that human society places on the environment. It requires reduced energy and resource use; less toxic production and products; shorter individual worktime; and less production for war. But it requires vast growth in education, health care, human caring, recycling, rebuilding an ecologically sound production and consumption system, and time available for self-development, community life, and democratic participation.

Do you believe that such human cooperation is possible? Will it be possible for a new generation of political leaders to separate *politics* from *policy* and focus on discovering the best courses of action for the country and the world? Where do ideas regarding possible social policies come from? Some of the ideas and policies of tomorrow are being developed today in public policy organizations and think tanks (see Table 18.3). If, as some analysts believe, these think tanks are increasingly setting the U.S. government's

TABLE 18.3 Examples of Public Policy Organizations and Think Tanks

Action Institute for the Study of Religion and Liberty	Family Research Council
Adam Smith Institute	Fight Internet Taxes!
The AFL-CIO	Frontiers of Freedom Institute
Alliance for America	Galen Institute
American Civil Liberties Union	Goldwater Institute
American Conservative Union	Heartland Institute
American Enterprise Institute	Heritage Foundation
The American Institute for Full Employment	Hoover Institute
Americans for a Balanced Budget	Hudson Institute
Americans for Democratic Action	Independence Institute
Americans for Hope, Growth and Opportunity	Institute for Civic Values
Americans for Tax Reform	Institute for Economic Analysis, Inc.
Amnesty International	Institute for First Amendment Studies
Atlas Economic Research Foundation	Institute for Global Communications
Brookings Institution	Institute for Justice
Campaign for America's Future	Institute for Policy Innovation
The Carter Center	Leadership Institute
Cascade Policy Institute	League of Conservative Voters
Cato Institute	League of Women Voters
Center of the American Experiment	Ludwig von Mises Institute
Center for Defense Information	Madison Institute
Center for Equal Opportunity	Manhattan Institute
Center for Individual Rights	National Organization for Women
Center for Law and Social Policy	National Rifle Association
Center for Policy Alternatives	OMB Watch
Center to Prevent Handgun Violence	People for the American Way
Center for Public Integrity	Pioneer Institute for Public Policy Research
Center for Responsive Politics	Planned Parenthood
Century Foundation	Progress and Freedom Foundation
Children's Defense Fund	Project for Defense Alternatives
Christian Coalition	Public Citizen
Citizens Against Government Waste	RAND Corporation
Citizens for an Alternative Tax System	Reason Foundation
Citizens for Tax Justice	Tax Reform NOW!
Clare Boothe Luce Policy Institute	Union of Concerned Scientists
Claremont Institute	U.S. Term Limits
Discovery Institute	Worldwatch Institute
Economic Policy Institute	Young America's Foundation
Empower America	

agenda, how much do we know about these groups, their spokespersons, and the causes they advocate?

Perhaps gaining more information about the current state of U.S. and global affairs is the first step toward our individual efforts to be part of the solution rather than part of the problem in the future.

Limitations of the Macrolevel Solutions Approach

As C. Wright Mills stated, social problems by definition cannot be resolved without organizational initiatives that bring about social change. Therefore, macrolevel approaches are necessary for reducing or eliminating many social problems. However, some analysts believe that macrolevel approaches overemphasize structural barriers in society and give people the impression that these barriers are insurmountable walls that preclude social change. Macrolevel approaches might also deemphasize the importance of individual responsibility. Reducing the availability of illegal drugs, for example, does not resolve the problem of the individual drug abuser who still needs a means to eliminate the problem in her or his personal life. Similarly, macrolevel approaches usually do not allow for the possibility of positive communication and the kind of *human cooperation* that transcends national boundaries (Brecher and Costello, 1998). Experience, however, has shown us that positive communication and global cooperation are possible.

According to sociologist Immanuel Wallerstein, a former president of the International Sociological Association:

> We live in an imperfect world, one that will always be imperfect and therefore always harbor injustice. But we are far from helpless before this reality. We can make the world less unjust; we can make it more beautiful; we can increase our cognition of it. We need but to construct it, and in order to construct it we need but to reason with each other and struggle to obtain from each other the special knowledge that each of us has been able to seize. We can labor in the vineyards and bring forth fruit, if only we try. (Wallerstein, 1999:250)

In the two decades since this statement was made, Wallerstein has reaffirmed these beliefs on numerous occasions, namely that social justice is the way to improve life for more people around the world. In any case, a sociological approach to examining social problems provides us with new ideas about how to tackle some of the most pressing issues of our times (see Box 18.2).

We have seen that different theoretical approaches to analyzing social problems bring us to a variety of conclusions about how we might reduce or eliminate certain problems. Let's take a last look at the major sociological theories we have studied so that we can relate them one more time to social problems, an activity which you will hopefully continue in the future as new challenges arise and older problems continue to need resolution.

FINAL REVIEW OF SOCIAL THEORIES AND SOCIAL PROBLEMS

The underlying theoretical assumptions that we hold regarding social problems often have a profound influence on what we feel may be the best solution for a specific problem. Do we believe society is based on stability or conflict? Is conflict typically good for society or bad for society? According to the functionalist perspective, society is a stable, orderly system that is composed of a number of interrelated parts, each of which performs a function that contributes to the overall stability of the society. From the functionalist perspective, social problems arise when social institutions do not fulfill the functions they are supposed to perform or when dysfunctions (undesirable consequences of an activity or social process that inhibit a society's ability to adapt or adjust) occur. For example, in the aftermath of Hurricane Katrina, all levels of government were severely criticized for the excessive amount of time it took to get military personnel and emergency evacuation crews to disaster sites and to provide food, water, sanitation, and transportation for those who were displaced by the storm. If the vast problems experienced by individuals living in the Gulf Coast states are symptomatic of larger gaps in national emergency preparedness, the U.S. government will continue to be accused of indifference, incompetence, or even worse. According to the functionalist approach, dysfunctions create social disorganization, which in turn causes a breakdown in the traditional values and norms that serve as social control mechanisms. As shown in Table 18.4 on page 422, the social disorganization approach traces the causes of social problems to social

Critical Thinking and You

Box 18.2

Applying Sociology to the Ordinary and the Extraordinary in Everyday Life

[In the aftermath of Hurricane Katrina in New Orleans], you're now looking at a situation in which, when people return, they may have to find work. . . . Both close ties [with others] and extended relationships will be very important, and it's likely the people who have both will do best.

—Jeanne Hulbert, a sociologist at Louisiana State University in Baton Rouge, talks about studies on hurricane disasters she and her colleagues conducted that show a clear link between people's mental health and the kinds of social relationships they have (Carey, 2005:A20).

People don't know until something like this comes along how much the shape of their house, the texture of their house, the mood of their neighborhood, are important parts of who they are. People take all of this so much for granted that when they return and the house is gone or not habitable it disorients them, makes them more lonely and more afraid, and they don't know why. This is true of public spaces and streets, too. You have no idea how much they mean to you until they are gone or permanently altered.

—Kai Erikson, a sociologist at Yale University and author of several books about disasters, including Everything in Its Path: Destruction of Community in the Buffalo Creek Flood, *looks at the sociological psychology of how people deal with disasters (Carey, 2005:A20).*

In times of crisis, including natural disasters, terrorist attacks, war, and other cataclysmic events, sociologists are often called on to discuss these events as they affect individuals, groups, and nations. Because sociologists in academic and research settings are continually engaged in research in their areas of specialization, they are authorities on topics such as the social psychology of survival. As a result of years of theorizing and research, scholars such as Jeanne Hulbert and Kai Erikson (quoted previously) gain and share with others significant insights on social phenomenon such as how people react to disasters.

However, we do not necessarily need to be experts in order to put basic sociological ideas into practice. Sociological insights on social problems can be used in a variety of fields, including criminal justice, community and human services, health care and substance abuse programs, and disaster relief efforts. But, perhaps more importantly to each of us, sociology can be used in our everyday life to help us understand what is going on around us and to evaluate the quality of life in our own community. As a final critical thinking activity in this course, let's take a new look at the city where you live.

Questions for Consideration

1. Media discussions about the disaster in New Orleans often called attention to a "rich section" or "poor section" of the city. Can you identify areas of your city that could be classified as upper, middle, or lower class? If so, what sociological factors did you use to distinguish among the various areas and the people who live in each?

2. Can you identify distinct racial or ethnic patterns with regard to where people live in your city? If a reporter asked you the following question, how would you answer: "Do you think that race or class is the most important factor in determining where people in your community live?" In answering this question, is it possible that race and class are so intertwined as factors relating to privilege or deprivation that giving the reporter an "either/or" answer is virtually impossible?

change that leaves existing rules inadequate for current conditions. In societies undergoing social change—for example, high rates of immigration, rapid changes in technology, and increasingly complex patterns of social life—social disorganization produces stress at the individual level and inefficiency and confusion at the institutional and societal levels. Thus, the functionalist approach to reducing social problems has as central factors the prevention of rapid social changes, the maintenance of the status quo, and the restoration of order.

In contrast, the conflict perspective assumes that conflict is natural and inevitable in society. Value conflict approaches focus on conflict between the values held by members of divergent groups. These approaches also highlight the ways in which cultural, economic, and social diversity may contribute to misunderstandings

Table 18.4   Perceived Problems and Possible Solutions

Perspective	Causes	Possible Solutions
Functionalist:		
Social disorganization	Social change; inadequacy of existing social rules	Developing and implementing social rules that are explicit, workable, and consistent
Conflict:		
Value conflict	Conflict between different groups' values; economic, social, and cultural diversity	Groups confronting opponents and working for lasting changes in policy or legislation
Critical conflict (Marxist)	Relations of domination and subordination are reinforced by the global capitalist economy and political leaders who put other priorities ahead of the good of the people	Changing the nature of society, particularly inequalities that grow more pronounced as the wealthy grow richer and the poor worldwide become increasingly impoverished
Symbolic Interactionist:		
Deviant behavior	Inappropriate socialization within primary groups	Resocializing or rehabilitating people so that they will conform
Labeling	How people label behavior, how they respond to it, and the consequences of their responses	Changing the definition through decriminalization; limiting labeling

Source: Based on Weinberg et al., 1981; Feagin et al., 2006.

and problems. According to Marxist (or critical-conflict) theorists, groups are engaged in a continuous power struggle for control of scarce resources. As a result of the unjust use of political, economic, or social power, certain groups of people are privileged while others are disadvantaged. Thus, for critical-conflict theorists, social problems arise out of major contradictions that are inherent in the ways in which societies are organized. When this approach is used, the root causes of social problems—patriarchy, capitalism, and massive spending on the U.S. military-industrial complex at the expense of human services, for example—must be radically altered or eliminated altogether. Focusing on the political economy, one critical-conflict approach states that the capitalist economy, which is now global, maintains and reinforces domination and subordination in social relations. This approach also examines how political leaders might put their own interests ahead of any

common good that might exist. Clearly, any solutions to social problems by this approach would require radical changes in society and thus are not always viewed positively in societies in which economic prosperity based on individual attributes rather than collective activities is considered a mark of personal and social achievement. Other conflict theorists view the interlocking nature of race, class, and gender as systems of domination and subordination as central concerns to social problems. Therefore, their solutions for reducing or eliminating social problems that are embedded in racial and ethnic relations, class relationships, and gender inequalities also require dramatic changes in society.

At the macrolevel, globalization theories make us aware that many social problems transcend the borders of any one nation and are often international in their causes and consequences. As some social scientists have suggested, any solution to global social problems will require new thinking about how business, politics, and civil society ought to work together and how nation-states worldwide must establish policies and enact legislation that will benefit not only their own constituents but also the global community (Richard, 2002).

If we shift to the microlevel, the symbolic interactionist perspective focuses on how people act toward one another and make sense of their daily lives. From this perspective, society is the sum of the interactions of individuals and groups. Thus, symbolic interactionists often study social problems by analyzing the process whereby a behavior is defined as a social problem and how individuals and groups come to engage in activities that a significant number of people view as major social concerns. Symbolic interactionist theories of deviance note that inadequate socialization or interacting with the "wrong" people may contribute to deviant behavior and crime. Similarly, interactionists who use the labeling framework for their analysis of social problems study how people label behavior, how they respond to people engaged in such behavior, and the consequences of their behavior. Essentially, a symbolic interactionist approach helps us understand why certain actions are significant to people and how people communicate what these actions mean to them. For example, fear of potential terrorism can affect how people think and behave, whether or not they are actually in harm's way and have real cause to modify their daily routines and encounters with others.

A symbolic interactionist approach can also help us understand how some low-income people caught up in a natural disaster such as Hurricane Katrina might engage in illegal behavior that they otherwise might never have considered, such as pilfering and looting, because of the magnitude of the tragedy facing them and the brief opportunity that presents itself to get "free" food, supplies, and perhaps "luxury" items such as expensive television sets or jewelry they otherwise would never have been able to afford. Moreover, only limited plans had been made by officials to successfully evacuate these individuals should the need ever arise, as one journalist stated:

> The victims . . . were largely black and poor, those who toiled in the background of the tourist havens, living in tumbledown neighborhoods that were long known to be vulnerable to disaster if the levees failed. Without so much as a car or bus fare to escape ahead of time, they found

Why were some people referred to as "looters" in the aftermath of Hurricane Katrina while others were described as "appropriating what they needed to survive"? According to symbolic interactionists, social problems may be viewed differently based on who is participating in the activity and what is believed to be the cause of their conduct.

> themselves left behind by a failure to plan for their rescue should the dreaded day ever arrive. (Gonzalez, 2005:A1, A19)

And, indeed, when that day did arrive, the majority of the victims who were hardest hit were those who lived at the margins of society and who were left behind not only when people initially evacuated from the city before the storm hit but also when initial rescue efforts were so slow getting started. From a symbolic interactionist perspective, an ordeal such as resulted from Hurricane Katrina is likely to affect how people think and feel about themselves and others, how they view "reality," and the labels they use to identify themselves and their needs in relation to others. For example, some of the poor and black victims who prior to the disaster were struggling mightily now find themselves with new labels, including "homeless," "destitute," and "refugee."

Each of these sociological perspectives suggests ways in which social problems may be identified and remedies may be sought. In doing so, these theories provide divergent views on social change that might reduce or eliminate social problems. We are left with one final question as we conclude this book and our time together: Won't you join with sociologists and others who seek to face up to one of the greatest challenges of the twenty-first century, which is how to bring peace, justice, and greater social equality to as many of the world's people as possible?

SUMMARY

✔•⌐ **Study** and **Review** on **mysoclab.com**

■ **Why is it difficult to reduce or eliminate social problems?**
According to social scientists, reducing or solving social problems is more complex than simply identifying such problems and pinpointing their social locations because many obstacles, delays, and frustrations confront those who attempt to bring about social changes that might alleviate the problems. Solving a problem can entail prohibitive costs and may only give rise to a whole new set of problems.

■ **What is social change and why is it important in reducing social problems?**
Social change refers to the alternation, modification, or transformation of public policy, culture, or social institutions over time. Social change is important in reducing social problems because a combination of strategies, some previously untried, are usually required to reduce major social problems.

■ **What are microlevel solutions to social problems? What are the limitations of this approach?**
Microlevel solutions to social problems focus on how individuals operate within small groups to try to remedy a problem that affects them, their family, or friends. Most people turn to their primary groups to help them deal with a problem. However, solving social problems one person at a time does not take into account the fact that secondary groups and societal institutions play a significant part in creating, maintaining, and exacerbating many social problems.

■ **What are midrange attempts to deal with social problems? What are the limitations of this approach?**
Midrange attempts to deal with social problems focus on how secondary groups and formal organizations deal with problems or seek to assist individuals in overcoming problems such as addiction to drugs or alcohol. Grassroots groups often work to change a perceived wrong in their neighborhood, city, state, or nation. Although local efforts to reduce problems that affect individuals and collectivities in a specific city or region have brought about many improvements in the social life of individuals and small groups, they usually lack the sustained capacity to produce the larger systemic changes needed at the national or international levels to reduce or eliminate the problems.

■ **What are macrolevel attempts to deal with social problems? What are the limitations of this approach?**
Macrolevel solutions to social problems focus on how large-scale social institutions such as the government and the media can become involved in remedying social problems. Some people work through social movements, others through special-interest groups, and still others through various forms of collective behavior. Although macrolevel approaches are necessary for reducing or eliminating many social problems, some analysts believe that these approaches overemphasize structural barriers in society and give people the impression that these barriers constitute insurmountable walls that preclude social change. Macrolevel approaches can also deemphasize the importance of individual responsibility.

■ **What are three key factors that can be used to differentiate special-interest groups?**
The three factors by which special-interest groups may be categorized are (1) issues (single issue versus multiple demands), (2) view of the present system of wealth and power (positive versus negative), and (3) beliefs about elites (whether to try to influence elites or seek to replace them).

■ **What is collective behavior? How does civil disobedience occur?**
Collective behavior is voluntary, often spontaneous activity that is engaged in by a large number of people and typically violates dominant-group norms and values. As a form of collective behavior, civil disobedience refers to nonviolent action that seeks to change a policy or law by refusing to comply with it.

■ **What are the key characteristics of the five major categories of national social movements?**
National social movements are divided into five major categories: reform, revolutionary, religious, alternative, and resistance movements. Reform movements seek to improve society by changing some specific aspect of the social structure. Revolutionary movements seek to bring about a total change in society. Religious movements seek to renovate or renew people through "inner change." Alternative movements seek limited change in some aspects of people's behavior and currently include organizations such as Mothers Against Drunk Driving (MADD).

■ **What is a human agenda? What might be the major criteria for such an agenda?**
According to some analysts, we need to develop a human agenda that focuses on the needs of people and offsets the corporate agenda that is currently taking precedence over other issues and concerns. Social activists Jeremy Brecher and Tim Costello suggest that any proposed human agenda should (1) improve the lives of the great majority of the world's people, (2) correspond to widely held common interests, as well as integrate the interests of people worldwide, (3) provide handles for action at a variety of levels, (4) include elements that can be implemented independently, at least in part, but that are compatible or mutually reinforcing, (5) make it easier to solve noneconomic problems such as environmental pollution, and (6) grow out of social movements and coalitions that have developed in response to the needs of diverse peoples.

■ **What is the primary focus of functionalist, conflict, and interactionist approaches to solving social problems?**
From the functionalist perspective, social problems arise when social institutions do not fulfill the functions they are supposed to or when dysfunctions occur; therefore, social institutions need to be made more effective, and social change needs to be managed carefully. According to critical-conflict theorists, social problems arise out of the major contradictions inherent in the way societ-ies are organized (particularly factors such as patriarchy and capitalism). Consequently, attempting to solve social problems requires major changes in the political economy. Symbolic interactionists focus on how certain behavior comes to be defined as a social problem and why some individuals and groups engage in that behavior. To reduce problems entails more adequate socialization of people as well as a better understanding of how labeling affects people's behavior.

KEY TERMS

civil disobedience, p. 416
collective behavior, p. 416
grassroots groups, p. 413

infrastructure, p. 406
primary groups, p. 411
secondary groups, p. 411

social change, p. 410
social movement, p. 413
special-interest group, p.416

QUESTIONS FOR CRITICAL THINKING

1. Do you believe that corporations can be trusted to do the right thing when it comes to reducing or eliminating existing social problems? Is good corporate citizenship a possibility in the global economy today? Why or why not?

2. Suppose that you were given the economic resources and political clout to reduce a major social problem. Which problem would you choose? What steps would you take to alleviate this problem? How would you measure your success or failure in reducing or eliminating the problem?

3. What is most useful about applying a sociological perspective to the study of social problems? What is least useful about a sociological approach? How can you contribute to a better understanding of the causes, effects, and possible solutions to social problems?

Succeed with MySocLab® www.mysoclab.com

The new MySocLab delivers proven results in helping students succeed, provides engaging experiences that personalize learning, and comes from a trusted partner with educational expertise and a deep commitment to helping students and instructors achieve their goals.

Here are a few activities you will find for this chapter:

Watch on **mysoclab.com**

Core Concepts video clips feature sociologists in action, exploring important concepts in the study of Social Problems. Watch:
• Grievances, Anger, and Hope

Explore on **mysoclab.com**

Social Explorer is an interactive application that allows you to explore Census data through interactive maps. Explore:
• Social Explorer Activity: Transportation and Social Status

Read on **mysoclab.com**

MySocLibrary includes primary source readings from classic and contemporary sociologists. Read:
• Community Building: Steps Toward a Good Society

Glossary

absolute poverty   a condition that exists when people do not have the means to secure the most basic necessities of life.

acid rain   rainfall containing large concentrations of sulfuric and nitric acids (primarily from the burning of fuel and car and truck exhausts).

acquaintance rape   forcible sexual activity that meets the legal definition of rape and involves people who first meet in a social setting.

acute diseases   illnesses that strike suddenly and cause dramatic incapacitation and sometimes death.

ageism   prejudice and discrimination against people on the basis of age.

amalgamation (the melting-pot model)   a process in which the cultural attributes of diverse racial-ethnic groups are blended together to form a new society incorporating the unique contributions of each group.

Anglo-conformity model   a pattern of assimilation whereby members of subordinate racial-ethnic groups are expected to conform to the culture of the dominant (white) Anglo-Saxon population.

anti-Semitism   prejudice and discriminatory behavior directed at Jews.

assimilation   the process by which members of subordinate racial and ethnic groups become absorbed into the dominant culture.

blaming the victim   a practice used by people who view a social problem as emanating from within the individual who exhibits the problem.

blended family   a family that consists of a husband and wife, children from previous marriages, and children (if any) from the new marriage.

capitalism   an economic system characterized by private ownership of the means of production, from which personal profits can be derived through market competition and without government intervention.

chronic diseases   illnesses that are long-term or lifelong and that develop gradually or are present from birth.

civil disobedience   nonviolent action that seeks to change a policy or law by refusing to comply with it.

class system   a system of social inequality based on the ownership and control of resources and on the type of work people do.

codependency   a reciprocal relationship between the alcoholic and one or more nonalcoholics who unwittingly aid and abet the alcoholic's excessive drinking and resulting behavior.

cohabitation   two adults living together in a sexual relationship without being legally married.

collective behavior   voluntary, often spontaneous, activity that is engaged in by a large number of people and typically violates dominant-group norms and values.

collective violence   organized violence by people seeking to promote their cause or resist social policies or practices that they consider oppressive.

comparable worth   the belief that wages ought to reflect the worth of a job, not the gender or race of the worker.

conflict perspective   a framework for viewing society that is based on the assumption that groups in society are engaged in a continuous power struggle for control of scarce resources.

contingent work   part-time work, temporary work, and subcontracted work that offers advantages to employers but can be detrimental to workers' welfare.

core nations   dominant capitalist centers characterized by high levels of industrialization and urbanization.

corporate crime   illegal acts committed by corporate employees on behalf of the corporation and with its support.

crime   a behavior that violates criminal law and is punishable by a fine, a jail term, or other negative sanctions.

criminal justice system   the network of organizations, including the police, courts, jails, and prisons, involved in law enforcement and the administration of justice.

crude birth rate   the number of live births per 1,000 people in a population in a given year.

cultural capital   social assets, such as values, beliefs, attitudes, and competencies in language and culture, that are learned at home and required for success and social advancement.

culture   the knowledge, language, values, customs, and material objects that are passed from person to person and from one generation to the next in a human group or society.

deinstitutionalization   the practice of discharging patients from mental hospitals into the community.

democracy   a political system in which the people hold the ruling power either directly or through elected representatives.

demographic transition theory   the process by which some societies move from high birth and death rates to relatively low birth and death rates as a result of technological development.

demography   the study of the size, composition, and distribution of populations.

dependency ratio   the number of workers necessary to support people under age fifteen and over age sixty-three.

desertification   the process by which usable land is turned into desert because of overgrazing, harmful agricultural practices, or deforestation.

deviance   a behavior, belief, or condition that violates social norms.

differential association theory   the belief that individuals have a greater tendency to deviate from societal norms when they frequently associate with people who tend toward deviance rather than conformity.

disability   a restricted or total lack of ability to perform certain activities as a result of physical limitations or the interplay of these limitations, social responses, and the social environment.

discrimination   actions or practices of dominant-group members (or their representatives) that have a harmful impact on members of subordinate groups.

domestic partnership   a household partnership in which an unmarried couple lives together in a committed, sexually intimate relationship and is granted the same rights and benefits accorded to a married couple.

427

dominant (majority) group   a group that is advantaged and has superior resources and rights in a society.

drug   any substance—other than food or water—that, when taken into the body, alters its functioning in some way.

drug addiction (or drug dependency)   a psychological and/or physiological need for a drug to maintain a sense of well-being and avoid withdrawal symptoms.

drug subculture   a group of people whose attitudes, beliefs, and behaviors pertaining to drug use differ significantly from those of most people in the larger society.

dual-earner marriages   marriages in which both spouses are in the labor force.

economy   the social institution that ensures that a society will be maintained through its production, distribution, and consumption of goods and services.

edge city   an area of middle- to upper-middle-class residences with complete working, shopping, and leisure activities so that it is not dependent on the central city or other suburbs.

education   the social institution responsible for transmitting knowledge, skills, and cultural values in a formally organized structure.

elite model   a view of society in which power in political systems is concentrated in the hands of a small group, whereas the masses are relatively powerless.

environmental degradation   disruptions to the environment that have negative consequences for ecosystems.

environmental racism   the intentional or unintentional enactment of a policy or regulation that has a negative effect on the living conditions of low-income individuals and/or persons of color as compared to those from more affluent communities.

environmental tobacco smoke   the smoke in the air as a result of other people's tobacco smoking.

erotica   materials that depict consensual sexual activities that are sought by and pleasurable to all parties involved.

ethnic group   a category of people who are distinguished, by others or by themselves, as inferior or superior, primarily on the basis of cultural or nationality characteristics.

ethnic pluralism   the coexistence of diverse racial-ethnic groups with separate identities and cultures within a society.

ethnocentrism   the assumption that one's own group and way of life are superior to all others.

extended family   a family unit composed of relatives in addition to parents and children, all of whom live in the same household.

families   relationships in which people live together with commitment, form an economic unit and care for any young, and consider the group critical to their identity.

family of orientation   the family into which a person is born and in which early socialization takes place.

family of procreation   the family that a person forms by having or adopting children.

felony   a serious crime, such as murder, rape, or aggravated assault, that is punishable by more than a year's imprisonment or even death.

feminization of poverty   the trend whereby women are disproportionately represented among individuals living in poverty.

fertility   the number of children born to an individual or a population.

fetal alcohol syndrome (FAS)   a condition characterized by mental retardation and craniofacial malformations that may affect the child of an alcoholic mother.

field research   the study of social life in its natural setting: observing and interviewing people where they live, work, and play.

forcible rape   the act of forcing sexual intercourse on an adult of legal age against their will.

framing   the manner in which news content and its accompanying visual images are linked together to create certain audience perceptions and give specific impressions to viewers and readers.

functionalist perspective   a framework for viewing society as a stable, orderly system composed of a number of interrelated parts, each of which performs a function that contributes to the overall stability of society.

functionally illiterate   being unable to read and/or write at the skill level necessary for carrying out everyday tasks.

gender   culturally and socially constructed differences between females and males that are based on meanings, beliefs, and practices that a group or society associates with "femininity" or "masculinity."

gender bias   a situation in which favoritism is shown toward one gender.

gendered division of labor   the process whereby productive tasks are separated on the basis of gender.

gendered racism   the interactive effect of racism and sexism in exploiting women of color.

gender gap   the difference between a candidate's number of votes from women and men.

genocide   the deliberate, systematic killing of an entire people or nation.

gentrification   the process by which people renovate or restore properties in city centers.

glass ceiling   the invisible institutional barrier constructed by male management that prevents women from reaching top positions in major corporations and other large-scale organizations.

government   a formal organization that has legal and political authority to regulate relationships among people in a society and between the society and others outside its borders.

grassroots groups   organizations started by ordinary people who work in concert to change a perceived wrong in their neighborhood, city, state, or nation.

greenhouse effect   an environmental condition caused by excessive quantities of carbon dioxide, water vapor, methane, and nitrous oxide in the atmosphere.

hate crime   a physical attack against a person because of assumptions regarding his or her racial group, ethnicity, religion, disability, sexual orientation, national origin, or ancestry.

health maintenance organization (HMO)   an organization that provides, for a fixed monthly fee, total health care with an emphasis on prevention to avoid costly treatment later.

hegemony theory   the view that the media are instruments of social control and are used by members of the ruling classes to create "false consciousness" in the working classes.

hidden curriculum   how certain cultural values and attitudes, such as conformity and obedience to authority, are transmitted through implied demands in the everyday rules and routines of schools.

high-income nations countries with highly industrialized economies; technologically advanced industrial, administrative, and service occupations; and relatively high levels of national and per capita (per person) income.

homophobia excessive fear or intolerance of homosexuality.

hospices organizations that provide a homelike facility or home-based care (or both) for people who are terminally ill.

illegitimate opportunity structures circumstances that allow people to acquire through illegitimate activities what they cannot achieve legitimately.

income the economic gain derived from wages, salaries, income transfers (governmental aid such as Temporary Aid to Needy Families, known as TANF), or ownership of property.

individual discrimination one-on-one acts by members of the dominant group that harm members of the subordinate group or their property.

industrialization the process by which societies are transformed from a dependence on agriculture and handmade products to an emphasis on manufacturing and related industries.

infant mortality rate the number of deaths of infants under one year of age per 1,000 live births in a given year.

infrastructure a framework of support systems, such as transportation and utilities, that makes it possible to have specific land uses and a built environment that facilitate people's daily activities and the nation's economy.

institutional discrimination the day-to-day practices of organizations and institutions that have a harmful impact on members of subordinate groups.

interactionist perspective a framework that views society as the sum of the interactions of individuals and groups.

internal colonialism a process that occurs when members of a racial-ethnic group are conquered or colonized and forcibly placed under the economic and political control of the dominant group.

juvenile delinquency a violation of law or the commission of a status offense by a young person under a specific age.

kinship a social network of people based on common ancestry, marriage, or adoption.

labeling theory the proposition that delinquents and criminals are those people who have been successfully labeled as such by others.

latent functions hidden, unstated, and sometimes unintended consequences of activities in an organization or institution.

life chances the extent to which individuals have access to important societal resources such as food, clothing, shelter, education, and health care.

life expectancy an estimate of the average lifetime of people born in a specific year.

lifestyle-routine activity approach the belief that the patterns and timing of people's daily movements and activities as they go about obtaining the necessities of life—such as food, shelter, companionship, and entertainment—are the keys to understanding violent personal crimes and other types of crime in our society.

low-income nations primarily agrarian countries with little industrialization and low levels of national and personal income.

macrolevel analysis focuses on social processes occurring at the societal level, especially in large-scale organizations and major social institutions such as politics, government, and the economy.

managed care any system of cost containment that closely monitors and controls health care providers' decisions about medical procedures, diagnostic tests, and other services that should be provided to patients.

manifest functions open, stated, and intended goals or consequences of activities within an organization or institution.

mass murder the killing of four or more people at one time and in one place by the same person.

master status the most significant status a person possesses because it largely determines how individuals view themselves and how they are treated by others.

mechanical solidarity social bonds based on shared religious beliefs and a simple division of labor.

media concentration the tendency of the media industries to cluster together in groups with the goal of enhancing profitability.

media industries major businesses that own or own interests in radio and television production and broadcasting; motion pictures, movie theaters, and music companies; newspaper, periodical (magazine), and book publishing; and Internet services and content providers that influence people and cultures worldwide.

medical-industrial complex a term that encompasses both local physicians and hospitals as well as global health-related industries such as the pharmaceutical and medical supply companies that deliver health care today.

megalopolis a continuous concentration of two or more cities and their suburbs that have grown until they form an interconnected urban area.

melting-pot model see amalgamation.

microlevel analysis focuses on small-group relations and social interaction among individuals.

middle-income nations countries undergoing transformation from agrarian to industrial economies.

migration the movement of people from one geographic area to another for the purpose of changing residency.

military-industrial complex the interdependence of the military establishment and private military contractors.

misdemeanor a relatively minor crime that is punishable by a fine or less than a year in jail.

mixed economy an economic system that combines elements of both capitalism (a market economy) and socialism (a command economy).

monogamy a marriage between one woman and one man.

monopoly a situation that exists when a single firm controls an industry and accounts for all sales in a specific market.

mortality the number of deaths that occur in a specific population.

murder the unlawful, intentional killing of one person by another.

norms established rules of behavior or standards of conduct.

nuclear family a family unit composed of one or two parents and their dependent children who live apart from other relatives.

obscenity the legal term for pornographic materials that are offensive by generally accepted standards of decency.

occupational (white-collar) crime illegal activities committed by people in the course of their employment or normal business activity.

oligopoly   a situation in which a small number of companies or suppliers control an entire industry or service.

organic solidarity   social bonds based on interdependence and an elaborate division of labor (specialization).

organized crime   a business operation that supplies illegal goods and services for profit.

patriarchy   a hierarchical system of social organization in which cultural, political, and economic structures are controlled by men.

peripheral nations   nations that depend on core nations for capital, have little or no industrialization (other than what may be brought in by core nations), and have uneven patterns of urbanization.

permanent government   the top-tier civil service bureaucrats who have a strong power base and play a major role in developing and implementing government policies and procedures.

perspective   an overall approach or viewpoint toward some subject.

pink-collar occupations   relatively low-paying, nonmanual, semi-skilled positions that are held primarily by women.

plea bargaining   a process in a criminal trial whereby the prosecution negotiates a reduced sentence in exchange for a guilty plea.

pluralistic model   the view that power is widely dispersed throughout many competing interest groups in our political system.

political action committees (PACs)   special-interest groups that fund campaigns to help elect (or defeat) candidates based on their positions on specific issues.

political economy   the interdependent workings and interests of political and economic systems.

political party   an organization whose purpose is to gain and hold legitimate control of government.

politics   the social institution through which power is acquired and exercised by some people and groups.

population composition   the biological and social characteristics of a population, including such attributes as age, sex, race, marital status, education, occupation, income, and size of household.

pornography   the graphic depiction of sexual behavior through pictures and/or words—including by electronic or other data retrieval systems—in a manner that is intended to be sexually arousing.

poverty rate   the proportion of the population whose income falls below the government's official poverty line—the level of income below which a family of a given size is considered to be poor.

power   the ability of people to achieve their goals despite opposition from others.

power elite   rulers of the United States, which at the top is composed of business leaders, the executive branch of the federal government, and the military (especially the "top brass" at the Pentagon).

prejudice   a negative attitude based on faulty generalizations about members of selected racial and ethnic groups.

prestige   the respect, esteem, or regard accorded to an individual or group by others.

primary deviance   the initial act of rule breaking.

primary groups   small, less specialized groups in which members engage in face-to-face, emotion-based interactions over an extended period of time.

primary prevention   programs that seek to prevent drug problems before they begin.

primary-sector production   the extraction of raw materials and natural resources from the environment.

property crime   the taking of money or property from another without force, the threat of force, or the destruction of property.

prostitution   the sale of sexual services (of oneself or another) for money or goods and without emotional attachment.

punishment   any action designed to deprive a person of things of value (including liberty) because of an offense the person is thought to have committed.

racial group   a category of people who have been singled out, by others or themselves, sometimes as inferior or superior, on the basis of subjectively selected physical characteristics such as skin color, hair texture, and eye shape.

racism   a set of attitudes, beliefs, and practices used to justify the superior treatment of one racial or ethnic group and the inferior treatment of another racial or ethnic group.

relative poverty   a condition that exists when people may be able to afford basic necessities, such as food, clothing, and shelter, but cannot maintain an average standard of living in comparison to that of other members of their society or group.

repressive terrorism   terrorism conducted by a government against its own citizens for the purpose of protecting an existing political order.

revolutionary terrorism   acts of violence against civilians that are carried out by internal enemies of the government who want to bring about political change.

scapegoat   a person or group that is blamed for some problem causing frustration and is therefore subjected to hostility or aggression by others.

secondary analysis of existing data   a research design in which investigators analyze data that originally were collected by others for some other purpose.

secondary deviance   the process that occurs when a person who has been labeled a deviant accepts that new identity and continues the deviant behavior.

secondary groups   larger, more specialized groups in which members engage in impersonal, goal-oriented relationships for a limited period of time.

secondary-sector production   the processing of raw materials (from the primary sector) into finished products.

second shift   the domestic work that many employed women perform at home after completing their work day on the job.

segregation   the spatial and social separation of categories of people by race-ethnicity, class, gender, religion, or other social characteristics.

self-fulfilling prophecy   the process by which an unsubstantiated belief or prediction results in behavior that makes the original false belief come true.

semiperipheral nations   nations that are more developed than peripheral nations but less developed than core nations.

serial murder   the killing of three or more people over more than a month by the same person.

sex   the biological differences between females and males.

sexism   the subordination of one sex, usually female, based on the assumed superiority of the other sex.

sex trafficking situations in which an adult is coerced, forced, or deceived into prostitution, or maintained in prostitution through coercion.

sexual harassment unwanted sexual advances, requests for sexual favors, or other verbal or physical conduct of a sexual nature.

sexuality attitudes, beliefs, and practices related to sexual attraction and intimate relationships with others.

sexual orientation a preference for emotional-sexual relationships with individuals of the same sex (homosexuality), the opposite sex (heterosexuality), or both (bisexuality).

situational approach the belief that violence results from a specific interaction process, termed a "situational transaction."

social bond theory the proposition that criminal behavior is most likely to occur when a person's ties to society are weakened or broken.

social change the alteration, modification, or transformation of public policy, culture, or social institutions over time.

social control the systematic practices developed by social groups to encourage conformity and discourage deviance.

social disorganization the conditions in society that undermine the ability of traditional social institutions to govern human behavior.

social gerontology the study of the social (nonphysical) aspects of aging.

socialism an economic system characterized by public ownership of the means of production, the pursuit of collective goals, and centralized decision making.

social learning theory a theory that is based on the assumption that people are likely to act out the behavior they see in role models and media sources.

social movement an organized group that acts collectively to promote or resist change through collective action.

social problem a social condition (such as poverty) or a pattern of behavior (such as substance abuse) that people believe warrants public concern and collective action to bring about change.

social stratification the hierarchical arrangement of large social groups on the basis of their control over basic resources.

society a large social grouping that shares the same geographic territory and is subject to the same political authority and dominant cultural expectations.

sociological imagination the ability to see the relationship between individual experiences and the larger society.

sociology the academic and scholarly discipline that engages in systematic study of human society and social interactions.

special-interest group a political coalition composed of individuals or groups sharing a specific interest they wish to protect or advance with the help of the political system.

state-sponsored terrorism political terrorism resulting from a government providing financial resources, weapons, and training for terrorists who conduct their activities in other nations.

statutory rape the act of having sexual intercourse with a person who is under the legal age of consent as established by state law.

stereotypes overgeneralizations about the appearance, behavior, or other characteristics of all members of a group.

strain theory the proposition that people feel strain when they are exposed to cultural goals that they cannot reach because they do not have access to culturally approved means of achieving those goals.

strategically significant weapon one that brings force to bear in such a way that it decisively erodes the war-making capability of the enemy.

subculture a group of people who share a distinctive set of cultural beliefs and behaviors that set them apart from the larger society.

subculture of violence hypothesis the hypothesis that violence is part of the normative expectations governing everyday behavior among young males in the lower classes.

subordinate (or minority) group a group whose members, because of physical or cultural characteristics, are disadvantaged and subjected to unequal treatment by the dominant group and regard themselves as objects of collective discrimination.

survey research a poll in which researchers ask respondents a series of questions about a specific topic and record their responses.

symbolic interactionist perspective views society as the sum of the interactions of individuals and groups.

terrorism the use of calculated, unlawful physical force or threats of violence against a government, organization, or individual to gain some political, religious, economic, or social objective.

tertiary-sector production providing services rather than goods as the primary source of livelihood.

theory a set of logically related statements that attempt to describe, explain, or predict social events.

theory of limited effects a theory that states that the media have a minimal effect on the attitudes and perceptions of individuals.

theory of racial formation a theory that states that the government substantially defines racial and ethnic relations.

tolerance a condition that occurs when larger doses of a drug are required over time to produce the same physical or psychological effect that was originally achieved by a smaller dose.

total institution a place where people are isolated from the rest of society for a period of time and come under the complete control of the officials who run the institution.

tracking assigning students to specific courses and educational programs on the basis of their test scores, previous grades, or both.

transnational corporation a large-scale business organization that is headquartered in one country but operates in many countries, which has the legal power (separate from individual owners or shareholders) to enter into contracts, buy and sell property, and engage in other business activity.

unemployment rate the percentage of unemployed persons in the labor force actively seeking jobs.

urbanization the process by which an increasing proportion of a population lives in cities rather than in rural areas.

values collective ideas about what is right or wrong, good or bad, and desirable or undesirable in a specific society.

victimless crime a crime that many people believe has no real victim because it involves willing participants in an economic exchange.

violence the use of physical force to cause pain, injury, or death to another, or damage to another's property.

violent crime actions involving force or the threat of force against others.

wage (pay) gap the disparity between women's and men's earnings.

war an organized, armed conflict between nations or distinct political fractions.

war system components of social institutions (e.g., the economy, government, and education) and cultural beliefs and practices that promote the development of warriors, weapons, and war as a normal part of the society and its foreign policy.

wealth the value of all economic assets, including income, personal property, and income-producing property.

weapons of mass destruction (WMDs) nuclear, biological, chemical, or radiological weapons that can kill thousands of people and destroy vast amounts of property at one time.

weapons system military technology comprising a weapons platform (e.g., a ship, aircraft, or tank), a weapon (e.g., a gun, missile, or torpedo), and the means of command and communication.

welfare state a program under which the government takes responsibility for specific categories of citizens by offering them certain services and benefits, such as employment, housing, health, education, or guaranteed income.

withdrawal a variety of physical and/or psychological symptoms that habitual drug users experience when they discontinue drug use.

zero population growth a situation in which a population is totally stable, one that neither grows nor decreases from year to year because births, deaths, and migration are in perfect balance.

References

NOTE: References in blue are new to the Sixth Edition.

Abbott, Sharon. 2000. "Motivation for Pursuing an Acting Career in Pornography." In Ronald Weitzer (Ed.), *Sex for Sale: Prostitution, Pornography, and the Sex Industry.* New York: Routledge, pp. 17–34.

Adams, Karen L., and Norma C. Ware. 1995. "Sexism and the English Language: The Linguistic Implications of Being a Woman." In Jo Freeman (Ed.), *Women: A Feminist Perspective* (5th ed.). Mountain View, CA: Mayfield Publishing, pp. 331–346.

Adams, Tom. 1991. *Grass Roots: How Ordinary People Are Changing America.* New York: Citadel Press.

Adorno, Theodor W., Else Frenkel-Brunswick, Daniel J. Levinson, and R. Nevitt Sanford. 1950. *The Authoritarian Personality.* New York: Harper & Row.

Agency for Healthcare Research and Quality. 2011. "Healthcare Quality and Disparities in Women: Selected Findings from the 2010 National Healthcare Quality and Disparities Report." Retrieved July 10, 2011. Online: http://www.ahrq.gov/qual/nhqrwomen/nhqrwomen.pdf

Allen, Robert L. 1974. *Reluctant Reformers.* Washington, DC: Howard University Press.

Almaguer, Tomás. 1995. "Chicano Men: A Cartography of Homosexual Identity and Behavior." In Michael S. Kimmel and Michael A. Messner (Eds.), *Men's Lives* (3rd ed.). Boston: Allyn and Bacon, pp. 418–431.

American Association of Community Colleges. 2011. "2011 Fact Sheet." Retrieved April 18, 2011. Online: http://www.aacc.nche.edu/AboutCC/Documents/FactSheet2011.pdf

American Association of University Women. 1992. *The AAUW Report: How Schools Short-Change Girls.* Washington, DC: The AAUW Educational Foundation and National Educational Association.

American Association of University Women. 2008. "Where the Girls Are: The Facts about Gender Equity in Education." Retrieved July 17, 2011. Online: http://www.aauw.org/learn/research/upload/whereGirlsAre.pdf

American Association of University Women. 2011. "The Simple Truth about Gender Pay Gap." Retrieved June 9, 2011. Online: http://www.aauw.org/learn/research/upload/SimpleTruthAboutPayGap1.pdf

American Association of University Women Dialog. 2009. "Harassed on the Way to School," blog posted by hollykearl (September 16). Retrieved June 8, 2011. Online: http://blog-aauw.org/2009/09/16/harassed-on-the-way-to-school/

American Association of University Women Educational Foundation. 2001. *Hostile Hallways: Bullying, Teasing, and Sexual Harassment in School.* Washington, DC: American Association of University Women Educational Foundation.

American Heritage Dictionary. 2000. *American Heritage Dictionary of the English Language.* Boston: Houghton Mifflin.

American Library Association. 2005. "USA PATRIOT Act and Intellectual Freedom." Retrieved August 29, 2005. Online: http://www.ala.org/ala/oif/fissues/usapatriotact.htm

American Library Association. 2011. "The USA PATRIOT ACT: Why Does It Matter to Libraries?" Retrieved February 4, 2012. Online: http://www.ala.org/advocacy/advleg/federallegislation/theusapatriotact

American Psychiatric Association. 2000 *Diagnostic and Statistical Manual of Mental Disorders (DSM-IV-TR).* Washington, DC: American Psychiatric Association.

American Red Cross. 2010. "Bringing Help, Bringing Hope: The American Red Cross Responds to Hurricanes Katrina, Rita and Wilma." American Red Cross. Retrieved: August 6, 2011. Online: http://www.redcross.org/www-files/Documents/pdf/corppubs/Katrina5Year.pdf

American Society for Aesthetic Plastic Surgery. 2011. "Highlights of the 2010 Cosmetic Surgery Statistics." Retrieved: June 12, 2011. Online: http://www.consultingroom.com/Statistics/Display.asp?Statistics_ID=48&Title=2010%20ASAPS%20U.S.A.%20Cosmetic%20Surgery%20Statistics

Andersen, Margaret L., and Patricia Hill Collins (Eds.). 2009. *Race, Class, and Gender: An Anthology* (7th ed.). Belmont, CA: Cengage/Wadsworth.

Anderson, Elijah. 2011. *The Cosmopolitan Canopy.* New York: Norton.

Angel, Ronald J., and Jacqueline L. Angel. 1993. *Painful Inheritance: Health and the New Generation of Fatherless Families.* Madison: University of Wisconsin Press.

Apple, Michael W. 1982. *Education and Power: Reproduction and Contradiction in Education.* London: Routledge & Kegan Paul.

Arnett, Jeffrey Jensen. 2004. *Emerging Adulthood: The Winding Road from the Late Teens Through the Twenties.* New York: Oxford University Press.

Arnold, Regina A. 1990. "Processes of Victimization and Criminalization of Black Women." *Social Justice,* 17(3):153–166.

Ashton, Paul, and Amanda Petteruti. 2011. "Gaming the System: How the Political Strategies of Private Prison Companies Promote Ineffective Incarceration Policies." Justice Policy Institute (June). Retrieved July 8, 2011. Online: http://www.justicepolicy.org/uploads/justicepolicy/documents/gaming_the_system.pdf

AspiringDocs.org. 2011. "America Needs a More Diverse Physician Workforce." Association of American Medical Colleges. Retrieved July 10, 2011. Online: http://www.aspiringdocs.org/download/127316/data/america_needs_a_more_diverse_physician_workforce.pdf

Association of American Medical Colleges. 2010. "U.S. Medical School Applicants and Students: 1982–1983 to 2010–2011." Retrieved July 10, 2011. Online: https://www.aamc.org/download/153708/data/charts1982to2011.pdf

Association of Certified Fraud Examiners. 2010. "Report to the Nations on Occupational Fraud and Abuse." Retrieved July 25, 2011. Online: https://www.acfe.com/rttn/rttn-2010.pdf

Atwood, Nina. 2008. "The Bachelor: Does Matt Have a Broken Chooser?" singlescoach.com (April 2). Retrieved June 4, 2008. Online: http://www.singlescoach.com/blog/?p=293

Austin American-Statesman. 1995. "Abuse of Elderly Is Increasing, Report Says" (May 2):A6.

Austin American-Statesman. 1997b. "Nation Needs Readers" (April 21):A6.

Avorn, Jerry, and Aaron Kesselheim. 2011. "Editorial: A Hemorrhage of Off-Label Use." *Annals of Internal Medicine* (April):566–567.

Baker, Kellan, and Jeff Krehely. 2011. "Changing the Game: What Health Care Reform Means for Gay, Lesbian, Bisexual, and Transgender Americans." Center for American Progress, National Coalition for LGBT Health (March). Retrieved

June 19, 2011. Online: http://www.americanprogress.org/issues/2011/03/aca_lgbt.html

Ballantine, Jeanne H., and Floyd M. Hammack. 2009. *The Sociology of Education: A Systematic Analysis* (6th ed.). Upper Saddle River, NJ: Prentice Hall.

Balsa, Ana I., Laura M. Guiliano, and Michael T. French. 2011. "The Effects of Alcohol Use on Academic Achievement in High School." *Economics in Education Review* (February):1–15.

Bandura, Albert. 1973. *Aggression: A Social Learning Analysis.* Upper Saddle River, NJ: Prentice Hall.

Bandura, Albert, and R. H. Walters. 1977. *Social Learning Theory.* Upper Saddle River, NJ: Prentice Hall.

Banta, Carolyn. 2005. "Trading for a High." *Time* (August 1):35.

Barber, Benjamin R. 1996. *Jihad vs. McWorld: How Globalism and Tribalism Are Reshaping the World.* New York: Ballantine Books.

Barboza, David. 2010. "After Suicides, Scrutiny of China's Grim Factories." *New York Times* (June 6). Retrieved July 19, 2011. Online: http://www.nytimes.com/2010/06/07/business/global/07suicide.html

Barnett, James H. 1954. *The American Christmas: A Study in National Culture.* New York: Macmillan.

Baron, Harold M. 1969. "The Web of Urban Racism." In Louis L. Knowles and Kenneth Prewitt (Eds.), *Institutional Racism in America.* Upper Saddle River, NJ: Prentice Hall, pp. 134–176.

Barrows, Sydney Biddle, with William Novak. 1986. *Mayflower Madam: The Secret Life of Sydney Biddle Barrows.* New York: Ivy Books.

Basken, Paul. 2010. "Pell Grant Increase Could Be Cut as Talks Intensify on Student-Aid Bill." *The Chronicle of Higher Education* (March 12). Retrieved July 17, 2011. Online: http://chroniclecareers.com/article/Pell-Grant-Increase-Could-Be/64666/

Bater, Jeff. 2011. "Budget-Deficit Figures Narrow From a Year Ago." *Wall Street Journal* (July 13). Retrieved July 18, 2011. Online: http://online.wsj.com/article/SB10001424052702304911104576444202308329060.html#printMode

Bawer, Bruce. 1994. *A Place at the Table: The Gay Individual in American Society.* New York: Touchstone.

BBC News. 2010. "China Faces Growing Sex Imbalance." BBC News. Retrieved June 11, 2011. Online: http://news.bbc.co.uk/2/hi/asia-pacific/8451289.stm

BBC News. 2011. "as It Happened: Norway Attacks." BBC News (July 22). Retrieved August 2, 2011. Online: http://www.bbc.co.uk/news/world-europe-14254705

Becker, Howard S. 1963. *Outsiders: Studies in the Sociology of Deviance.* New York: Free Press.

Belkin, Lisa. 2010. "Child Care Costs More Than College." *New York Times* (August 9). Retrieved February 3, 2012. Online: http://www.parenting/blogs.nytimes.com/2010/08/09/child-care-costs-more-than-college/

Belkin, Lisa. 2011. "The Nanny at the Wedding." *New York Times* (April 29). Retrieved July 14, 2011. Online: http://parenting.blogs.nytimes.com/2011/04/29/the-nanny-at-the-wedding/?scp=5&sq=foreign%20nannies%20that%20take%20care%20of%20American%20children%202011?&st=cse

Bennhold, Katrin. 2011. "From Afar, Moneymaker and Mother." *New York Times* (March 7). Retrieved July 14, 2011. Online: http://www.nytimes.com/2011/03/08/world/europe/08iht-ffhelp08.html?ref=thefemalefactor

Berger, Peter. 1963. *Invitation to Sociology: A Humanistic Perspective.* New York: Anchor.

Berger, Peter, and Hansfried Kellner. 1964. "Marriage and the Construction of Reality." *Diogenes,* 46:1–32.

Berger, Peter, and Thomas Luckmann. 1967. *The Social Construction of Reality: A Treatise in the Sociology of Knowledge.* Garden City, NY: Anchor Books.

Bergmann, Barbara R. 1986. *The Economic Emergence of Women.* New York: Basic Books.

Bernard, Jessie. 1982. *The Future of Marriage.* New Haven, CT: Yale University Press.

Bernhardt, Annette, Heather Boushey, Laura Dresser, and Chris Tilly (Eds.). 2008. *The Gloves-Off Economy: Workplace Standards at the Bottom of America's Labor Market.* Ithaca, NY: Cornell University Press.

Bernstein, Jared. 2010. "The Lift: Recovery Act Moderates 2009 Poverty Results." The White House Blog (September 16). Retrieved May 29, 2011. Online: http://www.whitehouse.gov/blog/2010/09/16/lift-recovery-act-moderates-2009-poverty-results

Best, Joel. 1999. *Random Violence: How We Talk about New Crimes and New Victims.* Berkeley: University of California Press.

Best, Joel. 2001. *Damned Lies and Statistics: Untangling Numbers from the Media, Politicians, and Activists.* Berkeley: University of California Press.

Biagi, Shirley. 2012. *Media Impact: An Introduction to Mass Media* (10th ed.). Belmont, CA: Cengage/Wadsworth.

Bilirakis, Gus M., and Daniel E. Lundgren. 2011. "Addressing the Threat of Weapons of Mass Destruction." *The Hill: Congress Blog* (June 21). Retrieved August 2, 2011. Online: http://thehill.com/blogs/congress-blog/homeland-security/167543-addressing-the-threat-of-weapons-of-mass-destruction

Blauner, Robert. 1972. *Racial Oppression in America.* New York: Harper & Row.

Block, Jerald J. 2008. "Editorial: Issues for *DSM–V*: Internet Addiction." *American Journal of Psychiatry* (March). Retrieved July 21, 2011. Online: http://ajp.psychiatryonline.org/cgi/content/full/165/3/306

Bloomberg News. 2011. "People's Daily May Lead China's State-Run Media to Market." Bloomberg.com (January 5). Retrieved July 23, 2011. Online: http://www.bloomberg.com/news/2011-01-05/people-s-daily-website-ipo-may-lead-to-a-wave-of-state-run-media-listings.html

Blumerman, Lisa M. 2011. "Public Education Finances: 2009." U.S. Census Bureau (May). Retrieved July 17, 2011. Online: http://www2.census.gov/govs/school/09f33pub.pdf

Bonacich, Edna. 1972. "A Theory of Ethnic Antagonism: The Split Labor Market." *American Sociological Review,* 37:547–549.

Bonacich, Edna. 1976. "Advanced Capitalism and Black White Relations in the United States: A Split Labor Market Interpretation." *American Sociological Review,* 41:34–51.

Bonanno, George A. 2009. "Grief Does Not Come in Stages and It's Not the Same for Everyone." *Psychology Today* (October 26). Retrieved March 25, 2011. Online: http://www.psychologytoday.com/blog/thriving-in-the-face-trauma/200910/grief-does-not-come-in-stages-and-its-not-the-same-everyone

Bonanno, George A. 2010. *The Other Side of Sadness: What the New Science of Bereavement Tells Us about Life after Loss.* New York: Basic Books.

Bonger, Willem. 1969. *Criminality and Economic Conditions* (abridged ed.). Bloomington: Indiana University Press (orig. published in 1916).

Botvin, Gilbert. 2011. "Botvin LifeSkills Training: Overview." Retrieved June 30, 2011. Online: http://www.lifeskillstraining.com/overview.php

Boudreau, John. 2011. "Cyberattacks Have Been Targeting Government and Financial Institutions, McAfee Says." *Contra Costa*

Times (August 3). Retrieved August 4, 2011. Online: http://www.contracostatimes.com/news/ci_18609065?source=rss

Bourdieu, Pierre, and Jean-Claude Passeron. 1990. *Reproduction in Education, Society, and Culture.* Newbury Park, CA: Sage.

Bovino, Arthur. 2003. "Offering a Hand, and Hope, in a Year of Record Homelessness in New York." *New York Times* (November 2):A25.

Bowers, William J. 1984. *Legal Homicide: Death as Punishment in America, 1864–1982.* Boston: Northeastern University Press.

BP. 2010. "Annual Report." Retrieved August 6, 2011. Online: http://www.bp.com/assets/bp_internet/globalbp/globalbp_uk_english/set_branch/STAGING/common_assets/downloads/pdf/BP_Annual_Report_and_Form_20F.pdf

Brandon, Emily. 2009. "Save for College or Retirement?" *U.S. News and World Report* (September 8). Retrieved June 13, 2011. Online: http://money.usnews.com/money/retirement/articles/2009/09/08/save-for-college-or-retirement_print.html

Brecher, Jeremy, and Tim Costello. 1998. *Global Village or Global Pillage: Economic Reconstruction from the Bottom Up* (2nd ed.). Cambridge, MA: South End Press.

Broder, John M. 2010. "'Cap and Trade' Loses Its Standing as Energy Policy of Choice." *New York Times* (March 25). Retrieved July 29, 2011. Online: http://www.nytimes.com/2010/03/26/science/earth/26climate.html?pagewanted=print

Brody, Jane E. 1996. "Good Habits Outweigh Genes as Key to a Healthy Old Age." *New York Times* (February 28):B9.

Buechler, Steven M. 2000. *Social Movements in Advanced Capitalism: The Political Economy and Cultural Construction of Social Activism.* New York: Oxford University Press.

Bullard, Robert D., and Beverly H. Wright. 1992. "The Quest for Environmental Equity: Mobilizing the African-American Community for Social Change." In Riley E. Dunlap and Angela G. Mertig (Eds.), *American Environmentalism: The U.S. Environmental Movement, 1970–1990.* New York: Taylor & Francis, pp. 39–50.

Burke, Daniel. 2011. "Bishops Push Back on Gay Couples in Housing." *National Catholic Reporter* (March 29). Retrieved June 19, 2011. Online: http://ncronline.org/print/23749

Burleigh, Nina. 1991. "Watching Children Starve to Death." *Time* (June 10):56–58.

Burns, Crosby, and Jeff Krehely. 2011. "Gay and Transgender People Face High Rates of Workplace Discrimination and Harassment." Center for American Progress (May). Retrieved June 19, 2011. Online: http://www.americanprogress.org/issues/2011/06/pdf/workplace_discrimination.pdf

Bush, George W. 2003a. "President Bush Addresses the Nation." Retrieved September 3, 2005. Online: http://www.whitehouse.gov/news/releases/2003/03/20030319-17.html

Bush, George W. 2003b. "President Says Saddam Hussein Must Leave Iraq within 48 Hours. Remarks by the President in Address to the Nation, March 17, 2003." Retrieved September 3, 2005. Online: http://www.whitehouse.gov/news/releases/2003/03/20030317-7.html

Bushman, Brad J., Hannah R. Rothstein, and Craig A. Anderson. 2010. "Much Ado About Something: Violent Video Games Effects and a School of Red Herring: Reply to Ferguson and Kilburn." *Psychological Bulletin* 136(2):182–187.

Butler, Robert N. 1969. "Ageism: Another Form of Bigotry." *The Gerontologist,* 9:243–246.

Bynum, Jack E., and William E. Thompson. 1996. *Juvenile Delinquency: A Sociological Approach.* Boston: Allyn and Bacon.

Byrd, Jim. 2007. "Welfare Ain't What It Used to Be." *A Skewed View* (December 22). Retrieved May 20, 2011. Online: http://www.jimbyrd.com/welfare-aint-what-it-used-to-be

Cable, Sherry, and Charles Cable. 1995. *Environmental Problems, Grassroots Solutions: The Politics of Grassroots Environmental Conflict.* New York: St. Martin's Press.

Camarota, Steven A. 2006. "Immigration's Impact on Public Coffers." Center for Immigration Studies (August 24). Retrieved July 29, 2011. Online: http://www.cis.org/articles/2006/sactestimony082406.html

Cancian, Francesca M. 1990. "The Feminization of Love." In C. Carlson (Ed.), *Perspectives on the Family: History, Class, and Feminism.* Belmont, CA: Wadsworth, pp. 171–185.

Cancian, Francesca M., and James William Gibson. 1990. *Making War, Making Peace: The Social Foundations of Violent Conflict.* Belmont, CA: Wadsworth.

Capek, Stella M. 1993. "The 'Environmental Justice' Frame: A Conceptual Discussion and an Application." *Social Problems,* 40:5–24.

Carey, Benedict. 2005. "Storm Will Have a Long-Term Emotional Effect on Some, Experts Say." *New York Times* (September 4):A20.

Carmichael, Stokely, and Charles V. Hamilton. 1967. *Black Power: The Politics of Liberation in America.* New York: Vintage.

Carpenter, Rachel. 2010. "How to Share Your Pregnancy News on Facebook." Associated Content. Retrieved July 13, 2011. Online: http://www.associatedcontent.com/article/7756736/10_facebook_status_updates_and_ideas_pg2.html?cat=5

Cass, Vivien C. 1984. "Homosexual Identity Formation: Testing a Theoretical Model." *Journal of Sex Research,* 20:143–167.

Castells, Manuel. 1977. *The Urban Question.* London: Edward Arnold.

Casualties.org. 2011. "Operation Iraqi Freedom/Operation Enduring Freedom/Afghanisan." Retrieved November 21, 2011. Online: http://www.icasualties.org

Cavender, Gray. 1995. "Alternative Approaches: Labeling and Critical Perspectives." In Joseph F. Sheley (Ed.), *Criminology: A Contemporary Handbook* (2nd ed.). Belmont, CA: Wadsworth, pp. 349–367.

CBSLosAngeles. 2011. "Report: Tainted Cocaine in LA, NY Linked to Flesh-Eating Disease." Retrieved June 29, 2011. Online: http://losangeles.cbslocal.com/2011/06/28/report-tainted-cocaine-in-la-ny-linked-to-flesh-eating-disease/

cdc.gov. 2011. "Smoking and Tobacco Use." Youth and Young Adult Data Fact Sheets. Retrieved February 2, 2012. Online: http://www.cdc.gov/tobacco/data_statistics/fact_sheets/youth_data/tobacco_use/index.htm

CDC Morbidity and Mortality Weekly Report. 2011. "CDC Health Disparities and Inequalities Report—United States, 2011." Retrieved May 29, 2011. Online: http://www.cdc.gov/mmwr/pdf/other/su6001.pdf

census.gov. 2011. "Census Bureau Reports 55 Percent Have Married One Time." U.S. Census Bureau (May 18). Retrieved July 12, 2011. Online: http://www.census.gov/newsroom/releases/archives/marital_status_living_arrangements/cb11-90.html

Center for American Women and Politics. 2010. "Gender Gap Widespread in 2010 Elections: Women Less Likely Than Men to Support Republican Candidates." Rutgers University (November 4). Retrieved July 18, 2011. Online: http://www.cawp.rutgers.edu/press_room/news/documents/PressRelease_11-04-10-GG.pdf

CDC, NCHS.

Centers for Disease Control and Prevention. 2010a. "Early Release of Selected

Estimates Based on Data from the 2009 National Health Interview Survey." Retrieved June 27, 2011. Online: http://www.cdc.gov/nchs/data/nhis/early release/earlyrelease201006.pdf

Centers for Disease Control and Prevention. 2010b "Use of Contraception in the United States: 1982-2008." Vital and Health Statistics Series 23, Number 29 (May). Retrieved January 19, 2011. Online: http://www.cdc.gov/nchs/pressroom/data/Contraception_series_Report.pdf

Centers for Disease Control and Prevention. 2011a. "HIV in the United States." National Center for HIV/AIDs, Hepatitis, STD, and TB Prevention (July). Retrieved July 10, 2011. Online: http://www.cdc.gov/hiv/resources/factsheets/PDF/us.pdf

Centers for Disease Control and Prevention. 2011b. "National Vital Statistics Report: Deaths—Preliminary Data for 2009" (March 16). Retrieved July 9, 2011. Online: http://www.cdc.gov/nchs/data/nvsr/nvsr59/nvsr59_04.pdf

Centers for Medicare and Medicaid Services. 2011. "National Health Expenditures Fact Sheet: 2009." Retrieved February 3, 2012. Online: http://www.cms.gov/NationalHealthExpendData/25_NHE_Fact_Sheet.asp

Central Intelligence Agency. 2011. *The World Factbook*. Retrieved May 12, 2011. Online: https://www.cia.gov/library/publications/the-world-factbook/rankorder/2091rank.html

Century Council. 2010. "State of Drunk Driving Fatalities in America." Retrieved June 27, 2011. Online: http://www.centurycouncil.org/learn-the-facts/drunk-driving-research

Chan, Sucheng (Ed.). 1991. *Entry Denied: Exclusion and the Chinese Community in America, 1882–1943*. Philadelphia: Temple University Press.

Chartier, Karen, and Raul Caetano. 2010. "Ethnicity and Health Disparities in Alcohol Research." *Alcohol Research & Health*, 33(1–2):152–160.

Chavez, Linda. 1991. *Out of the Barrio: Toward a New Politics of Hispanic Assimilation*. New York: Basic Books.

Cherlin, Andrew J. 1992. *Marriage, Divorce, and Remarriage* (rev. and enlarged ed.). Cambridge, MA: Harvard University Press.

Children's Defense Fund. 2008. "State of America's Children: 2008 Report." Retrieved April 15, 2009. Online: http://www.childrensdefense.org/child-research-data-publications/data/state-of-americas-children-2008-report.pdf

Children's Defense Fund. 2010. "State of America's Children: 2010 Report." Retrieved June 12, 2011. Online: http://www.childrensdefense.org/child-research-data-publications/data/state-of-americas-children-2010-report-child-poverty.pdf

Chin, Rockwell. 1999. "Long Struggle for Justice." *ABA Journal* (November):66–67.

Chronicle of Higher Education. 2008. "Should Prostitution Be Legalized?" (March 28):B4.

CIA. 2011. CIA World Factbook. Retrieved May 12, 2011. Online: https://www.cia.gov/library/publications/the-world-factbook/

"Classy Black Lady" blog. 2011. "Racist Super Bowl Commercial—Pepsi Ad Stereotypes Black Women." Written by Tabitha Soren. Retrieved May 31, 2011. Online: http://blog.classyblacklady.com/2011/02/racist-superbowl-commercial-pepsi-ad.html

Cloud, John. 2011. "How the Casey Anthony Murder Case Became the Social-Media Trial of the Century." *Time* (June 16). Retrieved July 5, 2011. Online: http://www.time.com/time/printout/0,8816,2077969,00.html

Coale, Ansley. 1973. "The Demographic Transition." Proceedings of the International Population Conference, Liege. Vol. 1, pp. 53–72 (cited in Weeks, 1992).

Cock, Jacklyn. 1994. "Women and the Military: Implications for Demilitarization in the 1990s in South Africa. *Gender and Society*, 8(2):152–169.

Cody, Edward. 2010. "France Moves to Fine Muslim Women with Full-Face Islamic Veils." *Washington Post* (May 20):A9.

Cohen, Patricia. 2011. "Genetic Basis for Crime: A New Look." *New York Times* (June 19). Retrieved July 9, 2011. Online: http://www.nytimes.com/2011/06/20/arts/genetics-and-crime-at-institute-of-justice-conference.html?_r=1&scp=1&sq=crime%20gene?&st=cse

Cohn, Jonathan. 1997. "Reform School." *Mother Jones* (May–June):62.

Colbert, Chuck. 2011. "Presbyterians Open Door to Gay Clergy." Windy City Media Group (May 18). Retrieved June 16, 2011. Online: http://windycitymediagroup.com/gay/lesbian/news/ARTICLE.php?AID=31814

Cole, Thomas B., and Annette Flanagin. 1999. "Editorial: What Can We Do About Violence?" *Journal of the American Medical Association* (August 4):481–482.

Coleman, Eli. 1981–1982. "Developmental Stages of the Coming Out Process." *Journal of Homosexuality,* 7:31–43.

Colhoun, J. 1992. "Census Fails to Quash Report on Iraqi Deaths." *The Guardian* (April 22):5.

Collins, James. 1997. "Day of Reckoning." *Time* (June 16):27–29.

Collins, Patricia Hill. 1991. *Black Feminist Thought: Knowledge, Consciousness, and the Politics of Empowerment*. New York: Routledge.

Collins, Patricia Hill. 2005. *Black Sexual Politics: African Americans, Gender, and the New Racism*. New York: Routledge.

Collins, Randall. 1979. *The Credential Society: An Historical Sociology of Education*. New York: Academic Press.

Coltrane, Scott. 2004. "Fathering: Paradoxes, Contradictions and Dilemmas." In Marilyn Coleman and Lawrence Ganong (Eds.), *Handbook of Contemporary Families: Considering the Past, Contemplating the Future*. Thousand Oaks, CA: Sage, pp. 224–243.

Committee on Ways and Means, U.S. House of Representatives. 2011. "Linder Statement on Report Showing Rise in Poverty, Despite Record Government Benefits." Retrieved May 29, 2011. Online: http://republicans.waysandmeans.house.gov/News/DocumentSingle.aspx?DocumentID=206862

Conan, Neal. 2011. "More States Consider Stricter Medical Pot Rules." Talk of the Nation: National Public Radio (June 30). Retrieved July 3, 2011. Online: http://www.npr.org/2011/06/30/137529482/more-states-consider-stricter-medical-pot-rules

Connelly, Marjorie. 2011. "Few Americans Familiar with Title IX, Though Most Approve of It." *New York Times* (April 26). Retrieved June 10, 2011. Online: http://www.womenssportsfoundation.org/~/media/Files/Research%20Reports/Whos%20Playing%20College%20Sports/fullreport.pdf

COPS. 2011. "Community Policing Defined." U.S. Department of Justice. Retrieved July 9, 2011. Online: http://www.cops.usdoj.gov/Default.asp?Item=36

Coser, Lewis A. 1969. "The Visibility of Evil." In William K. Bunis, Angela Yancik, and David Snow, "The Cultural Patterning of Sympathy toward the Homeless and Other Victims of Misfortune." *Social Problems* (November):387–402.

Cowgill, Donald O. 1986. *Aging around the World*. Belmont, CA: Wadsworth.

Cox, Oliver C. 1948. *Caste, Class, and Race*. Garden City, NY: Doubleday.

Crossette, Barbara. 1996. "Agency Sees Risk in Drug to Temper Child Behavior: Worldwide Survey Cites Overuse of Ritalin." *New York Times* (February 29):A7.

Crossette, Barbara. 1997. "Democracies Love Peace, Don't They?" *New York Times* (June 1):E3.

Cumming, Elaine C., and William E. Henry. 1961. *Growing Old: The Process of Disengagement.* New York: Basic Books.

Curran, James, Michael Gurevitch, and Janet Woollacott. 1982. "The Study of the Media: Theoretical Approaches." In Michael Gurevitch, Tony Bennett, James Curran, and Janet Woollacott (Eds.), *Culture, Society and the Media.* London: Methuen, pp. 5–35.

Dahl, Robert A. 1961. *Who Governs?* New Haven, CT: Yale University Press.

Dalaker, Joseph. 2001. *Poverty in the United States.* Current Population Reports, Series P60-214. Washington, DC: U.S. Census Bureau.

Daly, Kathleen, and Meda Chesney-Lind. 1988. "Feminism and Criminology." *Justice Quarterly,* 5:497–533.

Dao, James. 2011. "Cost of Treating Veterans Will Rise Long Past Wars." *New York Times* (July 27). Retrieved August 2, 2011. Online: http://www.nytimes.com/2011/07/28/us/28veterans.html

Davey, Monica, and Emma G. Fitzsimmons. 2011. "Ex-Governor Found Guilty of Corruption." *New York Times* (June 28): A1, A16.

Davis, Kingsley. 1937. "The Sociology of Prostitution." *American Sociological Review,* 2:744–755.

De Castro, Steven. 1994. "Identity in Action: A Filipino American's Perspective." In Karin Aguilar-San Juan (Ed.), *The State of Asian America: Activism and Resistance in the 1990s.* Boston: South End Press, pp. 295–320.

Defensetech.org. 2011. "U.S. Using Armed Predator Drones Over Libya." Retrieved August 3, 2011. Online: http://defensetech.org/2011/04/21/u-s-using-armed-predator-drones-over-libya/

DeNavas-Walt, Carmen, Bernadette D. Proctor, and Jessica C. Smith. 2010. "Income, Poverty, and Health Insurance Coverage in the United States: 2009." U.S. Census Bureau (September). Retrieved June 5, 2011. Online: http://www.census.gov/prod/2010pubs/p60-238.pdf

Denoble, Damjan. 2010. "Seriously, the Chinese Aren't Okay with Aborting Their Baby Girls." Asia Healthcare blog (May 31). Retrieved June 11, 2011. Online: http://www.asiahealthcareblog.com/2010/05/31/seriously-the-chinese-arent-okay-with-aborting-their-baby-girls/comment-page-1/

Dewan, Shaila. 2010. "Southern Schools Mark Two Majorities." *New York Times* (January 6). Retrieved February 4,

2012. Online: http://www.nytimes.com/2010/01/07/us/07south.html

DeWolf, Christopher. 2007. "Where Latinos Speak Korean" (June 4). Retrieved June 6, 2011. Online: http://www.urbanphoto.net/blog/2007/06/04/where-latinos-speak-korean/

Diamond, Jared. 2000. "The Greening of Corporate America." *New York Times* (January 8):A31.

Dillon, Sam. 2010. "12th-Grade Reading and Math Scores Rise Slightly After a Historic Low in 2005." *New York Times* (November 18). Retrieved July 17, 2011. Online: http://www.nytimes.com/2010/11/19/education/19education.html?ref=nationalassessmentofeducationalprogress

Dillon, Sam. 2011a. "Failing Grades on Civics Exam Called a 'Crisis'" (May 4). Retrieved July 17, 2011. Online: http://www.nytimes.com/2011/05/05/education/05civics.html?_r=1&ref=nationalassessmentofeducationalprogress

Dillon, Sam. 2011b. U.S. Students Remain Poor at History, Tests Show." *New York Times* (June 14). Retrieved July 17, 2011. Online: http://www.nytimes.com/2011/06/15/education/15history.html

Dollard, John, Neal E. Miller, Leonard W. Doob, O. H. Mowrer, and Robert R. Sears. 1939. *Frustration and Aggression.* New Haven, CT: Yale University Press.

Domhoff, G. William. 1978. *The Powers That Be: Processes of Ruling Class Domination in America.* New York: Random House.

Domhoff, G. William. 1990. *The Power Elite and the State: How Policy Is Made in America.* New York: Aldine De Gruyter.

Domhoff, G. William. 2011. "Wealth, Income and Power" (January). *Who Rules America?* Retrieved May 27, 2011. Online: http://sociology.ucsc.edu/whorulesamerica/power/wealth.html

Drew, Christopher. 2011. "Under an Unblinking Eye: A Costly Drone Is Poised to Replace the U-2." *New York Times* (August 3):B1, B4.

Duke, Rachel B. 2010. "Epidemic Growth of Net Porn Cited." *Washington Times* (June 15). Retrieved June 26, 2011. Online: http://www.washingtontimes.com/news/2010/jun/15/epidemic-growth-of-net-porn-cited/

Dull, Diana, and Candace West. 1991. "Accounting for Cosmetic Surgery: The Accomplishments of Gender." *Social Problems,* 38(1):54–70.

Dunlap, Riley E. 1992. "Trends in Public Opinion toward Environmental Issues: 1965–1990." In Riley E. Dunlap and Angela G. Mertig (Eds.), *American*

Environmentalism: The U.S. Environmental Movement, 1970–1990. New York: Taylor & Francis, pp. 89–113.

Durkheim, Emile. 1933. *Division of Labor in Society.* Trans. George Simpson. New York: Free Press (orig. published in 1893).

Durkheim, Emile. 1964. *The Rules of Sociological Method.* Trans. Sarah A. Solovay and John H. Mueller. New York: Free Press (orig. published in 1895).

Duster, Troy. 1995. "Symposium: The Bell Curve." *Contemporary Sociology: A Journal of Reviews,* 24(2):158–161.

Dye, Thomas R., Harmon Zeigler, and Louis Schubert. 2012. *The Irony of Democracy: An Uncommon Introduction to American Politics* (15th ed.). Belmont, CA: Cengage.

Dynes, Wayne R. (Ed.). 1990. *Encyclopedia of Homosexuality.* New York: Garland.

Eaton, Danice K., Laura Kann, Steve Kinchen, Shari Shanklin, James Ross, and others. 2010. "Youth Risk Behavior Surveillance—United States, 2009" (June 4). Retrieved June 29, 2011. Online: http://www.cdc.gov/mmwr/pdf/ss/ss5905.pdf

Eckhard, Mimi. 2011. "Glass Ceiling Exists for Women Surgeons." Research News at Vanderbilt University (February 21). Retrieved June 11, 2011. Online: http://news.vanderbilt.edu/2011/02/glass-ceiling-women-surgeons/

Eckholm, Erik. 2011. "Southern Baptists Approve an Appeal to Minorities." *New York Times* (June 16):A20.

The Economist. 2002. "Over 60 and Overlooked" (August 10):51.

Edwards, Laurie. 2011. "A Chronic Dose: A Blog about Chronic Illness, Health Care, and Writing." Retrieved July 9, 2011. Online: http://www.achronicdose.com

Ehrenreich, Barbara. 1997. *Blood Rites: Origins and History of the Passions of War.* New York: Metropolitan Books.

Ehrenreich, Barbara, and Arlie Russell Hochschild. 2002. "Introduction." In Barbara Ehrenreich and Arlie Russell Hochschild (Eds.), *Global Woman: Nannies, Maids, and Sex Workers in the New Economy.* New York: Metropolitan/Owl, pp. 1–13.

Ehrlich, Paul R., and Anne H. Ehrlich. 1991. *The Population Explosion.* New York: Touchstone/Simon & Schuster.

Ehrlich, Paul R., and Anne H. Ehrlich. 2009. "The Population Bomb Revisited." *Electronic Journal of Sustainable Development* 1(3):63-71. Retrieved February 2, 2010. Online: http://www.ejsd.org

ELCA World Hunger. 2005. "World Hunger Facts." Retrieved August 20, 2005.

Online: http://www.elca.org/hunger/printfriendly/facts.html

Elliott, Marta, and Lauren J. Krivo. 1991. "Structural Determinants of Homelessness in the United States." *Social Problems*, 38(1):113–131.

Engels, Friedrich. 1972. *The Origins of the Family, Private Property, and the State.* (Ed. Eleanor Burke Leacock). New York: International.

Enloe, Cynthia H. 1987. "Feminists Thinking about War, Militarism, and Peace." In Beth Hess and Myra Marx Ferree (Eds.), *Analyzing Gender: A Handbook of Social Science Research.* Newbury Park, CA: Sage, pp. 526–547.

Ennis, Sharon R., Merarys Rios-Vargas, and Nora G. Albert. 2011. "The Hispanic Population: 2010" (May). Retrieved June 5, 2011. Online: http://cafefuerte.com/wp-content/uploads/2011/05/PoblacionHispana2010.pdf

Environmental Protection Agency. 2010. "Municipal Solid Waste Generation, Recycling, and Disposal in the United States: Facts and Figures for 2009." Retrieved July 29, 2011. Online: http://www.epa.gov/wastes/nonhaz/municipal/pubs/msw2009-fs.pdf

Epstein, Cynthia Fuchs. 1988. *Deceptive Distinctions: Sex, Gender, and the Social Order.* New Haven, CT: Yale University Press.

Equal Employment Opportunity Commission. 2002. "Facts about Sexual Harassment." Retrieved October 16, 2002. Online: http://www.eeoc.gov/facts/fs-sex.html

Erikson, Kai T. 1962. "Notes on the Sociology of Deviance." *Social Problems*, 9:307–314.

Erikson, Kai T. 1991. "A New Species of Trouble." In Stephen Robert Crouch and J. Stephen Kroll-Smith (Eds.), *Communities at Risk: Collective Responses to Technological Hazards.* New York: Peter Land, pp. 11–29.

Erikson, Kai T. 1994. *A New Species of Trouble: Explorations in Disaster, Trauma, and Community.* New York: Norton.

Erowid.org. 2009. "Marijuana Myths, Claim No. 2." The Vaults of EROWID: Exposing Marijuana Myths" (April 23). Retrieved June 29, 2011. Online: http://www.erowid.org/plants/cannabis/cannabis_myth2.shtml

Espiritu, Yen Le. 1995. *Filipino American Lives.* Philadelphia: Temple University Press.

Essed, Philomena. 1991. *Understanding Everyday Racism.* Newbury Park, CA: Sage.

Factbook on Global Sexual Exploitation. 1999. "United States of America: Facts on Trafficking and Prostitution." Retrieved

December 3, 1999. Online: http://www.uri.edu/artsci/wms/hughes/catw/usa.htm

Farley, Melissa, and Victor Malarek. 2008. "The Myth of the Victimless Crime." *New York Times* (March 12):A27.

FBI. 2009. "2009 Financial Crimes Report." U.S. Department of Justice. Retrieved July 9, 2011. Online: http://www.fbi.gov/stats-services/publications/financial-crimes-report-2009

FBI. 2010a. "Crime in the United States, 2009." U.S. Department of Justice. Retrieved July 9, 2011. Online: http://www2.fbi.gov/ucr/cius2009/index.html

FBI. 2010b. "Hate Crime Statistics, 2009: Incidents and Offenses." U.S. Department of Justice (November). Retrieved June 19, 2011. Online: http://www2.fbi.gov/ucr/hc2009/documents/incidentsandoffenses.pdf

FBI. 2011a. "Organized Crime: 'It's Not Just the Mafia Anymore." U.S. Department of Justice. Retrieved July 9, 2011. Online: http://www.fbi.gov/about-us/investigate/organizedcrime/organized_crime

FBI. 2011b. "Preliminary Report: Crime in America, 2010." U.S. Department of Justice. Retrieved July 9, 2011. Online: http://www.fbi.gov/about-us/cjis/ucr/crime-in-the-u.s/2010/preliminary-annual-ucr-jan-dec-2010

Feagin, Joe R., and Clairece Booher Feagin. 2011. *Racial and Ethnic Relations* (9th ed.). Upper Saddle River, NJ: Prentice Hall.

Feagin, Joe R., David Baker, and Clairece Booher Feagin. 2006. *Social Problems: A Critical Power-Conflict Perspective* (6th ed.). Upper Saddle River, NJ: Prentice Hall.

Feagin, Joe R., and Hernán Vera. 1995. *White Racism: The Basics.* New York: Routledge.

Feagin, Joe R., and Robert Parker. 1990. *Building American Cities: The Urban Real Estate Game* (2nd ed.). Upper Saddle River, NJ: Prentice Hall.

Federal Trade Commission. 2011. "FTC Releases List of Top Consumer Complaints in 2010; Identity Theft Tops the List Again." Federal Trade Commission, U.S. Government. Retrieved July 4, 2011. Online: http://ftc.gov/opa/2011/03/topcomplaints.shtm

Ferguson, Christopher J., and John Kilburn. 2010. "Much Ado about Nothing: The Misestimation and Overinterpretation of Violent Video Game Effects in Eastern and Western Nations: Comment on Anderson, et al." *Psychological Bulletin* 136(2):174–178.

Ferran, Lee. 2011. "Former CIA Counter-Terror Chief: Al Qaeda Will Go Cyber." ABC

News (August 4). Retrieved August 4, 2011. Online: http://abcnews.go.com/Blotter/cia-counter-terror-chief-al-qaeda-cyber/story?id=14224256

Fine, Gary Alan. 1987. *With the Boys: Little League Baseball and Preadolescent Culture.* Chicago: University of Chicago Press.

Finkelhor, David, and Kersti Yllo. 1985. *License to Rape: Sexual Abuse of Wives.* New York: Free Press.

Firestone, Shulamith. 1970. *The Dialectic of Sex.* New York: Morrow.

Fisher, Lawrence M. 1996. "Health on Line: Doctor Is in, and His Disk Is Full." *New York Times* (June 14):C1, C8.

Fleming, Justin. 2010. "College Shootings Shock Nation." *Campus Times,* University of Rochester (September 30). Retrieved May 25, 2011. Online: http://www.campustimes.org/2010/09/30/college-shootings-shock-nation/

Foner, Philip S., and Daniel Rosenberg (Eds.). 1993. *Racism, Dissent, and Asian Americans from 1850 to Present.* Westport, CT: Greenwood Press.

Food and Agricultural Organization. 1995. *FAO Yearbook 1995.* Rome, Italy: Food and Agricultural Organization of the United Nations.

Food and Agriculture Organization of the United Nations. 2011. "Global Food Losses and Food Waste: Extent, Causes and Prevention." Retrieved May 30, 2011. Online: http://www.fao.org/fileadmin/user_upload/ags/publications/GFL_web.pdf

Forbes. 2008a. "The Forbes 400: A Billion Dollars Is No Longer Enough." Retrieved July 5, 2008. Online: http://www.forbes.com/2007/09/19/richest-americans-forbes-lists-richlist07-cx_mm_0920rich_land.html

Forbes. 2008b. "World's Billionaires." Retrieved April 18, 2008. Online: http://www.forbes.com/2008/03/05/richest-billionaires-people-billionaires08-cx_lk_0305intro.html

Forbes. 2010. *The Forbes 400: 2010.* Retrieved February 4, 2012 *Online*: http://finance.yahoo.com/news/pf_article_110765.html Ford, Peter. 2001. "Injustice Seen as Fertile Soil for Terrorists." *The Christian Science Monitor* (November 28). Retrieved December 12, 2002. Online: http://www.csmonitor.com/2001/1128/p7s1woeu.html

Foreman, Judy. 1996. "Caring for Parents Long-Distance Is a Baby Boomer's Nightmare." *Austin American-Statesman* (November 3):E1, E14.

Fortune. 2005. "Women CEOs of *Fortune* 500 Companies." Retrieved August

27, 2005. Online: http://www.fortune.com/fortune/subs/fortune500/women-ceos/0,23621,,00.html

Forum on Child and Family Statistics. 2010. "America's Children in Brief: Key National Indicators of Well-Being, 2010." Retrieved February 3, 2012. Online: http://www.childstats.gov/pdf.ac2010/ac_10.pdf

FOXNews.com. 2005. "Justifiable Shooting?" *The O'Reilly Factor* (July 15). Retrieved July 20, 2005. Online: http://www.foxnews.com/story/0,2933,162806,00.html

Franklin, John Hope. 1980. *From Slavery to Freedom* (3rd ed.). New York: Knopf.

French, Dolores, with Linda Lee. 1988. *Working: My Life as a Prostitute.* New York: E.P. Dutton.

French, Howard W. 2005. "A Village Grows Rich Off Its Main Export: Its Daughters." *New York Times* (January 3). Retrieved June 2, 2008. Online: http://www.nytimes.com/2005/01/03/international/asia/03china.html

Freudenberg, Nicholas, and Carl Steinsapir. 1992. "Not in Our Backyards: The Grassroots Environmental Movement." In Riley E. Dunlap and Angela G. Mertig (Eds.), *American Environmentalism: The U.S. Environmental Movement, 1970–1990.* New York: Taylor & Francis, pp. 27–37.

Freund, Matthew, Nancy Lee, and Terri Leonard. 1991. "Sexual Behavior of Clients with Street Prostitutes in Camden, New Jersey." *Journal of Sex Research,* 28(November 4):579–591.

Friedlander, Whitney. 2011. "Gay and Lesbian Characters Are Popping Up on Shows for Young People." *Los Angeles Times* (January 3). Retrieved June 20, 2011. Online: http://articles.latimes.com/2011/jan/03/entertainment/la-et-gay-characters-20110103

Friedman, George, and Meredith Friedman. 1996. *The Future of War.* New York: St. Martin's Griffin.

Friedman, Thomas L. 2000. "Boston E-Party." *New York Times* (January 1):A31.

Friedman, Thomas L. 2008. *Hot, Flat, and Crowded.* New York: Farrar, Straus and Giroux.

Fritze, John. 2010. "Medical Expenditures Have 'Very Steep' Rate of Growth." *USA Today* (Feb. 4). Retrieved June 7, 2010. Online: http://www.usatoday.com/cleanprint/?1275957329928

The Future of Children. 2001. *Caring for Infants and Toddlers.* Retrieved March 27, 2005. Online: http://www.futureofchildren.org/pubsinfo2825/pubsinfo_show.htm?doc_id=79324

Gabriel, Trip. 1995. "Some On-Line Discoveries Give Gay Youths a Path to Themselves." *New York Times* (July 2):1, 9.

Galbraith, John Kenneth. 1985. *The New Industrial State* (4th ed.). Boston: Houghton Mifflin.

Galbraith, Kate. 2011. "Budget Fight Hurts U.S. Climate Effort." *New York Times* (April 18). Retrieved July 29, 2011. Online: http://www.nytimes.com/2011/04/18/business/energy-environment/18green.html

Gamson, Joshua. 1994. *Claims to Fame: Celebrity in Contemporary America.* Berkeley: University of California Press.

Gans, Herbert. 1982. *The Urban Villagers: Group and Class in the Life of Italian Americans* (updated and expanded ed.; orig. published in 1962). New York: Free Press.

Gardiner, Maria, Marika Tiggermann, Hugh Kearns, and Kelly Marshall. 2007. "Show Me the Money! An Empirical Analysis of Mentoring Outcomes for Women in Academia." *Higher Education Research & Development,* 26(4):425–442.

Gardner, Tracey A. 1994. "Racism in Pornography and the Women's Movement." In Alison M. Jaggar (Ed.), *Living with Contradictions: Controversies in Feminist Social Ethics.* Boulder, CO: Westview, pp. 171–176.

Garner, Abigail. 2005. *Families Like Mine.* New York: HarperCollins.

Garreau, Joel. 1991. *Edge City: Life on the New Frontier.* New York: Doubleday.

Gates, Gary J. 2011. "How Many People Are Lesbian, Gay, Bisexual, and Transgender?" Williams Institute, UCLA School of Law (April). Retrieved June 16, 2011. Online: http://www3.law.ucla.edu/williamsinstitute/pdf/How-many-people-are-LGBT-Final.pdf

Gelfand, Donald E. 1994. *Aging and Ethnicity: Knowledge and Services.* New York: Springer.

Gerbner, George, 1995. "Television Violence: The Power and the Peril." In Gail Dines and Jean M. Humez (Eds.), *Gender, Face, and Class in Media: A Text-Reader.* Thousand Oaks, CA: Sage, pp. 547–557.

Gibbs, Lois Marie, as told to Murray Levine. 1982. *Love Canal: My Story.* Albany: State University of New York Press.

Gibson, James William, and Francesca M. Cancian. 1990. "Is War Inevitable?" In Francesca M. Cancian and James William Gibson (Eds.), *Making War, Making Peace: The Social Foundations of Violent Conflict.* Belmont, CA: Wadsworth, pp. 1–10.

Ginsburg, Ruth Bader. 2011. Opinion in *Wal-Mart Stores, Inc., Petitioner v. Betty Dukes et al.* U.S. Supreme Court. Retrieved June 20, 2011. Online: http://www.supremecourt.gov/opinions/10pdf/10-277.pdf

Glaeser, Edward. 2011. *Triumph of the City.* New York: Penguin.

Glaser, Barney, and Anselm Strauss. 1968. *Time for Dying.* Chicago: Aldine.

globalissues.org. 2011. "Corporate Profits Trumping Public Health (September 21). Retrieved February 4, 2012. Online: http://www.globalissues.org.news/2011/09/21/11262

GlobalSecurity.org. 2011. "World Wide Military Expenditures 2011." Retrieved August 2, 2011. Online: http://www.globalsecurity.org/military/world/spending.htm

Goffman, Erving. 1961. *Asylums: Essays on the Social Situation of Mental Patients and Other Inmates.* Chicago: Aldine.

Goffman, Erving. 1963. *Stigma: Notes of the Management of Spoiled Identity.* Upper Saddle River, NJ: Prentice Hall.

Golay, Michael, and Carl Rollyson. 1996. *Where America Stands: 1996.* New York: John Wiley.

Goldstein, Joseph, and Al Baker. 2011. "For Prostitutes, the Discovery of Bodies on Long Island Is Stoking Fear." *New York Times* (May 30). Retrieved June 25, 2011. Online: http://www.nytimes.com/2011/05/31/nyregion/prostitutes-fears-grow-as-remains-on-long-island-are-identified.html?_r=1&ref=prostitution

Gonzalez, David. 2005. "From Margins of Society to Center of the Tragedy." *New York Times* (September 2):A1, A19.

Goode, William J. 1982. "Why Men Resist." In Barrie Thorne with Marilyn Yalom (Eds.), *Rethinking the Family: Some Feminist Questions.* New York: Longman, pp. 131–150.

Goodman, Emily Jane. 1999. "Seducers, Harassers, and Wimps in Black Robes." *New York Times* (December 19):AR47, 51.

Gordon, Milton M. 1964. *Assimilation in American Life: The Role of Race, Religion, and National Origins.* New York: Oxford University Press.

Gorman, Siobhan, and Julian E. Barnes. 2011. "Cyber Combat: Act of War." *Wall Street Journal* (May 31). Retrieved August 4, 2011. Online: http://online.wsj.com/article/SB10001424052702304563104576355623135782718.html

Gottdiener, Mark. 1985. *The Social Production of Urban Space.* Austin: University of Texas Press.

Graham, Paul. 2004. *Hackers & Painters: Big Ideas from the Computer Age.* Sebastopol, CA: O'Reilly.

Greenhouse, Linda. 2008. "Supreme Court Upholds Child Pornography Law." *New York Times* (May 20). Retrieved June 26. 2011. Online: http://www.nytimes.com/2008/05/20/washington/20scotus.html

gulfspilloil.com 2011. "BP's Oil Spill Costs Look Manageable (January 9). Retrieved February 4, 2012. Online: http://www.gulfspilloil.com/ap-bps-oil-spill-costs-look-manageable

Guttmacher Institute. 2011. "Facts on Induced Abortion in the United States." Guttmacher Institute (May). Retrieved July 13, 2011. Online: http://www.guttmacher.org/pubs/fb_induced_abortion.html

Hamper, Ben. 1991. *Rivethead: Tales from the Assembly Line.* New York: Warner Books.

Haney, Craig, Curtis Banks, and Philip Zimbardo. 1984. "A Study of Prisoners and Guards in a Simulated Prison." In E. Aronson (Ed.), *Readings about the Social Animal.* New York: W.H. Freeman.

Hardy, Jackie. 2010. "Charter Schools Closing the Achievement Gap among Minority Students." *North Dallas Gazette* (March 3). Retrieved April 29, 2011. Online: http://northdallasgazette.com/2010/03/charter-schools-closing-the-achievement-gap-among-minority-students/

Harrison, Todd. 2011. "Analysis of the FY 2011 Defense Budget." Center for Strategic and Budgetary Assessments. Retrieved February 4, 2012. Online: http://www.csbaonline.org/wp-content/uploads/2010/06/2010.06.29-Analysis-of-the-FY2011-Defense-Budget.pdf

Hartmann, Heidi. 1976. "Capitalism, Patriarchy, and Job Segregation by Sex." *Signs: Journal of Women in Culture and Society,* 1(Spring):137–169.

Hauchler, Ingomar, and Paul M. Kennedy (Eds.). 1994. *Global Trends: The World Almanac of Development and Peace.* New York: Continuum.

Hauser, Robert M. 1995. "Symposium: The Bell Curve." *Contemporary Sociology: A Journal of Reviews,* 24(2):149–153.

Havighurst, Robert J., Bernice L. Neugarten, and Sheldon S. Tobin. 1968. "Disengagement and Patterns of Aging." In Bernice L. Neugarten (Ed.), *Middle Age and Aging.* Chicago: University of Chicago Press, pp. 161–172.

Hawley, Amos. 1950. *Human Ecology.* New York: Ronald Press.

Hawley, Amos. 1981. *Urban Society* (2nd ed.). New York: Wiley.

Healy, Patrick O'Gilfoil. 2007. "Run! Hide! The Illegal Border Crossing Experience."

New York Times (February 4). Retrieved September 10, 2008. Online: http://travel.nytimes.com/2007/02/04/travel/04HeadsUp.html

Heffernan, Virginia. 2011. "Miss G.: A Case of Internet Addiction." Opinionator: Exclusive Online Commentary from the *Times. New York Times* (April 9). Retrieved February 4, 2012. Online: http://www.opinionator.blogs.nytimes.com/2011/04/09miss-g-a-case-of-internet-addiction/

Heilbrunn, Leslie. 2000. "Mind Control?" *Brill's Content* (January):105–109.

Helms, Marisa. 2005. "Shooting Fuels Debate over Safety of Prozac for Teens." Minnesota Public Radio: News & Features (March 25). Retrieved July 25, 2005. Online: http://news.minnesota.publicradio.org/features/2005/03/25_helmsm_prozacfolo/

Henig, Robin Marantz. 2010. "What Is It about 20-Somethings?" *New York Times* (August 18). Retrieved June 12, 2011. Online: http://www.nytimes.com/2010/08/22/magazine/22Adulthood-t.html?scp=1&sq=emerging%20adulthood&st=cse

Herrnstein, Richard J., and Charles Murray. 1994. *The Bell Curve: Intelligence and Class Structure in American Life.* New York: Free Press.

Herz, Diane E., and Barbara H. Wootton. 1996. "Women in the Workforce: An Overview." In Cynthia Costello and Barbara Kivimae Krimgold (Eds.) for the Women's Research and Education Institute, *The American Woman 1996–97: Women and Work.* New York: Norton, pp. 44–78.

Higginbotham, Elizabeth. 1994. "Black Professional Women: Job Ceilings and Employment Sectors." In Maxine Baca Zinn and Bonnie Thornton Dill (Eds.), *Women of Color in U.S. Society.* Philadelphia: Temple University Press, pp. 113–131.

Hill, Catherine, and Elena Silva. 2005. *Drawing the Line: Sexual Harassment on Campus.* American Association of University Women Educational Foundation. Retrieved June 11, 2011. Online: http://www.aauw.org/learn/research/upload/DTLFinal.pdf

Hirsch, Amanda. 2008. "Confessions of an Internet Addict." Retrieved August 31, 2008. Online: http://www.creativedc.org/blog/2008/07/confessions-of-internet-addict.html

Hirschi, Travis. 1969. *Causes of Delinquency.* Berkeley: University of California Press.

Hirschi, Travis, and Michael J. Hindelang. 1977. "Intelligence and Delinquency: A Revisionist Review." *American Sociological Review,* 42:571–586.

Hirshon, Robert E. 2010. "Legalizing Marijuana: An Issue That Just Won't Go Away." *CNBC Special Report: Marijuana and Money* (April 20). Retrieved July 2, 2011. Online: http://www.cnbc.com/id/36267224

Hispanic Association on Corporate Responsibility. 2004. "Corporate Governance Report 2004." Retrieved July 23, 2005. Online: http://www.hacr.org/mediacenter/pubID.21/pub_detail.asp

Hochschild, Arlie Russell, with Ann Machung. 1989. *The Second Shift: Working Parents and the Revolution at Home.* New York: Viking/Penguin.

Hodson, Randy, and Teresa A. Sullivan. 2008. *The Social Organization of Work* Belmont: Wadsworth.

Hodson, Steven. 2011. "Fake Apple Store Employees Believe They Work for Apple." The Inquisitr (July 20). Retrieved July 20, 2011. Online: http://www.inquisitr.com/127725/fake-apple-store-employees-believe-they-work-for-apple/

Hoffman, Andrew J. 1994. "Love Canal Lives." *E Magazine* (November–December):19–22.

Holmes, Robert M. 1988. *Serial Murder.* Beverly Hills, CA: Sage.

Holt, John C. 1964. *How Children Fail.* New York: Dell.

Homeland Security. 2011. "Refugees and Asylees: 2010." U.S. Department of Homeland Security (May). Retrieved February 4, 2012. Online: http://www.dhs.gov/xlibrary/assets/statistics/publications/ois_rfa_fr_2010.pdf

Hooker, Evelyn. 1957. "The Adjustment of the Male Overt Homosexual." *Journal of Projective Techniques,* 21:18–31.

Hooker, Evelyn. 1958. "Male Homosexuality and the Rorschach." *Journal of Projective Techniques,* 22:33–54.

Hooyman, Nancy, and H. Asuman Kiyak. 2008. *Social Gerontology: A Multidisciplinary Perspective* (8th ed.). Boston: Allyn and Bacon.

Horowitz, Allan V. 1982. *Social Control of Mental Illness.* New York: Academic.

HUD. 2009. "2009 Annual Homeless Assessment Report to Congress." Retrieved August 1, 2011. Online: http://www.hudhre.info/documents/5thHomelessAssessmentReport.pdf

Hudson, Kenneth. 2008. "Dual Labor Market and Its Work–Family Implications." Retrieved June 1, 2011. Online: http://wfnetwork.bc.edu/encyclopedia_entry.php?id=15159&area=All

Hughes, Diane, James Rodriguez, Emilie P. Smith, Deborah J. Johnson, Howard C. Stevenson, and Paul Spicer. 2006. "Parents' Ethnic-Racial Socialization Practices: A Review of Research and Directions for Future Study." *Developmental Psychology*, 42(5):747–770.

Human Rights Watch. 2011. "World Report: 2011." Retrieved July 23, 2011. Online: http://www.hrw.org/en/world-report-2011

Humes, Karen R., Nicholas A. Jones, and Roberto R. Ramirez. 2011. "Overview of Race and Hispanic Origin: 2010." U.S. Census Bureau. Retrieved June 1, 2011. Online: http://www.census.gov/prod/cen2010/briefs/c2010br-02.pdf

Hunnicutt, Gwen. 2009. "Varieties of Patriarchy and Violence Against Women." *Violence Against Women* 15(5; May). Retrieved May 25, 2011. Online: http://vaw.sagepub.com/content/15/5/553.abstract

Hynes, Samuel. 1997. *The Soldiers' Tale: Bearing Witness to Modern War.* New York: Allen Lane/Penguin.

International Organization for Migration. 2010. *World Migration Report: 2010.* Retrieved July 29, 2011. Online: http://publications.iom.int/bookstore/free/WMR_2010_ENGLISH.pdf

International Organization for Migration. 2011. "Facts & Figures." Retrieved July 5, 2011. Online: http://www.iom.int/jahia/Jahia/about-migration/facts-and-figures/lang/en

Jack, Dana Crowley. 1993. *Silencing the Self: Women and Depression.* New York: HarperPerennial.

Jacobs, Jane. 1961. *The Death and Life of Great American Cities.* New York: Random House.

Jaffee, David. 1990. *Levels of Socio-economic Development Theory.* Westport, CT: Praeger.

Jakes, Lara. 2011. "Iraq War Review: U.S. Finds Country Is Deadlier Now Than a Year Ago" (July 30). Retrieved August 3, 2011. Online: http://www.huffingtonpost.com/2011/07/30/iraq-war-review-deadlier-now-than-year-ago_n_913928.html

Javelin Strategy and Research. 2010. "Identity Fraud Survey Report, 2009." Retrieved July 5, 2011. Online: https://www.javelinstrategy.com/research/brochures/Brochure-170

Jerrard, Jane. 2007. "Psychiatric Hospitalists Diagnose, Treat Mental Illness." *The Hospitalist* (October). Retrieved July 10, 2011. Online: http://www.the-hospitalist.org/details/article/233885/Psychiatric_hospitalists_diagnose_treat_mental_illness.html

Johnson, Bruce D., Paul J. Goldstein, Edward Preble, James Schmeidler, Douglas S. Lipton, Barry Spunt, and Thomas Miller. 1985. *Taking Care of Business: The Economics of Crime by Heroin Abusers.* Lexington, MA: Lexington Books.

Johnson, Reed. 2008. "Mexican Town Offers Illegal Immigration Simulation Adventure." *Los Angeles Times* (May 24). Retrieved September 10, 2008. Online: http://www.latimes.com/news/nationworld/nation/la-et-border24-2008may24,0,4295754,print.story

Johnston, Lloyd D., Patrick M. O'Malley, Jerald G. Bachman, and John E. Schulenberg. 2011. *Monitoring the Future: National Results on Adolescent Drug Use.* Ann Arbor: Institute for Social Research, University of Michigan. Retrieved June 27, 2011. Online: http://monitoringthefuture.org/pubs/monographs/mtf-overview2010.pdf

Jones, Jeffrey M. 2011. "Budget Rises as Most Important Problem to Highest Since '96." Gallup.com (April 13). Retrieved May 26, 2011. Online: http://www.gallup.com/poll/147086/Budget-Rises-Most-Important-Problem-Highest.aspx

Jones, Owen. 2011. *Chavs: The Demonization of the Working Class.* London: Verso. Excerpt from Chapter 7: Broken Britain. Reprinted at nytimes.com (July 12). Retrieved July 19, 2011. Online: http://www.nytimes.com/2011/07/13/books/excerpt-chavs-by-owen-jones.html?scp=4&sq=long%20term%20unemployment?&st=cse

Jordans, Frank. 2011. "UN Backs Gay Rights for First Time Ever." Latimes.com (June 18). Retrieved June 20, 2011. Online: http://www.latimes.com/news/nationworld/world/la-fgw-un-gay-rights-20110619,0,6160506,print.story

Journalism.org. 2011. "Eight Things to Know about How the Media Covered the Gulf Disaster." Pew Research Center's Project for Excellence in Journalism (August 25). Retrieved August 6, 2011. Online: http://www.journalism.org/analysis_report/100_days_gushing_oil

Jung, John. 1994. *Under the Influence: Alcohol and Human Behavior.* Pacific Grove, CA: Brooks/Cole.

Kaiser Family Foundation. 2003. "Key Facts: TV Violence" (Spring). Retrieved May 25, 2011. Online: http://www.kff.org/entmedia/upload/Key-Facts-TV-Violence.pdf

Kaldor, Mary. 1981. *The Baroque Arsenal.* New York: Hill and Wang.

Kalish, Richard A. 1985. *Death, Grief, and Caring Relationships* (2nd ed.). Monterey, CA: Brooks/Cole.

Kantrowitz, Barbara. 1993. "Live Wires." *Newsweek* (September 6):42–48.

Karcher, Richard T. 2009. "Tort Law and Journalism Ethics." *Loyola University Chicago Law Journal*, 40:781–845. Retrieved July 21, 2011. Online: http://www.luc.edu/law/activities/publications/lljdocs/vol40_no4/vol40_issue4/Karcher.pdf

Kasarda, John D., and Greg Lindsay. 2011. *Aerotropolis: The Way We'll Live Next.* New York: Farrar, Straus and Giroux.

Kasperowicz, Pete. 2011. "Republicans Push English-Only Bill, Requires Language Tests" (March 12). Retrieved June 4, 2011. Online: http://thehill.com/blogs/floor-action/house/149049-republicans-push-english-only-bill-requiring-language-tests

Katz, Janet, and William J. Chambliss. 1995. In Joseph F. Sheley (Ed.), *Criminology: A Contemporary Handbook* (2nd ed.). Belmont, CA: Wadsworth, pp. 275–303.

Kaysen, Susanna. 1993. *Girl, Interrupted.* New York: Vintage.

Kazemi, Darius. 2005. "I Love It Here: The Secret Maps of Worcester." *WPI Tech News* (April 12). Retrieved August 20, 2005. Online: http://www.wpi.edu/News/TechNews/article.php?id=973

Kearl, Holly. 2010. "Sexual Harassment during Commute Hurts Performance at Work." abcnews.com (July 14). Retrieved June 10, 2011. Online: http://abcnews.go.com/Business/sexual-harassment-work-hurts-performance/story?id=11165814

Kearns-Bodkin, Jill N., and Kenneth E. Leonard. 2008. "Relationship Functioning Among Adult Children of Alcoholics." *Journal of Studies on Alcohol and Drugs* (November):941–950. Online: http://www.ncbi.nlm.nih.gov/pmc/articles/PMC2583382/pdf/jsad941.pdf

Kelso, William A. 1994. *Poverty and the Underclass: Changing Perceptions of the Poor in America.* New York: New York University Press.

Kempe, C. Henry, F. Silverman, B. Steele, W. Droegemueller, and H. Silver. 1962. "The Battered-Child Syndrome." *Journal of the American Medical Association*, 181:17–24.

Kendall, Diana. 2002. *The Power of Good Deeds: Privileged Women and the Social Reproduction of the Upper Class.* Lanham, MD: Rowman & Littlefield.

Kendall, Diana. 2011. *Framing Class: Media Representations of Wealth and Poverty in America* (2nd ed.). Lanham, MD: Rowman & Littlefield.

Kennedy, Kelly. 2011. "Up to $49 Billion Unpaid by Uninsured for Hospitalizations." *USA Today* (May 9). Retrieved July 11,

2011. Online: http://www.usatoday.com/news/washington/2011-05-09-uninsured-unpaid-hospital-bills_n.htm#

Kerry, John F. 2006. "Merits of 'Masha's Law.'" *Washington Times* (July 18). Retrieved June 26, 2011. Online: http://www.washingtontimes.com/news/2006/jul/18/20060718-083427-1343r/

Kessler, Ronald C. 2011. "FBI: 100 Percent Chance of WMD Attack." Newsmax.com (February 14). Retrieved August 2, 2011. Online: http://www.newsmax.com/PrintTemplate.aspx?nodeid=386055

Kessler-Harris, Alice. 1990. *A Woman's Wage: Historical Meanings and Social Consequences.* Lexington: University Press of Kentucky.

Kimmel, Michael S. (Ed.). 1990. *Men Confront Pornography.* New York: Crown Books.

Kimmel, Michael S., and Abby L. Ferber (Eds.). 2009. *Privilege: A Reader* (2nd ed.). Boulder, CO: Westview.

King, Leslie, and Madonna Harrington Meyer. 1997. "The Politics of Reproductive Benefits: U.S. Insurance Coverage of Contraceptive and Infertility Treatments." *Gender and Society,* 11(1):8–30.

Kinsey, Alfred C., Wardell B. Pomeroy, Clyde E. Martin, and Paul H. Gebhard. 1948. *Sexual Behavior in the Human Male.* Philadelphia: Saunders.

Kitano, Harry H. L., and Roger Daniels. 1995. *Asian Americans: Emerging Minorities* (2nd ed.). Upper Saddle River, NJ: Prentice Hall.

Klaus, Rikki. 2010. "University of Texas Student Talks about Shooting." whnt.com (September 28). Retrieved May 26, 2011. Online: http://www.whnt.com/news/whnt-university-of-texas-shooting-092810,0,1061492.story?track=rss

Klockars, Carl B. 1979. "The Contemporary Crises of Marxist Criminology." *Criminology,* 16:477–515.

Knox, Paul L., and Peter J. Taylor (Eds.). 1995. *World Cities in a World-System.* Cambridge, England: Cambridge University Press.

Kolata, Gina. 1996a. "New Era of Robust Elderly Belies the Fears of Scientists." *New York Times* (February 27):A1, B10.

Kolata, Gina. 1996b. "On Fringes of Health Care, Untested Therapies Thrive." *New York Times* (June 17):A1, C11.

Kort-Butler, Lisa A., and Kelley J. Sittner Hartshorn. 2011. "Watching the Detectives: Crime Programming, Fear of Crime, and Attitudes about the Criminal Justice System." *Sociological Quarterly* 52(1):36.

Kosmin, Barry A., and Seymour P. Lachman. 1993. *One Nation under God: Religion in Contemporary American Society.* New York: Crown Trade Paperbacks.

Kouri, Jim. 2011. "La Cosa Nostra Bosses, Members Charged in RICO Case." Examiner.com. Retrieved July 8, 2011. Online: http://www.examiner.com/public-safety-in-national/la-cosa-nostra-bosses-members-charged-rico-case

Kozlowski, Lori. 2011. "On Race in Commercials: Was Pepsi Offensive, Funny, or Both?" *Los Angeles Times/Community* (February 9). Retrieved May 31, 2011. Online: http://latimesblogs.latimes.com/chatter/2011/02/superbowl-commercials-race-pepsi-offensive-or-not.html

Kramer, Peter D. 1993. *Listening to Prozac.* New York: Viking.

Kreider, Rose M. 2010. "Increase in Opposesex Cohabitating Couples from 2009 to 2010." Retrieved July 13, 2011. Online: http://www.census.gov/population/www/socdemo/Inc-Opp-sex-2009-to-2010.pdf

Kristof, Nicholas D. 2009. "The Hidden Hunger." *New York Times* (May 23). Retrieved May 30, 2011. Online: http://www.nytimes.com/2009/05/24/opinion/24kristof.html?pagewanted=print

Kristof, Nicholas D. 2011. "Raiding a Brothel in India." *New York Times* (May 25). Retrieved June 26, 2011. Online: http://www.nytimes.com/2011/05/26/opinion/26kristof.html?_r=1&pagewanted=print

Krohn, Marvin. 2000. "Sources of Criminality: Control and Deterrence Theories." In Joseph F. Sheley (Ed.), *Criminology: A Contemporary Handbook* (3rd ed.). Belmont, CA: Wadsworth, pp. 373–399.

Krugman, Paul. 2005a. "A Can't Do Government." *New York Times* (September 2):A23.

Krugman, Paul. 2005b. "Passing the Buck." *New York Times* (April 22):A23.

Kübler-Ross, Elisabeth. 1969. *On Death and Dying.* New York: Macmillan.

Kurtzleben, Danielle. 2010. "Data Show Racial Disparity in Crack Sentencing." *U.S. News and World Report* (August 3). Retrieved June 29, 2011. Online: http://www.usnews.com/news/articles/2010/08/03/data-show-racial-disparity-in-crack-sentencing

Kurz, Demie. 1989. "Social Science Perspectives on Wife Abuse: Current Debates and Future Directions." *Gender and Society,* 3(4):489–505.

Kurz, Demie. 1995. *For Richer, for Poorer: Mothers Confront Divorce.* New York: Routledge.

Lacey, Marc. 2008. "Across Globe, Empty Bellies Bring Rising Anger." *New York Times* (April 18):A1, A11.

Lakoff, George. 2002. *Moral Politics: How Liberals and Conservatives Think.* Chicago: University of Chicago Press.

Lamanna, Mary Ann, and Agnes Riedmann. 2012. *Marriages and Families: Making Choices in a Diverse Society* (11th ed.). Belmont, CA: Wadsworth/Cengage.

Lane, Michael, Amanda Ryan, Shelly Wilson, and Taylor Yeftich. 2004. "A Path to Renewal: The Revitalization of North Lawndale." DePaul University PPS (Winter 2007). Retrieved September 5, 2008. Online: http://condor/depaul.edu/~fdemissi/lawndale1.pdf

Lappé, Frances Moore. 2008. "World Hunger: Its Roots and Remedies." In John Germov (Ed.), *A Sociology of Food and Nutrition: The Social Appetite* (3rd ed.). New York: Oxford University Press. Retrieved April 18, 2008. Online: http://www.smallplanet.org/worldhungerchapter.pdf

Lappé, Frances Moore, and Paul Martin Du Bois. 1994. *The Quickening of America: Rebuilding Our Nation, Remaking Our Lives.* San Francisco: Jossey-Bass.

Lasswell, Harold D. 1969. "The Structure and Function of Communication in Society." In Wilbur Schramm (Ed.), *Mass Communications.* Urbana: University of Illinois Press, pp. 103–130.

Lattman, Peter, and Azam Ahmed. 2011. "Galleon's Rajaranam Found Guilty." *New York Times* (May 11). Retrieved July 3, 2011. Online: http://dealbook.nytimes.com/2011/05/11/rajaratnam-found-guilty/?ref=rajrajaratnam

Lauber, Almon W. 1913. *Indian Slavery in Colonial Times within the Present Limits of the United States.* New York: Columbia University Press.

Laumann, Edward O., John H. Gagnon, Robert T. Michael, and Stuart Michaels. 1994. *The Social Organization of Sexuality: Sexual Practices in the United States.* Chicago: University of Chicago Press.

learn-about-alcoholism.com, 2011. "Alcoholism in the Workplace." Retrieved June 27, 2011. Online: http://www.learn-about-alcoholism.com/alcoholism-in-the-workplace.html

Lehmann, Jennifer M. 1994. *Durkheim and Women.* Lincoln: University of Nebraska Press.

Lemert, Edwin. 1951. *Social Pathology.* New York: McGraw-Hill.

Levin, William C. 1988. "Age Stereotyping: College Student Evaluations." *Research on Aging,* 10(1):134–148.

Levine, Peter. 1992. *Ellis Island to Ebbets Field: Sport and the American Jewish Experience*. New York: Oxford University Press.

Levinthal, Charles F. 2011. *Drugs, Behavior, and Modern Society* (7th ed.). Upper Saddle River, NJ: Pearson.

Lewis, Denise C., Katalin Medvedev, and Desiree M. Seponski. 2011. "Awakening to the Desire of Older Women: Deconstructing Ageism within Fashion Magazines." *Journal of Aging Studies* 25(2):101–109.

Lewis, Oscar. 1966. *La Vida: A Puerto Rican Family in the Culture of Poverty—San Juan and New York*. New York: Random House.

Libraries Linking Idaho. N.d. "USA PATRIOT Act." Retrieved August 4, 2011. Online: http://lili.org/forlibs/ce/able/course12/s3-patriot-17.htm

Lifton, Robert Jay. 1997. "Doubling: The Faustian Bargain." In Jennifer Turpin and Lester R. Kurtz (Eds.), *The Web of Violence: From Interpersonal to Global*. Urbana and Chicago: University of Illinois, pp. 31–44.

Lindenberger, Michael A. 2011. "Health Reform: SCOTUS to Dial Back Federal Power?" *Time* (February 2). Retrieved July 10, 2011. Online: http://www.time.com/time/nation/article/0,8599,2045553,00.html

Lindsey, Linda L. 1994. *Gender Roles: A Sociological Perspective* (2nd ed.). Upper Saddle River, NJ: Prentice Hall.

Liptak, Adam. 2008. "Same-Sex Marriage and Racial Justice Find Common Ground." *New York Times* (May 17):A10.

Liptak, Adam. 2011. "Justices Rule for Wal-Mart in Bias Case." *New York Times* (June 20):A1.

Lorber, Judith. 1994. *Paradoxes of Gender*. New Haven, CT: Yale University Press.

Lorenz, Konrad. 1966. *On Aggression*. New York: Bantam.

Lubrano, Alfred. 2004. *Limbo: Blue-Collar Roots, White-Collar Dreams*. Hoboken, NJ: John Wiley.

Luckenbill, David F. 1977. "Criminal Homicide as a Situated Transaction." *Social Problems*, 25:176–186.

Luker, Kristin. 1996. *Dubious Conceptions: The Politics of Teenage Pregnancy*. Cambridge, MA: Harvard University Press.

Lynn, Richard. 2008. *The Global Bell Curve: Race, IQ, and Inequality Worldwide*. Whitefish, MT: Washington Summit Publishers.

MADD. 1999. "Rating the States 2000 Report Card." Mothers Against Drunk Driving and the GuideOne Foundation.

Retrieved December 4, 1999. Online: http://www.madd.org

Madden, Patricia A., and Joel W. Grube. 1994. "The Frequency and Nature of Alcohol and Tobacco Advertising in Televised Sports, 1990 through 1992." *The American Journal of Public Health*, 84(2):297–300.

Malinowski, Bronislaw. 1964. "The Principle of Legitimacy: Parenthood, the Basis of Social Structure." In Rose Laub Coser (Ed.), *The Family: Its Structure and Functions*. New York: St. Martin's Press.

Malthus, Thomas R. 1965. *An Essay on Population*. New York: Augustus Kelley, Bookseller (orig. published in 1798).

Marcus, Eric. 1992. *Making History: The Struggle for Gay and Lesbian Equal Rights*. New York: HarperCollins.

Marquart, James W., Sheldon Ekland-Olson, and Jonathan R. Sorensen. 1994. *The Rope, the Chair, and the Needle*. Austin: University of Texas Press.

Marshall, Victor W. 1980. *Last Chapters: A Sociology of Aging and Dying*. Monterey, CA: Brooks/Cole.

Marshall, Victor W., and Judith Levy. 1990. "Aging and Dying." In Robert H. Binstock and Linda George (Eds.), *Handbook of Aging and the Social Sciences* (3rd ed). New York: Academic Press.

Martin, Philip, and Elizabeth Midgley. 2010. "Immigration in America 2010" (June). Population Reference Bureau. Retrieved May 15, 2011. Online: http://www.prb.org/Publications/PopulationBulletins/2010/immigrationupdate1

Marx, Karl, and Friedrich Engels. 1971. "The Communist Manifesto." (orig. published in 1847). In Dirk Struik (Ed.), *The Birth of the Communist Manifesto*. New York: International.

Marx, Karl, and Friedrich Engels. 1976. *The Communist Manifesto*. New York: Pantheon (orig. published in 1848).

Massey, Douglas S., and Nancy A. Denton. 1992. *American Apartheid: Segregation and the Making of the Underclass*. Cambridge, MA: Harvard University Press.

Massey, James L., and Marvin D. Krohn. 1986. "A Longitudinal Examination of an Integrated Social Process Model of Deviant Behavior." *Social Forces*, 65:106–134.

Matsueda, Ross L., Kevin Drakulich, and Charis E. Kubrin. 2006. In Ruth D. Peterson, Lauren J. Krivo, and John Hagan (Eds.), *The Many Colors of Crime: Inequalities of Race, Ethnicity and Crime in America*. New York: New York University Press, pp. 549–584.

Matthew's Place (matthewsplace.com). 1999. "Dennis Shepard's Statement to the Court" (November 4). Retrieved November 15, 1999. Online: http://www.matthewsplace.com/dennis2.htm

Mayall, Alice, and Diana E. H. Russell. 1993. "Racism in Pornography." In Diana E. H. Russell (Ed.), *Making Violence Sexy: Feminist Views on Pornography*. New York: Teachers College Press, pp. 167–177.

Maynard, Joyce. 1994. "To Tell the Truth." In Jay David (Ed.), *The Family Secret: An Anthology*. New York: William Morrow, pp. 79–85.

McCall, Nathan. 1994. *Makes Me Wanna Holler: A Young Black Man in America*. New York: Vintage.

McChesney, Robert W. 1999. *Rich Media, Poor Democracy: Communication Politics in Dubious Times*. Urbana: University of Illinois Press.

McClellan, Scott. 2008. *What Happened: Inside the Bush White House and Washington's Culture of Deception*. New York: PublicAffairs Books.

McDonnell, Janet A. 1991. *The Dispossession of the American Indian, 1887–1934*. Bloomington: Indiana University Press.

McKinlay, John B. 1994. "A Case for Refocusing Upstream: The Political Economy of Illness." In Peter Conrad and Rochelle Kern (Eds.), *The Sociology of Health and Illness*. New York: St. Martin's, pp. 509–530.

McKinley, Jesse. 2011. "California Raids Net Dozens Suspected of Being Gang Members." *New York Times* (June 8). Retrieved July 4, 2011. Online: http://www.nytimes.com/2011/06/09/us/09gang.html?ref=gangs

Medpagetoday.com. 2005. "Coffee Sends Wake Up Call to the Brain." Retrieved July 25, 2005. Online: http://www.medpagetoday.com/PrimaryCare/SleepDisorders/TB/927

Melendez, Edgardo. 1993. "Colonialism, Citizenship, and Contemporary Statehood." In Edwin Melendez and Edgardo Melendez (Eds.), *Colonial Dilemma: Critical Perspectives on Contemporary Puerto Rico*. Boston: South End Press, pp. 41–52.

Menchaca, Martha. 1995. *The Mexican Outsiders: A Community History of Marginalization and Discrimination in California*. Austin: University of Texas Press.

Merchant, Carolyn. 1983. *The Death of Nature: Women, Ecology, and the Scientific Revolution*. San Francisco: Harper and Row.

Merton, Robert. 1938. "Social Structure and Anomie." *American Sociological Review,* 3(6):672–682.

Merton, Robert King. 1968. *Social Theory and Social Structure* (enlarged ed.). New York: Free Press.

Meserve, Jeanne, and Mike M. Ahlers. 2009. "Marijuana Potency Surpasses 10 Percent, U.S. Says." Cnn.com (May 14). Retrieved June 29, 2011. Online: http://edition.cnn.com/2009/HEALTH/05/14/marijuana.potency/index.html

Messer, Ellen, and Kathryn E. May. 1994. *Back Rooms: Voices from the Illegal Abortion Era.* Buffalo, NY: Prometheus.

Michael, Robert T., John H. Gagnon, Edward O. Laumann, and Gina Kolata. 1994. *Sex in America: A Definitive Survey.* New York: Warner Books.

Michigan Department of Education. 1990. *The Influence of Gender Role Socialization on Student Perceptions.* Lansing: Michigan Department of Education, Office of Sex Equity in Education.

Mies, Maria, and Vandana Shiva. 1993. *Ecofeminism.* Atlantic Highlands, NJ: Zed Books.

Milgram, Stanley. 1974. *Obedience to Authority.* New York: Harper & Row.

Miller, Casey, and Kate Swift. 1991. *Words and Women: New Language in New Times* (updated). New York: HarperCollins.

Miller, Patricia G. 1993. *The Worst of Times.* New York: HarperCollins.

Mills, C. Wright. 1959a. *The Power Elite.* Fair Lawn, NJ: Oxford University Press.

Mills, C. Wright. 1959b. *The Sociological Imagination.* London: Oxford University Press.

Mills, C. Wright. 1976. *The Causes of World War Three.* Westport, CT: Greenwood Press.

Moeller, Susan D. 2004. "Media Coverage of Weapons of Mass Destruction." Center for International Security Studies at Maryland, University of Maryland, College Park. Retrieved August 28, 2005. Online: http://www.cissm.umd.edu/documents/WMDstudy_full.pdf

Mohawk, John. 1992. "Looking for Columbus: Thoughts on the Past, Present, and Future of Humanity." In M. Annette Jaimes (Ed.), *The State of Native America: Genocide, Colonization, and Resistance.* Boston: South End Press, pp. 439–444.

Molnar, Alex, Gary Miron, and Jessica L. Urschel. 2010. "Profiles of For-Profit Education Management Organizations, 2009–2010." National Education Policy Center, University of Colorado at Boulder. Retrieved April 29, 2011. Online:

http://nepc.colorado.edu/files/EMO-FP-09-10.pdf

Moore, Malcolm. 2010. "Chinese Hiding Three Million Babies a Year." *The Telegraph* (May 30). Retrieved June 11, 2011. Online: http://www.telegraph.co.uk/news/worldnews/asia/china/7787661/Chinese-hiding-three-million-babies-a-year.html

Morgenson, Gretchen. 2010. "Housing Policy's Third Rail." *New York Times* (August 7). Retrieved July 30, 2011. Online: http://www.nytimes.com/2010/08/08/business/08gret.html

Morial, Marc. H. 2011. "National Urban League Trains African Americans for Corporate Boards" (April 15). Retrieved June 5, 2011. Online: http://www.sacobserver.com/2011/04/national-urban-league-trains-african-americans-for-corporate-boards/

msnbc.com 2007. "Witness: Gunman 'Didn't Say a Single Word.'" msnbc.com (April 16). Retrieved March 24, 2008. Online: http://www.msnbc.msn.com/id/18139889

Muro, Mark, and Christopher W. Hoene. 2009. "Fiscal Challenges Facing Cities: Implications for Recovery." Blueprint for American Prosperity published by National League of Cities (November). Retrieved July 29, 2011. Online: http://www.brookings.edu/~/media/Files/rc/papers/2009/1118_cities_fiscal_challenges_muro_hoene/1118_cities_fiscal_challenges_paper.pdf

Myers, Steven Lee. 1997. "Converting the Dollar into a Bludgeon." *New York Times* (April 20):E5.

NACCRRA.org. 2011. "Women with Children Are Entering the Workforce in Greater Numbers Than Ever Before." National Association of Child Care Resource and Reference Agencies. Retrieved July 13, 2011. Online: http://www.naccrra.org/policy/background_issues/working-mothers-need-child-care

National Alliance to End Homelessness. 2011. "State of Homelessness in America 2011" (January 11). Retrieved May 29, 2011. Online: http://www.endhomelessness.org/content/article/detail/3668

National Center for Biotechnology Information. 2009. "Fetal Alcohol Syndrome." Retrieved June 27, 2011. Online: http://www.ncbi.nlm.nih.gov/pubmedhealth/PMH0001909/

National Center for Education Statistics. 2010a. "Indicators of School Crime and Safety: 2010." Retrieved July 16, 2011. Online: http://nces.ed.gov/programs/

crimeindicators/crimeindicators2010/key.asp

National Center for Education Statistics. 2010b. "The Nation's Report Card: Reading 2009." Retrieved July 18, 2011. Online: http://nces.ed.gov/nationsreportcard/pdf/main2009/2010458.pdf

National Center for Education Statistics. 2011. "The Condition of Education: 2011." Retrieved May 29, 2011. Online: http://nces.ed.gov/pubs2011/2011033.pdf

National Center for Health Statistics. 2010. Health, United States, 2010. Hyattsville, MD: National Center for Health Statistics.

National Center for Legal and Economic Justice. 2010. "Poverty in the United States: A Snapshot." Retrieved May 28, 2011. Online: http://www.nclej.org/poverty-in-the-us.php

National Center for Statistics and Analysis. 2010. "Traffic Safety Facts: Alcohol-Impaired Driving." Retrieved June 27, 2011. Online: http://www.nhtsa.gov/staticfiles/ncsa/pdf/2010/811385.pdf

National Center on Elder Abuse. 2005. "Elder Abuse Prevalence and Incidence." Retrieved July 28, 2005. Online: http://www.elderabuse-center.org/pdf/publication/FinalStatistics050331.pdf

National Gang Intelligence Center. 2009. "Criminal Activity." *National Gang Threat Assessment* (January). U.S. Department of Justice. Retrieved July 4, 2011. Online: http://www.justice.gov/ndic/pubs32/32146/activities.htm#start

National Institute of Mental Health. 2010. "Mental Healthcare Cost Data." Retrieved July 10, 2011. Online: http://www.nimh.nih.gov/statistics/4COST_AM2006.shtml

National Institute on Aging. 2010. "Alzheimer's Disease: General Information." Retrieved June 12, 2011. Online: http://www.nia.nih.gov/Alzheimers/AlzheimersInformation/GeneralInfo/NIH, 2010

National Institute on Drug Abuse. 2010. "NIDA Info-Facts: Cigarettes and Other Nicotine Products." Retrieved June 27, 2011. Online: http://www.drugabuse.gov/infofacts/tobacco.html#References

National Law Enforcement Officers. 2011. "Law Enforcement Facts." Retrieved July 8, 2011. Online: http://www.nleomf.org/facts/enforcement/

National League of Cities. 2010. "State of America's Cities Survey on Jobs and the Economy (May). Retrieved February 4, 2012. Online: http://www.nlc.org/

state-of-americas-cities-survey-jobs-economy-rpt-may10.pdf

National Oceanic and Atmospheric Administration. 2011. "Ozone Layer's Future Linked Strongly to Changes in Climate, Study Finds." *ScienceDaily* (February 17). Retrieved July 29, 2011. Online: http://www.scienceday.com/releases/2011/02/110217003347.htm

National Vital Statistics System. 2011. "Deaths: Preliminary Data for 2009." National Vital Statistics Reports, Vol. 59, No. 4 (March 16). Retrieved February 4, 2012. Online: http://www.cdc.gov/nchs.data/nvsr/nvsr59/nvsr59_04.pdf

National Television Violence Study. 1998. "Executive Summary," *National Television Violence Study,* vol. 3. Retrieved October 31, 1999. Online: http://www.ccsp.ucsb.edu/execsum.pdf

Nelson, Margaret K. 2010. "Parenting out of Control: Anxious Parents in Uncertain Times." New York: New York University Press.

Newman, Katherine S., Cybelle Fox, David J. Harding, Jal Mehta, and Wendy Roth. 2004. *Rampage: The Social Roots of School Shootings.* New York: Basic Books.

News Corporation. 2010. "Annual Report: 2010." Retrieved July 23, 2011. Online: http://www.newscorp.com/Report2010/report/NewsCorp2010AR.pdf

New York Times. 1996a. "Aging World, New Wrinkles" (September 22):E1.

New York Times. 1996b. "Where the Drugs Come From" (March 2):5.

New York Times. 2007. "High Cost of Health Care." Editorial, *New York Times* (November 25):WK9.

Nieves, Evelyn. 1995. "Wanted in Levittown: One Little Box, with Ticky Tacky Intact." *New York Times* (November 3):A12.

Norman, Michael. 1993. "One Cop, Eight Square Blocks." *New York Times Magazine* (December 12):62–90, 96.

Nyhart. Nick. 2001. "Raising Hard-Money Limits: An Incumbent Protection Plan." Retrieved December 14, 2002. Online: http://www.rollcall.com/pages/columns/observers/01/guest0329.html

Oakes, Jeannie. 1985. *Keeping Track: How Schools Structure Inequality.* New Haven, CT: Yale University Press.

Obama, Barack. 2011. "Remarks by the President on the Way Forward in Afghanistan (June 22). Retrieved February 4, 2012. Online: http://www.whitehouse.gov/the-press-office/2011/06/22/remarks-president-way-forward-afghanistan

Okie, Susan. 2009. "The Epidemic That Wasn't." *New York Times* (January 27). Retrieved June 29, 2011. Online: http://www.nytimes.com/2009/01/27/health/27coca.html?pagewanted=print

Oliver, Melvin L., and Thomas M. Shapiro. 2006. *Black Wealth/White Wealth: A New Perspective on Racial Inequality* (2nd ed.). New York: Routledge.

Olzak, Susan, Suzanne Shanahan, and Elizabeth H. McEneaney. 1996. "Poverty, Segregation, and Race Riots: 1960 to 1993." *American Sociological Review,* 61(August):590–613.

Omi, Michael, and Howard Winant. 1994. *Racial Formation in the United States: From the 1960s to the 1990s* (2nd ed.). New York: Routledge.

Oppel, Richard A., Jr. 2011. "Steady Decline in Major Crime Baffles Experts." *New York Times* (May 23). Retrieved May 24, 2011. Online: http://www.nytimes.com/2011/05/24/us/24crime.html?_r=1&scp=1&sq=violent%20crime%20rates%20down&st=cse

Orfield, Gary, and Chungmei Lee. 2007. "Historic Reversals, Accelerated Resegregation, and the Need for New Integration Strategies" (August 29). Retrieved June 5, 2011. Online: http://civilrightsproject.ucla.edu/research/k-12-education/integration-and-diversity/historic-reversals-accelerating-resegregation-and-the-need-for-new-integration-strategies-1

Ortner, Sherry B. 1974. "Is Female to Male as Nature Is to Culture?" In Michelle Rosaldo and Louise Lamphere (Eds.), *Women, Culture, and Society.* Stanford, CA: Stanford University Press.

Orum, Anthony M. 1995. *City-Building in America.* Boulder, CO: Westview.

Ott, Thomas. 2011. "Cleveland Students Hold Their Own with Voucher Students on State Tests." Cleveland.com (February 22). Retrieved April 27, 2011. Online: http://blog.cleveland.com/metro/2011/02/cleveland_students_hold_own_wi.html

Oxendine, Joseph B. 1995. *American Indian Sports Heritage.* Lincoln: University of Nebraska Press (orig. published in 1988).

Palen, J. John. 2012. *The Urban World* (9th ed.). Boulder, CO: Paradigm Publishers.

Palmer, Griff. 2010. "Decision Could Allow Anonymous Political Contributions by Businesses." *New York Times* (February 27). Retrieved July 18, 2011. Online: http://www.nytimes.com/2010/02/28/us/28donate.html?scp=31&sq=Citizens+United&st=nyt

Pappas, Stephanie. 2011. "Despite Aging Readership, Magazines Feature More Young Women." msnbc.com (June 12). Retrieved June 14, 2011. Online: http://today.msnbc.msn.com/id/43360848/ns/health-skin_and_beauty/#

Parenti, Michael. 1998. *America Besieged.* San Francisco: City Lights Books.

Parker-Pope, Tara. 2008. "Drinking to Extremes to Celebrate 21." *New York Times* (April 8):A1.

Parsons, Talcott. 1951. *The Social System.* New York: Free Press.

Parsons, Talcott. 1955. "The American Family: Its Relations to Personality and to the Social Structure." In Talcott Parsons and Robert F. Bales (Eds.), *Family, Socialization, and Interaction Process.* Glencoe, IL: Free Press, pp. 3–33.

Pateman, Carole. 1994. "What's Wrong with Prostitution?" In Alison M. Jaggar (Ed.), *Living with Contradictions: Controversies in Feminist Social Ethics.* Boulder, CO: Westview, pp. 127–132.

Pearce, Diana. 1978. "The Feminization of Poverty: Women, Work, and Welfare." *Urban and Social Change Review,* 11:28–36.

Perkins, Daniel F. 2011. "What Are the Development Tasks Facing Adolescents?" University of Florida IFAS Extension. Retrieved June 12, 2011. Online: http://www.education.com/reference/article/Ref_Adolescence/

Perry, David C., and Alfred J. Watkins (Eds.). 1977. *The Rise of the Sunbelt Cities.* Beverly Hills, CA: Sage.

Petersen, John L. 1994. *The Road to 2015: Profiles of the Future.* Corte Madera, CA: Waite Group Press.

Pettigrew, Thomas. 1981. "The Mental Health Impact." In Benjamin Bowser and Raymond G. Hunt (Eds.), *Impacts of Racism on White Americans.* Beverly Hills, CA: Sage, p. 117.

Pew Hispanic Center. 2009. "Statistical Portrait of Hispanics in the United States, 2009." Retrieved June 6, 2011. Online: http://pewhispanic.org/files/factsheets/hispanics2009/Table%2022.pdf

Pew Hispanic Center. 2010. "Hispanics and Arizona's New Immigration Law" (April 29). Pew Research Center. Retrieved June 2, 2011. Online: http://pewresearch.org/pubs/1579/arizona-immigration-law-fact-sheet-hispanic-population-opinion-discrimination

Pew Research Center. 2009. "Growing Old in America: Expectations vs. Reality." Retrieved June 13, 2011. Online: http://pewsocialtrends.org/2009/06/29/growing-old-in-america-expectations-vs-reality/

Pew Research Center Project for Excellence in Journalism. 2011. "Afghanistan War Jumps Back into Headlines" (June 20–26). Retrieved August 4, 2011. Online: http://www.journalism.org/

index_report/pej_news_coverage_index_june_2026_2011

Phillips, Kevin. 1995. *Arrogant Capital: Washington, Wall Street, and the Frustration of American Politics.* Boston: Little, Brown.

Phillips, Peter. 2011. "Big Media Interlocks with Corporate America." Project Censored: Media Democracy in Action. Retrieved July 23, 2011. Online: http://www.projectcensored.org/top-stories/articles/big-media-interlocks-with-corporate-america/

Picca, Leslie Houts and Joe R. Feagin. 2007. *Two-Faced Racism: Whites in the Backstage and Frontstage.* New York: Routledge.

Pilkington, Ed. 2011. "Washington Moves to Classify Cyber-Attacks as Acts of War." Guardian.co.uk (May 31). Retrieved August 4, 2011. Online: http://www.guardian.co.uk/world/2011/may/31/washington-moves-to-classify-cyber-attacks

Polakow, Valerie. 1993. *Lives on the Edge: Single Mothers and Their Children in the Other America.* Chicago: University of Chicago Press.

The Polling Report. 2005. "Problems and Priorities." Retrieved June 23, 2005. Online: http://www.pollingreport.com/prioriti.htm

Ponse, Barbara. 1978. *Identities in the Lesbian World: The Social Construction of Self.* Westport, CT: Greenwood Press.

Popenoe, David. 1996. *Life without Father: Compelling New Evidence That Fatherhood and Marriage Are Indispensable for the Good of Children and Society.* New York: Martin Kessler/Free Press.

Population Institute. 2010. "Maternal and Child Health" (August). Retrieved February 4, 2012. Online: http://www.populationinstitute.org/external/files/Fact_Sheets/maternal_and_child_health.pdf

Presidency of the Republic of Turkey. 2010. "Business World Should Always Be Consolidated" (February 11). Retrieved July 18, 2011. Online: http://www.tccb.gov.tr/news/397/77861/busineb-world-should-always-be-consolidated.html

ProLiteracy.org. 2010. "The Impact of Literacy." Retrieved July 16, 2011. Online: http://www.proliteracy.org/NetCommunity/Page.aspx?pid=345&srcid=191

Prud'Homme, Alex. 2011. "Drought: A Creeping Disaster." *New York Times* (July 16). Retrieved August 1, 2011. Online: http://www.nytimes.com/2011/07/17/opinion/sunday/17drought.html?scp=1&sq=worldwide%20water%20shortage?&st=cse

Qiuping, Gu, Charles F. Dillon, and Vicki L. Burt. 2010. "Prescription Drug Use Continues to Increase: U.S. Prescription Drug Data for 2007–2008." U.S. Department of Health and Human Services (September). Retrieved June 28, 2011. Online: http://www.cdc.gov/nchs/data/databriefs/db42.htm

Quattrochi, Regina. 2001. "Homeless with AIDS: Letter to the Editor." *New York Times* (June 9):A14.

Raddatz, Martha, and Kirit Radia. 2011. "Obama Approves Use of Armed Predator Drones over Libya." *ABC News* (April 21). Retrieved August 2, 2011. Online: http://abcnews.go.com/Politics/obama-approves-armed-predator-drones-libya/story?id=13429788

Radley, David C., Stan N. Finkelstein, and Randall S. Stafford. 2006. "Off-Label Prescribing among Office-Based Physicians." *Archives of Internal Medicine,* 166:1021–1026.

Rahn, Will. 2011. "Prime Minister Cameron Plans to Reform Britain's Government-Run Health-Care System. *The Daily Caller* (January 17). Retrieved July 11, 2011. Online: http://dailycaller.com/2011/01/17/prime-minister-cameron-plans-to-reform-britains-government-run-health-care-system/

Rape, Abuse, and Incest National Network. 2011. "Reporting Rates." Retrieved July 4, 2011. Online: http://www.rainn.org/get-information/statistics/reporting-rates

Rashbaum, William K. 2011. "Nearly 125 Arrested in Sweeping Mob Roundup." *New York Times* (January 20). Retrieved July 8, 2011. Online: http://www.nytimes.com/2011/01/21/nyregion/21mob.html

Reckless, Walter C. 1967. *The Crime Problem.* New York: Meredith.

Renner, Michael. 1993. *Critical Juncture: The Future of Peacekeeping.* Washington, DC: Worldwatch Institute.

Renzetti, Claire M., and Daniel J. Curran. 1995. *Women, Men, and Society* (3rd ed.). Boston: Allyn and Bacon.

Reporters without Borders. 2011. "Introduction." Retrieved July 23, 2011. Online: http://en.rsf.org/introduction-24-03-2011,32617.html

Reskin, Barbara F., and Heidi Hartmann. 1986. *Women's Work, Men's Work: Sex Segregation on the Job.* Washington, DC: National Academy Press.

Reskin, Barbara F., and Irene Padavic. 1994. *Women and Men at Work.* Thousand Oaks, CA: Pine Forge.

Resnick, Barbara, Lisa P. Gwyther, and Karen A. Roberto, eds. *Resilience in Aging: Concepts, Research, and Outcomes.* New York: Springer Science + Business Media, 2011.

Reuters. 2011. "Rural Americans Face Greater Lack of Healthcare Access: Report." The Raw Story (July 27). Retrieved July 30, 2011. Online: http://www.rawstory.com/rs/2011/07/27/rural-americans-face-greater-lack-of-healthcare-access-report/

Richard, J. F. 2002. *High Noon: Twenty Global Problems, Twenty Years to Solve Them.* New York: Basic.

Risling, Greg. 2005. "Autopsy Shows LAPD Gunfire Killed Toddler." *MercedSun-Star.com* (July 13). Retrieved July 30, 2005. Online: http://www.mercedsun-star.com/24hour/nation/story/2553521p-10958581c.html

Rogg, E. 1974. *The Assimilation of Cuban Exiles: The Role of Community and Class.* New York: Aberdeen.

Romo, Harriett D., and Toni Falbo. 1996. *Latino High School Graduation.* Austin: University of Texas Press.

Rowley, Ian, and Kiroko Tashiro. 2005. "Japan: Crazy for Cramming." *BusinessWeek.com* (April 18). Retrieved August 1, 2005. Online: http://www.businessweek.com/magazine/content/05_16/b3929071.htm

Rubin, Jennifer. 2011. "For Obama, It's All about Getting Out of Afghanistan" (June 22). Retrieved August 4, 2011. Online: http://www.washingtonpost.com/blogs/right-turn

Rubin, Lillian B. 1976. *Worlds of Pain: Life in the Working-Class Family.* New York: Basic Books.

Rubin, Lillian B. 1994. *Families on the Fault Line.* New York: HarperCollins.

Ruggles, Patricia. 1990. *Drawing the Line: Alternative Policy Measures and Their Implications for Public Policy.* Washington, DC: Urban Institute Press.

Ruggles, Patricia. 1992. "Measuring Poverty." *Focus,* 14(1):1–5.

Russell, Diana E. H. 1993. "Introduction." In Diana E. H. Russell (Ed.), *Making Violence Sexy: Feminist Views on Pornography.* New York: Teachers College Press, pp. 1–20.

Rutenberg, Jim, and Corey Kilgannon. 2005. "2 More White Men Are in Custody in Attack on Black MAN." *New York Times* (July 1):A15.

Ryan, William. 1976. *Blaming the Victim* (rev. ed.). New York: Vintage.

Saad, Lydia. 2010. "Americans' Acceptance of Gay Relations Crosses 50% Threshold." Gallup.com (May 25). Retrieved June 20, 2011. Online: http://www.gallup.com/poll/135764/americans-acceptance-gay-relations-crosses-threshold.aspx?version=print

Sadker, Myra, and David Sadker. 1994. *Failing at Fairness: How America's Schools Cheat Girls.* New York: Scribner.

Safilios-Rothschild, Constantina. 1969. "Family Sociology or Wives' Family Sociology? A Cross-Cultural Examination of Decision-Making." *Journal of Marriage and the Family,* 31(2):290–301.

Safire, William. 1993. *Safire's New Political Dictionary.* New York: Random House.

Sale, Kirkpatrick. 1990. *The Conquest of Paradise.* New York: Knopf.

Saltmarsh, Matthew. 2011. "Dior Fires John Galliano after Bigotry Complaints." *New York Times* (March 1). Retrieved June 1, 2011. Online: http://www.nytimes.com/2011/03/02/fashion/02dior.html

Sampson, Robert J. 1986. "Effects of Socioeconomic Context on Official Reactions to Juvenile Delinquency." *American Sociological Review,* 51 (December):876–885.

Sanday, Peggy Reeves. 2007. *Fraternity Gang Rape: Sex, Brotherhood, and Privilege on Campus* (2nd ed.). New York. New York University Press.

Sang-Hun, Choe. 2008. "A Taste of Failure Fuels an Appetite for Success at South Korea's Cram Schools." *New York Times* (August 13). Retrieved August 17, 2008. Online: http://www.nytimes.com/2008/08/13/world/asia/13cram.html

Santiago, Anna M., and George Galster. 1995. "Puerto Rican Segregation in the United States: Cause or Consequence of Economic Status?" *Social Problems,* 42:361–389.

Santiago, Anna M., and Margaret G. Wilder. 1991. "Residential Segregation and Links to Minority Poverty: The Case of Latinos in the United States." *Social Problems,* 38:701–723.

Sassler, Sharon. 2010. "The Higher Risk of Cohabitation." *New York Times* (December 20). Retrieved July 13, 2011. Online: http://www.nytimes.com/roomfordebate/2010/12/19/why-remarry/the-higher-risks-of-cohabitation

Saulny, Susan. 2008. "Financial Crisis Takes a Toll on Already-Squeezed Cities." *New York Times* (October 7). Retrieved July 29, 2011. Online: http://www.nytimes.com/2008/10/07/us/07citybudgets.html

Savage, Charlie, and Sheryl Gay Stolberg. 2011. "In Shift, U.S. Says Marriage Act Blocks Gay Rights." *New York Times* (February 23). Retrieved June 17, 2011. Online: http://www.nytimes.com/2011/02/24/us/24marriage.html

Sayare, Scott. 2011. "French Provocateur Enters Battle over Comments." *New York Times* (February 12):A5.

Schmidle, Nicholas. 2011. "Getting bin Laden: What Happened That Night in Abbottabad." *New Yorker* (August 8). Retrieved August 3, 2011. Online: http://www.newyorker.com/reporting/2011/08/08/110808fa_fact_schmidle?currentPage=all

Schoenbrod, David, and Melissa Witte. 2011. "Rescuing the Clean Air Act from Old Age." *The American* (March 16). American Enterprise Institute. Retrieved July 29, 2011. Online: http://www.american.com/archive/2011/march/rescuing-the-clean-air-act-from-old-age

Schur, Edwin M. 1965. *Crimes without Victims: Deviant Behavior and Public Policy.* Upper Saddle River, NJ: Prentice Hall.

ScienceDaily. 2009. "Iraq Troops' PTSD Rate as High as 35 Percent Analysis Finds." Institute for Operations Research and the Management Sciences (September 15). Retrieved August 2, 2011. Online: http://www.sciencedaily.com/releases/2009/09/090914151629.htm

Seelye, Katharine Q. 2011. "Detroit Census Confirms a Desertion Like No Other." *New York Times* (March 22). Retrieved July 19, 2011. http://www.nytimes.com/2011/03/23/us/23detroit.html

Segal, Lynn. 1990. "Pornography and Violence: What the 'Experts' Really Say." *Feminist Review,* 36:29–41.

Seligman, Martin E. P. 1975. *Helplessness: On Depression, Development and Death.* San Francisco: Freeman.

Shane, Scott. 2011. "Killings Spotlight Anti-Muslim Thought in U.S." *New York Times* (July 25):A1, A7.

Shane, Scott, and Eric Lipton. 2005. "Storm Overwhelmed Government's Preparation." *New York Times* (September 2):A1, A14.

Shapira, Ian. 2010. "Infertile Couples Cope with Prolific Facebook Friends." *Washington Post* (October 25). Retrieved July 13, 2011. Online: http://www.washingtonpost.com/wp-dyn/content/article/2010/10/24/AR2010102402642_pf.html

Sharam, Charles. 2011. "Native Americans in Video Games: Racism, Stereotypes, and the Digitized Indian" (April 4). Retrieved June 7, 2011. Online: http://www.projectcoe.com/2011/04/04/native-americans-in-video-games-racism-stereotypes-and-progress/

Shaw, Randy. 1999. *Reclaiming America: Nike, Clean Air, and the New National Activism.* Berkeley: University of California Press.

Shedler, J., and J. Block. 1990. "Adolescent Drug Users and Psychological Health." *American Psychologist,* 45:612–630.

Sheldon, William H. 1949. *Varieties of Delinquent Youth: An Introduction to Constitutional Psychiatry.* New York: Harper.

Shelton, Beth Ann. 1992. *Women, Men and Time: Gender Differences in Paid Work, Housework and Leisure.* Westport, CT: Greenwood.

Shenon, Philip. 1996. "Jet Makers Preparing Bids for a Rich Pentagon Prize." *New York Times* (March 12): A1, C4.

Shibutani, Tamotsu. 1970. "On the Personification of Adversaries." In Tamotsu Shibutani (Ed.), *Human Nature and Collective Behavior.* Upper Saddle River, NJ: Prentice Hall, pp. 223–233.

Shilts, Randy. 1993. *Conduct Unbecoming: Lesbians and Gays in the U.S. Military, Vietnam to the Persian Gulf.* New York: St. Martin's Press.

Simmel, Georg. 1950. *The Sociology of Georg Simmel.* Trans. Kurt Wolff. Glencoe, IL: Free Press (orig. written in 1902–1917).

Sivard, Ruth L. 1991. *World Military and Social Expenditures—1991.* Washington, DC: World Priorities.

Sivard, Ruth L. 1993. *World Military and Social Expenditures—1993.* Washington, DC: World Priorities.

Skolnick, Jerome H. 1975. *Justice without Trial* (2nd ed.). New York: Wiley.

Sleeter, Christine E. 1996. "White Silence, White Solidarity." In Noel Ignatiev and John Garvey (Eds.), *Race Traitor.* New York: Routledge, pp. 257–265.

Smith, A. 2002. "Effects of Caffeine on Human Behavior." Food and Chemical Toxicology (September): 1243–1255. Retrieved June 29, 2011. Online: http://www.ncbi.nlm.nih.gov/pubmed/12204388

Smith, M. Dwayne. 2000. "Capital Punishment in America." In Joseph F. Sheley (Ed.), *Criminology: A Contemporary Handbook* (3rd ed.). Belmont, CA: Wadsworth, pp. 621–643.

Smith, Tracy. 2011. "Baby Boomers: America's New Unemployables." CBS News (April 3). Retrieved June 12, 2011. Online: http://www.cbsnews.com/stories/2011/04/03/sunday/main20050117.shtml?tag=contentBody;featuredPost-PE

Snyder, Benson R. 1971. *The Hidden Curriculum.* New York: Knopf.

Snyder, Karrie Ann, and Adam Isaiah Green. 2008. "Revisiting the Glass Escalator: The Case of Gender Segregation in a Female Dominated Occupation." *Social Problems,* 55(2):271–299.

Soble, Alan. 1986. "Pornography in Capitalism: Powerlessness." In Alan Soble, *Pornography: Marxism, Feminism and the Future of Sexuality.* New Haven, CT: Yale University Press, pp. 78–84.

Sommers, Christina Hoff. 2001. *The War against Boys: How Misguided Feminism Is Harming Our Young Men.* New York: Simon & Schuster.

Spendonlife.com. 2011. "Official Identity Theft Statistics." Retrieved July 4, 2011. Online: http://www.spendonlife.com/guide/identgity-theft-statistics

Stanley, Julia P. 1972. "Paradigmatic Woman: The Prostitute." Paper presented at South Atlantic Modern Language Association, Jacksonville, FL, cited in Jessie Bernard, *The Female World.* New York: Free Press, 1981.

Starr, Paul. 1982. *The Social Transformation of American Medicine.* New York: Basic Books.

Steinberg, Jacques. 2011. "SAT's Reality TV Essay Stumps Some." *New York Times* (March 16). Retrieved July 24, 2011. Online: http://www.nytimes.com/2011/03/17/education/17sat.html

Stern, Christopher. 1998. "Researchers Shocked to Find—TV Violence." *Variety* (April 20–26):24.

Stevens, Jane Ellen. 2001. In "Reporting on Violence: New Ideas for Television, Print and Web" (Ed. Lori Dorfman). Berkeley: Berkeley Media Studies Group. Retrieved June 30, 2005. Online: http://www.bmsg.org/content/handbook2ndEd.pdf

Stevens, William K. 1997. "How Much Is Nature Worth? For You, $33 Trillion." *New York Times* (May 20):B7, B9.

Stewart, Charles T., Jr. 1995. *Healthy, Wealthy, or Wise? Issues in American Health Care Policy.* Armonk, NY: M.E. Sharpe.

Stolberg, Sheryl Gay. 1997. "Breaks for Mental Illness: Just What the Government Ordered." *New York Times* (May 4):E1, E5.

Stoller, Robert J. 1991. *Porn: Myths for the Twentieth Century.* New Haven, CT: Yale University Press.

Stransky, Michelle, and David Finkelhor. 2008. "How Many Juveniles Are Involved in Prostitution in the U.S.?" Crimes Against Children Research Center, University of New Hampshire. Retrieved June 24, 2011. Online: http://www.unh.edu/ccrc/prostitution/Juvenile_Prostitution_factsheet.pdf

Substance Abuse and Mental Health Services Administration. 2010. *Results from the 2009 National Survey on Drug Use and Health: Vol. 1. Summary of National Findings* (Office of Applied Studies, NSDUH Series H-38A, HHS Publication No. SMA 10-4586Findings). Rockville, MD. Retrieved June 27, 2011. Online: http://www.oas.samhsa.gov/NSDUH/2k9NSDUH/2k9ResultsP.pdf

Sullivan, Oriel. 2008. "Men's Changing Contribution to Housework and Childcare." Council on Contemporary Families.

Retrieved July 13, 2011. Online: http://www.contemporaryfamilies.org/marriage-partnership-divorce/menchange.html?q=coltrane

Sutherland, Edwin H. 1939. *Principles of Criminology.* Philadelphia: Lippincott.

Sutherland, Edwin H. 1949. *White Collar Crime.* New York: Dryden.

Sweet, Frank W. 2005. *Legal History of the Color Line: The Rise and Triumph of the One-Drop Rule.* Palm Coast, FL: Backintyme.

Takaki, Ronald. 1993. *A Different Mirror: A History of Multicultural America.* Boston: Little, Brown.

Tatum, Beverly Daniel. 2003. *Why Are All the Black Kids Sitting Together in the Cafeteria? And Other Conversations about Race.* New York: Basic Books.

Tavernise, Sabrina. 2011. "Parenting by Gays More Common in the South, Census Shows." *New York Times* (January 18). Retrieved June 18, 2011. Online: http://www.nytimes.com/2011/01/19/us/19gays.html

Taylor, Howard F. 1995. "Symposium: The Bell Curve." *Contemporary Sociology: A Journal of Reviews,* 24(2):153–157.

Terzis, Gillian. 2011. "Indonesia's Looming AIDS Crisis." *The Diplomat* (February 3). Retrieved June 23, 2011. Online: http://the-diplomat.com/2011/02/03/indonesia%E2%80%99s-looming-aids-crisis/

theathleticmindset.com 2011. "15 *Fortune* 500 CEO Women with the Athletic Mindset. Retrieved June 10, 2011. Online: http://theathleticmindset.com/2011/01/fortune-500-ceo-women-with-the-athletic-mindset/

thetaskforce.org. 2011. "Groundbreaking Study Finds Pervasive Discrimination Against Transgender People." National Gay and Lesbian Task Force (February 4). Retrieved June 19, 2011. Online: http://www.thetaskforce.org/press/releases/pr_study_020411

theweek.com. 2010. "The Internet Porn 'Epidemic': By the Numbers." Retrieved June 26, 2011. Online: http://theweek.com/article/index/204156/the-internet-porn-epidemic-by-the-numbers

Thomas, Katie. 2011a. "College Teams, Relying on Deception, Undermine Gender Equity." *New York Times* (April 25). Retrieved June 11, 2011. Online: http://www.nytimes.com/2011/04/26/sports/26titleix.html

Thomas, Katie. 2011b. "Colleges Cut Men's Programs to Satisfy Title IX." *New York Times* (May 1). Retrieved June 9, 2011. Online: http://www.nytimes.

com/2011/05/02/sports/02gender.html?scp=1&sq=title%20IX&st=cse

Thornton, Russell. 1984. "Cherokee Population Losses during the Trail of Tears: A New Perspective and a New Estimate." *Ethnohistory,* 31:289–300.

Thornton, Russell. 1987. *American Indian Holocaust and Survival.* Norman: University of Oklahoma Press.

354gay.com. 2010. "Half LGBT, HIV+ Surveyed Report Health Discrimination." Press release from Lambda Legal (February 4). Retrieved June 19, 2011. Online: http://www.365gay.com/news/half-lgbt-hiv-surveyed-report-health-discrimination/

Tierney, John. 1994. "Porn, the Low-Slung Engine of Progress." *New York Times* (January 9):H1, H18.

Tierney, John. 2005. "Fight Floods Like Fires, without the Feds." *New York Times* (September 3):A29.

Tierney, John. 2008. "Greens and Hunger." *New York Times* (May 19). Retrieved July 25, 2011. Online: http://tierneylab.blogs.nytimes.com/2008/05/19/greens-and-hunger/

Times of India. 2011. "Women Plagued by Double-Shift Stress." Retrieved June 11, 2011. Online: http://articles.timesofindia.indiatimes.com/2011-03-24/work/28215548_1_neck-pain-stress-double-shift

Tower, Cynthia Crosson. 1996. *Child Abuse and Neglect* (3rd. ed.) Boston: Allyn and Bacon.

Trejos, Nancy. 2008. "Identity Theft Gets Personal." *Washington Post* (January 13). Retrieved July 4, 2011. Online: http://www.washingtonpost.com/wp-dyn/content/story/2008/01/12/ST2008011201190.html

Truman, Jennifer L., and Michael R. Rand. 2010. "Criminal Victimization, 2009." *National Crime Victimization Survey* (October). U.S. Department of Justice. Retrieved July 4, 2011. Online: http://bjs.ojp.usdoj.gov/content/pub/pdf/cv09.pdf

Turk, Austin T. 1966. "Conflict and Criminality." *American Sociological Review,* 31:338–352.

Turk, Austin T. 1971. *Criminality and Legal Order.* Chicago: Rand McNally.

Turpin, Jennifer, and Lester R. Kurtz. 1997. "Introduction: Violence: The Micro/Macro Link." In Jennifer Turpin and Lester R. Kurtz (Eds.), *The Web of Violence: From Interpersonal to Global.* Urbana and Chicago: University of Illinois, pp. 1–27.

Tyre, Peg. 2008. *The Trouble with Boys: A Surprising Report Card on Our Sons, Their Problems at School, and What Parents and*

Educators Must Do. New York: Crown Archetype.

United Nations. 1995. *The World's Women 1995: Trends and Statistics*. New York: United Nations Publications.

United Nations Children's Fund. 2009. "Facts on Children: Child Protection from Violence, Exploitation, and Abuse." Retrieved June 26, 2011. Online: http://www.unicef.org/protection/index_exploitation.html?q=printme

United Nations Educational, Scientific and Cultural Organization. 2011. "Literacy." UNESCO Institute for Statistics (March 29). Retrieved June 11, 2011. Online: http://www.uis.unesco.org/ev.php?ID=2867_201&ID2=DO_TOPIC

United Nations Environmental Program. 2002. *Global Environmental Outlook 3*. Retrieved December 14, 2002. Online: http://www.unep.org/geo/geo3/english/overview/020.htm

United Nations Population Division. 2010. "World Urbanization Prospects: The 2009 Revision." United Nations (March 25). Retrieved August 1, 2011. Online: http://esa.un.org/unpd/wup/Documents/WUP2009_Press-Release_Final_Rev1.pdf

UnityFirst.com. 2011. "Corporate Board Census Shows Significant Decline in Seats Held by African Americans: Blacks, Women and Other Minorities Remain Seriously Underrepresented" (May). Retrieved June 10, 2011. Online: http://www.unityfirst.com/2011specialelcok.pdf

unwater.org. 2011. "Water Resources: Statistics." United Nations Water. Retrieved July 29, 2011. Online: http://www.unwater.org/statistics_res.html

U.S. Bureau of Justice Statistics. 2010a. "Local Police Departments, 2007." U.S. Department of Justice (December). Retrieved July 8, 2011. Online: http://bjs.ojp.usdoj.gov/content/pub/pdf/lpd07.pdf

U.S. Bureau of Justice Statistics. 2010b. "Total Correctional Population." U.S. Department of Justice. Retrieved July 8, 2011. Online: http://bjs.ojp.usdoj.gov/index.cfm?ty=tp&tid=11

U.S. Bureau of Labor Statistics. 2010. "Women in the Labor Force: A Databook." U.S. Bureau of Labor Statistics (December). Retrieved June 10, 2011. Online: http://www.bls.gov/cps/wlf-databook-2010.pdf

U.S. Bureau of Labor Statistics. 2011a. "Employment Status of the Civilian Population by Race, Sex, and Age." Retrieved June 5, 2011. Online: http://www.bls.gov/news.release/empsit.t02.htm

U.S. Bureau of Labor Statistics. 2011b. "Real Earnings—April 2011" (May 13). Retrieved May 29, 2011. Online: http://

www.bls.gov/news.release/pdf/realer.pdf

U.S. Census Bureau. 2008a. "Health Insurance Coverage: 2006." Washington, DC: U.S. Census Bureau. Retrieved July 8, 2008. Online: http://www.census.gov/hhes/www.hlthins/hlthin06/hlth06asc.html

U.S. Census Bureau. 2008b. *Statistical Abstract of the United States: 2008* (127th ed.). Washington, DC: U.S. Government Printing Office. Online: http://www.census.gov/statb/www/

U.S. Census Bureau. 2010. "The Black Population." Retrieved June 12, 2011. Online: http://www.census.gov/prod/cen2010/briefs/c2010br-06.pdf

U.S. Census Bureau. 2011a. "Older Americans Month: May 2011." Retrieved June 12, 2011. Online: http://www.census.gov/newsroom/releases/pdf/cb11-ff08_olderamericans.pdf

U.S. Census Bureau. 2011b. *Statistical Abstract of the United States: 2010* (130th ed.). Washington, DC: U.S. Government Printing Office. Online: http://http://www.census.gov/compendia/statab/2011edition.html

U.S. Conference of Mayors. 2010. "Hunger and Homelessness Survey" (December). Retrieved February 4, 2012. Online: http://www.usmayors.org/pressreleases/uploads/2010_Hunger-Homelessness_Report-final%20Dec%202010.pdf

U.S. Department of Education. 2010. "A Blueprint for Reform: The Reauthorization of the Elementary and Secondary Education Act" (March). Retrieved February 4, 2012. Online: http://www2.ed.gov/policy/elsec/leg/blueprint/blueprint.pdf

U.S. Department of Health and Human Services. 2010. *Child Maltreatment 2009*. Administration for Children and Families. Retrieved July 14, 2011. Online: http://www.acf.hhs.gov/programs/cb/pubs/cm09/index.htm

U.S. Department of Health and Human Services. 2010. *Infertility Fact Sheet*. Retrieved February 3, 2012. Online: http://www.womenshealth.gov/publications/our-publications/fact-sheet/infertility.cfm

U.S. Department of State. 2011. "International Narcotics Control Strategy: Vol. 1. Drug and Chemical Control." Bureau of International Narcotics and Law Enforcement Affairs (March). Retrieved July 2, 2011. Online: http://www.state.gov/documents/organization/156575.pdf Online: http://www.ilo.org/public/english/dialogue/actrav/publ/129/129.pdf

Venkatesh, Sudhir. 2006. *Off the Books: The Underground Economy of the Urban Poor*. Cambridge, MA: Harvard University Press.

Venkatesh, Sudhir. 2010. "Five Myths about Prostitution." *Washington Post* (September 12):B3. Retrieved June 24, 2011. Online: http://www.washingtonpost.com/wp-dyn/content/article/2010/09/10/AR2010091002670.html

Vertuno, Jim. 2011. "Texas Legislature Set to Allow Guns on College Campuses." Star-Telegram.com (February 21). Retrieved May 26, 2011. Online: http://www.star-telegram.com/2011/02/20/v-print/2863470/texas-legislature-appears-set.html

Wagner, David. 1993. *Checkerboard Square: Culture and Resistance in a Homeless Community*. Boulder, CO: Westview.

Walker-Rodriguez, Amanda, and Rodney Hill. 2011. "Human Sex Trafficking." Federal Bureau of Investigation (March). Retrieved June 26, 2011. Online: http://www.fbi.gov/stats-services/publications/law-enforcement-bulletin/march_2011/human_sex_trafficking

Wallerstein, Immanuel. 1984. *The Politics of the World Economy*. Cambridge, England: Cambridge University Press.

Wallerstein, Immanuel. 1999. *The End of the World as We Know It: Social Science for the Twenty-First Century*. Minneapolis: University of Minnesota Press.

Wall Street Journal. 2011. "Research Highlights the Glass Ceiling in Investment Banking." Retrieved June 11, 2011. Online: http://blogs.wsj.com/source/2011/03/29/research-highlights-the-glass-ceiling-in-investment-banking/?KEYWORDS=glass+ceiling

Wapner, Scott. 2011. "One Nation Overweight: Fat Facts" cnbc.com. Retrieved February 4, 2012. Online: http://www.cnbc.com/id/36919883/

Watney, Murdoch. 2004. "Identity Theft—The Dangerous Imposter." *De Rebus: South African Attorney's Journal* (July):20. Retrieved July 30, 2005. Online: http://www.derebus.org.za/archives/2004Jul/articles/identitytheft.htm

Watson, Bruce. 2010. "The 10 Biggest Corporate Campaign Contributors in U.S. Politics." Dailyfinance.com (October 13). Retrieved July 19, 2011. Online: http://www.dailyfinance.com/2010/10/13/the-10-biggest-corporate-campaign-contributors-in-u-s-politics/

Weeks, John R. 2012. *Population: An Introduction to Concepts and Issues* (11th ed.). Belmont, CA: Cengage/Wadsworth.

Weinberg, Martin S., Earl Rubington, and Sue Kiefer Hammersmith. 1981. *The Solution of*

Social Problems: Five Perspectives (2nd ed.). New York: Oxford University Press.

Weinberg, Martin S., Colin J. Williams, and Douglas W. Pryor. 1994. *Dual Attraction: Understanding Bisexuality*. New York: Oxford University Press.

Weiten, Wayne, and Margaret A. Lloyd. 1994. *Psychology Applied to Modern Life: Adjustment in the 90s*. Pacific Grove, CA: Brooks/Cole.

Weitz, Rose. 2010. *The Sociology of Health, Illness, and Health Care: A Critical Approach* (5th ed.). Belmont, CA: Cengage/Wadsworth.

Wheeler, David L. 1997. "The Animal Origins of Male Violence." *Chronicle of Higher Education* (March 28):A15–A16.

Whitaker, Bill. 2011. "Summer Job Bummer: Teen Unemployment 24 Percent." CBS News (June 4). Retrieved June 12, 2011. Online: http://www.cbsnews.com/2102-18563_162-20069017.html?tag=content Main;contentBody

Whitesides, John. 2005. "Katrina Devastation Highlights Poverty of U.S. Blacks." Reuters.com (September 2). Retrieved September 3, 2005. Online: http://today.reuters.com

Whitmire, Richard. 2010. *Why Boys Fail: Saving Our Sons from an Educational System That's Leaving Them Behind*. New York: AMACOM.

Williams, Christine L. 1995. *Still a Man's World: Men Who Do Women's Work*. Berkeley: University of California Press.

Williams, Gregory Howard. 1996. *Life on the Color Line: The True Story of a White Boy Who Discovered He Was Black*. New York: Plume/Penguin.

Williams, Robin M., Jr. 1970. *American Society: A Sociological Interpretation* (3rd ed.). New York: Knopf.

Williamson, Robert C., Alice Duffy Rinehart, and Thomas O. Blank. 1992. *Early Retirement: Promises and Pitfalls*. New York: Plenum Press.

Willis, Ellen. 1981. *Beginning to See the Light*. New York: Knopf.

Wilson, David (Ed.). 1997. "Globalization and the Changing U.S. City." *The Annals of the American Academy of Political and Social Science*, 551(May; special issue). Thousand Oaks, CA: Sage.

Wilson, Edward O. 1975. *Sociobiology: A New Synthesis*. Cambridge, MA: Harvard University Press.

Wilson, William Julius. 1996. *When Work Disappears: The World of the New Urban Poor*. New York: Knopf.

Winters, Marcus A. 2010. "For Minorities, a Charter-School Boost." *New York Post* (April 27). Online: http://www.manhattan-institute.org/cgi-bin/apMI/print.cgi

Wirth, Louis. 1938. "Urbanism as a Way of Life." *American Journal of Sociology*, 40:1–24.

Wirth, Louis. 1945. "The Problem of Minority Groups." In Ralph Linton (Ed.), *The Science of Man in the World Crisis*. New York: Columbia University Press, p. 38.

Witteman, P. 1991. "Lost in America." *Time* (February 11):76–77.

Wolfers, Justin. 2008. "Misreporting on Divorce." Freakonomics: The Hidden Side of Everything. Retrieved February 3, 2012. Online: http://www.freakonomics.com/2008/03/21/misreporting-on-divorce/

Wolfgang, Marvin E., and Franco Ferracuti. 1967. *The Subculture of Violence: Towards an Integrated Theory in Criminology*. Beverly Hills, CA: Sage.

Women for Sobriety. 2011. "Motto of Women for Sobriety." Retrieved July 2, 2011. Online: http://womenforsobriety.org/beta2/

World Bank. 2011. "How We Classify Countries." *World Development Indicators: 2011*. Retrieved May 27, 2011. Online: http://data.worldbank.org/about/country-classifications?print&book_recurse

World Health Organization. 1946. *Constitution of the World Health Organization*. New York: World Health Organization Interim Commission.

World Health Organization. 2009. "Global Health Risks: Mortality and Burden of Disease Attributable to Selected Major Risks." Retrieved July 10, 2011. Online: http://www.who.int/healthinfo/global_burden_disease/GlobalHealthRisks_report_full.pdf

World Health Organization. 2011. "Reproductive Health." Retrieved February 3, 2012. Online: http://www.who.int/topics/reproductive_health/en/

Wrangham, Richard, and Dale Peterson. 1996. *Demonic Males: Apes and the Origins of Human Violence*. New York: Houghton Mifflin.

Wright, Erik Olin. 1979. *Class Structure and Income Determination*. New York: Academic Press.

Wright, Erik Olin. 1985. *Class*. London: Verso.

Wright, Erik Olin. 1997. *Class Counts: Comparative Studies in Class Analysis*. Cambridge, England: Cambridge University Press.

Wright, Erik Olin, and Joel Rogers. 2010. *American Society: How It Actually Works*. New York: Norton.

Yong, Ed. 2011. "New Evidence That IQ Is Not Set in Stone." cbsnews.com (April 26). Retrieved April 28, 2011. Online: http://www.cbsnews.com/stories/2011/04/26/scitech/main20057536.shtml

Yost, Carol, and Barbara Rodriguez. 2010. "U.S. Congress Reintroduces Act to Address Violence against Women around the World" (March 7). Asia Foundation. Retrieved June 11, 2011. Online: http://asiafoundation.org/in-asia/2010/03/07/u-s-congress-reintroduces-act-to-address-violence-against-women-around-the-world/

Young, Michael Dunlap. 1994. *The Rise of the Meritocracy*. New Brunswick, NJ: Transaction.

Zate, Maria. 1996. "Hispanics Struggle for Corporate Stature." *Austin American-Statesman* (August 11):H1, H3.

Zephyr (A pseudonym). 2008. "Would You Wear … Designer Knockoffs?" College Fashion—College Girl Blog and Fashion Blog with Fashion Tips for the College Fashionista. Retrieved February 4, 2012. Online: http://www.collegefashion.net/would-you-wear/would-you-wear-designer-knockoffs/

Zernike, Kate, and Megan Thee-Brenan. 2010. "Poll Finds Tea Party Backers Wealthier and More Educated." *New York Times* (April 14). Retrieved July 21, 2011. Online: http://www.nytimes.com/2010/04/15/us/politics/15poll.html

Name Index

Note: Page numbers are annotated with b for boxes, t for tables, and f for figures, where appropriate.

Subject Index

Note: Page numbers are annotated with b for boxes, t for tables, and f for figures, where appropriate.